Political Violence in the Weimar Republic, 1918–1933

Studies in German History

Published in Association with the German Historical Institute, Washington, DC

General Editors: **Hartmut Berghoff**, Director of the German Historical Institute, Washington D.C.
Uwe Spiekermann, Deputy Director of the German Historical Institute, Washington D.C.

Volume 1
Nature in German History
Edited by Christof Mauch

Volume 2
Coping with the Nazi Past: West German Debates on Nazism and Generational Conflict, 1955–1975
Edited by Philipp Gassert and Alan E. Steinweis

Volume 3
Adolf Cluss, Architect: From Germany to America
Edited by Alan Lessoff and Christof Mauch

Volume 4
Two Lives in Uncertain Times: Facing the Challenges of the 20th Century as Scholars and Citizens
Wilma Iggers and Georg Iggers

Volume 5
Driving Germany: The Landscape of the German Autobahn, 1930–1970
Thomas Zeller

Volume 6
The Pleasure of a Surplus Income: Part-Time Work, Gender Politics, and Social Change in West Germany, 1955–1969
Christine von Oertzen

Volume 7
Between Mass Death and Individual Loss: The Place of the Dead in Twentieth-Century Germany
Edited by Paul Betts, Alon Confino, and Dirk Schumann

Volume 8
Nature of the Miracle Years: Conservation in West Germany, 1945–1975
Sandra Chaney

Volume 9
Biography between Structure and Agency: Central European Lives in International Historiography
Edited by Volker R. Berghahn and Simone Lässig

Volume 10
Political Violence in the Weimar Republic, 1918–1933: Fight for the Streets and Fear of Civil War
Dirk Schumann

Political Violence in the Weimar Republic, 1918–1933

Fight for the Streets and Fear of Civil War

Dirk Schumann

Translated by Thomas Dunlap

Berghahn Books
NEW YORK • OXFORD

Published in 2009 by
Berghahn Books
www.berghahnbooks.com

First published in Germany as
Politische Gewalt in der Weimarer Republik, 1918–1933

First paperback edition published in 2012

Library of Congress Cataloging-in-Publication Data

Schumann, Dirk.
[Politische Gewalt in der Weimarer Republik, 1918–1933. English]
Political violence in the Weimar Republic, 1918–1933 : fight for the streets and fear of civil war / Dirk Schumann ; translated by Thomas Dunlap. — 1st ed.
p. cm. — (Studies in German history ; v. 10)
Includes bibliographical references and index.
ISBN 978-1-84545-460-9 (hbk.) -- ISBN 978-0-85745-314-3 (pbk.)
1. Germany—Politics and government—1918–1933. 2. Political violence—Germany—History—20th century. 3. Social conflict—Germany—History—20th century. I. Title.

DD240.S41613 2009
943.085—dc22

2008032619

British Library Cataloguing in Publication Data
A catalogue record for this book is available from the British Library.

Printed in the United States on acid-free paper

ISBN 978-0-85745-314-3 (paperback)

Contents

List of Illustrations and Tables

Preface to the English Edition

This is the translation of the revised and shortened version of my book *Politische Gewalt in der Weimarer Republik 1918–1933: Kampf um die Straße und Furcht vor dem Bürgerkrieg,* which was published by Klartext-Verlag, Essen, in 2001. Unlike most similar studies, it focuses neither on one side of the radical political spectrum alone nor on only the early or the late years of the Weimar Republic but provides a comprehensive analysis of political violence in Weimar Germany with particular emphasis on the political culture from which it emerged. It is based on a case study of the socially diverse and politically important Prussian province of Saxony, where the Communist uprising of March 1921 took place and two Combat Leagues (*Wehrverbände*) were founded, the right-wing Stahlhelm and the Social Democratic Reichsbanner.

The book takes issue with two key explanations of political radicalism and violence in post-1918 Germany: the thesis that the Bolshevik revolution was the prime cause of Fascism and violence, and the argument that an all-encompassing "brutalization" by the experience of the First World War determined and doomed post-1918 German political life from the very beginning. Instead, following the first turbulent years of the Weimar Republic that did see a civil war in some regions and cities, political violence was, I argue, the by-product of a fight for public space that never amounted to a civil war again, not even in 1932. While the extreme right became its driving force by "inventing" the Combat Leagues and forcing the moderate and radical left to react, claiming public space for organizations of all sides meant a symbolic show of force rather than a direct physical threat to their opponents. Political violence, therefore, was controllable, if governments had the political will to do so. The study will thus help contribute to a view of the Weimar Republic as a state in severe crisis but with alternatives to the Nazi takeover.

The publication of this translation would not have been possible without the help and support of many people. I want to thank first and foremost Tom Dunlap for doing an excellent job in translating the manuscript. I greatly appreciated his flexibility and responsiveness when we discussed the many nuances of meaning and terminological details that such an undertaking invariably raises. Many thanks also go to Marion Berghahn, who accepted the manuscript for publication in her press, and to the German Historical Institute in Washington, D.C., for making the translation and the publication possible. Jaime Taber has been a very meticulous editor and always quick in responding to my questions. Lena Elisa Freitag and Sandra Wenk have read the proofs and prepared the indices with great care. I am also grateful to an anonymous reader for thoughtful comments on the original German version and to the participants in talks I gave at Emory University and the University of Maryland at College Park. All their ideas and remarks have greatly helped me in clarifying my arguments and making the painful decisions on what parts of the original text to drop from the final version.

The publication of this book comes not long after the conclusion of more than seven years of work and life in the U.S., first as a German Studies Visiting Professor at the History Department of Emory University and then as Deputy Director of the German Historical Institute in Washington, D.C. These years have immensely enriched my life and that of my wife Katrin, both professionally and personally. I am grateful to many friends and colleagues for numerous conversations at Emory, in Washington, and at the meetings of the German Studies Association and the American Historical Association. They have reinforced my conviction that American and German academic cultures can tremendously benefit from each other. I want to mention in particular Heide Fehrenbach and Jamie Melton, whose friendship I have greatly appreciated and enjoyed ever since we first met at Emory in the fall of 1999. It would have been a great pleasure to send one of the first copies of this book to Gerry Feldman. I will always remember with fondness and gratitude his sharp wit, kindness, and support.

List of Abbreviations

AAU	Allgemeine Arbeiter-Union: General Workers' Union
ADGB	Allgemeiner Deutscher Gewerkschaftsbund: General German Union League
AfA	Arbeitsgemeinschaft Freier Angestelltenverbände: Consortium of Free Employees' Associations
AfS	*Archiv für Sozialgeschichte*
AHR	*American Historical Review*
BASF	Badische Anilin- und Sodafabrik
CEH	*Central European History*
CNBLP	Christlich-Nationale Bauern- und Landvolkpartei: Christian-National Peasants and Farmers' Party
DDP	Deutsche Demokratische Partei: German Democratic Party
DLV	Deutscher Landarbeiterverband: German Rural Workers' League
DMV	Deutscher Metallarbeiterverband: German Metal Workers' League
DNVP	Deutschnationale Volkspartei: German National People's Party
DVFP	Deutschvölkische Freiheitspartei: German-*Völkisch* Freedom Party
DVP	Deutsche Volkspartei: German People's Party
DVSTB	Deutschvölkischer Schutz- und Trutz-Bund: German-*Völkisch* Protective and Resistance League
GG	*Geschichte und Gesellschaft*
GSTA PK	Geheimes Staatsarchiv Preußischer Kulturbesitz
GWU	*Geschichte in Wissenschaft und Unterricht*
HZ	*Historische Zeitschrift*
IWK	*Internationale Wissenschaftliche Korrespondenz zur Geschichte der deutschen Arbeiterbewegung*
JbW	*Jahrbuch für Wirtschaftsgeschichte*
KAPD	Kommunistische Arbeiterpartei Deutschlands: Communist German Workers' Party
KK	*Klassenkampf* (Halle)
KPD	Kommunistische Partei Deutschlands: German Communist Party
KZfSS	*Kölner Zeitschrift für Soziologie und Sozialpsychologie*

LAG	Landesarchiv Gotha
LAMe	Landesarchiv Merseburg
LR	Landrat
LHAM	Landeshauptarchiv Magdeburg
MGM	*Militärgeschichtliche Mitteilungen*
MSPD	Mehrheitssozialdemokratische Partei Deutschlands: Majority German Social Democratic Party
MZ	*Magdeburgische Zeitung*
NSBO	Nationalsozialistische Betriebszellen-Organisation: National Socialist Organization of Works Cells
NSDAP	Nationalsozialistische Deutsche Arbeiterpartei: National Socialist German Workers' Party
OP	Oberpräsident
Orgesch	Organisation Escherich
ÖZG	*Österreichische Zeitschrift für Geschichtswissenschaften*
PP	Polizeipräsident
PVS	*Politische Vierteljahrschrift*
RP	Regierungspräsident
RGI	Rote Gewerkschaftsinternationale: Red Union International
RFB	Roter Frontkämpferbund: Red Front Fighters' League
RGO	Revolutionäre Gewerkschaftsopposition: Revolutionary Union Opposition
RKO	Reichskommissar für Überwachung der öffentlichen Ordnung: Reich Commissioner for the Supervision of Public Order
SA	Sturmabteilung: Storm Troopers (of the Nazi Party)
SAPMO	Stiftung Archiv der Parteien und Massenorganisationen der DDR (im Bundesarchiv)
Schufo	Schutzformationen: Protective Formations
SPD	Sozialdemokratische Partei Deutschlands: German Social Democratic Party
SS	Schutzstaffel: Security Squad
StakoöO	Staatskommissar für Überwachung der öffentlichen Ordnung: State Commissioner for the Supervision of Public Order, Berlin
Stat.Dt.R., N.F.	*Statistik des Deutschen Reiches, Neue Folge*
SZ	*Saale-Zeitung* (Halle)
Teno	Technische Nothilfe: Technical Emergency Assistance
USPD	Unabhängige Sozialdemokratische Partei Deutschlands: Independent German Social Democratic Party
VB	*Volksblatt* (Halle)
VKPD	Vereinigte Kommunistische Partei Deutschlands: United German Communist Party
VS	*Volksstimme* (Magdeburg)
ZfG	*Zeitschrift für Geschichtswissenschaft*

Note on the Administrative Structure of Prussia under the Weimar Republic

Prussia (technically The Free State of Prussia) was the largest of the federal states of the Weimar Republic, comprising about 60 percent of its territory and also of its population. Administratively, it was broken down into fourteen provinces: Berlin, Brandenburg, East Prussia, Hanover, Hesse-Nassau, Hohenzollern, Lower Silesia, Pomerania, Posen-West Prussia, Rhine Province, **Saxony**, Schleswig-Holstein, Upper Silesia, and Westphalia.

Each province was headed by a provincial governor, called *Oberpräsident* (his office was referred to as the *Oberpräsidium*). Each province was in turn subdivided into *Regierungsbezirke* (governmental districts), each headed by a *Regierungspräsident.* A *Regierungsbezirk* was subdivided into *Kreise* (counties) headed by a *Landrat* (county executive). There were two different kinds of *Kreise*: *Landkreise* (rural counties) and *Stadtkreise* (urban counties). The province of **Saxony** (capital city: Magdeburg) was divided into three *Regierungsbezirke* (Magdeburg, Merseburg, Erfurt) and into thirty-nine *Landkreise* and sixteen (in 1920, thirteen) *Stadtkreise.*

Introduction

> In the paradoxes of today lies the truth of tomorrow. And so one may venture to say that violence has become obsolete. It was a way in the feudal and early capitalist world to bring about a new distribution of social power, but its time is past.
>
> Emil Lederer (1921)[1]

Introduction

Emil Lederer—a Heidelberg professor, Social Democratic intellectual, and future emigrant—was right: after the Revolution of 1918/19, political violence in Germany was in fact an anachronism. The new Weimar Republic was based on a compromise between the moderate right, the political center, and the moderate left. By granting the workers' movement equal rights without fundamentally altering the social order, it offered German society the chance to pursue conflicts between classes, interest groups, and ideological camps within democratic forms. That chance, however, was squandered. Political violence accompanied the Weimar Republic from the civil war battles in its early years to the bloody clashes between National Socialists and Communists in its final phase.

Yet I shall argue that the bloody battles between 1919 and 1921 did not make the subsequent development inevitable. After the phase of civil war, political violence assumed a distinctly limited form. It was no longer aimed at killing or wounding as many opponents as possible; instead, it served political parties and organizations as an instrument for exerting pressure in the struggle over control of the street. This development was driven by the Combat Leagues (*Wehrverbände*) of all political camps, who, with their uniforms and marches, injected militaristic elements into the political culture. However, since the violence they perpetrated followed a political and not a military logic, it was, as I will show, in principle controllable and did not pose a fundamental threat to the political order, not even in 1932, that particularly turbulent year before Hitler's assumption of power. Still, in the increasingly polarized society of Weimar Germany, such "small" violence pervaded an ever growing number of places and regions. This helped the extreme right to instrumentalize violence for its campaign against the Weimar democracy, which ended in victory in 1933. It stoked the fear of a civil war the Communists were allegedly preparing, and to that end it picked

---

Notes from this section begin on page xxxviii.

up and radicalized interpretive schemes that had served to discredit the workers' movement before the First World War. The Communists' aggressive propaganda and readiness to engage in violence contributed to this development, but at no time did they pose a serious threat. It was not political violence as such that forced the Weimar Republic into a position where abandoning democracy seemed a way out, but its use as an argument by forces on the right intent on transforming the Republic into an authoritarian state.

By investigating the causes and effects of political violence in the Weimar Republic, the present study sheds new light on the first German democracy's chances of survival. The Weimar Republic has been the topic of intensive research for a long time.[2] And for quite some time that research has been dominated by the question about the reasons behind its failure. Scholars searched for missed opportunities in the Revolution of 1918/19 and for the factors that led to the rise of the Nazi Party (NSDAP) and Hitler's assumption of power in 1933. From that perspective, the Weimar Republic seemed nothing more than a transitional stage, a mere prehistory to the "Third Reich" and its horrors. This perception changed in the wake of Detlev Peukert's groundbreaking study of the Weimar Republic as an experiment with modernity (1987). The years between 1918/19 and 1933 are now seen as a time of a massive push toward modernization, one that triggered enormous changes in the political system, the welfare state, relations between classes and genders, and the culture at large, spawning fierce resistance in the process. Special attention is paid to the effects of the inflation that began with the outbreak of war in 1914 and reached its catastrophic climax in 1923.[3]

This does not mean that the question about the causes behind the failure of Weimar has been abandoned. But it has been placed within a more complex framework. The interest is now directed at the multiplicity of designs and interpretations generated by the modernizing thrust, especially in the first years of Weimar, and the reasons for why and when they became more constricted and polarized in the years that followed. The presumption, then, is of a certain openness in Weimar's development: the Republic no longer appears doomed from the very start. The present study embraces this kind of perspective. By examining political violence, a particularly dangerous element of political culture, it probes into the severity of political conflicts and the ways in which they were carried out, into the social conflicts underlying them, and into the cultural processes of interpretation that helped to either heighten or diffuse these conflicts, processes that included, not least, the definition of gender roles in the Weimar Republic. In the end, our picture of Weimar will become clearer insofar as we will get a better sense of the options that were available in Weimar's crisis and could have been used to save democracy.

The State of Scholarship

In spite of the numerousness of studies on the Weimar Republic, to date there is none that has examined, alongside the organizations by which political violence was perpetrated, this violence itself for the entire period from 1918/19 to 1933. The present book is intended to close this gap, and to show that a careful look at the contexts that gave rise to violence, at the way in which it unfolded, at its victims, and at the damage it caused is indispensable for a thorough understanding of the interpretations and actions that followed in its wake.

Among the outstanding events in the history of Weimar violence, the Kapp Putsch and the subsequent fighting in the Ruhr region have been analyzed especially closely. In the 1970s, Erhard Lucas interpreted these events rather sweepingly as the "March revolution," seeing in them a syndicalist alternative to both the government's policy and to the line of the German Communist Party (KPD).[4] However, most of the studies on political violence focus on only one side of the political spectrum. A number of older studies examined the organizational structure, the ideology, and the political behavior of the Free Corps, the Home Guards (*Einwohnerwehren*), and the Combat Leagues of all political camps; among them, Karl Rohe's work on the Reichsbanner Schwarz-Rot-Gold (Reich Banner Black-Red-Gold) stands out.[5] In his synthesis of these studies, James Diehl interpreted the history of the paramilitary units on the right as a continuation of the bourgeois *Sammlungspolitik* (policy of concentration) of the prewar period, with the Vaterlandspartei (Fatherland Party) as an intermediate stage. The Free Corps and the Home Guards—whose importance Diehl overestimates—in his view carried the militarization of politics into wide circles of the citizenry, thus preparing the ground for the right-wing Combat Leagues and, finally, the Nazi Sturmabteilung (SA, Storm Troopers).[6]

Since the late 1970s, a more refined methodology has been used to examine especially National Socialist and Communist violence in the end phase of the Weimar Republic after 1929. Following in the footsteps of Richard Bessel's penetrating study on the National Socialist SA in the eastern regions of Prussia, Sven Reichardt has most recently studied the SA in Berlin. He explains the readiness of SA men to become violent by their habituation to violence in the male bonding world of the SA tavern. In this world, ideological driving forces were of less importance than the self-affirmation and the recognition from SA comrades that was sought in day-to-day acts of violence. In contrast to Reichardt, however, Bessel emphasizes the relatively limited character of the confrontation between the SA and its opponents.[7]

Peter Merkl's analysis of the biographies of SA men also ascribes great importance to long-term learning processes of violence in conjunction with experiences of social decline.[8] Communist violence in the final phase of the Weimar Republic has been examined in detail by Eve Rosenhaft, who looked at the example of Berlin. She interprets this violence primarily as defensive behavior by the party rank and file, which sought to prevent the National Socialists from invading its territory and was only in part amenable to control by the party's central organization.[9] Pamela Swett, focusing also on Berlin in the final years of the Weimar Republic, has recently taken Rosenhaft's argument even further. Her explanation of street violence as product of a "neighborhood-based radical culture" that lacked clear-cut party allegiances, however, fails to examine and therefore underestimates the influence of radical party leaders and organizations at the neighborhood level.[10]

The heroization of the radical left—which can be found in Lucas, for example, but still shines through in Rosenhaft, as well—is no longer convincing today. Equally to be rejected is the contrary position advanced by Ernst Nolte, namely that the violence of the radical right in the "European civil war" after 1917 was merely the inevitable response to the desire of the radical left to destroy them.[11] It readily equates Communist propaganda with the Communist rank and file's readiness to take action, completely overlooks the causes of right-wing violence that are rooted in an authoritarian conception of order, and in the final analysis takes an apologetic stance toward that violence. Not long ago, Andreas Wirsching, following Nolte's lead but also engaging his views critically, examined the radical political currents and the violence they spawned in Berlin and Paris in the period between the wars.[12] His approach, which is based on a modified, "historical-genetic" theory of totalitarianism, avoids the implicit value judgment of Nolte's position. But it, too, does not escape the danger of painting an excessively monolithic picture of the Communist movement, or of downplaying the radical right prior to the rise of National Socialism.

The study by Wirsching and many others of recent date proceed on the assumption that the First World War "brutalized" European societies, and they see in this a primary cause behind the political violence of the interwar period. For the most part, the core of this brutalization is located in the violent experiences of front-line soldiers, which supposedly lowered the inhibitory threshold to the use of violence in a lasting way.[13] At first glance, this thesis seems plausible. Political violence characterized the interwar period not only in Germany. However, recent studies have shown that the violence was perpetrated by only a minority of the returning front-line soldiers. Moreover, the old nation states of France and England were able to keep this violence within very tightly drawn limits.[14] An automatic connection between the war experience and political violence after the war therefore did not exist. What was crucial is how the war experience was interpreted and employed as an argument in the political clashes.

Approach

A study of political violence requires an explicit definition of its subject, for it is not self-evident. What is violence in the first place, and what is "political" violence? These questions are the subject of controversy and debate not only within the historical profession.[15] The most recent contributions to the scholarly discussion—which a single scholar can no longer even begin to keep track of—insist on taking seriously the physical act of violence as the impact upon the body, as the sensation of pleasure and pain. I try to do this here in the sense that a close look at the unfolding of specific violent events and the behavior of those who participated forms a crucial part of the account. However, one cannot get around the fact that an approach focused on the emotions connected with violence is confronted with historical sources that often contain so little information when it comes to individual feelings that any interpretation faces clear limitations. Moreover, such an approach is not immune from describing violence too quickly as a constant that is resistant to civilization, as one can see in Wolfgang Sofsky's "tractate on violence."[16]

The attribute "political" indicates that the violence of interest to me here is not a matter of individuals, which means that in the final analysis it is not the motives and feelings of individual actors that are at the center of the analysis, but the factors and circumstances decisive for their collective action. In this context, Johan Galtung's concept of "structural violence," which was highly influential for a while and is still occasionally used today, turns out not to be useful. Galtung argued that violence is present "if humans are influenced in such a way that their current physical and intellectual self-realization is less than their potential self-realization." It can take the form of directly experienced, "personal" violence, or of indirect, "structural" violence, which Galtung also defined as "social injustice."[17] Critics have generally objected that his definition lacks specificity and is not very useful analytically.[18] If in principle nearly every form of social inequality is violence, it is no longer possible to draw meaningful distinctions between the varying degrees of legitimacy of such inequalities, between the different ways in which they are perceived and the resulting consequences for social action; the concept of violence dissolves into the concept of society. Moreover, this kind of notion of violence suggests a fluid transition between indirect "structural" and direct "personal" violence. By contrast, what I try to do in the present study is, on the one hand, to take seriously the act of physical violence itself, and on the other, to elucidate the processes that mediate between social pressures and personal violence and identify the latitudes for action that exist along the way.

It therefore seems more workable to place physical violence at the center of the conceptual definition I am after. In the present context, "political violence" shall thus be understood as *the exercise of physical coercion that essentially takes place collectively, can be aimed at both objects as well as individuals or groups, and whose actors seek—by selecting a specific target—to simultaneously strike a blow against the political system as a whole or against a political concept regarded as hostile.*

This definition covers a broad spectrum of motives, forms, and behaviors. The acts of violence it includes can be carefully planned and deliberately carried out, but they can also arise rather spontaneously from a specific confrontational situation and elude control. These acts can pursue a clear goal, though they may also seek to express nonspecific demands and moods; their primary purpose could also be to consolidate the group that is engaged in the action.[19] They can be planned and carried out by a great many persons or a small group, employ arms on a massive scale or engage in limited physical violence, and be brief or long in duration. The bearers of such violence can be "normal" citizens (male and female) as well as members of state-run organizations charged with maintaining order.

While the proposed definition draws a relatively wide circle of persons involved in political violence, it substantially limits the sphere of the political. This, too, is not self-evident. To be sure, a number of recent works have shown that collective acts of protest by the lower classes that involved moderate acts of violence, for example, by women against the dismal food supply during the First World War, certainly could force officials and government to respond, even though these actions were in no way directed or influenced by political organizations. Since they altered the balance of power between "above" and "below," even if they usually did so only for a brief period, recent scholarship has defined them as "political."[20] The Weimar Republic, especially in its early years, also witnessed such bread-and-butter protests (*Subsistenzproteste*),[21] which occupied officials and the public and prompted reactions. As the present study will show, however, the special quality of the history of violence during the Weimar Republic lay in the fact that the confrontations between opposing political groups or between them and the state's forces of public order essentially revolved always around the foundations of the political system, and not merely around specific demands. By contrast, bread-and-butter protests were concerned primarily with the rapid improvement of the food supply. This distinction also shaped the public discussion. Moreover, many women participated in the bread-and-butter protests, whereas the clashes between political organizations were almost exclusively an affair of men. When bread-and-butter protests led to violence, it was directed chiefly against things and ranked far below the violence engendered by the other clashes. It therefore makes sense to draw an analytic distinction between bread-and-butter protests and political violence. Still, the present study will also deal with these protest actions. The crucial point is to determine why they remained limited and did not turn into political violence.

It is not only the definition of political violence that is controversial in the literature. Attempts at devising a typology of political violence have also failed to produce clear results.[22] At best two different types of political violence have been defined with some clarity: *assassination* as a carefully planned action, prepared and carried out by a small group of perpetrators with a high degree of organization; and *uprising* as an event of longer duration, with a large number of participants, with fighting on a larger scale that sometimes assumes military forms and involves corresponding weapons, and with at least part of the actors displaying a high level of organization; the *coup* contains elements of both types. These forms comprise what is in a sense the most spectacular part of the political violence in the Weimar Republic: examples are the murders of Erzberger and Rathenau in 1921 and 1922, the Ruhr uprising in 1920, or the Hitler putsch in 1923.

However, the vast majority of acts of political violence in the Weimar Republic should be assigned to the category of "unrest," which is difficult to grasp and has for the most part not been described in detail in the existing literature: these acts arose in a comparatively spontaneous manner, were shorter in duration, and unfolded in a variety of ways. They include *clashes* between groups of political opponents and between these groups and the police, for example in connection with public rallies and marches; *assaults* on political opponents, which often took place at night; and *brawls* during political meetings. Those who were involved, who numbered at most in the dozens, could use a wide variety of weapons, have ties to organizations that varied in their closeness, and have pre-planned the use of violence to a greater or lesser degree. On the whole, the violence was rather limited, and the number of victims and the damage tended to be minor. The starting position of the present study is that these acts, which were "small" violence[23] *("kleine" Gewalt)* compared to civil war fighting and assassinations, are especially suited for identifying the causes and effects of political violence in the Weimar Republic, and showing how it gradually took root in the political culture.

No satisfactory explanatory model for why political conflicts turn violent has been devised to date, but the classical models of the systematic social sciences are useful in developing a heuristic concept. Robert Gurr's notion of "relative deprivation" has an opposing idea in Charles Tilly's "collective action."[24] At the center of his model, Gurr places the discrepancy between a social group's expectations of material well-being and political influence, on the one hand, and the perceived chances of realizing these expectations, on the other. Underlying it is the basic assumption that rapid social change leads to the collapse of civilizing control mechanisms and thus turns into a cause of political violence. The transformation of "relative deprivation" into violence requires mediating factors, which also include norms and historical experiences, for example, but the model does not describe how this mediation takes place.[25]

Against Gurr, Charles Tilly has sought to explain violence as arising from the mechanisms of the struggle for power, and to decouple it from a direct link with abrupt changes in a social structure.[26] Political violence occurs, according to Tilly, when newly emerging or declining groups struggle for shares of power in such a system and the regime responds to this challenge with repression on a moderate level.[27] The potential with which a group enters the struggle over power grows primarily from two elements: its organizational strength, and its ability to mobilize.[28]

There is no doubt that the early years of the Weimar Republic, especially, were rife with experiences of "relative deprivation." But Tilly's model helps us to understand why the shocks of military defeat, revolution, and inflation on the side of the bourgeoisie, but also the disappointed hopes on the other side in 1919/20, did not lead invariably to violence. Tilly's category "organization" underscores the importance attached to the development of membership numbers, local groups, and auxiliary organizations within the radical parties and the Combat Leagues close to them. The category "mobilization" directs our attention, first, at the availability of material resources such as weapons, means of transportation, and tools of communication, and second, at the willingness of an organization's members and supporters to take on tasks in accordance with the directives of the leadership. As we shall see especially in the case of the Communists, this willingness to follow had very clear limits.

For all its differentiation, Tilly's model lacks a dimension that a modern social history can no longer ignore: that of culture.[29] Scholars have emphasized how important images, symbols, and the political language were especially for the Weimar Republic. Useful in this regard is the concept of "political culture" developed by the American scholars Almond and Verba;[30] important contributions in Germany have come especially from Karl Rohe.[31] The concept embodies those fundamental attitudes, emotions, and actions that are determinative for the actors in a political system over a longer period of time. In its ideal form, political culture can be divided, according to Rohe, into the areas of "social culture" and "interpretive culture." While "social culture" refers to the practices and ritual of everyday political life, "interpretive culture" refers to the processes of reflection and discussion in which these behaviors are debated and affirmed, but also newly defined. This distinction does not necessarily coincide with that between a party's "base" and its leading thinkers.[32]

The present study will examine political language as an important part of the political culture of the Weimar Republic. It will probe the guiding concepts and core arguments that were used to discuss political violence, the ways in which its causes and presumed consequences were articulated, and what recommendations for action were derived from this understanding.[33] A second focus will be on the forms and content of public political self-representation. Here the study will examine the references to violence found in the rituals and in the world of images and symbols, with special attention given to the gender-specific attribution of spheres of action and characteristics. Political violence was a phenomenon molded by men, yet the "manliness" that all political camps called for displayed important differences alongside common elements.[34] To reiterate: the study of political culture as a whole is thus concerned with both patterns of interpretation and modes of behavior. My intention here is neither to pursue a pure history of concepts and political discourse, on the basis of lead articles, for example,[35] nor to concentrate solely on symbolic practices.[36]

The political culture of the Weimar Republic was not a homogeneous whole. In fact, it is precisely its "fragmentation"[37] into several hostile subcultures that seems to have been characteristic of the unstable republic. So far, however, scholarship has not been able to determine the precise boundaries of these subcultures, the boundaries of the political milieus.[38] Only the continued existence of a Catholic milieu, though diminished, appears to be uncontested. By contrast, whether a separate Communist milieu took shape—clearly distinct from the Social Democratic milieu—is as controversial as the question of which political milieu(s) the bourgeoisie established. Harder still is the allocation of the NSDAP to one or several milieus, especially if—as scholars have been doing increasingly—one conceives of it as a kind of mass party.[39] However, as the basic framework for the present study I use the three-camp model that Karl Rohe proposed on the basis of election analyses. According to this model, the electoral landscape had been dominated since the Empire by a Catholic, a Socialist, and a National camp (which might better be called the "bourgeois-national" camp). Using this approach, Rohe is better able than the previous milieu models to explain especially the disintegration within the bourgeois party spectrum and the rise of the NSDAP.[40]

The present study examines the issue of political violence by looking at one larger German region. It is easier to achieve greater empirical depth by narrowing to this mid-size level than by encompassing all of Germany. At the same time, the important differences between city and countryside and between various sociopolitical milieus are more visible on this scale than with the focus on a large city. Because of its diversity of milieus, its importance to the history of violence in the Weimar Republic, and the quality of the available sources, I have chosen the Prussian province of Saxony as the region to study. The province included areas that were predominantly agricultural as well as important industrial regions. Some of the industrial sectors and enterprises had been around for quite some time by the beginning of the 1920s and employed many skilled workers; others had received the decisive growth impulse only during the First World War and were home to many unskilled and semiskilled workers. While the KPD had one of its strongholds in Germany around Halle-Merseburg, in the heart of the province, the Social Democratic Party (SPD) was dominant in the north. Magdeburg was the founding city of the Stahlhelm (Steel Helmet), soon to be the largest of the right-wing Combat Leagues, and later of the Republican Reichsbanner; Halle, the bastion of the right wing of the Stahlhelm, was the birthplace of the Wehrwolf (Werewolf), another large Combat League of the right. In 1919 and 1920, the region witnessed bloody clashes between workers and Free Corps, and in 1921 the KPD staged its only attempt at a larger uprising here, the "March action"; in addition, there were numerous clashes between members of the various Combat Leagues and later with the SA.

The state of research and scholarship on this politically highly interesting region does not reflect the very good overall availability of sources, for reasons that are not difficult to see. The studies that were undertaken in the German Democratic Republic (GDR), especially in the 1960s and 1970s, examined the emergence and further development of the KPD, its influence on industrial and rural workers, and its program.[41] Separate studies were devoted to the defeat of the Kapp putsch and the "March action," as well as to the history of individual enterprises, especially the Leuna Works and the Mansfeld Combine.[42] These studies contain a wealth of valuable source references and a lot of useful, detailed information on the organizational and political history of the workers' movement. However, since they were interested solely in the rise of the KPD, in keeping with the official guidelines for East German historiography, the insights we can derive from them are, on the whole, clearly limited. Alongside the "treason" of the SPD and the Independent Social Democratic Party (USPD), these studies mention at most internal organizational shortcomings and the insufficiently enlightened consciousness of the masses as obstacles to the rise of the party.[43] The studies on the province of Saxony that have been published since the end of the GDR have continued to focus largely on its political history.[44]

The present study is based largely on government files. Especially well preserved for the Weimar period are the files of the *Oberpräsidium* (provincial government), which received copies of all the reports sent by the presidents of the administrative districts (*Regierungspräsidenten*) to the Prussian Minister of the Interior. The great majority of sources that I have used come from this collection. I have also drawn on the files of the *Regierungspräsidium* of Merseburg and Erfurt (those in Magdeburg are missing for the period of the Weimar Republic) and the files of the Prussian Ministries of the Interior and Justice. In individual cases I was also able to evaluate files from the *Landratsämter* (rural county offices). As a whole, the official files yielded a wealth of information on larger and smaller incidents of violence, on the general mood within the population, and on the structure and propaganda activity of the radical parties and organizations, most abundantly for the years from 1920 to 1923. Since all state agencies of the province at all levels were in the hands of republicans officials until the late summer of 1932, their reports are highly credible, especially with respect to the extreme right. Of course, this observation needs to be qualified for parts of the rural areas, especially the Altmark, where it is possible that the authorities did not become aware of all the subversive activities by the radical right. Their reports need to be read through critical lenses, especially when they deal with the Communists.

Another source I have drawn on is court files, though their availability is much more limited. Preserved in their entirety are only the files of the extraordinary courts that were set up after the "March action" of 1921. In addition to the sentences, they contain reports about the trials, sometimes also detailed records of interrogations, variously detailed information about the biographies of the accused, and frequently also information about the subsequent pardon process. Otherwise, large collections of files can be found only for individual prosecutor's offices, such as those in Halberstadt and Naumburg; these merely document selected cases of violence and contain large gaps.

A not very extensive but very informative source of nongovernmental files I evaluated is the reports of the KPD district leadership in Halle-Merseburg and other material from the internal communication of the party. Though likewise riddled with large gaps, they contain important data on the movement of membership and assessments of the actual political situation. Another central source is the daily newspapers of the region. Here I had to take into account their very uneven survival, and at the same time be selective for practical reasons. I drew closely on the Magdeburg *Volksstimme* as the leading Social Democratic paper, the Halle *Volksblatt* as the most important organ of the USPD until 1920, the *Klassenkampf* as the organ of the KPD district Halle-Merseburg, and, finally, the *Magdeburgische Zeitung* and the *Saale-Zeitung* (Halle) as the leading, opinion-shaping papers of the bourgeois press.[45] All the papers listed have survived with only minor gaps for the entire period of the Weimar Republic.[46] I evaluated reports and commentaries on local and supraregional incidents of violence[47] and on celebrations and rallies the Combat Leagues organized or participated in, as well as the lead articles and commentary on political events of central importance, such as Reichstag elections or changes in the government.

The Prussian Province of Saxony up to 1918

With the exception of Anhalt, some parts of Thuringia, and a strip of land around Eilenburg and Torgau that was assigned to the Free State of Saxony, the Prussian province of Saxony was largely equal to the modern federal state of Saxony-Anhalt. Great differences characterized its economic and social structure. The deepest agricultural imprint was found in the *Regierungsbezirk* (administrative district) of Magdeburg, which had nearly 1.3 million inhabitants in 1925 and was the second largest of the three administrative districts. A quarter of the population (25.5 percent) was still within the agricultural sector. But while the Altmark (the *Landkreise* [rural counties] of Salzwedel, Osterburg, Stendal, and Gardelegen) was dominated by medium- and large-sized peasant holdings,

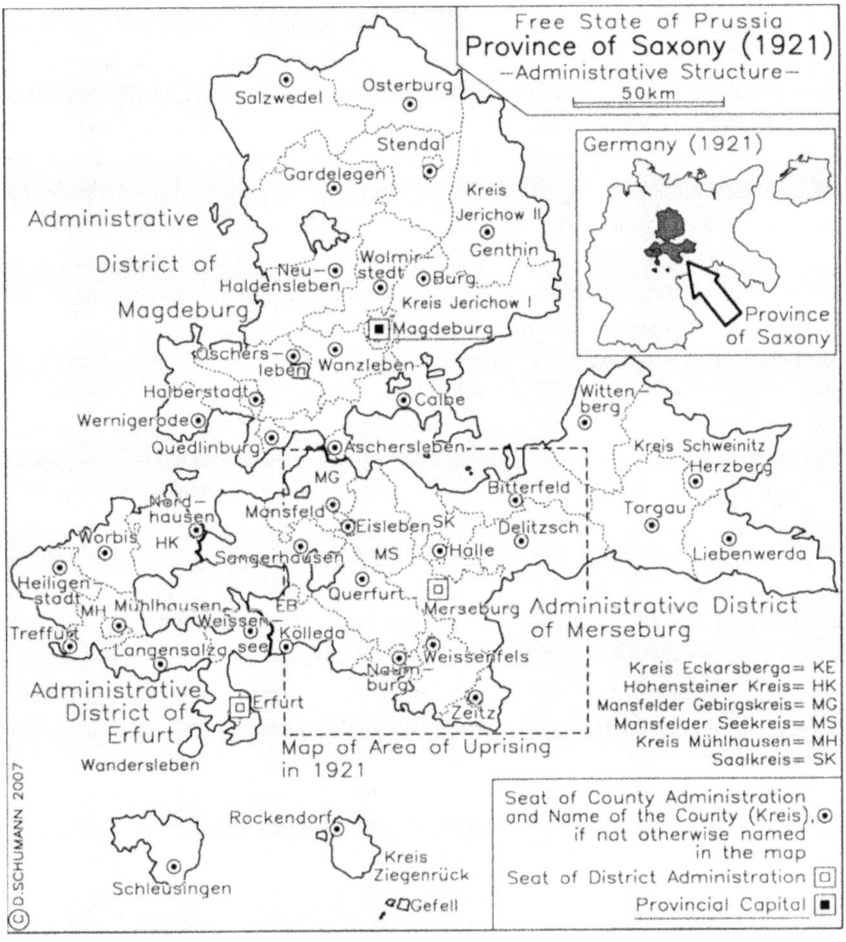

Map I.1 Prussian Province of Saxony, 1921

large estates prevailed in the very fertile Magdeburg Börde (the counties of Neuhaldensleben, Wolmirstedt, Calbe, and Wanzleben) and in the foothills of the Harz; a substantial portion of their arable land was devoted to sugar beets. For example, in the county of Salzwedel, medium- and large-scale peasant farms (5–100 hectares) controlled more than 82.8 percent of the acreage, while owners of large estates (more than 100 acres) held only 7.5 percent of the land; by contrast, in the county of Wanzleben the corresponding figures were 31.2 and 54.1 percent.[48] Over a third of the population (36.6 percent) lived from work in trade and industry, concentrated in the southern portion of the administrative district. Large potash salt deposits and processing enterprises were found in the area around Staßfurt, and brown coal was extracted in the counties of Calbe and Neuhaldensleben.[49] Magdeburg itself was by far the most important center of machine building in the entire province. Three-fifths of all workers in the mechanical engineering industry in the administrative district (and more than one-quarter of all those in the province), a total of nearly 21,000 in 1925, were employed in the city.[50] The First World War led to a strong rise in the number of those employed in the metal processing and machine building industries. That was true not only for the largest enterprise, the Gruson Works, since the 1880s part of the Krupp conglomerate, but also for smaller firms like the Poltesche Patronenfabrik (cartridge factory), which employed only 568 workers at the outbreak of the war, more than 5,000 by the end of 1914, and eventually 10,000 by 1918.[51] Other centers of machine building lay in the environs of Magdeburg; in the north of the province there was only Stendal, which was in fact the only city with any industry to speak of in this area.[52]

The industrial heart of the province beat in the administrative district of Merseburg, which counted 1.4 million inhabitants and was thus the district with the largest population. The development of the very abundant brown coal deposits had begun around 1800; after 1900 they were extracted chiefly by open-pit mining. Most important were the Bitterfeld and Zeitz-Weißenfels mining areas, alongside the Liebenwerda area that was located entirely in the east; in the 1920s, the newly opened mining area of the Geisel Valley between Merseburg and Querfurt topped the list.[53] By contrast, the extraction of copper ore in the Mansfelder Land had been going on for centuries. The pits and smelting works were owned by the Mansfeld Combine, which was notorious for its low wages and harsh working conditions.[54] In the entire administrative district, more than 45,000 workers were employed in mining in 1925, surpassing any other industrial sector.[55]

In second place (or third, after the construction industry) stood the chemical industry, which employed nearly 35,000.[56] It had received its decisive developmental boost during the First World War. The salt and brown coal deposits of the region supplied cheap raw materials and energy. Its location at a considerable distance from the borders offered protection against enemy attacks, and after 1914 this prompted the establishment of large enterprises that initially produced military goods but were able to retool quickly after the end of the war, manufacturing chiefly nitrogen and fertilizer. Far and away the largest among them was the Leuna Works near Merseburg (founded in 1916), a branch of the Badische Anilin- und Sodafabrik (BASF), that employed about 14,000 by the end of the war. The factory was notable not only for its exceptional size, but also for the fact that even years after the war it was as much a construction site as a production site. Because of the steady expansion of the installations, about half of the workers in the first years after 1918 were construction workers, and supervising them proved especially difficult for the company's management.[57]

Another important wartime creation was the Nitrogen Works Piesteritz near Wittenberg, which employed 2,700 workers in 1918/19. Massive expansion occurred during the war at the chemicals plant Griesheim Elektron in Bitterfeld and the neighboring paint factory Wolfen, both of which were later part of I. G. Farben. The chemicals industry in the Bitterfeld region employed more than 13,000 workers in 1918/19, more than three times as many as before 1914.[58] The number of workers had risen dramatically, not only but especially in the chemicals industry (and in mining); many came from the countryside and were first-generation unskilled or semiskilled industrial workers.[59] They were less willing to follow the party or union leadership and were more inclined to political radicalism than were workers from the traditional Social Democratic milieu.[60]

All other sectors lagged far behind. Among them, machine building topped this list with more than 24,000 workers in 1925. About half were employed in Halle itself, where, as in Magdeburg, chiefly agricultural machines were manufactured, and in neighboring Ammendorf, where railroad cars were built.[61] Of some importance was also the soil and rock industry with nearly 15,000 workers, which had large production sites in the Bittterfeld earthenware pipe industry.[62]

The distribution of brown coal deposits and other mineral resources ensured that the industrial workers in the Merseburg administrative district were not concentrated in a few locations. Only in the rural counties of Eckartsberga (at the border with Thuringia) and in Schweinitz (at the border with Brandenburg north of the Torgau) was the ratio of the industrial population—at 24.1 and 20.9 percent, respectively—far below the district average of 46.1 percent. In three rural counties it was above 50 percent (Weißenfels, Merseburg, and Saalkreis, i.e., the rural county around Halle), in two it was even above 60 percent (Zeitz and Bitterfeld).[63] Moreover, many industrial workers did not live in cities but in villages, where they often owned a small piece of land. In 1925, fields of less than 2 hectares (the smallest pieces included in the statistics) made up 7.3 percent of all the agricultural land in the Merseburg administrative district, which was well above the average for Prussia. There were hardly any large settlements of purely rural character.[64] For that reason alone, peasants played no more than a subordinate role here, unlike in the north of the province; added to this is the fact that large-scale landholdings—most of which, incidentally, were in bourgeois hands—accounted for a share of agricultural land that was only slightly less than that in the administrative district of Magdeburg. In 1925, enterprises with a size of over 100 hectares controlled more than 26.6 percent of agricultural acreage, the soil of which in the larger environs of Halle had the same excellent quality as in the Magdeburg Börde.[65]

The administrative district of Erfurt, the smallest with a population of 570,000, had a level of industrialization that was nearly as high as that of the administrative district of Merseburg, but it lacked the latter's giant enterprises. In 1925, 45.7 percent of its population lived from industry and trades, and only 21.5 percent from agriculture.[66] Large landholdings accounted for only a little more than 10 percent of the agricultural acreage, while nearly half (43.4 percent) was cultivated by medium-sized farms (5–20 hectares).[67] The most heavily agricultural rural district was that of Erfurt, with a corresponding population ratio of nearly half (45.8 percent), but even here the industrial population accounted for one-third (33.0 percent) and was thus substantially higher than in the counties of Eckartsberga and Schweinitz in the administrative district of Merseburg.[68]

Mining played no role in the administrative district of Erfurt; industry itself was dominated by consumer sectors. In 1925 about 20,000 were employed in each of the apparel business (with the center of shoe manufacturing in Erfurt), food processing, and luxury goods production (chiefly tobacco), while around 16,000 worked in the textile industry.[69] About 14,000 each worked in machine and equipment buildings and in metal goods manufacturing, with precision mechanical goods playing a preeminent role. A politically explosive combination of several factors occurred in the rural county of Schleusingen. Its chief town of Suhl was home to the rifle factory Simson & Co., a central armaments enterprise during the war, when its workforce grew from around 1,000 to 5,500. After 1918 it became a factory for hunting weapons, though needless to say, its highly qualified skilled workers would find it easy to turn them into "real" rifles. If that alone was reason for vigilance by the authorities, it seemed all the more necessary as Schleusingen formed an exclave surrounded completely by Thuringian territory about 50 kilometers south of Erfurt: this would make it more difficult to control than other danger spots in case of unrest.[70]

Another special feature of the Erfurt administrative district was politically relevant. In the rural counties of Heiligenstadt (including the Eichsfeld) and Worbis, Catholics accounted for nine-tenths and three-quarters of the population, respectively, which guaranteed the Center Party the dominant position here until the end of the Weimar Republic, and nearly half of the population in the rural county of Mühlhausen. In the entire administrative district, however, their share was no greater than one-fifth, and in the other two administrative districts only around a tenth, which meant that the identity of the province as a whole was unquestionably Protestant.[71]

The province of Saxony had developed into a bastion of the workers' movement long before 1914. On the eve of the First World War, the Magdeburg SPD could look back upon a decades-long tradition. As early as 1884, a Social Democrat was elected to the Reichstag for the city. The long-term continuity of leadership by representatives of the right wing of the party (men like the future Reich Justice Minister Otto Landsberg), together with a high degree of union organization among the local industrial workforce, ensured that the Magdeburg SPD developed into a solid and well-organized bastion of the party's right wing. Between 1906 and 1914, membership in the SPD district of Magdeburg-Anhalt rose to nearly 38,000, an increase of nearly fivefold. In 1912, five of its eight electoral districts were represented in the Reichstag by Social Democrats.[72]

On the eve of the First World War, the SPD district of Halle could also look back upon its party work with much satisfaction. It had more than 26,000 members, nearly three times as many as in 1906. The party had three of the eight Reichstag seats after the 1912 election, two of which, for Halle and the Saalkreis and for Naumburg-Weißenfels-Zeitz, it had held since 1893. In Halle, which had the strongest organization in the district in terms of members, conditions were similar to Magdeburg: a large number of skilled workers, especially in the metal industry, and a high degree of union organization. In 1914, however, the local party was clearly on the left wing of the SPD, which was working for a revolution that would be triggered by a mass strike, and which was suspicious of any rapprochement with the bourgeois parties. Since 1905 there had been clashes in the district between the two wings of the party, from which the left—centered on the Reichstag delegates Kunert and Albrecht and the new editor-in-chief of the *Volksblatt,* Hennig—emerged the winners once and for all. As the holder of a Reichstag seat, Kunert had been exerting influence on the Halle party since the 1890s, while the moderate Adolf Thiele had been at the head of the *Volksblatt* until 1907, after which he withdrew to his electoral district of Naumburg-Weißenfels-Zeitz, which he had represented since the 1890s.[73] This configuration continued during the Weimar years, when the districts of Zeitz and Weißenfels—following the intermezzo of the USPD—remained Social Democratic bastions in a region otherwise dominated by the KPD. Thus long before the sociostructural conditions in the industrial region of central Germany underwent massive change, the stage in the Halle district had been set for the split of the party in the First World War and the rise of the KPD. But it was only the changes produced by wartime that imparted the real dynamic to this development.[74]

Since Erfurt was located in the Thuringian-Saxon land that gave birth to the SPD, it could also look back on a long party and union tradition in 1914. The local SPD had 2,500 members, and the unions had 10,000. In the northwestern part of the administrative district in the workers' villages around Nordhausen, the party was able to knit an especially dense network of precursor organizations, thus laying the foundation for a consistently strong position right up to the end of the Weimar Republic. The political position of the district could not be clearly determined, even if its long-term chairman, Paul Reißhaus, who simultaneously represented the electoral district of Saxony-Meiningen 2 in the *Reichstag,* was close to the left wing of the party.[75]

On the other side of the political spectrum, the three large bourgeois parties were about equal in strength, though with regionally distinct centers of gravity. In the district of Magdeburg, the field was headed by the National Liberals, who won just under a fifth of the votes in the first round of voting in the elections of 1912, followed directly by the Conservative Party, which was closely allied to the Bund der Landwirte (Farmers' League). In the district of Merseburg, on the other hand, the leading role clearly belonged to the left-leaning Liberals, who captured nearly a quarter of the ballots in the 1912 elections. A distant second was the other conservative party, the Reichspartei. In the district of Erfurt, the National Liberals lost their leading position in 1912 to the Conservative Party. There was hardly another Prussian province in which conservative and liberal parties were similarly more or less equally balanced, with the two conservative parties at 22.2 percent across the province, and the two liberal parties with exactly 25.0 percent.[76]

In spite of the pronounced political tensions in the authoritarian empire, whose leading strata saw themselves confronted by a Social Democratic movement that was steadily growing right up to 1912, confrontations between the two sides remained relatively free of violence. Beginning in 1906, the SPD, notwithstanding all official restrictions, used the public sphere of the street to articulate its demands in a previously unknown manner. It called for large gatherings on 21 January 1906 in many places throughout Prussia to protest the three-class suffrage system, which weighted the ballots of voters according to their tax returns and strongly disadvantaged workers. In anticipation of the large crowds that would be marching through the streets on this occasion, the authorities made provisions for a massive show of force. On instructions from the Prussian Minister of the Interior, the military kept handguns at the ready for the police and prepared to intervene itself; lists of party and union leaders who were to be arrested should the situation warrant it were compiled.[77]

What actually transpired on 21 January in the streets of the cities in the province of Saxony and other parts of Prussia was far removed from the horror scenario that the authorities had laid out. In Magdeburg, about 10,000 workers marched peacefully around the blocked-off central part of the city to the site of the meeting. Later, 200 of them tried to get to the center of town, though they were prevailed upon to turn around by police, who brandished—but did not use—their weapons. Halle offered a similar picture: mounted police "cleared" the street near the market and arrested thirty-four individuals, but here, too, there were no clashes. Reports from Erfurt spoke of complete calm at all the events.[78] When the SPD announced similar gatherings for March of the same year, Interior Minister Bethmann Hollweg considered precautionary measures by the police to be entirely sufficient.[79]

Even when the demonstrations reached their climax at the beginning of 1910 in the "suffrage storm," there were no incidents in Magdeburg.[80] Not so in Halle: on 13 February, following the end of several meetings, about 2,500 individuals—almost exclusively men, in contrast to previous demonstrations—congregated for an unauthorized march through the downtown. The police officers tried to stop and disperse them. When mounted officers advanced on the crowd from several sides, they were heckled as "bloodhounds" and then pelted with stones. Finally, the policemen drew their swords and moved against the demonstrators with few inhibitions; even uninvolved bystanders who were unable to escape quickly enough were brutally beaten. This day, which became known as "Bloody Sunday" in the collective memory of the workers' movement in Halle, resulted in: five slightly injured police officers, forty injured demonstrators, among them three with serious injuries, and eighty arrests.[81] The responsibility for what had happened lay largely with the police, whose response had been completely disproportionate. In part, however, the demonstrators themselves were also responsible, for their behavior was noticeably more aggressive than on previous occasions.

Anger at what had happened and with what was perceived to have been a departure from the previous conduct of the police was reflected in the editorial statement of the Halle *Volksblatt*. The actions of the police were described in detail and in harsh words—but the reason behind their deployment and the cause of what the commentator called the "outrageous bloodshed" were not mentioned. Anyone who had seen the "atrocities yesterday," the paper thundered, could not but "feel unquenchable hatred" and the "utmost contempt towards people who were willing to commit such outrages." But the following day the paper sounded a different tone and reaffirmed the party's fundamental position on the instrument of street demonstrations: equal suffrage would be won only if demonstrations were "calm and disciplined"; one's own discipline had to become "unshakable."[82] During new gatherings on voting rights at the beginning of March, the local party leadership made every effort to prevent clashes with the police under any circumstances.[83] Even if the leadership approved of the "street politics" of mass demonstrations as the first step toward a mass strike and ultimately revolution, it could not expect any benefit from violent confrontations with the police, notwithstanding the urgings of the party rank and file to pursue a more aggressive line.

The liberal press of the province, which set the tone in the middle-class public, took the street demonstrations of the Social Democrats as an occasion to demarcate very clearly what separated it from them. The left-liberal *Saale-Zeitung* referred explicitly to Berlin Police President Jagow, who was not known for his liberal attitudes, in noting in a commentary on the events of 13 February 1910 that it was "unwise and fundamentally wrong to carry politics into the street." Harsher still was the characterization of the actors at the demonstration by the National-Liberal *Magdeburgische Zeitung:* behind it all there stood, in the final analysis, the Social Democratic leaders, who were able to slip into the role of "inciters" and "agitators." Although the masses they directed comprised for the most part "very decent, conscientious, and hard-working men" (the women who also participated in the demonstration do not appear in this categorization), there was also a minority of "rowdies, toughs," and "anarchists," the very "riffraff" that the Social Democrats themselves should keep at arm's length.[84] True, the *Saale-Zeitung* had to acknowledge that "deeply regrettable missteps" had been made by the police in Halle. Yet some members of the bourgeoisie had been at the receiving end of the sword not purely by accident, but because they had watched as "idle gawkers" and had thus contributed to politicizing the street.[85]

Of course, not only was Social Democracy responsible for these kinds of disturbances, but it constituted a threat to the state, pure and simple. On this point, though, the accents in the papers deviated more strongly in line with their respective party-political sympathies. In the eyes of the *Magdeburgische Zeitung*, the SPD, which sought to deprive the citizens "of everything … that makes live worth living in the first place," simply stood for "subversion." The acknowledged discipline of the Social Democratic demonstrators was therefore not exactly a good sign, for it merely revealed the degree to which the party leadership controlled its followers.[86] By contrast, while the *Saale-Zeitung* denounced the SPD's "revolutionary phrases" and its unrealistic radicalism, it did believe that the party was fully capable of "positive participation" in the Reichstag.[87] Fear of the SPD thus had two components: the Social Democratic movement was dangerous, first because it challenged the state and society of the empire in principle, and second because it bore responsibility for what were directly experienced as disturbances of "peace and orderliness." After the war and the Revolution, the second point would come to dominate bourgeois criticism of the Communists, while the first provided the basis for it and in the end also defined the relationship to the SPD.

The relationship between the middle class and the Social Democrats was also influenced by labor struggles. At the end of September 1909, the workers in one shaft of the Mansfeld Combine walked off the job after management had fired a number of miners because of their party and union membership. To the surprise of the company management, the strike, led by the national chairman of the Social Democratic Miners Association, spread quickly and eventually involved more than half of the 21,000 workers of the combine, in which a strict "master-of-the-house" regiment had prevailed, and where a "yellow" work association had organized the most workers. The work stoppage had to be terminated on 13 November without any immediate success, though it did lead to a wave of new members for the party and the union and provided the impetus behind a reversal of the political majorities in the Mansfeld region. Although the conservative Reichspartei won the mandate in the 1912 elections, the SPD was able to force a second ballot and to nearly double its votes to just under 50 percent. The work stoppage itself was a largely peaceful affair, even though the Prussian military was in action alongside the police beginning on 22 October.[88] The strike leadership employed monitors chosen by the miners themselves in order to avoid clashes, and by and large it was successful in doing so. However, the day before the arrival of the military witnessed a clash when a group of "laborers willing to work" (*Arbeitswillige*) encountered a larger number of strikers who were returning home from a film showing; the strikebreakers were insulted, pelted with rocks and dirt, and punched. Twelve strikers were later put on trial for breach of the public peace, and despite the efforts of their prominent defense attorneys, the SPD politicians Landsberg and Heine, they were sentenced to prison terms ranging from six months to a year.[89]

The trial and its outcome expressed the dilemma in which the leadership of the SPD and the Free Unions, which were affiliated with the party, found themselves time and again. On the one hand, they tried, with a good deal of success, to emphasize the respectability of the workers' movement and to avoid violence against the authorities and other opponents like the strikebreakers as much as possible, that is, to pursue a "policy of peacefulness and lawfulness," as the *Volksstimme* put it in a commentary on the Ruhr miners' strike in 1912.[90] On the other hand, "small violence," the goal of which was not to inflict serious harm on the person targeted but to drive home the reprehensible nature of his wrongdoing, was part of the social culture of the lower classes. Beating strikebreakers was a common method in this repertoire of behavior, though it could occasionally lead to more serious violence.[91] An authoritarian state that used its security forces (and later its judicial system) to "protect those willing to work," without at the same time acting vigorously to make sure that a powerful company took seriously the right of association, which had long since been granted by law, was certainly not doing anything to contain this kind of violence "from below." The SPD, for its part, if it did not want to lose credibility, could not abandon those who vented their anger in such "small" violence, even as it did everything in its power to undercut their behavioral tradition in the long run. In so doing, however, it provided fodder to the hostile image in the bourgeois camp of a party that failed to distance itself clearly enough from the "rabble" (*Janhagel*).[92] Here was a potential for conflict that was covered up by the outbreak of the First World War, though by no means did it disappear.

"We are not jubilant, we know that, in spite of everything, a serious struggle awaits us, but the time of hesitation is over. Now the fatherland is calling. We all will follow."[93] These lines from the lead article of the *Saale-Zeitung*'s morning edition of 2 August 1914 convey a better sense of the general mood at the outbreak of war than does the conventional picture of overwhelming enthusiasm among the population. Although the further right–leaning *Magdeburgische Zeitung* saw a "storm wind of enthusiasm" blow through the city when the kaiser's mobilization order was made public on 1 August, it arose out of an atmosphere of "utmost tension" and was not able to sweep away the "fateful seriousness of these hours."[94] In the previous week, the paper had initially expressed the hope that the expected confrontation could be limited to the Balkans and pled for "calm composure" with which to face all other eventualities. Then, when the outbreak of the Great War was expected any hour, the paper noted that a "breath of relief" ran "through the doubts of the days and weeks."[95] To be sure, the enthusiasm that coursed through streets and squares on the day of mobilization—at least in the cities—was not invented, but neither was it the expression of a sustained mood that had slowly built up over the preceding four weeks; rather, it was above all the release of a tension that seemed to have become nearly unbearable by the end. It was "nervous unease,"[96] a mix of the most diverse emotions, that had been spreading in the weeks since the beginning of July—not exuberant patriotic enthusiasm.[97] Moreover, it was more likely the members of the bourgeoisie who were filled with this kind of elation. "Our heart knows nothing of a war enthusiasm," wrote the *Volksstimme* on 2 August, but if it was no longer possible to stop the calamity, and if one imagined what a victorious czarism would do in Germany, one could not refuse to join in. Yet the price for relenting was immediately stipulated and to the point: "A free German people that conquers its fatherland by defending its country."[98]

On 9 August, the *Magdeburgische Zeitung* looked back at the first week of war and noted with satisfaction: "Here a *Volk* rose up as *one* man … here every barrier that otherwise separates us disappeared … *a united* Volk *of brothers.*"[99] The evoked unity was the dominant motif in the articles and commentaries when war broke out. This unity was, notwithstanding all political differences, chiefly a unity of men, and the virtues assigned to it were primarily masculine. The "hardening of the ideal of manhood" since the turn of the century had carried the day for good.[100] However, determination and courage were demanded not only from soldiers on the front line, but also from those at home; the model was the uprising of 1813.[101]

As the war dragged on and a growing disillusionment set in about its consequences and the inability of the empire to reform itself, the unity of the SPD fractured. At the beginning of April 1917, its left wing split off and formed the Independent Social Democratic Party (USPD). The USPD refused to continue supporting the policy of the "truce" (*Burgfrieden*), the SPD's compromise course toward the leadership of both the Reich and the moderate bourgeois parties, and urged the immediate conclusion of a peace. In the province of Saxony, the split ran along the lines of conflict that had existed within the party before the war. While the USPD was able to win only insignificant influence in Magdeburg—even though Alwin Brandes, Reichstag delegate for Halberstadt and a leading member of the metal workers' association, joined the party at the beginning of 1918[102]—the district organization of Halle-Merseburg switched to the new party almost in its entirety in July 1917, with only twenty local organizations remaining with the old SPD (now called the Majority Social Democratic Party, MSPD). This was also important in that here, the new party had at its disposal a well-functioning organizational structure and the important newspapers, including the *Volksblatt.*

This move was prepared through the establishment of a network of trusted individuals in the large armament plants, in which the brothers Wilhelm and Bernhard Koenen had played an important part. In March of 1917, they set up the first Social Democratic factory-based organization at the Leuna Works, and a month later they brought it into the new party.[103] The balance of power within the Social Democratic movement was less clear-cut in the administrative district of Erfurt. In the city itself there was a two-thirds majority in favor of joining the USPD in May 1917, though the youth and educational activities continued to be run together with the MSPD. Although the editorial office of the *Tribüne* was now in the hands of the USPD, the MSPD was allowed to continue publishing reports of its meetings and announcements.[104] A similar picture emerged in Nordhausen, where the movement toward the USPD was even stronger, though the press organ also continued to be available also to the MSPD.[105]

The split within the party was also the result of the growing war-weariness on the part of the population, which manifested itself, especially after the "starvation winter" of 1916/17, in food unrests and strikes, and which undercut the basis of legitimacy of the political system of the empire to the point where the latter collapsed without any meaningful resistance in November 1918.[106] Women and youths, who could not be threatened with being dispatched to fight at the front, were prominent participants in food protests. These kinds of protests developed spontaneously. A "crowd" would gather in front of city halls or bakeries, officials were insulted and called upon to do something to improve the food situation, shop owners were harassed and compelled to sell food at reduced prices, and sometimes rocks were thrown through shop windows and goods hauled off without payment. Still, these disturbances were *not* marked by unbridled violence. It was also typical that no party-political demands were put forth and "ringleaders" could not be identified among the ranks of the radical left.[107] In this sense, the protests did not have a political character because they lacked the link to a specific political organization or a specific political program. Their long-term effects, however, were political. They made the authoritarian state that was no longer able to secure the material existence of its population the subject of public criticism. In so doing, they expressed a new conception of "nation" that had been taking shape since the beginning of the war, one that placed the class-transcending exertions and sufferings of the mobilized national community (*Volksgemeinschaft*) front and center, and demanded in return that the state provide certain services (of providing for their livelihood). The failure of the (authoritarian) state that was now defined increasingly as a welfare state stripped it of its political legitimacy.[108]

Much the same is true for strikes during the war, which increased sharply in number in 1917 and 1918. The wave of strikes in April 1917, triggered by the February revolution in Russia and the kaiser's half-hearted "Easter message," seems to have largely missed the province of Saxony, including the Leuna Works, where the influence of the radical left was already strongest.[109] However, the middle of August 1917 saw the first mass strikes since the beginning of the war at the Leuna Works, as well as in Halle and at other armament plants. Set off by the announcement of a cutback in food rations, they were able to force through some material demands like special food allotments.[110] The great wave of strikes at the end of January 1918 gripped the entire province. In Halle, the strikers were already drawing up lists of names for a workers' council.[111] In Magdeburg, where Alwin Brandes assumed the leadership, 23,000 workers walked off the job on 29 January; the following day, the MSPD and the union cartel got involved to slow the movement.[112] At the rifle factory in Erfurt, a part of the workforce under the leadership of supporters of the Spartacus League, the germ cell of the later KPD, went on strike, but here the MSPD and the USPD were able to keep the action from spreading.[113]

For the bourgeois public of the province, this development was for a long time no topic at all. The otherwise commentary-happy *Magdeburgische Zeitung* had only brief reports about the January strikes, while the *Saale-Zeitung*, in a lead article, criticized the MSPD's decision to join the Berlin strike committee as "politically unwise," though not so much because this move strengthened the radical forces of the left as because it provided ammunition to the right for its strategy of blocking domestic political reforms.[114] The primary concern had to be the preservation of domestic unity. But while the paper from Halle emphatically supported the reforms in the spirit of the left-liberals and backed the peace resolution of the Reichstag majority, the Magdeburg paper advocated a cautious reform course while—still confident of victory—rejecting a "peace of surrender (*Verzichtfrieden*)."[115] Both papers agreed, however, that the Germans must "not lose their nerve." "The people will keep its nerve, only let us take it like a nation of men, not like a nation of neurasthenics!" demanded the Magdeburg paper. Statements like these reflect the emphasis—further reinforced since the beginning of the war—of the political value of "masculinity," while at the same time mirroring the fears emanating from the "femaleness" of the subsistence protests.[116]

But when the *Magdeburgische Zeitung* gave voice, with enormous bitterness, to the realization in the middle of October that the war was lost, it set its sights not at this mental state of society, but at the political institutions of the empire. Never before had "such a great and brave people not only been left in the dark so irresponsibly, but also, through the abuse of the press from the prewar period until now, been misled about its place in the world."[117] Following the offer of truce from the German military leadership, which came as a complete surprise to the public, one must not nurse any more illusions, the paper declared. The war was lost, the Germans would have to pay its costs, and because of that "heavy burdens will weigh on our children and their future."[118] The responsibility lay first and foremost with those politicians who had spoken untruly during the war, and before the war had charted a course that was characterized by the "immense misperception of reality," the overestimation of German strength, and the false interpretation of the alliance system. Now the Germans were experiencing nothing less than the "collapse of our entire policy of illusion since Bismarck's dismissal." Even if part of the blame had to be assigned to Social Democracy—its stance on foreign policy had been too weak, its critique of the inner condition of the Empire sometimes too harsh[119]—the paper was by no means articulating a "stab-in-the-back legend"; instead, leaving aside all tactical considerations for the MSPD that it might have entertained in the first days of November, it was unambiguous in assessing the primary responsibility for Germany's collapse. The *Magdeburgische Zeitung*, the leading bourgeois press organ in the province of Saxony, had essentially given up on the empire once the inevitability of military defeat was obvious, and it clearly identified the consequences that would flow from this situation for the foreseeable future.

The lead articles and commentaries of the *Volksstimme* as of the beginning of October reflected the dilemma of the Majority Social Democrats. The party's goal was to democratize the empire in an evolutionary way, yet it had to take up the revolutionary sentiment among the masses and demand comprehensive as well as rapid domestic political reforms if it wanted to continue to play a leadership role.

In the process, it had to avoid being forced onto a radical track, for otherwise it would be playing into the hands of the USPD and the Spartacus League, and the result could be the kind of chaos that happened in Russia after the Bolshevik revolution. Thus the *Volksstimme* on 30 October called on the German people to now "make a clean sweep" of the guilty, "autocracy and class rule,"[120] and yet three days later, following the abdication of the kaiser and the crown prince, it still considered a representative monarchy a possibility. But then, on 8 November, the paper, having warned three days earlier—with an eye toward Berlin—about "hotheads," demanded: "Open the valves!" for "the revolution is sweeping across the land from Kiel." Of course, the paper wanted nothing to do with "Russian methods"—Germany "was not a Tartar state, but a European one."[121]

As for the *Magdeburgische Zeitung,* it believed that the only thing at stake at the end of October and the beginning of November was to preserve at least the foundations for a revival of Germany. The important thing was to remain "proud and undaunted," to preserve "the calm in the land" and stand side by side "in shared work." To that end, one must not impede Social Democracy if it turned against the radical left. But if the Majority Social Democrats did not prevail, one had to expect Russian conditions, with the "possibility of a civil war, a war of all against all with chaos as the backdrop."[122] It was only now that a domestic political enemy was coming to the fore, though not as a cause of the defeat, but a danger to the reconstruction.

When the Revolution actually came, the fears of the bourgeois press, like those in Germany in general, at first proved groundless. "The movement, which began suddenly, had quickly carried the day without running into opposition," noted Merseburg Regierungspräsident von Gersdorff on 14 November 1918, summarizing his impressions in the observation that the "sweeping change" had "occurred for the most part without notable unrests or excesses."[123] The same was true in the other two districts. The collapse of the old order took place everywhere in a similarly calm manner, regardless of the social and political developments that had preceded it locally.

Even in Halle, the strongest bastion of the USPD, the party had made no preparations for the Revolution. It was not workers who set things in motion, but soldiers of the air force reserve unit, who disarmed their officers on 7 November. The next day, a workers' and soldiers' council dominated by the USPD was set up and confirmed by a mass assembly. The chairmanship was assumed by the editor of the *Volksblatt,* Otto Kilian, a leading member of the left wing of the USPD and later of the KPD in the district. Although pressure was soon exerted on the bourgeois newspapers of the city, which went so far as individual censorship measures, beyond that the workers' and soldiers' council made no attempt until December to establish its own instrument of military power or interfere in the local administration in more than a merely supervisory capacity.[124] At the neighboring Leuna Works, the revolutionary movement grew out of gradually intensifying demands for higher wages, shorter hours, and a better supply of food, which were articulated by the full assembly of shop stewards (*Vertrauensmänner-Vollversammlung*) that was in permanent session beginning 3 November. The demands were presented to the managing board on 9 November in the form of an ultimatum; at the top of the list stood the call for an eight-hour day. Management quickly accepted. That same day, a workers' council was set up (which also included salaried employees) and elected an executive committee. The work of the committee ran along the lines of the previously formulated demands. The talks with management in the following days revolved around "clothing allowance, worker protection regulations, kitchen supervision, overtime," and similar demands, but of course also around the recognition of the Free Unions, which was now pushed through.[125] General political demands were not advanced, and not yet raised was the call for socialization, which would dominate the revolutionary movement in the central German industrial region as of the beginning of 1919. The workers' councils movement was comparatively well developed, though the focus of its activities was not the political system, but the factory.[126]

In Magdeburg, too, which was in the hands of the Majority Social Democrats, the Revolution was initiated by the military: on the morning of 8 November, sailors from Kiel prevailed upon the men of several artillery units to refuse to obey orders; afterward, the soldiers marched into the center of the city. A mass assembly, at which representatives from the MSDP and the USPD spoke, agreed to form a workers' and soldiers' council. From the very beginning its members also included a number of white-collar workers, civil servants, and representatives of the bourgeois parties. On 11 November, a "burghers' council" (*Bürgerrat*) was added with the consent of all the parties. In Magdeburg as well, the workers' and soldiers' council limited itself to supervising the bureaucracy. The USPD council member Albert Vater, later one of the co-founders of the local KPD, was assigned to the police president, and the city delegate and future SPD Lord Mayor Beims was assigned to the municipal authorities.[127] In the Erfurt workers' and soldiers' council, representatives of the right wing of the USPD were in charge along with the MSPD and also charted a moderate course.[128]

Things remained quiet during the November days on the great estates in the province of Saxony. The revolutionary movement barely took hold of the rural workers, whose Social Democratic Deutscher Landarbeiterverband (DLV, German Rural Workers' League) had only limited influence. Workers' and soldiers' councils were initially set up in county cities and smaller towns that were also home to large numbers of industrial workers, as for example in the Mansfeld Gebirgskreis. In addition to supervising the bureaucracy, their chief concern here was a secure food supply, which is why the council in Nordhausen, for example, took pains to maintain close contact to the farmers in the county. Although the Landrat in Eisleben, the center of the Mansfeld Seekreis, noted the existence of "strong differences of opinions between the independents and the governing socialists (!)," both parties were promoting "peace and order in every way," and in the workers' and soldiers' council they had agreed on an appeal directed at all communities that also called "for protection of property and obedience toward the authorities."[129] Councils of farmers and rural laborers were slow to form. The initiative came from estate owners and from associations of rural workers that denounced strikes and sought to establish a counterweight to the workers' and soldiers' councils, which were dominated by the Socialist parties. In the process, the large landowners behaved in a fairly flexible fashion. As early as the middle of December 1918 they recognized the DLV as a partner in wage negotiations and agreed upon regulations that later became part of the labor regulations for all of Germany in January of 1919. The position of the organized rural workers was thus noticeably strengthened, though it still lagged far behind that of the industrial workers.[130]

Although the collapse of the old system in the November days of 1918 did not take place without violence, it was not the kind of harsh and costly violence that pervaded later confrontations. If there was violence, it was directed—as often in later years—primarily against symbols. Shoulder straps were torn from the uniforms of officers and their swords taken away—that covered most cases in which force was used.[131] The point was to dismantle the military hierarchy at least momentarily and thereby symbolically abolish the social order of the fallen empire, which found its most memorable expression in the red banners newly hoisted over city halls or factories. However, in the November days there was neither organized resistance to the revolutionary movement nor any attempt on the part of the revolutionaries to set up their own instruments of military power.[132] The first new security organ reported in the sources was a "citizens' militia" (*Bürgerwehr*) of 300–400 men set up by the Magdeburg workers' and soldiers' council (which by now had been joined by a council of officers alongside the council of citizens).[133]

The language with which the mouthpiece of the USPD, the *Volksblatt* in Halle, praised and defended the Revolution was, though harsh, still very different from the later civil war rhetoric of the KPD. A few days after the formation of the workers' and soldiers' council, the paper emphasized that the issue now was "to nip all assaults upon the achievements of the Revolution in the bud! Ruthlessly!" At the same time, it reproached the Prussian Conservative Party for using the threat of "civil war," while the Liberals were judged to be balanced and fair.[134] Once the Revolution was secure, democracy would exist "also for our harshest opponents!" but should they choose a different path, "they are playing with fire," the paper declared at the end of November.[135] The harsh tone in such declarations of willingness to fight, especially if it was combined with censorship measures by the workers' and soldiers' council, certainly did not help allay the fears in the bourgeois camp. However, this rhetoric was not backed by any potential threat of military force, nor was there any call to establish such a force.

The anxieties that were articulated within the bourgeois public were therefore far more varied than the argument of the fear of Bolshevism suggests. They were initially fed by incidents like the freeing of inmates from the military jail in Halberstadt, who then used force to procure foodstuffs from a sausage factory, or the refusal of peasants to live up to their delivery obligations—"it is now Revolution, they say, and one does not have to make any more deliveries."[136] These kinds of behaviors did not have a thrust that could be identified with any particular party politics. Still, they seemed to indicate profound threats to the general order, especially a further intensification of the conflict—stoked by the command economy and inflation—between rural producers and urban consumers.[137]

The *Magdeburgische Zeitung* picked up on this when it warned that an excessively radical course of the Revolution, by sparking resistance in the countryside, would give rise first "to economic conditions of a Russian nature" and then related political conditions, which would be followed, finally, by a "period of the harshest reaction"—though the paper hoped that the German people would be spared such "dishonor, shame, and misery." This was the often invoked and highly emotionally charged fear of chaos that was shared by the Social Democratic *Volksstimme* and expressed itself, for example, in that paper's warning that a hasty socialization of mining and industry would mean "chaos … famine, revolts, civil war, and economic anarchy."[138] Of course, the model of how the Revolution would unfold was based not only on contemporary events in Russia, but also on the French Revolution, and it was—as the reference to the danger of "reaction" showed—therefore based on a liberal foundation.[139] One aspect from the prewar period that returned in the argumentation of the *Magdeburgische Zeitung* was the notion of an easily swayed "mass" and its leaders who therefore had to be made all the more aware of their responsibility to save their followers from radical "excesses," especially in the face of a "national body (*Volkskörper*)" as economically and socially complex as the German one.[140] The mass-leader argument and the concept of the *Volkskörper* were subsequently picked up by the bourgeois press time and again, with increasingly anti-liberal connotations.

Notes

1. Emil Lederer, "Soziologie der Gewalt: Ein Beitrag zur Theorie der gesellschaftsbildenden Kräfte," in E. Lederer, ed., *Soziologische Probleme der Gegenwart,* (Berlin, 1921), 16–29, here 16.
2. Recent introductions: Eric D. Weitz, *Weimar Germany: Promise and Tragedy* (Princeton, 2007); Eberhard Kolb, *The Weimar Republic*, trans. P. S. Falla, 2nd ed. (New York, 2004); Detlev J. K. Peukert, *Die Weimarer Republik: Krisenjahre der klassischen Moderne* (Frankfurt, 1987), English edition, *The Weimar Republic: The Crisis of Classical Modernity,* trans. Richard Deveson (New York, 1992); see also Ian Kershaw, ed., *Weimar: Why Did German Democracy Fail?* (New York, 1990).
3. See, for example, Richard J. Bessel, *Germany after the First World War* (Oxford, 1993); Martin H. Geyer, *Verkehrte Welt: Revolution, Inflation und Moderne. München 1914–1924* (Göttingen, 1998); Bernd Widdig, *Culture and Inflation in Weimar Germany* (Berkeley, 2001); Janet Ward, *Weimar Surfaces: Urban Visual Culture in 1920s Germany* (Berkeley, 2001); Julia Sneeringer, *Winning Women's Votes: Propaganda and Politics in Weimar Germany* (Chapel Hill, NC, 2002).
4. Johannes Erger, *Der Kapp-Lüttwitz-Putsch* (Düsseldorf, 1967); Erhard Lucas, *Märzrevolution im Ruhrgebiet: Vom Generalstreik gegen den Militärputsch zum bewaffneten Arbeiteraufstand*

März–April 1920, 3 vols. (Frankfurt a. M., 1970–78); Johannes Gorlas and Detlef J. K. Peukert, eds., *Ruhrkampf 1920* (Essen, 1986); Erwin Könnemann and Hans-Joachim Krusch, *Aktionseinheit contra Kapp-Putsch: Der Kapp-Putsch im März 1920 und der Kampf der deutschen Arbeiterklasse sowie anderer Werktätiger gegen die Errichtung der Militärdiktatur und für demokratische Verhältnisse* (East Berlin, 1972); Sigrid Koch-Baumgarten, *Aufstand der Avantgarde: Die Märzaktion der KPD 1921* (Frankfurt, 1986); Stefan Weber, *Ein kommunistischer Putsch? Märzaktion 1921 in Mitteldeutschland* (Berlin, 1991); Martin Sabrow, *Der Rathenaumord: Rekonstruktion einer Verschwörung gegen die Republik von Weimar* (Munich, 1994); Harold J. Gordon, *Hitler and the Beer Hall Putsch* (Princeton, N.J., 1972); Thomas Kurz, *Blutmai: Sozialdemokraten und Kommunisten im Brennpunkt der Berliner Ereignisse von 1929* (Berlin, 1988); Richard Bessel, "The Potempa Murder," *CEH* 10, no. 3 (1977): 241–254.

5. Robert G. L. Waite, *Vanguard of Nazism: The Free Corps Movement in Postwar Germany* (Cambridge, MA, 1952); Hagen Schulze, *Freikorps und Republik 1918–1920* (Boppard, 1969); Erwin Könnemann, *Einwohnerwehren und Zeitfreiwilligenverbände: Ihre Funktion beim Aufbau eines neuen imperialistischen Militärsystems (November 1918 bis 1920)* (East Berlin, 1971); David Clay Large, *The Politics of Law and Order: A History of the Bavarian Einwohnerwehr, 1918–1921* (Philadelphia, 1980); Volker Berghahn, *Der Stahlhelm: Bund der Frontsoldaten 1918–1935* (Düsseldorf, 1966); Alois Klotzbücher, "Der politische Weg des Stahlhelm, Bund der Frontsoldaten, in der Weimarer Republik: Ein Beitrag zur Geschichte der 'Nationalen Opposition' 1918–1933," PhD diss., University of Erlangen-Nuremberg, 1964; Klaus Hornung, *Der Jungdeutsche Orden* (Düsseldorf, 1958); Kurt Finker, "Die militaristischen Wehrverbände der Weimarer Republik und ihre Rolle bei der Unterdrückung der Arbeiterklasse und bei der Vorbereitung eines neuen imperialistischen Krieges (1924–1929)," habilitation thesis, PH Potsdam, 1964; Karl Rohe, *Das Reichsbanner Schwazr-Rot-Gold: Ein Beitrag zur Geschichte und Struktur der politischen Kampfverbände zur Zeit der Weimarer Republik* (Düsseldorf, 1966); Kurt G. P. Schuster, *Der Rote Frontkämpferbund 1924–1929: Beiträge zur Geschichte und Organisationsstruktur eines politischen Kampfbundes* (Düsseldorf, 1975). Only the most important works are listed here and in the following footnotes.
6. James M. Diehl, *Paramilitary Politics in Weimar Germany* (Bloomington, IN, 1977). So far, the history of the police in the Weimar Republic has also been written primarily as an institutional history. The existing studies emphasize the continuity in terms of personnel and ideology with the imperial army, stress the orientation of police training along military lines, and point to the crumbling of the esprit de corps and the growing right-wing orientation of policemen since the beginning of the economic crisis: Peter Leßmann, *Die preußische Schutzpolizei in der Weimarer Republik: Streifendienst und Straßenkampf* (Düsseldorf, 1989); Richard Bessel, "Militarisierung und Modernisierung: Polizeiliches Handeln in der Weimarer Republik," in A. Lüdtke, ed., *'Sicherheit' und 'Wohlfahrt': Polizei, Gesellschaft und Herrschaft im 19. und 20. Jahrhundert* (Frankfurt a. M., 1992), 323–343; see also Johannes Buder, *Die Reorganisation der preußischen Polizei 1918–1923* (Frankfurt, 1986); Jürgen Siggemann, *Die kasernierte Polizei und das Problem der inneren Sicherheit in der Weimarer Republik: Eine Studie zum Auf- und Ausbau des innerstaatlichen Sicherheitssystems in Deutschland 1918/19–1933* (Frankfurt, 1980); His-Huey Liang, *Die Berliner Polizei in der Weimarer Republik* (Berlin, 1977); completely inadequate: Johannes Schwarze, *Die bayerische Polizei und ihre historische Funktion bei der Aufrechterhaltung der öffentlichen Sicherheit in Bayern von 1919–1933* (Munich, 1977).
7. Richard Bessel, *Political Violence and the Rise of Nazism: The Storm Troopers in Eastern Germany, 1925–1934* (New York, 1984); Sven Reichardt, *Faschistische Kampfbünde: Gewalt und Gemeinschaft im italienischen Squadrismus und in der deutschen SA* (Cologne, 2002).
8. Peter H. Merkl, *The Making of a Stormtrooper* (Princeton, N.J., 1980); idem, *Political Violence under the Swastika: 581 Early Nazis* (Princeton, N.J., 1975) (Merkl's work is based on a problematic source: a collection, compiled after 1933, of the biographies of Nazi activists who had joined the movement before September 1930); Conan Fischer, *Stormtroopers: A Social, Economic and Ideological Analysis, 1929–1935* (London, 1983), is an unpersuasive attempt to

demonstrate that the SA had a particularly high ratio of workers; as a synthesis see Peter Longerich, *Die braunen Bataillone: Geschichte der SA* (Munich, 1989). Schematic in nature is the approach of Hans-Joachim Mauch, *Nationalistische Wehrorganisation in der Weimarer Republik: Zur Entwicklung und Ideologie des "Paramilitarismus"* (Frankfurt, 1982), who, with reference to Geiger, Freud, and Adorno, argues that the reason why the right-wing Combat Leagues attracted so many followers lies in the "authoritarian character" of the panic-stricken members of the middle class.

9. Eve Rosenhaft, *Beating the Fascists? The German Communists and Political Violence, 1929–1933* (London, 1983); idem, "Links gleich rechts? Militante Straßengewalt um 1930," in T. Lindenberger and A. Lüdtke, eds., *Physische Gewalt: Studien zur Geschichte der Neuzeit* (Frankfurt, 1995), 238–275. Hans-Ulrich Ludewig, *Arbeiterbewegung und Aufstand: Eine Untersuchung zum Verhalten der Arbeiterparteien in den Aufstandsbewegungen der frühen Weimarer Republik 1920–1923* (Husum, 1978), sees in economic and social conditions an explanatory factor of only limited reach and points to genuinely political causes. The quantifying counterpart, as it were, to Ludewig's study, which is based on arguments drawn from the history of ideas, is Gerhard Botz, *Gewalt in der Politik: Attentate, Zusammenstöße, Putschversuche, Unruhen in Österreich 1918 bis 1938,* 2nd ed. (Munich, 1983); according to Botz, unemployment provides the key to explaining the violence.
10. Pamela E. Swett, *Neighbors and Enemies: The Culture of Radicalism in Berlin, 1929–1933* (Cambridge, 2004).
11. Ernst Nolte, *Der europäische Bürgerkrieg 1917–1945: Nationalsozialismus und Bolschewismus* (Berlin, 1987). Dissertations written under Nolte's supervision have illustrated his basic thesis with additional material, but have not developed it further: Christian Striefler, *Kampf um die Macht: Kommunisten und Nationalsozialisten am Ende der Weimarer Republik* (Berlin, 1993); Kai-Uwe Merz, *Das Schreckbild: Deutschland und der Bolschewismus 1917 bis 1921* (Berlin, 1995).
12. Andreas Wirsching, *Vom Weltkrieg zum Bürgerkrieg? Politischer Extremismus in Deutschland und Frankreich 1918–1933/39: Berlin und Paris im Vergleich* (Munich, 1999).
13. On the brutalization thesis see, for example, Eric J. Hobsbawm, *The Age of Extremes: A History of the World, 1914–1991* (New York, 1994), 125, who calls the First World War a "machine for brutalizing the world" but then proceeds to partly retract his sweeping thesis by noting that only a minority of radical right-wing supporters in Germany and elsewhere "gloried in the release of their latent brutality"; George L. Mosse, *Fallen Soldiers: Reshaping the Memory of the World Wars* (Oxford, 1990), esp. chap. 8; Hans Mommsen, "Militär und zivile Militarisierung in Deutschland 1914 bis 1938," in U. Frevert, ed., *Militär und Gesellschaft im 19. und 20. Jahrhundert* (Stuttgart, 1997), 265–276; Wirsching, *Weltkrieg,* 546; Eric D. Weitz, *Creating German Communism, 1890–1990: From Popular Protests to Socialist State* (Princeton, 1997), 135, 200; Klaus-Michael Mallmann, *Kommunisten in der Weimarer Republik: Sozialgeschichte einer revolutionären Bewegung* (Darmstadt, 1996), 109f.; Reichardt, *Kampfbünde,* 616.
14. See Dirk Schumann, "Europa, der Erste Weltkrieg und die Nachkriegszeit: Eine Kontinuität der Gewalt?" *Journal of Modern European History* 1, no. 1 (2003): 24–43, as well as the other contributions to this volume; also, Benjamin Ziemann, *Front und Heimat: Ländliche Kriegserfahrungen im südlichen Bayern 1914–1923* (Essen, 1997); see also Joanna Bourke, *Dismembering the Male: Men's Bodies, Britain, and the Great War* (Chicago, 1996). Bernd Weisbrod, "Gewalt in der Politik: Zur politischen Kultur in Deutschland zwischen den beiden Weltkriegen," *GWU* 43, no. 6 (1992): 391–404, places the accent on the interpretation processes after the war.
15. On the problems of definition see the detailed overview by Ekkart Zimmermann, *Political Violence, Crises, and Revolutions: Theories and Research* (Cambridge, MA, 1983), 6–15.
16. Thomas Lindenberger and Alf Lüdtke, eds., *Physische Gewalt: Studien zur Geschichte der Neuzeit* (Frankfurt, 1995); Trutz von Trotha, ed., *Soziologie der Gewalt* (Cologne, 1997); Wolfgang Sofsky, *Traktat über die Gewalt* (Frankfurt, 1996), English edition, *Violence: Terrorism, Genocide, War,* trans. Anthea Bell (London, 2003); on the historical study of violence in general see

Dirk Schumann, "Gewalt als Grenzüberschreitung: Überlegungen zur Sozialgeschichte der Gewalt im 19. und 20. Jahrhundert," *AfS* 37 (1997): 366–386.

17. Johan Galtung, *Strukturelle Gewalt: Beiträge zur Friedens- und Konfliktforschung* (Reinbek, 1975), here 9 and 12. Examples for the influence of Galtung's concept: Jörg Calließ, ed., *Gewalt in der Geschichte: Beiträge zur Friedenserziehung* (Düsseldorf, 1983); Udo Rauchfleisch, *Allgegenwart der Gewalt* (Göttingen, 1992).
18. For an overview with additional references: Wolf Dieter Narr, "Gewalt und Legitimität," *Leviathan* 1, no. 1 (1973): 7–42, reprinted in O. Rammstedt, ed., *Gewaltverhältnisse und die Ohnmacht der Kritik* (Frankfurt, 1974), 9–58; Terry Nardin, "Conflicting Conceptions of Political Violence," in C. P. Cotter, ed., *Political Science Annual: An International Review*, vol. 4 (Indianapolis, IN, 1973), 75–126, esp. 106–110; Friedhelm Neidhardt, "Gewalt: Soziale Bedeutungen und sozialwissenschaftliche Bestimmung des Begriffs," in Bundeskriminalamt, ed., *Was ist Gewalt?* vol. 1 (Wiesbaden, 1986), 109–147, esp. 128–131; Botz, *Gewalt in der Politik,* 13f.
19. See the list of the functions of political violence in Harold L. Nieburg, *Political Violence: The Behavioral Process* (New York, 1969), 14.
20. Belinda J. Davis, *Home Fires Burning: Food, Politics, and Everyday Life in World War I Berlin* (Chapel Hill, NC, 2000); on the concept of "street politics" see Manfred Gailus, *Straße und Brot: Sozialer Protest in den deutschen Staaten unter besonderer Berücksichtigung Preußens, 1847–1849* (Göttingen, 1990); Thomas Lindenberger, *Straßenpolitik: Zur Sozialgeschichte der öffentlichen Ordnung in Berlin 1900 bis 1914* (Bonn, 1995). Both are guided by the concept of *Eigensinn*, which Alf Lüdtke has developed (John Eidson has defined *Eigensinn* as "putting up with political power to the degree that one must, while pursuing one's own ends to the degree that one can"). Nieburg, *Political Violence,* 13, defines political violence in this kind of overly broad sense as "acts of disruption, destruction, injury whose purpose, choice of targets or victims, surrounding circumstances, implementation, and/or effects have political significance, that is, tend to modify the behavior of others in a bargaining situation that has consequences for the social system." For a critique see Zimmermann, *Political Violence,* 8.
21. The use of this word reflects the tendency of recent research into protest, following criticism of the vagueness of the concept of "social protest," to focus on acts of protest in connection with satisfying one's basic material needs, though in the process to increasingly include also the twentieth century. See Karin Hausen, "Schwierigkeiten mit dem 'sozialen Protest': Kritische Anmerkungen zu einem historischen Forschungsansatz," *GG* 3, no. 2 (1977): 257–263; Heinrich Volkmann and Jürgen Bergmann, eds., *Sozialer Protest: Studien zu traditioneller Resistenz und kollektiver Gewalt in Deutschland vom Vormärz bis zur Reichsgründung* (Opladen, 1980); Manfred Gailus and Heinrich Volkmann, ed., *Der Kampf um das tägliche Brot: Nahrungsmangel, Versorgungspolitik und Protest 1770–1990* (Opladen, 1994).
22. Ted Robert Gurr, drawing on older efforts, distinguished only three types (turmoil, conspiracy, internal war); Botz created a schema that is less clear-cut and uses new forms. Both use as their basic criteria only the degree of organization, the number of individuals involved, and the duration. While Gurr's definitions remain qualitative, Botz draws the lines when it comes to those involved at 10, 500, and more than 500. Apart from the fact that the sources rarely provide such specific information, a persuasive justification for these kinds of determinations is not apparent: Ted Robert Gurr, *Why Men Rebel* (Princeton, 1970), 11; Botz, *Gewalt in der Politik,* 14f.
23. Lindenberger and Lüdtke, *Physische Gewalt,* 22–27, also speak of "small" violence, though they relate the concept primarily to everyday violent practices such as slapping within the family or in closed institutions.
24. For a useful overview see Harry Eckstein, "Theoretical Approaches to Explaining Collective Political Violence," in T. R. Gurr, ed., *Handbook of Political Conflict* (New York, 1980), 135–166. The discussion has become too vast to keep track of: see Zimmermann, *Violence,* whose bibliography lists about 3,000 titles.

25. Gurr, *Why Men Rebel,* 12–25, 46–56, 105–109. See Zimmermann, *Violence*, 37–71. Needless to say, my brief remarks can only sketch the complexity of Gurr's concept. In the subsequent empirical study of the model, the mediating factors were moved into the foreground, though this did not lead to the presentation of a new concept. See Zimmermann, *Violence,* 48–50; Eckstein, "Theoretical Approaches," 160f.
26. Charles Tilly, Louise Tilly, and Richard Tilly, *The Rebellious Century, 1830–1930* (Cambridge, MA, 1975); Charles Tilly, *From Mobilization to Revolution* (Reading, MA, 1978); idem, "Review of Ted Robert Gurr, *Why Men Rebel,*" *Journal of Social History* 4, no. 4 (1971): 416–420. See Eckstein, "Theoretical Approaches," 147–149, on related approaches.
27. Tilly, Tilly, and Tilly, *Rebellious Century,* 239–244, 285–287; Tilly, *Mobilization,* 16–51, 172–188.
28. Tilly, *Mobilization,* 62–84. See Zimmermann, *Violence,* 424. As "organization" Tilly defines the strength of shared convictions, the strictness of the demarcation against the outside world, and the network of relationships between the members of an organized group (with no requirement that formal structures and institutions must have been created in the process); "mobilization" is the availability and usability of various resources, which in turn depend on the maintenance of group coherence. As further factors of importance to collective action, Tilly lists common interests within group and the external conditions ("opportunities"), which are above all the product of a particular political system. Tilly, *Mobilization,* 7f., 52–62, 98–142. Tilly's approach was developed further by Sidney Tarrow, *Power in Movement: Social Movements, Collective Action, and Politics* (New York, 1994), who also works with the concept of "protest cycle." See Erich Weede and Edward N. Muller, "Rationalität, Repression und Gewalt," *KZfSS* 42, no. 2 (1990): 232–247, who in a comparative study on the basis of international data from the 1970s support Tilly's thesis that a moderate level of repression is responsible for an especially high level of political violence, while indicators of "relative deprivation," such a low life expectancy and a low GDP, reveal no significant correlation with political violence.
29. Fruitful attempts at linking cultural and social history can be found in the work of William H. Sewell: see his essay "The Concept of Culture" in V. E. Bonnell and L. Hunt, eds., *Beyond the Cultural Turn: New Directions in the Study of Society and Culture* (Berkeley, 1999), 35–60; on the discussion in Germany in general see Thomas Mergel and Thomas Welskopp, eds., *Geschichte zwischen Kultur und Gesellschaft: Beiträge zur Theoriedebatte* (Munich, 1997); Ute Daniel, *Kompendium Kulturgeschichte: Theorien, Praxis, Schlüsselwörter* (Frankfurt, 2001).
30. The best introduction is by Wolf M. Iwand, *Paradigma Politische Kultur: Konzepte, Methoden, Ergebnisse der Political-Culture Forschung in der Bundesrepublik. Ein Forschungsbericht* (Opladen, 1985); see Dirk Berg-Schlosser and Jakob Schissler, eds., *Politische Kultur in Deutschland: Bilanz und Perspektiven der Forschung* (Opladen, 1987), with important contributions by Almond, Rohe, and the editors. See also the informative though in the final analysis unsatisfying outline of the problem by Carola Lipp, "Politische Kultur oder das Politische und Gesellschaftliche in der Kultur," in W. Hardtwig and H.-U. Wehler, eds., *Kulturgeschichte heute* (Göttingen, 1996), 78–110. For criticism of this concept by political scientists who fault its flexibility—which is helpful to historians—as a lack of clarity, see especially Max Kaase, "Sinn oder Unsinn des Konzepts Politische Kultur für die vergleichende Politikforschung, oder auch: Der Versuch, einen Pudding an die Wand zu nageln," in M. Kaase and H. D. Klingmann, eds., *Wahlen und Politisches System: Analysen aus Anlaß der Bundestagswahl 1980* (Opladen, 1983), 144–172; David J. Elkins and Richard E. B. Simeon, "A Cause in Search of Its Effect, or What Does Political Culture Explain?" *Comparative Politics* 11, no. 2 (1979): 127–145.
31. Karl Rohe, "Politische Kultur und der kulturelle Aspekt von politischer Wirklichkeit: Konzeptionelle und typologische Überlegungen zu Gegenstand und Fragestellung Politischer Kulturforschung," in Berg-Schlosser and Schissler, *Politische Kultur,* 39–48; idem, "Politische Kultur und ihre Analyse: Probleme und Perspektiven der politischen Kulturforschung," *HZ* 250 (1990): 321–346; idem, *Wahlen und Wählertraditionen in Deutschland: Kulturelle Grundlagen deutscher Parteien und Parteiensysteme im 19. und 20. Jahrhundert* (Frankfurt, 1992), 9–18,

19–29; see also his "Regionalkultur, regionale Identität und Regionalismus im Ruhrgebiet," in W. Lipp, ed., *Industriegesellschaft und Regionalkultur* (Munich, 1984), 123–154.

32. Rohe, "Kulturelle Aspekt," 42f. Political culture "consists, for one, of those things that are undiscussed and self-evident, which mark the latent or dormant part of political culture; at the same time, however, it also consists of cultural discussions that challenge precisely these self-evident realities and make up the manifest realm, as it were, of political culture" (42).
33. This also picks up on the reflections by Thomas Childers, "The Social Language of Politics in Germany: The Sociology of Political Discourse in the Weimar Republic," *AHR* 95, no. 2 (1990): 331–358. What I am concerned with here are the fundamental elements of everyday political language. It would therefore be inappropriate to concentrate on the thought world of individual intellectuals.
34. For an introduction into the male-specific aspects of gender history see Thomas Kühne, ed., *Männergeschichte – Geschlechtergeschichte: Männlichkeit im Wandel der Moderne* (Frankfurt, 1996).
35. This was the narrow approach of a Berlin project on the political culture of the Weimar Republic: Detlef Lehnert and Klaus Megerle, eds., *Politische Identität und nationale Gedenktage: Zur politischen Kultur in der Weimarer Republik* (Opladen, 1984); idem, *Politische Teilkulturen zwischen Integration und Polariesierung: Zur politischen Kultur in der Weimarer Republik* (Opladen, 1990); Dietmar Schirmer, *Mythos-Heilshoffnung-Modernität: Politisch-kulturelle Deutungscodes in der Weimarer Republik* (Opladen, 1992).
36. This is the tendency in the otherwise very stimulating study by Rohe's student Andreas Dörner, *Politischer Mythos und symbolische Politik: Der Hermannmythos. Zur Entstehung des Nationalbewußtseins der Deutschen* (Reinbek, 1996). The more recent theoretical discussion about the meaning of cultural history as a supplement to social history or as a competing approach, as well as the more specific question about the role that discourses should play in it, cannot be pursued further here. See Wolfgang Hardtwig and Hans-Ulrich Wehler, eds., *Kulturgeschichte heute* (Göttingen, 1996); Mergel and Welskopp, *Geschichte.* Incidentally, it would be a rewarding undertaking to examine the discourses on violence in the Weimar Republic in the pertinent disciplines such as criminology, sociology, or psychology.
37. This is the starting hypothesis of Lehnert and Megerle, *Teilkulturen.*
38. Fundamental to the political milieus is still M. Rainer Lepsius, "Parteiensystem und Sozialstruktur: Zum Problem der Demokratisierung der deutschen Gesellschaft," in M. R. Lepsius, *Demokratie in Deutschland: Soziologisch-historische Konstellationsanalysen. Ausgewählte Aufsätze* (Göttingen, 1993 [1966]), 25–50.
39. Jürgen W. Falter, *Hitlers Wähler* (Munich, 1991).
40. For a summary of the dicussion about political milieus and the counter-model of "camps" see Rohe, *Wahlen.* For a recent monograph see Siegfried Weichlein, *Sozialmilieus und politische Kultur in der Weimarer Republik: Lebenswelt, Vereinskultur, Politik in Hessen* (Göttingen, 1996); however, political culture in the sense I have just discussed is dealt with only marginally. The better studies of political milieus have examined above all the most clearly demarcated Catholic milieu; see, for example, Doris Kaufmann, *Katholisches Milieu in Münster 1928–1933: Politische Aktionsformen and geschlechtsspezifische Verhaltensräume* (Düsseldorf, 1984); Cornelia Rauh-Kühne, *Katholisches Milieu und Kleinstadtgesellschaft: Ettlingen 1918–1939* (Sigmaringen, 1991); Oded Heilbronner, *Catholicism, Political Culture, and the Countryside: A Social History of the Nazi Party in South Germany* (Ann Arbor, 1998). The study of the bourgeois camp or bourgeois milieu is getting off the ground only slowly. See, for example, Peter Fritzsche, *Rehearsals for Fascism: Populism and Political Mobilization in Weimar Germany* (New York, 1990); Rudy Koshar, *Social Life, Local Politics, and Nazism: Bourgeois Marburg 1880–1935* (Chapel Hill, NC, 1986); Helge Matthiesen, *Bürgertum und Nationalsozialismus in Thüringen: Das bürgerliche Gotha von 1918 bis 1930* (Jena, 1994).
41. Karl-Heinz Leidigkeit and Jürgen Herrmann, *Auf leninistischem Kurs: Geschichte der KPD-Bezirksorganisation Halle-Merseburg bis 1933* (Halle, 1979); Eberhard Schultz, "Rolle und

Anteil des linken Flügels der USPD im ehemaligen Regierungsbezirk Halle-Merseburg bei der Herausbildung und Entwicklung der KPD zur revolutionären Massenpartei (1917–1920)," PhD diss., University of Halle, 1969; Helga Schubert, "Der mitteldeutsche Generalstreik 1919," PhD diss., University of Leipzig, 1963; Willi Tonn, "Der Kampf der KPD um die Aktionseinheit der Arbeiterklasse im Bezirk Merseburg in den Jahren 1921–1923," PhD diss. (A), Martin Luther University, Halle-Wittenberg, 1973; Wilhelm Vogler, "Probleme des Klassenkampfes zwischen den Landarbeitern und Gutsbesitzern im Regierungsbezirk Merseburg (1918–1923)," PhD diss. (A), Martin Luther University, Halle-Wittenberg, 1973; Willibald Gutsche, *Die revolutionäre Bewegung in Erfurt während des 1. imperialistischen Weltkrieges und der Novemberrevolution* (Erfurt, 1963).

42. Joachim Schunke, *Schlacht um Halle* (East Berlin, 1956), on the battles in March of 1920; *Die Märzkämpfe 1921,* ed. Marx-Engels-Lenin-Stalin Institut (East Berlin, 1956); S. Weber, *Ein kommunistischer Putsch?* (based on a work from the period before 1989); *Kämpfendes Leuna: Die Geschichte des Kampfes der Leuna-Arbeiter,* Part I, vol. 1 (1916–1933) (East Berlin, 1961); Werner Imig, *Streik bei Mansfeld 1930: Der Streik der Mansfeld-Arbeiter im Jahre 1930 und seine Unterdrückung mit Hilfe des Staatsapparates der Weimarer Republik* (East Berlin, 1958); Karl Lärmer, *Vom Arbeitszwang zur Zwangsarbeit: Die Arbeitsordnung im Mansfelder Kupferschieferbergbau von 1673–1945* (East Berlin, 1961); Wolfgang Jonas, *Das Leben der Mansfeld-Arbeiter, 1924 bis 1945* (East Berlin, 1957).
43. One exception is the project—undertaken from the perspective of folklore studies—on the social structure and way of life of the workers in the Magdeburg Börde, although its central focus is on the nineteenth century: Hans-Jürgen Rach and Bernhard Weissel, eds., *Landwirtschaft und Kapitalismus: Zur Entwicklung der ökonomischen und sozialen Verhältnisse in der Magdeburger Börde vom Ausgang des 18. Jahrhunderts bis zum Ende des Ersten Weltkrieges,* 2 vols. (East Berlin, 1978–79); idem, eds., *Bauer und Landarbeiter im Kapitalismus der Magdeburger Börde: Zur Geschichte des dörflichen Alltags vom Ausgang des 18. Jahrhunderts bis zum Beginn des 20. Jahrhunderts* (East Berlin, 1982); Hans-Jürgen Rach, Bernhard Weissel, and Hainer Plaul, eds., *Die werktätige Dorfbevölkerung in der Magdeburger Börde: Studien zum dörflichen Alltag vom Beginn des 20. Jahrhunderts bis zum Anfang der 60er Jahre,* 2 vols. (East Berlin, 1986–87).
44. Ingrun Drechsler, "Die Magdeburger Sozialdemokratie vor dem Ersten Weltkrieg," PhD diss., University of Magdeburg, 1992; idem, "Die Rote Stadt im Roten Land: Die Magdeburger Soziademokratie unter besonderer Berücksichtigung ihrer Gründungsphase und Entwicklung vor dem Ersten Weltkrieg, als sozialdemokratische Hochburg im Spiegel ihrer Wahlergebnisse während der Weimarer Republik und ihrer erfolgreichen kommunalen Wohnungsbaupolitik," *IWK* 29, no. 2 (1993): 177–194; idem, "Von Fehden und Kämpfen: Der schwierige Weg der Magdeburger Arbeiter bis zur Gründung einer sozialdemokratischen Partei 1900," in H. Grebing, H. Mommsen, and K. Rudolph, eds., *Demokratie und Emanzipation zwischen Elbe und Saale: Beiträge zur Geschichte der sozialdemokratischen Arbeiterbewegung bis 1933* (Essen, 1993), 42–53; Hans-Dieter Klein, "Zwischen Burgfrieden und Komintern: Die Unabhängige Sozialdemokratie in Halle-Merseburg 1917–1920," in Grebing, Mommsen, and Rudolph, *Demokratie und Emanzipation,* 181–195; Klaus Schmidtke, "Die Sozialdemokratie in Nordhausen und Salza-Bürgerstadt und Arbeiterdorf zwischen Kaiserreich und DDR," in F. Walter, T. Dürr, and K. Schmidtke, eds., *Die SPD in Sachsen und Thüringen zwischen Hochburg und Diaspora: Untersuchungen auf lokaler Ebene vom Kaiserreich bis zur Gegenwart* (Bonn, 1993), 183–286; Steffen Raßloff, *Flucht in die nationale Volksgemeinschaft: Das Erfurter Bürgertum zwischen Kaiserreich und NS-Diktatur* (Cologne, 2003). Hans-Ulrich Ludewig wrote his essay without consulting primary sources: "Unruhen, Aufstand und Bürgerkrieg 1918–1923 im mitteldeutschen Raum," in W. Freitag, K. E. Pollmann, and M. Puhle, eds., *Politische, soziale und kulturelle Konflikte in der Geschichte von Sachsen-Anhalt* (Halle, 1999), 164–174. Weitz, *German Communism,* takes a broader approach that deals with both the Ruhr region and the central German industrial region around Halle-Merseburg.

45. See Fritz Faber, "Magdeburgische Zeitung, Magdeburg (1664–1945)," in H.-D. Fischer, ed., *Deutsche Zeitungen des 17. bis 20. Jahrhunderts*, vol. 2 (Pullach, 1972), 57–73; *Sperlings Zeitschriften- und Zeitungsadreßbuch: Handbuch der deutschen Presse*, 52nd ed. (Leipzig, 1926), 420–422, 53rd ed. (Leipzig, 1927), 469, 55th ed. (Leipzig, 1929), 497f., 57th ed. (Leipzig, 1931), 539. Each of the papers I have listed had a circulation of about 40,000 copies. The region lacked a large conservative or German-national paper, at least in the years up to 1923. After that date, however, the initially left-liberal *Saale-Zeitung* (and part of the Hugenberg group) moved increasingly to the right.
46. Most critical is the absence of the months November and December 1918 for the *Saale-Zeitung*, and that of the months of January and February 1933 for the *Volksstimme;* in the latter case, I was able to use the *Volksblatt* in Halle, which was by then part of the SPD again.
47. I should emphasize here that even with the addition of the official files, this did not yield a data base of all cases of violence that would have allowed any kind of valid quantification. To that extent, the goal here can be only to describe trends and examine typical cases.
48. Author's calculations based on Erwin Haneke, "Die Bodennutzung, das Personal, die Vieh- und Maschinenhaltung der landwirtschaftlichen Betriebe im Freistaat Preußen, in seinen Provinzen, Regierungsbezirken und Kreisen nach den Ergebnissen der landwirtschaftlichen Betriebszählung vom 16. Juni 1925," *Zeitschrift des preußischen statistischen Landesamtes* 68 (1929): 89–219, here 174f. On the economic development of Börde counties up to the First World War see Sieglinde Bandoly, "Veränderungen der sozialökonomischen Struktur in der Magdeburger Börde von dem ersten Weltkrieg," in H.-J. Rach and B. Weissel, *Landwirtschaft und Kapitalismus*, vol. 1, 233–262, and the other essays in this collection. On the social structure of the province as a whole see also Table 1 in Chapter 1.
49. Hans Thormann and Erich Staab, *Der mitteldeutsche Raum: Seine natürlichen, geschichtlichen und wirtschaftlichen Grenzen* (Merseburg, 1929), 78–83, 72; Friedrich-Wilhelm Henning, "Ansätze der industriellen Entwicklung in Sachsen-Anhalt im 19. und 20. Jahrhundert," *Forschungen zur Brandenburgischen und Preußischen Geschichte, Neue Folge* 4, no. 1 (1994): 1–30, here 14f.
50. In precise numbers there were 20,842, which accounted for 61.5 percent of all machine builders in the administrative district and 29 percent of all machine builders in the province. Author's calculations based on *Statistik des Deutschen Reiches, Neue Folge* 403, part 9, 74–164, here 76f., 88, 100.
51. Martin Lichtenberg, "Entwicklungstendenzen in der Magdeburger Industrie," PhD diss., University of Jena, 1934, 53–55.
52. Thormann and Staab, *Mitteldeutscher Raum*, 93f.
53. Henning, "Industrielle Entwicklung," 11–16; Thormann and Staab, *Mitteldeutscher Raum*, 72.
54. Beginning in 1921, the "Mansfeldsche Kupferschiefer bauende Gewerkschaft" operated as the "Mansfeld A.G." The extraction of potassium that was begun in 1897 was henceforth in the hands of the "Mansfeld Kaliwerke A.G."; added to this was the "Mansfeldsche Metallhandel A.G." in Berlin. The seat of the enterprise was in Eisleben. For the development of the company see Walter Hoffmann, *Der Mansfelder Kupferschieferbergbau: Ein Beitrag zur mitteldeutschen Wirtschaftsgeschichte* (Meisenheim a. Gl., 1957); on working conditions see Karl Lärmer, *Vom Arbeitszwang zur Zwangsarbeit*, and Waltraud Robbe, *Die Knappschaftsfessel von Mansfeld: Ein Beitrag zur Geschichte der Lage und des Kampfes der deutschen Arbeiterklasse in der Zeit von 1850 bis 1900* (East Berlin, 1958).
55. *Stat. Dt. R., N. F.* 403, part 9, 86.
56. *Stat. Dt. R., N. F.* 403, part 9, 86, 88.
57. *Jahresberichte der preußischen Regierungs- und Gewerberäte und Bergbehörden für 1914–1918* (Berlin, 1919), 553; *Kämpfendes Leuna, part I, 1 (1916–1933)*, 145.
58. Erich Knabe, "Die mitteldeutsche chemische Industrie in ihrer standortmäßigen Bedingtheit," PhD diss., University of Halle, 1927; *Jahresberichte*, 553f.; Thormann and Staab, *Mitteldeutscher Raum*, 103.

59. Compare with additional figures in Klein, "Burgfrieden," 182f. According to these data, the number of chemical workers in the Bitterfeld region rose by another 1,500 to 10,000 between 1905 and 1919, the number of miners in the Geisel Valley (where the coal for Leuna was being extracted) grew between 1916 and 1919 alone from 2,844 to 9,815.
60. On the disposition of workers in such monoindustrial sites with extremely rapid growth toward radical behavior, see the fundamental observations by Klaus Tenfelde, *Proletarische Provinz: Radikalisierung und Widerstand in Penzberg/Oberbayern 1900–1945* (Munich, 1982), 4–6.
61. Thormann and Staab, *Mitteldeutscher Raum,* 94, 96; *Stat. Dt. R., N. F.,* 403, part 9, 88f., 94.
62. Thormann and Staab, *Mitteldeutscher Raum,* 84.
63. Author's calculations based on *Stat. Dt. R., N. F.,* 403, part 9, 89, 93; Thormann and Staab, *Mitteldeutscher Raum,* 65.
64. Thormann and Staab, *Mitteldeutscher Raum,* 131; Vogler, "Probleme des Klassenkampfes," 8.
65. Thormann and Staab, *Mitteldeutscher Raum,* 131; also see Vogler, "Probleme des Klassenkampfes," 13. In the administrative district of Magdeburg, the figure was 27.5 percent. On the structure of agriculture in the province in general see also Thomas Nabert, *Der Großgrundbesitz in der preußischen Provinz Sachsen 1913–1933: Soziale Struktur, ökonomische Position und politische Rolle* (Cologne, 1992), esp. 12ff., 57ff.
66. *Stat. Dt. R., N. F.,* 403, part 9, 98.
67. Thormann and Staab, *Mitteldeutscher Raum,* 131.
68. *Stat. Dt. R., N. F.,* 403, part 9, 98.
69. Ibid., 99f.; Thormann and Staab, *Mitteldeutscher Raum,* 126, 112, 110. See also Raßloff, *Flucht,* 41–60.
70. Thormann and Staab, *Mitteldeutscher Raum,* 92–94, 96; *Jahresbericht,* 583.
71. *Stat. Dt. R., N. F.* 401, 363f. (results of the census of 1925).
72. The preceding discussion is based on Drechsler, "Rote Stadt," 177–190; idem, "Fehden," 42–53; idem, "Sozialdemokratie."
73. Roswitha Mende, „Geschichte der Sozialdemokratie im Regierungsbezirk Merseburg von der Jahrhundertwende bis 1917," PhD diss. (B), University of Halle, 1984.
74. The debate over when precisely the development that led to the party split in 1917 began and which specific factors were decisive cannot be pursued here. On this see Dieter Groh, *Negative Integration und revolutionärer Attentismus: Die deutsche Sozialdemokratie am Vorabend des Ersten Weltkrieges* (Frankfurt, 1973); Carl E. Schorske, *Die große Spaltung: Die deutsche Sozialdemokratie 1905–1917* (Berlin, 1981); most recently Wolfgang Kruse, *Krieg und nationale Integration: Eine Neuinterpretation des sozialdemokratischen Burgfriedensschlusses 1914/15* (Essen, 1993).
75. Ulrich Heß, "Entwicklung zur Industriestadt und zu einem Zentrum der Arbeiterbewegung (1871 bis 1897/98)," in W. Gutsche, ed., *Geschichte der Stadt Erfurt* (Weimar, 1986), 281–320; Willibald Gutsche, "Übergang zum Imperialismus und Erster Weltkrieg (1897/98 bis 1917)," in W. Gutsche, *Geschichte der Stadt Erfurt,* 321–358; Franz Walter, "Sachsen und Thüringen: Von Mutterländern der Arbeiterbewegung zu Sorgenkindern der SPD: Einführung und Überblick," in F. Walter, T. Dürr, and K. Schmidtke, eds., *Die SPD in Sachsen und Thüringen zwischen Hochburg und Diaspora: Untersuchungen auf lokaler Ebene vom Kaiserreich bis zur Gegenwart* (Bonn, 1993), 11–38; Schmidtke, "Sozialdemokratie," 183–213.
76. *Stat. Dt. R., N. F.* vol. 250, 22–25. Given the complete lack of studies on the bourgeois parties in this region, these brief indications must suffice.
77. See on this the correspondence in LHAM C 20 Ib 202/I. At that time, the commanding general of the IVth Army Corps headquartered in Magdeburg was Paul von Hindenburg, the future Reich President.
78. LHAM C 20 Ib 202/II, fol. 16f. (Regierungspräsident (RP) of Magdeburg to the Oberpräsident (OP), 21 January 1906), fol. 20–22 (RP Merseburg to OP, 25 January 1906), fol. 23f. (RP Erfurt to OP, 22 January 1906).
79. LHAM C 20 Ib 202/I, fol. 44 (Ministry of the Interior to all Oberpräsidenten, 7 March 1906).

80. LHAM C 20 Ib 202/II, fol. 78 (Polizeipräsident (PP) of Magdeburg to OP, 16 March 1910). However, the "soft" line of the police president was harshly criticized by the Regierungspräsident, who was not interested in the fact that there had not been any clashes, but merely held that the mob had "ruled the street." The real problem was the symbolic victory of the demonstrators, their occupation of public space (ibid., fol. 81f., RP to OP, 30 March 1910).
81. LHAM C 20 Ib 202/II, fol. 62f. (RP Merseburg to OP, 25 January 1910); LAMe C 48 Ia 217, fols. 104–107 (Police Administration of Halle to RP, 14 February 1910); *VB* no. 38, 15 February 1910. Eighty-eight individuals were later sentenced to prison terms and seventy-five were fined, with not a single policeman among them.
82. *VB* no. 38, 15 February; no. 39, 16 February 1910. In an editorial, the *Volksstimme* in Magdeburg also criticized the arbitrary conduct of the police in Halle and elsewhere, but at the same time it warned against a "blue rage" (*VS* no. 41, 18 February 1910).
83. LAMe C 48 Ia 217, fol. 126f. (Police Administration of Halle to RP, 7 March 1910). See the account of the events in Mende, "Sozialdemokratie," 225–232, who does not mention the dominance of the men among the demonstrators, a critical difference from earlier demonstrations. Weitz, *German Communism*, 43–45, suggests that the experience with police brutality pushed the Social Democrats in Halle to the left. He overlooks, first, the development since the 1890s I have sketched above, and, second, the fact that the brutality of the police response on 13 February was not the rule, but the exception.
84. *SZ* no. 74, 14 February 1910; *MZ* no. 37, 21 January 1906.
85. *SZ* no. 74, 14 February 1910. On the demonstrations over voting rights in Berlin and the reactions to them see Lindenberger, *Straßenpolitik,* 304–351.
86. *MZ* no. 20, 12 January 1912; no. 48, 26 January 1912; no. 37, 21 January; no. 40, 23 January 1906.
87. *SZ* no. 38, 24 January 1910; no. 21, 13 January 1912.
88. *VS* no. 65, 17 March 1912. For the long-term significance of this and other strikes in the area under investigation see the apt comment by Weitz, *German Communism,* 40–43.
89. Mende, "Sozialdemokratie," 205–212; *VB* no. 39, 16 February; no. 40, 17 February; no. 41, 18 February 1910. On the relationship between the authoritarian Wilhelminian state, the police, and the workers' movement in general, see Gerhard A. Ritter and Klaus Tenfelde, *Arbeiter im deutschen Kaiserreich 1871 bis 1914* (Bonn, 1992), 682–684; Hans-Ulrich Wehler, *Deutsche Gesellschaftsgeschichte, vol. 3: Von der „Deutschen Doppelrevolution" bis zum Beginn des Ersten Weltkriegs, 1849–1914* (Munich, 1995), 1045–1050. Ralph Jessen, *Polizei im Industrierevier: Modernisierung und Herrschaftspraxis im westfälischen Ruhrgebiet 1848–1914* (Göttingen, 1991) emphasizes especially the indirect effect of police action: although it could intervene palpably in the daily life of the proletariat again and again, it prompted especially the SPD to distance itself clearly from violent forms of action.
90. *VS* no. 64, 16 March 1912.
91. See, for example, the minor clashes during a lockout of several hundred tobacco workers in Nordhausen in 1901, LAG Reg. Erfurt 8793 (not paginated), passim; on the background see Schmidtke, "Sozialdemokratie," 188f. During a strike of construction workers in Erfurt in 1907, Italian workers, who had been brought in as strikebreakers, shot at the strikers with revolvers, but nobody was hurt (LAG Reg. Erfurt 12354, fols. 3, 8, 9f.); during a strike of metal workers in Erfurt in 1911, two strikebreakers were assaulted in the dark of night and severely beaten, and here, too, shots were fired (ibid., fol. 85, Polizei Erfurt to RP, 12 September 1911). For a detailed discussion of the various forms of this "small" violence see Lindenberger, *Straßenpolitik,* passim, on the strike esp. 233–240.
92. See, for example, *MZ* no. 132, 12 March 1912, where the miners' strike in the Ruhr was described as a "frivolous strike," one that revolved in the final analysis around questions of political power; the "most serious danger," however, was that the strikers, "under the pressure of hatred and hunger, will eventually lose any discipline and therefore try to block the entrance into the mines by force."

93. *SZ* no. 357, 2 August 1914.
94. *MZ* no. 565, 2 August 1914. It should also not be forgotten that after 1 August 1914, all newspapers were subject to censorship; their reports about war enthusiasm must also be evaluated from this perspective.
95. *MZ* no. 546, 26 July; no. 547, 27 July; no. 562, 1 August 1914.
96. *SZ* no. 355, 1 August 1914.
97. Christian Geinitz and Uta Hinz have argued along the same lines: "Das Augusterlebnis in Südbaden: Ambivalente Reaktionen der deutschen Öffentlichkeit auf den Kriegsbeginn 1914," in G. Hirschfeld et al., eds., *Kriegserfahrungen: Studien zur Sozial- und Mentalitätsgeschichte des Ersten Weltkriegs* (Essen, 1997), 20–35, here 20–28; Christian Geinitz, *Kriegsfurcht und Kampfbereitschaft: Das Augusterlebnis in Freiburg. Eine Studie zum Kriegsbeginn 1914* (Essen, 1998).
98. *VS* no. 178, 2 August 1914. As late as 28 July (no. 173), the paper had opposed the "politics of the street" that bourgeois papers were trying to generate by disseminating exaggerated reports about a mood of enthusiasm in the streets. See Kruse, *Krieg,* 54ff., who has argued convincingly against the older thesis of a wave of patriotism also among the workers; also see his "Die Kriegsbegeisterung im Deutschen Reich zu Beginn des Ersten Weltkriegs: Entstehungszusammenhänge, Grenzen und ideologische Strukturen," in G. Mergner and M. van der Linden, eds., *Kriegsbegeisterung und mentale Kriegsvorbereitung* (Berlin, 1991), 73–81. On the lack of enthusiasm in the countryside see Ziemann, *Front,* 39ff.; of course, it should be tested to what extent Ziemann's findings for a Catholic region apply to rural Protestant areas. For a comprehensive look at the mood at the outbreak of the war, see Jeffrey Verhey, *The Spirit of 1914: Militarism, Myth and Mobilization in Germany* (Cambridge, 2000), who sees the enthusiasm that can be found as above all a phenomenon in the large cities, carried by young men from the bourgeoisie.
99. *MZ* no. 584, 9 August 1914; emphases in original.
100. Thus the tenor of the reflections by Joachim Radkau, *Das Zeitalter der Nervosität: Deutschland zwischen Bismarck und Hitler* (Munich, 1998), 389ff., quote on 389. On the practice of "hard" masculinity in the prewar society see Ute Frevert, *Ehrenmänner: Das Duell in der bürgerlichen Gesellschaft* (Munich, 1991), English edition, *Men of Honour: A Social and Cultural History of the Duel,* trans. Anthony Williams (Cambridge, MA, 1995), esp. chaps. 3 and 4; on the hardening of the ideal of manhood see also Svenja Goltermann, *Körper der Nation: Habitusformierung und die Politik des Turnens 1860 –1890* (Göttingen, 1998), 126ff., 290ff.
101. *MZ* no. 565, 2 August; no. 573, 5 August 1914; *SZ* no. 537, 2 August; no. 361, 5 August 1914. By comparison, the notion of war as a bath of steel that purified man was secondary. See on this the recent, detailed analysis of the press by Thomas Raithel, *Das „Wunder" der inneren Einheit: Studien zur deutschen und französischen Öffentlichkeit bei Beginn des Ersten Weltkriegs* (Bonn, 1996), esp. 467ff.; in the same spirit Geinitz and Hinz, "Augusterlebnis," 28.
102. Susanne Miller, *Burgfrieden und Klassenkampf: Die deutsche Sozialdemokratie im Ersten Weltkrieg* (Düsseldorf, 1974), 339.
103. Mende, "Sozialdemokratie," 411–429; Schultz, "USPD," 45–49; Klein, "Burgfrieden," 181–186. Both men later played leading roles in the KPD.
104. Gutsche, *Bewegung,* 84–91.
105. Schmidtke, "Sozialdemokratie," 209. Crucial in this case were the aftershocks from the "second ballot quarrel" in 1912, when the local party organization was unwilling to adhere to the "restraining agreement" (*Dämpfungsabkommen*) made by the SPD and the liberal Fortschrittliche Volkspartei and was able to push through its own candidate, Cohn; Cohn, like the Reichstag delegates Reißhaus from Erfurt and Kunert from Halle, was an early opponent of approving additional war bonds.
106. The study by Jürgen Kocka remains of fundamental importance: *Klassengesellschaft im Krieg: Deutsche Sozialgeschichte 1914–1918,* 2nd ed. (Göttingen, 1978); for two syntheses see Thomas Nipperdey, *Deutsche Geschichte 1866–1918, vol. 2: Machtstaat vor der Demokratie* (Munich,

1992), 778ff., 850ff.; Roger Chickering, *Imperial Germany and the Great War, 1914–1918* (Cambridge, 1998).

107. Examples of such protests in LHAM C 28 If 2269, fols. 105ff. (in Magdeburg on 28 March 1917); fols. 173ff. (in Gardelegen on 30 and 31 July 1917). See the detailed account of a food disturbance in Tangermünde in Ute Daniel, *Arbeiterfrauen in der Kriegsgesellschaft: Beruf, Familie und Politik im Ersten Weltkrieg* (Göttingen, 1989), English edition, *The War From Within: German Working-Class Women in the First World War,* trans. Margaret Ries (Oxford, 1997), 247f. However, Daniel's statement that such protests had "brought the governability of the cities into question" (p. 247) seems overdrawn.
108. For general discussions see Peter Fritzsche, *Germans into Nazis* (Cambridge, MA, 1998), 11ff.; Davis, *Home Fires Burning;* Geyer, *Verkehrte Welt,* 28ff.
109. LHAM C 28 If 2269, fol. 25 (work stoppages in several Magdeburg machine factories in protest against a cut in the bread ration and additional holiday shifts, PP Magdeburg to RP, 6 April 1917); Mende, "Sozialdemokratie," 434; Gutsche, *Bewegung,* 87f.
110. Schultz, "USPD," 58f., Mende, "Sozialdemokratie," 441f.; Klein, *Burgfrieden,* 186f.; *Kämpfendes Leuna,* 88–91.
111. Schultz, "USPD," 67–70; Klein, "Burgfrieden," 187; *Kämpfendes Leuna,* 96.
112. LHAM C 28 If 2269, fols. 220–229 (several reports by PP Magdeburg to RP).
113. Gutsche, *Bewegung,* 106f.
114. *SZ* no. 54, 1 February 1918.
115. *SZ* no. 185, 8 April; no. 166, 10 April; no. 318, 10 July; no. 334, 19 July 1917; no. 429, 13 September 1918; *MZ* no. 244, 1 April; no. 261, 8 April; no. 715, 25 September; no. 971, 31 December 1917.
116. *SZ* no. 455, 28 September 1918; *MZ* no. 500, 8 July 1917 (quote); no. 528, 18 July 1918. On the broad debate over "nervousness" in Germany before 1914 see Radkau, *Zeitalter der Nervosität,* 389ff., 416ff., esp. 428, who puts forth the thesis that until 1914, the problem of a lack of nervous strength was certainly discussed with a sense of ambivalence and that people were skeptical of draconian treatments; it was only during the war itself that a tendency toward toughness prevailed in the scientific discussion. On fear of the "female" subsistence protests see Davis, *Home Fires Burning;* Geyer, *Verkehrte Welt,* 48f.
117. *MZ* no. 767, 14 October 1918. The paper was paraphrasing a statement from the Association of German Newspaper Publishers.
118. Ibid.
119. *MZ* no. 802, 27 October; no. 818, 2 November 1918.
120. *VS* no. 255, 30 October 1918 (here the last quote); see no. 221, 20 September; no. 239, 11 October; no. 250, 24 October ("remain firm"); no. 252, 26 October 1918.
121. *VS* no. 258, 2 November; no. 260, 5 November; no. 262, 7 November ("Tartar state"); no. 263, 8 November 1918 (here the longer quote). On the position of the SPD leadership in October 1918 see Susanne Miller, *Die Bürde der Macht: Die deutsche Sozialdemokratie 1918–1920* (Düsseldorf, 1978), 62–69.
122. *MZ* no. 767, 14 October; no. 825, 5 November; no. 833, 7 November; no. 834, 8 November (here the last quote). Incidentally, the *Saale-Zeitung* fell largely silent from the second half of October onward, limiting itself to very brief reporting of the events. There is a gap in the surviving editions of the paper for the months of November and December.
123. LHAM C 20 Ib 4786/I, fol. 7.
124. Eberhard Kolb, *Die Arbeiterräte in der deutschen Innenpolitik 1918–1919* (Düsseldorf, 1962), 93; Leidigkeit and Herrmann, *Leinistischer Kurs,* 31–36; Schultz, "USPD," 87–89; "Anklagerede des Staatsanwalts im Kilian-Prozeß," in *SZ* no. 577, 10 December 1919; according to this statement by the prosecutor, Lord Mayor Rive was, by his own account, not impeded in the exercise of his official duties until 23 December.
125. *Kämpfendes Leuna,* 102–106, quote on 106; see Leidigkeit and Herrmann, *Leninistischer Kurs,* 38; Schultz, "USPD," 96–100.

126. Peter von Oertzen, *Betriebsräte in der Novemberrevolution: Eine politikwissenschaftliche Untersuchung über Ideengehalt und Struktur der betrieblichen und wirtschaftlichen Arbeiterräte in der deutschen Revolution 1918/19,* 2nd ed. (Berlin, 1976), 133f., emphasizes both of these factors as specific to the workers' councils movement in central Germany compared to the workers' councils in the Ruhr region. On the development in the other cities of the district of Merseburg during the November days see Schultz, "USPD," 90–96; David Morgan, *The Socialist Left and the German Revolution: A History of the German Independent Social Democratic Party, 1917–1922* (Ithaca, 1975), 173–176. Only in Weißenfels did the workers' and soldiers' council co-founded by Alfred Oelßner (later KPD) have a leadership as radical as that in Halle; elsewhere, the MSPD had greater influence.
127. LHAM C 20 Ib 4786/I, fols. 4–6 (Report of RP Magdeburg to OP, 13 November 1918), which also gives a report of the unfolding of the movement in the other cities of the region; Manfred Wille, "Grundzüge der Entwicklung Magdeburgs von 1917 bis 1945," in Rach, Weissel, and Plaul, *Dorfbevölkerung,* vol. 2, 255–279, here 256–258; *VS* no. 263, 9 November 1927 ("Days of Revolution in Magdeburg," remembrances by the SPD district chairman Ernst Wittmaack).
128. Gutsche, *Bewegung,* 127–50; Raßloff, *Flucht,* 155–163.
129. The reports of the Landräte in LHAM C 20 Ib 4786/I, fols. 34, 36, 37, 46, 50, 53; the quote is from the report by the Landrat in Eisleben dated 12 November 1918, fol. 37.
130. Vogler, "Klassenkampf," 71–88, 93–116, 151–156; on the details of the agreement of 13 December see 116–132. Martin Schumacher, *Land und Politik: Eine Untersuchung über politische Parteien und agrarische Interessen 1914–1923* (Düsseldorf, 1978), 85ff. (on the rural laborer regulations of 24 January 1919 see 105–116), criticizes the overly accommodating attitude of the DLV during the negotiations at the Reich level. The eight-hour day was not achieved during the negotiations in the province of Saxony (instead, work shifts between eight and eleven hours, changing depending on the time of year, were stipulated), wages in kind were not abolished, child labor was not limited, and no regulations were made about vacation.
131. Examples in LHAM C 20 Ib 4786/I, fol. 9 (RP Erfurt to OP, 12 November 1918); fol. 6 (RP Magdeburg to OP, 13 November 1918); *VS* no. 263, 9 November 1927.
132. This is also true, for example, for Suhl and its weapons factories, the most likely place where (as in Halle) one might have expected such efforts among the workers who tended toward the left-wing USPD; it was not until 16 January 1919 that the workers' and soldiers' council, now completely under the control of the USPD, set up a force of its own: Heinz Oeckel, *Die revolutionäre Volkswehr 1918/19: Die deutsche Arbeiterklasse im Kampf um die revolutionäre Volkswehr, November 1918 bis Mai 1919* (East Berlin, 1968), 119.
133. LHAM C 20 Ib 4786/I, fol. 6 (RP Magdeburg to OP, 13 November 1918). In Magdeburg, however, just as in Stendal and Quedlinburg, for example, the local police force was able to resume its armed service after only a few hours of interruption (ibid., fol. 5).
134. *VB* no. 268, 14 November 1918.
135. *VB* no. 278, 27 November 1918.
136. LHAM C 20 Ib 4786/I, fol. 4 (RP Magdeburg to OP, 13 November 1918), fol. 7 (RP Merseburg to OP, 14 November 1918). Military jails were also opened in Quedlinburg and Magdeburg. Examples for the problems in the countryside, ibid., fols. 34ff. For example, the Landrat of Nordhausen reported that by 14 November, "the storage rooms for the separators for goat and cow farmers had already been stormed in three villages and the separators had been removed" (fol. 50). The Landrat of Schleusingen believed that especially the supply of potatoes to the industrial communities was "most seriously" imperiled by the possible formation of farmers' councils, and he pointed to the refusal of smaller farmers to fulfill their obligations (fol. 53).
137. For a general account of these disturbances of 'peace and order' see Bessel, *Germany after the First World War,* 81, and on the city-countryside conflict during the war and the immediate postwar period see Ziemann, *Front,* 308ff.; Robert G. Moeller, *German Peasants and Agrarian Politics, 1914–1924: The Rhineland and Westphalia* (Chapel Hill, NC, 1986); Geyer, *Verkehrte Welt,* 40ff.

138. *MZ* no. 940, 10 November 1918; *VS* no. 293, 14 December 1918, compare no. 269, 15 November. Heinrich August Winkler, *Weimar, 1918–1933: Die Geschichte der ersten deutschen Demokratie* (Munich, 1993), 32.
139. On the comparison with the French Revolution see also *SZ* no. 18, 11 January 1919. For a clear separation from the empire in Germany's liberal press (*Münchener Neueste Nachrichten, BZ am Mittag, Frankfurter Zeitung*), see the not very insightful work by Burkhard Asmuss, *Republik ohne Chance? Akzeptanz und Legitimation der Weimarer Republik in der deutschen Tagespresse zwischen 1918 und 1923* (Berlin, 1994), 89f., 100f., 115–118.
140. *MZ* no. 840, 10 November 1918. On the concept of the *Volkskörper* and its male connotations see Goltermann, *Körper der Nation,* esp. 333–336.

Part I

The Circumscribed Civil War 1919–1921

Following the largely bloodless collapse of the old order in the fall of 1918, intense political violence left its mark on the province of Saxony in the first months of 1919 and continued to do so for another two years. A circumscribed civil war developed, triggered by a confrontation about the future course of the Revolution. When many workers heeded the call in February 1919 for a general strike to bring about the socialization of industry, the middle classes in the province sought to prevent such a radical measure. While they employed new forms of protest such as street demonstrations and counter-strikes and forming Home Guards (*Einwohnerwehren*) in many locations, they mostly shied away from taking up arms against the radical left themselves. Fighting broke out between the military and groups of armed workers as a result of military action in the wake of the general strike in 1919. In March 1920, the Kapp Putsch again resulted in bloody battles between armed workers and the military. A year later, the Communist "March action," which saw fighting between young radical workers and the Prussian police, concluded the circumscribed civil war of the early Weimar years in the province of Saxony. While these massive and deadly confrontations served to solidify the status of the leaders of the radical left as outcasts, their followers met with partial understanding in the bourgeois and the Social Democratic press, which explained much of the political and social chaos after 1918 as a result of the devastating effects of the First World War.

Chapter 1

Radicalization and Violence, 1919

General Strike, Bourgeois Counter-Strike (*Bürgerstreik*), and Armed Clashes

At the turn of 1918/19, the Revolution entered its second phase, one dominated by bloody confrontations. While the beginnings of a reform of the military bogged down, the old elites in the military and the bureaucracy were able to consolidate their position once again. The decision of the Berlin Rätekongress in December 1918 to hold the election for a National Assembly soon followed the course of compromise charted by the Majority Social Democrats and was intended to allay the bourgeoisie's fears of Russian-style chaos. At the same time, this decision also signaled that there would be hardly any radical social changes. The improvised attempt by the Spartacus League at the beginning of January 1919 to advance the Revolution through an uprising in Berlin was put down bloodily by the newly formed Free Corps, and Karl Liebknecht and Rosa Luxemburg, the intellectual leaders of the Spartacus League, were brutally murdered.

The events in Berlin contributed to radicalizing the mass movement among the workers, who were demanding a socialization of key industries along with a substantial improvement in working conditions and massive wage hikes, though beyond that they were not pursuing any clear political goals. The movement found expression in large strikes, in some places also in attempts by the radical left to organize uprisings. Although these uncoordinated insurrections were the work of only a minority, the Reich government allowed the military to quash them with uncompromising severity.[1] This deepened the rift between the MSPD and segments of the working class in a lasting way.

Even if a large segment of the workers in the province of Saxony opted to continue the Revolution, as would become apparent in the February strikes, there was little willingness to pursue this through the path of armed struggle. It was only after the events in Berlin in January 1919 that the workers' and soldiers'

Notes from this chapter begin on page 25.

councils seriously pursued the establishment of their own militias. In Halle, the creation of such a unit had been under way since the end of November. However, three of the four companies of the "security regiment" (*Sicherheitsregiment*) gradually moved toward the positions of the Majority Social Democrats, while only the sailors' company of 280 men declared its loyalty to the newly founded KPD at the beginning of January.[2] Incidentally, the local KPD group that was set up here was the first of its kind in the district of Merseburg; it was only in the spring and summer that the KPD was able to establish additional groups.[3] At the Suhl weapons factory, the workers' and soldiers' council, now dominated by the USPD, created a "people's militia" (*Volkswehr*) in the middle of January, though it comprised no more than 70–80 men. In neighboring Erfurt, where a local KPD group had been in existence since the beginning of January,[4] the workers' and soldiers' council—where the USPD had also become the majority—began at the end of January to hand out weapons to about 2,500, and possibly as many as 5,000, workers.[5] The militias in Naumburg and Halberstadt, meanwhile, followed the course of the Majority Social Democrats, as did the Magdeburg citizens' militia, which was composed de facto chiefly of workers, and the "guard regiment" (*Wachtregiment*) set up there by the local soldiers' council.[6] Although since December fairly large and potent formations had emerged under the control of radical leftists near the provincial borders, in Gotha, and in Leipzig, all in all the militias—in part also because of a lack of coordination[7]—were far from constituting a serious factor of military power.[8]

The clashes between armed workers and Free Corps units that soon occurred in Halle and other cities therefore did not result from the attempt by the radical left to stage an uprising, but from a process of escalation in which the crucial impulses came from the government troops. This process reflects the radicalization of the revolutionary mass movement[9] as well as the countermobilization by the bourgeoisie; while revealing the growing tensions it simultaneously showed just as clearly the possible ways to contain the civil war–like violence.

The January fighting in Berlin was the trigger for the events in the province. In the days following 6 January, trains that were supposed to transport troops to the capital were blocked in Halle. In the process, the company of sailors took a large number of weapons and a large amount of ammunition for itself.[10] On 10 January, the citizens of Halle held a large demonstration in support of the Reich government, in the course of which there were fights with followers of the USPD; circles of the latter party, in turn, had launched attacks on printing shops, during which election posters of the German Democratic Party (DDP) had been destroyed.[11] The atmosphere in the run-up to the National Assembly elections scheduled for 19 January was tense. Two days later, the escalating violence led to the first fatality. More than ten thousand bourgeois demonstrators, singing "patriotic" songs and waving the new black-red-gold Reich flag, as well as the old black-white-red flag of the empire, marched through downtown Halle. For the bourgeoisie, this occupation of the public space was a very new way of articulating its political opinion[12] and of presenting itself as a unified force that was essentially the equal of the workers' movement (even if that unity remained fragile, as is evident from the appearance of the two competing flags side by side).[13] The violence was triggered—as so often in later years—by the fight over a symbol, in this case the black-white-red flag. Several attempts to steal the flag had failed when a shot was suddenly fired, possibly from within the ranks of the demonstrators.[14] In response, soldiers from the company of sailors opened fire on the procession with a machine gun. Several people were injured, one fourteen-year-old boy so severely that he died a short time later. What prevented the situation from getting worse was an agreement immediately after the incident between the garrison troops and the workers' council, to the effect that guard duty in the city would henceforth be undertaken jointly by the security regiment and the troops of the garrison, which found itself increasingly in opposition to the course of the local USPD.[15] The military balance of power had thus shifted in favor of the radicals.

The perception of the bourgeois public was shaped, however, by the battles in Berlin and the military weakness of the government they exposed. For the *Magdeburgische Zeitung,* a possible takeover of power by the Spartacists opened up "the most dreadful prospects," and the *Saale-Zeitung* noted with relief, once it became apparent that the uprising would be defeated, that the "general civil war" had not materialized.[16] Once again the danger of general "chaos" was evoked also by the Social Democratic *Volksstimme,* which believed at the end of December 1918 that Berlin was on the verge of "unrestrained gang rule."[17] For the *Magdeburgische Zeitung* there was no question that the Revolution was a "power struggle" and that the government now had to take steps to set up an effective body of troops—and therein lay a critique of the behavior of the Social Democrats in November of 1918 that was not identical to the "stab-in-the-back legend" but compatible with it in the long run, namely that "the Revolution broke up the German army."[18] And it had no effect that the *Volksblatt,* too, sharply criticized the actions of the Spartacus supporters as "terroristic" and the "road to perdition," demanding that the revolutionary struggle be carried on with "weapons of the mind" and "economic weapons," but not with violence.[19]

When it came to the elections for the National Assembly, however, the intensifying political situation was only just beginning to show its effects. While the MSPD got 58.3 percent of the votes in Electoral District 12 (district Magdeburg and Anhalt) and the USPD only 3.0 percent, in Electoral District 13 (district Merseburg), the MSPD could not get above 16.3 percent, while the USPD won 44.1 percent of the votes, by far its best showing in any of the electoral districts in Germany. In the district of Erfurt, the USPD was also ahead of the MSPD in all of the counties (*Kreise*), except those dominated by the Catholic Center Party, with the final tally ranging from 35.9 percent (rural county Langensalza) to 56.9 percent in the county of Schleusingen, the heart of weapons manufacturing. Its strongest competitor on the bourgeois side was the left-liberal DDP with a total of around one-quarter of the votes; it was barely edged out by the conservative DNVP in only a few rural counties dominated by medium-size and large-scale farmers.[20]

Tensions grew further as a result of the course that the conflict over the socialization of mining took. At the end of January, the workers' and soldiers' councils of the administrative district of Merseburg and the newly constituted district workers' council (*Bezirksarbeiterrat*) voted to join the socialization movement of the Ruhr region. The core of the concept of socialization in central Germany was a "Preliminary Directive for Works Councils (*Betriebsräte*)." Drafted by the USPD politician Wilhelm Koenen, it granted the works councils extensive oversight authority also when it came to the decisions by management on investments and personnel.[21] On 13 and 14 February, representatives of the Reich government and delegations from Essen and Halle held talks in Weimar. The government declared its willingness to accept works councils, which would be given limited access to business records, though no general supervisory rights. Even before the results of the conference became known, the hurried actions by the military commander in the Ruhr region triggered a general strike there; after several days of bloody clashes, it was suspended on 21 February.[22]

In the region as well, provocative actions by the authorities incited further escalation. On 17 February, one of the four members of the district workers' council was arrested, as was the commander of the security regiment in Halle a few days later.[23] In response, the miners in the mining district of Zeitz went on strike on 22 February, and on the following day a district conference of miners that was meeting in Halle decided almost unanimously to call for a general strike.[24] Negotiations with the government were now pointless and it was time to resort to "self-help," declared the chairman of the Miners' Association. The strike also pursued political goals. A statement by the action committee described co-determination (*Mitbestimmung*) by works councils as the "precondition for Socialism" and demanded that the "recognition of workers' and soldiers' councils" be secured. However, to counteract any fears of chaos, it was emphasized at the same time that water works, slaughterhouses, and bakeries were excluded from the strike and food warehouses were to be guarded, and it was emphatically demanded that there should "be no violence of any kind." The general strike was described as "the final, terrible weapon" of the workers, which underscored the position that the *Volksblatt* had taken in January on the question of violence. In addition, Koenen, the main speaker at the conference, had explicitly rejected the use of armed force.[25]

The call for a strike met with broad resonance. In Halle itself, the workers of the metalworking industry walked off the job, and they were joined by the miners in numerous brown coal pits, especially in the districts of Zeitz and Bitterfeld and in the Mansfeld area, and by workers from the Leuna Works. The front of strikers extended via Erfurt to Thuringia and all the way into the Free State of Saxony, where the general strike was proclaimed on 27 February. What made the action especially explosive was the fact that it was joined, as early as 25 February, by railroad and transportation workers, and by the employees at the Zschornewitz power plant, which supplied electricity to Berlin.[26] This cut the link between the National Assembly that was in session in quiet Weimar and Berlin, and the capital itself was now affected by the action. Here and there, agricultural workers also joined the strike.[27]

The situation intensified further when a "general strike" of the bourgeoisie was proclaimed in Halle on 26 February. Like the demonstration in January, this was a new form of activism for the middle class, borrowed once again from the workers' movement.[28] An appeal to the population identified as its goal the quickest possible end to the "general strike of the Independents," for whom, as the *Saale-Zeitung* opined, this was really a "test of power."[29] The appeal seems to have elicited widespread response, especially from civil servants of the postal service and the railroad and from teachers, less so from shop owners, bakers, and butchers. Tension was ratcheted up substantially by a telegram that the action committee of the bourgeoisie sent to the Reich government in Weimar and printed in the *Saale-Zeitung:* the dispatch asked for "the swiftest possible aid measures."[30] Given the state of affairs, this could only mean military action: a few days before, the Landesjägerkorps (Landesjäger Free Corps), commanded by General Maercker, had occupied the city of Gotha at the command of Reich Minister of Defense Noske (MSPD) in order to break the power of the soldiers' council that was dominated by the leftist USPD.[31] No clashes of any kind had occurred until then in Halle, but now tensions in the city grew. The evening edition of the *Saale-Zeitung* on 26 February was censored by the workers' council, after which the editors felt compelled to suspend publication of the paper for the time being.[32]

On 27 February General Maercker received orders to occupy Halle, and two days later his troops were ready to move into the city. In this situation, the soldiers' council of Halle, which was dominated by the Majority Social Democrats and rejected the general strike, tried to avoid a violent confrontation. It sent a delegation to General Maercker, pointing to the calm in the city and warning against the possible consequences of an occupation by his troops. Maercker, however, rebuffed its overtures and ordered his troops to move in.[33] In response, the workers' and soldiers' council decided to refrain from any resistance, especially since no preparations had been made.[34] Maercker's own report confirms this: he occupied the train station without incident, and after emplacing artillery and machine guns, he forced the unconditional handover of the Charlotten School, where the company of sailors was headquartered.[35]

Violent clashes occurred only when units of the Landesjägerkorps pushed into the city center and a small number of radical activists made a poorly coordinated attempt to put up armed resistance. The streets filled with a growing "crowd," some of whom insulted and spat at the soldiers. At the Charlotten School, the crowd that had gathered there after the withdrawal of the sailors refused to disperse; suddenly the ominous "first shot" rang out—from which side is impossible to determine—and triggered a brief exchange of fire, with casualties on both sides. Shooting also occurred at the main post office after soldiers there had been attacked and stripped of their arms. Gunfire continued through the following night. A kind of military stalemate took place: the Landesjägerkorps had barricaded itself in the main post office, while the enemy had turned the theater located on the other side of the square into the center of the resistance and set up an improvised battle command. Both sides limited themselves to securing their position. One result of this stalemate and the resulting security vacuum was that numerous shops were looted.[36]

The atmosphere was extremely tense, for the often invoked "chaos" now had been directly experienced. Nevertheless, the following day the elections for the city council (*Stadtverordnetenversammlung*) went ahead without any serious incidents, and—remarkably enough—the results differed but little from the elections for the National Assembly in January. Once again, the USPD became the strongest party with 42.2 percent of the votes, while the MSPD dropped to only 10.2 percent (from 16.3 percent). Among the bourgeois parties, the German People's Party (DVP) and the Center Party each gained a few hundred votes, coming in at 2.7 percent and 2.0 percent, respectively; the DNVP polled 11.9 percent, exactly the same result as in January, and the DDP, with a slight gain to 29.6 percent, defended its position as the leading party in the bourgeois camp.[37] While the MSPD was the real loser of the elections, the insignificant change in the position of the USPD and a noticeably lower voter turnout reveal that there was certainly no further radicalization of the workers as a whole; likewise, the experience of anarchy and chaos had not had a direct radicalizing effect on bourgeois voters.

But the situation in Halle was not calm. While on a stroll through the city on the afternoon of the Sunday elections, Lieutenant Colonel von Klüber, an officer who was serving with Maercker at the behest of the Reich government, was recognized in spite of his civilian clothes, seized upon, and maltreated by a "crowd" in which a 24-year-old disabled veteran played a leading role. Members of the security regiments tried in vain to come to his aid. Twice he tried to flee but was thrown into the Saale. Eventually he was killed by a gunshot to the neck, and his body was cast back into the river.[38] This act and its repulsive brutality were not typical, however, of the resistance to the government troops. The way it had unfolded resembled in part the "lynching actions" of the prewar period in large cities, where the intent had been to punish violations of moral rules in front of a larger (street) public with clear but limited physical violence.[39] In this particular instance, though, the boundary of the use of violence was crossed: the attack on Klüber punished the military for intervening—with its arrival in the city and its implicit threat of force—in a conflict that had been peacefully negotiated until then. By contrast, in spite of the tense situation, no one from Halle's bourgeoisie became the target of an attack.

The following nights saw more looting, on an even larger scale than before. As the *Saale-Zeitung* conceded, it was not only members of the lower classes who participated.[40] Several looters were shot and killed during exchanges of gunfire with patrols of the Landesjägerkorps. The next day, Maercker imposed martial law on the city, after which the fighting ceased. All in all, thirty-six people were killed in the clashes, of whom seven were members of the Landesjägerkorps; eighty-seven were wounded, among them twenty soldiers.[41] After minimal concessions by the Reich government and the employers, the general strike was ended on 8 March.[42]

This, however, did not yet put an end to the violence. Maercker disbanded the security regiment of the workers' and soldiers' council and replaced it with the Freikorps Halle (Free Corps Halle), a temporary unit of volunteers that reached a strength of over 400 men after a few days, though it was recruited from among students more than from the propertied middle class.[43] Larger quantities of weapons and looted goods were secured during house searches, and an unknown number of persons were arrested. More than a few of them were maltreated by soldiers of the Landesjägerkorps.[44] Karl Meseberg, the leader of the disbanded company of sailors, was arrested by several members of the new Free Corps acting on their own; during an "escape attempt" at the banks of the Saale he was shot and badly wounded, then thrown into the river, where he died.[45] The chief culprit, a medical student, was able to flee abroad. His accomplices initially took off to Berlin, where they joined the infamous Garde-Kavallerie-Schützendivision (Guard Cavalry Riflemen Division) but were arrested soon after; all had belonged to the garrison troops in Halle.[46] These were the first cases of "white" terror in the province. Others would follow after the Kapp Putsch and the "March action" of 1921.

Even though strikes by the bourgeoisie and the entry of troops occurred in other places, gun battles and massive looting remained confined to Halle. The much-invoked "chaos" had truly broken out only in that city. Maercker's intervention had first triggered and then put an end to it, and it had helped the government to come out on top in the power struggle with those elements of the mass movement in the radical heart of the province who were determined to push the Revolution ahead. For the bourgeois public as well as the Majority Social Democrats, these events, the interpretation of which was influenced by the bloody battles in Berlin and in the Ruhr region, seemed to confirm their worst fears. Political radicalism had cleared the way for the mob and had caused the general order to collapse. For the *Saale-Zeitung,* only a "handful of men" had driven the masses into the general strike; thereafter, "wild hordes" and "bands of riffraff" had moved through Halle, and the only reason they were unable "to go from house to house, robbing, burning, and murdering" in keeping with "a plan worked out in detail by the nests of Spartacists in Halle," was that the Landesjägerkorps took timely action to stop them.[47] The USPD and the KPD were not perceived as the representatives of a political camp, but as the instigators of crimes: the old fear of the masses that could be seduced and misled was thereby driven to an extreme. The sometimes hysterical quality of this fear is explained by the prediction of what the future would bring, a prediction that seemed to make perfect sense in March of 1919. The *Magdeburgische Zeitung* believed it was possible that "the Russian chaos with its danger of contagion" could spread to "all of central Europe"; the *Saale-Zeitung,* meanwhile, noted not only that a "wave of Bolshevism" had "flooded" Germany, but went so far as to express fear that it could turn into a "dangerous rush of madness."[48] The *Volksstimme* also warned against "terrible bloodshed" and predicted that hundreds of thousands would die of starvation during the transformation of Germany into a Bolshevist state.[49] After the end of the March fighting in Berlin, the *Magdeburgische Zeitung* declared that anyone who proceeded in this manner was "not open to reason" and "can therefore be fought only by force."[50] The fear that was articulated here—and which revolved around the notion of "chaos"—concerned not so much the dictatorship that was expected to follow a Bolshevist takeover of power, but rather referred to the expectation that the takeover attempt would utterly destroy the state and the economy, making a revival of Germany impossible for the foreseeable future.[51]

However, highly emotional charges and horror scenarios were not the final word in the interpretation of the events. As early as April, the hysterical fear of Bolshevism gave way once again to more differentiated perspectives on the situation in Germany. That change must be borne in mind: even though the equation "Communists = criminals" proved to have the greater potency over the long run, still that equation was not the only perspective from which the events were perceived, and it pushed others aside only gradually. In the middle of April, the *Magdeburgische Zeitung* also shifted its attention back to the radical right and returned to an assessment of the political state of affairs that was guided by the course of the French Revolution. The "extreme left and the extreme right" were working "hand in hand," the paper argued, the "chaotization" of Germany pursued by the "hyper-radicals" on the left was creating the desire for a strong man in the first place, and meanwhile the plans for a putsch on the right were kindling the "fear of counterrevolution" among the workers.[52] By the time the fighting in Berlin had ended, the paper had called upon the citizenry to show good sense by participating in concrete steps toward socialization and thus cooperate with the MSPD; another appeal for cooperation was issued in the middle of April.[53] Immediately after the clash with Maercker's troops, the *Saale-Zeitung* published the words of the DDP politician and university professor Emil Abderhalden, who wanted to help overcome the "hatred between brothers" of the previous days and demanded that the bourgeoisie agree to the "socialization of a number of enterprises."[54] To be sure, these statements were not without a certain tactical element, but they also reflected a mood that extended beyond the working class and demanded a fundamental change in the economic system, a change that took its cues from the "wartime socialism."[55]

In the wake of the armed clashes, the USPD's *Volksblatt* also made every effort not to pour more oil onto the fire. To be sure, it was harshly critical of the actions of the government, holding it responsible for the subsequent violence because of its decision to use troops. However, it called the counterviolence by the workers "understandable but misguided," and reiterated that the struggle against capitalism had to be waged with peaceful means, for "militarism and brutal physical force" stood on a historical level that had been transcended.[56] The *Volksstimme* was also concerned to calm the situation, and in spite of the sharp separation that the MSPD drew between itself and the USPD and KPD, it campaigned for understanding for the workers who had been drawn into the fighting and looting by those two parties. The paper pointed to the youth and quick politicization of many of the strikers, which had supposedly turned them into "enthusiastic supporters of the wild confusion."[57] However, it believed that the deeper reason for the outbreaks of violence since December 1918 lay in the war. That "organized act of violence of indescribable scope and bestiality" had "emotionally torn apart" the soldiers and the people at home and created the very "fever bacillus" that was now threatening the "body of the nation (*Volkskörper*)."[58] While this line of argumentation suggested, on the one hand, a sympathetic and careful policy, the notion of the "*Volkskörper*," with its medical overtones, could on the other hand justify demands for harsh measures that were allegedly driven by "objective" necessity.

There is no question that the clashes during the first few months of 1919 marked a profound turning point in the province of Saxony, as they did in other parts of Germany. For the first time, contemporaries witnessed a sharp confrontation between the workers' movement and the state, a confrontation in which a mobilized middle class intervened, actual battles were fought between security forces and striking workers, and large-scale looting took place. For the first time, this kind of confrontation killed a number of people on both sides, and it showed, if only briefly here and there, that a general collapse of order could become terrible reality. Such experiences transpired in the province of Saxony, in Berlin, in the Ruhr region, and—finally—in Munich and a number of other places.[59]

The notion of "civil war" encapsulated these experiences in the public discussion. However, in contrast to the perspective usually taken by scholarship, which tends to place these experiences of civil war front and center, it is important to bear in mind the limits of this process so as not to overlook the chances of political agreement that still existed.[60] There were no serious preparations in the camp of the radicals for a "second Revolution" pursued with force of arms, as scholarship has noted for some time now.[61] Moreover, nowhere did the armed clashes develop into larger battles of longer duration, nor was there any ad hoc formation of meaningful armed units on the part of the radical left. The "masses" that took to the street in the days of February and March chose the peaceful mass action of the strike to push through their demands, which is why the situation typically turned violent when the military seemed intent on taking this public space away from the "masses."[62] Revealingly enough, there were no attacks anywhere on prominent citizens such as the chairmen of burghers' councils or of bourgeois associations and parties, although the middle-class counter-strikes interfered massively in the daily lives of workers too when physicians refused to treat patients, or bakers and butchers closed their shops. But like their models from the workers' movement, these were in principle peaceful actions that left room for negotiations and did not force a military solution to the conflict.[63]

Subsistence Protest, Violence, and Criminality

What worried contemporaries beyond the conflicts with the USPD and KPD and made those political fears even more explosive was the material condition of the population. Under the impact of the continuing Allied blockade it remained precarious, while the accelerating inflation was producing ambivalent effects. As subsistence protests and property crime pervaded the year 1919, new ways of spending one's leisure time and new possibilities of consumption also appeared. Not a few contemporaries saw all of this as moral decay and a threat to the social order, though it was distinguished from the dangers posed by political radicalism.

One protest action in the industrial city of Tangermünde in the northern part of the province had deadly consequences. The headquarters of the IV Army Corps had set up a food depot there in November of 1918, but in spite of the dire supply situation it had not handed over even some of the stocks to the city. Thus, as the Landrat of Stendal later recounted, "the view slowly spread in wide circles of the population that one had to take what was being kept from them." As was so often the case in the years of inflation, society resorted to "self-help."[64] A small group of looters was able to make off with supplies on the night of 24/25 March without being stopped by the guard detail of the workers' and soldiers' council. In response, the corps headquarters posted additional troops at the depot and set up a machine gun. But these measures did not have the hoped-for effect. On the evening of 26 March, a crowd of 500–800 people gathered in front of the warehouse, having previously armed itself with rifles from the guardroom of the workers' and soldiers' council. The troops fired warning shots, and some in the crowd fired back, wounding one officer and a police constable. The soldiers then opened fire with the machine gun, killing five people and injuring a larger number. The crowd ultimately overpowered the troops, but no soldier was maltreated. It was only on the afternoon of the following day that outside troops regained control of the now looted depot, and there were no further clashes.[65]

The "crowd" that stormed the depot wanted to remedy what it perceived to be an unfair supply situation and was willing to use force to achieve its goal. Yet this force did not turn into an uncontrolled eruption, even after the other side had used deadly force of its own. In spite of the widespread fear of the "Spartacists" in the spring of 1919, the Landrat that reported on the incident refrained from holding Communist machinations responsible for what had happened. Instead, he pointed to an administrative injustice: with respect to the allocation of food, Tangermünde was still placed into a rural classification, which had resulted in the city being inadequately supplied. Peace would return only if this situation were remedied.[66]

Two months later, Magdeburg was the site of a market riot. The *Volksstimme* referred to it—semi-ironically—as the "cherry revolt," thus underscoring that it was different in character from the political unrest of the previous months. In spite of a good harvest, prices for fruits and vegetables remained high in the city. On 28 June, consumers at the weekly market resorted to "self-help." The merchants, probably out of fear of actions by the consumers, had shown up with an unusually small quantity of produce and eventually began to declare that items that were in especially short supply and expensive—like cherries and strawberries—were "already sold," thus taking them out of circulation altogether. Tensions erupted around ten o'clock. Market booths were trashed and the displayed wares were looted, but the tumultuous phase of the action was only brief and ended when security guards appeared on the scene. At the request of the customers they acted as mediators and prevailed upon the merchants to sell their fruits and vegetables at much lower prices. At the same time, the radius of the action expanded. Smaller bands from the crowd made their way to grocery stores in the suburbs and demanded lower prices. Almost everywhere, the action was peaceful and orderly; in most cases the goods were actually paid for and thefts were rare. In the suburb of Buckau, the wares of a merchant who refused to lower his prices were tossed into the street, and a meat shop was demolished, though the shop owner himself was not harmed. Violence against persons occurred only when the police tried to disperse crowds with a show of force and then called in the military. Insults were hurled at the soldiers, who fired warning shots into the air and eventually took aim at the crowd; fortunately, only two people were injured.[67]

The "crowd" in the marketplace of Magdeburg drew on a repertoire of behaviors that had been used by others decades before.[68] They intimidated grocers with measured violence against property and then continued the action with representatives of the authorities, who took the side of the consumers while initially calming the conflict. There is no need to assume the existence of deeply rooted and complex ideas about a "moral economy" as the driving force behind this action and others like it.[69] In the face of a good harvest and lower prices elsewhere, the consumers believed they were being cheated and resorted to "self-help." That there were no eruptions of violence—at least over a longer period—was owed to the relative levelheadedness on all sides, as well as the skillful intervention by the police. Had the police used force right away, it is likely that the subsequent course of the events would have all but run out of control (as they did in Tangermünde). Political slogans were not heard during the incident. The "cherry revolt" was an uprising by consumers, not a political demonstration.

The Magdeburg "cherry revolt" and the looting of the warehouse in Tangermünde—though different in the way they unfolded—were both palpable disturbances of "peace and order." Yet the public reacted differently than it had during the political unrest in the preceding months and was eager to find common ground. In Tangermünde (where the USPD had won only 124 votes—less than 1.7 percent—in the elections to the National Assembly),[70] the whole city mourned when the victims of the assault on the food depot were laid to rest. Larger businesses closed, and a firemen's escort and delegations from various clubs and organizations accompanied the funeral procession. Pastor König, who spoke at the graves, "was trying," according to the *Volksstimme,* "to reconcile Socialism and Christianity."[71] Moreover, although all of the dead were workers, two of them were older than fifty, and one was a married woman;[72] they could not be dismissed as hotheaded rabble-rousers.

The press, too, was essentially unanimous. The *Volksstimme* identified the cause of both incidents much as the authorities had done—inflated prices, an inadequate food supply resulting from an improper classification—and emphasized, especially in the case of Tangermünde, that these were "absolutely not Spartacist machinations." The behavior of people who had resorted to "self-help" was understandable, the paper maintained with respect to the "cherry revolt," for there was certainly such a thing as "just self-help." However, in this case it had eventually degenerated into "common looting and robbery."[73] The *Magdeburgische Zeitung*, too, spoke of "justified outrage" about the high food prices. Although it labeled the looters themselves a "gang" and a "horde" and considered the behavior of the crowd an action that had been planned days ahead in the "Magdeburg underworld," thus associating it with criminals, it did not place any blame on the USPD or the KPD.[74]

The three Regierungspräsidenten of the province, looking back at the year 1919, also made a clear distinction between food riots and political clashes. They were still the old officials appointed under Kaiser Wilhelm II,[75] who could hardly be accused of being inattentive to "Spartacist machinations." The top official in Magdeburg pointed to high prices and discontent over the food situation as the causes behind the self-help actions in Tangermünde, Magdeburg, and elsewhere.[76] His colleague in Merseburg suspected that "unrests (*Tumulte*) that were inherently political in nature … cause less concern than those whose cause … should be looked for in economic pressures, and which are then politically exploited." The Regierungspräsident of Erfurt, meanwhile, referred merely to "larger groups of reckless elements" who were to blame for the unrests (on the whole few in number) in his district.[77] Although the "Spartacists" might try to take advantage of the testy mood of the population, they were not the driving force behind it.

One thing all three Regierungspräsidenten considered especially worrisome was the strong rise in crime since the war. They were unanimous in noting a dramatic surge in property crimes. In Magdeburg, where 3,315 individuals had been sentenced for such crimes in 1913, their number had more than doubled to 8,417 between the beginning of July 1918 and the end of June 1919, while in Halberstadt it had grown fourfold from 309 to 1,468. Two Landräte of the district of Merseburg believed that the crime rate had surged no less than tenfold.[78] All three Regierungspräsidenten agreed that the problem of property crime was made worse by the fact that in many cases the felonies were committed by armed gangs that did not shy away from using violence—here the boundary between understandable "self-help" and outright criminal behavior deserving of condemnation blurred.[79] There was also agreement that young people were responsible for a considerable share of the rising criminality. There was disagreement, however, about the importance of strikes and the dangers they posed. While the Regierungspräsident of Magdeburg saw strikes as "the order of the day," which he claimed almost entailed "violence against those willing to work" and "unrests," his two colleagues—who had to deal with a more radical workers' movement—remarkably enough took the opposite position. "Acts of violence, sabotage, and so on" had not occurred during strikes, noted the Regierungspräsident of Erfurt, and his counterpart in Erfurt believed that the "period of wild strikes" had been overcome for the time being and the influence of "criminal circles" was on the wane.[80]

In the retrospective assessment of the events of 1919 by the three Regierungspräsidenten, the danger to public safety over the medium term thus arose not from Bolshevist machinations, but from the ominous surge in crime. As was true for unrests and riots, all were in agreement that the chief cause of the rise in criminal behavior was the shortage and high prices of food and other important goods. The deeper reason, however, lay in the "moral nadir of the people." After the war and especially the Revolution had "dissolved all bonds," "most people" believed "they could do whatever they pleased." "Law and justice" were "often shunted aside to obtain personal advantages,"[81] and not only to satisfy basic necessities of life. The Regierungspräsidenten also denounced the fact that neither tavern keepers nor their clientele were willing to observe closing time during "carousals" and "dances." They were especially troubled by young people, whose "depravity and brutalization" had increased "markedly" during the war, as reflected in an "excessive craving for pleasure, rude behavior on the street, thefts from garden and fields, as well as in disregard for directives from parents and the authorities." These manifestations were especially evident in the countryside, because the presence of police was more diffuse.[82] A remedy was possible only if the police were strengthened and the food supply improved—which latter measure was, in the view of the Regierungspräsident of Merseburg, the "best defensive measure."[83]

What the Wilhelminian officials perceived as a general social crisis was the result of a broad variety of factors. The collapse of the old authorities in the fall of 1918, political radicalism, and the difficult food situation were part of the mix. However, what also found expression was a new way of dealing with work and leisure, a changed way of shaping one's life. Returning soldiers were looking for the happiness that had been denied them, work was relatively easy to find (after a phase of high unemployment in the winter of 1918/19), the eight-hour day pushed through by the unions allowed for more leisure, and the advancing inflation also made it seem reasonable to spend a part of one's earnings on short-lived pleasures. As Richard Bessel has observed, in the period after the First World War, Germany became a "consumer society."[84] Though this development was already under way in 1919, it certainly did not take hold of all workers, but primarily involved well-paid younger workers with no family obligations yet. Those "masses" and "crowds" who participated in food protests, on the other hand, did so to satisfy basic necessities of life. At the same time, their actions articulated public criticism of the actions of the public authorities, who seemed incapable of dealing adequately with the supply problems. Indirectly, the political movement that found expression in the spring strikes also received a boost from the food protests. However, the two are by no means coincident. The supporters of the workers' council in Halle who were determined to offer armed resistance to Maercker's troops were *not* elderly men or housewives, who had led the assault on the food warehouse in Tangermünde. Chronologically the subsistence protest overlapped the political movement, which it had initially helped to advance, and eventually it shaped the picture of public order in the summer of 1919 more than the political movement did.[85]

The bourgeois public could clearly identify the most important means for overcoming the moral decay, the general crisis in society and state: work. "Work, unceasing work is the slogan of 1919," demanded the *Saale-Zeitung* as early as the beginning of the year.[86] On the one hand, this notion of work reflected the greatly enhanced importance that a society mobilized during wartime now ascribed to "work" in all spheres of employment;[87] on the other hand, it formed the opposite of the strike and was thus given a coloring that was potentially directed against the entire workers' movement, not only against the radical left. For example, after the battles in March, the newspaper in Halle demanded that everything be done "to make clear to the masses the necessity of work."[88] This argument gained new weight after the acceptance of the Versailles Treaty at the end of June 1919. For the *Magdeburgische Zeitung,* there now began a "time of misery" that could be endured only through work. From this perspective, it then accused the supporters of Social Democracy, on the occasion of the first anniversary of the Revolution, of seeing the Revolution as a "naked wage movement" while at the same time displaying "a disinclination to work and be productive."[89] A review of the year placed this idea at the forefront. Here, it was not the bloodshed of the first half of the year that dominated the picture, but "wild strike insanity" and "crass materialism," which had convulsed Germany like a "fever" and attested to the nadir of public morality. Fears of a civil war, anxiety about Bolshevism—none of this was mentioned any longer. "Positive work" was the slogan for the new year, though it was combined with an appeal to unity, both "in the will to engage in reconstruction and work" and "in mutual understanding and mutual respect."[90]

Militarized Citizens? The Home Guards (*Einwohnerwehren*)

Were such pronouncements of a willingness to cooperate merely tactical, intended to help conceal the preparations for a counterrevolution? Scholarship has long adduced the Home Guards as the chief evidence for an extensive mobilization of the middle classes in the cities and the countryside for this purpose. Historians have pointed especially to the activities of the Pommerscher Landbund (Pomeranian Agrarian League) in setting up the guards in eastern Prussia, which in fact led to a coup attempt in the summer of 1919, and to the participation of the Bavarian guards (under the strict leadership of *Forstrat* Georg Escherich) in toppling the Social Democratic–led state government during the Kapp Putsch. Scholars disagree only on whether the militias were already seen by their members as "counterrevolutionary civil war troops" (Könnemann) during their founding phase, or whether they developed such goals only gradually, especially in response to pressure from the Allies to disband.[91]

Most recently, however, scholars have emphasized the profound skepticism, especially of the rural population, toward an institution that seemed to introduce a new kind of obligatory military service shortly after the end of the war.[92] It is therefore not easy to characterize the Home Guards with precision, because various motivations blended during their creation and the perspectives of the organizers "from above" were not necessarily those of the individuals running them on the ground or of individual members. An auxiliary group to fight an uprising was not the same as a hidden military reserve force, and both were in turn very different from a local self-help formation to protect house and farm. What remains unclear, especially, is where the guards were most strongly represented—in the areas strongly affected by the unrests in the spring of 1919 or outside of them—and whether the followers of the Socialist parties generally rejected the guards, or whether their attempts to join were rebuffed by the bourgeoisie and the farmers.[93]

As it was, the formation of Home Guards took several attempts and ran into difficulties. In the first days of the war, the Prussian Minister of the Interior had ordered the establishment of citizens' militias as an auxiliary police, especially in larger communities. On 6 November 1918, with the Revolution imminent, his successor issued a similar decree that envisaged citizens' militias to protect food stocks, though in larger and industrial cities it was left to the local police whether or not to raise such auxiliary units. Only nine days later, the new Social Democratic Minister of the Interior, Hirsch, issued another decree to the effect that the citizens' militias should be used chiefly to disarm soldiers returning from the front who had not been properly demobilized.[94] The March fighting in Berlin was followed on 18 March 1919 by another ministerial decree that described the units, now called *Einwohnerwehren,* as an urgently needed defensive measure against Bolshevism and Spartacism as well as "the very closely related activity of looting and robbing gangs," and urged collaboration with the Schutzverband deutscher Landwirtschaft (Protective League of German Agriculture) in setting up the militias. After the Social Democrats' fierce criticism of the decree, especially of the selection mechanisms that were skewed to the political right, Hirsch's successor Heine repealed it and, on 15 April 1919, issued directives for setting up Home Guards that remained in force for a longer period. According to these directives, the local authorities were to form the guards—with the participation of the workers,' farmers,' and rural workers' councils—from all segments of the population, and the guards were to be sworn to uphold the Republican form of government. The military was to provide them with weapons, and the Oberpräsidenten were to control them.[95]

The fact that the Prussian Minister of the Interior had to issue four calls for the establishment of armed self-help units at a time of great political tension does not indicate that large segments of the population were necessarily ready and eager to participate. Were the ministerial decrees merely intended to direct a movement that was surging ahead onto the right paths? The sources provide no evidence. It would appear that the establishment of Home Guards was rather the result of a longer process in which fears of chaos merged with persuasion by the authorities.

In the province of Saxony, it was General Maercker who provided the impetus for the formation of Home Guards. After marching into Halle at the beginning of March 1919, he also had a "city protective guard" (*städtische Schutzwehr*) set up, whose deployment was explicitly limited to the protection of life and property in Halle itself. This guard proved to be, in his own words, a "very desirable relief" for the Landesjägerkorps.[96]

Outside of Halle, the establishment of Home Guards began in the civil servant town of Naumburg. In the wake of looting in the surrounding area, three corporals had taken it into their own hands to set them up in March. The man who soon emerged as the central organizer was a former captain in the general staff, Jüttner, who lived in Naumburg; from there, at the behest of the authorities, he promoted the establishment of militias in other parts of the district of Merseburg. According to Maercker, by mid April 400 guard units existed in the entire district.[97] Two years later, Jüttner took over as leader of the Stahlhelm local group in Halle,[98] the seat of the right wing of the Stahlhelm headed by Theodor Duesterberg. In the upcoming elections, Naumburg would prove a stable bastion of the extreme right. Here there is clearly a direct line of continuity from the Home Guards to organized opposition to the Republic.

Massive concerns about the new militia units were voiced by the local and regional councils, independent of their political orientation. The workers' councils expressed their fear that the units could be misused for reactionary political purposes, as well as the fear that the armed farmers could refuse to make their obligatory deliveries. By comparison, protecting the land against plundering seemed a secondary, though legitimate, purpose. The workers' council in the Altmark county of Gardelegen, for example, wanted to authorize Home Guards outside of cities in only a few rural locations that were close to the railroad tracks.[99] The formation of guard units ran into especially considerable difficulties in those areas in which industrial workers were mixed with the agrarian population. Here the fear was that the tensions between the workers and the small landholders, on the one hand, and between the larger farmers and the industrialists, on the other hand, could be dangerously exacerbated by arming only one camp. That was especially true if there had not been any unrest so far in the area in question. As the Erfurt police saw it, the establishment of a Home Guard would lead to "considerable uneasiness," and the town council of Mühlhausen expressed a similar concern. The town council of Bitterfeld, under repeated pressure from higher authorities, persisted in its refusal to set up a guard unit that would divide "the population into two parts, which was undesirable," claiming that so far "order has by and large prevailed." For that reason, the council said that it would merely reinforce the existing field guards (*Flurschutz*). The Landrat of Nordhausen went so far as to voice the fear that there would be a "battle of all against all."[100]

Did the bourgeoisie in the cities abandon its restraint once it had experienced chaos and plundering directly? In Tangermünde, whose food warehouse, as we have seen, was stormed twice within six weeks, the formation of a guard unit got off the ground very slowly. On 20 May, two weeks after the first assault on the warehouse, the first mayor believed that the establishment of a Home Guard was imminent, but by the middle of July he was not at all satisfied with the progress that had been made. Although the local sugar factory now commanded a factory guard, linked to which was a general Home Guard of forty men, all members were workers, most belonging to the MSPD, though a few to the DDP. The Regierungspräsident reported that the bourgeoisie was still holding back out of fear of the radicals among the workers.[101]

On the whole, though, the setting up of Home Guards in the province proceeded apace. According to the first complete survey for the districts of Magdeburg and Merseburg, compiled in the middle of August 1919, the guard units in the district of Magdeburg had 19,626 members and those in the district of Merseburg 17,795, each of which was equipped with at least a newer army rifle.[102] By the beginning of August, the General Command of the IV Army Corps had distributed 46,718 rifles, 264 light and 66 heavy machine guns, 5,300 steel helmets, and several thousand waist belts, pouches, and bayonets.[103] Like many other regions in Prussia and Germany, the province of Saxony had turned into a large weapons depot. The weapons, however, were very unevenly distributed. The main concentrations were in the rural areas—exactly where they would also remain four months later, after a massive expansion and before Social Democrats entered the guards in larger numbers beginning in December of 1919. Within the district of Magdeburg, the most heavily armed (not in terms of absolute numbers but relative to the population) were the Altmark rural counties of Osterburg, Salzwedel, and Stendal, and in the district of Merseburg the list was headed by the rural counties of Naumburg, Eckartsberga, and Weißenfels (which was the only one with an above-average number of industrial workers). In fact, the Magdeburg Home Guard, with 4,346 members, was even smaller in absolute numbers than its counterpart in the county of Salzwedel (4,689), even though the population of Magdeburg was nearly five times larger. The guard unit in Halle was the largest in its district in absolute numbers (2,486), but even so, it had only 700 more men than the unit of the purely agrarian county of Eckartsberga (1,760), whose population was less than one-fourth that of Halle.[104] Within the various counties, the units were widely dispersed: hardly a single unit had more than hundred members, most had around thirty, and occasionally they had as few as ten.

Although the sources do not contain any detailed information about the professions of the members of the guards, the clues that we do have indicate that their social profile was, on the whole, as lopsided as scholarship has previously assumed. It is exceedingly rare to find a "worker" among the local leaders of the guard units. By far the largest number were farmers, the rest estate owners, teachers and other civil servants, master craftsmen, and merchants and tavern keepers; in a number of cases they were the mayors. The guard in Halle was commanded by a mining engineer and a factory director, who had served in the war as captain and lieutenant colonel, respectively. We have detailed information about the composition of the Home Guard in the town of Brumby in the Börde county Calbe/Saale south of Magdeburg: the thirty-nine members included eighteen farmers, nine estate owners, six merchants and craftsmen, five civil servants, and one "administrator"; no one was working-class.[105] Where they existed, the Home Guards were chiefly organizations of the propertied in town and country.

However, the willingness of the Home Guards to take offensive action against striking workers allied with the radical left was weak. The summer and fall of 1919 saw a series of strikes by rural workers in various locations in the province of Saxony, especially in the county of Sangerhausen and in the Mansfelder Seekreis; their goal was higher wages and better working conditions, and most lasted only a few days. On the grounds that the harvest was imperiled, steps were taken to intervene in the strikes, not by the Home Guards but by Maercker's Landesjägerkorps, with the general eventually deploying his entire force as strikebreakers.[106]

At the end of October 1919, the workers of the Zschornewitz power plant in the county of Bitterfeld, which supplied part of Berlin's electricity, walked off the job in a show of solidarity with the striking Berlin metal workers. A week later, the work force at the Leopold brown coal pit, which was important to the coal supply for Zschornewitz, also went on strike for higher wages and the dismissal of unpopular bosses. In mid November, the workers at the Wolfen aniline factory tried to push through the demand that the Day of Prayer and Repentance be made a paid holiday and exerted massive pressure on the director of the factory with a large demonstration in front of the management building; similar events took place at the neighboring electronics factory. In response, the Reich government had Maercker's Landesjägerkorps occupy the two factories and keep them running with the help of the Technische Nothilfe (Teno, Technical Emergency Assistance) that had been set up in September.[107] The strike was abandoned a few days later, without incident. Neither the Home Guards from County Bitterfeld, which had over 300 members by now, nor other guard units from neighboring counties were involved in any way in the actions taken against the strikers; at least, they are not mentioned at all in Maercker's exhaustive account of the events.[108]

That the main burden of the action in County Bitterfeld was borne by the professional military comes as no surprise. The fact that neither a single Home Guard of the region nor the Freikorps Halle appeared on the scene certainly allows for various interpretations. Perhaps the scope of the action did not seem large enough to justify their participation, or perhaps the townspeople and farmers in the Home Guards wanted to avoid exacerbating the situation and the conflicts in their own communities—at any rate, their reluctance does not bespeak a great readiness to take offensive action against the opponent on the left.

By the middle of December 1919, Home Guards could be found in nearly all counties of the province of Saxony. Two months before, new guidelines from the Prussian Ministry of the Interior had gone into effect: they extended the principles articulated in April, underscored even more emphatically the function of the guard units as "emergency defense organizations" whose primary mission was to defend against local threats, and created separate positions for "land protection officials" (*Landesschutzbeamte*) with the Oberpräsident and all Landräte as a way of consolidating the guard units organizationally.[109] In late November and early December 1919, the MSPD called upon its members—long skeptical towards the Home Guards—to join the units so they might finally take on a balanced political profile. By the time a review of the developments to date was undertaken in the Magdeburg Oberpräsidium in mid December, the appeal had produced the first successes, though the basic structure of the guard units had not changed.[110] Membership in the units had risen noticeably since summer and now stood at 56,277, of which 29,822 were in the district of Magdeburg, 20,945 in the district of Merseburg, and 5,510 in the district of Erfurt. At first glance the absolute numbers make the guard units seem like a significant force: in the province alone, it could muster half as many men as the future Reichswehr would have soldiers and about one-tenth of all militiamen in all of Prussia;[111] however, the numbers alone do not tell us anything about the strength of the units relative to the size of the population.

To determine the rate of participation, it makes little sense to use as the basis the entire population or even the entire male population. It is more informative to measure the strength of the guard units against the part of the population to which they were tailored first and foremost: the numbers of self-employed males and of employees and civil servants in agriculture, trade, commerce, and industry, and in the administration as recorded in the occupations census of 1925. Relative to size, the rate of participation in the Home Guards in the district of Magdeburg stood at 18.1 percent in December 1919. In the district of Merseburg it was already significantly lower at 13.2 percent, and in the district of Erfurt lower still at 7.2 percent (Table 1.1).[112] The bastions of the Home Guards were found in the rural counties of the northern district: in Osterburg, 58.2 percent of the self-employed, employees, and civil servants were members of the guard units, in Salzwedel 52.2 percent, in Stendal 51.5 percent. By contrast, the relatively strongest units in the rural counties of the district of Merseburg had significantly lower rates (with the exception of the rural county of Naumburg, which as the center of Captain Jüttner's organizational work reached a participation rate of 66.1 percent): 34.6 percent in Eckartsberga, 27.4 percent in Weißenfels, and 26.1 percent in Querfurt. The figures were lower still in the district of Erfurt: here the highest participation rate was achieved in the rural county of Mühlhausen with 27.5 percent, while all other counties came in at below 20 percent. The cities in all three districts were able to recruit members for the units only at much lower rates. With Naumburg again forming the exception (20.1 percent), participation rates were significantly above 10 percent only in Quedlinburg (17.0 percent). Magdeburg had 10.2 percent and Halle 8.4 percent, while Erfurt, along with Nordhausen, Merseburg, Eisleben, and other cities, did not show up at all in the survey from the middle of December 1919.

The foundation of the Home Guards was thus the countryside, not the cities. We can put this in more precise terms. In the five counties with the strongest Home Guards in relative terms—Osterburg, Salzwedel, Stendal, Naumburg, and Eckartsberga—the ratio of independent farmers was far above, and that of industrial workers far below, the average for the district. For example, in County

Table 1.1 Strength of the Home Guards in the Province of Saxony

District/County	Rate of participation (percent)	Membership number in December 1919	Number of male self-employed and civil servants/ white collar workers 1925	Farmers within the population (occupational classification) 1925 (percent)	Share of agricultural land held by medium-sized and large-scale farmers (5–100 hectares) 1925 (percent)	Industrial workers within the population (occupational classification) 1925 (percent)
a) District Magdeburg						
Osterburg	58.2	3,661	6,285	14.9	65.7	12.3
Salzwedel	52.5	4,998	9,513	20.6	82.8	12.4
Stendal (countryside)	51.5	3,194	6,203	10.4	66.9	27.3
Jerichow I	31.6	2,177	6,900	10.5	60.7	21.1
Gardelegen	26.0	2,343	9,010	16.8	71.0	16.8
Quedlinburg (countryside)	24.8	1,126	4,537	5.9	43.9	43.0
Halberstadt (countryside)	22.1	1,029	4,657	9.3	51.2	19.7
Quedlinburg (city)	17.0	650	3,826	1.3	14.9	28.7
Jerichow II	15.9	1,318	8,297	11.6	60.8	20.1
Oschersleben	14.1	857	6,073	5.6	43.0	26.6
Wanzleben	11.7	750	6,403	4.3	31.2	33.0
Stendal (city)	10.2	400	3,910	1.1	64.6	23.4
Magdeburg (city)	10.2	4,804	47,042	0.3	53.8	33.9
Calbe/Saale	9.6	1,079	11,242	4.0	43.6	39.3
Neuhaldensleben	9.5	626	6,603	5.3	43.9	33.1
Aschersleben	6.0	210	3,506	1.4	66.6	42.8
Halberstadt (city)	4.7	350	7,580	0.6	15.8	27.7
Wolmirstedt	3.7	200	5,414	8.0	57.7	26.6
Grafschaft Wernigerode	1.1	50	4,558	4.5	77.2	34.9
Burg (city)	–	–	3,506	1.5	63.7	50.6
District total	**18.1**	**29,822**	**164,799**	**6.2**	**60.4**	**29.2**
b) District Merseburg						
Naumburg (countryside)	66.1	1,200	1,816	12.6	64.6	26.5
Eckartsberga	34.7	1,872	5,392	16.3	55.3	18.0
Weißenfels (countryside)	27.4	1,908	6,968	5.8	67.8	51.1
Querfurt	26.1	1,777	6,816	7.8	51.8	33.6
Wittenberg (countryside)	22.1	1,296	5,850	10.9	75.2	39.2
Schweinitz	21.9	1,274	5,817	23.0	70.8	15.9
Zeitz (countryside)	21.4	654	3,054	5.8	75.8	54.6

District/County	Rate of participation (percent)	Membership number in December 1919	Number of male self-employed and civil servants/ white collar workers 1925	Farmers within the population (occupational classification) 1925 (percent)	Share of agricultural land held by medium-sized and large-scale farmers (5–100 hectares) 1925 (percent)	Industrial workers within the population (occupational classification) 1925 (percent)
Naumburg (city)	20.1	872	4,328	1.3	74.0	30.8
Mansf. Gebirgskreis	16.7	901	5,193	5.9	46.0	47.6
Merseburg (countryside)	16.3	1,291	7,898	6.9	60.9	43.3
Delitzsch	14.5	1,207	8,351	6.8	63.4	35.5
Torgau	13.5	1,020	7,580	11.9	56.5	24.9
Saalkreis	13.0	902	6,958	3.6	41.0	45.9
Liebenwerda	11.8	1,100	9,239	10.7	67.6	36.5
Halle (city)	8.4	2,475	29,567	0.1	30.4	34.5
Bitterfeld	8.3	781	9,381	4.3	52.7	51.4
Mansf. Seekreis	6.5	372	5,745	3.3	29.3	45.3
Sangerhausen	0.5	43	8,629	9.2	58.9	29.1
Eisleben (city)	–	–	2,841	0.7	33.2	46.1
Merseburg (city)	–	–	3,870	0.4	48.9	43.3
Weißenfels (city)	–	–	4,776	0.3	71.1	48.6
Wittenberg (city)	–	–	3,638	2.3	71.4	40.2
Zeitz (city)	–	–	4,489	0.2	39.4	50.3
District total	**13.2**	**20,945**	**158,196**	**6.0**	**58.7**	**39.3**
c) District Erfurt						
Mühlhausen (countryside)	27.5	1,419	5,168	15.5	62.0	36.1
Erfurt (countryside)	19.9	766	3,846	16.6	70.7	27.3
Langensalza	17.7	1,074	6,055	16.3	68.8	23.9
Worbis	12.9	701	5,440	14.6	48.8	36.4
Mühlhausen (city)	9.6	475	4,931	0.8	15.3	45.9
Schleusingen	9.1	596	6,560	5.0	49.3	51.5
Heiligenstadt	6.8	369	5,425	15.0	63.4	31.0
Grafschaft Hohenstein	1.9	110	5,843	8.6	51.0	38.1
Erfurt (city)	–	–	20,914	0.4	51.2	34.3
Nordhausen (city)	–	–	5,861	0.4	55.0	30.3
Weißensee	–	–	3,902	14.2	49.7	27.8
Ziegenrück	–	—	2,135	11.0	71.9	43.5
District total	**7.2**	**5,510**	**76,080**	**8.2**	**58.0**	**35.9**

Sources: column 2 calculated on the basis of columns 3 and 4; column 3: LHAM C 20 Ib 4582, fol. 41f.; columns 4, 5, 7: *Stat. Dt. R., N. F.*, vol. 403, part 9, 74–104 (column 4: A-F, a+b, col. 1 - A-F, a+b, col. 2; column 5: A, a, col.3 : A-F, Zus., col. 3; colunn 7: B, c, col. 3 : A-F, Zus., col. 3); column 6: Haneke, "Die Bodennutzung," 89–219, here 102, 172–179. The counties are listed in order of the relative strength of their Home Guards (i.e., the participation rate).

Salzwedel, 20.5 percent of those with an occupational classification were independent farmers, but only 12.4 percent were industrial workers—the averages for the district were 6.2 percent and 29.2 percent, respectively. Among the farmers, the medium-sized and large-scale farmers dominated, owning 32.0 percent and 50.8 percent of the total acreage, respectively. Comparable figures apply to the other four counties. In County Naumburg-Land, the ratio of farmers was twice the district average (12.6 percent vs. 6.0 percent) while that of industrial workers was below average (26.5 percent vs. 39.3 percent); here, the medium-sized and large-scale farmers owned two-thirds of the agricultural land. In County Eckartsberga, the share of farmers stood at 16.3 percent and that of industrial workers at a mere 18.0 percent, while medium-sized and large-scale farmers owned well over 50 percent of the land. Analogous ratios are found in the rural counties of Mühlhausen and Erfurt.

What can we infer from all these numbers? The typical member of a Home Guard was a farmer with a medium-sized or larger farmstead, though not a large landowner—the Home Guards were especially weak in the counties of the Magdeburger Börde—and tended to live at a distance from urban centers and from the industrial regions of the province. It was not the farmers who frequently had to deal with the theft of produce from the fields by industrial workers nearby, or the urban propertied bourgeoisie that was anxious about its stores being looted that flocked en masse to the guard units, but precisely those rural inhabitants who rarely ever saw a true "Spartacist" or worker plundering the fields. If some incident did occur in the few urban centers in the north of the province, such as the assault on the food depot in Tangermünde, it may have served as an especially potent reinforcement of the fear of the "Spartacists" residing there because it remained a rare event in an otherwise quiet environment. The Home Guards were not so much the sign of a class struggle—now heightened "from the right"—between the "haves" and the working class, as they were an expression of the deepening opposition between city and countryside.[113]

Do these—at first glance—striking figures on the overall strength of the Home Guards mean that they were, after all, a breeding ground for a counterrevolutionary potential, especially in the countryside, that should not be underestimated? The conclusion by the Oberpräsidium in December 1919 does not support such an assumption. A review of the units had shown, so we read, that "a large part exist only on paper. These units were formed in the Spring of 1919 under the impression of a threat, but then they slowly fell dormant, since nobody looked after them. The indifference of the middle class (*Bürgertum*), however, necessitates that the units are constantly agitated." But the rural population, too, in the estimation of the report's author, did not seem sufficiently enthusiastic to serve. He complained about their "aversion to any military service" and their fear of the hidden introduction of a new "compulsory service." In addition, he pointed to their reluctance to bear the costs for ammunition and equipment: "Especially the farmer avoids any expense and prefers to forego the Home Guard if it costs him anything."[114] It is evident that divergent and hard-to-reconcile conceptions of the guard units clashed: most of their members saw them at best as a short-term, necessary instrument to protect house and farm against plundering and vandalism, while the organizers within the bureaucracy and the Central Office in Berlin had in mind a permanent militarization of the "order-loving" segments of the population (leaving aside the even more far-reaching plans of the leader of the Bavarian units, Escherich). The failure of that concept started to become apparent in December of 1919. It is doubtful that, as James Diehl has surmised, the guard units "brutalized and militarized the political mentality of its members"[115] the way the Free Corps did.

The impossibility of shaping the Home Guards into a uniform and potent organization became evident when the number of joining MSPD members rose sharply at the end of 1919 and the beginning of 1920. In December, following appeals in the *Vorwärts,* "a great many" members of the MSPD had joined the guard units in several counties, which made the expert official in the Oberpräsidium express his concern that the units there could "turn into a party-political organization."[116] The problem became more acute in the first two months of 1920. Now the fear was that the arrival of so many MSPD members had also brought into the units those "who in fact have independent positions," that is, supported the USPD. Especially in the countryside there was no strict separation between the three socialist parties, an official noted.[117] In various counties the USPD called on its members to join the units en masse, in response to which the councils of Halle and Mansfeld requested an official clarification that USPD members should not be admitted under any circumstances.[118] On the other hand, there was criticism once again that the bourgeoisie was lacking "determination and vigor" when it came to the Home Guards, from either fear or laziness.[119]

Some of these statements from the period before the Kapp Putsch may be seen as attempts by officials sympathetic to the putschists to keep the guard units as "pure" as possible as a potential weapon in a coup d'état. However, they show above all else that beginning in December 1919, the units not only required a kind of permanent mobilization, but that they also began to become more diverse in their social makeup.[120] How profound the mutual distrust had continued to be would be revealed by the Kapp Putsch. However, those March days would also prove that the Home Guards did not contain meaningful potential for a putsch from the right.

Notes

1. For a survey of the second phase of the Revolution and the military policy that preceded it see Ulrich Kluge, *Die deutsche Revolution 1918/19: Staat, Politik und Gesellschaft zwischen Weltkrieg und Kapp-Putsch* (Frankfurt, 1985), 83ff., 138ff.; Winkler, *Weimar,* 73–83.
2. Oeckel, *Volkswehr,* 120f.

3. Leidigkeit and Herrmann, *Leninistischer Kurs,* 65; Schultz, "USPD," 140; *Kämpfendes Leuna,* 147 (local group established here in March 1919). In October 1919, the paper *Klassenkampf* had 7,000 subscribers.
4. Gutsche, *Bewegung,* 175–181.
5. Oeckel, *Volkswehr,* 118. See the reports by the Erfurt Regierungspräsident Count Pückler to the Oberpräsident on 1 and 5 February 1919, in which he expressed his concern about the arming of workers in Erfurt, Suhl, and other locations in the surrounding area. It was not possible to force them to hand over the weapons, though no excesses had taken place so far. However, the new workers' and soldiers' council in Erfurt would urge a handover of the weapons if the People's Plenipotentiaries (*Volksbeauftragte*) in Weimar would provide assurances regarding the troops stationed there (LHAM C 20 Ib 1996/I, fols. 9–11). We have no information about the size of the milita in Zeitz, which was also dominated by the radicals (Oeckel, *Volkswehr,* 122).
6. Oeckel, *Volkswehr,* 122–124.
7. Oeckel, *Volkswehr,* 133, who cites for this assessment the military leader of the sailors' company in Halle, Hugo Pfeiffer. The Braunschweig "people's militia" (*Volkswehr*), which was also strong and controlled by the leftist USPD and the KPD, seems to have served as a model more for the Ruhr area (ibid., 94–97).
8. For a discussion about the role of violence in the Revolution that took place at the founding party meeting of the KPD see Ludewig, *Arbeiterbewegung,* 34–38. Here the KPD saw violence fundamentally as the last resort, necessary only to fight off a counterrevolution, which is why it did not develop a concept for the use of force and for the establishment of its own military apparatus. Ludewig's work is, strangely enough, not drawn upon by Wirsching, *Weltkrieg.*
9. The work of Gerald D. Feldman, Eberhard Kolb, and Reinhard Rürup, „Die Massenbewegungen der Arbeiterschaft in Deutschland am Ende des Ersten Weltkrieges (1917–1920)," *PVS* 13, no. 3 (1972): 84–105, remains essential reading.
10. Oeckel, *Volkswehr,* 121. The sailors took more than 2,800 rifles, as well as thirty-six heavy and additional light machine guns.
11. Such actions in the run-up to the elections were also reported from other parts of the province. Demonstrators participating in a 14 January rally staged by the USPD and the KPD to oppose the election of a National Assembly stormed the offices of the German National People's Party (DNVP) and the DDP in Erfurt, seized their campaign material, and burned it in the streets. The editor-in-chief of the *Allgemeiner Anzeiger* in Erfurt was forced to print a leaflet in which he acknowledged that the paper had lied (LHAM C 20 Ib 1996/II, fol. 46, RP Erfurt to OP, 4 December 1919). Similar pressures on the bourgeois press and the bourgeois parties in the run-up to the elections were reported from Staßfurt in the district of Magdeburg, from Suhl, and from Langensalza. The demonstrators in Langensalza went a step further: on 13 January, a "popular crowd" (*Volksmenge*) forced the first mayor to resign (ibid., fols. 96f.; ibid., fol. 90, RP Magdeburg to OP, 2 December 1919; these reports were reviews of the year).
12. For a detailed account see Hans-Joachim Bieber, *Bürgertum in der Revolution: Bürgerräte und Bürgerstreiks in Deutschland 1918-1920* (Hamburg, 1992), 180–182. Incidentally, in Halle the bourgeoisie embraced this form early, compared to the rest of Germany, a circumstance that attests to the high degree of political mobilization in January 1919.
13. On the pressure toward a unity of the bourgeoisie in the political language see Dirk Schumann, „Einheitssehnsucht und Gewaltakzeptanz: Politische Grundpositionen des deutschen Bürgertums nach 1918 (mit vergleichenden Überlegungen zu den britischen „middle classes")," in H. Mommsen, ed., *Der Große Krieg und die Nachkriegsordnung: Politischer und kultureller Wandel in Europa 1914–1924,* (Stuttgart, 2000), 83–105.
14. The *Volksblatt,* the paper of the USPD (no. 10, 13 January 1919) was certain of that; the bourgeois *Saale-Zeitung* (no. 19a, 13 January 1919) hesitated to lay blame, which at least makes the version in the *Volksblatt* seem plausible. The *Saale-Zeitung,* incidentally, spoke of "Bloody Sunday," and it was no doubt consciously using the label that the *Volksblatt* had given to the conduct of the police in 1910, though the target was reversed.

15. This account of the events is based on *SZ* no. 19a, 13 January 1919; see Georg Maercker, *Vom Kaiserheer zur Reichswehr: Geschichte des freiwilligen Landesjägerkorps. Ein Beitrag zur Geschichte der deutschen Revolution* (Leipzig, 1921), 132f.; Oeckel, *Volkswehr,* 123.
16. *MZ* no. 966, 29 December 1918; *SZ* no. 21, 14 January 1919.
17. *VS* no. 303, 28 December; no. 304, 29 December 1918.
18. *MZ* no. 7, 3 January 1919. See *MZ* no. 967, 30 December 1918; no. 26, 10 January 1919; no. 801, 9 September 1919; no. 38, 16 January 1920. The difference between the actual "stab-in-the-back legend," which blamed the agitation of the left for the defeat in the war, and the argument presented here, which emphasized Germany's military weakness after November 1918, is overlooked by Detlef Lehnert, "Propaganda des Bürgerkriegs? Politische Feindbilder in der Novemberrevolution als mentale Destabilisierung der Weimarer Demokratie," in Lehnert and Megerle, *Teilkulturen,* 61–101, here esp. 63–68; Lehnert draws also primarily on conservative and Center Party papers. On the "stab-in-the-back" legend see also Felix Höffler, "Kriegserfahrungen in der Heimat: Kriegsverlauf, Kriegsschuld und Kriegsende in württembergischen Stimmungsbildern des Ersten Weltkriegs," in G. Hirschfeld et al., eds., *Kriegserfahrungen: Studien zur Sozial- und Mentalitätsgeschichte des Ersten Weltkriegs* (Essen, 1997), 68–82, here 80–82, who emphasizes the processes of interpretation and propaganda efforts that led to its diffusion in the first place; and, most recently, the voluminous study by Boris Barth, *Dolchstoßlegenden und politische Desintegration: das Trauma der deutschen Niederlage im Ersten Weltkrieg 1914–1933* (Düsseldorf, 2003).
19. *VB* no. 14, 17 January 1919; no. 23, 28 January 1919.
20. Jürgen Falter, Thomas Lindenberger, and Siegfried Schumann, *Wahlen und Abstimmungen in der Weimarer Republik: Materialien zum Wahlverhalten 1919–1933* (Munich, 1986), 67; LAG Reg. Erfurt No. 12784, fol. 275. No detailed record of the election results exists in contemporary statistics. In the press, the results from the urban and rural counties were reported only in part; those from individual towns are even more fragmentary. The *Magdeburgische Zeitung* was fairly precise in its reporting about the election results in the district of Magdeburg (no. 50, 20 January; no. 53, 21 January 1919). According to its figures, the dominance of the SPD was nearly as pronounced in the countryside as it was in the cities. Although the USPD was able to exceed its average showing significantly in Magdeburg itself (6.3 percent), in Staßfurt (7.1 percent), and in Aschersleben (7.0 percent), even in the cities it came in far behind the SPD. For the district of Merseburg, by contrast, we have only a few, largely local, partial results (*SZ* no. 31a, no. 32, 20 January; no. 34, 21 January 1919). They suggest not that the USPD owed its excellent results to a few strongholds, but that it was the strongest party across the board, though it did show greater local variation than the SPD in the northern area of the district. For example, in the Halle suburb of Ammendorf, which was dominated by railway carriage manufacturing, it won no less than 66.2 percent, in the old workers' county of Eilenburg 59.5 percent, in the traditional mining town of Eisleben 50.3 percent (also above average), in Liebenwerda in the brown coal region 47.1 percent, and in Bitterfeld, a site of the chemical industry, 44.0 percent. The USPD had been able to establish itself as by far the strongest workers' party in both the traditional and the relatively new industrial areas. In the district of Erfurt, which was part of Electoral District 36 (Thuringia), the SPD achieved its best result in the urban county Mühlhausen with 37.9 percent of the ballots (vs. 19.8 percent for the USPD), while in the urban county Erfurt it won only 21.2 percent (vs. 37.3 percent for the USPD), and in the urban county Nordhausen a mere 11.0 percent (vs. 39.5 percent for the USPD). Its weakest showing was 7.2 percent in the rural county Weißensee, site of a factory of the armament company Rheinmetall; the USPD won 47.0 percent here (LAG Erfurt no. 12784, fol. 275). Apart from the rural counties Osterburg and Stendal—later strongholds of Home Guards (*Einwohnerwehren*)—the DDP was overtaken by the DNVP in six rural counties of the district of Erfurt, though just barely.
21. Schubert, "Generalstreik," 34–38, the wording of the directive on page 174; Leidigkeit and Herrmann, *Leninistischer Kurs,* 73–76; see Heinrich August Winkler, *Von der Revolution zur Stabilisierung: Arbeiter und Arbeiterbewegung in der Weimarer Republik 1918 bis 1924* (2nd

ed. Berlin, 1985), 168, 175f. On the course of the negotiations and the subsequent events see Oertzen, *Betriebsräte,* 133–147.

22. Winkler, *Revolution,* 169f.
23. Schubert, "Generalstreik," 48–50.
24. According to a report by the *VB* no. 48, 26 February 1919.
25. *VB* no. 46, 24 February 1919; Schubert, "Generalstreik," 57–62; Winkler, *Revolution,* 175f. For the text of the appeal see *SZ* no. 94, 25 February 1919.
26. Schubert, "Generalstreik," 63–65, who has a detailed list of all the places that joined the strike, though without the number of participating workers. See Raßloff, *Flucht,* 184–190, for details on the strike and the counterstrike in Erfurt.
27. Vogler, "Klassenkampf," 167–172; Schubert, "Generalstreik," 75f.
28. Bieber, *Bürgertum,* 204ff.
29. *SZ* no. 94, 25 February; no. 95, 26 February 1919; on the conduct of the physicians see *SZ* no. 94, 25 February 1919.
30. That is clear from the information in *SZ* no. 96, 26 February 1919.
31. Helge Matthiesen, "Zwei Radikalisierungen—Bürgertum und Arbeiterschaft in Gotha 1918–1923," *GG* 21, no. 1 (1995): 32–62, here 44.
32. According to the retrospective report in *SZ* no. 98, 4 April 1919.
33. *SZ* no. 98, 4 April 1919. See Kolb, *Arbeiterräte,* 297–301, who believes that the unresolved security problems in the bastions of the radicals played a key role in the actions of the Reich government, while conceding, however, that "serious unrests" developed in Halle only after Maercker's entry into the city and that the workers' council in Erfurt had disciplined troops at its command.
34. Schubert, "Generalstreik," 105f.; Gertrud Kling, *Die Rolle des Arbeiter- und Soldatenrats von Halle in der Novemberrevolution (November 1918 bis März 1919)* (Halle, n.d. [1960]), 49; Maercker, *Kaiserheer,* 136ff.
35. Maercker, *Kaiserheer,* 137; see Schubert, "Generalstreik," 107f.
36. *SZ* no. 98, 4 March 1919; Maercker, *Kaiserheer,* 138–140; Schubert, "Generalstreik," 178 (Gustav Borrmann's recollections of the fighting in Halle: according to Borrmann, the attempts to offer armed resistance to the occupying soldiers were poorly coordinated); see the vivid account of the nighttime reconnaissance car trip by Curt Geyer—one of the leading members of the workers' and soldiers' council in Leipzig—to Halle, where Geyer made his way to the theater and spoke with the battle leadership and tried to prevent looting in the city: Curt Geyer, *Die revolutionäre Illusion: Zur Geschichte des linken Flügels der USPD,* ed. W. Benz and H. Graml (Stuttgart, 1976), 99–102. Maercker, *Kaiserheer,* 143f., reports that as a form of "deterrence," the names of looters sentenced by an extraordinary military court were publicly posted. They included many who were "not part of the actual mob." Moreover, many looters were informed against, especially by women.
37. Author's calculations based on *SZ* no. 114, 8 March 1919. A total of 79,588 ballots were cast, compared to 97,807 in January. The contention by Kling, *Arbeiter- und Soldatenrat,* 50, that the USPD had gained votes compared to the elections for the National Assembly is wrong. According to *SZ* no. 98, 4 March 1919, voting was not possible in some electoral districts because the board and the assessors were not at hand, while in others the balloting had to be stopped because of firefights. Maercker claims, without providing any details, that the other side did not adhere to the restraint imposed on his own troops and fired upon his soldiers with machine guns, wounding four (Maercker, *Kaiserheer,* 140). In Erfurt, where no fighting had taken place but the water works had been shut down, the DDP lost a considerable number of voters to the DVP and DNVP. See Raßloff, *Flucht,* 186–187, 190.
38. Maercker, *Kaiserheer,* 144f.; *SZ* no. 100, 5 March 1919; *VB* no. 57, 8 March 1919. The main culprit was sentenced to death a few months later, and several other participants were sentenced to long jail terms. See the "Bericht des Untersuchungsausschusses über die Unruhen in Mitteldeutschland vom November 1918 bis zum 19. März 1919," in *Sammlung der*

Drucksachen der verfassungsgebenden preußischen Landesversammlung, Tagung 1919/21, vol. 10, no. 3227 (Berlin, 1921), 5577–5579. Nearly all those involved belonged to "front line age cohorts," though the report does not reveal whether they had actually been soldiers.

39. Thomas Lindenberger, "Die 'verdiente Tracht Prügel': Ein kurzes Kapitel über das Lynchen im wilhelminischen Berlin," in T. Lindenberger and A. Lüdtke, eds., *Physische Gewalt: Studien zur Geschichte der Neuzeit* (Frankfurt, 1995), 190–212.
40. *SZ* no. 98, 4 March 1919; see *VB* no. 56, 7 March 1919, according to which "upstanding burghers" had also taken part in the looting alongside the "so-called mob."
41. Maercker, *Kaiserheer,* 140–142 (where the date is erroneously given as 2 March instead of 3 March); see Oeckel, *Volkswehr,* 184, who takes his casualty figures from Maercker.
42. Winkler, *Revolution,* 176–178; Schubert, "Generalstreik," 129–143, whose confused accounts reveal neither the reasons for the end to the strike nor the precise time when it ended; Maercker, *Kaiserheer,* 154f. In central Germany, works councils were generally recognized beyond mining, their incorporation into the constitution was promised, and their right to information was expanded. Still, the right of entrepreneurs to run their businesses on their own was not changed; see Oertzen, *Betriebsräte,* 145f.
43. *SZ* no. 102, 6 March 1919; Maercker, *Kaiserheer,* 149–151; Könnemann, *Einwohnerwehren,* 102; Maercker, *Kaiserheer,* 150f. Maercker reports that when he set up the Free Corps, he had been "deeply disappointed" by the "conduct of the young men of Halle, especially from commercial circles." Evidently, the direct if short-lived experience of chaos and anarchy had not aroused the willingness among future shopowners to join a paramilitary unit, one that could also have been used outside of Halle. Temporary volunteers had to commit to serving for several months and were trained by regular army units, though they continued to pursue their jobs or studies and were only activated if the military needed additional forces for a deployment. See Könnemann, *Einwohnerwehren,* 157–185; Diehl, *Paramilitary Politics,* 30–32.
44. Maercker admitted this indirectly at a press conference on 8 March (*SZ* no. 114, 8 March 1919); see Maercker, *Kaiserheer,* 144, 152. For details about the mistreatment see *VB* no. 63, 15 March 1919, according to which detainees were beaten by the soldiers with whips and clubs, slapped and kicked, given inadequate food, and made to spend the night on the bare floor without blankets.
45. Schubert, "Generalstreik," 114f., 180f.; see Maercker, *Kaiserheer,* 152. In this context Maercker also mentions that the "known Spartacist leader" Pludra was found one morning on the street shot to death. Whether this, too, was a political murder remained unresolved; Maercker himself seems to have assumed that it was.
46. GSTA PK I. HA Rep. 84a no. 10432 (Preliminary proceedings concerning the murder of KPD–leader K. Meseberg). The file does not reveal whether the culprits had been front line soldiers during the war who may have been "brutalized" by their experience. The trial against the four men was later suspended, but that against the fugitive primary culprit was continued. In 1922, one of the accomplices, Felix Claus, wrote an open letter to the DNVP, which the *Vorwärts,* the national paper of the Social Democrats, printed a few days after the murder of Walter Rathenau under the title "Protection of criminals by the German Nationals" (no. 302, 29 June 1922). In this letter, Claus recounted his experiences as a member of the "Organisation Consul," an infamous clandestine right-wing terror organization, and the financial support as well as other help he supposedly received from members of the DNVP, including also in Halle itself. How credible Claus was is an open question, however. According to information from the police administration in Zeitz, prior to November 1918 he had lived in Berlin for a long time and had worked there as a pimp; at the outbreak of the Revolution, he became a member of the workers' and soldiers' council, though he was soon expelled (GSTA PK I. HA Rep. 84a no. 10432, fol. 12, Report, 17 June 1920).
47. *SZ* no. 100, 5 March 1919; no. 102, 6 March 1919. At the beginning of April, the *Volksstimme,* too, identified as those responsible for the unrest in Halle "independent and communist instigators (*Drahtzieher*)," who had then brought "dubious elements," indeed, "criminal riffraff,"

into the plan (*VS* no. 84, 9 April 1919; no. 85, 10 April 1919). The *Magdeburgische Zeitung* saw the "wildest chaos" prevailing in Berlin at the beginning of March (*MZ* no. 179, 8 March 1919).

48. *MZ* no. 176, 7 March 1919; *SZ* no. 102, 6 March 1919; see *MZ* no. 165, 3 March 1919, in which a special correspondent from the Baltic front line reported a new large-scale offensive by Russian troops, spoke of the "immense danger" that this posed to Germany, and quoted General Groener as saying that Bolshevism was today as strong as Islam was at its height.
49. *VS* no. 82, 6 April 1919.
50. *MZ* no. 179, 8 March 1919; in the same vein *VS* no. 85, 10 April 1919.
51. Jürgen Zarusky, *Die deutschen Sozialdemokraten und das sowjetische Modell: Ideologische Auseinandersetzung und außenpolitische Konzeptionen 1917–1933* (Munich, 1992), 85–95, who makes clear that for Social Democracy during the revolutionary period, "Bolshevism" did not mean "dictatorship" as much as "chaos." See also Peter Lösche, *Der Bolschewismus im Urteil der deutschen Sozialdemokratie 1903–1920* (Berlin, 1967). Lehnert, "Propaganda," 73–78, who calls anti-Bolshevism the "propaganda tool of the general enmity toward Socialism and the Republic," cites only two Center Party papers in support of this contention, the *Germania* and the *Kölnische Volkszeitung.* Ute Döser, "Das bolschewistische Rußland im Urteil der deutschen Rechtspresse 1918–1925," PhD diss., Free University of Berlin, 1961, esp. 40–46, 124, highlights the emotionally charged reporting on events in Russia, which involved variations on the "chaos" theme and that of the decline of Western culture and did not lack anti-Semitic undertones. However, she also notes that enmity to the Entente ranked higher than hostility to Bolshevist Russia. Michael Trauthig, *Im Kampf um Glauben und Kirche: Eine Studie über Gewaltakzeptanz und Krisenmentalität der württembergischen Protestanten zwischen 1918 und 1933* (Leinfelden-Echterdingen, 1999), 242–260, shows the apocalyptic charge of the Bolshevist picture of the enemy in Württemberg Protestantism; it weakened after 1922.
52. *MZ* no. 283, 16 April 1919. Following the entry of troops into the city at the beginning of April, the paper also noted that while "subversive endeavors" had existed in Magdeburg, they had been "far removed from Hallean models" and that in spite of all the disturbances of order, "there were still elements that were eager to prevent chaos from taking hold" (*MZ* no. 265, 9 April 1919).
53. *MZ* no. 179, 8 March 1919; no. 283, 16 April 1919.
54. *SZ* no. 118, 11 March 1919. Abderhalden also underscored that the bourgeoisie had to show a general willingness to come to an "understanding" with the workers, which presupposed that each side know more about the other; so far, the "so-called bourgeois camp … was not learning what the workers wanted," and vice versa.
55. Martin H. Geyer, „Teuerungsprotest und Teuerungsunruhen 1914–1923: Selbsthilfegesellschaft und Geldentwertung," in M. Gailus and H. Volkmann, eds., *Der Kampf um das tägliche Brot: Nahrungsmangel, Versorgungspolitik und Protest 1770–1990* (Opladen, 1994), 319–345, esp. 337, who speaks of a "popular anti-capitalism" (though here with reference to the situation of the beginning hyperinflation in 1922/23).
56. *VB* no. 57, 8 March 1919; cf. *VB* no. 48, 24 February 1919.
57. *VS* no. 89, 15 April 1919; no. 85, 10 April 1919.
58. *VS* no. 47, 25 February 1919; no. 89, 15 April 1919.
59. On the fighting in other places and the use of the Free Corps there see Diehl, *Paramilitary Politics,* 38–42.
60. To that extent it is also important to emphasize the limited transferability of what was experienced in Berlin; Wirsching, *Weltkrieg,* 128, points to the "language of violence and civil war that was systematically carried into the public arena … by the Communists," which he regards as a "decisive factor." That certainly does not apply to the fighting in the province of Saxony.
61. Kluge, *Revolution,* 111.
62. The conflicts were "political" in the sense that the striking "masses" wanted to structure the economic and social order of the new Republic in a way that was fundamentally different from

where it seemed to be heading. It does not matter how detailed the program they were pursuing was, or how accurately each striker was able to grasp it. Here Weitz, *German Communism,* 91, is right; he criticizes, among others, the position of Wolfgang J. Mommsen, "Die deutsche Revolution 1918–1920: Politische Revolution und soziale Protestbewegung," *GG* 4, no. 3 (1978): 362–391. Mommsen (381f.) ascribes to the strike movement in the industrial region of central Germany a more pronounced political character than that of its counterpart in the Ruhr region, but here, too, he emphasizes the great importance of the demands that were directly related to the industrial enterprises in question.

63. On the stages of the mobilization of the middle class see Bieber, *Bürgertum,* 182ff., 212ff., who emphasizes that the individual strikes by the bourgeoisie were not coordinated.
64. For an incisive discussion see Geyer, "Teuerungsprotest."
65. LHAM C 20 Ib 1996/I, fols. 148–151 (LR to OP, 29 March 1919); *VS* no. 76, 30 March 1919.
66. LHAM C 20 Ib 1996/I, fols. 150f., fols. 331–336 (RP Magdeburg to the Prussian Ministry of the Interior, 25 October 1919). Over the medium term the conditions in Tangermünde do not seem to have improved. On 5 May, the warehouse was stormed and looted a second time by a larger, partially armed crowd, which suspected that the goods there were being used for profiteering. There were no clashes, since the guards did not take any action this time (LHAM C 20 Ib 1996/I, fol. 216, LR to OP, 6 June 1919).
67. *VS* no. 149, 29 June 1919; *MZ* no. 458, 28 June 1919. The article in the *Volksstimme* says nothing about the deployment of the military; otherwise, the reports are largely consistent, though their assessments of the events diverge in part.
68. Gailus, *Straße und Brot.*
69. On the debate about E. P. Thompson's influential concept of a "moral economy," see Manfred Gailus, "Food Riots in Großbritannien, Frankreich und Deutschland. Anmerkungen zu neueren Forschungsergebnissen," *AfS* 33 (1993): 586–604; Manfred Gailus and Thomas Lindenberger, "Zwanzig Jahre 'moralische Ökonomie.' Ein sozialhistorisches Konzept ist volljährig geworden," *GG* 20, no. 3 (1994): 469–477.
70. *MZ* no. 50, 20 January 1919.
71. *VS* no. 79, 3 April 1919. But see the contrasting interpretation of two incidents of unrest over rising prices in Altona by Anthony McElligott, "Petty Complaints, Plunder and Police in Altona 1917–1920: Towards an Interpretation of Community and Conflict," in P. Assion, ed., *Transformationen der Arbeiterkultur* (Marburg, 1985), 110–125, esp. 121, who sees them as manifestations of proletarian solidarity against the claims to power on the part of the police and (petty) capitalists.
72. LHAM C 20 Ib 1996/I, fol. 159 (Police of Tangermünde to LR Stendal, 31 March 1919).
73. *VS* no. 79, 3 April; no. 149, 29 June; no. 150, 1 July 1919.
74. *MZ* no. 458, 28 June 1919.
75. For this see the information in Joachim Stang, *Die Deutsche Demokratische Partei in Preußen, 1918–1933* (Düsseldorf, 1994), 402f.
76. LHAM C 20 Ib 1996/I, fols. 334–336 (RP Magdeburg to the Prussian Ministry of the Interior, 25 October 1919).
77. LHAM C 20 Ib 1996/I, fol. 341 (RP Merseburg to the Prussian Ministry of the Interior, 17 November 1919), fol. 325 (RP Erfurt to the Prussian Ministry of the Interior, 8 September 1919).
78. LHAM C 20 Ib 1996/I, fol. 331 (RP Magdeburg to the Prussian Ministry of the Interior, 25 October 1919), fol. 340 (RP Magdeburg to the Prussian Ministry of the Interior, 17 November 1919). The report does not identify the rural counties in question. See Franz Exner, *Krieg und Kriminalität* (Leipzig, 1926); Moritz Liepmann, *Krieg und Kriminalität in Deutschland* (Stuttgart, 1930), esp. 33ff., 55ff.; for a summary account, with further sources, see Bessel, *Germany,* 240ff.
79. On such cases of collective theft especially of potatoes and other field crops, see the reports in

LHAM C 20 Ib 1996/I, fols. 175f., 184–186, 224–229, 322f., 333f., 375–377. In Magdeburg at the beginning of February, a group of 50–60 men, chiefly soldiers, roamed through the city at night, attacked a police station where they procured weapons, and then opened the prison, all without encountering any opposition. This was followed by the looting of a watch and clothing store (LHAM C 20 Ib 1996/I, fols. 69–74, 334f.; *MZ* no. 93, 4 February 1919; *VS* no. 31, 6 February 1919). On this special, briefly important mixture of protest and criminality among young, still-unmarried soldiers, who were waiting to be demobilized and who expressed their discontent and fear of an uncertain future in a way that was especially provocative to the authorities but nonpolitical, see Bessel, *Germany,* 79–81.

80. LHAM C 20 Ib, 1996/I, fol. 334 (RP Magdeburg to the Prussian Ministry of the Interior, 8 September 1919); fols. 325f. (RP Erfurt to the Prussian Ministry of the Interior, 8 September 1919); fol. 341 (RP Merseburg to the Prussian Ministry of the Interior, 8 September 1919).
81. LHAM C 20 Ib 1996/I, fols. 332, 336 (RP Magdeburg to the Prussian Ministry of the Interior, 8 September 1919); fols. 340f. (RP Merseburg to the Prussian Ministry of the Interior, 8 September 1919).
82. LHAM C 20 Ib 1996/I, fols. 336, 332f. (RP Magdeburg to the Prussian Ministry of the Interior, 8 September 1919); fol. 341 (RP Merseburg to the Prussian Ministry of the Interior, 8 September 1919); fol. 323 (RP Erfurt to the Prussian Ministry of the Interior, 8 September 1919); see Bessel, *Germany,* 246ff.
83. LHAM C 20 Ib 1996/I, fol. 342 (RP Merseburg to the Prussian Ministry of the Interior, 8 September 1919).
84. Bessel, *Germany,* 250; figures on the unemployment trend, 129. For a vivid account of the mood of a new departure and the critique of authority that went hand in hand with the new possibilities of consumption see Geyer, *Verkehrte Welt,* 70–75.
85. In this way one could today reformulate the thesis by Wolfgang J. Mommsen, who argued in 1978 that the "political Revolution" was overlaid by a "social protest movement." By "social protest," Mommsen meant the elevated rank of the goals of the strike movement in the spring of 1919 that were directly related to the business enterprises and which played a prominent role especially in the syndicalist-tinged strike movement in the Ruhr region; the subsistence protests, on the other hand, he leaves out completely.
86. *SZ* no. 1, 1 January 1919.
87. Geyer, *Verkehrte Welt,* 76–79.
88. *SZ* no. 102, 6 March 1919.
89. *MZ* no. 459, 29 June; no. 801, 9 November 1919. The *Volksstimme,* too, underscored the importance of work, an assertion that was directed against the radical left: "general work" was needed, not a general strike, the paper declared in the middle of April 1919. However, this notion of work meant, alongside "work for the German economy," also "work for the family" and "work … for the party" (*VS* no. 89, 15 April 1919).
90. *MZ* no. 1, 1 January 1920. In its review of the year, the *Saale-Zeitung* pointed generally to the "chaos" at the beginning of the year, which fortunately had been overcome, and it then went on to speak about the "desperate situation" in which the people had to be brought together in "positive work" (*SZ* no. 610, 31 December 1919).
91. Könnemann, *Einwohnerwehren,* quote on 129; Diehl, *Paramilitary Politics,* 32–38, 55–74; Jens Flemming, "Die Bewaffnung des 'Landvolks': Ländliche Schutzwehren und agrarischer Konservatismus in der Anfangsphase der Weimarer Republik," *MGM* 26, no. 2 (1979): 7–36; Large, *The Politics of Law and Order;* Peter Bucher, "Zur Geschichte der Einwohnerwehren in Preußen 1918–1921," *MGM* 9, no. 1 (1971): 15–59; Bieber, *Bürgertum in der Revolution,* 246–252; cf. Kolb, *Arbeiterräte,* 385–393; on Bavaria see now also Geyer, *Verkehrte Welt,* 117–123; on Berlin, Wirsching, *Weltkrieg,* 300–312.
92. Ziemann, *Front,* 394–413; Fritzsche, *Rehearsals for Fascism,* 56–65, also emphasizes the low levels of participation; see already the brief indications in Bucher, "Einwohnerwehren," 50–53.
93. A good example of this lack of clarity is Bieber, *Bürgertum in der Revolution,* 366f.

94. Könnemann, *Einwohnerwehren,* 45f.
95. On the decrees see Diehl, *Paramilitary Politics,* 33f.; Könnemann, *Einwohnerwehren,* 31f., 45, 117–121, for the decrees of 18 March and 15 April 1919 see 357–359. Also see LHAM C 20 Ib 1820, fol. 1 (Decree by Loebell, 7 August 1914), fol. 19 (Decree of 6 June 1918). Könnemann, *Einwohnerwehren,* 117f., points out that the decrees of 6 November, 15 November, and 18 March went back to the same three imperial ministerial officials.
96. Maercker, *Kaiserheer,* 150f. It would appear that Maercker had no problem recruiting for the Home Guard, in contrast to the formation of the Freikorps Halle.
97. Ibid., 329f.
98. Berghahn, *Stahlhelm,* 38, 47.
99. LHAM C 20 Ib 1997/II (LR Gardelegen to OP, 21 May 1919); C 20 Ib 1997/I, fols. 27–29 (RP Magdeburg to the Prussian Ministry of the Interior, 30 March 1919); fol. 37 (RP Erfurt to OP, 3 April 1919); fol. 55 (County farmers' and rural workers' council to LR of Nordhausen, 8 May 1919); fols. 87f. (LR Liebenwerda to OP, 18 June 1919). In the small Thuringian town of Heiligenstadt, which was dominated by the Center Party, the old workers' council was opposed to the Home Guard in May 1919, whereas the newly elected one was in favor; however, the representatives of the radicals did not go beyond threats of violence in their unsuccessful opposition; LHAM C 20 Ib 1997/I, fols. 61–64, (LR Heiligenstadt to RP Erfurt, 19 May 1919); see LAG Reg. Erfurt no. 1352, fol. 83 (LR Heiligenstadt to RP, 26 June 1919).
100. LHAM C 20 Ib 1997/I, fols. 53f. (LR Nordhausen to RP, 13 May 1919); fols. 87f. (LR Liebenwerda to RP, 18 June 1919); fol. 119 (LR Halberstadt to RP, 12 July 1919); fols. 139f. (RP Magdeburg to OP, 10 July 1919); on Bitterfeld: fol. 80 (General Command IV Army Corps to OP, 13 June 1919); fol. 180 (RP Merseburg to OP, 12 July 1919); LAG Reg. Erfurt no. 1352, fol. 34 (Police of Erfurt to RP, 10 May 1919); fol. 75 (Town council of Mühlhausen to RP, 22 May 1919); LAMe C 47 Ie 919/II, fol. 63 (Town council of Bitterfeld to LR, 6 September 1919). In the Free State of Saxony, the initiative to form Home Guards was taken by its burgher leagues, but such attempts ran into firm resistance from the Social Democrats and the other Socialist parties. See Benjamin Nathan Lapp, *Revolution from the Right: Politics, Class, and the Rise of Nazism in Saxony, 1919–1933* (Atlantic Highlands, NJ, 1997), 37f.
101. LHAM C 20 Ib 1996/I, fols. 278f. (First Mayor to LR Stendal, 20 May 1919); 1997/I, fols. 167f. (RP Magdeburg to the General Command IV Army Corps, 17 July 1919). According to a list of all Home Guards in the county of Stendal on 24 May 1919, the guard unit in Tangermünde had a total of 127 members, who were armed with an equal number of rifles; its leader was a "boatman" (*Schiffer*) (C 20 Ib 1997/II, fol. 3). However, a survey from August gives no membership number and equipment of only twenty pistols (C 20 Ib 1997/II, fol. 176).
102. LHAM C 20 Ib 1997/II, fols. 173–183 (General Command IV Army Corps to OP, 17 August 1919).
103. LHAM C 20 Ib 1997/I, fol. 271 (General Command IV Army Corps to OP, 6 August 1919).
104. LHAM C 20 Ib 1997/II, fols. 172, 174f., 178, 182. Population figures in *Stat. Dt. R., N. F.,* vol. 40: 54f. (1925 census).
105. Lists of a number of guard units in the counties with information about their leaders are found in LHAM C 20 Ib 1997/II, passim; on Halle: fol. 114 and 1997/I, fols. 118, 120, 158; on Brumby: fol. 198. The lists were apparently drawn up between the end of May and the end of June 1919. On the social profile of the guards see Könnemann, *Einwohnerwehren,* 202–212.
106. Maercker, *Kaiserheer,* 333–335; Vogler, "Klassenkampf," 178–182.
107. The Technische Nothilfe was a volunteer organization under the control of the Reich Ministry of the Interior. Originally intended to provide technical expertise in emergency situations, it became an organization of mainly bourgeois members that played a substantial part in strikebreaking. See Winkler, *Revolution,* pp. 407–412.
108. *SZ* no. 552, 25 November; no. 554, 26 November; no. 570, 5 December 1919; *VB* no. 276, 25 November 1919; Maercker, *Kaiserheer,* 338–344; LHAM C 20 Ib 1997/II, fols. 180f.

(General Command IV Army Corps to OP, 17 August 1919, overview of the state of the Home Guards).

109. Text in Könnemann, *Einwohnerwehren,* 377–385, see 135f.
110. The following is based on LHAM C 20 Ib 4582, fols. 39–42 (Expert for Home Guards with the OP to the Prussian Ministry of the Interior, Central Office for Home Guards, 23 December 1919).
111. According to Könnemann, *Einwohnerwehren,* 139, as of 1 October 1919, 626,764 men were registered in the Home Guards in Prussia.
112. This and the following calculations are based on LHAM C 20 Ib 4582, fols. 41f., and *Stat. Dt. R., N. F.,* vol. 403, party 9, 74ff.
113. For a general account of the development of this opposition during the inflation period see Klaus Tenfelde, "Stadt und Land in Krisenzeiten: München und das Münchener Umland zwischen Revolution und Inflation 1918 bis 1923," in K. Tenfelde and W. Hardtwig, eds., *Soziale Räume in der Urbanisierung: Studien zur Geschichte Münchens im Vergleich 1850 bis 1933* (Munich, 1990), 37–57; Ziemann, *Front,* 401, 405.
114. LHAM C 20 Ib 4582, fols. 39f. (Expert for Home Guards with the OP to the Prussian Ministry of the Interior, Central Office for Home Guards, 23 December 1919). An official at Langensalza noted that the sentiment among the population toward the Home Guards was "indifferent;" the Landrat of Worbis noted "excuses like 'I spent four years lying in the trenches and am not interested in putting my life at risk again'" (LAG Reg. Erfurt no. 1352, fol. 337, *Kreisrat* of Langensalza to RP, 24 November 1919; fol. 261, LR Worbis to RP, 6 October 1919). See Könnemann, *Einwohnerwehren,* 218, who refers to similar complaints, for example in Hamburg; Ziemann, *Front,* 403f.
115. Diehl, *Paramilitary Politics,* 38. Fritzsche, *Rehearsals,* 56–65, also rejects the thesis of the radicalization of the citizenry by the Home Guards.
116. LHAM C 20 Ib 4582, fols. 39f. (Expert for Home Guards with the OP to the Prussian Ministry of the Interior, Central Office for Home Guards, 23 December 1919). See also the appeal in the *Volksstimme* that its readers join the units in no. 281, 2 December 1919.
117. LHAM C 20 Ib 4582, fols. 51–54 (Expert for Home Guards with the OP to the Prussian Ministry of the Interior, 3 February 1920).
118. LHAM C 20 Ib 4582, fols. 88f. (Expert for Home Guards with the OP to the Prussian Ministry of the Interior, 3 March 1920); fol. 93 (*Kreisrat* Halle/Saalkreis to Expert for Home Guards with the OP, 4 March 1920); fol. 95 (*Kreisrat* Mansfeld to Expert for Home Guards with the OP, 12 March 1920). However, in some cities (Bitterfeld and Eisleben, for example), the resistance of the USPD remained massive and went so far as threats of boycott against shop owners, which is why no Home Guards existed there yet (LHAM C 20 Ib 4582, fols. 39f., Expert for Home Guards with the OP to the Prussian Ministry of the Interior, 23 December 1919).
119. LHAM C 20 Ib 4582, fols. 39f. The expert also noted that "some circles on the right" had concerns about the joining oath for the guard units and rejected them for that reason (fols. 40f.).
120. See also Könnemann, *Einwohnerwehren,* 237ff., who describes the eventually failed attempts by the head of the central office in Berlin, Runkel, to impart a uniform ideological foundation to the units. Runkel's construction of an idea of a *Volk* community aimed against both "individualistic Bolshevism" and capitalism, Könnemann tells us, was received with skepticism especially by the right.

Chapter 2

NEW MISTRUST, OLD ENEMIES

The Massive Experience of Violence during the Kapp Putsch of 1920 and Its Aftermath

On 13 March 1920, a circle of right-wing conspirators sought to seize power in Germany. Free Corps units occupied the government buildings in Berlin, and when the leadership of the Reichswehr gave no indication that it was willing to take vigorous countermeasures, the Reich government fled the capital. Nevertheless, the putsch, named after one of its two leaders, ended in failure after only four days: the upper-level civil servants of the Berlin ministries refused to cooperate with the putschists, and the unions called for a general strike throughout Germany. In a few regions, the strike turned into clashes with units of the Reichswehr. This included above all the Ruhr region, where a "Red Army" had formed: for several weeks it ruled large sections of the industrial area and it was eventually crushed by the military in brutal fighting. These clashes have been interpreted as the third and last phase of the Revolution, in which another attempt was made to prevent it from getting bogged down, without there being any clarity about the goals of the movement.[1]

In the province of Saxony, which also saw intense fighting in March of 1920, this interpretation is only partially true. Here, where the struggle was chiefly over not yielding the street to the military, many workers had their first experience of violent clashes with the state's security forces. This experience did not so much end a process as trigger a push toward radicalization: over the medium term this push turned the KPD into a mass party, while also promoting the formation of organizational structures with counterrevolutionary intent on the part of the urban bourgeoisie and the farmers.

Notes from this chapter begin on page 49.

Passive Burghers, Trigger-Happy Soldiers, Distrustful Workers: The Escalation of Violence after 13 March 1920

The province of Saxony saw the first organized reactions to the putsch only a few hours after the government buildings in Berlin had been occupied. The disagreements between the MSPD, USPD, and KPD receded into the background. Action committees of the three workers' parties formed first in the district of Magdeburg, where the MSPD assumed the leadership of the movement from the outset and was also able to largely control it to the end. In the provincial capital Magdeburg itself, as in Stendal, a rapidly formed action committee proclaimed an immediate general strike.[2] Action committees calling for a general strike were also set up in Erfurt and in Suhl on 13 and 14 March, respectively.[3]

The response was slower and more hesitant in the district of Merseburg. On 13 March, the workers of the Zschornewitz power plant went on strike, and that afternoon the works councils in the Bitterfeld coal mining district called for a general strike and formed an action committee. Workers also walked off the job in the Geisel Valley, Halle, at the Leuna Works, and in Merseburg, though action committees seem to have formed here only a day later. It is possible that the disagreements between the MSPD and the USPD and KPD were so deep, and the skepticism of the radical left toward the previous Reich governments so profound, that the leaders of the various parties could not immediately bring themselves to issue a call for a strike in support of the old government; tellingly, the central office of the KPD had also initially rebuffed the proclamation of a general strike by the leadership of the MSPD.[4] In the end, though, the various calls for a strike differed only in nuances. All emphasized the defensive goal of the work stoppage (defeating the putsch in Berlin), appealed for calm and levelheadedness, and declared explicitly that the essential utilities would continue operating. No proclamation mentioned arming the workers or taking violent action against the putschists or their sympathizers. But they all underscored—as had been the case in the spring of 1919—that the general strike constituted the use of the "most potent" (Halle) or the "most terrible weapon of the entire proletariat" (Aschersleben).[5]

Initially, the initiative in most places lay with the organized workers. Following the proclamation of a general strike, the Home Guards were disarmed almost everywhere and the workers were armed. In the garrison town of Stendal this was done as early as noon on 13 March. The action committee seized the centrally stored weapons of the guard unit without opposition—including 77 rifles, 3 machine guns, and more than 80,000 cartridges—and distributed them to trusted members of all three parties. A cavalry unit from the local garrison sought to disarm the workers, but it withdrew without firing a shot after Ernst Brandenburg, the chairman of the action committee, reached an agreement with its commanding officer that the issued weapons would remain in the hands of the workers "until the old government has been restored to its full rights." There was no pressing need for the steps taken by the action committee, but concerns that the Home Guard and the local garrison might support the putschists seemed to call for quick action.[6] The guard unit itself—in a rural county with the strongest guards overall—was completely taken by surprise and was evidently not prepared to offer any kind of help to the putschists in Berlin. The disarming of the Home Guards went just as smoothly in many other places.[7]

Only in a few instances did such disarming actions lead to violent confrontations. Most casualties occurred in Heldrungen, a rural community in the south of the district of Merseburg. On 18 March, armed workers prevailed upon the mayor to call for a handover of weapons at the town hall "through bell ringing and a public announcement." When members of the Home Guard appeared on the scene, the workers left the center of the town and regrouped at its outskirts. When a part of the Home Guard confronted them there, a firefight ensued, which left two dead among the Heldrungers, and one dead and one seriously injured among the workers.[8] At other locations in the county houses were forced open, and the few communities that initially refused to hand over weapons witnessed threats to burn down farms or shoot members of the units, a few of whom were roughed up.[9]

Such clashes and attacks notwithstanding, the main line of conflict was not between the workers on one side and the middle-class citizens and farmers in the Home Guards on the other, but between the workers and the military. To be sure, the central Reich office of the Home Guards came out openly for the conspirators, and in the province of Saxony as well, individual leaders of the guard units, chief among them Captain Jüttner in Naumburg, were clearly supportive of the coup in Berlin.[10] However, a broad mobilization of the Home Guards on the side of the putschists did not even get off the ground.[11] As the case of Heldrungen shows, even in a region that was one of the strongholds of the guard units and was not far from the center of the civil war–like clashes (described below), the units were prepared neither for intervention in the conflict nor for an effective defense against an attack.

Still, in a few locations in the province of Saxony fighting broke out on a larger scale. Here it was the military that triggered the clashes by its conduct or had a crucial influence on how they unfolded. Violent confrontations occurred in all garrison towns where entire units declared open allegiance to the putschists. The first fatality came on 14 March, when soldiers of the Reichswehr fired unprovoked into a crowd that was gathering on the market square of Bitterfeld for a rally.[12] A firefight in Suhl lasted several hours and left six soldiers dead.[13] In Zeitz, where the Moritzburg garrison had joined the side of the putschists, a firefight killed four soldiers and one female bystander. Fifteen workers and several soldiers died on the same day in Weißenfels during an attempt to disarm the putsch-friendly troops stationed at the railway station: a firefight broke out in front of the castle, and eventually the troops had to withdraw to Naumburg. Fighting left several dead and seriously injured in its wake in and around Naumburg.[14] Intense fighting unfolded on 16 and 17 March in Eisleben, where the Reichswehr even deployed an armored car.[15]

The Zeitz-Weißenfels brown coal mining district, Eisleben, Bitterfeld, and Suhl were strongholds of the USPD, yet there are no indications that the initiative for the violent confrontations came from the armed workers. Although the workers in Weißenfels received help from the surrounding area, no concerted leadership of the fighting was set up for the entire region; in fact, there was not even an attempt to do so. The workers were not fighting *for* a specific political program, but *against* the hated military. And they were generally successful—a circumstance that boosted their will to resist and gave meaning to the considerable number of casualties.

The longest and bloodiest clashes developed in and around Halle. Here, too, the spiral of violence was set in motion by the behavior of the military.[16] On 14 March, the garrison commander, Colonel v. Czettritz, issued a general appeal to maintain calm and order, which had to be interpreted as approval for the putsch. That same day he had the temporary volunteers activated, even though the situation in Halle was completely quiet. All workers went on strike on 15 March. Czettritz sent armored cars through the center of the city, outlawed meetings, and arrested the strike leadership of the railroad workers, the city councilors of the USPD and KPD, and leading members of the DDP—among them the later civilian commissioner Schreiber—as well as the editors of the *Volksblatt.* On 16 March, soldiers occupied the union building and the editorial offices of the *Volksblatt* and the *Saale-Zeitung.* However, the previous day the USPD paper had still managed to publish an article that not only called on the Kapp government to step down, but also issued an appeal to prevent a "return of the old Noskean despotism." The "path for socialization" had to be cleared, a "self-government of the working German people" had to be brought about. The article had articulated a political perspective; though still rather vague, it went much further than the call for a general strike on 13 March. However, there was no mention of violent action: the general strike remained the "most potent weapon that the working class possesses."[17] Thus the workers who disarmed the Home Guards around Halle (the Halle guard unit itself made no appearance at all[18]) behaved in a relatively spontaneous manner and were not following a script laid out by the USPD.

In the meantime, Czettritz had blocked off important locations in the center of the city, posted guards armed with machine guns, and stepped up patrol activities. The Reichswehr soldiers and the temporary volunteers found themselves exposed to insults and threats in the increasingly tense atmosphere, and they were the occasional target of random shots. However, their behavior, especially that of the volunteers who were recruited mostly from among students, exceeded, in the view of the *Saale-Zeitung,* all reasonable bounds and caused "intense outrage ... among the citizens."[19] Uncontrolled shots from nervous soldiers killed the wife of a shop owner as she stood by the register, an old woman was killed by wild firing from an armored car, and a nun serving in a children's home was fatally shot while on the way to church with her charges.

The situation relaxed briefly when, following the collapse of the putsch in Berlin, the arrested party leaders were released on 18 March and public meetings were once again permitted. The Social Democrat Hörsing, installed as Reich commissioner for the province, appointed Schreiber as civil commissioner. The three Socialist parties and the DDP agreed on a catalogue of demands that included, among other things, the resignation of the garrison commander, the demobilization of the temporary volunteers, and the formation of a new, Republican Home Guard. The military, however, did not accept these demands. In response, 19 March saw the first larger clashes in the city and the suburb of Ammendorf with the armed workers, who had by now surrounded Halle on all sides and clearly outnumbered the 1,500 soldiers in the city. Action committees in the villages around Halle had decreed the formation of a "Red Guard" for which all male residents between the ages of 17 and 45 were to register, and the large majority complied.[20] The bloody fighting lasted until the afternoon of 22 March, with both sides able to report victories. Talks between the garrison leaders and representatives of the armed workers finally stopped the clashes. Twenty-seven soldiers had been killed, and more than 100 civilians are presumed to have lost their lives in Halle alone.[21]

There is no doubt that the events of March 1920 added new dimensions to the experiences with violence from the previous year. This was the first time the counterrevolutionary forces had tried to change the state of affairs by force, the first time a general strike had paralyzed life in the entire province, and the first time there had been larger, warlike clashes between workers and the military that left many dead. Many more towns had now undergone these kinds of experiences than in 1919. Still, one must note the limits on violence even in the conflict over the Kapp Putsch. The mobilization of the workers who opposed it remained defensive and local. It was party-spanning contacts at work and in the neighborhood that brought them together, not specific political programs. Although the tensions between the military and the armed workers were apparently greater and the outbreak of violence more likely where the USPD and the KPD were dominant, that is the only significant difference from regions ruled by the MSPD. Even in Halle, an explicit program that picked up on still-unmet demands from the revolution existed only in its infancy.[22] The force employed by the workers was overwhelmingly defensive in nature. Thus the fighting was not the result of long-term planning, but of specific circumstances and processes of escalation that were driven, not least, by "the endless rumors ... and the general state of agitation."[23]

The citizens in the towns and the farmers remained largely passive during the days of the putsch. The far-flung and in some locations tight-knit network of Home Guards quickly unraveled. While in some places this breakdown may have been the result of what was by now a fairly mixed political membership, it was due more to the fact that their members saw themselves not as the auxiliary troops of the counterrevolution, but as the instrument for the locally limited protection of property. The putsch and its aftereffect were registered by most men of the Home Guards as remote political events that did not concern them directly. Moreover, the bourgeoisie was ambivalent in its attitude toward the Republic.

Even the direct experience with violence did not change this ambivalence or lead to its turning against the entire workers' movement.

Among the bourgeois public, the coup d'état was sharply and unequivocally condemned, though understanding was also voiced for the sympathizers among the population. The putschists themselves were clearly dissociated from the right and denounced as a "pan-German-conservative-antisemitic clique"[24] and "the worst kind of political criminals."[25] At the end of March, after the fighting in Halle, the *Saale-Zeitung* went so far as to speak of a "stab in the back of the *Volk*," which had triggered the "bloodiest civil war," leading in the Ruhr region and just now in its own city to "boundless misery."[26] The sort of highly emotional charges that were usually leveled against the radical left were thus redefined and now aimed at the radical right. In its review of the events, however, the *Magdeburgische Zeitung* described the putsch as the expression of the desperation of "those segments of our worthiest circles" who had been "internally and economically uprooted by the Revolution."[27] At the same time, though, it praised the bourgeoisie's sense of realism overall, which in the end had thwarted the putsch, and it defined the instrument of the strike—"the sole means of defense of the majority of the *Volk* against the attempts by minorities to oppress them"—as something positive in this context.[28] Of course, this was an ambivalent argument that justified the general strike against the Kapp Putsch as well as the bourgeois strike in 1919 against the revolutionary mass movement.

The continuation of the armed resistance in the Ruhr region and in the industrial region of central Germany was as harshly condemned as the putsch itself. The *Magdeburgische Zeitung* called it a "crime" equal in seriousness to the coup d'état that was being used by "dark elements to carry out their pernicious plans to overthrow the government." While there was no reason to fear a Bolshevist takeover, as the actions of armed resistance were merely the "spasms of local agitation," it was still permissible to remove such "evil on the body of the *Volk*," if necessary through a "strong surgical intervention"—a medical analogy that depoliticized the enemy and legitimated violence against him as "objectively" justified.[29] Although the *Saale-Zeitung* believed that the "dictatorship of soviets" was the goal of the fighting in and around Halle, it did strike a calming tone by blaming the violent clashes on the workers' agitated state of mind and the confusing information they received.[30] Seeing, alongside "a lot of rabble," chiefly "very young men" involved in the agitation, the paper noted that "[t]he vast majority of the workers of Halle did not participate in the attacks on the military."[31] Reference to the special circumstances and the distinction between dangerous foreign and "good" native workers made the situation seem less threatening.[32]

How ambivalently the bloody fighting was perceived and interpreted is also evident from the fact that on 29 March, the workers as well as the soldiers and temporary volunteers who had been killed were put to rest in the Getrauden cemetery in Halle in separate ceremonies. In the morning, delegations from the Reichswehr, representatives of the city administration, and Civil Commissioner Schreiber paid the last honors to the slain soldiers and volunteers; the Reich

Central Office for Home Guards, which had been actively involved in the putsch, sent a wreath, as did the DDP. The division chaplain praised the willingness with which the dead had done their duty in order to preserve "calm and order … in days of Germany's severest internal convulsions," which made them into even greater heroes than those killed in the war. The *Saale-Zeitung* not only reported this but used the word "hero" itself; on the other hand, in a lengthy account of the "days of terror" it criticized the volunteers for their uncontrolled use of firearms, although it then went on to praise their efforts once the "putsch from the left" had replaced that "from the right."[33] The notion of "order," which could have various meanings, was able to bridge this tension, though it could never make the DDP politician Schreiber and the *Saale-Zeitung,* which was close to his party, forget the behavior of the military.

On the afternoon of 29 March, about 30,000 people—among them delegations from surrounding communities—gathered at the cemetery to honor the slain workers. No representative of the city or the bourgeois parties was present; the MSPD had sent a wreath but no speaker. Alongside workers' songs, "I Had a Comrade" was played, as it had been during the military funerals. The chief speaker from the USPD saw the fighting of the previous days as the continuation of the Revolution of March 1848 and the Paris Commune in March 1871. As a "fight for freedom" it represented another step in the proletariat's great struggle for emancipation. Here, too, mention was made of "heroes" of whom the living had to prove themselves worthy. The old Social Democratic tradition of remembering the "March casualties" of 1848 and 1871 was thus infused with a new meaning by which the radical left claimed the tradition for itself.[34] Martyrs of freedom stood opposed to defenders of order, both were honored as though they had been killed in a war, and the grieving communities were strictly separated from each other. The great political camps—the bourgeois-national, on the one hand, and the proletarian, on the other—that had confronted each other before the war became once again visible in outline. Still, the fault lines were not yet unbridgeable. Both the *Volksblatt* and the *Saale-Zeitung* spoke of the dead of the other side as "*Gefallene,*" fallen soldiers, and refrained from any negative judgment in their brief reports on the memorial services. Both ceremonies' speeches eschewed characterizing the opponent. As with the great funerals put on by the Social Democrats during the Empire, the state refrained from interfering in its opponent's ceremonies.[35] A basic respect for the dead of the other side remained.

Vague Dangers: The After-Effects of the March Fighting

With the end of the fighting in the wake of the Kapp Putsch, the situation calmed down only on the surface. The events had aroused new distrust and promoted a political radicalization with at times diffuse traits. Nervous fears were attached to the weapons that had fallen into the hands of the workers, fears that did not correspond to the actual dangers, while attempts continued on the radical right to build up a military potential.

In the spring and summer of 1920, the authorities repeatedly took note of rumors and indications that the radical left was setting up a "Red Army" and would soon use it in an attempt to overthrow the government.[36] However, none of the investigations was able to confirm this. Although there had been signs of coordinated action during the fighting in the wake of the Kapp Putsch, the armed units had been set up ad hoc, the official reports noted. The Regierungspräsident of Merseburg, usually the most vociferous voice to warn of putsch intentions on the part of the Communists, conceded that while the investigations by his officials had produced "numerous indications" that a "Red Army" actually existed, they had not found any "direct evidence."[37] The new Oberpräsident Hörsing (MSPD) eventually summed up the hodgepodge of clues and speculations in one terse statement: "A Red Army does not exist."[38]

By contrast, a direct, if less serious, threat emanated from the activist Communist German Workers' Party (KAPD), a left-wing splinter group of the KPD that had been founded in Berlin at the beginning of April.[39] The founding conference for the district of Central Germany took place on 16 May in Halle; by this time, the district organization had more than 2,300 members, especially from the mining areas and the chemical triangle around Halle.[40] The progressive radicalization in the industrial region of central Germany channeled to the political forces pushing for "direct action" a certain number of supporters that were largely recruited from among workers who lacked a well-developed Social Democratic and unionist tradition; compared to the USPD, however, these forces remained in a marginal position.

Partly responsible for this marginalization was also the image that the KAPD presented with its peculiar public actions, which were a blend of social protest, common criminal behavior, and revolutionary play-acting. In the middle of May, the county town of Sangerhausen, neighbor to the Mansfelder counties, got a taste of this. On the afternoon of 13 May, a meeting of the local KAPD organization—which had about thirty members—had taken place there with an outside speaker. Around midnight, the mayor of Sangerhausen—as he later recounted—was awakened by suspicious noises. He found the streets empty, but in the brightly lit town hall he encountered a number of armed men who were not locals; they had detained several policemen and presented themselves as the "Red Executive Council" (*Roter Vollzugsrat*). Also present was a local KAPD leader, who assured the mayor that at this very hour, town halls were being occupied all over Germany and the "dictatorship of the proletariat" was being proclaimed. The funds at the local savings bank would not be touched, though the revolutionaries intended to sell eggs and butter in the stores at "peace prices." It later turned out, however, that the intruders had robbed two banks in town, stolen money from the town hall, and also seized shoes, bread, and tobacco from various shops. They had also destroyed the voter list for the upcoming Reichstag elections. By the next morning, most of the "putschists" had disappeared, and the others were arrested without offering any resistance. There were no casualties. All told, the mayor estimated that "50–60 persons participated in the action, the majority unemployed men." It is notable that at least two leaders called themselves "Max Hoelz," thus trying to appropriate the prestige of a leader of armed actions who became known in the Vogtland as a kind of Robin Hood after the Kapp Putsch.[41]

In the following months, the KAPD attracted attention with additional actions of this sort. Officials in the Oberpräsidium believed that they were not centrally directed, though they all followed the same pattern. Because the KAPD supposedly admitted its members without any background check, any radical agitator could easily attain a leading position—as could every "agent provocateur" of the radical right. These actors could then easily prevail upon a small group of party members to embark on a putsch-like enterprise, which would then always attract hangers-on from among the young and the *lumpenproletariat.* All in all, this was a "blend of politics and crime" with which "the entire working class, including the Independents and even a part of the Communists," wanted nothing to do.[42] This assessment was accurate. The KAPD managed to acquire a measure of influence once more during the "March action" of 1921, but after that it declined into irrelevance. Of course, its actions—because they so closely linked politics and criminal behavior—further helped to associate the radical left with criminals, and to provide their radical enemies on the right with reasons to prepare their own violent measures. That is precisely what the *Volksstimme* meant when it warned insistently against the "phony, putsch-crazy radicalism" of the KAPD and denounced its supporters as "traitors to the counterrevolution."[43]

Thus the fears of an attempted putsch from the left in the weeks and months following March 1920 expressed more an imagined than a real danger. Although the isolated actions of the KAPD supporters were not seen as a warning of an impending proletarian revolution, they did fuel a diffuse sense of insecurity and, not least, gave new nourishment to the fears of the bourgeoisie and farmers about the radical left. For that same reason, the officials were initially unsure about what course they should take toward the Home Guards. When the government decreed on 8 April 1920 that the guards in Prussia should be dissolved, it was not so much reacting to the conduct of some units during the days of the putsch as yielding to pressure from the Allies, who would not tolerate any military reserves prohibited in the Versailles Treaty. Thus the dissolution order initially merely put an end to the centralization of the units and stripped them of their quasi-military character. Then, in a decree of 16 May, the Ministry of the Interior gave the Oberpräsidenten the option of setting up local units to protect towns and fields, with their members to be recruited from all parties loyal to the constitution.[44]

Oberpräsident Hörsing, however, hewed to a restrictive course. He was aware that the chief threat to the Republic emanated from the radical right, which in the province of Saxony had by now also begun to set up an organizational network intended to provide propaganda, logistics, and armed support for a new putsch. A few days before Reichstag elections on 6 June, the deputy Landrat of County

Weißenfels reported a conversation he had had with a local delegate of the DNVP who had warned of a putsch by the left in connection with the elections, describing conditions in Bavaria as the model (a right-wing government had come to power there with the support of the Home Guards, led by Georg Escherich).[45] The German National politician had gone on to explain that the *Forstrat* Escherich was now setting up an organization throughout the Reich whose goal was a change of government in Berlin without a putsch. If that happened, resistance was expected in central Germany, but it would be met with force. The Catholic clergy in Eichsfeld was already preaching along the lines of what Escherich was planning, other organizational successes had also been achieved, and here it was possible to draw on the new town and field protection units.[46] A Bund der Kaisertreuen (League of Those Faithful to the Kaiser) had formed in the rural county of Wolmirstedt; during the Kapp Putsch it had evidently taken the side of the putschists, and most of its members also belonged to the new veterans' organization Stahlhelm. The chairman of the latter, the Magdeburg factory owner and former officer Seldte, had been in contact with Escherich since January 1920 and was giving him active support. In a few places in the county so-called "riding clubs" were set up, though their connections to the Organisation Escherich (Orgesch) were still unclear. At the beginning of June, twenty-five members of the Orgesch from the region, including the chairman of the Landbund Sachsen (Saxon Agrarian League), met in Magdeburg.[47]

The organizational efforts of the radical right continued in the following months, though they now encountered determined opposition from officials. Indications of secret weapons caches, for example in Salzwedel or in Stendal (in the post office), that is, places where the Home Guards had been particularly strong, led to searches, though these only occasionally turned up anything. At the beginning of October 1920, police found a substantial stash of weapons in a school complex in Halle, including 6 heavy machine guns and 211 rifles. The weapons belonged to a volunteer unit and had been hidden there by two of its officers following the Kapp Putsch. At the beginning of December, the security police raided a weapons depot on an estate in County Naumburg, consisting of 2 mine throwers, 8 heavy and 10 light machine guns, 381 rifles, and larger quantities of cartridges. The trail led to the Home Guard of Naumburg.[48]

At the beginning of August, the Oberpräsidium uncovered a conspiratorial circle that maintained contact with the Landbund of the province and especially with the Reichswehr. A former agent from military counterintelligence and a teacher, working from Magdeburg, had set up a network of spies with at least tacit support from the Reichswehr Brigade IV. Among other places, it reached into the KAPD, and its members—including two Reichswehr soldiers—were soon no longer content to report on the activities of the leftist organization, but invented Communist plans for a putsch and funneled them to the authorities. The teacher had close contact with the office of the Orgesch in Berlin, while the head of the Orgesch branch office in Halle, who turned out to be a lieutenant of a disbanded unit of temporary volunteers, continued to recruit volunteers clandestinely from his office in a barracks in Halle and was in touch with the managing director of the Landbund.[49] At the same time, the representative of the DLV for the counties of Liebenwerda and Schweinitz in the district of Merseburg reported that self-defense organizations were being set up on two estates and many former fighters from the Baltics were being housed there.[50] The "'national' reaction (is arming) for civil war," declared the *Volksstimme*, which went on to denounce the accomplices of the Orgesch who had been unmasked in Magdeburg as "bandits."[51]

The Prussian authorities eventually responded by outlawing all self-protection organizations, and the authorities in the neighboring Free State of Saxony soon followed suit.[52] However, the organizational activities of the radical right by no means ground to a halt. At the beginning of December, the Landrat of Naumburg reported on meetings in several locations that discussed joining up with the Orgesch. Those involved included a retired major and a functionary of the Landbund for the provinces of Saxony and Anhalt. A few days later, a search of the house of the managing director of the Landbund turned up pertinent material.[53]

The shift to the right within the urban bourgeoisie and the rural population, which was evident in the results of the Reichstag elections on 6 June, was also manifested in the attempts to preserve the military potential of the Home Guards, the temporary volunteers, and individual Free Corps units in a different form. Such activities were alarming especially because of the cooperation with offices of the Reichswehr. Still, these efforts did not cover the entire province, as had been the case with the formation of the Home Guards, but were concentrated, in addition to various urban bases, in those agrarian districts in which the militia units had been especially strong.[54] The emphatic actions of the police authorities prevented the Orgesch from putting down firm roots in the province. However, right-wing combat leagues would soon pick up where it had left off.

In the Reichstag elections, the "Weimar Coalition" of the MSPD, DDP, and Center Party lost its majority also in the province of Saxony, though there were enormous regional variations in the results. As elsewhere, the main losers in the province of Saxony were once again the MSPD and the DDP, with both parties suffering losses at roughly the same rate as in Germany overall. The main winner on the bourgeois side in all three electoral districts, as in the Reich in general, was the German People's Party (DVP); in addition, the DNVP, who was further to the right of the political spectrum, was able to make gains that were above the average for the Reich as a whole. However, the violent events of 1919 and the spring of 1920 generated new support not only for the most radical of the bourgeois parties in those areas that had experienced these events directly. In Halle, for example, the DNVP increased its votes from 11.9 percent at the elections for the National Assembly in 1919 to now 16.3 percent, but the DVP surged from 1.6 percent to 18.7 percent. In the countryside, as well, the DVP made stronger gains relative to the DNVP, though the latter party was able to further consolidate its leading position here. In County Salzwedel, the DNVP polled 35.3 percent of the votes compared to 18.7 percent in 1919 while the DVP now had 16.7 percent (vs. 3.8 percent); in County Stendal, the DNVP stood at 31.8 percent (previously 21.3 percent) and the DVP at 7.0 percent (2.6 percent).

Without a doubt, the bourgeoisie in the province of Saxony, as in many other German regions, had clearly moved to the right in response to the experiences of chaos and violence between 1919 and 1920. It must be noted, though, that this move to the right stopped halfway, as it were, and that the uncompromisingly anti-Republican DNVP benefited from it only to some extent. Moreover, the shift to the right did not level out the differences between city and countryside. Party preferences were still different, as was the willingness to become active in self-defense organizations against the threat that was believed to emanate from the radical left.

On the left, the USPD (together with the KPD, which remained a splinter party in all three electoral districts) made gains especially in the electoral district of Magdeburg-Anhalt, the old MSPD bastion, where it was able to raise its share of the votes—against a backdrop of consistently low voter turnout—from 3.0 percent in 1919 to 19.2 percent (KPD: 1.1 percent). The gains were especially strong where the USPD had been particularly weak in 1919 and slightly weaker where its results had already been somewhat better in 1919, but they did not depend on whether the region in question had been directly involved in the violent events. In the city of Magdeburg, for example, the USPD boosted its share of the vote from 6.3 percent to 20.2 percent, and in County Stendal from 0.5 percent to 18.4 percent. In the electoral district of Merseburg, as well, the USPD was able to improve slightly from its results in 1919 to 45.2 percent (KPD: 1.6 percent), while it posted solid gains in the electoral district of Thuringia and in counties where the MSPD had been the majority party in 1919; here the party now had a total of 30.6 percent (KPD: 1.9 percent) as opposed to 22.5 percent in 1919.[55] The gains for the USPD and the KPD resulted less from the direct experience of violence two months earlier, and more from the general disappointment over the governing policies of the Social Democrats.

Lastly, at the end of 1920 the KPD benefited from the radicalization of wide segments of the working class, while the USPD succumbed to its internal tensions. In October 1920, the USPD held a party conference in Halle, its strongest party district, to decide whether or not to join the Third International and thus subordinate itself to the Soviet Communists. An overwhelming majority of the party members of the district voted to accept the "21 admission conditions," though at least one-sixth cast "no" votes. The number of "yes" votes was especially high in the counties of the Mansfeld region and in the counties of Merseburg-Querfurt, dominated, respectively, by mining and the chemical industry; in the region of Naumburg-Weißenfels-Zeitz, where a majority voted against the proposal, the supporters also came from the mining industry. The thesis that it was chiefly younger workers who had not been politicized for very long and tended to be less qualified who voted in favor of joining Moscow (and that more men did so than women) remains, on the whole, plausible.[56] By contrast, there was evidently no direct connection with the bloody fighting six months earlier and in 1919. Especially in Halle and the surrounding Saalkreis, the minority that voted against the proposal made up a solid one-fifth of the votes, which was higher than the average for the district as a whole; the stronghold of those opposed to joining Moscow was in the region around Naumburg, where the Home Guards had been particularly strong and had been set up by a committed enemy of the Republic.[57]

The USPD rank and file in the party districts of Magdeburg and Thuringia voted to join the Third International, though with only a bare majority. When the leftist USPD and the KPD subsequently merged into the United German Communist Party (VKPD) in early December 1920, the new party had around 430,000 members, nearly six times as many as the old KPD. In the district Halle-Merseburg it had around 66,000 members, which made it the largest party district in Germany. However, 15,000 USPD members refused to join the new party. Finally, in the districts of Magdeburg and Thuringia, a majority did not join the KPD. In the industrial region of central Germany, the KPD would never again attain the strength of the old USPD.[58]

Following the decision in Halle, the lead article in the *Volksblatt* declared on Revolution Day that an "immense responsibility" was weighing on the German proletariat. Since the Russian proletariat could not defend Socialism on its own, the goal had to be a "dictatorship of soviets in Germany." In Russia, that dictatorship had been forced through by a "small band of heroes … who proceeded with ruthless energy against all enemies of the Revolution."[59] The lead article at the turn of 1920/21 was even blunter. The class struggle character of history had become apparent precisely in the violent events of the past year. The more "rotten" the capitalist system was on the whole, the more violently it behaved, and the greater the "mountains of corpses" it heaped up. Consequently, political action could take its cues only from the conditions posed by the "unavoidable civil war that can be fought—for all practical purposes—only internationally." That gave rise to the following conclusion: "Dealing the bourgeoisie the death blow means preventing the gradual suicide of all of mankind."[60]

This was clear and unambiguous language. Violence was now no longer defined as a means of last resort, to be used only after a general strike and as a defense against the counter-revolution, but as an offensive tool, one that accelerated the necessary development of history and culminated in civil war. The notion of civil war thus referred no longer to the deeply abhorred actions by the enemies of the proletariat, but was given a new, positive spin. At the same time, it was clearly stated that the Russian way was seen as a model.

The Magdeburg *Volksstimme* reacted with stinging criticism to the leftward shift of the USPD, though it continued to underscore that the chief threat came from the right. A commentary on the USPD party convention, titled "Mass murderer Zinoviev," accused the leader of the Comintern of having employed a tone in his speech that was once used in Russia to call for the "slaughter of the Jews." The notion of a bloody revolution, however, belonged to an obsolete "stage of culture."[61] The new Bolshevist Russia was in truth the old czarist Russia. According to this critique, the left wing of the USPD was oriented toward a system that all of Social Democracy had roundly condemned until 1917. A clear decision was now called for. Any notion of a middle way was an illusion, for there "is no such thing as rationed terror," the *Volksstimme* declared succinctly, just as there was no halfway dictatorship.[62] However, the paper believed that "the capitalist world no longer has anything to fear from a Bolshevist uprising, but all the more to hope for," namely the chance to set up "a regulatory state (*Ordnungsstaat*) on the Hungarian model." For that reason the KPD would move steadily to the right and attempt to prevent the "worst follies" of groups like the KAPD; eventually, the Social Democratic party organ was convinced, this would lead to its demise.[63]

Among the bourgeois public, the USPD's embrace of the Communists led to even more vehement reactions, but these did not rise to the level of the—at times—hysterical fears that had been voiced at the beginning of 1919. The "terror" recommended by Zinoviev meant convincing the masses by "murdering all those who are unwilling to go along," the *Saale-Zeitung* wrote. In fact, the Moscow leadership were "preachers of hatred who no longer have a sense for humanity and humaneness," and who wished to "put into practice an impossible idea with the most brutal instruments of violence."[64] The Magdeburg paper seconded this with the warning that the defeated right wing of the USPD also sympathized with Bolshevism "in its heart of hearts" and was willing "to join Communist steps toward open acts of violence."[65] There was only one answer to this, according to the *Saale-Zeitung:* "human society" had the "duty to protect itself with all means against elements who in their madness can become a threat to it, if they are unable at the last moment to bring them to their senses."[66] Any kind of engagement with the political program of left-wing radicalism was therefore out of the question.

The fear that was expressed here was not so much the fear of a successful power grab by the Communists in Germany, but the fear of the chaos they would produce in the attempt to do so. At the time of the USPD convention in the middle of October, the *Saale-Zeitung* believed that Bolshevism was about to collapse in Russia itself; it would be able to hang on to power for a little longer only through bloody terror.[67] In a lead article the *Magdeburgische Zeitung* described the state Germany was in at the turn of 1920/21 as follows: while the enemies in the West were getting ready "to pounce like predators," in the East there were gathering "the poisonous vapors of culture-destroying Bolshevism, which today, thank God, are able to ignite what are for now only scattered concentrations of the swamp gas of Communism in Germany."[68] The menacing nature metaphors and the indirect reference to the use of poison gas in the war show how deep-seated the fears were that the paper was touching on. However, the danger emanating from Bolshevism did not seem any bigger than the threat posed by France. In the end, both had to be answered in the same way. The "spirit of community" had to be awakened, declared the *Magdeburgische Zeitung* at the turn of 1920/21, and the Halle paper called for "the tormented German people to stand together united and unified" and for an end to "party bickering."[69] From this perspective, which invoked the "national community" (*Volksgemeinschaft*) of August 1914 and the war years, the Communists were above all "troublemakers" impeding the work of reconstruction who had to be neutralized. That the number of "troublemakers" who were receptive to the KPD's violent slogans was relatively small would soon be revealed.

Notes

1. Kluge, *Deutsche Revolution,* 195–199; Feldman, Kolb, and Rürup, "Die Massenbewegungen," 84–105, here 101–103; Mommsen, *Revolution,* 388f.; Winkler, *Weimar,* 135.
2. Könnemann and Krusch, *Aktionseinheit,* 112–114; LHAM C 20 Ib 4776, fol. 94 (Police administration of Stendal to RP Magdeburg, 17 March 1920); *VS* no. 65/66, 21 March 1920.
3. Report by the KPD district organization of Thuringia to the central office, end of March 1920, in *Arbeiterklasse siegt über Kapp und Lüttwitz.* Sources selected and edited by Erwin Könnemann, Brigitte Berthold, and Gerhard Schulze (East Berlin, 1971), 532; Könnemann and Krusch, *Aktionseinheit,* 104.
4. Könnemann and Krusch, *Aktionseinheit,* 108–111, 115; see also Winkler, *Revolution,* 303f.; Erger, *Kapp-Lüttwitz-Putsch,* 196–202.
5. The texts of the various calls for a general strike can be found in *Arbeiterklasse,* 375 (District Merseburg), 376f. (Magdeburg), 377f. (Stendal), 378f. (Halle), 379f. (Dessau), 380f. (Aschersleben).
6. LHAM C 20 Ib 4776, fol. 94 (Police administration Stendal to RP Magdeburg, 17 March 1920).
7. LHAM C 20 Ib, 4776, fol. 91 (LR Neuhaldensleben to RP Magdeburg, 17 March 1920); C 20 Ib 4777, fol. 55 (RP Merseburg to OP, 28 March 1920); C 20 Ib 5212/I, fol. 12 (RP to OP, 7 April 1920). See the similar findings in Fritzsche, *Rehearsals,* 56–65.
8. LHAM C 20 Ib 1996/II, fols. 203f. (LR Eckartsberga to OP, 6 April 1920). The rural county was second within the district in terms of the strength of its Home Guards.
9. LHAM C 20 Ib 1996/II, fols. 205f. (LR Eckartsberga to OP, 6 April 1920).
10. See one letter by Jüttner to Kapp, dated 24 February 1920, in which he asks "whether the time has come to move Your Honor's name to the fore," in Könnemann and Krusch, *Aktionseinheit,* 69.
11. We know that in the town of Worbis there was a one– or two–day counter–strike by the bourgeoisie and the civil servants (LHAM C 20 Ib 4778, fols. 39f., Report on the mood among the population by RP Erfurt, 20 March and 21 March 1920). Bieber, *Bürgertum,* 314, claims—without evidence—that "large parts" of the Home Guards had also supported the putsch.
12. Könnemann and Krusch, *Aktionseinheit,* 111.
13. LHAM C 20 Ib 5212/I, fols. 14f. (RP Erfurt to OP, 7 April 1920); Könnemann and Krusch, *Aktionseinheit,* 210–212. Some of the workers then entered the fighting that was raging in and around Gotha. The clashes, which also involved many members of the bourgeoisie, were especially bloody in this small, USPD-dominated state, where a Red Army of several thousand men was assembled on the military training grounds of Ohrdruf under the leadership of the USPD and the KPD. Moreover, the Gotha action committee soon imparted a revolutionary perspective to the fighting. See Könnemann and Krusch, *Aktionseinheit,* 210–212; "Aufruf des Aktionsauschusses Gotha v. 19. März," in *Arbeiterklasse,* 491. On the clashes in detail see Matthiesen, *Bürgertum,* 89–102; idem, "Radikalisierungen," 47.

14. Adolf Leopoldt, Rote Chronik der Kreise Zeitz, Weißenfels, Naumburg (Zeitz, 1931), 151f.
15. Könnemann and Krusch, *Aktionseinheit,* 219–221.
16. This account of the events is based on *SZ* no. 125, 14 March; no. 152, 30 March (the paper was not published between these two dates); no. 154, 31 March 1920, and *VB* no. 77, 31 March 1920.
17. *VB* no. 63, 15 March 1920.
18. The *Volksblatt,* no. 63, 15 March 1920, mentioned that the Home Guard had been called out but many members had not answered the call and some officers had resigned. A "strong disintegration" was noted. The statement is credible, for in a situation in which the paper was at pains to mobilize the workers for the imminent confrontation, it would have made no sense to downplay the threat posed by the other side.
19. *SZ* no. 152, 30 March 1920. The assessment is all the more credible as it was made after the fact.
20. LHAM C 20 Ib 4786/III, fol. 77 (Rural Police of Nietleben to LR Saalkreis, 27 March 1920).
21. *SZ* no. 152, 30 March 1920; the Report of the Civil Commissioner in *SZ* no. 154, 31 March 1920; *VN* no. 77, 31 March 1920; see Könnemann and Krusch, *Aktionseinheit,* 403–407; on the fighting itself see also Schunke, *Schlacht um Halle,* who emphasizes the role played by the temporary volunteers. Weitz, *German Communism,* 96f., mentions only the fighting that occurred in the Ruhr region after the Kapp Putsch; however, the fighting in Halle was surely more important than the "Bloody Sunday" of 1910 in driving the USPD in the district closer to the KPD.
22. Mommsen, *Revolution,* 388f.
23. These are the words of the Regierungspräsident of Erfurt in his summary report on the events. While he did plead for punishment for the leaders of the radical workers, he also noted other causes for what had happened (LHAM C 20 Ib 5212/I, fol. 15, RP Erfurt to OP, 7 April 1920). On the events in Erfurt, where fighting left eight dead and almost eighty severely wounded, see Raßloff, *Flucht,* 199–207.
24. *SZ* no. 152, 30 March 1920.
25. *MZ* no. 221, 27 March 1920.
26. *SZ* no. 152, 30 March 1920. Similarly, the *Volksstimme* also spoke of a "stab-in-the-back" that had been aimed "at the heart of the Republic," and it accused Kapp and his followers of "having brought civil war to the country" (*VS* no. 63, 14 March; no. 71, 24 March; no. 263, 9 November 1920).
27. *MZ* no. 204, 21 March 1920.
28. *MZ* no. 221, 27 March, no. 223, 29 March 1920. At least the paper, which was otherwise close to the DVP, assumed a position that was clearly to the left of the DVP leadership, which even in retrospect and in spite of its ambivalent conduct during the putsch days was unable to arrive at a positive assessment of the general strike. See Wolfgang Hartenstein, *Die Anfänge der deutschen Volkspartei 1918–1920* (Düsseldorf, 1962), 182f.; on the position of the DVP and that of the DDP, which supported the general strike with a certain delay, see also Lothar Albertin, *Liberalismus und Demokratie am Anfang der Weimarer Republik: Eine vergleichende Analyse der Deutschen Demokratischen Partei und der Deutschen Volkspartei* (Düsseldorf, 1972), 371–375; Larry Eugene Jones, *German Liberalism and the Dissolution of the Weimar Party System, 1918–1933* (Chapel Hill, NC, 1988), 62–66.
29. *MZ* no. 204, 21 March; no. 205, 22 March 1920. At the same time, the paper warned—as it had done in 1918/19—against any ideas on the extreme right that would see a Bolshevist dictatorship as useful for its own plans; that would only spur the Entente to march into the country and cast Germany "completely into the abyss."
30. *SZ* no. 152, 30 March 1920.
31. *SZ* no. 156, 1 April 1920. In its review of the year, the paper also spoke in a fairly neutral tone of how the defense against the putsch had turned into "highly regrettable power struggles by workers who were extremely agitated and incited by the Communists."

32. Of course, these kinds of dichotomies (leaders/masses, locals/outsiders, "roughs"/"respectables") place the issue beyond a genuine political analysis.
33. *SZ* no. 152, 30 March 1920.
34. *VB* no. 76, 30 March 1920.
35. On the honoring of the "March casualties" and the behavior of the police in the Empire see the vivid account by Alf Lüdtke, "Trauerritual und politische Manifestation. Zu den Begräbnisumzügen der Sozialdemokratie im frühen Kaiserreich," in B. J. Warnecken, ed., *Massenmedium Straße: Zur Kulturgeschichte der Demonstration* (Frankfurt, 1991), 120–148.
36. LHAM C 20 Ib 4776, fol. 104 (Report on public sentiment from RP Magdeburg, 1 April 1920); fol. 106 (Report, 11 April); fol. 109 (Report, 14 April); 4777, fol. 58 (Report on public sentiment from RP Merseburg, 18 April 1920); fol. 64 (Report, 16 May, here the quote); fol. 66 (Report, 30 May); 4778, fol. 52 (Report on public sentiment from RP Erfurt, 16 May 1920).
37. LHAM C 20 Ib 4786/III, fols. 72f. (RP Merseburg to OP, 12 June 1920); fol. 96 (RP Magdeburg to OP, 18 May 1920; according to this report, only the officials in Magdeburg itself and the counties of Calbe and Stendal had any clues to the existence of a fighting organization belonging to the radical left); fol. 99 (RP Erfurt to OP, 20 May 1920; here, too, there was no firm evidence, even though the Regierungspräsident believed that there was "little doubt" of the existence of a Red Army); see fol. 16ff. (Negative reports from lower offices in response to a relevant decree issued by the Oberpräsident, 10 June 1920); fol. 89 (PP Magdeburg to OP, 11 May 1920; precise evidence could be obtained only with the use of large amounts of money).
38. LHAM C 20 Ib 4786/III, fol. 601 (OP to Staaatskommissar für Überwachung der öffentlichen Ordnung [StakoöO, State Commissioner for the Supervision of Public Order], 29 August 1920). On the poor effectiveness of the fighting organizations of the USPD, KPD, and Communist German Workers' Party (KAPD) see also Hans-Manfred Bock, *Syndikalismus und Linkskommunismus von 1918 bis 1923: Ein Beitrag zur Sozial- und Ideengeschichte der frühen Weimarer Republik,* new ed. (Darmstadt, 1993 [1969]), 234–236.
39. On the brief history of the KAPD see Bock, *Syndikalismus,* esp. 225ff.; Winkler, *Revolution,* 266, 347–349.
40. LHAM C 20 Ib 4786/II, fols. 167f. (Report to OP, 31 May 1920). Leipzig accounted for 700 members. The numbers were mentioned at the meeting and recorded by a police spy. According to his report, the following towns were considered as the headquarters for a subdistrict: Halle, Merseburg, Weißenfels, Hettstedt, Aschersleben, Magdeburg, Bitterfeld, Leipzig. Bock, *Syndikalismus,* 239, provides the information about membership strength at the second party congress of the KAPD at the beginning of August. According to these figures, the party had a total of about 40,000 members, 3,200 of whom were now to be found in "Central Germany." This would make it the third-largest district after Berlin and Rhineland-Palatinate.
41. LHAM C 20 Ib 4786/II, fols. 34–40, quote in fol. 39 (Mayor of Sangerhausen to OP, 17 May 1920). Similar "putsches" that had already occurred in the first week of April in Tangermünde, Delitzsch, and Bitterfeld all ended after a few hours without any bloodshed (*VS* no. 82, 8 April; no. 83, 9 April 1920). On Hoelz's actions in the Free State of Saxony see Lapp, *Revolution,* 39.
42. LHAM C 20 Ib 4786/III, fols. 603–606 (OP reporting office to StakoöO, 29 August 1920). Lemck, one of the leaders of the USPD in Halle, later of the KPD, arranged for the arrest of one of the instigators of the actions, an alleged senior teacher by name of Berg, who, according to the report of the reporting office, may have been a spy from the DNVP.
43. *VS* no. 196, 22 August; no. 197, 24 August 1920.
44. For a detailed account: Könnemann, *Einwohnerwehren,* 316ff., 324ff., 405–407; Michael Salewski, *Entwaffnung und Militärkontrolle in Deutschland, 1919–1927* (Munich, 1966), 119ff.; see also Bieber, *Bürgertum,* 324f.
45. On Escherich see Diehl, *Paramilitary Politics,* 69–74, 78–93; Large, *Politics;* Horst G. W. Nußer, *Konservative Wehrverbände in Bayern, Preußen und Österreich 1918–1933, mit einer Bio-*

graphie von Forstrat Georg Escherich 1870–1941 (2 vols. Munich, 1973); Ziemann, *Front und Heimat,* 402–413; Geyer, *Verkehrte Welt,* 117–123. Escherich had turned the Bavarian Home Guards into a tightly led organization and committed them to an anti-Republican course. During the Kapp Putsch he urged the Social Democratic state government of Bavaria to step down and helped a right-conservative government under Gustav v. Kahr to come to power. To that extent, the Kapp Putsch was successful in Bavaria. In the summer of 1920, Escherich tried to reform the disbanded Home Guards of northern Germany into a network tied to Bavaria under the name Organisation Escherich (Orgesch), though he was thwarted by the determined position of the Prussian government. His Bavarian Home Guards were able to avoid disbanding until 1921.

46. LHAM C 20 Ib 4667, fols. 2f. (Deputy LR Weißenfels to OP, 3 June 1920).
47. LHAM C 20 Ib 4748, fol. 360 (OP to StakoöO, 21 August 1920); fol. 413 (OP to police headquarters Halle, 15 October 1910). On the contacts between Escherich and Seldte see Diehl, *Paramilitary Politics,* 79–81. On Seldte and the beginnings of the Stahlhelm see below, ch. 4.
48. LHAM C 20 Ib 4609, passim; LAMe C 48 Ie 242/I, fols. 310–312; LHAM C 20 Ib 4610 (not paginated), (Police Lieutenant Seidenschnur [a later member of the leadership of the Reichsbanner] to OP, 8 December 1920; OP to the Prussian Minister President, 1 February 1921). Rural county Naumburg had had the largest Home Guard in the district of Merseburg, and here the DNVP achieved its best result in the district in the Reichstag elections in June (41.4 percent).
49. The Oberpräsident regarded the affair as so important that he compiled all results of the investigation into a secret memorandum for the Prussian state government: LHAM C 20 Ib 4806, fols. 1–32 (Memorandum, 20 August 1920). See Diehl, *Paramilitary Politics,* 92. At the end of July 1920, the *Magdeburgische Zeitung* reported on preparations to proclaim a German-Russian soviet republic and on the organization of a "Red Army" in the province of Saxony, basing its coverage on what it called a "quite reliable source." When the "spy center" (*Spitzelzentrale*) was uncovered, however, the paper was reluctant to admit its mistake (*MZ* no. 447, 28 July; no. 449, 29 July; no. 472, 11 August 1920). The *Volksstimme* reported extensively on the "spy center" and its links to the Orgesch (*VS* no. 175, 29 July; no. 187, 12 August; no. 188, 13 August; no. 192, 18 August; no. 196, 22 August 1920).
50. LHAM C 20 Ib 4786/IV, fol. 4a (OP to LR Liebenwerda, 12 August 1920).
51. *VS* no. 187, 12 August 1920.
52. LHAM C 20 Ib 4580, fol. 103 (OP to the Ministry of the Interior, 17 June 1920); fol. 115 (Decree by the Ministry of the Interior, 23 August 1920); Lapp, *Revolution,* 62.
53. LHAM C 20 Ib 4669, LR of Naumburg to OP, 16 December 1920; 4667, Police report, 21 December 1920.
54. Diehl, *Paramilitary Politics,* 79, on the whole overestimates the influence of the Orgesch and overlooks the fact that it was chiefly a rural organization.
55. Results of the Reichstag elections of 6 June 1920: *Stat. Dt. R., N. F.,* vol. 291/2: 21–31; Falter, Lindenberger, and Schumann, *Wahlen und Abstimmungen,* 68. Results 1919 (incomplete especially for the district of Merseburg): *MZ* no. 50, 20 January; no. 53, 21 January 1919; *SZ* no. 31a, 20 January; no. 34, 21 January 1919; LAG Reg. Erfurt no. 12784, fol. 275; Falter, Lindenberger, and Schumann, *Wahlen und Abstimmungen,* 67; author's calculations based on this information.
56. On this see esp. Robert F. Wheeler, *USPD und Internationale. Sozialistischer Internationalismus in der Zeit der Revolution* (Frankfurt, 1975), 252–257; Hartfried Krause, *USPD: Zur Geschichte der Unabhängigen Sozialdemokratischen Partei Deutschlands* (Frankfurt, 1975), 205f.
57. Klein, *Burgfrieden,* 192f.
58. Klein, *Burgfrieden,* 193; Wheeler, *USPD,* 263; for an account of the merger of the USPD and the KPD see Winkler, *Revolution,* 468–477; Weitz, *German Communism,* 97f.
59. *VB* no. 261, 6 November 1920.

60. *VB* no. 306, 31 December 1920. On the conflict between the two wings of the USPD over the question of violence see Ludewig, *Arbeiterbewegung*, 87–90. While the right wing in principle wished to allow violence only as a defensive tool, the left wing dismissed the distinction between unavoidable violence in the transition phase to proletarian rule and terror as a means of securing power and dismissed the purely defensive use of violence.
61. *VS* no. 244, 17 October 1920. The reference to the "slaughter of the Jews" also implied a criticism of the anti-Semitism that was on the rise in the wake of the inflation; after the Reichstag elections of 6 June, the *Saale-Zeitung* also attacked the DNVP for its anti-Semitic propaganda (*SZ* no. 260, 7 June 1920).
62. *VS* no. 243, 16 October 1920.
63. *VS* no. 253, 28 October 1920.
64. *SZ* no. 487, 17 October 1920.
65. *MZ* no. 606, 15 October 1920.
66. *SZ* no. 487, 17 October 1920. By dangerous "elements" the paper meant not only the Communist leaders, but "all who are now joining the Third Communist International."
67. *SZ* no. 487, 17 October 1920.
68. *MZ* no. 1, 1 January 1921.
69. *MZ* no. 1, 1 January 1921; *SZ* no. 609, 30 December 1920. The *MZ* called for a "reaction" to defeat the revolution, infusing this word, as well, with new meaning, though not in the sense of a mere turn backward, but of an evolutionary path that would pave the way for reason, eliminate everything that was ossified, and replace the party man with the citizen.

Chapter 3

Preventive Offense and Improvised Uprising

The "March Actions" of the Prussian Government and the Communists 1921

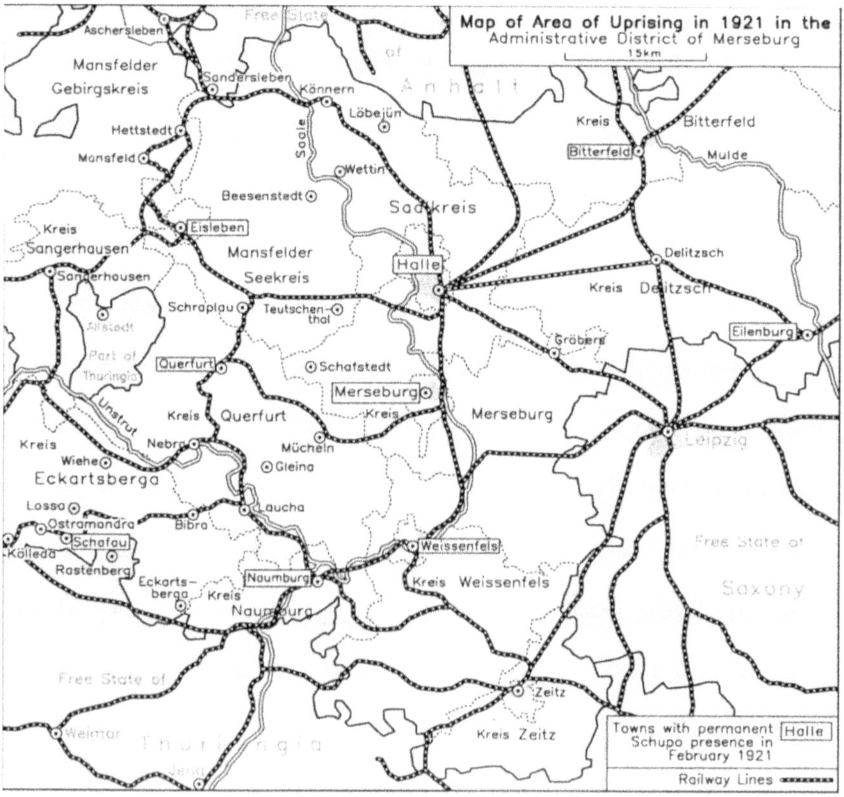

Map 3.1 Map of Area of Uprising in 1921

Notes from this chapter begin on page 76.

In the second half of March 1921, the province of Saxony became the stage for violent clashes that attracted attention far beyond the region. After units of the Prussian Schutzpolizei (Schupo, Security Police) had moved into the Mansfelder Land on 19 March, fights erupted between the security forces and armed workers, culminating on 29 March with police units firing on and then storming the Leuna Works.

Communist historiography has propounded the thesis that the actions by the armed workers should be seen primarily as a response to the "provocation" by the Prussian government, a puppet of big business. At the same time, the "March fighting 1921" is placed into a direct line with the resistance to the Kapp Putsch a year earlier and is regarded as part of a tradition of the legitimate exercise of force by the proletariat, which later continued in the anti-Fascist resistance. This interpretation was subsequently modified only to the extent that the "adventurous course" of the VKPD leadership in the spring of 1921 was credited with exercising a promoting influence on the events.[1]

Non-Communist scholarship has placed the primary responsibility for the events on the policy of the central leadership of the VKPD. At the beginning of January 1921, the party leadership around Paul Levi, which rejected putschist undertakings, had proposed joint actions to the unions and the Social Democrats in an "open letter," though without abandoning the goal of a dictatorship of the proletariat.[2] The party leadership was overthrown at the end of February and replaced with a new group, headed by Heinrich Brandler, that advocated the "offensive theory." According to this theory, the party should not wait to pursue revolutionary upheaval until after it had won over the masses through tenacious political work; rather, it was to move the masses by means of an armed uprising prepared by the party, a "revolt of the avant-garde" (Koch-Baumgarten). Pointing in the same direction were the activities of a delegation from the Comintern under Béla Kun that had been in Germany since the beginning of March. For a long time, scholarship regarded its influence as decisive. It is certainly true that a regime change in Germany would have provided a most welcome relief to the Bolshevik regime in Russia, which was then engaged in a sharp change of course in economic policy and found itself confronted by the Kronstadt uprising; however, it now seems far less certain that the VKPD leadership decided to take action only under pressure from the Comintern delegates. The most recent study of the "March action" emphasizes that while the Comintern leadership and the majority of the German party central office wanted to wait for the appropriate occasion to attempt an uprising, a minority in the top echelons of the VKPD as well as the three-man Comintern delegation advocated a swift strike.[3]

The segments of the VKPD that were pushing for rapid action had the opportunity to implement their plans sooner than expected because the Prussian government provided them with an occasion. Scholars agree unanimously that the justification given by Oberpräsident Hörsing both when the police were first deployed and after the fact—namely, that he wanted to move against the spreading wild strikes and the property crimes that were getting out of hand—was at best the partial truth. The primary goal of the action was to sharply curtail the power base that the VKPD seemed to possess in the industrial region of central Germany ever since the merger of the KPD and the USPD.[4] The supporters of the party were to be intimidated by the deployment of the police, and the weapons that had fallen into the hands of the workers after the Kapp Putsch were to be confiscated. What has drawn little interest from scholars, however, is the behavior of the workers themselves in the March days. Their reaction to the appearance of the Schupo and to the activities of the representatives of the VKPD and the KAPD shows that the "March action" was very different in character from the fighting in March 1919 and 1920. In contrast to these previous events, only workers from strongholds of the radical left took arms against the government forces. Most of them were young and had no roots in prewar Social Democracy. This aspect of the events will be the primary focus of the discussion that follows.

Overestimated Mobilization: The Communist Movement as of Fall 1920

Following the merger with the majority of the USPD, the VKPD in the district Halle-Merseburg had about 66,000 members—more than in any other party district.[5] The first test of the party's ability to mobilize supporters beyond its membership came in the Prussian Landtag elections on 20 February 1921. Across the state, the VKPD achieved an impressive success by winning 7.4 percent of the votes, the equivalent of 1.25 million ballots. It thus surpassed the remaining USPD (6.4 percent) and polled nearly one-third the votes that the SPD received (25.9 percent).[6] By far the best result came in the electoral district of Merseburg, which coincided with the party district Halle-Merseburg: 197,101 voters cast their ballots for the VKPD, equivalent to 29.8 percent. The party's results were far above this average in those counties that would later become focal points of the "March action." In the Mansfelder Seekreis it polled 47.9 percent (18,877 votes), in the Mansfelder Gebirgskreis 39.6 percent (11,597), and in the urban and rural county Merseburg, which included the Leuna Works, it came in at 34.0 percent (16,580).[7]

As impressive as these numbers are, the VKPD did not even come close to repeating the results that the USPD had achieved in the Reichstag elections of 1920. At that time, the USPD had won 60.3 percent in the Mansfelder Seekreis, 55.4 percent in the Mansfelder Gebirgskreis, and 48.3 percent in County Merseburg.[8] In addition, the USPD remained clearly ahead of the VKPD as the strongest party also in 1921 in the counties of Weißenfels and Zeitz, whose delegates had voted against the "21 Conditions" at the special party congress. Moreover, the SPD improved noticeably over its results from 1920 in all counties of the district and came overall to no less than 10.6 percent.[9] Since the participation rate in 1921 was slightly below that of 1920 (81.0 percent vs. 83.6 percent), with the number of eligible voters remaining nearly identical,[10] the VKPD won noticeably fewer votes than the USPD had in the Reichstag elections of 1920, not only percentage-wise, but also in absolute numbers. The same pattern is found in the electoral districts of Magdeburg and Erfurt, where the VKPD was able to attract even fewer voters away from the USPD. The larger part of USPD supporters switched to the VKPD, but the smaller part went back to the SPD, while the workers' parties on the whole mobilized fewer voters also in other Landtag elections in 1921 than had been the case a year before.[11] Although the bloody fighting of 1920 had driven many workers to the left, especially in the industrial region of central Germany, the VKPD was not able to repeat the success mobilizing voters that the USPD had had in 1920.

Still, the considerable influence of the VKPD is evident not only from the result of the elections on the level of the states and the Reich. The authorities were worried at least as much about the influence of the party on the local level. When large numbers of USPD members switched to the VKPD, it also meant that many official posts changed over to the Communists. At the beginning of 1921, the VKPD had, among others, 72 city commissioners, mayors, and lay judges, as well as more than 426 city councilors in the district of Merseburg, and the majority in many municipal councils.[12] The Prussian government sought to curtail the influence of the Communists by refusing to confirm elected mayors.

The VKPD gained additional influence in the unions. In December 1920, the Communists took over the leadership of the Deutscher Metallarbeiterverband (DMV, German Metal Workers' League) in Halle and of the Wood-Working and Construction Union, and on 7 January they took over the Halle union cartel. In the spring of 1921, the VKPD in the district held the leadership of most union associations on the level of the counties, though not the district level, and much the same was true for the consumer cooperatives and local health insurance funds.[13] By now the party had also won some influence among rural workers. The Freie Landarbeiterverband (Free Rural Workers' League), founded in the fall of 1920 to compete with the Social-Democratic dominated DLV, may have had up to 30,000 members. This organization, which was especially strong in the Mansfelder Seekreis, rejected the regulation of agricultural work for the province of Saxony agreed on in 1919 and was therefore not accepted as a partner to the wage agreement.[14]

The crucial point now was whether the party would be able to build upon its successful mobilization in this area. The opportunity to do so came with the conflicts over wages and working conditions that developed in the province of Saxony after September 1920, following the lifting of the state of siege. The operators of brown coal mines abrogated the wage agreement and tried to push through a cut in pay. After months of negotiations and massive threats of strike, the unions finally succeeded, in the middle of January, in extracting a wage increase. At the Leuna Works, a conflict over weekly work hours that had been going on since the end of 1920 and also involved strikes led to the company's introduction of the 48-hour work week.[15]

Another conflict, one that was part of the history immediately leading up to the deployment of the Schupo and the Communist "March action," unfolded in the Mansfeld Combine, by far the largest enterprise in the northwest of the district of Merseburg. A growing number of thefts, especially of mine timber, prompted management to take special security measures in November of 1920. The thefts were apparently a form of social protest against the continuing shortages and against the particularly poor wages and working conditions in the Mansfeld Combine.[16] Initially, management hired eight members of a Berlin detective agency to watch the grounds; then on 1 February 1921 it announced its intention to set up its own police force, without drawing protest from the works council. Opposition was voiced among the workers, however. A strike broke out at the Hermann mine and continued to spread. An assembly of several thousand workers elected an action committee, led by Josef Schneider, the editor of the Communist *Mansfelder Volkszeitung*. On 4 February, ten to fifteen thousand strikers marched behind Schneider to the office of management in Eisleben and prevailed upon the director-general to refrain from setting up a company police force. According to management, miners armed with clubs had appeared in the negotiation room.[17]

The Communists had been able to take the lead in the protest movement, but their success was short-lived. The Reich Labor Ministry got involved and summoned representatives of the company and the union cartel to Magdeburg to resolve the problem of how to pay for the strike days. Oberpräsident Hörsing sent his party comrade and confidant Kunzemann to Eisleben, where he established contact with management, the union cartel, and the two Social Democratic parties. On 8 February, the board of the union cartel and subdistricts of the SPD and the USPD issued an appeal to the "workers of Mansfeld," denouncing the management's plans as "unlawful" and "provocative" while at the same time trumpeting its own competence to resolve the crisis. The appeal sharply attacked the VKPD, without naming it directly, by pointing to alleged plans to refuse emergency work that would cause the shafts to fill with water and thus deprive the Mansfeld miners of any possibility of gainful employment for years to come.[18]

The appeal was effective: in a vote on 15 February, a clear majority of the workers in the Mansfeld Combine decided against continuing the strike and in favor of accepting the compromise arrived at in Magdeburg, which provided payment of half the wage for all days of the strike.[19] The Communists' attempt to turn the conflict over the company police into a great strike had failed. While the miners of Mansfeld were willing to trust and follow the elected works council and their union in a situation of conflict, they did not let the VKPD draft them into fighting for its larger goals. Giving the party the vote during an election was one thing, participating in an action initiated by it was another.

However, the consequences that Hörsing's confidant Kunzemann drew from the events were clear. He recommended that "tough action" be taken "at the appropriate time" against the VKPD, which could be expected to incite unrest first of all in the county of Mansfeld.[20] Representatives of the authorities were now also speaking out in favor of a tough course against the Communists. Eisleben's lord mayor, who had previously been restrained in his comments, now wanted the question of a heightened police presence to be reviewed.[21] The Regierungspräsident of Merseburg saw the establishment of a military organization by the Communists proceeding apace and feared larger unrest in the Mansfelder Seekreis and County Merseburg, home to the Leuna Works.[22] However, the main proponent of the thesis that a great uprising was imminent was the Prussian State Commissioner for the Supervision of Public Order, Weismann. It was evidently due to his influence that the Schupo action—originally planned, by Hörsing and Prussian Minister of the Interior Severing, only for the two Mansfeld counties and for Eisleben—was broadened on 14 March: police units were now to be stationed also at three locations in County Merseburg and additional units kept in reserve. Historians disagree on the significance in this context of a bombing of the Victory Column in Berlin by members of the KAPD, which was discovered on 13 March and found to have a trail leading back to the province of Saxony.[23] That this expansion of the original deployment plans was intended to directly trigger the expected uprising and thus allow the authorities to retain the initiative is speculation and, as the later events would show, rather unlikely. Retrospective statements by Severing in this direction should be seen more as attempts to justify what was done rather than as a faithful reflection of his original intentions.[24] Regardless of what were in the final analysis tactical differences, the authorities decided to respond to Communist influence not with genuinely political means, but with what was believed to be the simpler and safer instrument: the police.

According to the action plan, initially the units were merely to occupy and secure their quarters and await further instructions about the search for weapons and arrests. Saturday, 19 March, was carefully chosen as the day to begin the action, for Easter vacation had begun the day before, meaning that the schools would be available as quarters. Moreover, the run-up to the plebiscite in Upper Silesia on 20 March was not to be disturbed by excessive public attention to a police deployment. Almost simultaneously, on 16/17 March, the Central Committee of the VKPD decided on its offensive course, though at first it wanted to undertake an action only in the district Halle-Merseburg, at the beginning of which would be a general strike. However, a radical minority as well as the delegation from the Comintern advocated the immediate arming of the proletariat, and emissaries from the KAPD called upon party members in the central German industrial region to cooperate with the VKPD.[25] When the first groups of one hundred policemen arrived in and around Eisleben on 19 March, the sort of reaction their appearance would trigger remained a fairly open question.

Workers' Uprising or Schutzpolizei Campaign? The Fighting in the Industrial Region of Central Germany

Even before the police units arrived, an appeal from the Oberpräsident asking for understanding for the action reached the people of the Mansfelder Land. For two years, the appeal declared, "dreadful thefts" of the most varied kind had taken place, as had wildcat strikes during which the majority of workers had been terrorized by a small minority of "international criminals." The Communist Party itself, Hörsing continued, was not at fault, for the instigators were merely pretending to be Communists and may even be "spies and provocateurs." Pleas for help had reached him from all circles of the population. The police, however, would "not meddle in either political or union matters" and would take action "only against the criminals themselves."[26] The announcement said nothing about the length of the deployment or where it would take place, nor about the type of measures that were planned. Although the appeal painted a completely exaggerated picture of the security situation,[27] its argumentation was not without skill. The VKPD was not directly attacked; meanwhile the reference to "spies and provocateurs" could claim a good deal of credibility given the experiences with the real putsches of the KAPD the year before.

On the morning of 19 March, three hundred-man units of police moved into Eisleben, two into neighboring Hettstedt. There were no clashes of any kind. Not a single source reports "crowds" that gave the police deployments a hostile reception. However, the local VKPD under the leadership of the editor of the *Mansfelder Volkszeitung,* Schneider, reacted immediately. Together with the Mansfeld union cartel it issued a call for a general strike intended to force the withdrawal of the police. There was no talk of armed actions, though the workers were to be "armed, just in case." In Hettstedt, an ultimatum was issued for a withdrawal by noon on 20 March. However, by the morning of 21 March it was evident that the strike had not had much resonance; one reason may have been a conference held in Eisleben that Saturday between the leader of the Schupo, Kunzemann (the civil commissioner assigned to them), and various officials of the region to explain the action. Workers walked off the job at only a few mines and enterprises in the environs of Eisleben. A small number of agricultural workers also went on strike on 22 March.[28]

The response of the VKPD to the action of the Prussian government, which evidently caught it by surprise, was not uniform. On 18 March, the *Rote Fahne,* its central Berlin organ, published an appeal drafted by the activist minority in the party leadership. It attacked the Orgesch-friendly policy of von Kahr in Bavaria and explicitly called upon German workers to arm themselves: "No worker gives two hoots about the law and acquires a weapon wherever he can find it!"[29] The district leadership in Halle-Merseburg, meanwhile, took a much more cautious position. On 17 March, *Klassenkampf,* the new party organ of the VKPD in the district of Merseburg, dismissed Hörsing's justification for the police action as a lie and demanded that they be immediately withdrawn. At the same time, however, it warned the workers not to allow themselves to be provoked. On 19 March, the district leadership itself addressed the "workers of central Germany," spoke much like the central office in Berlin of the "bloody rule of the Orgesch" that conservative powers in Germany were seeking to establish with the help of the government, and called upon workers to resist the deployment of the police. In concrete terms, however, it demanded that workers walk off the job only where the Schupo had occupied businesses. Only on 21 March did the *Klas-*

senkampf speak more bluntly: an article under the title "Draw up the battalions!" accused Hörsing of assembling "White guardists" and called for arming oneself against the "counterrevolution." If the latter violated the disarmament laws, "the Revolution" must "follow its example."[30] Clearly, by invoking the Orgesch and its alleged accomplices among the Social Democrats, the VKPD leadership was hoping to brand the SPD once again as a "traitor" and thereby reach more workers than it could through offensive slogans alone.

The VKPD district leadership hesitated, however, to proclaim the general strike or to call for other concrete actions, because it was not quite convinced they would be successful. When it met in Halle on 19 March and was urged by two delegates from Berlin headquarters to take action, all agreed that the deployment of the police units was not sufficient by itself to mobilize the workers; the other side had to be provoked into "firing the first shot." The following day another meeting took place in Halle, this time with participation from representatives of the illegal military apparatus from all party districts in Germany. "The mood was so bad and miserable that some believed it would take artificial means to get the matter going," Lemck, a leading member of the Halle district leadership, later recalled. The call for a general strike by the comrades in Mansfeld was evidently an action they took on their own initiative, initiated by Schneider. Movement on the district level occurred only when Hugo Eberlein ("Hugo with the fuse"), dispatched by the Berlin headquarters as an expert in military technology, arrived in Halle on 23 March and began to make concrete plans for bomb attacks, which were supposed to become a signal for an uprising by the workers. However, his "actionism" went too far, in the eyes of some members of the district leadership, and some of his bombs failed to go off; as a result, not one of the planned operations succeeded. In the meantime, a top military leadership had been set up that also urged the district leadership in Halle to move at a faster pace. Within the VKPD there were several poorly connected centers of activism, and they were unable to agree on a unified approach.[31]

That was also true of the second focal point of the events, the Leuna Works. On 19 and 21 March, police units occupied six towns and villages in the vicinity of Merseburg, including Ammendorf and Teutschenthal, though not Leuna itself. Here, too, the arrival of the police took place without incident. Only the municipal council of Teutschenthal issued a unanimous call for the withdrawal of the police and demanded from the Oberpräsident an explanation of the action. On 21 March, ten thousand workers gathered at the Leuna Works for a workers' meeting, which was chaired by the KAPD leader Utzelmann (alias Kempin). The meeting, whose speakers called Hörsing's action a "provocation," adopted a resolution that demanded, in addition to the withdrawal of the Schupo from the entire industrial region of central Germany, the disarming of the Orgesch and the "arming of the workers to defend against all counterrevolutionary attacks"; it also threatened a strike should the police occupy the factory itself. The works' VKPD-dominated council was deposed, and an action committee under Kempin's leadership was elected.[32] How confusing the political situation in Leuna was can be seen from the fact that the new action committee, though dominated by the KAPD, appears to have been set up also with participation of delegates from the VKPD district leadership, who thereby disavowed their own comrades at the factory. It is therefore not surprising that the cooperation between the VKPD and the KAPD at the factory did not go smoothly. Offensive actions, which had the potential for considerable impact given the size of the workforce at Leuna, were initially not considered. As management refused to have contact with the action committee, work de facto ground to a halt on 22 March; further meetings were held, but for now nothing more happened.[33]

On the evening of the same day, the situation in the Mansfelder Land grew dangerously tense. Until then, the police had taken a wait-and-see attitude, refusing to be rattled even by insults. That would change after the arrival in Eisleben of Max Hoelz, who only the day before had decided spontaneously, and on his own initiative, to travel into this area. During the revolutionary months of 1918/19 and the days of the Kapp Putsch, Hoelz had attracted attention with spectacular liberations of prisoners and military actions in the Vogtland and enjoyed considerable popularity. He was a charismatic, captivating speaker, and at the same time a daredevil and skillful leader of small fighting units. Hoelz exuded, more so than almost anyone else, the attraction of "direct action": factory owners in the Vogtland had to pay for the upkeep of the "Red Army" set up by Hoelz, and when freeing prisoners, Hoelz made sure that their court files went up in smoke. In all he did, Hoelz seemed like his own man, not the representative of a party; and in fact, though he was a member of the USPD and then the VKPD, he was directly active at their behest only at times.[34]

Hoelz arrived in Eisleben in the late afternoon of 22 March, a day on which the action committee had summoned the strikers for a meeting. According to the plans of Eberlein and the military leadership in Halle, the meeting was to provide the occasion for violent intervention on the part of the police. Hoelz, who knew nothing about this, introduced himself to the assembled workers, issued a vigorous call for a struggle against the "haves," and promised to chase the police out of Eisleben with fifty courageous fighters. What happened next is not entirely clear. It would appear that two policemen in civilian dress, who, carrying VKPD membership books, were there to spy on the meeting, were arrested and taken to the offices of the *Mansfelder Volkszeitung*, where Schneider, the local leader of the movement, interrogated them. In downtown Eisleben, several policemen who were out shopping were attacked and beaten. In response, Major Folte, the squad leader, ordered his men to clear the streets, break into the editorial offices of the paper, and free the detained policemen. In the process, the police made two arrests. Following reports that groups of armed men could be seen in neighboring towns and villages, Folte placed guards at the access roads. The first shots were fired that night: the seminary building in which some of the police officers were housed came under fire from about fifty rifles. Because of the poor visibility, the police did not return fire and there were no casualties. However, it hardly seemed possible now to prevent a further escalation.[35]

The next day, nearly all mines around Eisleben had gone on strike. From Mansfeld and Helbra came reports from attacks on the district savings bank and the post office.[36] The Schupo suffered its first fatalities when a unit of twenty-five men at the Otto shaft in Eisleben tried to secure several trucks against attacks from the rebels and came unexpectedly under fire. Four officers were killed, five were wounded, and four were taken prisoner.[37]

In the meantime, the situation was also growing dangerously tense at the Leuna Works. On the day of 23 March, the first reports about the clashes in Eisleben arrived; rumors circulated of an imminent occupation of the factory and "provocative actions" by the Schupo. Under the leadership of Kempin, yet another meeting of workers decided to walk out. Strikes were also taking place at the brown coal mines of the neighboring Geisel Valley and in Schkeuditz, where action committees were formed the next day. Kempin began to divide the workers into military formations and to hand out weapons, some of which had evidently been brought in during the night; apart from rifles, there were probably a few machine guns. The following day saw the confiscation of bicycles and stretchers from the factory fire brigade, and of oil and gasoline. A locomotive and two wagons were turned into an armored train, though it did not see any real action. Massive reservations were voiced about these preparations for military clashes, and Kempin and his followers evidently responded to them also with threats of violence. Although the exits from the factory were manned by armed guards, most of the workers were able to leave. Initial reports that a "Red Army" of 12,000 men had formed soon turned out to be false; on the afternoon of 26 March, it was reported to the Oberpräsidium that at most 2,000 men were still at Leuna, and they did not possess very many weapons.[38]

The conflict now entered into its decisive phase. On 23 March, the USPD, SPD, and the local union cartel in Halle, who had previously been conferring with Oberpräsident Hörsing, issued an appeal to the workers of the industrial region of central Germany. It was mildly critical of the police deployment—Hörsing had not remained "in touch with the workers"—but then passed on the assurance of the Oberpräsident that the deployment was aimed only at pursuing criminals and that no factories or enterprises would be occupied. Finally, it called upon the workers to refuse to follow the VKPD and not let themselves by pushed into a putsch.[39]

The following day, the VKPD in Berlin and in the district responded by proclaiming a general strike. The Berlin headquarters of the party came out openly in favor of resisting the police action by force, and this defensive battle was then to move on to pushing through the goals that had not been realized in March 1920. However, there was no talk of a revolutionary reshaping of society, only assertions that the "power in the enterprises" had to be won. By contrast, the VKPD leadership in Halle put the strike itself front and center. Although it, too, called upon the workers to arm themselves, it asked them only to maintain a general readiness to fight.[40] Even the VKPD functionary Lemck, who tried from Halle to organize fighting groups to support the Mansfeld insurrectionists, expressed himself in restrained language in an appeal to the workers of Halle that was disseminated as a leaflet. Until now, Lemck declared, the workers of Mansfeld had successfully resisted the "provocation of the bloodthirsty Hörsing" and would soon chase the rest of his troops "from the Mansfeld lands with clubs"; the expectation now was that the workers of the city would rise up "like one man" and disarm "the gangs of the likes of Hörsing and Döltz [the police president of Halle]." The appeal did not say how that was supposed to be accomplished.[41] The district leadership was by no means unanimously behind the offensive tactics propagated by headquarters and some of its own members.

The edition of the *Klassenkampf* that contained the call for a general strike was at the same time the last to appear for a long time. On 24 March, the Reich president imposed a nonmilitary state of emergency throughout the entire province of Saxony. Outdoor meetings and demonstrations were banned, and the *Klassenkampf* and other Communist papers had to suspend publication. Hundreds of additional police officers were ordered into the central German industrial region as reinforcement, especially from Berlin and Düsseldorf; eventually, thirty-eight hundred-man units were operating there, their armament including mine throwers. If needed, individual Reichswehr units would also be called in. Oberpräsident Hörsing, who functioned as the Reich civil commissioner for the province, was in overall command of the police deployment; de facto, however, he was increasingly in the hands of those police leaders who commanded the deployment groups that were each composed of several hundred-man units. The police deployment took on an increasingly military character, even though the Reichswehr itself hardly saw any action.[42]

The VKPD's call for a strike on 24 March met with only weak resonance. The only new hot spot was the district of Bitterfeld, where all enterprises of the chemical industry except for Wolfen and a few construction companies were shut down, as was the Zschornewitz power plant (though not until 31 March). Eisleben and its environs remained the center of the strike, even though nearly a third of the workers at the Mansfeld Combine were on the job. Participation in the strike was massive in the brown coal mines of the Geisel Valley and in Querfurt; it was also pronounced in the Saalkreis (which bordered Halle), where the workforce of nearly all enterprises was on strike in Ammendorf and in Könnern. In Halle itself, most enterprises of the metal industry were hit with a strike, and for a short time beginning on 30 March so was the municipal electric company.

Beyond these locations, the strike appeal met with meaningful resonance only in the munitions factory of Piesteritz (County Wittenberg) and in County Sangerhausen, and to a smaller degree also in County Liebenwerda, while participation in the other counties of the district remained very anemic, especially in the brown coal field of Zeitz-Weißenfels. Rural workers walked off the job in only a few locations. It would seem that the strikes themselves were peaceful and did not involve attempts by the strikers to arm themselves. In only a few cases did entrepreneurs ask that Schupo or Teno be sent out.[43] Outside the district of Merseburg, the workers in only a few enterprises followed the Communists' call for a strike. In Suhl and its neighboring towns, work was suspended in twenty-five enterprises, though starting only on 29 March and then for just two days, "because the majority of the workers were opposed." In the administrative district of Erfurt, there seem to have been sympathy strikes in only a few smaller businesses in County Erfurt.[44] In the district of Magdeburg, sympathy strikes occurred only in one oil factory in Aken (County Calbe) and three salt mines in County Wanzleben, though they did not begin until 29 and 30 March, respectively, and lasted only one day each.[45]

All in all, the strike activity during the March fighting mirrored the political landscape of the province. Where the VKPD was particularly strong, the workers followed its call for a strike in large numbers. In addition to the Mansfelder Land and the Saalkreis, this was also true for the counties of Bitterfeld and Querfurt, where no Schupo had been initially deployed and the VKPD was noticeably stronger than elsewhere; the same was true for County Schleusingen, where it had won 34.0 percent in the Prussian Landtag elections, a result that was far higher than the average. In counties like Delitzsch, Torgau, or Wittenberg, which were not strongholds of the VKPD (although it was the strongest workers' party), the response to the strike appeal was much weaker or almost nonexistent.

If the VKPD was unable to mobilize all its supporters even in areas where it had achieved particularly good results in the previous elections, its attempt at mobilization failed especially where one of the other Socialist parties was dominant. In the Zeitz-Weißenfels brown coal field, which continued to be dominated by the USPD, the appeal of the VKPD met with no response, and the same was true in the greater part of the district of Thuringia, where the USPD had remained the strongest party (apart from County Schleusingen and the city of Erfurt). Thus, what characterized workers who joined sympathy strikes was not so much a particular social profile—although miners of the various sectors of the mining industry and chemical workers were prominent—as the fact that they lived in a region in which the VKPD had a clear hegemony. The strike was therefore not—or at least not primarily—a protest strike against the measures of the Prussian authorities and the actions of the Schupo, but an act of solidarity with the party.[46]

The armed clashes remained initially concentrated in the Mansfelder Land. The initiative was not yet with the police. Max Hoelz, who had set up his headquarters between Eisleben and Hettstedt, organized fighting units and tried to establish contact with higher party leaders of the VKPD, though without assuming any kind of subordinate relationship to the party either now or later. As early as 24 March, according to his own statements, he had at his disposal "four storm companies of a hundred men each and six machine gun units." They were, however, inadequately equipped with arms, most of which probably came from hidden caches. A runner service of bicycle patrols maintained contact between the units. Hoelz opted for surprise attacks by his fighters, who moved about like partisans. Twice—in small numbers on 23 March and with a force of several hundred men in the late evening of 25 March—they pushed into Eisleben, occupied buildings, and tried to lure Folte's policemen from their quarters. The second attempt led to an intense gun battle around city hall, with the insurrectionists forced to retreat after one of their ammunition boxes exploded. The Schupo continued to come under fire from the surrounding heights. During an attack on Hettstedt on 24 March, Hoelz himself blew up part of the train station, two villas, and a print shop near the quarters of the policemen. In this early phase of the fighting, Folte's men in part lacked the necessary coordination, and in part acted too cautiously. Even the curfew and the arrival of five hundred men from Halle at noon on 24 March did not change the situation decisively. For now there was a stalemate, but a turnaround could be expected given the approaching reinforcements of policemen from the northwest.

At this juncture, a delegation of Eisleben Communists, led by the second editor of the *Mansfelder Volkszeitung*, tried to negotiate with Folte. The latter declined, but after consulting with Hörsing he offered to let the insurrectionists get off without punishment if the fighting ceased, all weapons were handed over, and the workers returned to their jobs. Any possible agreement was thwarted by the fact that Hoelz had in the meantime launched his second attack against Eisleben, and the Reich Interior Minister and Prussian Interior Minister, Severing, upon hearing of this offer, sharply reprimanded Hörsing and forbade him to pursue any such negotiations. The Prussian government and the Reich government had now unambiguously chosen to resolve the conflict by force.[47]

When the reinforcements led by Count Poninski arrived in Eisleben and prepared to face the insurrectionists with their superior strength and armaments, which also included artillery, the writing was on the wall for the attempted uprising. In a series of smaller skirmishes, Poninski was able, with few casualties to his own forces, to defeat and disperse the armed groups in the Mansfeld region. On 27 March, Easter Sunday, he joined up with Folte's units, and together they combed the area between Eisleben and Merseburg until the evening of the following day. Hoelz himself—it would appear that only some of the groups of armed fighters active in the Mansfeld area considered themselves to be in some kind of command relationship to him—had withdrawn toward Sangerhausen with part of this troops in order to give them some rest and then move on to Leuna.[48]

Although the fighting headquarters of the Communists in Leipzig and Halle tried hard to coordinate the actions of the insurrectionists and to help the beleaguered men in Mansfeld, their efforts had no decisive success. It would appear that Bowitzki, whom the top leadership had appointed "political commissar" for the Mansfelder Land, was not able to establish contact with Hoelz until 26 March, and the latter was not willing to enter into any kind of binding agreement with him. Lemck, too, who was commanding the military actions around Halle, had trouble gaining Hoelz's support at a meeting on Easter Sunday.[49] The VKPD in Halle had some success at mobilizing on Good Friday, when a crowd of more than 10,000 at the Gertrauden cemetery remembered those who had died in March 1920, with Bowitzki and Lemck giving speeches. Bowitzki asked those present to give their "sacred oath" that they would hasten to the aid of the Mansfelders in their struggle; Lemck directly appealed to the mourners to arm themselves and proceed to the Mansfelder Land. It would appear that a larger number of younger workers did in fact set out that very day.[50]

A day later, Max Hoelz and his men arrived in Sangerhausen. Their behavior here, outside of the actual core region of the insurrection, was no different from that in the Mansfeld area. As early as 24 March, the local VKPD leadership had called for a general strike at a meeting; it formed an action committee, and the next day, Good Friday, it began preparations for providing active support to the Mansfeld fighters, though it was not moving as quickly as Max Hoelz had demanded in his telegram ("as quickly as possible"). In the early afternoon of 26 March, Hoelz's unit, a total of around 300 armed men, suddenly appeared in the city with several vehicles. The public buildings were occupied, and "money, clothing, and food was extorted from numerous residents of the city without payment." That evening, the telegraph office was blown up. Hoelz took fourteen hostages, including the first mayor and the postal director, though he released both of them after the postal director had handed over the hastily hidden contents of his cash box, a sum of about 200,000 marks. The other hostages later returned to Sangerhausen unharmed. The arrival of an armored train from the route protection division at the train station that same afternoon sparked an intense firefight, in which seven people were killed: one soldier, three insurrectionists, and three townspeople who had ended up in the crossfire out of curiosity or by accident. Hoelz and his people left the city in the evening. At noon the following day, a hundred-man unit of police from Kassel moved into Sangerhausen and immediately made a larger number of arrests. The strike ended on 29 March.[51]

Other counties were also affected by similar "visitations," though these did not lead to any fighting.[52] There, and in Sangerhausen, where the escalation of the events had not been preceded by the arrival of the Schupo, Hoelz's tactics had to seem even more terrifying to those parts of the population remote from the VKPD than they did in the Mansfeld area, the actual site of the uprising. It was not so much the actual fighting that was frightening (especially since the number of casualties in most other clashes during the conflict was not substantially higher than in Sangerhausen), but the visible loss of property caused by the bombings. Hoelz's method resembled the pseudo-putsches of the KAPD the previous year—on that occasion, as well, Sangerhausen had been affected—and to that extent did not seem all that far from ordinary crimes. The use of dynamite gave him an especially menacing aspect.

Added to this was the tone that Max Hoelz struck in his public pronouncements. For example, one proclamation, entitled "Dictatorship of the Proletariat!," declared: "I have occupied the town together with my troops and am herewith imposing proletarian martial law. This means that any citizen who does not follow the orders of the supreme military leadership will be shot. The very moment I am informed that *Sipo* or Reichswehr are approaching, I will immediately torch the entire town and slaughter the bourgeoisie, with no distinction as to gender and age (!). As long as no *Sipo* or Reichswehr advance, I will spare the lives of the residents and their houses."[53]

In an appeal that was circulated as a leaflet, Hoelz called upon the workers of Halle to follow his example there and then come to the Mansfeld area. He and his men were fighting "with all means against the executioners of the proletariat": "We are slaughtering the bourgeoisie ... we are blowing up their castles and palaces ... we are taking away the stolen goods, the money, the gold that they stole first from the workers through exploitation and usury ... Take action!"[54] Genuine political goals were not to be found in these appeals. They were marked entirely by wild tirades against the class enemy and calls for "direct action." This was not the language of the VKPD. Slogans like this had no meaningful attraction for workers with some capacity for political judgment, though they seemed attractive to many a youngster precisely because of their blunt language, no matter how seriously they took the call to "slaughter the bourgeoisie." In the bourgeois camp, Hoelz's threats reinforced the fears triggered by his attacks and bombings.

His actions and the accompanying language altered the very words that the bourgeois papers used to describe the uprising. Whereas in the first days of the armed clashes we still hear neutral words like "armed men" or "armed workers," occasionally also "insurrectionists," beginning on 26 March, the term "gangs" moved to the fore. "Red gangs" were setting up a "reign of terror," "gangs of criminals" were at work, led by the "chief bandit" or "robber captain Hoelz;" the region was in a "gang war."[55] The authorities, as well, used chiefly the term "gang" in their internal communications. Only occasionally did they speak of the "enemy" or the "opponent."[56] Not only was the police action mutating increasingly into a warlike operation; it was simultaneously losing the character of a "normal" military clash and developing into a punitive action against criminals—with brutalizing consequences, as we shall see.

In the process, no distinction was made between Max Hoelz and the VKPD in the public bourgeois arena. The events seemed to confirm the image of the dangerous Communist enemy, an image that had grown more menacing since the fall of 1920. A few days after the outbreak of the fighting there was a consensus that the Communists were acting on orders from Moscow and had carefully prepared this campaign. They were trying to "drive the workers into a civil war" and "Germany into general chaos."[57] By supporting "criminal gangs" they had put themselves "outside any state order." There was therefore little that separated them from ordinary criminals. The phrase "Muscovite gangsterism" (*moskowitisches Verbrechertum*) summed up these charges in a nutshell.[58] The picture of the enemy had become darker still. Even the Social Democratic *Volksstimme* was not far removed from such assessments when it spoke of "Muscovite vampires who want to suck the blood of German workers to engage in their own terroristic life" and let their German vassals start a "senseless civil war." For that reason they were "either criminals themselves" or were "favoring criminals."[59]

One result of this view was the notion that the Communist leadership had to be fought with all possible means. The *Magdeburgische Zeitung* demanded that the party leadership of the VKPD be arrested and its publications outlawed. Pointing to Zinoviev's statements at the Halle party congress of the USPD, the paper declared: "If the heralds of such doctrines are drowned in the bloodbath they have caused, we do not feel pity but satisfaction. It would be suicidal sentimentality to spare their lives." The *Saale-Zeitung* emphasized that Communists should no longer be allowed to hold public offices and that parliamentary immunity should not pose an insurmountable obstacle.[60] The *Volksstimme,* by contrast, dispensed with such recommendations for action and was content to express general agreement with the course of the Prussian government.[61]

There was disagreement within the bourgeois press about the possible widening of the uprising and the measures that should be taken in response. The left-liberal *Saale-Zeitung* believed on the whole that Germany was in danger only if "circles with a reactionary orientation" became active, and it maintained even at the height of the fighting that there was "no reason for special concern."[62] It therefore cautioned against an excessively harsh response, as it would only create "martyrs" and drive the masses toward radicalism, thus defending the Prussian government and its concept of a limited police action.[63] By contrast, the *Magdeburgische Zeitung,* which was close to the DVP, vehemently attacked the government and especially Oberpräsident Hörsing, criticizing him for his alleged offer of amnesty in Eisleben. The paper called on the Reich government to impose martial law and to intervene with the military means at its disposal, since a "policy of letting things take their course" was allowing Germany "to stumble into the abyss."[64] This put the paper on the side of demands for a harsher course toward the insurgents, which had been voiced since 26 March in a series of telegrams to the Oberpräsident. A "committee of the harmed" (*Geschädigtenausschuß*) in Eisleben was threatening a tax strike if the government failed to provide adequate protection for the city, a Mitteldeutscher Volksbund für Stadt und Land (Central German *Volksbund* for City and Countryside) and the local organization of the DVP Naumburg urged the deployment of the Reichswehr, while farmers from the Mansfeld counties were even calling for the use of courts-martial—as was the Erfurter Bürgerbund (Erfurt Civil League).[65] Some were also thinking about setting up self-protection leagues, but these plans were not put into practice.[66] The reflexive response against chaos that had been evident during the last few years played itself out once again and in a more acute form.

The defeat of the insurgents was sealed on 28 and 29 March. While Poninski's and Folte's units were moving southeast from Eisleben, other Schupo units were operating from Halle and Merseburg. By now, the situation that was typical of the events in March had developed in the Geisel Valley, the brown coal region between Merseburg and Querfurt: numerous action committees had sprung into being, and smaller groups of armed men crisscrossed the area requisitioning food and vehicles, stealing explosives, destroying telephone lines, and in some cases taking hostages. However, nobody was maltreated or killed. On 28 March, the insurgents' attempt to push toward Halle failed. Hoelz had agreed with Lemck and Bowitzki to concentrate all available fighters in the suburb of Ammendorf and then attack the artillery depots in Halle. Lemck and Bowitzki could muster about 200 men, Hoelz around 500. Kempin, however, refused to send reinforcements from Leuna, as he was unwilling to weaken its defenses. As a result, the offensive got bogged down in Ammendorf. Hoelz blew up the post office and parts of the railroad tracks, but then his men came under a pincer attack from 600 policemen. After some fierce house-to-house fighting, the insurgents were forced to admit defeat. A great many of them, including their leaders, managed to escape, but their vehicles and a large part of their weapons fell into the hands of the Schupo. Thirty fighters were killed on the Communist side and seventy were taken prisoner, while the police did not suffer a single fatality. For the time being, the insurgents no longer had a larger, mobile fighting unit at their disposal.[67]

The next day, police units took the Leuna Works, surrounding the facility with 2,100 men and one artillery unit of the Reichswehr. As a large number of the armed workers, Kempin among them, had left Leuna the night before, the remaining defenders were fighting a losing battle, with perhaps no more than fifty or sixty rifles at their disposal. The works council, which had been shunted aside by the action committee a few days earlier, made an offer to hand over the facility, but the leadership of the Schupo did not accept. Poninski wanted a demonstration of military strength. The police stormed the grounds after a brief artillery bombardment. The workers resisted vigorously in only a few places and were unable to do so for long. About fifty were killed, while only one of the attacking policemen lost his life. More than 1,000 rebels, Lemck among them, were captured and detained in the factory under degrading conditions.[68] With the capture of Leuna, the uprising had been quashed for good. The remnants of Hoelz's unit were surrounded and crushed by police units at Beesenstedt near the Saale on April 1. Eighteen insurgents were killed, many were taken prisoner, and most of the weapons and all vehicles fell into the hands of the Schupo. Hoelz and Schneider barely escaped.[69]

The strike movement felt the effects of these events. The Zschornewitz power plant had been up and running again since 30 March, a day later the enterprises in Halle resumed work, and gradually the brown coal pits around the city did the same. On the evening of 1 April the district leadership of the VKPD, after intense soul-searching, decided to call for an end to the general strike.[70] The deployment of Reichswehr troops—which so far had not been operating in the area of the uprising, with the exception of the battery attached to Count Poninski—did not alter the situation. Oberpräsident Hörsing and Minister of the Interior Severing were at pains to prevent the uprising from spreading beyond its initial area and therefore had central locations at the edges of the area occupied by Reichswehr units.[71] On 29 March a small group entered Naumburg, and on the following day Sangerhausen, Aschersleben, Bitterfeld, and Delitzsch were occupied. The entry of the troops went off without incident everywhere except in Delitzsch, which saw a minor exchange of gunfire. All told, the Reichswehr pulled together twelve battalions, five squadrons, thirteen batteries, two motorized columns, and two pioneer companies in the towns mentioned above—a considerable force.[72] The increasing military character of the entire deployment of the security forces was becoming clear once again.

Schupo units combed the area of the uprising until the middle of April and made about three hundred additional arrests. This put the total number of detainees at 3,470. The last units were withdrawn at the end of June, and martial law was lifted in all but the centers of the uprising, where it ended on 1 September. Most Reichswehr units had returned to their garrisons at the beginning of April, the rest by the end of the month. Oberpräsident Hörsing estimated that all told, no more than 3 percent of all VKPD members in the area of the uprising had joined an armed group. At the height of the unrest, hardly more than 3,000 insurgents had confronted the units of the Schupo and the Reichswehr. Their arms were a far cry from the horror scenario that Prussian State Commissioner Weismann had painted before the events. The police confiscated from the insurgents a total of 1,346 rifles, 34 machine guns, some of them nonfunctioning, and 10,000 rounds of ammunition. Even if one assumes that the insurgents were able to hide some of the weapons, this does not amount to a lot. Thirty-four police officers had been killed during the clashes; 67 had been wounded. According to Prussian Minister of the Interior Severing, 145 insurgents (or civilians in general) had been killed and 51 injured. Even if the information provided by Severing is unlikely to have included all casualties, one can say that the "March action" in 1921 had fewer casualties than the fighting the previous year.[73]

Some of those who lost their lives were killed outside of the actual fighting. The atrocities that can be attributed to the insurgents were limited to the events following a rear guard engagement on 29 March in Gröbers, south of Halle that proved costly for the Schupo. Among the eleven policemen who were killed, four had not succumbed to the injuries they sustained in the fighting but had been brutally tortured and then murdered. The incident was brought to light a week later. Two brothers among the insurgents, one of whom died shortly thereafter in a firefight with the police, had committed the sadistic acts. On 1 April the press reported in detail about the bodies found near Gröbers.[74] The resulting outrage was understandable, but it is at best a partial explanation for the subsequent brutality by members of the security forces.

The latter were charged with a series of murders and physical abuse. Most of these incidents were perpetrated by the Düsseldorf units. Müller, the chief magistrate of Klostermansfeld, a cofounder of the Freie Landarbeiterverband, and a member of the VKPD, was presumably killed on 25 March, even though he had in fact tried to prevent fighting in his town. Straube, the VKPD leader from Querfurt, who had participated actively in the uprising, was killed on Easter Monday. It is likely that both men were given up by informants. Each was shot in an isolated area after dark. Also on Easter Monday, a Schupo patrol arrested three residents of Schraplau (located between Eisleben and Halle) who had allegedly supported the rebels. With blows from rifle butts and rubber truncheons they were driven to a limekiln on the outskirts of town and shot, along with a fourth man. The shooters pulled the intestines from one of the bodies; a few days earlier this victim had allegedly called for "ripping the guts from the bellies" of the

Schupo.[75] That same day in Bischofsrode, ten kilometers to the west, nine rebels were taken prisoner and then killed by the police.[76]

The Communist mayor (*Amtsvorsteher*) of a community neighboring Gröbers was severely maltreated by the Schupo policemen, driven into a field, and shot to death. On 1 April, when police units moved into Beesenstedt following their victory and were given a friendly reception by the villagers, residents recognized in the crowd, which also included some rebels, the Communist mayor of a neighboring community. In the presence of numerous villagers, he was put against a wall at the edge of the village and shot. Command was here in the hands of a Lieutenant von der Tann, who—not only in this case—informed his subordinates in coded statements when he wanted someone dead.[77]

Numerous abuses and killings were also reported from the Leuna Works. The detainees there suffered kicks and blows from rifle butts and rubber truncheons, were given very little to eat or drink, and in some cases had to sleep on bare concrete floors. Schupo policemen threw wine bottles at them and forced them to sing "Deutschland, Deutschland, über alles" and to cheer the Düsseldorf Schupo. It is likely that a number of prisoners were randomly shot or beaten to death.[78]

Several officers and noncommissioned officers of the Schupo were questioned by the investigative committee about the events. Either they had not seen anything, could not remember anything, or tried to undermine the credibility of the witnesses. Lieutenant von der Tann denied all allegations, stating, moreover, that he knew from his time in the World War what trouble it spelled to have prisoners: "I can do this or I can do that, I cannot take all of them under my wings."[79] It is noteworthy that at the very end of the questioning of the Schupo policemen, it was discovered that some of the officers in the Düsseldorf unit had previously been part of the Free Corps deployed in the Baltic area. More detailed information was withheld, however. It should undoubtedly be seen as an indirect admission of guilt that the police leadership had by now dissolved a unit "for special assignments" that had been connected to the atrocities.[80]

Thus, the March fighting in 1921 saw a repeated pattern of behavior that one could have observed years before in the province of Saxony, in Munich, in the Ruhr region, and elsewhere. Of course, only a minority of the Schupo officers engaged in the atrocities and arbitrary killings. But the incidents in Bischofsrode, Schraplau, and Beesenstedt were the work of more than just a few sadists. They were the final consequence of an approach that took its cues from military ways of thinking instead of from police work. As I have already noted, there certainly were alternatives to the decision to deploy the Schupo on a large scale. If the issue was in fact to combat a massive surge in crimes, it would have been sufficient to provide better security arrangements in the enterprises in question and to back them up politically. It must be said, though, that the policy deployment initially unfolded in ways that were much more "civil" than the deployment of Maercker's troops in 1919. That this approach was abandoned was the result not so much of the actions of the insurgents, but above all of massive political pressure, especially on the Reich level. To be sure, Severing had succeeded in putting down a rebellious movement with the Schupo he had set up without having to resort to help from the Reichswehr on any substantial scale, thus proving that a Social Democratic state interior minister, too, could guarantee "law and order." However, the change in the deployment concept had long-term reverberations that ran counter to its original intentions. The approach of the security forces during the March uprising became the model for police training and contributed significantly to its "militarization."[81]

Moreover, it was alarming that even a man like Hörsing, who initially had wanted to pursue a more cautious path that did not rule out negotiations, eventually joined the chorus of those who considered the police action a complete success. At a press conference following the events, he summed up his stance this way: "You cannot go up against the enemy with a holy water sprinkler."[82] Such martial words were undoubtedly also intended as a response to pressure from the political right, which accused the Oberpräsident and his fellow party member Severing of being too hesitant during the March days. But describing the radical left was as the "enemy" contributed to marginalizing it further and lowering the inhibitory threshold for using violence against it.

The Communist activists, on the other hand, were not able to prevail upon the workers in the industrial region of central Germany and beyond to participate in the "March action" on a large scale, even though the police deployment was taking on increasingly military characteristics. Even some members of the district leadership were not convinced that the offensive course was the right approach. Without the appearance of Max Hoelz, it is likely that the armed actions against the Schupo would have remained limited to a few places and been quickly ended. Unlike what happened during the Kapp Putsch, there was no outrage among large sections of the workers. The solidarity strikes were limited to the Communist bastions and even there did not draw in all the workers. Moreover, it was only in the core area of the uprising that it served as a prelude to armed actions. In any case, what is striking are the large discrepancies between the number of Communist voters, the number of strikers, and the number of those actively involved in the fighting.[83] Most of those who cast their votes for the VKPD expected their party to chart a tough course of opposition to the policies of the government on the Reich and state levels, but certainly not to engage in putsch-like actions. As the conflict in the Mansfeld works had shown, there were other ways to resist the arbitrary will of employers. The methods of Max Hoelz resonated with only a very small segment of the Communist rank and file.

The "March Action": A Youth Rebellion? The Social Profile of the Actors

Who were the rebels? Occasional conjectures that foreigners had played a central role, especially Russians who had come to central Germany on orders from Moscow, soon turned out to be false.[84] But a series of accounts and reports, composed as early as during the events themselves, pointed to the prominent role of young men. Following the initial incidents in Eisleben and Hettstedt, the *Magdeburgische Zeitung* reported the impression of a business owner living in the area of the uprising, who asserted that in the Mansfelder Land "the carriers of the movement were in the beginning mostly young, immature lads." The *Volksstimme,* too, in one of its first reports, identified "mostly young people" as the attackers in Hettstedt. The town's mayor later stated that the unrest had begun when "a band of young, immature, mostly outside people," who were armed with clubs, came into town and extorted clothes and shoes.[85] On 26 March, the *Saale Zeitung* saw "crowds of young workers" on their way from Halle to the Mansfeld area. Three days later it reported that "21, mostly adolescent lads" who wanted to go from Leuna to Bitterfeld had been arrested at the main train station in Halle. In Bitterfeld itself, most workers as well as the local VKPD leadership resisted the call for a general strike, while "mostly adolescent lads led by a few fanatics" supposedly armed themselves and exerted pressure on the others.[86] Special emphasis was placed on the role played by younger men in the events at the Leuna Works. Shortly after the grounds had been stormed by the security forces, Director Oster noted that most of the unrest had originated with the construction workers employed on the site, among whom were "many juvenile (!) people." According to the Landrat, "lads of 16–17, armed with knives and rifles," had terrorized the other workers.[87] These were more than isolated remarks, and they referred, moreover, to the flashpoints of the clashes. Such unambiguous statements had not been made after the fighting in the spring of 1919 or after the Kapp Putsch. Is it true that the circle of fighters had shrunk to encompass especially the younger supporters of the Communists?

Clues about the social profile of those involved come from the files of the extraordinary tribunals that were set up by several state courts after the unrest.[88] The sample I analyzed[89] allows us to make precise statements especially about the age range of the actors, who, incidentally, did not include a single woman. The oldest had been born in 1856, the youngest in 1905. Three-fifths belonged to the age cohorts born between 1890 and 1900; that is, they were part of the actual front line generation of the First World War; however, no fewer than a quarter were younger and had experienced the war only at home. Mostly strongly represented were the birth years from 1899 to 1902, accounting for nearly half of those convicted by the courts in the sample. In 1921, they had attained the age of majority only a year earlier or had not yet reached adulthood. To them can be ascribed the youthfulness that contemporary sources speak of, especially since the judges as well were not very strict in the criteria they applied and ascribed a youthful age also to those born in 1899 and 1897.[90]

At least two-thirds of the actors were unskilled or semi-skilled "laborers," while fewer than one-fifth were trained tradesmen or had some other kind of higher qualification; a few worked in service jobs.[91] Considering where the centers of the uprising were, this is not a surprising occupational profile, but it provides further evidence for the thesis that it was especially workers barely reached by the Social Democratic workers' movement that tended toward radical political behavior. Only one-sixth of the actors in the sample had definitely served in the First World War, and one-sixth had definitely not served, apart from those who were too young to begin with. At least a quarter were single and at least a quarter were married. At least half were employed, and nearly two-thirds did not have a prior criminal record. Just under a third could be clearly identified as members or supporters of the Communists, for the most part the VKPD. The rebels thus did not represent a "conspicuous" group. They were not unemployed workers with prior criminal records, nor were they consistently young men in the life phase before marriage and family. Neither does the front line experience during the war constitute a shared characteristic.

Rather, what characterizes the majority of the actors, apart from their low professional qualifications, is the fact that it was only after 1918 that they had experienced a political system in times of peace. Nearly two-thirds had been born in 1897 or later, which means that they came of age during the war. They had therefore been barely aware of the Reichstag elections of 1912, and it was only afterward that they were politically socialized and became familiar with openly contested political conflicts since November 1918. The willingness to participate in an uprising had its primary roots in this political "youthfulness," but not in a specifically "criminal" profile or in a brutalization as a result of the use of violence on the front line during the war.[92]

When contemporary observers highlighted so emphatically the prominent role of younger men among the rebels, there was undoubtedly an element of wishful thinking in all of this, since they were reluctant to imagine older workers as followers of a man like Max Hoelz. On the whole, however, this emphasis was, as I have shown, not false. Yet still one must beware of seeing the "adolescents" in 1921 only as young men in the life phase before job, marriage, and family, even if some statements by observers point in this direction. To be sure, Hoelz's fighting methods also appealed to a sense of adventure, but those who joined an armed group in the March days of 1921 did so less from adolescent inclinations than because they had not developed any deeper bonds to the old Social Democracy and had early on experienced politics as violent confrontation with the state's agents of order.

The *Volksstimme* argued in this sense when it applied to the "March action" the tried-and-true argument about the masses and those who lead them astray. The "many hundreds of young people who, seduced by unscrupulous fellows … took up arms" should not "pay with inhuman punishments," for "in most cases" they were "the instrument of the crime, not its cause." One might even have to consider setting up special courts for them. After all, they were part of "Germany's hope for the future," especially since there were "honest enthusiasts and idealists" among them.[93] The *Saale-Zeitung* also advocated understanding for some of the rebels. A large segment of the population was still suffering the "aftereffects of the war" and was "out of balance both physically and emotionally." The need for punishment, however, was underscored with reference to the "youth that grew dissolute in the war" as the main carriers of the armed groups.[94]

Shortly before, the paper had also described the rebels as a minority characterized by "stupidity, a passion devoid of any will to self-control, and criminal inclination," and as "vermin" (*Schädlinge*). The use of a biologism in this context was new.[95] This language reflects the notion of a national body (*Volkskörper*) that needed to be treated in ways that were borrowed from medical categories. Curing its sickness implied, in the most extreme case, the elimination of the "vermin" threatening it, a concept that stripped the latter of their human character. The other side of the healing process consisted of "educating the elements that were misguided but not yet entirely lost to the people as a whole." That also included, as both the *Saale-Zeitung* and the *Magdeburgische Zeitung* emphasized, recognizing the legitimate social demands of the workers, and refraining from any revenge or any "efforts at reaction and triumphal urges" after the failure of the Communist uprising.[96] This stance made it possible to continue to find areas of agreement with the SPD. The Magdeburg paper, however, contrasted Severing's and Hörsing's hesitant fight against the radical left with conditions in Bavaria, where the government and *Forstrat* Escherich were protecting the population from such dangers.[97] Invoking the Bavarian model, the paper advocated new "self-protection" units. Though Communists may have lost much ground after their failed uprising, "the substratum remains volcanic, and the strongest eruptions come after what seems like a long period of calm."[98]

Notes

1. *Die Märzkämpfe 1921,* ed. Marx-Engels-Lenin-Stalin Institut (East Berlin, 1956); Leidigkeit and Herrmann, *Leninistischer Kurs,* 126–150; the modified version of the old thesis in Weber, *Putsch.* Weber's work draws on numerous sources that were not available to Western scholars until 1989, though he ignores the findings of non-Communist scholarship and therefore arrives at a distorted conclusion, especially in interpreting the attitude of the VKPD leadership and the influence of the envoys of the Communist International. Another factor that renders his analysis only partially convincing is that he draws an impermissibly sharp distinction between the course of the VKPD and the actions of the KAPD. Above all, he largely excludes the behavior of the rank and file. The KPD added the "V" after its merger with the USPD.
2. Winkler, *Revolution,* 507–513.
3. See Werner T. Angress, *Stillborn Revolution: The Communist Bid for Power in Germany, 1921–1923* (Princeton, 1963), 110ff.; Ludewig, *Arbeiterbewegung,* 186–200; a summary overview in Winkler, *Revolution,* 514–518; most recently Koch-Baumgarten, *Avantgarde.*
4. Koch-Baumgarten, *Avantgarde,* 141–143; Weber, *Putsch,* 35–48; Winkler, *Revolution,* 514.
5. See above, ch.2.; Koch-Baumgarten, *Avantgarde,* 88f.; Mallmann, *Kommunisten in der Weimarer Republik,* 33, 90. The membership numbers that were reported immediately after the merger of the parties were presumably too high, but after the loss of members in the wake of the "March action" the central leadership strongly revised them downward in order to conceal these very losses. That is the line taken by Weber, *Putsch,* 24–27, who assumes a membership figure of "about 30,000" in "the first months after the merger," though he also presents evidence against his own thesis. Without any indication of the source, he provides information

from a questionnaire that was evidently filled out at the end of July and signed off by district leader Georg Schumann: according to this questionnaire, 66,000 members were registered in the district on 1 January, with the number dropping to 19,344 on 1 April and rising again to 25,105 on 1 July.

6. Falter, Lindenberger, and Schumann, *Wahlen,* 101.
7. All numbers from *Preußische Statistik,* vol. 251: 30–32.
8. *Stat. Dt. R., N. F.,* vol. 291/2: 26.
9. *Preußische Statistik,* vol. 251: 32, 30. In County Weißenfels, the USPD polled 35.5 percent compared to the VKPD's 19.5 percent; in County Zeitz the respective figures were 48.6 percent and 10.7 percent. Incidentally, in these two counties the SPD gained votes as well.
10. *Stat. Dt. R., N. F.*, vol. 291/2: 24; *Preußische Statistik,* vol. 251: 30.
11. Winkler, *Revolution,* 482f.; see Koch-Baumgarten, *Avantgarde,* 88f.
12. Weber, *Putsch,* 28.
13. Weber, *Putsch,* 28f.; Vogler, "Klassenkampf," 258–262; Winkler, *Revolution,* 422f.
14. The Landrat of the Seekreis recommended a pragmatic approach to the organization, which it hoped would one day recognize the regulations after all, for it was "a completely intolerable situation in the long run" that an association representing so many workers was not being accepted as a negotiating partner. LHAM C 20 Ib 4699/VIII, fol. 6 (LR Eisleben to OP, 18 December 1920; fol. 23, LR Eisleben to OP, 24 January 1921). On the short history of the Freie Landarbeiterverband, whose remnants were absorbed into the Union der Hand- und Kopfarbeiter in the fall of 1921, see Eberhard Voss, „Revolutionäre Ereignisse und Probleme des Klassenkampfes zwischen Landarbeitern und Gutsbesitzern in den Jahren 1921 bis 1923 in Deutschland," PhD diss. (A), University of Rostock, 1964, 82; Vogler, "Klassenkampf," 373–387.
15. Weber, *Putsch,* 30–32; see Koch-Baumgarten, *Avantgarde,* 144f.
16. LHAM C 20 Ib 4699/IX, fol. 11 (Minutes of a meeting with OP, 9 February 1921). In the investigating committee of the Prussian Landtag that was set up after the March fighting, Morgenstern, a former member of the works council, used concrete numbers to show that wages were comparatively bad and lagged behind inflation, and that the supply of coal had been inadequate since the war. According to his information, the average wage per shift (with six shifts per week) stood at 40 marks at the beginning of 1921, while at the Leuna Works it was 57 marks („Niederschriften über die von dem Untersuchungsausschuß zur Nachprüfung der Ursachen, des Umfangs und der Wirkungen des kommunistischen Aufstandes in Mitteldeutschland im März 1921 in mündlicher Verhandlung erhobenen Beweise," *Sammlung der Drucksachen des Preußischen Landtages,* 1. Wahlperiode, 1. Tagung, vol. 8, no. 4140361f.). A similar conflict developed at the Leuna Works shortly before the deployment of the police. Here the issue was the taking of scrap lumber, which was apparently getting out of hand.
17. LHAM C 20 Ib 4699/IX, fols. 1–4 (Lord Mayor of Eisleben to OP, 4 February 1921); fol. 7 (Appeal by the provisional action committee, 2 February 1921); fols. 11f. (Minutes of a meeting with OP, 9 February 1921). Schneider later expressed the plausible conjecture that the chief task of the new security force would have been to identify the Communist shop stewards. Joseph Schneider, *Die blutige Osterwoche im Mansfelder Land: Tatsachenmaterial aus der Märzaktion* (Vienna, 1922), 28f..
18. LHAM C 20 Ib 4699/IV, fol. 8.
19. Ibid., fol. 23 (Kunzemann to OP, 11 February 1921). According to the information given here, 6,448 workers voted against and 4,328 for a strike. Weitz, *German Communism,* 105, who does not mention the efforts at mediation, describes the conflict merely as an example of businesses' growing desire to deploy state security forces in the region.
20. LHAM C 20 Ib 4699/IV, fol. 22 (Kunzemann to OP, 11 February 1921).
21. Ibid., fol. 4 (Lord Mayor of Eisleben to OP, 4 February 1921). During questioning by the investigative committee of the Prussian Landtag, the director-general of the Mansfeld Combine would not rule out the possibility that the police deployment came in response also to

reports by his company about the events concerning the new security service, though he himself had not directed any such demand to the Oberpräsident ("Niederschriften," 366–380).

22. LHAM C 20 Ib 5217/Ib, fol. 32 (RP Merseburg to OP, 15 January 1921).
23. Angress, *Revolution,* 130–135, maintains that the bombing was central to the change in plans. Koch-Baumgarten, *Avantgarde,* 149, attributes only a "secondary role" to it, whereas she sees a letter by Weismann to the Reich government as the decisive factor. Her contention that Hörsing and Severing now embraced Weismann's position that a large-scale uprising was imminent seems doubtful, for the reason alone that Hörsing as late as 22 March, that is, after the beginning of the police action, told Weismann that there was no definitive information about the existence of armed workers' militias. There was, at best, evidence of "illegal organizations" under the radical workers, "who intend to unite into military units in case of an armed uprising by the proletariat." LHAM C 20 Ib 4610 (OP to the StaköoO, 22 March 1921; with the same tenor 4627, fols. 55–60, 7 March 1921). Even the Reichskommissar für Überwachung der öffentlichen Ordnung (RKO, Reich Commissioner for the Supervision of Public Order), who had repeatedly noted the signs of an imminent Communist uprising, was still skeptical as late as 15 March whether the bombing of the Victory Column (and a bombing of the Berlin-Halle express train on the night of 15/16 March) were the signal for the great uprising (RKO, Report of 15 March 1921, p. 43f.).
24. For a detailed discussion see Koch-Baumgarten, *Avantgarde,* 146–150, who suspects such a triggering intention. However, what argues against it is the behavior of the police, who in the first days after their deployment were concerned to avoid any provocation, as well as the improvised deployment of Reichswehr units a few days later, which was something the authorities had been determined to avoid.
25. Angress, *Revolution,* 123–126, 128–133; Koch-Baumgarten, *Avantgarde,* 127–137, 149–156; not entirely clear, by contrast, are the statements of Weber, *Putsch,* 74–81, 264–267 (wording of the deployment order for the police, 18 March 1921).
26. LHAM C 20 Ib 4797/IV, fols. 10f. The appeal is reprinted in its entirety in Weber, *Putsch,* 259–262.
27. Hörsing's exaggerated account has been adopted by scholarship. Winkler, *Revolution,* 515, says that the region had "not settled down" since the Kapp Putsch and maintains that "wild strikes, plundering, and robberies" had been "daily fare" since the beginning of 1921. The inaccuracy of Hörsing's official justification for the police deployment can also be seen from the restrained responses to his inquiry to the large companies—*after* the events—about the extent of the thefts that had occurred up to March 1921. The Mansfeld Combine now mentioned merely a sum of 191,836 marks, more than half of which was accounted for by a theft of 70 kilograms of silver, and did not know of any attacks on officials worth mentioning, and the Riebeschen Montanwerke mentioned only smaller thefts of material and a single insignificant walkout. Only the management of the Leuna Works emphasized a steady increase in the pilfering of lumber, abusive treatment of porters, and unruliness—expressed in wild strikes—especially of workers with construction companies working at Leuna. LHAM C 20 Ib 4797/IV, fols. 41–53 (Inquiry by Hörsing, 11 April 1921, responses dated 27 April, 4 May, and 11 May 1921).
28. LHAM C 20 Ib 4797/IV, fol. 24 (Report from the reporting office of OP to the StakoöO, March 1921, n.d.); *KK* no. 67, 21 March 1921; *SZ* no. 134, 21 March; no. 136, 22 March 1921; see LHAM C 20 Ib 4797/X, fol. 194 (Report from Comrade Lemck from Halle, undated, part of the material later confiscated from Clara Zetkin). The sources do not reveal who exactly had formulated the ultimatum. Both the *Klassenkampf* and Lemck, in his report after the fact, speak only in general terms of the Mansfeld workers. It is likely that here, too, Schneider, who is described as impulsive and forward-pushing, was the initiator. Koch-Baumgarten, *Avantgarde,* 160, claims that the Schupo behaved provocatively when they took up positions; for example, they supposedly seized their quarters in both Hettstedt and Eisleben, and they threatened to depose the mayor of Hettstedt. This is not true: the mayor of Hettstedt, a member of the VKPD, was in jail, which is why his office was exercised only temporarily

by a town councilor; the report cited above makes no mention that the school in Eisleben was seized.

29. On the background to this article and the discussion it triggered at VKPD headquarters see Koch-Baumgarten, *Avantgarde,* 154–156. The author of the article, which was written in muddled German, was presumably Béla Kun himself.
30. *KK* no. 64, 17 March; no. 66, 19 March; no. 67, 21 March 1921. Additional examples of the use of the Orgesch motif: no. 68, 22 March; no. 69, 23 March; no. 70, 24 March 1921; LHAM C 20 Ib 4797/VI, fol. 29 (Leaflet, n.d.), fol. 43 (Leaflet, n.d.). The district leadership of the VKPD, as well, justified the proclamation of a general strike chiefly by citing the "provocations by the Orgesch and its servant (*Büttel*) Hörsing," and listed, among the goals for which it was to be waged, the "disarming of the Orgesch" (LHAM C 20 Ib 4797/VI, fols. 34, 43, Leaflets, n.d.). Koch-Baumgarten, *Avantgarde,* 216–218, likewise points to the central role of the Orgesch argument, though not to its wider context.
31. LHAM c 20 Ib 4797/X, fols. 192f. (Bowitzki report, 12 April 1921); fols. 194f. (Lemck report, undated); Angress, *Revolution,* 142-146; Koch-Baumgarten, *Avantgarde,* 158–164; she presumably overestimates the role that Guralski ("Schmidt from the executive") played as a military leader within the top leadership in Leipzig.
32. LHAM C 20 Ib 4797/IV, fols. 24f. (Report from the reporting office of OP to the StaköoO, March 1921, n.d.); 4797/V, fol. 2 (Telegram from the municipal council Teutschenthal to OP, 20 March 1921); LHAM C 20 Ib 4797/XVI, fols. 5–7 (LR Merseburg to OP, 10 April 1921). The initiative on the part of Kempin, who had been active at Leuna since the summer of 1920 and was agitating for his party, initially met with such resonance not only because Leuna was already a bastion of the radical wing of the workers' movement, but also because at the Leuna Works, like the Mansfeld Combine, a conflict had been brewing for some time over the taking of scrap lumber, with the amount apparently rising steadily. LHAM C 20 Ib 4795/I, fols. 63f., (Report of a trip through the area of the uprising in central Germany, 7 April 1921). See also the statements by director Oster and various members of the works council to the investigative committee ("Niederschriften," 283–303, 336–353).
33. Angress, *Revolution,* 150f.; Koch-Baumgarten, *Avantgarde,* 164f., who presumably strongly overestimates the influence of the Halle VKPD district leadership on developments in Leuna. Neither Lemck nor Bowitzki mentioned in their later reports any influence on the workers there prior to 23 March. On the emissaries from the Berlin KAPD headquarters, who were also active in the area of the uprising though likely without attaining any great importance, see Koch-Baumgarten, *Avantgarde,* 156. On the disagreements between the VKPD and the KAPD at the Leuna Works see also Bock, *Syndikalismus,* 303. In 1966, Utzelmann told Bock that he had been convinced an armed uprising would be doomed to failure, which was why he had pursued only a general strike.
34. On Hoelz's life see especially his autobiography, *Vom 'Weißen Kreuz' zur roten Fahne: Jugend-, Kampf- und Zuchthauserlebnisse* (Berlin, 1929; reprint Leizpig, 1984), here 70–192. See the precise notes by Angress, *Revolution,* 146f.
35. LHAM C 20 Ib 4797/IV, fol. 35 (Report from the Schupo unit Eisleben, 23 March 1921); fol. 25 (Supplementary report by the reporting office of OP to the StaköoO, 22 March 1921); SAPMO Ry 1/I 3/11/21, fol. 3a (Report from comrade Klenzer, Mansfeld, undated); LHAM C 20 Ib 7497/X, fol. 192 (Bowitzki report, 12 April 1921); fol. 197 (Report from Comrade Merker, Mansfeld, undated); GSTA PK I.HA Rep. 90a D I 4c no. 16, vol. 1, fol. 160 (Telegram from "Heinrich" to unknown recipient, undated, part of the material confiscated from the military leadership in Halle and later published by the StakoöO); *SZ* no. 138, 23 March 1921; "Niederschriften," 390 (Folte testimony). All the sources I have mentioned agree that the violence did not originate with the Schupo. The escalation of the events seems to have been the result of the confluence of two factors: the more or less accidental discovery of the two spies, and the charged mood among the strikers, fired up by Hoelz and the actions of the police; both factors together provided the impetus for those activists willing to engage in

violence to take action. Koch-Baumgarten, *Avantgarde,* 169f., does not mention the intentions of the VKPD military leadership on 22 March, but provides an exaggerated account of the police action. Contrary to what she claims, the meeting in Eisleben was not "broken up" by the police, which would have in fact contributed substantially to the escalation. The meeting was already over when the attacks in the street occurred.

36. LHAM C 20 Ib 479/IV, fol. 35 (Report from the Schupo Eisleben, 23 March 1921).
37. Walter Drobnig, *Der mitteldeutsche Aufstand 1921: Seine Bekämpfung durch die Polizei* (Lübeck, 1929), 11f.
38. LHAM C 20 Ib 4797/XVI, fols. 7–10 (LR Merseburg to OP, 10 April 1921); 4797/V, fol. 36 (Schupo Major Fendel-Sartorius to OP, 23 March 1921, afternoon: the major fears that the rebels at Leuna want to open the prisons in Naumburg and Halle and demands that artillery be brought in); fol. 54 (RP Merseburg to OP, 24 March, noon: a Red Army of 12,000 men supposedly exists at Leuna); fol. 60 (Call from a farmer to OP, 24 March, evening: there are only 2,000 armed men); fol. 110 (Afternoon report to OP, 26 March: at most 2,000 men, poorly armed); on the armored train: *Kämpfendes Leuna,* 241.
39. *Vorwärts,* no. 138, 23 March 1921, quoted in Koch-Baumgarten, *Avantgarde,* 165; *SZ* no. 139, 24 March 1921. On the history leading up to this see Koch-Baumgarten, *Avantgarde,* 165f.
40. LHAM C 20 Ib 4797/VI, fol. 36 (Appeal of VKPD headquarters, which was evidently also disseminated in the district in leaflet form; also printed in Weber, *Putsch,* 275–278); *KK* no. 70, 24 March 1921; criticism of the "lagging behind" of the "class warfare": LHAM C 20 Ib 4797/X, fol. 198 (Report from Comrade Schmidt, chairman of the Halle party leadership). In its call for a general strike, the Halle district leadership even dispensed with any reference to the works councils and demanded only an "appropriate wage increase."
41. LHAM C 20 Ib 4797/VI, fol. 29. Bowitzki, who was acting as the "political commissioner for the Mansfeld districts," declared in an appeal to the population there that "any resistance to the power of the working class ...will be broken with all means" and he called upon the workers to act in accordance with the "example ... provided to you by the reaction in previous fighting" (ibid., fol. 30). On the ambivalence of the VKPD language see Ludewig, *Arbeiterbewegung,* 195–198.
42. Angress, *Revolution,* 152f.; Koch-Baumgarten, *Avantgarde,* 149, 173; Weber, *Putsch,* 271–274. The leadership for the police action was first in the hands of the Merseburg Regierungspräsident, who set up a police leadership staff under Colonel Klüfer. The most important leadership figure among the police was the Schupo Colonel Count Poninski, who was initially entrusted with heading the operation in the Mansfeld area; from there he was to move on the Leuna Works. On the technical details of the planning for the deployment see Drobnig, *Aufstand,* 48–57.
43. See on this the documentation of strikes in LHAM C 20 Ib 4699/I-XVII, esp. I, fols. 8-45 (County Bitterfeld); IV, fols. 32-34 (Urban county Eisleben); V, fols. 9-25 (Halle and Saalkreis), VII, fols. 2f. (Mansfelder Gebirgskreis); XVI, fols. 13f. (County Wittenberg); *SZ* no. 142, 26 March; no. 145, 30 March 1921; Vogler, "Klassenkampf," 275ff. Schmidt, head of the Halle district leadership, confirms the impression of the files in his look back at the event: "The general strike did not become effective at all. It happened at the Leuna Works, but nowhere else. In Halle, half were out of the enterprises. Life and the goings on the city were the same. We in Halle had a sense of the general strike for only half a day" (LHAM C 20 Ib 4797/X, fol. 198, Report by Comrade Schmidt, 13 April 1921, part of the material later confiscated from Clara Zetkin). It is difficult to determine the total number of strikers, since reliable information is missing in the sources. Greatly exaggerated seems the claim in East German scholarship that 150,000–200,000 workers were on strike, 40,000 alone at the Mansfeld Combine (on this see Koch-Baumgarten, *Avantgarde,* 174, who still posits about 120,000 strikers). In LHAM C 20 Ib 4699/VII, , fols. 2f. (Report, 2 May 1921), we hear of only 4,570 strikers among 6,637 workers of the Mansfeld Combine in total. This seems more plausible in view of the fact that Thormann and Staab, *Mitteldeutsche Raum,* 83, mention fewer than 15,000 workers total in

the ore mining industry in the district of Merseburg in 1921. There is also reason to doubt that 22,000 workers at the Leuna Works supposedly went on strike. It is likely that most of the workers who left after the events of 23 March did so primarily out of fear of the imminent fighting. Thormann and Staab mention a total of fewer than 37,000 workers in 1921 in the chemical industry of the district of Merseburg, which included, in addition to Leuna, the not exactly small enterprises in the Bitterfeld area and the nitrogen plant (*Stickstoffwerk*) Piesteritz. However, at Leuna there were about 8,000 construction workers in addition to employees of the plant itself. According to a rough estimate by the author, on the basis of the unquestionably incomplete and imprecise information in the sources, the total number of strikers was probably a little over 75,000.

44. LHAM C 20 Ib 4700/I–X, esp. I, fols. 1–3 (LR Schleusingen to the Reich President, 1 April 1921). On Mühlhausen see LHAM C 20 Ib 4797/XV, fol. 18 (Mayor of Mühlhausen to OP, 8 April 1921). Thereafter the VKPD issued leaflets calling upon workers to join the general strike, but it met with clear rejection from the other Socialist parties. Workers also removed the notices posted by the VKPD.
45. LHAM C 30 Ib 4698/I–XV, esp. II, fols. 8f. (Report from LR Calbe, 1 April 1921); XIII, fols. 2f. (Report from Mayor of Westeregeln, 15 April 1921).
46. On the electoral results see *Preußische Statistik,* vol. 251, 27ff. In Erfurt the general strike, proclaimed on 26 March following consultations of the district leadership with the higher-ups in Leipzig, did not get beyond some beginnings, since the USPD and the SPD joined forces against it and also circulated leaflets calling on workers to keep working. Nor did the occupation of a few enterprises by the Schupo and the arrest of Communist functionaries lead to an expansion of the strike. SAPMO Ry 1/I 3/13/9 (Report by the district leadership Thuringia, no date); LHAM C 20 Ib 4797/IV, fol. 39 (Report on meeting, 25 March 1921).
47. Hoelz, *Weißes Kreuz,* 202–216, quote on 210; *SZ* no. 142, 26 March 1921; "Niederschriften," 396–402 (Folte testimony); LHAM C 20 Ib 4797/I, fol. 18 (Offer from Hörsing to Folte, 25 March); fols. 43f. (Telegram from the Reich Interior Minister to Hörsing, 26 March); fol. 50 (Telegram from Severing to Hörsing, 26 March); fol. 63 (Telegram from Hörsing to Folte, 26 March 1921); Drobnig, *Aufstand,* 12, 18–24, 29–42. The units coming from Halle clashed with the insurrectionists near Helfta, where three policemen and eleven of their opponents were killed.
48. Drobnig, *Aufstand,* 57–77; Weber, *Putsch,* 137f.; see Hoelz, *Weißes Kreuz,* 216f.
49. GSTA PK I. HA Rep. 90a D I 4c no. 16, vol. 1, fol. 156 (Telegram from Bowitzki to headquarters, 27 March 1921) and passim; LHAM C 20 Ib 4797/X, fol. 195 (Lemck report, undated); fol. 193 (Bowitzki report, 12 April 1921). Hoelz, *Weißes Kreuz,* 218f., merely comments tersely that Lemck and Bowitzki had no directives from headquarters for their military action.
50. LHAM C 20 Ib 4797/X, fol. 193 (Bowitzki report, 12 April 1921), here the quote; fol. 195 (Lemck report, undated); *SZ* no. 142, 26 March 1921, which speaks of "bands (*Scharen*) of young workers," though it attributes their march to an appeal from the Communist Youth on 22 March (see *KK* no. 68, 22 March 1921). In spite of the ban on assemblies, the police president of Halle allowed the memorial rally on the condition that the participants would not form a solid column. Drobnig, *Aufstand,* 78, mentions a number "of about 2,000 young lads and men."
51. LHAM C 20 Ib 4797/XVI, fols. 263–267 (The Commissioned LR of Sangerhausen to OP, 11 April 1921); fol. 273 (Mayor of Sangerhausen to OP, 19 April 1921); GSTA PK I. HA Rep. 90a D I 4c no. 16, vol.1, fol. 161 (Hoelz to action committee Sangerhausen, 24 March 1921); LHAM C 20 Ib 4797/V, fol. 134 (Note by Syffert, 27 March 1921); fol. 171 (Evening report about fighting, 27 March 1921).
52. LHAM C 20 Ib 4797/V, fol. 134 (Note by Syffert, 27 March 1921); fol. 171 (Evening report about fighting, 27 March 1921). According to statements by the Landrat, the eastern part of the county bordering the Mansfeld area saw a series of further requisitions of foodstuffs, automobiles, and gasoline by smaller groups of armed men, without force being directly used in the

process. Railroad tracks were blown up at three locations. On the other counties see LHAM C 20 Ib 4795/I, fols. 47–71 (Report about a trip through the area of uprising in central Germany, 7 April 1921, in which the Oberpräsident, three Schupo officers, and one editor each of the *Volksstimme* and the *Berliner Tageblatt* participated).

53. LHAM C 20 Ib 4797/VI, fol. 33. It is not clear when and where the announcement was disseminated.
54. Ibid., fol. 34.
55. *SZ* no. 134, 21 March; no. 138, 23 March; no. 140, 24 March; *MZ* no. 209, 24 March; no. 211, 25 March; "Gangs" dominate: *SZ* special edition, 29 March; no. 44, 29 March; no. 147, 31 March; no. 149, 1 April; no. 151, 2 April; *MZ* no. 212, 25 March; no. 220, 31 March; no. 223, 1 April 1921. Hoelz's actions in the wake of Kapp Putsch in the Free State of Saxony had very similar effects on how the middle class perceived the dangers emanating from the radicalized workers (see Lapp, *Revolution,* 39).
56. Major Klüfer from the staff of the Regierungspräsident in Merseburg reported on the evening of 27 March that "the mood of the civil servants is particularly good and combative toward the gangs of robbers"; the Erfurt government reported about the fight near Bachra, where "a gang of Red Guardists … were finished off"; in Eisleben the Schupo had dispersed "gangs of rebels" on 1 April (LHAM C 20 Ib 4797/V, fol. 177). See also LHAM C 20 Ib 4797/V, fol. 305 (Report from RP Erfurt, 31 March 1921); fol. 324 (Report from Schupo Eisleben, 1 April 1921) and passim.
57. *SZ* no. 134, 21 March; no. 139, 24 March; *MZ* no. 213, 26 March 1921; see *SZ* no. 140, 24 March ("Fight of anarchy against state order as such").
58. *SZ* no. 144, 29 March; no. 146, 30 March; no. 150, 1 April; no. 152, 2 April 1921; see *MZ* no. 244, 9 April 1921.
59. *VS* no. 71, 25 March; no. 75, 1 April 1921.
60. *MZ* no. 221, 25 March; no. 244, 9 April; *SZ* no. 139, 24 March; no. 142, 26 March; no. 144, 29 March 1921.
61. See *VS* no. 70, 24 March; no. 74, 31 March 1921.
62. *SZ* no. 136, 21 March; no. 137, 23 March; no. 138, 23 March; no. 139, 24 March; no. 142, 26 March 1921.
63. *SZ* no. 146, 30 March 1921
64. *MZ* no. 213, 26 March; no. 217, 30 March; no. 220, 31 March; no. 228, 2 April; no. 212, 25 March 1921.
65. GSTA PK I. HA Rep. 90a D I 4c no. 16, vol. 1, fol. 37 (*Geschädigtenausschuss* to the Prussian Interior Ministry, 4 April 1921); fol. 42 (DVP Naumburg to the Prussian Minister President, 9 April 1921); LHAM C 20 Ib 4797/V, fol. 196 (Note, 28 March 1921); fol. 272 (Bürgerbund Erfurt to OP, 30 March 1921); fol. 331 (Mitteldeutscher Volksbund für Stadt und Land to the Reich Minister of Defense, 1 April 1921). See also Raßloff, *Flucht,* 230.
66. The Landbund of the province openly threatened to create such organizations in case no Reichswehr was deployed against the uprising; GSTA PK I. HA Rep. 90a D I 4c no. 16, vol.1, fol. 31 (Reichslandbund to the Reich Interior Ministry, 1 April 1921). See *MZ* no. 244, 9 April 1921, which speaks of the necessary cooperation between the police, the Reichswehr, and the self-defense forces. Hörsing reacted sharply. He pointed to the Reich president's prohibition against such organizations, which had been in force since the previous year, and accused the Landbund of disseminating a completely distorted picture of conditions in the province so it could expand the Orgesch to Prussia. With "the same harshness with which I have fought down the Communist madness … I will also fight down the Orgesch organization"; LHAM C 20 Ib 4797/III, fol. 16 (OP Hörsing to the Landbund of the province of Saxony, Halle, 2 April 1921).
67. LHAM C 20 Ib 4797/XVI, fols. 10–18 (Commissioned LR of Merseburg to OP, 10 April 1921); 4797/X, fols. 195f. (Lemck report, undated); *SZ* special edition, 29 March; no. 144, 29 March 1921; Weber, *Putsch,* 138–140, 145–147, 149–152; Hoelz, *Weißes Kreuz,* 219–221; Drobnig, *Aufstand,* 77–85, 89–93. Hoelz claims that he marshaled about 2,000 fighters; Weber, by contrast, assumes there were only around 500.

68. LHAM C 20 Ib 4797/X, fol. 196 (Lemck report, undated) speaks of 50–60 rifles; 4797/V, fol. 251 (RP Merseburg to OP, 29 March 1921, in the evening) speaks of fifty dead among the insurrectionists); fol. 278 (Morning report to OP, 31 March 1921) mentions 30–40 dead, 52 wounded; *SZ* nos. 145 and 146, 30 March 1921. On the offer of surrender, which the responsible Major Krey rejected with reference to the experiences of the Reichswehr during the fighting in the Ruhr region in 1920: "Niederschriften," 65f. (Liebknecht report); Drobnig, *Aufstand,* 96–112, according to whom 800 rifles and 3 machine guns were confiscated; Weber, *Putsch,* 161–163; Koch-Baumgarten, *Avantgarde,* 298.
69. LHAM C 20 Ib 4797/V, fol. 305 (RP Erfurt to OP, 31 March 1921); fol. 324 (Schupo Eisleben to OP, 1 April 1921); *SZ* no. 148, 31 March; nos. 149 and 150, 1 April; no. 151, 2 April 1921; Hoelz, *Weißes Kreuz,* 224–231; Drobnig, *Aufstand,* 124–126; Weber, *Putsch,* 174f.
70. *SZ* no. 146, 30 March; no. 148, 31 March; no. 151, 2 April 1921; Weber, *Putsch,* 175.
71. By now, both men no longer feared that the appearance of the Reichswehr would trigger a new, large insurrection. At a joint meeting of the Prussian and Reich cabinet on 28 March, Severing stated that "by now he had no objections to the deployment of military aid in individual cases." However, the state of civilian martial law should be retained. At a further meeting of both cabinets the following day, Colonel Hasse reported that the Reichswehr units would be ready for action on 30 March; see *Akten der Reichskanzlei: Weimarer Republik. Das Kabinett Fehrenbach, 25. Juni bis 4. Mai 1921,* ed. Peter Wulf (Boppard, 1972), 615f.
72. For a breakdown of the forces and the actions in detail see Drobnig, *Aufstand,* 115f.
73. "Niederschriften,“ 305; Reichskommissar für Überwachung der öffentlichen Ordnung, *Denkschrift über die Märzunruhen im Jahre 1921* (Berlin, n. d. [1921]), 167; Drobnig, *Aufstand,* 142–158; Koch-Baumgarten, *Avantgarde,* 172f. On martial law, see LHAM C 20 Ib 4797/I, fols. 265–268 (Correspondence between Hörsing and the Reich Interior Ministry). On the casualties: GSTA PK I. HA Rep. 90a D I 4c no. 16, vol.1, "Drucksache Nr. 1872 der Verhandlungen des preußischen Landtags, Antwort Severings auf eine parlamentarische Anfrage“; see Weber, *Putsch,* 179. The RKO estimated the hard-to-calculate property damage at 115,010,192 marks (*Denkschrift,* 243). The number of those arrested given by Winkler, *Revolution,* 517, 34,700, was the result of a misreading, as can be seen by a comparison with the figures given by Angress, *Revolution,* 166.
74. *Denkschrift,* 159f.; *SZ* no. 149, 1 April 1921. A survey drawn up in the Oberpräsidium also mentions the stripping of the corpse of one junior constable of the Schupo, the abuse of the two policemen detained in Eisleben and taken to the offices of the *Mansfelder Volkszeitung,* and the death of another policeman in the battle for Eisleben on 24 March; although he was seriously wounded, the insurgents did not allow him to be taken away by a medic; LHAM C 20 Ib 4797/X, fol. 144 (Undated list, presumably from the late summer 1921).
75. "Niederschriften,“ 485–489 (Müller case), 465–474 (Straube case); 446–451 (Schraplau case), quote on 450 (testimony of Dr. Gürig, physician in Schraplau). According to the testimony of the witness Feiger, a sergeant of the Schupo who had had Feiger repair his shoes stated the following: "If we get Müller, he's done for" (486). The detailed testimony of several witnesses in each case seems credible, while the monosyllabic and stereotyped statements by the policemen who came under attack do not. The plausibility of the charges is also underscored by the fact that they were also raised by former Schupo officers, who were apparently dismissed from the force after doing so.
76. "Niederschriften," 436–444.
77. "Niederschriften," 272–274; 489–495. Another man was recognized by a police officer as a participant in the fighting at Gröber's and was beaten to death with an iron rod. It is possible that additional detainees were killed. The witness Lichtenberger, a former member of the Schupo, testified that in the case of the one local Communist leader, von Tann had given the following order to an *Unterwachtmeister* (sergeant): "Lead the man through the defile; you know what to do. This was the man's method: indirectly he let the people know that they should kill the man" (ibid., 493).

78. "Niederschriften," 415–458. The company physician of Leuna, who issued the death certificates for the insurgents killed on the grounds of the company, conceded to the investigating committee that he examined the bodies only very superficially (ibid., 512–514). The other statements from Leuna, however, come exclusively from workers who were among the insurgents, in any case, not from neutral observers, and they are in some parts not credible. In his internal report, Lemck refused to address the "abuse" in detail and mentions only the Schupo officers throwing wine bottles; LHAM C 20 Ib 4797/X, fol. 196 (Lemck report, undated). The forced singing, but not the other accusations, was later confirmed by the delegate Krüger, who examined the matter at Hörsing's behest; LHAM C 20 Ib 4795/I, fol. 70 (Report of a press conference at the Leuna Works, 6 April 1921).
79. "Niederschriften," 514–519 (v.d.Tann, quote on 519); 510–512; 500–506, 523–527. See also Emil J. Gumbel, *Vier Jahre politischer Mord* (Berlin, 1922), 67f.; *Denkschrift,* 34f., 38f. Apparently only one of the trials brought against Schupo officers ended in a conviction: two officers who had taken money from detainees and who by then had been dismissed from the force were sentenced by the Halle criminal court to several months in jail; LHAM C 20 Ib 4797/X, fol. 142 (undated declaration by OP).
80. As one Schupo sergeant noted critically about this unit, its members were supposed "to look on the inside and the outside like the others. That certainly was a picture that the officers themselves did not like." "Niederschriften," 536 (*Wachtmeister* Bartling, here the quote); 532 (*Oberwachtmeister* Pfeiffer); 500–503 (Major Freiherr Wendt). On the atrocities committed by the Schupo as a whole see Weber, *Putsch,* 178–180. Drobnig, *Aufstand,* 75, who is silent about the abuses and assesses the Düsseldorf units as especially good, mentions that the unit "for special assignments" was a company from the old army that had been taken over into the Schupo en bloc under their old commanders. He also mentions (54) that Poninski's entire section had been expelled by the French occupation force from the Rhineland and had been forced to hand over most of their weapons. It is possible that the brutality was a kind of compensation for the humiliation it had suffered.
81. On this see Christian Knatz, "Ein Sieg über Aufrührer und Reformer: Der Mitteldeutsche Aufstand von 1921 als verpaßte Chance der preußischen Schutzpolizei," *ZfG* 46, no. 1 (1998): 28–39; Leßmann, *Preußische Schutzpolizei,* 103–120; Bessel, "Militarisierung."
82. LHAM C 20 Ib 4797/I, fols. 67–71, the quote fol. 69 (Report on the press conference at the Leuna Works on 6 April 1921); see "Niederschriften," 53, 159. I agree with Weitz, *German Communism,* 100–109, who sees the quashing of the "March action" as a test case for the functioning of a "coalition of order" between business owners, government authorities, and Social Democrats.
83. Weitz, *German Communism,* 106, conceals this distinction and, incidentally, adopts from Winkler the false number of 34,700 prisoners, which of course makes the degree of participation appear much greater than it actually was. Mallmann, *Kommunisten,* 76, is wrong in seeing the "March action" in the industrial region of central Germany "analogously to the Kapp Putsch, as a defensive battle and not a battle for power."
84. On these speculations see *SZ* no. 142, 26 March; *MZ* no. 247, 10 April 1921. In his testimony to the investigative committee, Interior Minister Severing stated that the participation of foreigners was insignificant, and *Regierungsrat* Freyseng from the Oberpräsidium said that the number of foreigners active as agitators in the area of the insurrection was not very large and far below the number of 2–3,000 previously mentioned by Oberpräsident Hörsing. In the district of Magdeburg, twelve foreigners had supposedly been active in that way; in Halle, thirty-three, of whom seven were Russians and eight Poles ("Niederschriften," 101, 196–200).
85. *MZ* no. 211, 25 March 1921. A special reporter from the *MZ* sent into the area of the insurrection noted that in Eisleben, "young lads armed with rifles" had been encountered looting (*MZ* no. 212, 25 March 1921); *VS* no. 72, 27 March 1921; see no. 73, 30 March 1921; LHAM C 20 Ib 4795/I, fol. 47 (Report about a trip through the area of uprising in central Germany, 7 April 1921), here the quote. According to the findings of the investigative committee, younger

workers had been especially noticeable as the driving force behind the strike in the Mansfelder Land at the beginning of 1921, in Helbra and Mansfeld itself they had attracted notice as the leaders of the insurgents; see "Niederschriften," 19, 73f. (Reports by the delegates Dr. Dryander and Liebknecht).

86. *SZ* no. 142, 26 March; special edition, 29 March 1921. A few days after the end of the fighting, the Landrat also reported that young people, in conjunction with outsiders, had played a key role in Bitterfeld itself, and that in the surrounding area agricultural workers had been forced to join the strike "by roving bands of youths," LHAM C 20 Ib 4797/II, fols. 1–4, the quote fol. 3 (LR Bitterfeld to OP, 9 April 1921).
87. LHAM C 20 Ib 4795/II, fol. 66 (Statement by Oster at the press conference, 6 April 1921); 4797/XVI, fol. 9 (LR Bitterfeld to OP, 10 April 1921); vgl. "Niederschriften," 78.
88. The State Archive in Merseburg has several hundred prosecutorial files from these courts, which were established in Halle and elsewhere on 1 April 1921 on orders from the Reich president. These courts had jurisdiction for treason and high treason, murder, manslaughter, robbery, blackmail, and all manner of violent crimes as well as violations of the explosives and disarmament law. There was no preliminary investigation and legal recourse was not allowed, though appeals for a retrial could be filed with the regular court (*SZ* no. 152, 2 April 1921).
89. From the files I pulled a random sample containing information about 184 persons whose trial ended with a conviction. The files vary in the quality of the information they contain. The year of birth is available for all, occupational information for all except one, data about marital status and employment for about half, information about party membership and war service for less than a third. The sample was drawn from the following files: LAMe C 133 Halle nos. 24, 27, 59, 78, 106, 185, 207, 250, 260, 293, 302, 348, 384, 421, 462, 466, 493, 494, 522, 526, 551, 569, 594; Torgau nos. 18, 35, 38, 80, 88, 102, 111, 149; Wittenberg nos. 83, 124, 137, 157, 158, 171, 177, 200, 225, 226, 232, 266, 289, 303, 305, 342, 344, 357.
90. For example, in LAMe C 133 Halle no. 59. On the problem of the definition of "youth" see Winfried Speitkamp, *Jugend in der Neuzeit: Deutschland vom 16. bis zum 20. Jahrhundert* (Göttingen, 1998), 9–12.
91. One hundred and eighteen actors were described as "workers," another 25 as "mine workers" or "miners," without any detailed information. Among the 31 qualified tradesmen, locksmiths formed the largest group with 8.
92. Here one should not forget that across all age groups, coercion played some kind of role in the decision to join an armed group. Most of the accused said something to this effect, the courts often saw this as a mitigating circumstance, and the press also noted repeatedly that the rebels had exerted pressure on other workers to go on strike or join the armed struggle. It is difficult to determine to what extent such statements should be seen as defensive assertions, and to what extent they are simply evidence for the bourgeois pattern of seeing a "mass" seduced by "instigators."
93. *VS* no. 78, 5 April 1921.
94. *SZ* no. 144, 29 March; no. 146, 30 March; see no. 152, 2 April 1921 ("Excessive nervousness as a result of the ruinous war").
95. *SZ* no. 139, 24 March 1921.
96. *SZ* no. 148, 31 March; *MZ* no. 244, 9 April 1921.
97. *MZ* no. 220, 31 March 1921.
98. *MZ* no. 244, 9 April 1921.

Part II

Symbolic Fighting and the Struggle for Territory 1921–1923

The "March action" was the last large-scale violent encounter in which larger groups of armed men confronted state security forces and fought regular battles with them. Thereafter, political violence took the form of smaller clashes during which the use of firearms and serious consequences tended to be rare. The place that had been hitherto occupied by the police and the military was now taken over by well-organized groups from the radical right, chief among them the Stahlhelm. With flag consecrations, marches, and rallies, they sought to occupy the public space physically and symbolically and challenge the presence of the left in that space. This deepened the rift within the political culture and consolidated the image that each side had of itself and its enemy. Competing designs for the political system tested their strength in street fighting. Political antagonisms intensified further in the wake of accelerating inflation, which eventually culminated in the hyperinflation of 1923. However, the exhaustion of the population and the fragmentation of society caused by the struggle to survive during the hyperinflation prevented the emergence of another civil war–like situation.

Chapter 4

The Political Murders of 1921/22 and Their Consequences in the Province of Saxony

Limiting the Damage and Regrouping: The Communists and the Stahlhelm in the Summer of 1921

The fiasco of the "March action" was a heavy blow to the KPD in the province of Saxony. Many members and functionaries went to jail for at least several months, and Oberpräsident Hörsing launched disciplinary proceedings against Communist mayors and their deputies, which ended in a number of dismissals. The martial law that was in force in the province until the end of August and the press censorship that extended all the way to the banning of some papers—the *Klassenkampf* did not appear again until 3 September—further hampered the work of the party.[1]

Added to this was the political repression in the factories. Many of the workers who had played an active role in the days of the uprising were fired—437 at the Mansfeld Combine, 300 in the Bitterfeld coal region—or disciplined. The toughest action was taken by the directors of the Leuna Works, who fired the entire workforce and made rehiring contingent on certain conditions. Excluded from returning were all workers under the age of twenty-five (further evidence of the prominent role of younger men among the rebels), members of the action committee, and all those who had already "attracted attention" before the March days by violating factory rules. All others had to declare their willingness to forgo any political activity at work, accept noticeable restrictions on the activities of the works council, and agree to being searched by the porter when leaving the factory. In addition, three hundred Schupo policemen remained stationed in the Mansfeld region for the time being, with the expense of maintaining them borne by the private sector. The Mansfeld Combine also tried to push through a general

Notes from this chapter begin on page 107.

cut in wages.[2] Lastly, the two Social Democratic parties now combined to oppose the KPD where it competed with them directly, in the unions. In May, the leadership of the Allgemeiner Deutscher Gewerkschaftsbund (ADGB, General German Union League) succeeded, with massive pressure, in reversing the takeover of the local union committee in Halle by the KPD, an event that sent a signal to the rest of the Germany.[3]

The consequences of the March events were most obvious in the loss of membership the party suffered. Koch-Baumgarten estimates that somewhere between one-half and two-thirds of all members left the KPD.[4] That was the magnitude of the losses suffered in the district of Halle-Merseburg, where in August 1921—that is, before the end of martial law—25,261 members were organized in 171 local groups, according to a report from the district leadership to headquarters. This would mean more than 40,000 members had turned their backs on the party since the beginning of the year. The KPD now had its weakest presence in the entire district in the subdistrict of Mansfeld, the center of the area of the uprising: only eight local groups were left, with no more than 267 members. By contrast, the subdistrict Halle-Saalkreis had the most members, a little more than half of those organized in the district, followed by the subdistricts Merseburg and Weissenfels, and—at a greater distance—Bitterfeld and Torgau-Liebenwerda. Percentage-wise, the loss of membership was even higher in the districts of Thuringia and Magdeburg-Anhalt, where the KPD had only a small following to begin with.[5]

The authorities, too, saw the KPD as noticeably weakened in the district. The Landrat of the Saalkreis reported in the middle of August that while Communist agitation had picked up again strongly during the previous weeks, it had met with little resonance: "Communism is finished as a mass movement in the Saalkreis." The police in Halle put the number of dues-paying KPD members in the city at no more than 1,500 to 2,000. The KAPD had in the meantime declined into insignificance.[6] In Suhl at the beginning of May, one-third of the members had left the KPD-dominated DMV.[7] The KPD had thus lost many members precisely in its bastions, where most of the fighting had taken place. The repression on the part of the states and the companies alone cannot explain this massive exodus. Many members turned away from the party because they were horrified at Hoelz's methods and the failure of the party leadership to distance itself from them. Generational differences also played a role. A situation report by the Oberpräsident to State Commissioner Weismann stated in the middle of May, without referring to a particular region, that "a strong exodus to the USPD and the SPD has begun … especially of the older workers, who form the local backbone of the party."[8] The continuous uptrend that the party had experienced since its founding was over; it now found itself at a crossroads, as Koch-Baumgarten has emphasized. The KPD had permanently discredited itself among large sections of the workers.[9]

The "March action" was of profound importance also for the leadership of the entire party. Prominent critics of the offensive course, chief among them the former party chairman Paul Levi, were pushed out of the party in the following months, which is why no potent opposition was able to form against the central leadership. No intensive debate about the debacle of the March uprising took place within the party; instead, under pressure from the Comintern, differences were papered over. The "March action" was redefined into a heroic defensive battle and defended as correct in principle. As Remmele, a member of the Reichstag, emphasized at a party meeting in Halle, the proletariat had been provoked by Hörsing and Severing and had responded "with proletarian instinct." In that situation, the party could not abandon the fighters. To be sure, one could not approve of all the methods that were used, but the most reprehensible had been merely adopted from the "bandits" on the other side.[10] Still, the offensive course was now replaced again by the previous united front. Of course, its goal was to separate the supporters of the SPD from its leadership and eventually bring them into the Communist camp. The party congress in Jena at the end of August 1921 decided on this process of internal consolidation by passing a program that raised a number of concrete demands on wage, economic, and social policy, demands that had to seem perfectly open to debate also to the two Social Democratic parties and the unions; in addition, however, it contained passages reflecting the position of the party's left wing. The party also returned to calling itself only "KPD," thus more strongly invoking its tradition before its union with the USPD majority. At the same time, the party tightened its organization, at the base of which were now "groups of ten" and work groups (*Betriebsfraktionen*), and created a "Polbüro" as a narrower decision-making body within the central leadership, modeled after the Soviet Union. The way had now been prepared for a rigid control of party work "from above," especially since the exodus involved above all those members and functionaries who had old experiences with a party that was not tightly run by the central leadership.[11]

For the time being, the new structures did not take effect in the district Halle-Merseburg. After district secretary Oelßner, Lemck, and Bowitzki had been arrested or forced to leave the country illegally, the central leadership first tried to hold the district to a line that hewed close to the offensive course by dispatching Arthur Ewert, a representative of the moderate left, to lead the party organization in the district, but he was arrested before the end of April. The job was then turned over to the experienced Georg Schumann, who had been among the more cautious members of the district leadership during the "March action."[12]

One promising starting point for the party's work was the fate of the workers sentenced by the extraordinary courts. According to estimates by the KPD, by June 1921 about 4,000 defendants had been sentenced by all the special courts set up in the Reich, which sentenced four workers to death, eight to life imprisonment, and others to jail, prison, and incarceration terms totaling more than 2,000 years. In some cases there were prison terms for minor transgressions.[13] Compared to the judicial response to the Kapp Putsch, in the wake of which only a few leaders were put on trial, this was an entirely disproportionate form of punishment. It is therefore not surprising that the KPD's protest against the sentences of the extraordinary courts found support from the other workers' parties, the unions, and even the left-liberal press. A newly established "Red Aid" collected money to provide legal defense to the imprisoned workers and support their families; in the district Halle-Merseburg and the surrounding areas it was able to spend more than 3 million marks in 1921.[14]

However, if one leaves aside the comparison with the Kapp Putsch, as important as it undoubtedly was in the political discussion, the verdicts of the courts after the "March action" seem less excessive than they might appear at first glance. Three-quarters of the defendants in the sample were sentenced—in keeping with the notion of the "misled masses"—to jail terms of up to twelve months;[15] the most frequent charge was breach of the public peace, combined with offenses such as joining an armed gang or violating the explosives and disarmament law. Although the courts frequently dispensed with witnesses, in determining the sentence they certainly did look at individual circumstances and did not proceed in a summary fashion. Moreover, there was hardly a punishment that was not reviewed by a clemency hearing in the summer of 1921—of course, thanks not least to the pressure brought to bear in the Reichstag and the Prussian Landtag by all three workers' parties—and commuted from a prison to a jail term, reduced, or converted to probation, often after six months. In this process, evaluations by municipal authorities and employers played an important role. They reveal that mere membership in the KPD was an obstacle to a reduced sentence only if the defendant had played a prominent role in the events, that is to say, if he had attracted special attention as an "instigator" or "ringleader." More important was a person's reputation, whether he had worked on a regular basis, cared for his family appropriately, and had no significant prior convictions.[16] A large number of the detained were therefore free again by the end of the year, and the amnesty in July 1922 closed the book on the "March action."[17] The legal prosecution of the March fighters was therefore not an issue the KPD could exploit propagandistically for very long.

Meanwhile, the radical right was continuing its efforts to establish self-defense organizations after the Bavarian model. Reports to that effect reached the Oberpräsident even before the beginning of the "March action" in the middle of March, and with greater frequency in the two months following.[18] However, nearly all reports concerned once again the northeastern part of the district of Magdeburg, the former bastion of the Home Guards, though not those areas in which the fighting of the "March action" had taken place. It was the old images of the enemy and deeply rooted political attitudes that lay behind these repeated attempts, not the recent experience of violence. Since the provincial authorities strictly enforced the prohibition of self-defense organizations, they prevented an Orgesch network from being set up in the province.[19]

At the same time, though, a new and, over the long term, very successful type of civic self-organization appeared in the Combat Leagues (*Wehrverbände*). It became a rallying point for war veterans who, in uniform and compact formation, sought to use the public space of the street to present themselves as the champions of a political and social order opposed to Weimar democracy. They picked up the attempts by the urban middle class from the beginning of 1919 to adopt forms of self-presentation from the workers' movement, but they gave them a military cast and disconnected them from short-lived political issues, thus trying to make the bourgeois conquest of the street permanent. However, rather than training as a paramilitary reserve for a new coup d'etat, the Combat Leagues primarily strove to be a political force of high visibility that aimed at unifying and strengthening the "national" camp. This placed limitations on the "militarization" of politics brought about by the Combat Leagues and prevented it from becoming uncontrollable.

The most prominent and largest of these new associations was the Stahlhelm, Bund der Frontsoldaten (Steel Helmet, League of Front Line Soldiers).[20] Its beginnings lay in Magdeburg, where a veterans' organization was formed in December 1918 at the initiative of Franz Seldte, a reserve officer who hailed from a local family of entrepreneurs and had been severely wounded in the war. Initially it was open to supporters of all parties except the radical left, and its purpose was to preserve the memory of the war and offer mutual aid to its members. A second local group was formed in August 1919; its leading figure soon became the former career officer Theodor Duesterberg. It was only now, after the signing of the Versailles Treaty, that the Stahlhelm began to develop a political profile that soon placed it squarely within the camp of the right. Political disagreements shaped the history of the organization from the very beginning, however. While Seldte, originally a member of the DVP, pursued a moderate though on the whole opportunistic course—after the motto that "in politics you sometimes have to gag down a toilet brush"[21]— the DNVP member Duesterberg and his followers from Halle took a decidedly anti-Republican and *völkisch* stance.

At the end of September 1919, the local groups that had been forming especially in northern Germany joined into a pan-German association, though its initial membership was only around 2,000. After the Kapp Putsch, during which the various groups had staked out different positions (the group in Magdeburg strictly rejected participation, whereas Halle supported the putsch), Seldte assumed the chairmanship for the national association. In 1920, he participated in the founding of the Orgesch, though the Stahlhelm as an organization did not yet play a prominent role. A number of its members had joined the Home Guards and had participated in the fighting in March 1920 in Halle, but here, too, the Stahlhelm hardly made an appearance as an organization. At any rate, the authorities in the province of Saxony did not become cognizant of it as an association of the radical right until the middle of 1921.

At first, the authorities had a difficult time figuring out what exactly the Stahlhelm was. What attracted attention was the willingness, repeatedly declared at meetings of the organization, "to stand up for peace and order, weapons in hand." In June 1921, the Oberpräsident believed that the local Magdeburg group had close ties to the Orgesch. Publicly it was the local group in Halle that forged ahead the furthest: at the beginning of April 1921, it proposed establishing self-protection organizations after the Bavarian model, called for a tough action against the Communist press, and demanded the expulsion of Jewish immigrants from Eastern Europe as the main culprits behind usury, black marketeering, and political "incitement." For now, however, such a clear borrowing from the Bavarian model and its anti-Semitism remained limited to Halle. The police saw the group as a potential threat, though it was unable to prove that they were guilty of any concrete violations of the law, such as the illegal possession of firearms.[22] More dangerous over the long term was the fact that the Stahlhelm as a whole developed into a catch basin for members of dissolved Orgesch formations and the likewise disbanded Verband nationalgesinnter Soldaten (Association of National-Minded Soldiers) as well as many former Free Corps soldiers, and that some of its local groups were systematically infiltrated.[23]

One of the first confrontations with the Stahlhelm occurred on 13 August in Stendal, where the local group wanted to hold a flag consecration ceremony. The participants intended to march to the cathedral in a closed column, celebrate a mass there, and then move, again in a solid column, to the tavern, where the day would end with a ball. The Stendal KPD and USPD, though not the much stronger SPD, had called for a counter-rally. Initially, about 1,000 people gathered in the market square, where the local KPD chairman denounced the Stahlhelm members as followers of Escherich, blamed them for rising food prices,[24] and demanded that their march be "broken up." While the police were taking a wait-and-see attitude, the counterdemonstrators, waving a red banner, moved toward the marchers and were able to interpose themselves between the marching band and the rest of the column. Although the police that now stepped in were able to keep the entrance to the cathedral clear, the Stahlhelm members had to pass by a row of opponents, and after the mass ended they were able to reach the site of the festivities only in small groups. In the meantime, the crowd in front of the cathedral had grown to 6,000; a representative of the local SPD had also appeared, and in a short speech he appealed for unity of the workers against the right. After that, the counterdemonstrators marched with their own band close to where the festivities were taking place; after another speech, their rally disbanded. A violent confrontation did not occur. Although the Stahlhelm opponents had removed several black-white-red flags in the streets of the town and had cut up a garland, the clash did not move beyond verbal insults. A fight nearly broke out that night, however. The police, summoned because the festivities were being interrupted, arrived in front of the tavern where the Stahlhelm held its ball to find fifteen to twenty members of the organization, armed with clubs, beginning to rush at the counterdemonstrators assembled outside. The police officers were able to prevent them from coming to blows, and there were no other incidents.[25]

The battle for the public space triggered by the Stahlhelm's display took place largely without any violence, but it contained the potential for a dangerous escalation. The activities of the Stahlhelm led to a countermobilization that was chiefly undertaken by—though not limited to—the radical left. Initially, the KPD and the USPD mobilized 1,000 demonstrators, about as many as they had received votes in the state parliamentary elections at the beginning of the year, but then they drew in many more and forced their Social Democratic competition to respond. The equation "inflation = Orgesch = Stahlhelm" seemed plausible especially in Stendal, the center of a region characterized by medium and large-sized farms, which a little earlier had had strong Home Guards and where activities were now under way to join the Orgesch. Still, all the tension notwithstanding, the actions by both sides had a clear symbolic component that was reflected, not least, in the use of marching bands. The primary goal was to demonstrate presence and strength in the public space; this could—but did not have to—turn into physical attacks on the opponent.

A week after the incident in Stendal, a flag consecration by the Stahlhelm in a village of the Börde county Calbe was disrupted by counterdemonstrators. Here, too, their attack was initially directed against the black-white-red banners. A fight followed, eventually shots were fired—details about the circumstances are unclear—and one woman from the ranks of the demonstrators was killed.[26] Three days later, on 24 August, retired General von Lettow-Vorbeck, the hero of East Africa in the First World War and a supporter of the Kapp Putsch, who was supposed to give a speech in Zeitz at the invitation of the Stahlhelm, was confronted with such a large protest rally that he chose to leave the city on the next train.[27] The atmosphere in the province was tense when, on 27 August, news spread that the Center Party politician Matthias Erzberger, deeply hated by the right-wing enemies of the republic as a signatory to the armistice of 1918 and a proponent of the "fulfillment policy" with regard to Allied demands for reparations, had been murdered by two assassins from their ranks while vacationing in the Black Forest.

Flag Stealing and Protests against Rising Prices: The Violence after the Murder of Erzberger

The assassination caused the three parties of the left to join forces. In many towns a joint protest rally was called for 28 August, a Sunday. Additional rallies and demonstrations occurred in the following days. In spite of the agitation among the population, they all went off surprisingly calmly, especially in the cities. Contrary to what the "Organization Consul," which was behind the assassins, had hoped, the murder did not trigger a large uprising by the left, the suppression of which the radical right had wanted to use to realize its plans of creating an authoritarian state. Violent clashes did occur in a few rural communities, but they did *not* follow the pattern of the civil war–like confrontations of the previous years. Instead, food protests caused by rising inflation and elements of the rural rebuke and festival culture were the key factor behind these clashes. The violence that was employed was political violence, because the existence of the republican constitution was at stake, but it was clearly contained. It served as a means of balancing the local power structures, not of destroying the opponent physically.

A large rally took place in Halle on 28 August. Three days later in Magdeburg, the largest demonstration the city had ever seen wound its way through the streets, lasting two and a half hours. In Aschersleben, Staßfurt, Halberstadt, und other cities, tens of thousands had followed the calls of the three parties.[28] Clashes occurred in the Börde county of Neuhaldensleben located northwest of Magdeburg, which included parts of the Helmstedt brown coal region and was solidly under Social Democratic control.[29] While all mines were idle, large protest rallies were held on 31 August in numerous towns.[30] Fights broke out in the village of Hundisburg when some of the 900 demonstrators there marched to the houses on several estates and large farms in an effort to force their owners to hand over black-white-red banners. When one farmer bolted his door and threatened the demonstrators with a rifle, the door was broken down and his estate manager was beaten. After that, the confiscated banners were taken to the village square and burned. In the meantime, the church bells were rung after several demonstrators broke into the church; the German National pastor and his wife had left the village earlier.[31]

The following day, the spark jumped to the surrounding villages. Workers in the small factories in Wedringen and Vahldorf, where no rallies had taken place yet, engaged in a "lively" discussion of the events in Hundisburg the next morning; they decided to hold a demonstration of their own and to ask for support from the neighboring village of Althaldensleben. Early in the evening, a group of 400–500 people, "among them many women," arrived from there in Wedringen along with a band. Smaller groups of demonstrators went to the homes of locals who were known to be supporters of right-wing parties while the rest of the crowd waited outside the properties. One tavern keeper was beaten and forced to march along carrying a gallows. One farmer had bacon, lard, and eggs stolen from his pantry, another was forced to join the demonstration, a third was beaten. The confiscation of flags continued in a neighboring village. Eventually, the demonstrators marched "with music" back to Althaldensleben, where all the flags were burned, including those of the Wedringen veterans' association (*Kriegerverein*).[32]

The same day, the situation also escalated in the small town of Neuhaldensleben, the chief town of the district. The events there were triggered by the behavior of the editor-in-chief of the *Stadt- und Landboten,* who early in the afternoon had posters edged in black-white-red, which bore the program of the party meeting of the DVP slated to begin the following day in Magdeburg, posted around town. Soon, a crowd gathered outside the newspaper building; a small group, led by the chairman of the union cartel and one town delegate, entered the business office and forced the editor-in-chief to step outside and remove the posters using a black-white-red flag and a bucket of water. After that, he was led through the town at the head of a column that kept continually growing as work in the factories ended. Along the way, the demonstrators pulled other leading figures of right-wing parties out of their homes, tied pieces of red cloth around their necks, and forced them to join the march. As in the neighboring villages, numerous black-white-red flags were confiscated and burned in the market square. Two banners of the veterans' association, which several younger workers had seized and taken to the square, were spared following protests by some of the demonstrators; only the black-white-red flag ribbons were thrown into the flames. The crowd then dispersed without any further incidents, and the harassed representatives of the right-wing parties were allowed to go home.[33]

The incidents in and around Neuhaldensleben were not excesses committed by a radical minority. Rather, the working people of these towns and villages—female workers among them, although men played the leading role—stood up against political forces that did not accept the Republic and seemed to be on the rise again. In the process, protest against the accelerating rise in food prices and the farmers who were held responsible played a growing role, but it was not central to the goal of the actions and the course they took. The workers' aim was above all to symbolically consolidate the shift in the balance of power that had occurred since 1918 and now seemed under threat. Unlike before the war, village officials often came from the Social Democratic camp, which meant that at least the position of political power held by the old village notables had been broken.

It was no accident that the actions of the workers were directed against the flags of the opposing camp. Flags were not only one of the most visible symbols, they were also the most important symbol of the veterans' associations, which prior to 1914 had sprung up in every village of Germany, including the province of Saxony. Under the Empire, the right to carry a flag was tied to certain conditions, which made the flag consecration an important act and simultaneously, as the yearly celebration of the anniversary of the founding of an organization shows, a central element in the rural calendar of festivals. The Social Democrats had an ambiguous relationship to the veterans' associations. On the one hand, they kept a distance from their officially declared nationalistic and militaristic intentions, especially since the authorities had tried to keep Social Democrats out of the organizations as best they could. On the other hand, Social Democrats could not resist the sociable aspects of these groups. Finally, these clubs were, not least, a chance for rural workers who had served in the military to assert their claim to social equality with the large landowners.[34] This ambivalent relationship is also evident in the varied behavior of the demonstrators in and around Neuhaldensleben. While the club banners landed on the bonfire in Wedringen and Althaldensleben, in Neuhaldensleben only the flag ribbons awarded on special occasions were consigned to the flames; here, some of the older participants in the protest action identified so strongly with the organization that they rejected the complete destruction of its symbols.

Moreover, the events in Wedringen, especially, show that the goal was not primarily the physical maltreatment of the enemies of the Republic, but their public humiliation. Although violence was part of the calculation, it was only an additional means of exerting pressure and did not really take on dangerous forms. Instead, the actions incorporated elements that were familiar to the villagers from their annual celebratory customs and from normal political rallies: the march, the band, the gathering on the market square. At the same time, they employed methods from the repertoire of traditional rural customs of rebuke.[35] When the bells were rung in Hundisburg, this was a mocking reversal of the pastor's position of power before 1914. The action in Neuhaldensleben developed relatively spontaneously from the obvious provocation by the editor-in-chief and went through several phases.

The SPD leadership in Magdeburg was caught in a dilemma. On the one hand, it wanted to accommodate the mood among the rank and file; on the other hand it tried to steer that mood in a different direction. Immediately after the assassination, the *Volksstimme* warned against "rash actions," but then it saw the "people's ire" flaring up and merely noted about the protest demonstration in Hundisburg that doors had been "forced open," without mentioning the violence against people.[36] After the paper had published calls for a boycott of right-wing businesses in several towns, the SPD in County Neuhaldensleben, and eventually the *Volksstimme* itself in an editorial, again warned the workers against allowing themselves to be provoked into committing acts of violence. It would be "absolutely no service" to the Republic "if, for example, people move from village to village, beat up farmers, pull the priest from his house, and try to extort food stocks." Finally, the paper drew a clear line of separation toward the left. The "justified outrage" of the workers must not be abused by "dubious elements," for that would in the end only help the reaction.[37] At the same time, the *Volksstimme* tried to turn a specific element of radical right propaganda against itself. A commentary on the protest rallies noted that "front line soldiers" had taken to the streets en masse; they had suffered for Germany for years, and they were not about to watch quietly as the monarchists destroyed the country.[38] Here, the front line experience was claimed for one's own side against the Stahlhelm, though with reference not to particular virtues of the veterans, but to the suffering they had experienced.

In the bourgeois public, the murder of Erzberger was unambiguously condemned, but the events of the following days led in some cases to even more intense reactions. The *Magdeburgische Zeitung* expressed "abhorrence" for the deed and affirmed its rejection of all "personal smear campaigns" against Erzberger, though it also called him a "political racketeer and gambler" and even a "pest" (*Schädling*). The *Saale-Zeitung,* however, warned against any rash judgments of the dead man and called his murderers "fanatics" who had acted in an "atmosphere of murder and violence" created by the radical right-wing press.[39] The harshest criticism of the excesses during the protest marches came from the *Magdeburgische Zeitung.* In fact, the paper went so far as to accuse the SPD of driving toward "open civil war" with "vicious incitement." The bourgeoisie had to face the "fight forced upon it" and engage in it "in the awareness of justified self-defense."[40] These words reflected a new harshness, though it should be interpreted primarily as a direct response to the confrontation between Social Democrats and DVP supporters in Neuhaldensleben. The *Saale-Zeitung,* by contrast, assigned blame for the excesses only to the "belligerent Communists" and called for a "Republican policy of unity" (*republikanische Sammlungspolitik*).[41] It would therefore be wrong to see the events as clear evidence of a polarization between the workers, on the one hand, and the bourgeoisie and farmers, on the other. To be sure, on the local level the DNVP and the DVP made common cause with the Stahlhelm and other right-leaning organizations. However, there was also the DDP, which had a noticeable presence, for example in Neuhaldensleben with 18 percent in the most recent elections, and whose members could be found in some places taking part in peaceful protest rallies.

It is striking that the violent confrontations shortly before and immediately after 27 August were concentrated largely in the central area of the district of Magdeburg, while no reports about clashes were received from the Communist bastions in the district of Merseburg and in the notorious centers of unrest in County Schleusingen. This speaks to the defensive basic character of the various actions and of the violence employed in them. The demonstrating workers went after the radical right in those areas where they were clearly aware of its organizational success and where, as in Neuhaldensleben, they were in a strong political position themselves.

Limited Mobilization during the Galloping Inflation: The Communists and the Radical Right between the Fall of 1921 and the Summer of 1922

After the London ultimatum of May 1921, which fixed German reparations at 132 billion gold marks, the devaluation of the currency entered into a state of galloping inflation. This increased the pressure from the rank and file on the unions, which had been forced, during the period of relative stability, to accept a restrained wage policy and an overall strengthening of the position of the employers. A wave of strikes was finally triggered by a 50 percent rise in the price of bread as well as price hikes for potatoes, vegetables, and milk, which were the result of poor weather, along with an announcement by the government that it would raise the indirect taxes.[42] Unlike the violent protest actions after the murder of Erzberger, the wave of strikes in the fall of 1921 swept across large areas of the province, though the KPD was not able to profit from it to any meaningful degree. The strikes, which no longer aimed merely at a balancing of monetary devaluation but had started to anticipate the inflation,[43] began mostly in early September but as early as August in a few places, including Halle. Participation was especially high in Magdeburg with 25,000 strikers, and in and around Suhl with 6,000 strikers.[44]

The KPD made progress rebuilding its organization, though it failed to come close to making up for the loss in members it had suffered after the debacle in March. In September, the district Halle-Merseburg once again had 178 local groups with nearly 26,000 members, an increase of 7 local groups and 600 members since August; by October there were 252 local groups with nearly 27,000 members. In the subdistrict of Mansfeld, where more than 1,000 members were organized once again, the KPD had been able to recover some of the lost ground, and in the subdistricts of Weißenfels-Zeitz, Torgau-Liebenwerda, and Bitterfeld, it had set up a number of new local groups; the organizational progress, however, was not matched by a larger rise in membership.[45] The authorities, too, did not see any noticeable upswing of the KPD following the events at the end of August and the beginning of September. Even the Regierungspräsident of Merseburg, who looked upon the KPD with even more critical eyes than his two colleagues, continued to believe at the end of October that the organization of the party had "suffered a heavy blow." At the Leuna Works, as well, the Communists had been unable to return to a dominant position.[46]

The general weakness of the Communists did not go unnoticed by the bourgeois public. A commentary by the *Magdeburgische Zeitung* on 9 November 1921 noted that the "flood waves of the Revolution" were in the process of subsiding, and at the beginning of 1922, the paper emphasized that the workers were no longer in the sort of "frenzy" of 1918, but were by now able to see the situation as "gray on gray."[47]

The following months, as well, saw only moderate successes for the KPD and its allied union organizations. In fact, its membership declined again slightly to stand at just under 25,000 in March 1922.[48] In February, the KPD won the majority in the Halle union cartel, and in Erfurt it dominated the union cartel, the metal workers' and railroad workers' organizations, and the works councils. In the town of Suhl, the KPD captured 55 of 80 seats on the works councils.[49] However, protest actions against the continuing incarceration of participants in the "March action" and wage strikes initiated by the party met with only weak resonance. The great railroad workers' strike in January 1922 skipped the province because in Halle and Magdeburg the majority of the workers voted against it.[50] In the Kreistag elections in the Mansfelder Seekreis, the KPD pulled in 6,800 votes, about 1,000 fewer than the two Social Democratic parties combined. This was a respectable showing, given the drastic decline in membership following the "March action," but a far cry from the nearly 19,000 votes the party had received in the Landtag elections at the beginning of 1921. The membership meetings of the KPD in the Mansfeld area, meanwhile, "especially also in the industrial cities and town," were "only sparsely attended," and the works councils of the region focused on internal tasks within the companies.[51] Large enterprises like the central German nitrogen works at Piesteritz also saw the influence of the Communists waning. The Westphalian-Anhaltian Explosives AG Reinsdorf near Wittenberg noted that while most of its workers were supporters of the KPD, "the better part should be seen merely as passive followers (*Mitläufer*)."[52] At the same time, the KPD stepped up its political agitation activities, especially in the district of Erfurt. For that reason, "because of the strong price increases and because of the wage movements," the KPD had "drawn more support," Oberpräsident Hörsing believed in March 1922. On the whole, though, he was convinced that the KPD "is not able to sweep the workers along in a general uprising, even if large-scale wage movements set in at the same time as a result of rising prices."[53]

It was obvious that the return of the KPD to the policy of a united front had by no means attracted new supporters in droves, in spite of the increasingly tense food supply situation in the wake of inflation. The party was able to more or less consolidate its position in its old bastions or make up some of the losses, in the process picking up the legacy of the ultra-radical and dubious KAPD. However, the votes that were cast for the KPD expressed not so much a solid commitment to the party as a protest against inflation and the governing parties that were held responsible for it.

Following the attacks on its meetings in the fall of 1921, the Stahlhelm initially reduced its activities, and in some places dispensed entirely with public meetings.[54] Within the organization, Seldte was by now trying to counteract radical tendencies. In his speech on the Front Line Veterans' Day in Magdeburg on 18 January 1922, he opposed putsch attempts from both the left and the right and declared that the activities of the Stahlhelm were not directed against either the workers or the SPD.[55] However, on 23 June 1922, only one day before the assassination of Walter Rathenau, the Schupo liaison Kunzemann observed in a report to the Oberpräsident that the province was now "in a similar state as before the Kapp putsch," the reason being that "[o]ne regimental celebration is followed by the next, war association festivals, flag consecrations, monument dedications, assemblies and demonstrations, camp services, and parades are daily occurrences." At the member meetings of the Stahlhelm, 11 and 12 July were being mentioned as the "date for a 'major thing.'" As a result, in many places there had already been meetings of the three Socialist parties to deliberate possible counterdemonstrations. Where the Communists were particularly strong, for example in Querfurt or Eisleben, the decision had already been made to respond to any action by the right with a counter-rally and to bring in support for that purpose from the surrounding towns and villages. In Eisleben, according to Kunzemann, the KPD had been able to recoup its losses after the "March action"; because of the "most recent events"—the first public appearance of the new local Stahlhelm group in May—a "rise in membership has occurred everywhere here."[56] The new mobilization on the part of the radical right was triggering a countermobilization with potentially violent consequences.

A Heightened Struggle over Symbols: The Violence after the Murder of Rathenau

The assassination of Reich Foreign Minister Walter Rathenau (DDP) on the morning of 24 June 1922 shocked the German public as did almost no other event in the history of the Weimar Republic. His enemies on the right hated Rathenau for being both an "*Erfüllungspolitiker*" (a politician willing to fulfill the Versailles Treaty) and a prominent German Jew.[57] The wave of outrage that swept over Germany took hold also of segments of the population that had previously rejected the Republic. Tumultuous scenes took place in the Reichstag when news about Rathenau's murder arrived, and the German Nationals, especially their representative Helfferich, were accused of having prepared the ground for this act with their tirades of hate.[58] In the province of Saxony as well, the public was overwhelmingly united in responding with abhorrence and unambiguous condemnation. Even the *Magdeburgische Zeitung* now distanced itself clearly from the radical right. "Such despicable incitement," the paper declared, had to be opposed "with extraordinary means," and one should see to the "extermination" of the instigators behind the murder. Once "upright self-defense organizations" had by now turned into "secret leagues dangerous to the state." If necessary, one had to oppose "violence with violence."[59]

In the province of Saxony, as in Germany as a whole, the three workers' parties quickly agreed on joint actions with the Free Unions. After an initial protest rally in Halle on 25 June, rallies with large-scale participation took place in many places throughout the province on the afternoon of 27 June, the day of the country-wide protest strike. In the district of Magdeburg alone there were thirty-eight such rallies, with participation also from bourgeois supporters of the Republic. The *Volksstimme* declared that it was time to move beyond demonstrations and to make up for what had been neglected—the "Republicanization of the Reichswehr and of the civil service," though one should not proceed "with violence"; instead, in Reichstag elections that should be held soon, "the bands of murderers had to be neutralized by the millions with the ballot in hand."[60] The *Klassenkampf* called for the removal of "reactionary officers" and an end to "all monarchist rallies," without saying anything about how this was to be achieved.[61] The restrained rhetoric was matched by the peaceful unfolding of nearly all protest rallies. Despite the outrage that had taken hold not only of the workers, but also of wide segments of the bourgeoisie, there was no wave of attacks on leading representatives of the radical right or on the offices of their parties and organizations, and such incidents as did happen were most definitely not the result of any systematic or organized action.

Even the incidents that unfolded in Magdeburg—which was, after all, the seat of the Stahlhelm national leadership—took a relatively harmless course. About 200,000 responded to the call by the unions and the three Socialist parties and marched through the center of the city in a silent protest rally. The demonstrators carried not only numerous banners and signs bearing pro-Republican slogans, but also symbols of criticism aimed at the radical right: gallows from which black-robed figures were hanging—anti-Republican pastors and judges executed in effigy. A thick rope was identified as a rope for Helfferich, a large cross had a "young German man" nailed to it, and a poster carried by railroad workers showed a stop signal with the words "This far and no further!"[62] After the rally, more than 1,000 people gathered outside the Stahlhelm offices. A few demonstrators saw some Stahlhelm members waving mockingly from the windows; irritation was also aroused by the steel helmets painted on the window panes. An attempt to storm the houses was thwarted by members of the SPD, who formed a protective chain around the building. Police who hurried to the scene had the steel helmets on the windows covered up and detained the five members of the organization that were in the offices. When the Stahlhelm members were taken away, demonstrators kept pushing toward them and, as the police report described, tried to "lynch" them, but in the end the police were able to take the men to the station unharmed and the "crowd" dispersed without any further incidents.[63]

The demonstrators' symbolic threat of violence led to a violent confrontation only where the hegemony of the defenders of the Republic in the public space was challenged by the other side's blatant display of its symbols. But the level-headed behavior of the police, who did not rush to use weapons, helped to keep the situation from escalating. What happened when the Stahlhelm members were led to the station followed older patterns of behavior by urban underclasses, as is signaled not least by the term "lynching" used in the police report; it did not mean, as it does today, the attempt to kill them, but referred to physical abuse intended to clearly mark the target but not seriously injure him.[64] In this case the *Volksstimme,* too, expressed its understanding, though it felt that the "lynch justice" meted out to the "steel helmets" had been "much too lenient."[65]

Halle also saw clashes, though these were a far cry from the civil war scenarios of the previous years. Passers-by wearing Stahlhelm insignia were attacked on the fringes of the first rally on 25 June; the insignia were torn off and their bearers beaten. After that, members of a Communist youth group attacked participants in a celebration of the Bismarck League, whereupon the police that had been summoned arrested two of the youths. Following the memorial rally on the afternoon of 27 June, a part of the crowd marched to the police prison in the center of town to call for the release of the detainees. At the same time, a rumor spread that the Stahlhelm was planning to hold a counter rally that same afternoon. The police were able to prevent a storming of the station only by threatening to open fire. When the two youths were finally released, the police had to call in reinforcements and fire warning shots before the crowd dispersed. One demonstrator was injured by a sword blow.[66]

These incidents suggest that the local KPD leadership was promoting a limited escalation, but that alone does not explain them. The rumor about the planned Stahlhelm rally might have been planted deliberately, though in view of the known radical nature of the Halle Stahlhelm, it could have arisen without any special help. With the attempt to free the detainees, the "crowd" in the market square was following forms of behavior toward a distrusted police force that had been practiced in the previous years, as well as forms that reached back further in time. It is possible that the experiences with violence of 1919, 1920, and 1921 also played a role. Had the police not detained the youths, whom the crowd saw as political prisoners, the events would hardly have escalated. The *Saale-Zeitung,* in any case, did not blame the Communists, seeing this instead as the work of "youthful rowdies."[67]

Another brief work stoppage and rallies in support of the Republic were called by the ADBG and AfA, SPD, USPD, and KPD for 4 July, the day before debate was to begin in the Reichstag on the Law for the Protection of the Republic.

However, the first cracks became apparent in the action alliance, which the KPD had entered into with the other workers' organizations very much in the spirit of the tactic of presenting a united front. Responding to pressure from its left wing, party headquarters refused on 3 July to reach agreement on how excesses could be prevented during the demonstrations.[68] What made this refusal more explosive is the fact that right-wing extremists struck again on the evening of 3 July in Berlin: this time the target was Maximilian Harden, a prominent German-Jewish journalist who before 1914 had been the leading critic of Kaiser Wilhelm II. Harden suffered serious but not life-threatening head injuries.[69]

The next day, the province of Saxony, too, saw another large number of rallies that attracted once again tens of thousands of people. In some places, participation was higher still than it had been on 27 June; some rallies drew supporters of the DDP, even though the party leadership—like the Reich government—had spoken out against renewed demonstrations.[70] This time, too, nearly all events came off without any incidents; this applied to most of those in the district of Magdeburg as well as those in Halle, where more than 25,000 came out, and Erfurt, where 20,000 participated. In Eisleben, 5,000 workers marched behind a band through the bourgeois sections of town to the market square, where a representative of the KPD spoke out explicitly against violent excesses in his address to the crowd, and, very much in the spirit of the two other parties, warned against provocateurs.[71]

In Magdeburg, however, the KPD tried to attract attention to itself by being especially radical. Three of its functionaries led a larger group of demonstrators who tried to topple a statue of Wilhelm I, thus carrying out—in a kind of hasty "self-help" action—a decree by the Magdeburg city council calling for the removal of all monarchist monuments. Another group stormed the local savings and loan to prevail upon the employees still working there to walk off the job, and in the evening, streetcars were stopped on the Breiter Weg. The police, who eventually had a substantial presence, were confronted with vigorous resistance, but they were so cautious in the use of their weapons that all the actions eventually ended without anyone having been injured, let alone killed.[72]

Incidents reminiscent of what had happened after the murder of Erzberger occurred in several places in the district of Magdeburg. Once again, locally known representatives of the radical right were publicly humiliated and their symbols were destroyed, but even here the injuries were minor at most.[73] It was only in Sommerschenburg, a village in County Neuhaldensleben located at the edge of the Helmstedt brown coal region, that a confrontation of this kind led to lethal violence. On the afternoon of 4 July, several hundred miners and agricultural workers marched to the village estate with the intent of compelling its manager, von Rosenberg, to declare before the demonstrators his support for the Republic and the SPD. When the demonstrators arrived in front of the estate, they found the gate locked and forced their way in. Thereupon they came under fire from the house without warning; one young boy and two workers were killed instantly, another died from his injuries a short time later. What developed next was a veritable siege of the estate. The demonstrators opened fire on the castle, and von Rosenberg was badly injured by a bullet. Eventually, the crowed stormed the castle, beat to death the estate worker who, alongside von Rosenberg, had been firing at them, and plundered and ransacked the rooms for several hours. The gravely injured von Rosenberg himself was not harmed any further, nor were his wife and children, who were able to take themselves to safety in Magdeburg.[74] The escalation of violence, and this is beyond question, was triggered by von Rosenberg when he opened fire without warning. In response, the "crowd" engaged in self-justice, terrible but also measured. According to the Landrat, they "insisted on lynching" those who had fired on them.[75] The previously unharmed shooter was beaten and stabbed to death and the family's property was destroyed, though its remaining members were not harmed, for they had, after all, not engaged in any violence. The entire incident resembles more a castle storming in 1830 or 1848 than the violent confrontations during the "March action" or the symbolic fighting in the summers of 1921 and 1922.[76]

However, the bloodshed and the destruction of Sommerschenburg helped to rekindle older visions of terror among the public and once again weakened the sense of togetherness that had just been achieved. Moreover, there had been fatalities during clashes in other regions of Germany. The *Magdeburgische Zeitung* saw the demonstrations of 4 July as the work of "fanatic riffraff" who had been incited by Communist "instigators" and "rabble-rousers." As the *Saale-Zeitung* saw it, "thousands of workers … had gathered into a mob" in Sommerschenburg, and the "vilest terror" had then emanated from them.[77] The *Volksstimme,* too, distanced itself again from the Communists, whom it accused of having been behind the excesses everywhere.[78] The events led the *Magdeburgische Zeitung* to conclude that the new emergency laws had to be enforced just as harshly against the radical left as against the radical right. At the same time, the paper once again—as it had done after the Kapp Putsch—urged understanding for the supporters of a monarchy. Most of them, it argued, were not staunch enemies of the Republic, but merely wanted to see their good memories of the *Kaiserreich* preserved. That is why they sharply rejected the "street politics" of Social Democracy and the "iconoclastic assault" on the old monarchist symbols. These actions were an affront to the bourgeoisie. The paper concluded in a tone of disappointment: "The wedge that has been in the body of the German *Volk* since the November days of 1918 had been loosened by the shots on Rathenau. The great opportunity to pull it out with united strength was once again missed. On the contrary, it was driven in still further with blind fury."[79]

All in all, the violent events of 4 July followed largely the patterns known from the late summer of 1921, though cost-of-living protests evidently no longer played a role. Meanwhile the influence of the Communists was certainly stronger than it had been during the events of 27 June, most clearly so in Magdeburg. Once again, the regions that saw violence were those in which a strengthening radical right was confronted by a strong SPD and an especially weak KPD, rather than the bastions of the Communists or of the right in the north of the province.[80] Once again, young men seem to have played a prominent role as aggressive demonstrators who were also ready and willing to engage in violence, though a large segment of the working population either backed them or at least did not stop them. This certainly did not mean that their behavior gained the approval of the Social Democratic leadership, which, after the events at Sommerschenburg, once again urged discipline and restraint in the *Volksstimme* and warned against provocateurs.[81] The models for the demonstrations were the great voting rights demonstrations and May Day marches of the late *Kaiserreich,* which had been characterized precisely by their discipline and pronounced peacefulness.[82] This traditional part of the workers' movement's repertoire of behaviors was now combined, especially in the countryside, with elements of old customs of public rebuke, where the forced wearing of a red kerchief or the carrying of a red flag was especially humiliating to those affected. Needless to say, these ways of dealing with political opponents were not guided by the model of rational and peaceful discourse, and they surely did not help to calm the atmosphere. But they had nothing to do with putsch attempts or other armed actions against the political enemy. They represented a fallback into traditional forms of engaging in conflict rather than a step into an ideologically justified civil war.

In the midst of the fears triggered by the Rathenau murder and its aftershocks, such differentiations were not entirely lost. When the *Volksstimme* saw the Republic in "grave danger," and with it "the survival of Germany, the unity of the German tribes," it was talking not about the Communists but Bavaria, whose government was refusing to recognize the new Law for the Protection of the Republic. And the *Magdeburgische Zeitung* argued in a similar vein when it spoke of the potential "dissolution of the German Reich." Although the danger of civil war continued, it seemed that the central domestic political problem of the previous years, "the split between left and right in a struggle of life and death," could be healed once the SPD had again split off from "the incorrigibly foul (*wüst*) Communists" and the DVP had signaled that it wished to join the government.[83] For the *Volksstimme,* the Weimar Constitution had so far prevented a civil war. The *Magdeburgische Zeitung* had a similar take: the Weimar National Assembly had been the beginning of the political rebirth of the bourgeoisie, which was why it should certainly celebrate the 11 August.[84] There was also a consensus that the greatest threat to Germany emanated from the former wartime enemies, especially France, which wanted nothing other than the "destruction of the German Reich," as the *Magdeburgische Zeitung* put it.[85]

But consensus ended when the same paper defined the "national community" (*Volksgemeinschaft*) to be created against France not as a pragmatic political community, but as an "indestructible community of feeling" that had to be cleansed of "vain pleasure-seeking" and the "worship of mammon."[86] Such appeals invoked once again the "August experience" of 1914 and affirmed the calls for moral renewal that had been raised in the wake of inflation, but they were also directed against the goals and methods of the workers' movement. What was needed was "loyal German work by every *Volk* comrade," what was not needed was "the spirit of profiteering (*Schiebergeist*) or socialist phrases."[87] The *Volksstimme,* on the other hand, made a direct link between "unity, cohesiveness, and organization."[88] A strong party and strong unions, the paper argued, would provide the best protection against reactionary machinations and help the Social Democratic workers find the place to which they were entitled in the still-young Republic.

Notes

1. *Niederschriften,* 125; Weber, *Putsch,* 177–182; Koch-Baumgarten, *Avantgarde,* 316f.
2. Weber, *Putsch,* 182–191, the text of the Leuna agreement 293–295; for additional details of the strategy for disciplining workers at Leuna see Weitz, *German Communism,* 122–126. Moreover, henceforth the taking of even small objects from the factory would now be regarded as theft and lead to immediate dismissal. Weber, *Putsch,* 185, claims that all workers who had participated "actively in the fight against the Schupo" were also excluded from being rehired, but I was unable to find any evidence for this in the sources he cites. Management was evidently concerned to exclude from being rehired, in addition to the Communist leaders, the "rebellious" workers, and mere participation in the fight was not yet evidence of that.
3. Winkler, *Revolution,* 422f. Taken together, all these measures show the functioning of the "order coalition" made up of the state, businesses, Social Democracy, and unions, though the limitations of that coalition—and this is something Weitz does not make clear—became obvious in its dealings with the newly emerging radical right.
4. Koch-Baumgarten, *Avantgarde,* 323.
5. SAPMO Ry 1/I 3/11/31 (Organization report of the district leadership, 15–31 October 1921); see the very similar numbers on paying members at the KPD's party congress in Jena in August 1921 in Koch-Baumgarten, *Avantgarde,* 447. According to her, membership in August stood at 25,251 or 23,251; the figures are also similar in Leidigkeit and Herrmann, *Leninistischer Kurs,* 154; Tonn, "Kampf der KPD," 42f. See also the above-mentioned information from Weber, *Putsch,* 26, according to which there were 176 local groups with 25,105 members on 1 July. At the Kreistag elections in the Mansfelder Seekreis in June 1921, the SPD and the USPD together captured substantially more votes than the KPD (7,869 vs. 6,719), whereas they had still been far behind the KPD in the Landtag elections in February (Weber, *Putsch,* 210). Membership numbers in the district of Magdeburg-Anhalt now stood at 1,737 or 1,458 dues-paying members compared with 8,000 at the beginning of 1921; in the district of Thuringia there were 9,368 members, compared with 25,000 (Koch-Baumgarten, *Avantgarde,* 447).
6. LHAM C 20 Ib 5212/I, fol. 176 (LR Saalkreis to OP, 13 August 1921); fol. 255 (Police Administration Halle to OP, 14 September 1921); similarly the tenor in the reports of the Landräte of Mansfeld and Bitterfeld (fols. 185, 186).
7. LHAM C 20 Ib 4627, fol. 77 (Situation report of OP to the StaKoöO, 7 May 1921); same tenor in C 20 Ib 5221, fol. 193 (RP Erfurt to OP, 25 July 1921).
8. LHAM C 20 Ib 4627, fol/ 82 (Situation report, 17 May 1921). See Koch-Baumgarten, *Avantgarde,* 324, who also highlights the fact that it was above all older members, those who had been politically socialized prior to 1918, who left the party; that is true of both earlier members of the Spartacus League and former USPD members.
9. Koch-Baumgarten, *Avantgarde,* 318–321.
10. LHAM C 20 Ib 5218/I, fols. 17–20 (Police report about KPD member meeting of the local Halle group, 29 April 1921).
11. For details see Koch-Baumgarten, *Avantgarde,* 328ff.; Angress, *Revolution,* 167ff.; see also Winkler, *Revolution,* 519–530.

12. LHAM C 20 Ib 5212/I, fols. 262f. (OP to the StaKoöO, 15 October 1921); Weber, *Putsch,* 210–219; Tonn, "Kampf,“ 34f.; on Ewert see Angress, *Revolution,* 276.
13. Koch-Baumgarten, *Avantgarde,* 316; Jürgen Christoph, *Die politischen Reichsamnestien 1918–1933* (Frankfurt, 1988), 102. Outside of central Germany, extraordinary courts were found above all in Hamburg and in the Ruhr region. There the "March action" had met with some—though comparatively weak—resonance.
14. Weber, *Putsch,* 213–218; Koch-Baumgarten, *Avantgarde,* 316f.
15. We know the severity of the sentence in 182 of 184 cases. One-third of the accused were given a prison terms of up to six months, and fewer than one-tenth received more than two years.
16. Examples of such assessments in LAMe C 133 Halle nos. 185, 348, 384, 462, C 133 Torgau nos. 18, 80, 88, C 133 Wittenberg no. 124. Weber's criticism, which labels this as "outrageous arbitrariness and open perversion of justice“ (*Putsch,* 214), is completely overdrawn.
17. For a detailed discussion on how the judicial system dealt with the "March action" see Christoph, *Reichsamnestien,* 99ff. On 4 June 1921, the Reichstag decided that the Reich chancellor should see to a review of the sentences and recommend to the Reich president that he make "extensive use of a pardon“ in cases of those who were "merely passive followers.“ This was no real amnesty, but thanks especially to the liberal way the decree was implemented by Justice Minister Radbruch, it worked de facto as an amnesty. The Amnesty Law of July 1922 was connected with the Law for the Protection of the Republic following the murder of Walter Rathenau. Those who had participated in the fighting after the Kapp Putsch had already received amnesty in August 1920 (ibid., 44ff.).
18. LHAM C 20 Ib 4668, fol. 58 (LR Jerichow II to OP, 24 May 1921). Evidently there was also an attempt to place "working committees" of former soldiers who fought in the Baltic region in various places of the province, but the vigilance of the Landräte did not make this seem a very promising approach: ibid., fols. 41–44 (OP to the Prussian Minister of the Interior, 15 March 1921); fol. 81 (LR Jerichow II to OP, 18 April 1921); fol. 83 (PP Magdeburg to OP, 18 May 1921); see also LHAM C 20 Ib 4667, fols. 83f. (Report from LR Gardelegen, recorded with OP on 14 March 1921).
19. LHAM C 20 Ib 4667, fols. 137f. (OP to RKO, 4 July 1921); fol. 163 (RP Erfurt to OP, 16 July 1921); fol. 166 (RP Magdeburg to OP, 18 July 1921); fol. 167 (RP Merseburg to OP, 1 August 1921); LHAM C 20 Ib 4627, fol. 87 (OP to the StaKoöO, 27 May 1921). See Nußer, *Wehrverbände,* vol. 1, 183f. Authorities in the Free State of Saxony may have been less successful in suppressing Orgesch activities; see Lapp, *Revolution,* 63. On the fairly well-organized Orgesch in Baden see Johnpeter Horst Grill, *The Nazi Movement in Baden, 1920–1945* (Chapel Hill, NC, 1983), 41–52.
20. The following remarks on the founding history of the Stahlhelm are a summary of Berghahn, *Stahlhelm,* 1–32; Klotzbücher, "Stahlhelm,“ 1–12; see Diehl, *Paramilitary Politics,* 96f.
21. Walter Frhr. von Medem, *Männer und Mächte: Seldte, Duesterberg* (Leipzig, 1932), 44, quoted in Berghahn, *Stahlhelm,* 23.
22. LHAM C 20 Ib 4667, fols. 137f. (OP to RKO, 4 July 1921), here the quote; fol. 163 (RP Erfurt to OP, 16 July 1921); 166 (RP Magdeburg to OP, 18 July 1921); 167 (RP Merseburg to OP, 1 August 1921); LHAM C 20 Ib 4669, fol. 103 (Police of Halle to OP, 15 July 1921); *Hallesche Zeitung,* 8 April 1921, in LHAM C 20 Ib 4665/I, fol. 2; LHAM C 20 Ib 4627, fol. 91 (OP to the StaKoöO, 14 June 1921).
23. Klotzbücher, "Stahlhelm," 12f.
24. Since the London ultimatum in May 1921 by the victorious powers, which fixed the reparations Germany had to pay in accordance with the Versailles Treaty at the dizzying sum of 132 billion gold marks, inflation had picked up noticeably.
25. LHAM C 20 Ib 4613, fols. 148–150 (Police administration of Stendal to OP, 14 August 1921).
26. LHAM C 20 Ib 4627, fol. 143 (RP Magdeburg to OP, 24 September 1921); *SZ* no. 391, 23 August 1921.

27. LHAM C 20 Ib 4614, fols. 64–66 (Police administration of Zeitz to OP, 25 August 1921).
28. *VS* no. 205, 2 September 1921; *SZ* no. 402, 29 August 1921.
29. The SPD had won 54 percent of the votes in the Landtag elections here.
30. *VS* no. 206, 3 September; no. 207, 4 September 1921.
31. LHAM C 20 Ib 4613, fol. 15 (LR Neuhaldensleben to OP, 2 September 1921); *VS* no. 207, 4 September 1921, which mentions nothing about mistreatment of the steward.
32. LHAM C 20 Ib 4613, fols. 105–107 (Gendarme of Neuhaldensleben to LR Neuhaldensleben, 18 September 1921, copy).
33. LHAM C 20 Ib 4613, fols. 42–47 (Police report to RP Magdeburg, 5 September 1921); fol. 22 (LR Neuhaldensleben to OP, 3 September 1921); *SZ* no. 412, 3 September 1921.
34. See Gerhard Birk, "Das regionale Kriegervereinswesen bis zum ersten Weltkrieg, unter besonderer Berücksichtigung des Kreises Wanzleben," in H.-J. Rach and B. Weissel, eds., *Bauer und Landarbeiter im Kapitalismus in der Magdeburger Börde: Zur Geschichte des dörflichen Alltags vom Ausgang des 18. Jahrhunderts bis zum Beginn des 20. Jahrhunderts* (East Berlin, 1982), 265–297, 265–297; Ziemann, *Front,* 413ff., esp. 421.; Robert von Friedeburg, "Klassen-, Geschlechter- oder Nationalidentität? Handwerker und Tagelöhner in den Kriegervereinen der neupreußischen Provinz Hessen-Nassau 1890–1914," in U. Frevert, ed., *Militär und Gesellschaft im 19. und 20. Jahrhundert* (Stuttgart, 1997), 229–244. Placing the accent only on the ideological influencing of the members, as Thomas Rohkrämer does in *Der Militarismus der ‚kleinen Leute': Die Kriegervereine im deutschen Kaiserreich 1871–1914* (Munich, 1990), is too limited a perspective.
35. See Ernst Hinrichs, "Le charivari et les usages de réprimande en Allemagne: État et perspectives de la recherche," in J. Le Goff and J.-C. Schmitt, eds., *Le Charivari: Actes de la table ronde organisée à Paris* (Paris, 1981), 297–306, esp. 300f.
36. *VS* no. 201, 28 August; 205, 2 September; no. 207, 4 September 1921. Incidentally, the demonstrators had no doubt that their actions were legitimate. When the rumor spread in the middle of September that all those involved in the collection of the flags would be arrested, the calling of a general strike was debated in the affected villages, and people pointed to the exceedingly lenient treatment of the Kapp putschists. Great displeasure was also triggered by the trials against a number of the participants in the spring of 1922, which ended with jail terms of several months: LHAM C 20 Ib 4613, fols. 59f. (Deputy to the Schupo to OP, 21 September 1921); fols. 199–211 (Reports on trials, May/June 1922). The trial records themselves are no longer extant. It is likely that the punishment was included in the amnesty of July 1922, meaning that the defendants de facto did not have to spend much time behind bars.
37. *VS* no. 209, 7 September; no. 210, 8 September; no. 214, 13 September 1921 (here the longer quote); on the calls for a boycott no. 204, 1 September (Groß-Salze); no. 210, 8 September 1921 (Burg).
38. *VS* no. 205, 2 September 1921.
39. *MZ* no. 599, 27 August 1921; *SZ* no. 399, 27 August; no. 408, 1 September 1921.
40. *MZ* no. 601, 28 August; vgl. no. 603, 29 August; no. 610, 1 September; no. 618, 3 September 1921.
41. *SZ* no. 402, 29 August; no. 408, 1 September 1921. According to Trauthig, *Glaube,* 37–46, the murderous violence of both assassinations was downplayed in Württemberg Protestantism, while criticism was more likely to be directed against the excesses that followed and against the new Law for the Protection of the Republic.
42. Feldman, *Disorder,* 406–411.
43. Ibid., 409–411.
44. LHAM C 20 Ib 4698/VII, fols. 84–90, 93, 115–117 (Reports of Deputy Kunzemann to OP, 8 September, 10 September, 16 September 1921); LHAM C 20 Ib 4699/V, fols. 99-110 (Report and documented strikes in Halle); LHAM C 20 Ib 4700/I, fols. 52–54 (Documented strikes in Erfurt); LHAM C 20 Ib 4700/VII, fols. 32, 35, 38, 40 (Documented strikes for Suhl and Heinrichs), fols. 28–34 (Documented strikes in Mühlhausen).

45. SAPMO Ry 1/I 3/11/31 (Organizational report of the district of Halle-Merseburg, 15–31 October 1921).
46. LHAM C 20 Ib 4627, fols. 155–157 (OP to the StaKoöO, 9 September 1921); LHAM C 20 Ib 4647, fols. 12–14 (RP Merseburg to OP, 22 October 1921), the quote fol. 12; see LHAM C 20 Ib 5212/II, fols. 406–410 (Secret messages of detainees in custody to Erfurt Schupo, 31 August 1921); fols. 403–405 (Response by the Erfurt Schupo, 10 October 1921); fols. 466f., 469–471, 479 (Reports about investigations in Erfurt, Arnstadt, Ruhla, Gotha and Eisleben, 26/31 October 1921); fols. 412–415 (Interrogation record, 11 October 1921, on putsch plans in Halle and Eisleben).
47. *MZ* no. 787, 9 November 1921; no. 1, 1 January 1922.
48. Leidigkeit and Herrmann, *Leninistischer Kurs,* 154.
49. LHAM C 20 Ib 5218/I, fols. 137–139 (OP to the StaKoöO, 25 April 1922); Wilhelm Ersil, *Aktionseinheit gegen Cuno: Zur Geschichte des Massenkampfes gegen die Cuno-Regierung 1923 in Mitteldeutschland* (Berlin, 1963), 70.
50. LHAM C 20 Ib 4627, fols. 204f., 244–246 (OP to the StaKoöO, 3 December 1921, 5 January 1922); see LHAM C 20 Ib 5218/I, fols. 99f. (PP Magdeburg to OP, 22 November 1921). On the railroad workers' strike—the largest strike by civil servants in the Weimar Republic—see Winkler, *Revolution,* 406.
51. LHAM C 20 Ib 5217/II, fol. 59 (LR Eisleben to OP, 24 February 1922), here the quote; fol. 124 (RP Merseburg to OP, 12 May 1922).
52. LHAM C 20 Ib 5217/II, fols. 60f. (Central German Nitrogen Works Piesteritz to OP, 25 February 1922); fol. 62 (Westfälisch-Anhaltinische Sprengstoff-AG to OP, 25 February 1922); see fols. 64-74, 83f. (Statements by other enterprises).
53. LHAM C 20 Ib 4627, fols. 259–265 (OP to the StaKoöO, 13 March 1922), the quotes fols. 259, 263.
54. LHAM C 20 Ib 4665/I, fols. 66–68 (Reports by the three Regierungspräsidenten to OP, Jan. 1922). On Stahlhelm activities in Erfurt see Raßloff, *Flucht,* 253–257.
55. *MZ* no. 32, 18 January 1922; Klotzbücher, "Stahlhelm,"15f.
56. LHAM C 20 Ib 4647, fols. 34f. (Deputy Kunzemann to OP, 23 June 1922); Stahlhelm, ed., *Sechs Jahre Stahlhelm in Mitteldeutschland,* 2nd ed. (Halle, 1926), 170. According to this source, the local group of Eisleben was founded in August 1921. Kunzemann also noted in his report that according to very credible indications, the "greater part" of the Schupo officers in Eisleben were members of the Stahlhelm, many wearing swastikas and greeting each other in the offices with phrase "Treu-Deutsch"; to his knowledge, openly monarchist propaganda was being disseminated in the Schupo barracks in Naumburg.
57. What they did not know or did not want to acknowledge was Rathenau's activity as the founder of the Department of Military Raw Materials within the Prussian War Ministry in 1914/15, which saved the German war economy from an early collapse. On Rathenau's life see Christian Schölzel, *Walther Rathenau: Eine Biographie* (Paderborn, 2005).
58. On the background to the assassination see Sabrow, *Rathenaumord;* on the reactions see Winkler, *Revolution,* 427f.; idem, *Weimar,* 174f.
59. *MZ* no. 324, 30 June; no. 328, 2 July; no. 331, 4 July 1922; see *SZ* no. 196, 28 June ("insane political fanaticism"); no. 197, 29 June 1922; *VS* no. 147, 27 June ("murderous monarchistic rabble"); no. 150, 30 June 1922; *KK* no. 146, 26 June 1922 ("monarchist murder").
60. *VS* no. 147, 27 June; no. 148, 28 June 1922.
61. *KK* no. 146, 26 June 1922.
62. *VS* no. 148, 28 June 1922.
63. LHAM C 20 Ib 4621, fols. 29f. (Police of Magdeburg to OP, 28 June 1922); *VS* no. 148, 28 June 1922. According to the *Volksstimme,* the police president himself arrived by car at the end of the incident, gave a brief address, in which he announced the closing of the office, and thus helped to calm the situation down. The police report does not mention this.
64. On this see Lindenberger and Lüdtke, "Die 'verdiente Tracht Prügel.'"

65. *VS* no. 151, 1 July 1922.
66. LHAM C 20 Ib 4621, fol. 98 (Police of Halle to OP, 28 June 1922); *SZ* no. 196, 28 June 1922. The comment by Sabrow, *Rathenaumord,* 162, that "workers' patrols" had searched in Halle for the insignia of right-leaning groups implies a non-existent level of organization behind this searching. On the rallies see also Tonn, "Kampf," 74–81, who lauds them as a success of the unity front, which they certainly were not.
67. *SZ* no. 196, 28 June 1922.
68. Winkler, *Revolution,* 543.
69. Details in Sabrow, *Rathenaumord,* 169ff.
70. *VS* no. 155, 7 June; no. 156, 8 July 1922.
71. LHAM C 20 Ib 4621, fol. 104, fol. 106, fols. 108f. (Police report about Halle, Erfurt, Eisleben); fols. 364–367 (RP Magdeburg to OP, 28 November 1922); *SZ* no. 202, 5 July 1922; *VS* no. 155, 6 July; no. 156, 7 July 1922.
72. LHAM C 20 Ib 4621, fols. 99f. (PP Magdeburg to OP, 6 July 1922); *MZ* no. 333, 5 July 1922; *VS* no. 155, 6 July 1922. In his report, the police president proceeded from the assumption (as did the *Magdeburgische Zeitung* and the *Volksstimme*) that the excesses had been the result of a "unified plan," the "instigators of which were the Communists, who have clearly been identified in all the hot spots."
73. LHAM C 20 Ib 4621, fols. 225f. (Police administration of Genthin to LR, 7 July 1922); fols. 364–367 (RP Magdeburg to the Prussian Ministry of the Interior, 28 November 1922).
74. LHAM C 20 Ib 4621, fols. 240f. (Report of Schupo lieutenant Heyer, 5 July); fols. 248–250 (Report by the criminal police to OP, 7 July 1922); LHAM C 30 Neuhaldensleben I no. 1095, fol. 125 (*Feldschutzkommando* Hötensleben to Schupo-*Kommando* Magdeburg, 9 July 1922); *VS* no. 156, 7 July 1922; *MZ* no. 338, 8 July 1922. The files contain no information about the outcome of the investigation of the prosecutor's office. The proceedings against Rosenberg were evidently terminated.
75. LHAM C 20 Ib 4621, fols. 252f. (LR to RP, 6 July 1922).
76. The Sommerschenburg Castle, which belonged to the Gneisenau family, had in fact been the target of an attack by the village population on 1 May 1848. To what extent the memory was still alive in the village and whether the attack back then should be seen as providing a model in some way or another must remain speculation. On the behavior of the East Elbian agrarian workers during the Revolution of 1848/49 and the violence that was employed in Saxony see Helmut Bleiber, "Zum Anteil der Landarbeiter an den Bewegungen der Dorfbevölkerung in der deutschen Revolution 1848/49," *JbW* 4 (1975): 65–81.
77. *MZ* no. 333, 5 July 1922; *SZ* no. 203, 6 July 1922.
78. *VS* no. 156, 7 July 1922.
79. *MZ* no. 322, 29 June; no. 324, 30 June; no. 331, 4 July 1922.
80. The fact that the Rathenau killers, who were being hotly pursued by a large body of police and who had been initially spotted in Gardelegen, were able to escape from the Altmark all the way to Bad Kösen near Naumburg, where they were eventually caught on 18 July, surely had something to do not only with the difficult-to-control terrain, but also with help they received from sympathizers. This is probably part of the explanation for the comment by Sabrow, *Rathenaumord,* 99, that the initial lack of investigative success was "very difficult to fathom."
81. *VS* no. 156, 7 July 1922.
82. On this see, for example, Bernd Jürgen Warneken, *Als die Deutschen demonstrieren lernten: Das Kulturmuster 'friedliche Straßendemonstration' im preußischen Wahlrechtskampf 1908–1910* (Tübingen, 1986); idem, "'Die friedliche Gewalt des Volkes.' Muster und Deutungsmuster von Demonstrationen im deutschen Kaiserreich," in B. J. Warneken, ed., *Massenmedium Straße: Zur Kulturgeschichte der Demonstration* (Frankfurt, 1991), 97–119; for a summary view see Lindenberger, *Straßenpolitik,* 304ff.
83. *VS* no. 147, 27 June 1922; *MZ* no. 340, 9 July 1922.

84. *VS* no. 186, 11 August 1922; *MZ* no. 401, 11 August 1922. The Weimar Reich Constitution had taken effect on 11 August 1919.
85. *VS* no. 1, 1 January; no. 263, 9 November 1922; see also no. 186, 11 August 1922; *MZ* no. 658, 31 December 1922.
86. *MZ* no. 322, 29 June; no. 315, 25 June; no. 1, 1 January 1922.
87. *MZ* no. 32, 18 January 1922.
88. *VS* no. 305, 31 December 1922.

Chapter 5

The Catastrophe That Did Not Happen

Food Protests and Political Violence under Hyperinflation 1922/23

The German mark went into a free fall in July 1922. Until then, inflation had staved off mass unemployment with all its consequences, but now, in the form of hyperinflation, it produced that very crisis. After a final attempt at stabilizing the currency had failed in the fall of 1922, the occupation of the Ruhr region by French and Belgian troops and the passive resistance proclaimed by the Germans in response dealt the final blow to the German mark. By the fall of 1923—when the mark was barely accepted any longer as a means of payment, unemployment was surging, and radical right-wing groups were gathering in Bavaria for a march on Berlin, with Proletarian Hundreds (*Proletarische Hundertschaften*) in Saxony and Thuringia intent on blocking their way—Germany was finally in danger of sinking into the kind of chaos many had been warning against.[1]

The civil war feared by many and wished for by some seemed imminent.[2] However, Reich Chancellor Stresemann, who for a time had the support of a Grand Coalition, was able to master the general crisis with surprising speed. Measured against the events of the preceding years, the force that was employed and the casualties suffered were comparatively minor. This was not only because Chancellor Stresemann and Reich President Ebert were determined to preserve democracy and the forces heading toward an attempted overthrow of the government lacked sufficient resolve to succeed. Another crucial reason was the social atomization that went hand in hand with the radicalization of the population. The complete collapse of the value of the currency and mass unemployment forced people to focus their energy on the struggle for daily survival and prevented the formation of well-organized camps ready for civil war.

Notes from this chapter begin on page 134.

Extremism on the March: Communists and the Radical Right up to the Summer of 1923

After the wave of protest in the wake of the murder of Rathenau, the KPD maintained the policy of a united front, but following the 4th World Congress of the Comintern in November 1922, which took place in a relatively stable Soviet Russia, it took on a more offensive tone.[3] At the forefront of the propaganda, which was intended to put pressure on the SPD, there was now the demand for "workers' governments"; at the center of local party activities stood the workplace, with the goal of building up the works councils to form a counterweight to the influence of the SPD in the unions. And here the party did in fact have some success. In the middle of March 1923, it gained the majority among the works councils in large chemical plants, for example, the Piesteritz explosives plant, the two Wolfen factories, and the Electron Works I Bitterfeld, as well as in several brown coal pits, the Zschornewitz power plant, and several plants of the Mansfeld AG.[4] In the Halle union cartel, the party was able to repeat its victory from the previous year and win the majority also in the district cartel.[5]

These successes seemed to signal a steady rise in influence.[6] In reality, though, they rested on weak foundations. At the end of August 1922, the Oberpräsidium called the attention of the Regierungspräsidenten to the heightened "agitation work" of the Communists in the factories, but a few months later the KPD already seemed to be in decline again. The police president of Magdeburg attributed the "touchy mood" of the workers to the progressive inflation, not to the agitation by the KPD, and he described the party's week-long efforts to drum up support and new members as "a flop." His colleague in Halle was even more blunt in his assessment: "The KPD in central Germany does not seem to be the party with the masses behind it. In terms of the union it is as good as finished … One cannot speak of a readiness to fight."[7] By no means did the party leadership see a steady uptrend, either. In February 1923, the leadership of the district Halle-Merseburg noted with disappointment that the gains made in the works council movement had been lost again. Attempts to set up work cells were running into strong resistance nearly everywhere; successes could be reported only in a few scattered places.[8]

The difference between occasional electoral successes and a stable advance in mobilization is even more evident in the membership trend. In May 1923, membership in the district of Halle-Merseburg stood at 19,404 and the number of local groups at 251,[9] thirty-two local groups more than in July 1922. They were distributed more or less equally across the district and marked the progress in the territorial spread of the party organization. However, the number of members had declined noticeably since July 1922, when there still had been more than 22,000. The district leadership saw the reason in the massive increase in unemployment during the winter. In its report for April 1923, it noted a gain of 600 new members, but also the lack of any real growth in membership, since many members were being lost to unemployment.[10] The fluctuation of membership in the KPD was not a problem limited to the last years of Weimar.[11]

In addition to its "normal" party work, the KPD tried to boost its following by trying to set up Proletarian Hundreds (hundred-man units) and proposing, within the framework of the tactic of a united front, the establishment of "control committees" (*Kontrollausschüsse*). The control committees were to supervise the food retail business and prevail upon shop owners to offer their wares at affordable prices. Given the authorities' efforts to keep a lid on surging prices with the help, not least, of coercive measures, this was a strategy that could expect broad approval, especially from women. On the other hand, it betrayed an inadequate understanding of the mechanism of inflation and turned shopkeepers into scapegoats.[12]

In Eisleben, the KPD had been raising such demands since the end of August 1922; in November, a control committee came into existence. Initially, its work met with approval even from the bourgeoisie, but following an intervention by the authorities, it was largely suspended.[13] Suhl saw the establishment in mid February 1923 of a "housewives' commission," whose members did not shrink from becoming physical with an official of the local price control office in order to force through their recognition. The local police were very hesitant to get involved. Eventually, an additional Schupo unit was deployed to the notoriously restive town.[14] What was unusual about the incident is that in this case it was women themselves who resorted to violence. Precisely because the action could be defined only in part as "political," it was met with at least tacit approval from officials. On the whole, however, the control committees achieved only scattered importance in the spring of 1923, even though the KPD set up a body to coordinate the committees in the district of Halle-Merseburg.[15]

At first, calls for the establishment of Proletarian Hundreds that issued forth at the beginning of 1923 seemed to meet with a wider resonance. Conceived as anti-fascist defense units (they were given an explicitly offensive role only as of September 1923), the units, set up on the basis of the workplace,[16] were intended to draw in also hitherto non-organized workers and members of the SPD. At the end of April, the Berlin headquarters of the KPD painted a mixed picture of the result of the campaign to date. No units of any kind existed yet in the district of Magdeburg-Anhalt. In the district of Halle-Merseburg, however, the workers in "numerous large enterprises" and the union cartels "in smaller locations" had already adopted the requisite resolutions to set up such units, and the same had also been done in Halle, though the implementation had not proceeded very far. The situation was better in the district of Thuringia, which included, along with the district of Erfurt, the SPD-governed state of Thuringia itself. Here, "joint units of a hundred had formed in a number of smaller towns, in part with support by the authorities," while "party units of a hundred … in the larger local groups" were "already fairly well organized."[17] On 1 May, the leadership of the district Halle-Merseburg counted nine local units of a hundred and several work-based units in Halle itself. A few marched in the May rallies, as in Bitterfeld; others were in the process of being set up. The local SPD leadership had been only partly successful in preventing its supporters from participating.[18]

The authorities attentively registered the progress in the formation of Proletarian Hundreds, though they did not yet see any reason to intervene. It was their view, as well, that the development had progressed the furthest in the district of Erfurt, which led the police president of the district capital to see a "danger to the state" as early as the beginning of March, since the units "have been completely set up in nearly all large enterprises in Erfurt" and were divided "in strict military fashion into strike troops (*Stoßtrupps*)" exercising "almost daily." However, it appeared that they had no firearms, only rubber clubs.[19] In Suhl, a proletarian self-defense of "several hundred men" did not make an appearance until 11 March, though it did not seem to be organized any further.[20] In Magdeburg, by contrast, no such unit was detectable even at the beginning of April.[21] In Halle, the resolutions to set up these units, contrary to the report of the party's district leadership, encountered reluctance among the workers over the long term. At the beginning of May, the police president noted a "falling away" and no longer saw any real danger emanating from the units. He attributed this to the rising unemployment and generational differences: "To avoid losing their jobs, married or older workers are staying away from political events and are also refusing to join the Proletarian Hundreds. Only a few younger, unmarried workers and a few hotheads have been willing to join."[22] Oberpräsident Hörsing also vigorously dismissed any horror scenarios involving these proletarian defense units. He informed Interior Minister Severing at the beginning of April that reports claiming the existence in several cities of the district of Erfurt of formations totaling several thousand members armed with pistols were greatly exaggerated. The establishment of a proletarian self-defense had to be seen largely as a reaction to the gathering of right-wing defense leagues in not-too-distant Bavaria. In contrast to these organizations, the proletarian units had no real weapons, nor did they entertain intentions for a putsch.[23]

The KPD's reports of success were thus in good measure simple self-delusion. At the beginning of 1923, just as in March 1921, an appreciable number of the workers in the province were unwilling to be drafted into paramilitary activities, regardless of whether they were described as defensive.[24] Efforts by the KPD met with greater resonance only where a threat from the fascist danger in Bavaria seemed realistic, which was especially true of Suhl, with its southernmost location. Elsewhere it was once again younger workers who had not spent the war at the front lines that responded to mobilization into quasi-military formations. The organizations of the radical right continued to focus on specific locations and regions, though they now sought to expand their sphere of influence also to their enemies' strongholds and in this sense pursued a more offensive course than the KPD with its Proletarian Hundreds. The right-wing organizations were aided in their efforts by their relative cohesiveness.[25] By now, the Stahlhelm had new local groups in Communist strongholds in the district of Merseburg, as for example in the counties of Bitterfeld and Liebenwerda and in the two Mansfeld counties. In the district of Erfurt, on the other hand, it was represented only by three local groups.[26]

The primary reason for this was competition from the Jungdeutscher Orden (Jungdo, Order of Young Germans), the second large Combat League of the right wing in the Weimar Republic. It had emerged in March 1920 from a unit of temporary volunteers, but it was characterized by the spirit of the organized youth movement. It regarded itself as "national" and initially stood at arm's length from the Republic, but it was even more difficult to situate politically than the Stahlhelm, from which it distinguished itself by not defining itself as a veterans' organization.[27] Since it was headquartered in Kassel, it is no surprise that it was able to recruit a larger number of members especially in the district of Erfurt. Nearly all counties in the district had local groups, for example, in the city of Erfurt itself with 900 members and in County Weißensee, where 150 members were organized in the industrial town of Sömmerda. The leadership of the Jungdo was clearly drawn from the bourgeoisie and the farming class; farmers and merchants are mentioned as chairmen of the local groups alongside white-collar workers and teachers. The Jungdo was also present in Suhl and in other communities of County Schleusingen. In the district of Magdeburg, the organization had local groups in Magdeburg itself, in the Altmark, and at the edge of the Harz; by the middle of August 1922, these groups comprised a total of 700 members. In Halle, the Jungdo had 180 members, with local groups also found in Bitterfeld, Eisleben, and the Mansfelder Gebirgskreis. Unlike the Stahlhelm, however, the Jungdo had so far not made itself especially conspicuous anywhere.[28] Over the long term, its importance in the province of Saxony—successes in the southernmost administrative district notwithstanding—remained minor compared to the Stahlhelm.

After the murder of Rathenau, the radical right was initially the target of massive repression and, for the first time, careful surveillance by the authorities, though this was only a temporary impediment to its upswing. The measures of the state were aimed first at the Deutschvölkischer Schutz- und Trutz-Bund (DVSTB, German-*Völkisch* Protective and Resistance League), though it was in fact not very influential in the province; it was outlawed throughout Prussia on 1 July 1922.[29] The next blow fell on the much more important Stahlhelm. On 2 July 1922, Oberpräsident Hörsing ordered that the organization be disbanded in the province, on the grounds that it was a "cover for a putsch organization modeled after the Orgesch"; six days later, Interior Minister Severing extended the ban to all of Prussia. This move proved rather ineffective, though. A number of skat, bowling, and hiking clubs were set up as disguised successor organizations, while in Halle the Stahlhelm members joined the local DNVP branch, whose managing director Duesterberg later became Second Federal Leader (*Zweiter Bundesführer*) of the Stahlhelm. When the ban on the organization was lifted at the end of January 1923 by the High Court for the Protection of the Republic, the number of its local groups across the Reich had doubled to more than 1,200.

And the conflict within the organization between the radicals and the moderates continued. In a series of decrees, Seldte underscored the Stahlhelm's loyalty to the Republic, forbade contacts with the new Deutschvölkische Freiheitspartei (DVFP, German-*Völkisch* Freedom Party), and insisted that the group was not a self-defense organization, a comment that drew vehement internal criticism. At the beginning of March 1923, he even sought out Severing in person to assure him that his organization was no threat.[30] Seldte did in fact want to prevent the Stahlhelm from becoming embroiled in putschist adventures. However, this did not mean that he had transformed into a supporter of Weimar democracy, as the fall of 1923 would show.

Special efforts were made by the right to organize the youth. Given that the Reichswehr was limited to 100,000 men, the most important goal was to provide pre-military training to as many young men as possible so as to preserve the potential for a larger army.[31] In this regard the competition among the various organizations was greater, as a result of which clear structures were slow to emerge. The Deutschnationale Jugendbund (German National Youth League), which was part of the DNVP, and its closely allied Vaterländische Jugendbund (Fatherland Youth League) were centered in the Altmark, though they also had 225 members in Magdeburg, mostly *Gymnasium* students; smaller local groups existed—outside of the right-wing stronghold of Naumburg—in the area of Halle-Merseburg, in the north and east of the administrative district of Merseburg, and in Erfurt (160 members).[32]

In January 1923, shortly after the Allies occupied the Ruhr region, a new organization appeared on the scene, conceived as a branch organization of the Stahlhelm. The Wehrwolf, Bund deutscher Männer (Wehrwolf, League of German Men), as it soon came to be called, was founded in Halle by two members of the Stahlhelm, one of whom was the local vice-chairman, a few days before the lifting of the ban on that organization. The Wehrwolf's goal was to admit every "German man" who had reached the age of seventeen. Its bylaws identified its primary task as the formation of a "joint defensive front against the external enemy." At the beginning of March, the Wehrwolf in Halle had 165 members and had already set up a local group in Eisleben with thirty to forty members. At the beginning of May a local group was established in Eilenburg (75 members), followed in June by one in Erfurt, though Magdeburg did not have one until August. In Halle, the Wehrwolf had grown to 250 members by the middle of June, and twelve local groups had sprung up in the surrounding area. At a convention of delegates in Halle in mid May, *Studienrat* Fritz Kloppe, a retired captain and former front line soldier, was elected national chairman.[33]

Finally, mid June saw the founding in Halle of the Bund Scharnhorst (Scharnhorst League), another auxiliary organization of the Stahlhelm that accepted young men between the ages of thirteen and seventeen.[34] In this way, the Stahlhelm could continue to define itself as an organization of front line veterans while at the same time organizing the young men who had grown up during the war and those who had just missed war service because of their age. Against the backdrop of the struggle in the Ruhr region, its purpose was no longer merely to support "national" policies, but to prepare also for a potential military confrontation with France. Moreover, the successful "March on Rome" by the Italian Fascists in October 1922 provided a model for a takeover of power by a right-wing movement organized along military lines. The radical right was on its way toward organizing the (bourgeois) youth in addition to adults in a unified manner. In the process, its organizational progress, especially in workers' cities like Eisleben and Eilenburg, increased the likelihood of violent confrontations.

Serious clashes occurred on 10 May (Ascension Day) in Eilenburg.[35] Only a few days earlier the Wehrwolf had set up a local group here, while the KPD had held the majority in the union cartel for several months.[36] On the occasion of a flag consecration by a veterans' organization on 10 May, Wehrwolf groups with a total strength of 800–860 men joined Stahlhelm delegations from the districts of Delitzsch, Halle, and Torgau to march into the city in formation, accompanied by thirteen gendarmes (*Landjäger*), who later received only insignificant reinforcement. Members of the Combat Leagues were equipped with bayonets, heavy walking sticks, rubber truncheons, and wire whips. The unions' calls for a counterdemonstration met with little response, but many workers came as spectators to line the streets along which the column would pass on its way to the market square. The members of the Stahlhelm and the Wehrwolf were showered with jeers, insulted as "bloodhounds," "mass murderers," and "rear-echelon pigs (*Etappenschweine*)" and responded aggressively; it is also possible that the "crowd" tried to stop the march. The chairman of the union cartel, who tried to calm the situation, was beaten severely and received a stab wound to the neck. However, the police were able to escort the marchers into the church and prevent a major incident.

While the service was going on, a larger number of workers armed with sticks gathered in front of the church. When the celebrants left the church, the insults (leveled also by many women, as the police noted) continued. Fights broke out at several locations along the column that was forming again; one member of the Wehrwolf who had lost his insignia in the heat of the battle was beaten so badly by his own comrades that he ended up in the hospital. The police, who were trying to cover the return march of the nonlocal Stahlhelm and Wehrwolf, were now themselves insulted, and the column was pelted with rocks, to the point where the officers felt compelled to drive the "crowd" back by brandishing their weapons. After the combatants had been separated, the authorities counted a total of sixty slightly and—in addition to the badly beaten Wehrwolf member—three seriously injured: two Stahlhelm marchers and one worker who had suffered a stab wound to the lung. Neither side had made use of firearms; one retired officer who had pulled out a revolver was immediately disarmed by the police.

An opportunity for revenge came at the end of June in Eisleben.[37] Here, in the heart of the Mansfeld Land, the Stahlhelm had been making special recruiting efforts since the founding of a local group in August 1921. At the beginning of March, the *Untergau* (subdistrict) Mansfeld was set up with Eisleben as its seat.

A "German Day" with a flag consecration was set for 24 June, with Theodor Duesterberg as the featured speaker. Duesterberg, who since April had been the leader of the Stahlhelm Gau Halle, was far more radical than the national leader Seldte. In response, the KPD moved a celebration by the union cartel it dominated to the date of 24 June as well, and mobilized its entire district organization under the slogan "For Eilenburg-Eisleben." At the same time, the police received information that "the members of the Stahlhelm are looking for opportunities at public events to take bloody revenge on the Communists."[38] The authorities authorized both events on the condition that the two marches take place at different times and that the participants not show up in large numbers along the route of the other marchers. In the morning, the Stahlhelm and the formations of the Wehrwolf and the Jungdo marched into the city, a force of more than 3,000 men according to the more credible Communist estimates, about 12,000 according to the police and the Stahlhelm. At this point, the streets belonged to the veterans' organization and its largely bourgeois supporters. A festive service was held in the market square. Duesterberg gave his speech and had the units march past him in military formation and drill step; after that, the participants moved to the taverns. So far, there had been no disturbances. By early afternoon the streets of the city offered a very different sight: workers and their families lined the route that the procession of the union cartel would take to the market square. According to police estimates, about 10,000 people participated; the KPD put the figure at 7,000. Both sides had been able to mobilize a considerable number of supporters.

Violent clashes developed later that afternoon. Smaller groups of young members of the Combat Leagues lingered at an intersection that participants in the union festivities would have to pass on their way back to the train station. When 30–40 younger workers crossed the intersection, verbal insults led to a fight that quickly drew in larger groups from each side. According to the report of the KPD, party organizers sent "three five-man groups" out of a total of ten Proletarian Hundreds that were taking part in the festivities, most of them from Halle, into the fray. On the part of the Stahlhelm, one policeman heard the order "Sub-Gau Halle! Strike force to the Volkshaus!" Sticks and fence pickets were used in the brawl, and a few shots were fired on both sides, though fortunately they injured only one man in the posterior. The Schupo officers who hurried to the scene managed to separate the fighters only after brandishing their pistols, with the Stahlhelm members behaving much more aggressively than their opponents.[39] Rumors about fatalities and seriously injured men that circulated in the afternoon hours turned out to be false. All in all, nineteen union members, including the chairman of the Halle SPD, and eleven members of the Combat Leagues suffered minor injuries.

This time, the Stahlhelm and its allies had not won a victory, but neither had they suffered a clear defeat. Although they had been able to show their presence in the streets of Eisleben without interference, they were able to occupy the public space only temporarily. What was new about their behavior in both Eilenburg and Eisleben was that the bourgeois camp resorted to direct force against the workers' movement rather than merely calling for force and then delegating it to the state's security forces. The counterdemonstrators, who insulted the Stahlhelm members in Eilenburg as "bloodhounds" just as they had done with the police during the *Kaiserreich,* saw them precisely in this role, namely as executors of an authoritarian political concept. At the same time, by calling them "rear-echelon pigs (*Etappenschweine*)" they challenged their self-image as brave front line soldiers and laid claim to the war experience for themselves. In Eisleben, the violence clearly emanated from the members of the Combat Leagues. They intercepted the union men on their way home and attacked them even more vehemently than in Eilenburg.[40] Their opponents on the left were now much better organized than before, as the presence of the Proletarian Hundreds from Halle attests. Moreover, the direct resistance against the violence coming from the right-wing groups united the Communists and the Socialists. And once again it was younger men who could not have served at the front lines in the war that were especially prominent in the fighting. Violence was on both sides a calculated instrument for holding their ground, its goal being not to inflict serious injuries but to force the enemy to retreat; firearms were evidently merely an instrument of last resort.

The growing activities of the right-wing groups and the clashes in Eilenburg and Eisleben helped the KPD. In June and July, the party was able to boost its membership by about one hundred in each of the counties to which the two towns belonged (Delitzsch and Mansfelder Seekreis). It attracted even more supporters in the Saalkreis around Halle, while it lost members in other counties. On the whole, though, the changes were not major. Membership in the entire district rose by a little over 500 between May and June, and the following month by another 400 to eventually reach 20,399; in the same period the number of local groups grew by five to 256. All in all, this was hardly more than a consolidation on a higher level, not the influx that the party was hoping for in the face of the general economic and political crisis.[41] The Stahlhelm had also achieved some successes in recruiting members from among the working class. In its report for May, the district leadership complained that "in the entire Geisel Valley it is not possible to place a single comrade anywhere," since the owners of the brown coal pits there were demanding that their workers be members of one of the Combat Leagues or the Teno. Elsewhere, the Stahlhelm was trying to woo the unemployed with special deliveries of food. In June, following a works council election challenged by the Stahlhelm, in one mine of the Weißenfels mining district 82 votes were cast for the right-wing organization alongside 265 votes for the KPD.[42]

The district leadership was happier about the party's youth work. At the end of July, there were 90 youth groups with 2,700 members. However, one caveat had to be made even here: in addition to their work in the fields, "the fairs that are now taking place every Sunday are keeping people from their organizing work."[43] The young Communists wanted to take advantage of the possibilities of entertainment and consumption offered to them—they were not blindly obedient party soldiers.

The Proletarian Hundreds also did not develop as the party had hoped. Eleven days after their first large-scale appearance at the May Day celebrations, Interior Minister Severing had outlawed them throughout Prussia,[44] so the work of setting them up continued in secret. The violent clashes in May and June led the workers in a number of enterprises, especially in Eisleben and County Mansfeld, to adopt resolutions to that effect, and had helped to overcome the resistance within the unions as well as the opposition from the weak SPD. According to information provided by the leadership of the party district Halle-Merseburg, there were thirteen work-based Proletarian Hundreds at the end of July: five each in Eisleben and Halle and three in Wittenberg. Their members were recruited primarily from among miners, followed by workers from the chemical industry, while metalworkers were only weakly represented. There were also thirteen local Proletarian Hundreds: six in Halle, and the others equally distributed across the district. About half of the members belonged to the KPD, the "indifferent" made up another two-fifths, and only one-tenth were members of the SPD. That so few Social Democrats responded to the recruitment evidently had something to do with the Communist rank and file. The district leadership noted that many comrades refused "to set up the Hundreds in the sense of the united front tactic. Rather, many of them want to slip back into playing military games." Moreover, there were efforts to circumvent Severing's prohibition by setting up "hiking clubs," which meant "opening up any kind of military drill club."[45]

It would seem that the KPD members most likely to find their way into the Hundreds were those who had been politicized and incorporated into the workers' movement only after the war, while the workers with a longer union and party tradition kept away. Moreover, the interest of party comrades active in these units seemed to limit itself to their paramilitary aspects, while their political task receded into the background. The Rote Frontkämpferbund (RFB, Red Front Fighters' League) that was set up the following year was in part a response to these proclivities among party members. This reveals a militancy among segments of the party rank and file that the leadership could control only to some degree. While the better part of the party base—as the debacle of March 1921 had shown—rejected the offensive use of force, there was now a smaller group among the noticeably shrunken number of followers who were pushing for such actions. However, disciplined party soldiers were not what the central leadership found in the Proletarian Hundreds.

The KPD tried to style the "Anti-Fascism Day" on 29 July, for which it sought to mobilize members and supporters throughout the entire province, as an impressive demonstration of its strength and a recruiting tool for new members. Public rallies were held in a number of towns and cities, including—in addition to Halle—Bitterfeld, Hettstedt, Naumburg, and Wittenberg. In a communiqué to the central office in Berlin, the district leadership in Halle judged the event a complete success, though it conceded that participation had been lower than expected. In nine locations throughout the district, 30,000 people had gathered, that is to say, not many more than the party had members. Moreover, many local groups had been represented "in small numbers" because of the high travel costs.[46] The authorities came to the same conclusion. The Landrat of Liebenwerda spoke of "1,200 persons, at most, youths included," a number he regarded as "extremely low" given the long preparations of the KPD. Similar comments came from his colleagues in Eisleben and Querfurt.[47] Nearly all rallies went off without incident. At most there were minor scuffles between individual demonstrators and the police or members of right-wing Combat Leagues that had gathered in some locations but did not make an appearance in larger formations. The police themselves had a massive presence, especially in Halle, where—among other things—they stationed an armored vehicle at police headquarters; however, the *Klassenkampf* noted that on the whole, the conduct of the police was "exceedingly correct."[48] This was no doubt helped by the fact that while smaller groups of party members carrying heavy sticks were spotted at the rallies and marches, no larger military formations came out, even though the Berlin party leadership had called upon the Proletarian Hundreds to accompany the rallies.[49] In most cases, the Proletarian Hundreds were, after all, nothing more than resolutions by the workforce.

Thus Anti-Fascism Day was by no means the "highpoint of the pro-Communist mass movement in Germany,"[50] even if the *Klassenkampf* believed that the "workers' consciousness of power … has been strengthened immensely."[51] While it is true that the party was able to show a presence precisely in places that the radical right had previously tried to claim for itself, it was unable to mobilize any "masses" beyond its own supporters. Larger clashes might have happened if the Combat Leagues of the right had staged a large-scale countermobilization at the rally sites, but they did not feel strong enough (yet) to do so. Unlike the events of the summer of 1921 and 1922, Anti-Fascism Day—as well as the Communist meetings preceding it—saw no attacks on helpless representatives of the right. The contained "masses" that filled the streets in Halle and elsewhere on 29 July were not preparing for a "civil war" against the right; rather, they were expressing their desire to see a radical change in politics at the Reich level.

The "Cuno Strikes": At the Zenith of the Mobilization?

When the Regierungspräsident of Merseburg, on 31 August, looked back over the month that had just passed, he believed that the activities of the KPD had had "no meaningful success," and continued: "The most recent unrest has shown that it is easy for the Communist Party to whip up the masses by pointing to the surging prices, which it believes to be unjustified, and inadequate wages. Yet the past days have demonstrated that the stirred-up masses, most of whom are passive supporters of the German Communist Party, quickly come to their senses once they are enlightened by the unions and the press and turn away from the efforts of the KPD."[52] The verdict of the official reveals the explosive political power of the worsening hyperinflation. But it also shows that the KPD was not able to convert the growing misery and agitation into sustained political gains. No real danger emanated from the KPD even in its strongholds, in spite of the growing crisis. In view of what had transpired during the preceding weeks, this was remarkable.

In the middle of August 1923, a wave of strikes washed over Germany, their focal point in the central region. Directed against the thoroughly failed policies of Reich Chancellor Cuno, in office for a year, they forced him into resigning and have therefore come to be associated with his name.[53] The strikes began with work stoppages, not yet aimed at bringing down the government, but at cost-of-living allowances and stable wages. With these demands, the workers in brown coal mines in the county of Wanzleben staged a walkout on 4, 6, and 7 August; during the following days they were joined by agricultural workers on several estates in the surrounding area. There was "strong agitation" among the population, the Landrat noted on 7 August, though he emphasized that "excesses ... have so far not occurred"; four days later, too, he felt that "public order ... is not disturbed."[54] On 8 August in neighboring County Calbe, agricultural workers went on strike followed by industrial workers; the same happened in Staßfurt. The next day, rural and industrial workers in County Jerichow II followed suit. Here the Landräte and the Oberpräsident saw the influence of the Communists as crucial, but Hörsing also highlighted the connection between the "intolerable conditions in the marketplace for food" and the success of the KPD: "One could almost believe that the farmers were supporting the Communist propaganda." The authorities deployed the Teno and the Schupo to lend support. However, no significant incidents were reported.[55] The wave of strikes did not begin in the strongholds of the KPD but at the periphery of its sphere of influence and immediately involved, along with miners, rural workers, who usually could not be mobilized so quickly. This demonstrates that this was hardly a movement that was planned and directed from the beginning by the KPD, even if the party quickly inserted itself and sought to expand it.

In the following days, the wave of strikes took hold of broad segments of the province and most industrial areas, although it did not—contrary to the KPD's intention—develop into a general strike encompassing the entire region. The movement was driven by the miners in various counties of the districts of Magdeburg and Merseburg; workers from enterprises in other sectors in and around Halle joined in. It is revealing that although the strikers until 11 August did call for the resignation of Cuno's cabinet alongside their economic demands, they were not yet calling for a "government of workers and peasants."[56] This clearly offensive slogan was articulated by the KPD only in its appeal for a general strike throughout Germany issued on 12 August, a Sunday. The same day, Cuno resigned from his office. The next day, the strikes spread further and now took hold also of the Mansfelder Land and the large enterprises of the chemical industry. The employees of the transportation enterprises, the postal service, and the railroad did not join the strike, however.[57] On 14 August, according to information from Ersil, 200,000 workers in the district of Halle-Merseburg and 75,000 in the district of Magdeburg-Anhalt were on strike, a very large number, if one compares it, for example, to the participation in the sympathy strikes in March 1921.[58] However, cost-of-living allowances continued to be the chief goals of the strikes even after Cuno's resignation. That is why the KPD most likely exerted influence on the movement not by ratcheting up the political goals of the strikes, but primarily by seeking to up the material demands of the workers, to which companies were beginning to respond.[59] At the same time, party propaganda was trying to generate a revolutionary mood. The "hour of the decisive struggle" was now "closer than many believe," the *Klassenkampf* proclaimed after Stresemann had succeeded Cuno.[60]

In addition, the party leadership pushed the formation of control committees and Proletarian Hundreds with greater vigor, trying in this way to consolidate its mobilization gains. In the days leading up to the beginning of the strikes, a number of cities had witnessed demonstrations against rising prices by women at the weekly markets; the authorities had responded to them—in Bitterfeld, for example—by buying up food and selling it to the population at cheaper prices. In its summary of the "Cuno strikes," the KPD district leadership then claimed that "in very many places" control committees had now been "recognized and provided with ID cards."[61] However, it is doubtful whether the control committees in fact attained the importance ascribed to them here: they are not mentioned at all in the bourgeois and Social Democratic press, nor do they appear in the final report of the Oberpräsident, which means that—unlike in the Free State of Saxony[62]—they are not likely to have intervened in any meaningful way in the property rights of shop owners.[63]

Proletarian Hundreds were supposed to secure communications between the local strike leadership, respond to abuses by the Schupo, and above all, function as forces to maintain order. In mid August, however, when the "Cuno strikes" had just peaked, the police president of Halle noted that the Proletarian Hundreds in his city, all efforts by the KPD notwithstanding, had not progressed beyond the "development stage." Because of the state of the economy, "almost exclusively young KPD members and those eager for an adventure" were participating, members to whom the party's "educational work" seemed too much effort. His assessment agreed with that of the district leadership. According to the latter, the units had made an appearance only in smaller towns and in a few other places. Initially set up to prevent the theft of field crops, "they failed completely" when it came to "any kind of other political work," the Halle KPD district leadership noted.[64] Much like the fighting groups of the "March action," the Proletarian Hundreds thus attracted chiefly young, politically inexperienced and therefore more violence-prone men.

Moreover, the Hundreds saw themselves caught in a fundamental dilemma. They were supposed to defend the rights of workers against the power of the state and reactionary political forces, while at the same time preventing the strike and protest movement from sliding into chaos and maintaining an orderly food supply. However, this mission clashed with the methods employed by the population in its food protests. The result was the paradoxical situation that the units were trying to prevent the theft of field crops, while elsewhere fields were being systematically plundered under the leadership of control committees.[65] Moreover, crop theft was by now not an isolated phenomenon, but a daily occurrence. The authorities, however, did not blame the Communists for this: Oberpräsident Hörsing emphasized that "agriculture" itself was "more or less responsible" for the thefts, "since the withholding of food and the misery and hunger this creates was driving the agitated mood to the boiling point."[66]

In this "agitated atmosphere," however, only a few violent clashes occurred, in spite of a massive deployment of the Schupo and the Teno, the appearance of Proletarian Hundreds, and some larger "self-help" actions.[67] The only serious confrontation between the police and the strikers took place on 13 August in Zeitz. On 11 August, the jail in that city had been stormed; the next day, the KPD had set up a strike committee with the SPD and formed a workers' militia. In response, Oberpräsident Hörsing dispatched two hundred-man Schupo units to Zeitz, where they arrested the strike leadership. When the police officers were attacked by some participants in a larger demonstration, a few lost their nerve and fired into the crowd without warning. At least nine demonstrators were killed and at least as many were injured, while only one police constable was injured in the arm. The only recently created workers' militia did not make an appearance.[68] On the whole, however, the conduct of the police seems to have been more careful than it had been during the second phase of the "March action" in 1921, for example. That is why one must beware of exaggerating the militarization of the police caused by those earlier events.

The *Klassenkampf*, needless to say, saw in the actions of the authorities "brutal force and oppression … the last resort for the bankrupt capitalist state." After Anti-Fascism Day, the paper had declared that "proletarian self-help" was the only defense against the "bloody terror" of the right, since the police were failing to protect the workers. "No discussion helps against guns, knives, and blackjacks. Here it is an eye for an eye, a tooth for a tooth, blood for blood." The confrontation with the Stahlhelm thus had to be carried on "militarily and politically."[69] Here, the phrase that originally emerged in the context of the food protests was transferred to the political struggle.[70] With this shift, the KPD was trying to further exacerbate the already tense atmosphere even as it placated its particularly militant activists. As the course of the strikes showed, however, their violent slogans had no great effect, even though the Stahlhelm in some locations offered itself to the authorities as an additional security force.[71]

In reality, though, the Stahlhelm—like the groups affiliated with it—dispensed with making its presence known in larger formations and asserting, at least symbolically, its own claim to being a force for order and security. One reason for the Stahlhelm's restraint was that the group's leadership could not be sure where all its members stood, especially those who had only recently joined in areas that were strongholds of the workers' movement. In the Mansfelder Land, for example, Stahlhelm members acted as pickets, and in the brown coal region of the Geisel Valley, from which the KPD had been almost entirely expelled, they also went on strike, which meant that all mines of the area were idle. Even at the Leonhardt mine, most of whose workers were organized in the Stahlhelm and had received a special shipment of meat when the strikes began, 92 percent of the workers voted by secret ballot to go on strike.[72] This shows that the calculations of the business owners, who aimed to build up the Stahlhelm organizations in their enterprises as successors to the "yellow" unions, did not really work out. Many workers had presumably joined only under pressure, and in the existential crisis in the summer of 1923 they were guided by their own interests, which it seemed would be best served by participation in the strike.

The "Cuno strikes" did not end abruptly but petered out gradually. Cuno's resignation was less critical to bringing them to an end than were the concessions from the business owners. There was no termination at the direct initiative of the KPD. Rather, the KPD tried, after the end of the strike in Berlin, to move material goals to the fore again in the province of Saxony, while at the same time stoking the previously created mood that this was the final struggle. The *Klassenkampf* voiced its conviction that the "collapse" could only be "a question of a very short period of time," even as it had to concede that the "fighting ability of the mobilized masses" was not yet sufficient.[73] The KPD, however, had to fend off groups from the left who were pushing for "direct action," in Halle the KAPD and in Bitterfeld the syndicalist Allgemeine Arbeiter-Union (AAU, General Workers' Union), which experienced a brief revival.[74]

Not least the AAU saw to it that the KPD could claim the aftereffects of the "Cuno strikes" as only half a victory for itself. To be sure, the district of Halle-Merseburg noted a "strong surge in the membership numbers" of the party, especially where—as in the Mansfelder Land—disciplinary measures were taken on a large scale, but the "most aggressive effect" of the events was felt in the unions. There, an "immense mass exodus" was under way, the district leadership complained. Even in Zschornewitz, where the party comrades otherwise maintained good discipline, this movement could not be stopped even with the threat of expulsion from the party. Those who left did not remain indifferent, but flocked to the AAU.[75] Even if the KPD attracted a number of new members after the "Cuno strikes," they were not obedient party soldiers but had a mind of their own when it came to their own immediate material interests. What was articulated first and foremost in the strike movement was a massive discontent with the unions, who had failed to represent these interests adequately.[76] The turn toward the KPD and to the action-oriented groups of the extreme left also expressed a diffuse radicalization born of hyperinflation, one that lacked clear political perspectives. By no means did the "masses" pour into the Proletarian Hundreds, nor were they waiting for the signal from the KPD for a general uprising against the government in Berlin. A prerevolutionary situation did not develop.[77]

This was also noted in the bourgeois public. The *Magdeburgische Zeitung* saw "[l]ittle would-be revolutions (*Revoluzzereien*), no real revolution" in the KPD-influenced demonstrations, and "Communist instigations (*Zetteleien*)" in the clashes in Zeitz, though it ascribed only "local character" to them. Although the *Saale-Zeitung* also noted "serious incidents," as late as 14 August it considered the situation "calm," even though it now accused the Communists of "incitement toward the new civil war." Much as in March 1921, the paper now saw "Communists gangs … everywhere in the province" that were engaging in "terror," and in the view of the *Magdeburgische Zeitung,* "most youthful troublemakers" were using "terror" against the rural workers.[78] The *Volksstimme,* too, spoke of "terroristic rural worker strikes," though only a minority had joined them.[79] The Communists were described once again as dangerous troublemakers, but not as a genuine political threat. The real threat to Germany emanated from the "agitation and despair of the masses," which the *Magdeburgische Zeitung* noted not only among the workers. At the beginning of the year, the Halle paper, in an editorial on the anniversary of the founding of the Republic, had already declared that "the usurer is the mortal enemy of the *Volk,* the gourmand its disgrace."[80] Hyperinflation was creating a potential for crisis that found concise expression in the fear of a "civil war," but it was not subsumed in the opposition between the right and the left.

Diffuse Unrest: Political Violence and Food Protests in the Fall of 1923

When a cabinet of the Grand Coalition under Chancellor Stresemann assumed the reins of government in the middle of August, the political situation in Germany relaxed only momentarily. While the Separatists in the west were intensifying their efforts, the Communist leadership in Moscow instructed the KPD at the beginning of October to prepare for an armed uprising. In Saxony and Thuringia the party thereupon entered into coalition governments with the SPD and intensified its efforts to set up Proletarian Hundreds whose mission was now defined as offensive, even though the central party leadership was skeptical about the chances of an armed uprising.[81] On 26 September, Stresemann ended the passive resistance in the Ruhr and simultaneously imposed a state of emergency over the entire Reich. The Bavarian government responded with its own state of emergency, thus underscoring the danger of a putsch that emanated from the "order cell." In the middle of October, Stresemann's government was given extraordinary powers in the area of economic and social policy through an enabling act and announced the new *Rentenmark,* which would be issued the following month and was intended to arrest inflation. The Reich government now had the means to take effective steps against the general crisis of hyperinflation. Whoever had plans for a putsch would have to move swiftly.

By calling for a general strike, the KPD wanted to provide the starting signal for a "German October." But when a conference of works councils, unionists, and delegates from other workers' organizations came out *against* this suggestion from the KPD chief at a conference in Chemnitz on 22 October, the danger of a Communist revolution was essentially over. A day later, the Reich government sent troops into Saxony and relieved the minister president of his office without encountering any resistance. Because the Reich government and the leadership of the Reichswehr refused to take military action against Bavaria, the SPD left the Grand Coalition. Had there really been a threat of Communist revolution until then? Was it a real possibility that a spark could have jumped from the Free State of Saxony to the province of Saxony and the rest of Germany?[82]

After Stresemann came into office, the *Klassenkampf* had continued its efforts to stoke a revolutionary mood, but its slogans lacked the final resolve and conviction. After the imposition of the state of emergency in the Reich and in Bavaria, the paper argued, the "dry putsch" had occurred there, soon to be followed by the "bloody putsch, the bloody terror against the entire Bavarian working class." The workers could oppose this only through the use of "extra-parliamentary means of power, the weapon of the strike and the weapon of their physical force."[83] On 16 October, an appeal from the central office of the KPD began with the words "Weapons into the hand of the entire proletariat!" and this demand was voiced again on 9 November. On Revolution Day, after the decision had been made in Chemnitz and the Reichswehr had occupied Saxony, the paper warned again: "We are only in the prelude to the revolution and tend to overestimate the situation with respect to how mature it is." At the same time, however, it declared that "a worker's fist" should "shut up every Fascist provocateur."[84] With the Hitler putsch on 9 November in Munich, the situation had now finally been reduced to the alternative "fascism or dictatorship of the proletariat," and there was "counterrevolution and civil war in the country." In the view of the *Klassenkampf*, after the defeat of the putschists the danger for the proletariat had actually grown, for now, with the handing over of executive power to the head of the Reichswehr, there was a "white dictatorship." A week later the paper called for "the masses" of the workers "to march out" and to show "in the street that they are here and are ready to fight for their vital rights not only with words, but with deeds."[85] This could be interpreted in various ways, though it was, at any rate, not as direct a call for force as that on Revolution Day.[86] We hear nothing more of the Proletarian Hundreds. The half-hearted rhetoric of the final battle was supposed to have a mobilizing effect, and yet time and again it betrayed the party's own weakness.

To be sure, the Halle district leadership of the KPD noted at the beginning of October that the "sentiment of the workers … is inclined to us to an overwhelming degree" and declared on 10 November, that is, immediately *after* Hitler's failed putsch attempt, that "the broadest strata of the have-nots have lost confidence in the November Republic."[87] In addition, the number of party members had risen steadily in nearly all counties between July and October by around 1,400 and now stood at 22,000, while the number of local groups had grown by 4 to 260. Still, membership was still noticeably below the previous year's level, when it had been more than 25,000.[88]

Other shortcomings were even more grievous. Although the district leadership believed by the middle of November that preparing the party apparatus "for the final struggle" had been a success, those within the party were "very cool" toward the events that were expected to unfold. Had it been necessary to employ force, the prospects would have been very bad, for "general Hundreds are almost completely nonexistent," the district leadership reported on 10 November, whereas during the previous months the formation of these units had been seen as progressing well. The existing armament, too, was "very poor." There was only a well-organized party self-defense force of 500 men.[89] Neither the occupation of Saxony by the Reichswehr on 22 October, which triggered only scattered local protest rallies, nor the Hitler putsch in Munich led to surges in mobilization that the party could have exploited for its further political aims.[90] In a meeting of the district committee on 11 November, Wilhelm Koenen put the situation in a nutshell: a call for a general strike would have not have been met with a great response given the massive unemployment. The party now had to focus on capturing the unions and, moreover, to counter the "social illusions of the fascists."[91]

It is likely that the "masses" would have risen up if Hitler and his allies had in fact tried a "march on Berlin" and entered the province of Saxony in the process. That would have created a situation similar to March of 1920. However, the KPD could hardly have succeeded in pushing such a defensive movement to the point of a second revolution. Had the conference in Chemnitz come to a different decision, the response would have been anemic in the province of Saxony, and no doubt not only there. There was no danger of a Germany-wide uprising by the workers under the leadership of the KPD in the fall of 1923.

Were their enemies on the radical right willing to go further? One thing that was clearly evident in the fall of 1923 was an increase in anti-Semitism and the violence connected with it. In Halberstadt, the only town of the province with a large Jewish community, the Alldeutscher Verband (Pan-German League), which had been insignificant there before the war,[92] experienced a remarkable surge that manifested itself also in anti-Semitic excesses. Initially, the driving force behind the party had been the educated bourgeoisie, the mayor reported in mid December; now, however, their place was being taken by smaller shopkeepers "who are being given a helping hand … by envoys from the Hitler movement." The party was meeting with particular resonance "among young people eighteen to twenty years of age, largely from the class of clerks and shop assistants." For a long time, their actions had been limited to the singing of "abusive songs," insults on the street, and rocks thrown through windows. For the last "few weeks," however, there had also been attacks on younger Jews, though stepped-up police deployment had been able to put a stop to this.[93] Anti-Jewish graffiti and the smashing of windows in Jewish houses had also been witnessed in Gardelegen and Nordhausen.[94] It would appear that these actions in the province of Saxony, reminiscent of the anti-Jewish "excesses" of the nineteenth century,[95] were nothing more than isolated incidents. However, in the general crisis in the fall of 1923 anti-Semitic views surely found a growing number of supporters, as is reflected not least in the electoral success of the explicitly anti-Semitic DNVP in 1924.[96]

Meanwhile, the Combat Leagues continued their intensive activities. In County Nordhausen, the Stahlhelm established "local groups everywhere" and was having a "very inflammatory" effect "with its provocative behavior ... There is avid recruitment among young people," noted the Regierungspräsident of Erfurt.[97] Moreover, the Stahlhelm and the Wehrwolf were attracting attention with a growing number of field exercises, and not only in the radical Gau Halle.[98] These exercises repeatedly led to clashes with their enemies on the left. In general, though, they remained limited to smaller brawls fought with fists, sticks, and fence pickets, and left no dead or seriously injured in their wake.[99] Meanwhile, the Stahlhelm leadership could not arrive at a unanimous stance on the plans for a putsch being discussed behind the scenes. While Duesterberg supported the intentions of Hitler and Ludendorff and was already in discussions with the circle of conspirators, Seldte and Kloppe backed the policy of Stresemann, though they tried to push him toward an even more authoritarian course. As of the beginning of November, Seldte developed sympathies for a scenario contemplated by General von Seeckt, the commander-in-chief of the Reichswehr, namely to govern Germany in authoritarian fashion at the head of a directory.[100] In the fall of 1923, the radical right of the province was undoubtedly in a heightened state of mobilization. It did not, however, pose a genuine threat to the Republic.

At the same time, a sharp attack was launched against the SPD within the bourgeois public as a whole. The reason was the situation in Saxony, where the collaboration between Social Democrats and Communists was kindling fears similar to those that had existed after the murder of Rathenau the previous year. In the middle of September, following a muster of Proletarian Hundreds in Dresden, the *Magdeburgische Zeitung* spoke of a "parade of Communist hordes" and called upon the Social Democratic Minister of the Interior, Zeigner, to deal with "a terror movement clearly bent on revolution," a movement, as the paper noted two weeks later, that had led to "lawlessness in all bourgeois circles." After the Communist minister Böttcher had called for the arming of the proletarian units, the *Saale-Zeitung* warned against the "fire of insurrection" that was "flaring up brightly everywhere" and saw the danger emanating from Communism as growing "to enormous size." A few days before the Reichswehr entered the province, the *Magdeburgische Zeitung* took an even sharper tone: the "conditions demonstrably beggar any description," which was why the bourgeoisie, "defenseless" in the face of numerous "acts of terror," had already turned to Bavaria; now it was time to reestablish "order" here.[101]

The criticism became even more heated at the beginning of November, when the conflict between Bavaria and the Reich had intensified considerably. Whereas at the end of June the *Saale-Zeitung* had still warned against the "suicidal urge" generated by the "Bolshevism of the left and the right" whipping each other up, it now characterized the situation in Northern Bavaria, where right-wing units were gathering for a "March on Berlin," as merely "unpleasant" but necessary as a "counterblow against ... the Bolshevist danger in central Germany." The paper now even went so far as to accuse the SPD of being willing to "risk a civil war" to defend the sinecures it had carved out for itself since 1918. The party was now reaping the "storm wind" it had sown through its doctrine of class warfare.

After the failure of the Hitler putsch, the *Magdeburgische Zeitung* chimed in by pointing out that the SPD had recommended a policy vis-à-vis Bavaria that had led to "civil war." By contrast, criticism of the events in Bavaria was more restrained. "A second edition of Kapp" and a "crime against Reich and *Volk*" is what the *Saale-Zeitung* called the attempted putsch, but not without noting that a dictatorship of the kind sought by the putschists was at least possible in a united people. The *Magdeburgische Zeitung* ran the headline "Hitler-Ludendorff betray Bavaria and the Reich" on 9 November, but it did not discuss the putschists in any detail.[102]

What was remarkable about these positions was not merely the sharp turn against a further participation in the government by the SPD, but above all—and especially in the left-liberal *Saale-Zeitung*—its justification. Accusing the Social Democrats of pursuing a course of civil war meant putting them on a par with the Communists. But there was another reason why the political course of the SPD met with sharp criticism from the two bourgeois papers. In the final stages of hyperinflation, which seemed to dissolve all order, they discussed the creation of a "dictatorship," demanded by many, and went so far as to ponder a fundamental revamping of the political system.[103] At the same time, they called upon the Chancellor and his government to show "ruthlessness, indeed, brutality."[104] This was a plea not for an absolute dictatorship, but for more power for Stresemann. The Enabling Act, passed by the Reichstag in mid October, struck the Magdeburg paper as inadequate, for it had merely created a "dictatorship in quotation marks." However, the paper maintained that such a "dictatorship" had to be bound to the constitution and that—in contrast to the *Kaiserreich*—the political power had to stand above military power.[105] The expectations placed on Stresemann were laid out once again in more detail in an editorial penned by the editor-in-chief on 11 November. Within the German *Volk,* the understanding for a "national dictatorship" had grown more and more, "not in the sense of a military dictatorship, but one borne by the broadest strata of the German *Volk,* by the entire citizenry, among which we count the moderate German Nationals as much as the worker from the Social Democratic camp, who is desperately looking about for the stability (*Halt*) that his party no longer affords him." Once again the chancellor was urged to use the situation for his own purposes by "taking ruthless advantage of it" and by mustering the "brutal will to power."[106]

To what extent the two bourgeois papers would have supported a dictatorship by Seeckt or anyone else remains unclear. What is clear is that in the fall of 1923, both had moved far away from approving a Grand Coalition, which had still seemed of central importance in the middle of the year. The reason was not only the fear of cooperation between the SPD and the KPD, or of another—possibly successful—attempt at a putsch by the Communists. Rather, in the situation in the fall of 1923, exceedingly ominous and at the same time marked by confused lines of conflict, liberal convictions eroded, especially in the left-liberal Halle newspaper.[107] The chaos and the feared struggle of "all against all" during the hyperinflation stoked the bourgeois camp's fundamental mistrust of both liberal capitalism and any socialism of Marxist provenance. In this situation, an authoritarian state like the ones recently created by Mussolini in Italy and General State Commissioner von Kahr in Bavaria seemed models at least worth discussing. The issue was not merely their structure as such, for the demand for "ruthlessness" and "brutality" did not rule out that violent measures might also be appropriate within the framework of a political reorganization.

The deep divide between the bourgeoisie and the Social Democrats receded into the background, however, when it came to an assessment of the food protests. In the later summer and early fall of 1923, hardly a day went by when the papers did not report on unrest over rising prices, crop thefts, and forms of criminal behavior that could be interpreted as the consequence of inflation. Moreover, the number of unemployed surged.[108] In Magdeburg, a "crowd" of eight hundred plundered the stalls at the meat market on 20 October and eventually clashed with the police, who used their swords. The confrontation was dragged out into the evening hours, and one worker was killed in an exchange of gunfire between the police and armed looters. The police president did not blame Communist machinations for the unrest, but the fact was that "the desperate state of the people's food supply had caused the deepest despair also in circles of the population that are otherwise quiet."[109]

In spite of the tense political climate, this view was also shared by the public. "The hungry and the desperate are not amenable to reason," noted the *Magdeburgische Zeitung,* which was harshly critical of the farmers. If the latter did not make concessions, the city dwellers would help themselves. "We know that this would trigger chaos, a war of all against all." There was no mention in this context of the Communists, only of "elements that like to stir up trouble," "so-called 'rowdies,'" and "disreputable elements," which had been joined by "dissolute characters."[110] The *Volksstimme* characterized the actors in the same way and saw the cause of the rioting in an elemental distress: "Desperation sinks its claws into the brain and creates a mood that leads to terrible outbursts." However, "violent self-help" could not be tolerated, for the "danger of bloodshed is incredibly high."[111]

The unrest over higher prices in Magdeburg, followed over the next few days by unrest in Burg, Wolmirstedt, Halle, and Halberstadt, was only part of the new wave of collective self-help action that washed over Germany with particular vehemence in October 1923.[112] Typically, the number of participants was large, and the actions of the "crowd" over large stretches were controlled, involved little violence, and were aimed at acquiring necessary foodstuffs at prices deemed to be appropriate or without any payment at all. Vandalism or massive violence against persons was part of the behavioral repertoire of the "crowd" only in exceptional cases, and in most instances it was the security forces who set off the violence. The majority of those involved were not a "mob," but a lower class pushed into existential distress by galloping inflation and the now surging unemployment.[113] What the police president of Halle had written in the middle of October about the mood of the population applied to them, as well: the catastrophic economic situation (by now there were 12,000 unemployed in Halle alone) had "thrown the population into a kind of political stupor, and it faces the shocking political events apathetically."[114] The last stage of hyperinflation did not create a revolutionary situation. Rather, it cast people back into worrying about daily survival, fracturing society not along class lines, but into a multitude of smaller parts.[115] The widely evoked "civil war" took place largely in people's heads.

Notes

1. On the end phase of the inflation see Feldman, *Disorder,* 457ff.; on what was in essence a similar strategy to fight the inflation under contrary political background conditions see his "Bayern und Sachsen in der Hyperinflation 1922/23," *HZ* 238 (1984): 569–609.
2. On this problem see Dirk Schumann, "Der aufgeschobene Bürgerkrieg: Sozialer Protest und Politische Gewalt in Deutschland 1923," *ZfG* 44, no. 6 (1996): 526–544.
3. Angress, *Revolution,* 241–253; Winkler, *Revolution,* 544–549.
4. Ersil, *Aktionseinheit,* 87f. At the Leuna Works, by contrast, it remained in the minority.
5. Ibid., 84f.
6. This is the picture consistently painted by the East German literature (e.g., Ersil, Leidigkeit and Herrmann), which describes the workers as part of "masses" that needed to be led "correctly," being incapable of engaging on their own the political offers from the parties.
7. LHAM C 20 Ib 5215, fol. 238 (OP to Regierungspräsidenten, 30 August 1922); fol. 266 (PP Magdeburg to OP, 30 October 1922); fol. 290 (PP Halle to OP, 8 November 1922).
8. SAPMO Ry I 3/11/18, fol. 62 (Monthly report for February 1923).
9. SAPMO Ry 1/I 3/11/18, fol. 143 (Monthly report for May 1923).
10. SAPMO Ry 1/I 3/11/18, fol. 118 (Report for April 1923). On the development of unemployment see Carl-Ludwig Holtfrerich, *Die deutsche Inflation 1914–1923* (Berlin, 1980), 195.
11. This is overlooked by Mallmann, *Kommunisten,* 87–93.
12. Tonn, "Kampf," 118ff. On the control committees in general see Geyer, "Teuerungsprotest," 339–341. There is still no monographic treatment of the topic.
13. LHAM C 20 Ib 5217/II, fols. 168f., 241–244, 216–268 (Meeting reports of 29 August, 13 October, 4 November, 11 November 1922); fol. 289 (RP Merseburg to OP, 31 January 1923). According to the Regierungspräsident, in January 1923 the population saw the committee as merely an "empty, useless entity."
14. LAG Reg. Erfurt 12354, fol. 257 (LR Schleusingen to RP, 7 March 1923). Control committees were also set up in Genthin and Halberstadt, though they did not lead to any lasting membership growth for the KPD: LHAM C 20 Ib 5213/II, fols. 39f., 74 (LR Jerichow II to RP, 16 November and 28 November 1922); fols. 80f. (Police administration of Halberstadt to RP, 22 February 1923).
15. Ersil, *Aktionseinheit,* 89f. Tonn, "Kampf," 126, speaks of the "often times inadequate activity by the various control committees."
16. Diehl, *Paramilitary Politics,* 130–136; Helmut Gast, "Die proletarischen Hundertschaften als Organe der Einheitsfront im Jahre 1923," *ZfG* 4, no. 3 (1956): 439–465; Wilfried Hanisch, *Die Hundertschaften der Arbeiterwehr: Die proletarischen Hundertschaften in Sachsen* (East Berlin, 1958).
17. SAPMO Ry 1/I 2/705/9, fols. 92f. (Situation report, 25 April 1923); Ersil, *Aktionseinheit,* 82–84.
18. SAPMO Ry 1/I 3/11/18, fols. 94–99 (Special report from the district leadership Halle-Merseburg on the movement to establish Proletarian Hundreds, 3 May 1923); Ersil, *Aktionseinheit,*

94–98; see Diehl, *Paramilitary Politics,* 133–136. In some places the KPD members had clear reservations about the Social Democrats; the tactic of a united front was thus not persuasive for all parts of the rank and file.

19. LHAM C 20 Ib 5228, fols. 9f. (PP Erfurt to RP, 10 March 1923).
20. LAG Landratsamt Schleusingen no. 585, fols. 17f. (Police administration Suhl to LR Schleusingen, 23 March 1923).
21. LHAM C 20 Ib 5228, fol. 21 (PP Magdeburg to RP, 4 April 1923).
22. Ibid., fol. 28 (PP Halle to RP Merseburg, 8 May 1923).
23. LHAM C 20 Ib 2002/I, fols. 1–16 (OP to the Prussian Minister of the Interior, 3 April 1923, attachments).
24. Wirsching, *Weltkrieg,* 234–239, avoids an unambiguous statement about the effective strength of the Proletarian Hundreds in Berlin and elsewhere, though he emphasizes that regardless of their strength and a Communist uprising's chances of success, one must not neglect the effects of Communist propaganda on the political culture. In response it should be noted that one must distinguish between such effects and a basic hostility to the workers' movement; such a distinction, however, requires an assessment of Communist strength.
25. The following discussion is based on reports from August-October 1922 and a number of additions in LHAM C 20 Ib 4687 and 4685. Apart from the reports of the police authorities, the files also contain extensive material on the various organizations, especially their bylaws.
26. LHAM C 20 Ib 4685, fol. 205 (RP Merseburg to OP, 16 August 1922); fol. 242 (RP Erfurt to OP, 4 September 1922). Veterans' organizations other than the Stahlhelm were found in very few places; also negligible were explicitly anti-Semitic organizations like the Hellmuth-von-Mücke Bund, which attracted about 100 *Gymnasium* students in Magdeburg but made an appearance in only one other place, Mühlhausen, or the Deutscher Herold, which had local groups only in Halle and Magdeburg (with 100 and 75 members, respectively).
27. On the founding history of the Jungdo see Hornung, *Jungdeutscher Orden,* 23–33; Finker, "Wehrverbände," 220–238, 247–250; also see Diehl, *Paramilitary Politics,* 97–100, 119.
28. LHAM C 20 Ib 4687, fols. 240–241, fol. 381 (RP Erfurt to OP, 4 and 21 September 1922); fol. 197 (PP Magdeburg to OP, 16 August 1922); fol. 213 (RP Magdeburg to OP, 21 August 1922); fol. 387 (RP Magdeburg to OP, 2 October 1922); fol. 8 (PP Halle to OP, 4 August 1922); fol. 205 (RP Merseburg to OP, v. 16 August 1922). See also Raßloff, *Flucht,* 258–260.
29. Uwe Lohalm, *Völkischer Radikalismus: Die Geschichte des Deutschvölkischen Schutz- und Trutz-Bundes 1919–1923* (Hamburg, 1970), 246ff. The DVSTB focused its propaganda on the big cities of Magdeburg and Halle but failed to attract a large following. In Magdeburg, where a local group did not appear until the end of 1919, the DVSTB at times had more than 1,200–1,500 members, though over the course of 1921 the number dropped to 400. Outside of the capital, following the league's disbanding after the murder of Rathenau, local groups in the district of Merseburg were found only in Halberstadt, Salzwedel, and two villages of the Börde: LHAM C 20 Ib 4627, fols. 263f. (OP to the StaKoöO, 13 March 1922); LHAM C 20 Ib 4680/I (not pag., PP Magdeburg to OP, 10 August 1922; RP Magdeburg to OP, 21 August 1922). There is no information on the presence of the DVSTB in the other administrative districts. Presumably it was somewhat stronger in the administrative district of Erfurt, since Thuringia was one of its bastions. A factory owner from Schleusingen was one of the financiers of the league (Lohalm, *Völkischer Radikalismus,* 102).
30. LHAM C 20 Ib 4665/I, fols. 195–197 (Dissolution decree from Hörsing, 2 July 1922) and passim; Klotzbücher, "Stahlhelm," 16–19; Berghahn, *Stahlhelm,* 36–39. It is possible that Seldte had made secret agreements with Stresemann.
31. Irmtraud Götz von Olenhusen, "Vom Jungstahlhelm zur SA: Die junge Nachkriegsgeneration in den paramilitärischen Verbänden der Weimarer Republik," in W. R. Krabbe, ed., *Politische Jugend in der Weimarer Republik* (Bochum 1993), 146–182.
32. A distant second was the more moderate Jungnationale Bund, which was present in Magdeburg (approx. 100 members), Halle (approx. 60), Naumburg, and Wittenberg. The Bismarck-

bund, which was also close to the DNVP, had a local group in Halberstadt and comprised 120 members in Halle but was outlawed at the end of September for engaging in military exercises. See the reports in LHAM C 20 Ib 4685, passim, esp. fol. 5; LHAM C 20 Ib 4687, passim, esp. fols. 174, 176.

33. LHAM C 20 Ib 4689, there a number of police reports from various locations; Finker, *Wehrverbände,* 312–314, 322; Diehl, *Paramilitary Politics,* 119f. The report from the police president of Halle mentions 22 January as the founding date, whereas Kloppe, in an informational booklet from May, gives 11 January, the day of the invasions of the Ruhr, as the date. The latter date was adopted by Berghahn, *Stahlhelm,* 33, and Finker, *Wehrverbände.* Berghahn overlooks the link to the Stahlhelm that existed from the very beginning, though it began to loosen in the summer of 1923. Kloppe himself belonged to the DVP, as he relates in a letter to Hörsing at the end of June 1923 (LHAM C 20 Ib 4689, fol. 38). The very sparse information about the social profile of the members indicates that the Wehrwolf and the Stahlhelm both were primarily bourgeois organizations.
34. LHAM C 20 Ib 4685, fols. 109f. (PP Halle to OP, 10 July 1923). Berghahn hints at an earlier founding of the Scharnhorst, though he offers no evidence.
35. What follows is taken from: LHAM C 20 Ib 5217/II, fol. 23 (Police administration of Eilenburg to LR Delitzsch, 12 May 1923); SAPMO Ry 1/I 3/11/18, fols. 106–109 (Special report for the district leadership, no date). According to this report ("According to a precise counting, there had appeared…") the Wehrwolf provided 650 participants, the Stahlhelm only 210. The police report, by contrast, does not mention the Wehrwolf at all, though the explanation is that the Wehrwolf was simply folded into the Stahlhelm, especially since the command is likely to have been with the leaders of the latter. On the events see Weitz, *German Communism,* 171–173, who draws only on the Communist sources.
36. Ersil, *Aktionseinheit,* 70; Stahlhelm, *Sechs Jahre Stahlhelm,* 126, 128; LHAM C 20 Ib 4689, fol. 36 (Police adminstration of Eilenburg to RP Merseburg, 6 June 1923). According to this report, the local Wehrwolf group comprised 75 members, chiefly "younger people (clerks, artisans, bank employees)."
37. The following is based on LHAM C 20 Ib 4665/II, fols. 37–39, 41–44, 45, 52–53 (Reports from the police administration and several police officers); SAPMO Ry 1/I 3/11/18, fols. 150–154 (Special report from the district leadership Halle-Merseburg, 9 July 1923); Stahlhelm, *Sechs Jahre Stahlhelm,* 170–174.
38. LHAM C 20 Ib 4665/II, fol. 45 (Command of the Eisleben Schupo to the Lord Mayor, 26 June 1923).
39. Ibid., fol. 53 (Testimony from police officers Flemming and Richter, 25 June 1923). During the clash, Duesterberg made an "offer of aid" to the police officer in charge: if he could not manage on his own, "I will put 1,000 men at your disposal, they will smash all of Eisleben into bits." The police officers as a whole certainly did not behave in a uniform way. The report from the KPD district leadership noted explicitly that the officers had acted in a "very loyal" way. On the other hand, pictures in Stahlhelm, *Sechs Jahre Stahlhelm,* 172, show several police officers saluting the military associations as they march by.
40. The claim by Berghahn, *Stahlhelm,* 34, that the members of the Stahlhelm had been instructed to defend themselves only against outright attacks and not to use offensive force themselves does not appear tenable.
41. SAPMO Ry 1/I 3/11/18, fols. 225f. (Report by the district leadership Halle-Merseburg for July 1923).
42. Ibid., fols. 144f., 172 (Reports by the district leadership Halle-Merseburg for May and June 1923). Another thing that was causing the district leadership headaches was the inadequate refocusing of the organizational work toward works cells: ibid., fol. 168 (Report for June 1923); fol. 224 (Report for July 1923). See Mallmann, *Kommunisten,* 306; also Lore Heer-Kleinert, *Die Gewerkschaftspolitik der KPD in der Weimarer Republik* (Frankfurt, 1983), 237f., according to whom the separation of party and union work merely caused confusion in the workplace.

43. SAPMO Ry 1/I 3/11/18, fols. 228f. (Report by the district leadership Halle-Merseburg for July 1923).
44. Gotthard Jasper, *Der Schutz der Republik: Studien zur staatlichen Sicherung der Demokratie in der Weimarer Republik 1922–1930* (Tübingen, 1963), 145f.
45. SAPMO Ry 1/I 3/11/18, fols. 158–162 (Special report by the district leadership on the Proletarian Hundreds, 10 July 1923); fols. 163f. (Situation report of the district leadership, 19 July 1923).
46. SAPMO Ry 1/I 3/11/18, fols. 223f. (Report of the district leadership for July 1923). By contrast, Ersil, *Aktionseinheit,* 163–174, claims that 45,000 workers participated in the district of Halle-Merseburg, while in the entire province the number was 70,000. He bases these tallies on the information in the Communist papers and "various police reports."
47. LHAM C 20 Ib 5217/II, fols. 347-350., the quote fol. 347 (LR Liebenwerda to RP Merseburg, 30 July 1923).
48. LHAM C 20 Ib 2003/I, fol. 9 (OP Hörsing to the Prussian Minister of the Interior, 1 August 1923); LHAM C 20 Ib 5218/II, fols. 5f. (PP Halle to RP Merseburg, 1 August 1923); *KK* no. 175, 30 July 1923; LAG Landratsamt Schleusingen no. 585, fols. 111–115 (Schupo command Suhl to LR Schleusingen, 1 August 1923). By contrast, Klotzbücher, "Stahlhelm," 23, claims, without offering any evidence, that there had been 350 slightly and seriously injured people in Halle, and follows this up with the untenable thesis that as early as summer 1923, the clashes between the Stahlhelm and its opponents on the left had reached "civil war–like levels." See Tonn, "Kampf," 178, according to whom Anti-Fascism Day came off quietly on the whole.
49. Angress, *Revolution,* 364. Ersil, *Aktionseinheit,* 175, merely mentions that proletarian hundreds appeared in various locations "in groups or as protection for the meetings."
50. That was still the verdict of Otto Wenzel, "Die kommunistische Partei Deutschlands im Jahre 1923," PhD dissertation, Free University of Berlin, 1955, 156. More skeptical is the assessment of Angress, *Revolution,* 361–366, who describes the result of the day as "far from overwhelming" (366).
51. *KK* no. 175, 30 July 1923.
52. LHAM C 20 Ib 5215, fol. 362 (RP Merseburg to OP, 31 August 1923).
53. Ersil, *Aktionseinheit,* 177ff.; Wenzel, "Kommunistische Partei,"164–175; Angress, *Revolution,* 369–375; Winkler, *Revolution,* 593ff.
54. LHAM C 20 Ib 4698/XIII, fols. 92, 93f., 96 (LR Wanzleben to OP, 7, 8, and 11 August 1923); Ersil, *Aktionseinheit,* 192–197.
55. LHAM C 20 Ib 1951/VII, fols. 6f. (LR Genthin to OP, 15 August 1923); fols. 24–26 (OP to the Prussian Minister of the Interior, 21 August 1923); LHAM C 20 Ib 4698/II, fols. 87–89 (LR Calbe to OP, 18 August 1923).
56. On the spread of the strike movement see Ersil, *Aktionseinheit,* 216ff., 228ff. Ersil based himself often on the statements of former activists of the KPD made after 1945 and ascribes to the party an influence it did not possess. However, he does not deny the largely defensive character of the movement. The evidence for the strikes in LHAM C 20 Ib 4698/I–XV, and 4699/I–XVII, is incomplete.
57. See LHAM C 20 Ib 1951/VII, fols. 27–29 (OP to the Prussian Minister of the Interior, 21 August 1923); fols. 72–87 (RP Erfurt to OP, 22 August 1923) on the calm events (including also Suhl) in the administrative district of Erfurt; Ersil, *Aktionseinheit,* 253ff., 308ff.; on the strikes of the rural workers see Vogler, "Klassenkampf," 318–321.
58. Ersil, *Aktionseinheit,* 357.
59. Such a case is described in detail in LAMe Rep. Mansfeldsche Kaliwerke AG Eisleben Va 1, vol. 1, fols. 119f. (Report by management on the strike at the Kali works Dittrichshall, no date).
60. *KK* no. 189, 15 August 1923.
61. SAPMO Ry 1/I 3/11/18, fols. 204–206, 211 (Complete report by the district leadership about the "Cuno strikes," 21 August 1923); Ersil, *Aktionseinheit,* 317, 328, does not provide very precise information.

62. Feldman, "Bayern und Sachsen," 601f.; idem, *Disorder,* 701f.; graphic examples are given by Lapp, *Revolution,* 85–93.
63. The findings of Tonn, "Kampf," 127–131, also do not suggest that the control committees had any greater importance.
64. LHAM C 20 Ib 5228, fols. 87f. (PP Halle to RP Merseburg, 17 August 1923); SAPMO Ry 1/I 3/11/18, fol. 207 (Complete report by the district leadership about the "Cuno strikes," 21 August 1923). Responding to a report that Proletarian Hundreds had assembled in the stadium of Halle, the police arrested 19 persons on 14 August and confiscated a number of sticks, knuckledusters, and cudgels. The previous day, the police had found 84 walking sticks and a smaller number of stabbing and striking weapons in the building of the Productiv cooperative: LHAM C 20 Ib 4699, fol. 291 (PP Halle to RP Merseburg, 16 August); fol. 287, (PP Halle to RP, 14 August 1923). It is obvious that people were preparing for violence, but this was a far cry from a terrifying weapons arsenal or intensive organizational preparations. See Gast, "Hundertschaften," 455f., who concedes that many members of the units had no interest in political training. Tonn, "Kampf," 131–147, repeats only the contemporary verdict of the district leadership when he attributes the weakness of the Proletarian Hundreds to a "lack of clarity" (145) and "absence of organization" (146) within the party when it came to armed struggle.
65. One example in Ersil, *Aktionseinheit,* 317.
66. LHAM C 20 Ib 1951/VII, fols. 33f. (OP to the Prussian Minister of the Interior, 21 August 1923).
67. Smaller clashes between the police and the strikers occurred in Aschersleben and Calbe; see *VS* no. 193, 21 August; no. 195, 23 August 1923.
68. LHAM C 20 Ib 1951/VII, fol. 27 (OP to the Prussian Minister of the Interior, 21 August 1923); LAMe C 141 Naumburg no. 42, vol. 3, fols. 138–142 (Verdict of district court of Naumburg, 1 March 1924); SAPMO Ry 1/I 3/11/18, fol. 208 (Complete report by the district leadership about the "Cuno strikes," 21 August 1923); Ersil, *Aktionseinheit,* 242–247, on the prehistory see 254–257, 285–287. The statements about the number of demonstrators who had been killed vacillated between nine and eleven, the number of injured demonstrators was given as high as twenty. Several demonstrators were later sentenced to prison terms ranging from several months to two years, and a number of others were acquitted in a retrial after the Reich Court noted flaws in the first verdict (LAMe C 141 Naumburg no. 42, vol. 1–6, the verdict in the retrial in vol. 4).
69. *KK* no. 188, 14 August; no. 181, 6 August; see no. 186, 11 August 1923, where the necessary "reckoning" with Cuno is described as paralleling the "self-help" of hungry workers who were looting the fields.
70. Geyer, "Teuerungsprotest."
71. For example in Genthin, where the group had had a "particularly strong organization" since Anti-Fascist Day, and in Halle. See LHAM C 20 Ib 1951/VII, fol. 6 (LR Jerichow II to OP, 15 August 1923); LHAM C 20 Ib 4699/V, fol. 289 (PP Halle to RP Merseburg, 14 August 1923).
72. SAPMO Ry 1/I 3/11/18, fol. 182 (District leadership of Halle-Merseburg to the central office, 13 August 1923); fol. 206 (Complete report by the district leadership about the "Cuno strikes," 21 August 1923).
73. *KK* no. 194, 21 August 1923.
74. SAPMO Ry 1/I 3/11/18, fols. 210–213 (Complete report by the district leadership about the "Cuno strikes," 21 August 1923); see Angress, *Revolution,* 374f., who puts forth the erroneous view that the influence of the SPD had brought the strike movement to an end. Winkler, *Revolution,* 603f., too, places the emphasis on the political events on the Reich level.
75. SAPMO Ry 1/I 3/11/18, fols. 213–216 (Complete report by the district leadership about the "Cuno strikes," 21 August 1923).
76. This is also pointed out by Mallmann, *Kommunisten,* 206f., though he does not mention the switch to syndicalist groups.

77. This is emphasized by Winkler, *Revolution,* 604.
78. *MZ* no. 400, 11 August; no. 404, 14 August; no. 406, 15 August 1923; *SZ* no. 188, 13 August; no. 189, 14 August; no. 190, 15 August 1923.
79. *VS* no. 187, 14 August; no. 188, 15 August; no. 189, 16 August 1923.
80. *MZ* no. 399, 11 August 1923; *SZ* no. 15, 18 January 1923. See also the detailed analysis of the diffuse protest mood in the summer of 1923 in Geyer, *Verkehrte Welt,* 319ff., esp. 328–345.
81. Winkler, *Revolution,* 619ff.; Angress, *Revolution,* 386f.; Ludewig, *Arbeiterbewegung,* 104ff., 142ff., 200; Wenzel, "Kommunistische Partei," 175ff.
82. Thus the thesis of Winkler, *Revolution,* 652
83. *KK* no. 228, 29 September; no. 231, 3 October; see nos. 235–241, 15 October 1923 (following a one-week ban).
84. *KK* no. 242, 16 October; no. 261, 7 November; no. 263, 9 November 1923. In its issue on Revolution Day, the *Klassenkampf* also pointed out that "the Fascist advance and Jewish pogroms" were "the two sides of one and the same plan of attack by the white hordes against the German working class." The KPD was evidently unsure about how to deal with the anti-Semitism. While the Halle paper distanced itself unambiguously from it, Asmuss, *Republik ohne Chance,* 535–542, has noted that the *Rote Fahne* "ignored it." On attempts by Ruth Fischers and other KPD leaders to use anti-Semitism for their own purposes, see Winkler, *Revolution,* 583f.
85. *KK* no. 263, 9 November; no. 264, 10 November; no. 231, 3 October; no. 271, 19 November 1923.
86. The tactical details and contortions of the Communist agitation have been described in detail elsewhere. See Ludewig, *Arbeiterbewegung,* 104–112, 122–126, 145–151.
87. SAPMO Ry 1/I 3/11/18, fol. 230 (District leadership Halle-Merseburg to the Central Office, 3 October 1923); fol. 262 (District leadership Halle-Merseburg to the Central Office, 10 November 1923).
88. SAPMO Ry 1/I 3/11/31, fol. 38 (Organizational report of the district Halle-Merseburg, 18 November 1923).
89. SAPMO Ry 1/I 3/11/18, fol. 277 (Political report of the district leadership of Halle-Merseburg for the months October to 15 November 1923, no date); fol. 262 (District leadership to the Central Office, 10 November 1923). This impression was confirmed in hindsight by Franz Modler, whom the district leadership had entrusted with the task of building up the hundred-man units. According to his recollections, in the fall of 1923 "only two proletarian hundreds well armed with rifles and Karabiner 98s and 0.8 pistols" had been ready: SAPMO Sq Y 30/2094/1, fol. 73 (Autobiographical recollections of Franz Modler, presumably completed at the beginning of 1985). In the light of this information, the official numbers of the KPD, repeated by Gast, "Proletarischen Hundertschaften," 452, according to which there were 800 Hundreds with about 100,000 members in all of Germany, seems very doubtful. On the military preparations of the KPD see Ludewig, *Arbeiterbewegung,* 200–205; Angress, *Revolution,* 417–425.
90. SAPMO Ry 1/I 3/11/18, fols. 244f. (District leadership of Halle-Merseburg to the Central Office, 29 October 1923); fols. 257f. (District leadership of Halle-Merseburg to the Central Office, 1 November 1923); fol. 261 (District leadership of Halle-Merseburg to the Central Office, 10 November 1923). On the intervention of the Reich government in the Free State of Saxony see Lapp, *Revolution,* 96–103.
91. SAPMO Ry 1/I 3/11/18, fols. 265–269 (Report about district committee meetings, 13 November 1923). According to Koenen, Otto Kilian and a few other speakers pointed out that the "mass flight" from the unions was continuing. See Heer-Kleinert, *Gewerkschaftspolitik,* 230–235, who emphasizes that the attempts by the party leadership to stop the mass exodus from the unions failed also, and precisely, because the party had paid no attention to union work in its concrete plans for an uprising, as a result of which it had moved further away from the mood among the rank and file.

92. On the role of the Pan-German League as an important organization of the radical right in the *Kaiserreich,* see the fundamental study by Roger Chickering, *We Men Who Feel Most German: A Cultural Study of the Pan-German League, 1886–1914* (Boston, 1984), and now most recently Rainer Hering, *Konstruierte Nation: Der Alldeutsche Verband 1890 bis 1939* (Hamburg, 2003).
93. LHAM C 20 Ib 4659 (not paginated, Lord Mayor of Halberstadt to OP, 16 December 1923).
94. Ibid., LR Gardelegen to RP Magdeburg, 24 February 1923; LAG Reg. Erfurt 7427, fols. 143f. (Police report and interrogation records, 31 October and 2 November 1922). The perpetrators were two *Gymnasium* students and one clerk apprentice. On other incidents of violence against Jews in 1923 see Cornelia Hecht, *Deutsche Juden und Antisemitismus in der Weimarer Republik* (Bonn, 2003), 168–186.
95. Stefan Rohrbacher, *Gewalt im Biedermeier: antijüdische Ausschreitungen in Vormärz und Revolution (1815–1848/49)* (Frankfurt, 1993).
96. For example, the extreme right demanded also in Halle the expulsion of "Eastern Jews": LHAM C 20 Ib 4663, fols. 105f. (Police report about a DNVP meeting on 6 February 1923); fols. 170–172 (Police report about a meeting of the Conservative League on 12 November 1923). For a detailed account of such measures in Bavaria and the excesses there in the fall of 1923, see Dirk Walter, *Antisemitische Gewalt und Kriminalität: Judenfeindschaft in der Weimarer Republik* (Bonn, 1999), 52ff., 111ff. On the comments regarding anti-Semitism in the press in the fall of 1923 see Asmuss, *Republik ohne Chance,* 549–551. On the general rise of anti-Semitism in Germany after the war see Werner Jochmann, "Die Ausbreitung des Antisemitismus in Deutschland 1914–1923," in W. Jochmann, *Gesellschaftskrise und Judenfeindschaft in Deutschland 1870–1945* (Hamburg, 1988), 99–170, here esp. 154–163.
97. LHAM C 20 Ib 4689, fol. 75 (PP Magdeburg to OP, 3 October 1923); fol. 64 (RP Erfurt to OP, 18 October 1923).
98. LHAM C 20 Ib 4665/II, fols. 191–212 (Reports about exercises in September 1923); fols. 131f. (LR Nordhausen to OP, 3 October 1923); SAPMO Ry 1/I 3/11/18, fol. 230 (District leadership Halle-Merseburg to the Central Office, 2 October 1923).
99. Examples in LHAM C 20 Ib 5218/II, fol. 29 (PP Halle to RP Merseburg, 19 August 1923); LAG Reg. Erfurt 7427, fol. 233 (Police administration of Langensalza to LR, 13 September 1923); LHAM C 20 Ib 5217/II, fol. 367 (Schupo command Eisleben to RP Merseburg, 28 September 1923); LHAM C 141 Staatsanwaltschaft Halberstadt no. 251.
100. Klotzbücher, "Stahlhelm," 25–27; Berghahn, *Stahlhelm,* 39–53; LHAM C 20 Ib 4689, fol. 58 (PP Magdburg to OP, 8 October 1923).
101. *MZ* no. 463, 14 September; no. 492, 30 September; no. 528, 19 October 1923; *SZ* no. 244, 3 October 1923.
102. *SZ* no. 148, 27 June; no. 261, 6 November; no. 264, 9 November 1923; *MZ* no. 567, 9 November; no. 570, 11 November 1923.
103. On these plans in Bavaria see Geyer, *Verkehrte Welt,* 328ff.
104. *MZ* no. 536, 24 October 1923.
105. *MZ* no. 516, 13 October; no. 508, 9 October 1923.
106. *MZ* no. 570, 11 November 1923.
107. The shift in the position of the *Saale-Zeitung,* especially toward the SPD, can hardly be explained by the change in ownership. Since 1919 the paper had been published by the Mitteldeutsche Verlagsanstalt, a company that was financed largely by Stinnes money and was part of the Hugenberg conglomerate, which was under both DVP and DNVP influence. On this see Heidrun Holzbach, *Das "System Hugenberg": Die Organisation bürgerlicher Sammlungspolitik vor dem Aufstieg der NSDAP* (Stuttgart, 1981), 91.
108. *MZ* no. 463, 16 September 1923; see in general Winkler, *Revolution,* 647; Feldman, *Disorder,* 609ff., 766–769.

109. LHAM C 20 Ib 4613, fols. 237f. (PP Magdeburg to OP, 22 October 1923); *MZ* no. 534, 23 October 1923.
110. *MZ* no. 532, 24 October; no. 532, 21 October 1923; *SZ* no. 253, 27 October 1923.
111. *VS* no. 246, 21 October; no. 247, 23 October; no. 248, 24 October 1923.
112. *MZ* no. 539, 25 October; no. 559, 5 November 1923; *VS* no. 247, 23 October; no. 249, 25 October 1923. See the account of different forms of food protests during the hyperinflation in Klaus Tenfelde, *Proletarische Provinz,* 135–141; idem, "La riscoperta dell' 'autodifesa colletiva.' Protesta sociale in Germania durante l'inflazione del 1923," *Annali dell' Istituto Storico Italo-Germanico Quaderno* 11 (1983): 379–422; Karin Hartewig, *Das unberechenbare Jahrzehnt: Bergarbeiter und ihre Familien im Ruhrgebiet 1914–1924* (Munich, 1993), 237–240.
113. On the participants in Magdeburg see LHAM C 20 Ib 4613, fols. 239–242 (Attachment to the report of the police president of Halle, 22 October 1923); see the case of field looting in Zeitz on 11 August 1923 (LAMe C 141 Naumburg no. 44), following which 69 defendants were brought before the court; they included 45 women and were born between 1866 and 1905; all were acquitted.
114. LHAM C 20 Ib 4663, fols. 176f. (PP Halle to RP Merseburg, 12 October 1923).
115. Thus the accurate main thesis of Geyer, "Teuerungsprotest," esp. 393.

Part III

Years of Calm? Political Violence 1924–1929

After 1921, political violence was above all a phenomenon that accompanied mobilization at the margins of the political spectrum. Whether it actually erupted depended also on situational factors. It was, however, accompanied by commentaries that reveal just how deeply an unspoken consensus about the legitimacy of violence had already penetrated into the political culture. And nothing would change this pattern during the putatively quiet years between 1924 and 1929. What is more, while there were hardly any spectacular incidents of violence to record, the continuity of violence on a small scale continued unabated, with its organizational basis solidifying and the references to violence in the political language intensifying. Well before the outbreak of the global economic crisis, the foundations of Weimar democracy had eroded, which was most evident in the decline of the liberal parties. This erosion was also driven forward by political violence; however, this violence still had clear limits and was not about to turn into civil war.

Chapter 6

The Rise of the Combat Leagues (*Wehrverbände*)

Bloody Prelude: German Day in Halle, 11 May 1924

One week after the Reichstag elections of 4 May 1924, which had brought striking losses to the parties of the middle and equally striking gains for the radical parties, especially those on the right, the events of 11 May in Halle demonstrated that violence would remain an element of political conflicts. The struggle over terrain and symbols that had developed since 1921 continued, and new organizations of the left soon became involved.

It was no coincidence that the city of Halle became the site of bloody clashes that left eight people dead. Following a bomb attack on the Kaiser Wilhelm monument the previous year,[1] the Moltke sculpture had been restored and was scheduled to be unveiled in a festive ceremony. The right-wing Combat Leagues and veterans' groups wanted to obliterate the disgrace that the bombing had inflicted on "patriotic circles." Following the end of the state of emergency across Germany and the elections, 11 May was the first possible date for the unveiling. Not only would the dishonor be expunged, but the strength that the radical right had by now attained could be publicly displayed. In Halle itself, the DNVP, the party of Stahlhelm leader Duesterberg, had won 24.3 percent of the votes, and the DVFP 7.6 percent; together, they had thus overtaken all other parties in the city, including the KPD, which polled 27.6 percent.[2] Moreover, the right-wing parade was a test of the movement's ability to assert itself against the Prussian authorities. After the state of emergency had been lifted, the government decreed a country-wide prohibition against open-air rallies and marches for the duration of the election campaign, and this prohibition was still in force for the province of Saxony. However, on orders from the German National Reich Minister of the Interior, the authorities had authorized a ceremony at the monument itself and

Notes from this chapter begin on page 164.

another one at a site outside the city, though on the condition that no organized marches be held.[3]

It was soon obvious that "German Day" would be an event of more than local significance. Since the middle of March, the right-leaning press throughout the Reich had been calling upon its readers to travel to Halle. The response was strong, and the number of participants exceeded the expectations of both the organizers and the authorities. The *Saale-Zeitung* estimated that there were more than 100,000, and 3,000 banners were carried along, according to information provided by the police.[4] While only local notables from the DNVP and the DVP made appearances, the presence of the former admirals Schröder and Scheer, Count Luckner, the retired generals Mackensen and Ludendorff, Free Corps leader Maercker, and Prince Oscar of Prussia attested to the importance that the military associations and veterans' organizations accorded this event.[5] In addition, many retired officers attended the ceremony dressed in uniform and steel helmets; the Reichswehr, too, had sent a delegation, without informing the authorities. The streets of Halle were festooned "abundantly, but not excessively" in banners of black-white-red.[6] The city was firmly in "patriotic" hands.

The ceremony itself went off without any larger incident. Duesterberg, who delivered the address, in recalling the bomb attack of the previous year, was not content to launch a sharp attack against its "intellectual authors," but also underscored—with remarkable frankness—that the act had provided the impulse in "all national circles" to take up the "struggle over equal treatment in the street." He noted with satisfaction: "The red terror has been successfully combated … in numerous clashes!"[7] The domestic political purpose of the Combat Leagues—to secure the right wing the necessary presence in the public arena—had thus been clearly articulated. Duesterberg did not even bother to make a special effort to conceal their activities as exclusively defensive, but allowed the offensive component to shine through as well.

During the second part of German Day, the differences between the "patriotic" groups became apparent. The marching troops were to be reviewed by Field Marshal Mackensen, though he had to bow out on short notice because of an accident and was replaced by the physically frail Colonel Heeringen, the former Prussian Minister of War and now chairman of the Kyffhäuser Association. After an hour, the exhausted Heeringen had to be carried off the field. Ludendorff, who was in command of the Bavarian participants, some of whom had shown up with swastika flags, now took his place, thus stepping into a position of prominence that was not welcomed by all. The *Saale-Zeitung*, however, gave him prominent coverage in its report about the "largest parade in Germany," thus demonstrating that the right wing in Halle no longer held the general's behavior in the coup attempt in November 1923 against him.[8] All in all, though, the *völkisch* organizations kept in the background. German Day brought together what was fundamentally the monarchist, Prussian-Protestant part of the right wing, not affiliated with any party, for one of its largest rallies. Duesterberg's blatant embrace of the violent street battle is therefore all the more remarkable.

By and large, however, there were no clashes between participants and their political opponents. Only in the morning had there been a small brawl at one place in the center of town and an exchange of gunfire between a counterdemonstrator and a police officer. The police, however, were able to prevent a column of 250 demonstrators from clashing with the participants; two people were injured when the demonstrators were dispersed by force.[9] While the better part of the police was dealing with the Communist demonstrators at the outskirts of the city, the right-wing associations, as they were leaving the square, now formed their parade into a few organized groups and carried unfurled flags. Given the large number of participants and the relative weakness of the security forces, this violation of the conditions imposed by the authorities had to be tolerated. The right-wing groups had achieved a complete success and had controlled Halle for a day.

Several weeks before German Day, the Communist press had already begun with propaganda for a counter-event. The Halle police president had outlawed a parade to celebrate May Day. As was to be expected, open-air rallies and marches for a planned "general German workers' day" were also prohibited. Still, the *Klassenkampf* continued to call for a large counterdemonstration and disseminated a kind of marching plan a few days before the event. In the process, the Communist paper picked up on the rhetoric of the final battle from the previous years, though it infused that rhetoric with a defensive note. The attempt, according to the paper, was "a final test of strength before the monarchist coup," in response to which 11 May had to become "the end to the advance of the reaction and the beginning of a victorious advance of the workers."[10] The KPD set its sights on two opponents: first, the assembled right wing, among whom it singled out the "*völkisch* Fascist groups" as especially dangerous; second, international, organized capitalism, whose intention was to make Germany into a staging ground against the Soviet Union with the help of the Dawes Plan, the "enslavement plan of the experts." This alluded also to the losses that, by all indications, the workers would suffer from the end of inflation, and it underlined the importance that attached to the appearance of the counterdemonstrators in Halle. As another reason for the necessity of resolute resistance to German Day, the *Klassenkampf* singled out the revolutionary tradition of central Germany. Its working class must "neither forget nor deny" that tradition, but had to prevent "Halle from becoming the final pillar of the Fascist triumph."[11] The suggestion here was that politics had in essence not changed since the failure of the plans for putsch and revolution in the fall of 1923.

Communist propaganda did not describe in detail the means that should be used to counter the parade of the right-wing organizations. This time, it was said, one would "not stand idly by and watch the impertinent and brutal provocation" but would "assert by force the right to the street," words that emphasized the willingness of one's own side to do battle and let the enemy know that offensive action was coming. These kinds of pronouncements were nothing new. What was new, however, was that the numerous articles in the run-up to 11 May contained a number of references to what was alleged to be the other side's particularly high willingness to engage in violence. "Fighting troops" had supposedly been set up to defend against attacks by workers; on 6 May, the paper also claimed that these troops were armed. In a circular that the Halle district leadership sent to all subdivisions of the party on the same day, it therefore demanded that all counterdemonstrators, "considering the long march, equip themselves with sturdy walking sticks," and that all "Fascists" who behaved provocatively should "be sent packing with the utmost ruthlessness." During the following days, note was made of special orders of rubber truncheons for the enemy organizations, and of their alleged orders to use not only striking weapons but also firearms—though later no indications of such orders could be found.[12] A meeting on 7 May between the police president and four leaders of the Halle KPD, to make the official prohibitions clear to them once again and to prevail upon them to honor them, that is, to make sure they limited the Communist counter-rally to the hall of the "Volkspark," was unsuccessful, as the articles in the *Klassenkampf* revealed over the following days.[13] It was clear that the leadership of the KPD was out for a test of strength and accepted at least the possibility of bloodshed.

The counter-rally by the Communists, however, turned into a fiasco. Although workers from more distant regions had followed the call to appear, their total number was probably barely 10,000. Marshals from the KPD that had been stationed at the Halle train station withdrew without offering any resistance when the police showed up. The center of the city lacked the expected demonstrators from the local working class, whose quarter was not festooned with red flags as the party leadership had asked. The exceedingly weak response to the leadership's directives stands in striking contrast to the success in the elections only a week earlier, when nearly 30,000 voters had cast their ballots for the KPD as an expression of their protest against the distribution of the burden of overcoming inflation.

The real confrontation with the police developed outside the gates of the city. Starting on the afternoon of 10 May, larger groups of counterdemonstrators had arrived to spend the night in various towns and villages on the outskirts of Halle. While the police were able to prevail upon most of them to leave, on the morning of 11 May a larger column formed southeast of Halle, composed of Leipzig workers and other counterdemonstrators. The police initially directed them to Ammendorf, from where the approximately 2,000 demonstrators tried to reach the center of the city in a closed formation. At Böllberg, eight police officers tried to block their further progress. Although they had bayonets planted and issued several threats to use their weapons, they were not able to stop the marchers. The officers slowly retreated for about 100 meters. Suddenly, a shot was fired. The police line was overrun, reinforcements arrived on the scene, and a firefight of approximately forty minutes ensued, during which several demonstrators and several police officers were killed and others wounded.[14] 467 demonstrators were briefly arrested; all but one were released again after a few days. A search of the arrested workers produced guns, knives, and clubs, and a search of the area at the Böllberg found four hand grenades.

Needless to say, the police maintained that the first shot had come from the ranks of the demonstrators. Remarkably enough, however, the *Klassenkampf*, in its account of the battle, avoided a clear statement, and an anonymous KPD functionary, who dealt with the events in a report to the district leadership, spoke only of a failed "breakthrough" and criticized various shortcomings among the "attackers." The position of the police is therefore entirely plausible in this case, to which we must add that, according to the police, whereas there were hardly any demonstrators at the Böllberg there were certainly marshals from Halle, who, according to a statement from an Erfurt Communist who was later arrested, were to divide the workers into companies. This also lends credence to the conclusion of the police that "a violent clash was expected from the beginning, and that for that purpose people were used who, ignorant of the balance of forces, marched blindly into disaster." The report from the KPD district leadership for its part found fault with the attackers for being unaware that reinforcements were posted behind the first, small line of police officers, and it criticized in general the inadequate preparations for the fight as well as the incompetence of the leadership and the poor fighting discipline of many workers. Thus it must remain speculation whether the bloody disaster was intentionally brought about by the KPD leadership in Berlin and in the district, or whether it was the result of a poorly prepared attack on the police. It seems certain, though, that the party leadership wanted a confrontation that would lead to casualties on the Communist side, whom their propaganda could then present as new heroes and martyrs.[15]

The assessment of the events was not long in coming. The following day, a Monday, the *Klassenkampf* opened with the headline "From blood and wounds to a new struggle." This allusion to the Passion of Christ was picked up again at a central place in the following article, which declared that the blood of the dead "is on the heads of the Social Democratic protectors of the Republic, Runge, Bergemann, Hörsing, and Severing." The thrust of the article, a mixture of report and appeal, was thus clear. Its primary target was not the Combat Leagues marching in the streets but the Social Democratic officeholders who had provoked the workers and thus triggered the "civil war against the supporters of the Republic." The demonstrators, who had opposed the "blood work of the Social Democratic-*völkisch*-national fascism," were proclaimed to be the real Republicans. At the same time, they were turned into heroes: forced into a battle, they had few weapons at their disposal, and yet they held out "heroically" and supposedly "for 2 1/2 hours … against a superior force a thousand times larger." But the "sacred proletarian blood" was not to have been shed in vain, the "heavy sacrifice of blood" not to have been for nothing. The article drew a line from the fighting in 1919 to the Communist electoral success at the beginning of May and the continuing lockouts in the Ruhr mining industry,[16] as a result of which it saw "avengers arising … by the thousands." However, the KPD did not even call for a protest strike, but was content with a general appeal to "complete the armaments for the final battle." No mention whatsoever was made of establishing a new organization, as would happen a few months later with the Red Front Fighters' League.[17] Thus, the primary purpose of the *Klassenkampf*'s reaction to the events was to assert the course that the ultra-leftist party leadership, in power since the beginning of April, was charting,[18] to stake out a position sharply opposed to the SPD, which was now accused of "social fascism," and at the same time to maintain its own supporters in a constant fighting mood. The bourgeois press reported in detail about German Day itself, but dealt only very briefly with the clash at Böllberg. A few days later, however, the *Saale-Zeitung* did take the events as an occasion to articulate, in two long articles, the kind of fundamental and vehement criticism of the Communists that the paper had hardly ever before voiced. The German people had "two enemies" and "must therefore fight against two fronts: outside, the Entente; inside, the Communist," the paper bluntly declared at the beginning of the lead article, which then focused on conditions in Russia. That country, readers were told, was in the thrall of a de facto tyranny, worse than earlier Asiatic despotisms, while the seductive slogans of the regime were mere deception, like the demands of the French Revolution propagated by Napoleon. The German Communists functioned only as the executive organs of a regime that was responsible for the "greatest theft of human rights known to human history" and was able to sustain itself only by force. The second article, in the form of fictitious speech, addressed what the *Klassenkampf* had caricatured a few days before as "cabbage-heads and fat-heads" who had greeted German Day with enthusiasm. It warned against cowardice and weakness in dealing with the Communists, who had "as little mercy with you and your women as they had with the poor Countess Hella von Westarp and the other hostages that were butchered by human jackals during the soviet regime in Munich." Ruthless action was called for: all Communist delegates should be put on trial for high treason, for they followed the directives of a foreign power, and locked up, "as should be done with all dangerous criminals and the insane"; that was the only way to bring the supporters to their senses.[19] Here, again, were assembled the topoi that had been used to attack the Communists since 1919: their anti-national attitude, their criminal character, which placed them outside the legal order, and the bloody traits of the Soviet dictatorship. The *Saale-Zeitung* did not address how great the immediate danger posed by the KPD was, whether it was necessary to take "self-help" against it, or what role the Combat Leagues that had just been parading would play in all this. The chief purpose of the two articles was to keep the picture of the Communist enemy from fading away now that the fears and hopes of the radical right had not materialized in the fall of 1923.

The *Volksstimme,* by contrast, sought to clarify, first of all, who was to blame for the bloody clash outside Halle; of course, this angle aimed not least to take the pressure off Social Democratic department chiefs who were responsible for the police. The paper assigned the lion's share of blame to the machinations of the "reactionaries around Ludendorff" and then to German National Reich Minister of the Interior Jarres, who had applied a "double standard" by allowing those who shared his views to engage in the demonstrations he prohibited to the workers. A substantial portion of the blame was also assigned to the new course of the Communists. The *Volksstimme,* too, spoke of a "provocation," though the workers were provoked not by the police, but by the parading of the "counter-revolution." However, the latter could not be fought with "rifles and blackjacks" as the KPD wanted, but only, as the Social Democratic paper concluded, with a "unified workers' movement."[20] A day later, the front page of the paper featured a new organization that the SPD had helped establish shortly before. The senior Saxon police officer Schützinger lamented the events in Halle as a "lost battle for the Republic" and encouraged participation in the Reichsbanner. He assigned two tasks to this organization: first, it had to serve Republican self-representation in forms that could compete with the right-wing groups; second, it had to be available as auxiliary troops to help the Republican police fight against a coup, and for that reason it should be given military and police training.[21]

The Republican Countermobilization: The Reichsbanner Schwarz-Rot-Gold

Schützinger's comments described precisely the two goals of the Reichsbanner Schwarz-Rot-Gold, Bund republikanischer Kriegsteilnehmer (Reich Banner Black-Red-Gold: League of Republican War Veterans), founded in Magdeburg on 22 February 1924. As Karl Rohe has noted in his fundamental study, there was no compelling necessity for the new organization to be set up in the capital of the province of Saxony, but neither was it an accident.[22] Magdeburg was the seat of the Stahlhelm, the main opponent and therefore in some respects also the model for the Reichsbanner, while not-too-distant Halle, with the more radical Stahlhelm group and the Wehrwolf, was another center of right-wing Combat Leagues. But Magdeburg was also a bastion of moderate Social Democracy, whose many members and voters provided a recruiting basis for an organization that was decidedly Republican, open also to bourgeois members, but above any suspicion of cooperating with the Communists.

Here, as elsewhere, the roots of the Reichsbanner can be traced back much further. The Republikanische Notwehr (Republican Self-Defense) had first appeared publicly in Magdeburg on 15 April 1923. Fifteen units of one hundred men each paraded past Oberpräsident Hörsing under the leadership of the political editor of the *Volksstimme,* Karl Höltermann. In his brief speech, Höltermann explained that the Notwehr was an "organ of the Social Democratic party … that extends over the entire province of Saxony, does not arrogate any policing or military authority, but simply intends to protect the Republic with all means available if the legitimate government calls upon it."[23] This organization thus saw itself not as a force providing protection for meetings or as propaganda auxiliaries for the party, but as a kind of police reserve in case of a putsch, which in April 1923 was surely expected to come from the right rather than the left. The reach of the Notwehr indicated by Höltermann was undoubtedly an exaggeration. It would appear that units existed above all in the Börde counties of Calbe and Wanzleben, in the more northerly country Jerichow I, and also in Aschersleben and Staßfurt, as well as in rural and urban regions of the administrative district of Magdeburg in which the SPD was particularly strong.[24] In the summer and fall of 1923, however, they did not make any meaningful public appearance. There is no evidence of any links to the proletarian hundreds that were active—though not very strong—in the administrative district of Merseburg. The Republikanische Notwehr was an organization set up merely to defend against a putsch; otherwise it had no function. This would change with the Reichsbanner, as Schützinger's statement already indicated. The new group had a genuinely political task from the very beginning: to finally allow the Republicans to assert the kind of presence in the public sphere that for many years only their enemies had commanded. Externally this was underscored not least by the fact that the founding meeting in February 1924 took place only about a month after the Front Line Veterans' Day of the Stahlhelm in Magdeburg, a turnout by the right wing that was accompanied by scuffles with the police.[25] Defense against a putsch took a back seat to this purpose of the organization. Scholars have so far probably underestimated that the Reichsbanner also had the function of offering veterans from the ranks of Social Democratic workers a space to cultivate their war memories, though this was always a secondary purpose.[26]

This is not contradicted by the fact that the Magdeburg founders of the Reichsbanner were mostly men, some of them highly decorated, who had spent the war at the front lines. That is true not least of Höltermann, who was the real driving force and acted first as the vice-chairman, and after 1932 as the federal chairman. It also applies to Gustav Ferl, the district secretary of the SPD, and to Dr. Horst Baerensprung, also a member of the SPD and later police president of Magdeburg. Oberpräsident Otto Hörsing, the first federal chairman, had also served in the war as a sergeant and commander of a prisoner-of-war camp. This list already makes clear that here, unlike in the case of the Stahlhelm, it was not "nameless" veterans distinguished only by their Republican sentiment that were coming together, but primarily the holders of important party and state offices, mostly from the ranks of the SPD—the major exception was Magdeburg Regierungspräsident Pohlmann, a member of the DDP. This points to the primarily political thrust of the organization from the time of its founding.[27]

The sources provide hardly any information about the growth of the Reichsbanner in the province of Saxony or about its organization and membership structure there. Because the leadership of the organization was in substantial part identical with the top administrative levels in the administrative district of Magdeburg, there was no cause to have it watched by the police. But also, the Reichsbanner as an organization was rarely put on record when cases of political violence were noted, and even its individual members on the whole did not end up in the files very often. The Reichsbanner did not become a prime target of either the right-wing Combat Leagues or the Communists,[28] but neither did it operate offensively against other organizations. Its marches, flag consecrations, and the Republican Days it helped to organize did not develop into scenes of larger physical confrontations with political opponents. Moreover, its activity as a protection force for meetings and as a propaganda troop was largely devoid of the kind of willingness to engage in violence that characterized the other organizations. This would change somewhat after 1930, but not fundamentally. Yet the organization was certainly able to mobilize large masses. For example, the pan-German meeting at the end of February 1925 drew well over 100,000 members to Magdeburg.[29] To be sure, the Reichsbanner further militarized the outward appearance of politics, galvanized the radical right in its attempts to control public space, and provided the Communists with a model of how to successfully build up a Combat League. However, given its restraint and largely defensive posture, it only made a very limited direct contribution to the continuity of political violence.[30]

Communist Reactions

The KPD found itself in a dilemma in 1924. With the lifting of the state of emergency at the end of February, it was quite clear that a revolutionary situation no longer existed in Germany, and that the KPD would not be able any time soon to achieve what it had failed to accomplish in October 1923. On the other hand, in the Reichstag elections at the beginning of May it was able to expand its position as a proletarian mass party alongside the SPD, achieving a top result in the district of Halle-Merseburg. More than 180,000 ballots were cast for the party, giving it an impressive share of 25.7 percent of the vote.

However, compared with the Prussian Landtag elections at the beginning of 1921—the first election after the formation of the VKPD—the picture is much less clear. Almost everywhere the KPD now failed to garner as many votes as in 1921, even with a substantially higher number of voters overall. In decided strongholds like the Saalkreis and the Mansfelder Seekreis the party dropped about by ten points (from 50.1 percent to 41.3 percent and from 47.9 percent to 34.0 percent, respectively), in County Bitterfeld by three (1921: 36.7 percent, 1924 I: 33.3 percent). But it also lost in weaker counties like Liebenwerda (1921: 26.9 percent, 1924 I: 24.9 percent) and Wittenberg (1921: 26.4 percent, 1924 I: 26.1 percent). It could post gains only where the remnant USPD had still been the strongest workers' party in 1921, for example in County Zeitz (1921: 10.7 percent; 1924 I: 16.6 percent). The same was true for the former USPD strongholds in the administrative district of Erfurt, though the KPD was not able to generally overtake the SPD here, and for the electoral district of Magdeburg, though the KPD did win 10.1 percent there.[31] The KPD had thus consolidated itself overall at a somewhat lower level; moreover, its losses compared to 1921 were greatest precisely where the failed "March action" had brought home to many workers the dangers of the offensive strategy. In spite of the unsettled recent years and the emerging stabilization crisis, the Communists were not as unchallenged as it might have appeared at first glance, even in one of their strongholds.

Although the founding of the Reichsbanner did not create a serious competitor in the heart of the central German industrial region, it did show generally how it was possible, under the conditions of a gradually stabilizing political situation, to successfully counter the right wing's attempt to control the street. If the KPD wanted to continue to attract masses instead of merely winning the protest votes of radicalized workers during elections, it had to respond in a similar way. The answer came in the form of the Roter Frontkämpferbund (RFB, Red Front Fighters' League). Contrary to what East German scholarship long suggested, its founding was by no means a direct reaction to the "bloody Sunday" of Halle, nor was it instigated "from below," as it were.[32] To be sure, the first local group of the RFB did in fact form in Halle, but the call to set up the organization, published in the *Klassenkampf* on 29 July 1924, made no mention whatsoever of the events two months earlier. Rather, we hear first of the "thousands of workers" who were still allowing themselves to be abused in the national organizations or misled by the pacifistic phrases of the Reichsbanner; they all are urged instead to join an organization that was fighting consistently against a new "imperialist world war." The second chief criticism of the other organizations was aimed at their structure. They were being led by officers who had harassed the workers during the war and had evaded the dangers of the front line as "rear-echelon pigs" (*Etappenschweine*). The only remedy for this was a true "workers' front-line veterans' league." As the goals of such an organization the appeal mentioned, first of all, cultivating "class consciousness and … war memories," and secondly, preserving the interests of disabled veterans and surviving dependents.[33] In this way one point of criticism—shared by most workers—about abuses in the army during the war was skillfully combined with core issues of Communist propaganda and with the promise of representing the interests of war victims and their social entitlements. The competition with other organizations is obvious, as is the effort to mobilize workers for the cause of the party beyond the closer circle of party supporters.[34]

Did this new organization of the KPD in fact enjoy the great success that scholarship has attributed to it?[35] In the founding district of Halle, the RFB seemed to be developing very well from the perspective of the party. By November 1924, the 400 members of the first local group in Halle had grown to ten times that number throughout the entire district; in March 1925, it had more than 6,500 members, and by September more than 7,000.[36] In 1928, the district had more than eighteen Untergaue with 144 local groups.[37] The opposition to the new organization within the party, emanating from the remnants of a clandestine military organization, the M-Apparat, which saw in the RFB the emergence of a competitor acting with the wrong means, had too small a basis.[38]

For the authorities, however, the picture was somewhat different. Only at the end of April 1925 did the Regierungspräsident of Merseburg note clear growth in the new organization. He originally had feared that the strict discipline of the RFB and the questions about previous military service rank suggested a new fighting organization analogous to the proletarian hundreds, though he did not repeat that concern later.[39] The authorities evidently saw no need to place the

RFB under closer observation. Until the end of 1924, no significant clashes with the police or the other military associations were recorded; even after that, reports emphasized the calm way in which the RFB's events were conducted.[40] RFB Day at the end of June 1925 in Magdeburg—in the "Diaspora," so to speak—for which the KPD assembled participants from all over the Reich, went off without any disturbances; ahead of the event the police had arranged agreements with the Stahlhelm and the Reichsbanner. Only 2,500–3,000 people, among them a strikingly large number of women and "young lads," marched through the streets, and red flags were rare in the working-class districts.[41] All in all, the RFB in the administrative district of Magdeburg was not able to confront the Reichsbanner with a potent organization of its own, even though the RFB had seventy-two local groups there by 1928.[42]

In the administrative district of Merseburg, the RFB enjoyed a more favorable position from the outset. At the end of 1926, the KPD district leadership regarded its rivals on the left as "very weak" and reported with satisfaction that a number of members of the Reichsbanner had demonstrated alongside the Communists during the referendum on the expropriation of the nobility, which had been jointly organized by the SPD and the KPD. But even shortly afterward, in spite of serious tensions within the Reichsbanner surrounding the resignation from the organization of Chancellor Marx (from the Center Party), the RFB was not able to lure members away from its competitor organization.[43] Evidently the slogan about a "unity front from below" propagated by the KPD, only briefly replaced during the referendum by agreement with the Social Democrats, did not make any headway against the Reichsbanner even where the KPD was the proletarian majority party and the SPD's internal resistance to cooperation with the Communists had begun to loosen.[44] The reason does not seem to have been the "battering tactics" of the RFB toward the Reichsbanner, repeatedly criticized elsewhere. On the other hand, members of the RFB and the Reichsbanner did cooperate informally to thwart the right-wing military associations.[45] All in all, the RFB was able to win members only within the immediate environs of the KPD.[46] It filled a gap in the Communist organizational network that had become apparent after the founding of the Reichsbanner. It provided, first, a forum for the exchange of war experiences, and second, an organizational backbone for the fight over terrain that had developed in the previous years. At the same time, the connection of the RFB to the Communist Party was so obvious that its attraction did not extend much beyond the party's own supporters.

The KPD was able to consolidate itself again in the province after the period of illegality in 1923/24, though it never again attained the membership numbers it had had at the height of the general crisis in the fall of 1923 or even before the "March action" at the beginning of 1921. The district leadership of Halle-Merseburg reported 11,181 members for September 1925, only about half as many as there had been two years before.[47] In the following years, party membership in the district settled down at around 10,000, in spite of larger fluctuations. At the end of 1926 it briefly passed the 11,000 mark, only to quickly drop back to 9,500. Although the referendum on the expropriation of the nobility had brought the workers' parties as a whole about 50,000 extra votes in comparison with the Reichstag elections in December 1924, the KPD added only about 500 new members. Between August and October 1928, the party was able to win 892 new members; in January 1929, membership was just below 12,000. By the end of the year it had fallen to a little over 9,000, only to rise once again to 12,000 at the beginning of 1930 and then drop just as quickly to below 10,000.[48] It would appear that the recruitment reservoir for party membership had clearly circumscribed boundaries.

What is also remarkable about these figures, however, is their relative constancy, which expresses a certain immunity toward the battles over the Bolshevization of the KPD that were raging within the party at this time. While the leftist opposition in its various flavors exerted no meaningful influence in the district of Halle-Merseburg, though it did gain control for some time of the Suhl KPD organ *Volkswille* in the neighboring district of Thuringia, Halle-Merseburg turned into a stronghold of the "reconcilers (*Versöhnler*)." This grouping of the party's right wing around Ernst Meyer, Hugo Eberlein, and the temporary district leader Georg Schumann, while accepting the leadership role of the Communist Party of the Soviet Union within the Comintern, supported the course of realpolitik pursued since 1926/27 and opposed Thälmann's radical line, which had prevailed in 1928.[49] When the conflict over the "reconcilers" reached its climax in 1928/29 and ended with their loss of power in late April 1929 at a district party meeting in Halle, all in all this does not seem to have had a significant influence on the development of membership. Although the number of members briefly dropped from 12,000 to 9,000 after the defeat of the "reconcilers," that only put it at the level it had had since the middle of 1928. But even before that, the district leadership had to admit to a strong fluctuation in membership, though it blamed this only on organizational shortcomings in party work.[50] In addition to a core of long-term members, a great many others bound themselves to the party only for a brief period.

An ambiguous picture also emerged when the KPD tried to mobilize the masses for commemorative days and campaigns. In 1925 the authorities recorded only 700 participants at a rally in Magdeburg for Communists killed during the March fighting in 1919, 1920, and 1921 and noted the weak response to a "school struggle week" in March 1925 in Halle, which took place only a few days before the election of the Reich president.[51] Turnout for the March commemorations in 1928 was particularly sparse in the administrative district of Merseburg, compared to the party's propaganda effort. For example, no rally took place at all in the Mansfelder Gebirgskreis, even though there was reason enough here to remember the "dead of March."[52] The same impression was conveyed by the anti-war rallies in the first week of August 1928, where, among others, Max Hoelz, who had just been released from prison, made an appearance. The Regierungspräsident of Merseburg noted that participation had been "low," the behavior of the spectators had been "generally reserved," and the result of the collection for "Red Aid" had been modest.[53]

The KPD district leadership, for its part, congratulated itself on the success of its March festivities in Leuna in 1927: 6,000 RFB members supposedly came out to march, and with them several thousand party members.[54] In 1929 it highlighted the great participation in the rallies on 1 May: about 10,000 workers had come out in Halle, 2,000 in Weißenfels, 1,400 each in Bitterfeld and Hettstedt. However, the assumption that this reflected also a special solidarity with the workers of Berlin, where the Social Democratic police president had, after all, imposed a prohibition against demonstrations, was deceptive. While it is true that protest rallies were held at many places throughout the district after the bloody fighting there, protest strikes were successful only in smaller enterprises in Halle, whereas the brown coal mines and the large chemical factories continued operating. One Leuna protest meeting "was by no means equal to the work force of several thousand." After the outlawing of the RFB, the party called for eight protest demonstrations, "though only two of these had reasonably good participation."[55] The willingness of workers who sympathized with the KPD to stand up for something that they did not regard as part of their own immediate interests was evidently weak.

The SPD members in the district drew a clear line of separation from the KPD, even though it briefly faded somewhat in the wake of the campaign for the referendum in 1926. This went so far that in Zeitz, for example, Social Democrats and Communists used different dressing and breakfast rooms or rode in separate compartments in the trains to the Leuna Works.[56] The result of the KPD's work in the factories was itself mixed. The formation of factory cells, something the party leadership had repeatedly demanded, just did not work, and it proved a "debacle" also in the province of Saxony.[57] However, the situation was different when it came to the KPD's influence on the unions. At the end of 1924, the union division in the district of Halle-Merseburg looked back on a difficult year. At the beginning of the year, the unions had suffered serious setbacks. The surging unemployment, especially in brown coal mining, which was affected by rationalization, led many workers to leave the unions and many employers to once again make membership in the Stahlhelm or the Wehrwolf a condition of employment. At the same time, the ADGB proceeded to attack Communist influence in the local union committees by dissolving the district committee of Halle-Merseburg in March and merging it with the committee of Magdeburg-Anhalt. At the end of the year, however, the KPD had succeeded in winning majorities in seventeen local committees, including Eisleben, Eilenburg, Weißenfels, and Querfurt.[58] The Communists reported further successes in 1927 and 1928. They now held the majority in the works councils of most metalworking enterprises in Halle and in the mining industry in the Mansfelder Land. Only Zeitz remained a bastion of the Social Democrats.[59]

After the 12th Party Congress in June 1929, which sealed a return to an ultraleftist policy and agreed—when it came to the unions—on a course of division and support for the Revolutionäre Gewerkschaftsopposition (RGO, Revolutionary Union Opposition), the limits of the influence of the KPD became apparent. A month later, the district leadership noted with disappointment that the union elections in the spring had brought no "meaningful increase in the positions held by us" and lamented a lack of commitment by party members when it came to union work. Members were behaving in a compromising manner toward the SPD and were capitulating to the "dictate of the bureaucracy." Moreover, district leadership detected a generational clash. The older union functionaries of the KPD were ensconced in their positions and blocking the rise of younger ones, thus reducing the general interest in union work.[60] The district leadership was unwilling to admit the real reason for the stagnation of Communist influence. During the years of KPD realpolitik in the mid 1920s, its union activity had been directed at the immediate interests of the workers and was rewarded correspondingly. By contrast, the change in course in the party's relationship to the unions, carried out under Thälmann long before the outbreak of the global economic crisis, failed to persuade the workers.[61]

The successes of the Communist realpolitik were undoubtedly also one reason behind the results the KPD achieved in the Reichstag elections during the middle years of the Weimar Republic. In December 1924 the KPD first lost some of the gains it had made in May. In the electoral district of Merseburg it lost about 20,000 votes and dropped three percentage points to 22.6 percent, while the SPD gained about the same number of votes. The party suffered setbacks also in the electoral district of Magdeburg and in the administrative district of Erfurt. But in May 1928, when both workers' parties were more successful than their bourgeois competitors at mobilizing their own supporters, the KPD posted clear gains. In the electoral district of Merseburg it garnered 176,113 votes, 12,000 more than in December 1924, which gave it 24.4 percent. However, the SPD was not far behind at 23.8 percent, which marked a difference of only 4,000 votes. A clear deviation from the general trend occurred only in the urban and rural county Zeitz, where the SPD was now able to succeed the USPD: in the urban county it even won more than 52 percent of the votes; the KPD, by contrast, suffered substantial losses at 8.6 percent and 9.2 percent, respectively. In the electoral district of Magdeburg as well, the KPD was able to post slight gains over December 1924 and now reached 7.2 percent, while the SPD reclaimed its old position with even stronger gains and a result of 43.0 percent. In the administrative district of Erfurt, by contrast, the KPD lost votes across the board, most dramatically in County Schleusingen, where it dropped from 38 percent to only 16.2 percent and had to relinquish leadership once again to the SPD, which now won 40.1 percent of the votes.[62] All in all, the KPD continued to have a considerable following in the province of Saxony during the period of relative stability for the Weimar Republic. However, while these followers certainly supported a course of limited participation in the political process that respected its rules, it proved difficult to mobilize them for party actions that attracted attention on the public stage.

Leadership Change on the Right: From the Stahlhelm to the Nazi Movement

The Stahlhelm continued to expand its organization throughout Germany between 1924 and 1929. In May 1924, the Landsturm Der Stahlhelm (Home Reserve Stahlhelm) was set up. It comprised men lacking front line experience but too old for the Jungstahlhelm, which meant that men from all age groups, veterans or not, could become members of the organization. By 1928/29, the postwar generation made up about half of all members in all divisions of the Stahlhelm. Among the new auxiliary organizations was the Stahlhelm Selbsthilfe (Stahlhelm Self-Help) created in Halle in 1928, a workers' organization that followed in the footsteps of the "yellow" unions[63] and helped to solidify the position of the group in various areas of the central German industrial region. The organizational expansion was accompanied by a rise in membership: at the beginning of 1927, it was 200–300,000 throughout the Reich, and by 1930 it had grown slightly larger. The Stahlhelm had thus definitively established itself as by far the largest of the "national" organizations in Germany.[64] The Wehrwolf, too, which broke from the Stahlhelm completely in 1924/25 and was now competing with it, was able to recruit new members and reached 40–50,000. With the establishment of the Jungwolf (Youngwolf) in 1925, it created a separate sub-organization for fourteen- to seventeen-year-olds. In addition, it set up a Wehrwolf-Hilfe (Werewolf Aid) as a relief fund during strikes. The Wehrwolf continued to be to the right of the Stahlhelm politically: it was clearly anti-Semitic, anti-capitalistic, and anti-Marxist. In this respect it was already anticipating the NSDAP, which most of its members later joined.[65]

Politically, the Stahlhelm was moving increasingly to the right, which was reflected outwardly in the election of Duesterberg as the Second Federal Leader (with authority equal to that of the First Leader) in March of 1927, and boldly proclaimed in September of 1928 in the "message of hatred from Fürstenwalde" delivered by Morosowicz, the leader of the organization in the state of Brandenburg. This now included also an open embrace of anti-Semitism: as of March 1924, Jews were no longer admitted into the Stahlhelm and Jewish members were slowly pushed out.[66] Moreover, the transfer of important offices of the federal leadership to Berlin, and the decision to move the Front Line Veterans' Days, always held in Magdeburg between 1919 and 1925, to a different large city every year—for example, to Berlin in 1927, and to Hamburg in 1928—reveals that the group saw itself increasingly as a political organization and no longer regarded the streets and squares of the province of Saxony as the main focus of its battle against the left and the Republic.[67]

The organizational expansion of the Stahlhelm and its growth in membership were put on display for the public above all in the yearly Front Line Veterans' Days, for which the organization was able to mobilize a growing number of participants in the middle years of the Weimar Republic. In January 1924, under the restrictive conditions of the state of emergency and the ongoing economic and social crisis, only about 10–15,000 members of the organization marched through downtown Magdeburg. In 1925, at the last Front Line Veterans' Days held here, the number had already risen to 25,000, while all other events drew a total of about 50,000. No fewer than 132,000 Stahlhelm members turned out for the Front Line Veterans' Days in Berlin at the beginning of May 1927, and a year later the number had risen to 138,000.[68] In Magdeburg itself, 40,000 participants still attended the celebrations of the anniversary of the founding of the Reich on 18 January 1926, and 8–9,000 marched through the streets. By the following year, however, participation had declined drastically: only 5,500 members of the organization marched through the city; the year after that it was no more than 1,500.[69] The Stahlhelm's capacity to mobilize its members thus did not grow across the board but was evidently greater on the national level, where the political significance of the meeting was obvious, than on the local level. Moreover, on the local level it now faced a potent opponent in the Reichsbanner. The political radicalization of the group since 1926 expressed not only disappointment over the behavior of Reich President Hindenburg, which conformed to the constitution, but was also a reaction to the presence of the new enemy. Thus, it was not only the political goals that became more radical, but also the conduct toward the enemy in the street: the result was violence.

The Stahlhelm and related associations reacted to the rise of the Reichsbanner with new paramilitary activities. As early as 1924 they set up their own small-caliber shooting clubs. Two years later, Interior Minister Severing believed that their efforts had reached the point where it was necessary to have the police authorities report to him about them. While the police president of Magdeburg still saw the shooting clubs as primarily a sporting activity in April 1926, his colleague from Halle was already noting that the Stahlhelm made up the largest such club in the city (with 100 members). Small-caliber gun clubs of right-wing organizations existed also in Naumburg, Zeitz, Erfurt, Mühlhausen, and other cities of the southernmost administrative district; plans to establish them existed in the Mansfelder Land.[70] Six months later, the Regierungspräsident noted "an enormous increase recently in small-caliber shooting," which he attributed to the "activities of the military associations." However, these had discovered their interest in shooting clubs only after they were confronted with a competing Republican organization: "It was only when the Reichsbanner held Republican Days against the German Days, and robbed the events of the right-wing groups of their mass-psychological effect through the mass turnout of uniformed Republicans, that the right-wing organizations resorted to a further military training of its members." However, he believed that this would sooner or later cause the Reichsbanner to follow suit and therefore posed a threat of armed clashes over the long term. The Regierungspräsident of Merseburg argued along the same line, and thus both men recommended a general prohibition of small-caliber shooting clubs.[71] Oberpräsident Hörsing, however, did not adopt this tough course, advocating, instead of a general prohibition, which would affect above all the gun trade and manufacture and the workers employed therein, careful supervision of the club boards especially.[72]

The Republican response to these developments got under way in March of the following year. The Republican shooting clubs that had sprung up in the meantime had formed into a Reich cartel, which set up its headquarters in Magdeburg.[73] Once the original fears about violent confrontations had come to seem unwarranted, the discussion of this issue waned. The small-caliber shooting clubs were thus largely instruments to enhance the attractiveness of one's own organization in competition with others, not a direct preparation for armed struggle against the enemy in a situation of civil war. But precisely because they grew out of such a situation of competition, they contributed to habituating people to violence as an element of political conflicts.

Such a contribution also came from the illegal military exercises held by the Stahlhelm and other right-wing military associations. In mid February 1925, members of the Wehrwolf were observed at a Magdeburg shooting range firing not small-caliber rifles, but regular infantry rifles, in the presence of a sergeant of the Reichswehr. When the police president asked for clarification, the local army commander referred him to his higher-ups. In April 1926, several Wehrwolf members attracted attention during a field exercise near Wernigerode. Investigating police uncovered not only a weapons cache in the house of a retired colonel in Quedlinburg, but also intensive connections between the Wehrwolf and the Halberstadt Reichswehr, which apparently instructed and supervised the exercises of the paramilitary group.[74] In October 1926, the Magdeburg Jungstahlhelm also held a larger field exercise. In response, the police president of Magdeburg wanted to outlaw the local Stahlhelm organization, whose growing "militarization" he had already criticized previously. However, Seldte managed to appease Prussia's Interior Minister Grzesinski: in an effective public relations move, he dismissed two Magdeburg functionaries and emphatically pointed to the prohibition against military exercises in the national paper.[75] These kinds of exercises excited especially explosive controversy if they were aimed directly at a domestic political enemy. In mid January 1926, the police in Magdeburg had reports that the Jungdo and other *völkisch* groups were readying themselves in the region around Staßfurt to fend off an allegedly imminent Communist putsch, were in contact with Nazi groups along the Bavarian-Thuringian border, and were planning to hold a field exercise in the near future near Calbe.[76]

The willingness to engage in violence on the right was furthered heightened by the fact that the established Combat Leagues faced a new kind of competitor in their own camp. The first indications came in early 1926: at the end of March, police authorities reported that the still small NSDAP had begun to set up "hall protection units" in Magdeburg, Halle, Erfurt, Mühlhausen, and Zeitz; the unit in Halle, for example, had thirty men.[77] A year later, the Erfurt SA already had fifty members, headed by a former group leader of the RFB. In addition, there was a ten-man SS unit.[78] The local Magdeburg group of the Stahlhelm found itself confronted, in the spring of 1926, with an offshoot of the Munich Frontkriegerbund (Front Line Warriors' League) (which had close ties to the Nazis); some members of the Stahlhelm who were unhappy with the restrained course of its leadership joined the new group. The radicalization of the Magdeburg Stahlhelm noted by the police president was the initially successful response to this development.[79] In January of 1928, the Regierungspräsident of Merseburg noted a clear waning of interest in the activities of the various right-wing groups, including in their sports exercises.[80] The Stahlhelm and the older Combat Leagues of the right were in a difficult position: their political offensive was failing, since the parties were able to avoid their attempts to influence them. The pragmatic response was therefore to radicalize the forms of action with which they were familiar. At the same time, they were coming under pressure from a new and even more extreme organization. Thus long before the global economic crisis, there were signs on the right of erosion of old structures, an erosion that pointed in the direction of a further radicalization.[81]

On the party level, this trend was only beginning to be felt. The Reichstag elections of 4 May 1924 reduced the DDP in the province of Saxony to about half of its previous votes, though the DVP suffered only relatively minor losses. At the same time, the German National People's Party (DNVP), which was agitating vehemently against the Dawes Plan, made gains that were above the Reich average, while to their right, the German-*völkisch* Freedom Party (DVFP) garnered a share of the votes greater than its Reich average. The bastions of this new party, as radically anti-Republican as it was anti-Semitic, were in part the places where the DNVP had its strongholds, as well, but in part also in the cities. In the Altmark county of Salzwedel, where the DNVP won 41.7 percent of the votes—its second-best result in the entire province—the DVFP polled 9.0 percent, in the neighboring County Gardelegen 12.0 percent (DNVP: 33.6 percent), in the neighboring County Osterburg still 6.7 percent (DNVP: 49.3 percent), and thus more than the average for the administrative district, which was 4.9 percent. It won 9.1 percent also in Halberstadt, 10.0 percent in Quedlinburg, and 7.5 percent in Aschersleben, while in Magdeburg it pulled in only 5.1 percent of the ballots.

Even more remarkable were the results for the DVFP in the administrative district of Merseburg, where it polled an average of 8.7 percent. Its uncontested stronghold was the city of Naumburg, an old bastion of right-wing radicalism, where it won 27.6 percent and thus almost caught up with the DNVP (31.0 percent), and the surrounding rural county, where it garnered 26.6 percent and was thus not all that far behind (DNVP: 40.9 percent); 23.3 percent was the result in the agrarian county of Eckartsberga (DNVP: 38.2 percent). But the DVFP also won 13.9 percent in Eisleben, just over 10 percent in the cities of Wittenberg and Zeitz, and 11.2 percent in the city of Weißenfels, while its showing in Halle was below average at only 7.6 percent. In the southernmost administrative district, its stronghold was the county of Langensalza, where it reached 19.3 percent (DNVP: 40.9 percent), followed by County Weißensee at 16.8 percent (DNVP: 41.8 percent); in third place was the city of Erfurt with 13.6 percent.[82] The *völkisch* parties thus were strong where—as in the Altmark or Naumburg—the Home Guards already had many members, but also in the smaller cities, though not in the real strongholds of the workers' movement. In the elections of 7 December 1924, their losses in urban areas were also relatively larger than in the rural counties.[83] The successes of the most radical of all right-wing parties were thus at most the partial reaction of a bourgeoisie confronted directly with the rise of the Communists and their activities. They reflect, first, the further intensified enemy images held by the farmers, and second, protest—most likely middle-class—against the economic and political repercussions of inflation.

This development was flagging in the Reichstag elections of 20 May 1928. The NSDAP was not able to pick up directly from the successes of the *völkisch* parties. In the province of Saxony, as well, it remained a splinter party, with results around the Reich average of 2.6 percent; only in a few places was it able to achieve a noticeably better showing. It did best in County Eckartsberga with 9.0 percent, followed by the city of Quedlinburg with 7.8 percent, rural Naumburg with 6.7 percent, and the city of Naumburg with 6.1 percent. The still-modest bastions of the Nazi party were to be found where the extreme right had already been particularly strong before. On the whole, the situation certainly did not stabilize for the bourgeois parties, since the DDP and the DVP continued to lose votes also in the province of Saxony.[84]

At the end of 1928, officials noted much stronger recruitment activity by the NSDAP, which was focused especially on the Altmark. At the end of 1929, the Regierungspräsident of Magdeburg reported that the National Socialist movement had been showing "a rising curve in recent times." Its membership was rising "day by day. The new members are chiefly from the Stahlhelm and the Communists … especially in the Altmark and the Harz region."[85] The intensive agitation continued and won the NSDAP additional members "from the camp of the German National People's Party and the KPD"; among others, the entire RFB band of the local group in Wernigerode had joined the Nazi party. In a different report we hear of the great resonance that the NSDAP rallies had among "officials of the judicial, postal, and financial departments, the Reich Autobahn, and teachers."[86] Evidently the NSDAP was developing, even before its great electoral successes, into a kind of catch-all party in the province of Saxony, a party that could speak to very different strata of the population—farmers as well as members of the "new middle class," along with miners, workers in the potash industry, and rural laborers, who did not hail from regions with a long tradition of Social Democracy or unions.[87] The fact that former Communists joined the NSDAP in large numbers would prove a temporary phenomenon, however.

It was not only the membership of the party that grew; its own Combat League also attracted new members. At the end of June 1929, the local party organization of Magdeburg had 100 members; three months later there were 450. Membership in the Magdeburg SA rose from 40 to 90, while the SS had 60 members in this city. A Hitler Youth organization was set up in June. In April of 1929, 1,000 members of the NSDAP were organized in the administrative district of Merseburg; the SA had a total of 200 members, though SS formations did not exist yet.[88]

In the referendum on the Young Plan in the fall of 1929, its initiators—the DNVP, the Stahlhelm, and the NSDAP—achieved a good, above-average result in the province of Saxony. The electoral districts of Magdeburg and Merseburg were among the nine districts of the Reich in which more than one-fifth of the eligible voters cast a "yes" ballot.[89] In the elections for the provincial parliament held shortly before, the NSDAP received 93,000 votes, or 5.3 percent.[90] That was not much, though still twice as high as the results in the Reichstag elections in 1928. A small incident that occurred at the beginning of January 1930 indicates how the weight had begun to shift within the radical right. On 7 January, Ernst Werner Techow, who had participated in the murder of Rathenau, was released from the prison in Halle thanks to the Amnesty Law of July 1928.[91] Waiting for him was a delegation from the local Stahlhelm with the *Untergauführer*, a uniformed band, and the seventy-man local NSDAP group, headed by their *Ortsgruppenführer* (local group leader) and the chief of the Halle-Merseburg Gau. The Stahlhelm members were left out in the cold: Techow had been released two hours earlier than announced and taken immediately to the train station, where he intended to wait for his mother. The Nazi Gau chief and the *Ortsgruppenführer* showed up at the station because they had been planning to escort the mother to the prison. Now they had the privilege of being able to spend some time with Techow, whereas the Stahlhelm delegation did not arrive at the station until he and his mother had already left.[92] That the NSDAP would openly embrace one of the accomplices to the murder of Rathenau came as no surprise; that a local organization of the Stahlhelm did so was less self-evident. The Halle Stahlhelm was honoring an accomplice to murder and showing, by this symbolic act, how close it had moved to the positions of the new competitor.

Notes

1. Four apprentices aged sixteen and seventeen, whom a twenty-year-old worker had put up to the act and supplied with the explosives, had chosen New Year's Eve of 1922 to take revenge for the alleged destruction of a monument to the fighters of the "March action" killed near Bachra in 1921. The instigator of the deed, Emil Werner, was sentenced to a prison term of several years, and the four apprentices received jail sentences of between three and nine months. Werner had returned to Germany from Russia in 1922 and had joined the Communist youth group in Halle, but according to the *Klassenkampf* (no. 6, 8 January 1923), he had been expelled for "unproletarian behavior and the suspicion of being an informant." There were no indications that the action had been encouraged by higher functionaries of the KPD: LHAM C 20 Ib 5218/I, fol. 293 (PP Halle to RP Merseburg, 2 January 1923); fol. 333 (PP Halle to RP Merseburg, 14 May 1923).
2. Calculated on the basis of the numbers in *Stat. Dt. R., N. F.*, vol. 315, II, S. 23. In the Reich-

stag elections of 1920, the USPD and the KPD together had still won 42.3 percent; the DNVP only 16.3 percent.

3. This and the following account of the events are based on LHAM C 20 Ib 1859/III, fols. 324–363 (PP Halle to the Prussian Minister of the Interior, 18 May 1924).
4. *SZ* no. 112, 14 May 1924; LHAM C 20 Ib 1859/III, fol. 325 (PP Halle to the Prussian Minister of the Interior, 18 May 1924). The report of the police president of Halle mentions no participant figure.
5. *MZ* no. 240, 12 May 1924.
6. LHAM C 20 Ib 1859/III, fol. 363 (PP Halle to the Prussian Minister of the Interior, 18 May 1924).
7. Stahlhelm, *Sechs Jahre Stahlhelm,* addendum 16.
8. *SZ* no. 112 , 14 May 1924.
9. LHAM C 20 Ib 1859/III, fols. 328f., 361f. (PP Halle to the Prussian Minister of the Interior, 18 May 1924).
10. *KK* no. 53, 5 May; no. 58, 10 May 1924.
11. *KK* no. 46, 25 April; no. 47, 26 April; no. 56, 8 May; no. 58, 10 May 1924.
12. *KK* no. 54, 6 May; no. 55, 7 May 1924; see LHAM C 20 Ib 1859/III, fols. 333f. (Circular of the KPD district leadership); fols. 340f. (PP Halle to the Prussian Minister of the Interior, 18 May 1924).
13. LHAM C 20 Ib 1859/III, fols. 337–340 (PP Halle to the Prussian Minister of the Interior, 18 May 1924).
14. The exact number of dead is unclear. The report of the police president explicitly mentions only one Communist who was shot dead. The *Klassenkampf* on 12 May (no. 59) spoke of four dead and six seriously injured on each side, while the *Volksstimme* on 13 May (no. 111), citing the police administration of Halle, suspected ten dead, though it could identify only the places where four had been killed. The *Magdeburgische Zeitung* reported on 12 May (no. 240) that a police officer had succumbed to his injuries in the hospital, though it did not know the precise number of dead on the Communist side. Evidently several of the demonstrators who had been killed were carried off by others and therefore not recorded by the police.
15. LHAM C 20 Ib 1859/III, fols. 345–354, 360 (PP Halle to the Prussian Minister of the Interior, 18 May 1924); SAPMO Ry 1/I 3/11/15, fols. 8–15 (Eyewitness report, undated). The author of the report evidently did not come from Halle, though he likely did not have a leading position at Berlin headquarters, either. Weitz, *German Communism,* 173–177, who did not consult the police report, does not address the events at Böllberg in his account of the incident.
16. On this conflict see Heinrich August Winkler, *Der Schein der Normalität: Arbeiter und Arbeiterbewegung in der Weimarer Republik 1924 bis 1930* (2nd ed. Berlin, 1988), 211–214.
17. *KK* no. 59, 12 May 1924.
18. For details see Winkler, *Schein,* 202–205.
19. *SZ* no. 115, 17 May 1924.
20. *VS* no. 112, 14 May 1924.
21. *VS* no. 113, 15 May 1924.
22. Rohe, *Reichsbanner,* 55, on the history of its founding, 29ff., specifically on Magdeburg, 39ff. See also the succinct account in Diehl, *Paramilitary Politics,* 176–184.
23. LHAM C 20 Ib 4654, fol. 1 (PP Magdeburg to OP, 17 April 1923). Rohe, *Reichsbanner,* 40, incorrectly gives the date as 19 April.
24. Indications to that effect in LHAM C 20 Ib 4654, fols. 11 and 12 (Report of the police administration Aschersleben to OP, 7 September, and of LR Calbe to OP, 27 September 1923).
25. On this see Chapter 7 in Part IV of this volume.
26. On this see Benjamin Ziemann, "Republikanische Kriegserinnerung in einer polarisierten Öffentlichkeit: Das Reichsbanner Schwarz-Rot-Gold als Veteranenverband der sozialistischen Arbeiterschaft," *HZ* 267 (1998): 357–398.

27. On the circle of the founders and the negotiations preceding the founding see Rohe, *Reichsbanner,* 55ff., 66ff.
28. On this see the following chapter.
29. *VS* no. 46, 24 February 1925. Here we hear of "one hundred thirty or one hundred forty thousand." On Constitution Day on 11 August 1927, 20,000 Reichsbanner men and other Republicans assembled in the square in front of the cathedral (*VS* no. 188, 13 August 1927).
30. Diehl's verdict about the Reichsbanner, *Paramilitary Politics,* 184, tends in this—exaggerated—direction.
31. *Stat. Dt. R., N. F.,* vol. 315, II, 20–27 (Reichstag elections of 4 May 1924), author's own calculations; *Preußische Statistik,* vol. 251, 27–34 (*Landtag* elections of 20 February 1921). Compare the analysis of the May elections in Winkler, *Schein,* 177–184; Charles Maier, *Recasting Bourgeois Europe: Stabilization in France, Germany, and Italy in the Decade after World War I* (Princeton, NJ, 1975), 450–455. Maier's thesis that the votes of the workers benefited the radical right is entirely plausible for the province of Saxony, since here, too, the SPD and the KPD together won far fewer votes than the three workers' parties in the previous Reichstag as well as Landtag elections in 1921, and since the number of eligible voters and voter participation were higher. For example, in the electoral district of Merseburg, the SPD, USPD, and KPD together had won 342,199 votes in 1921; in May 1924 the figure was only 294,938.
32. See Leidigkeit and Herrmann, *Leninistischer Kurs,* 203–205. Kurt Finker, *Geschichte des Roten Frontkämpferbundes* (East Berlin, 1981), 24, refers to the events of 11 May in Halle as "the final impetus" for the founding.
33. *KK* no. 124, 29 July 1924. At the founding meetings of the RFB in Halle on 31 July and in Erfurt on 15 August 1924, the idea of representing the party's interests did not appear; rather, opposition to the right-wing Combat Leagues, but chiefly to the Reichsbanner, was at the forefront: LHAM C 20 Ib 1960/I, fol. 9f. (PP Halle to RP Merseburg, 12 August 1924); fol. 16f. (PP Erfurt to RP Erfurt, 18 August 1924).
34. For a detailed account of the history of the RFB's founding see Schuster, *Roter Frontkämpferbund,* 23–34; see also Diehl, *Paramilitary Politics,* 184–190. Mallmann, *Kommunisten,* 193, rejects competition with the Reichsbanner as a motivation for its founding and, incidentally, simply posits—without any further differentiation—a military imprint on Communist workers by the veterans' organization of the *Kaiserreich* and the front line experience in World War I.
35. According to Mallmann, *Kommunisten,* 194, the RFB was an "unparalleled success"; Winkler, *Revolution,* 455–458, describes it as "by far the most important" mass organization of the KPD.
36. Leidigkeit and Herrmann, *Leninistischer Kurs,* 205; SAPMO Ry 1/I 3/11/31, fol. 56 (Organizational report of the district leadership for September 1925); see Schuster, *Roter Frontkämpferbund,* 35. Finker, *Geschichte,* 18, reports that in September 1924, there were 71 local groups with about 2,500 members in the district of Halle.
37. Schuster, *Roter Frontkämpferbund,* 245.
38. In October 1925, the head of the military organization in the district accused the RFB functionaries of political ignorance and claimed that "90 percent of the functionaries" of the party in the district lacked knowledge of the tasks of the M-Apparat, though he had to concede that this apparatus was "in complete disrepair" and in Halle had only "3 reliable groups of 20 men each": SAPMO Ry 1/I 3/11/21, fol. 83 (Situation report *Ordnungsdienst,* 15 October 1925). On the opposition to the founding of the RFB from representatives of the military apparatus within the party leadership see Schuster, *Roter Frontkämpferbund,* 31f.
39. LHAM C 20 Ib 1960/I, fol. 143f. (RP Merseburg to the Prussian Ministry of the Interior, 23 April 1925).
40. Ibid., fol. 172 (Banner consecration in Aken a. E. on 24 June 1925); fols. 190f. (Events for Anti-War Day at the end of July 1925 in Halle and Merseburg); fol. 214 (RFB Day in Halberstadt at the beginning of October 1925).

41. Ibid., fols. 173f. (PP Magdeburg to RP Magdeburg, 29 June 1925).
42. Ibid., fols. 103f. (RP Magdeburg to OP, 12 January 1925); Schuster, *Roter Frontkämpferbund,* 245f.
43. SAPMO Ry 1/I 3/11/16, fol. 16 (Report by the district leadership about the campaign for the referendum on 1 March 1926); fols. 43f. (Report by the district leadership, 12 November 1926), here the quote; fols. 61f. (Report by the district leadership, 11 February 1927).
44. For details on the RFB's tactic of a united front see Schuster, *Roter Frontkämpferbund,* 139–156, who also describes the overwhelming failure of this course. On the referendum see Winkler, *Schein,* 270–289.
45. On this see Chapter 7 of this volume. On the problem of the "battering tactic" see Rohe, *Reichsbanner,* 350f., who sees in this a main reason for the failure of the RFB's "subversion tactic"; Schuster, *Roter Frontkämpferbund,* 141ff.; Winkler, *Schein,* 208.
46. The internal problems of the RFB do not seem to have acquired any greater importance in the district of Halle-Merseburg in the process. The leftist opposition was quickly dealt with in 1927; it had been able to exert some influence only in Halle itself, and there only in the Rote Marine (Red Navy), an auxiliary organization of the RFB: SAPMO Ry 1/I 3/11/16, fol. 63 (Report by the district leadership, 11 February 1927); see Schuster, *Roter Frontkämpferbund,* 157–168. On the various "faces" of the RFB in Berlin—connecting to the old M-Apparat, "military games," strictly legal organizational and propaganda activity—see Wirsching, *Weltkrieg,* 246–251.
47. SAPMO Ry 1/I 3/11/31, fols. 56, 59 (Organizational report of the district leadership for September 1925).
48. SAPMO Ry 1/I 3/11/21 (not pag., Graphic overview of membership trend in the district to the end of 1930); 3/11/30, fol. 17 (Report by the district leadership on the campaign for the referendum, 14 July 1926); fol. 60 (Report by the organizational division for August-October 1928). Hermann Weber, *Die Wandlung des deutschen Kommunismus: Die Stalinisierung der KPD in der Weimarer Republik,* vol. 1 (Frankfurt, 1969), 370f., drawing on official sources, gives 1925 the much lower figure of 9,500, and 1929, 10,800. In the district of Thuringia, according to Weber (376), the number of members declined from 7,000 in 1925 to 5,000 in 1929, while in the district of Magdeburg-Anhalt (379) it rose from 2,000 to 3,000. In both cases it was substantially below the figures for 1923.
49. Still the fundamental work on the Bolshevization of the KPD in general is Weber, *Wandlung.* On Suhl, ibid., 178–180; on the "reconcilers" ibid., 17f., 219–223. Leidigkeit and Herrmann, *Leninistischer Kurs,* 308, concede, at least, that the district leadership found itself "temporarily in a complicated situation within the party."
50. SAPMO Ry 1/I 3/11/30, fol. 38 (Report by the organization division for August-October 1928). On the fluctuation in general see Mallmann, *Kommunisten,* 87–93.
51. LHAM C 20 Ib 2041/I, fol. 50 (PP Magdeburg to RP Magdeburg, 23 March 1925); fol. 53 (PP Halle to RP Merseburg, 25 March 1925).
52. Ibid., fol. 193 (RP Merseburg to OP, 1 May 1928).
53. LHAM C 20 Ib 1960/II, fol. 232 (RP Merseburg to OP, 14 August 1928).
54. SAPMO Ry 1/I 3/11/16, fol. 70 (Report of the district leadership for March/April 1927).
55. Ibid., fols. 138–144 (Special report by the district leadership about the May rallies 1929, 28 May 1929), the quotes fols. 139, 144.
56. SAPMO Ry 1/I 3/11/16, fol. 43 (Report by the district leadership, 12 November 1926).
57. Thus the assessment by Mallmann, *Kommunisten,* 306–312. See SAPMO Ry 1/I 3/11/16, fol. 143 (Special report by the district leadership, 28 May 1929); here we hear of the "serious deficiencies long since present in the work on work cells," and ibid., 3/11/25, fol. 125 (Report by the union leadership of the district Halle-Merseburg, 31 July 1929), which notes with regret that "in most companies the work of the work cells is inadequate, and, moreover, in very important companies the cells exist merely on paper."

58. SAPMO Ry 1/I 3/11/52, fols. 37–45 (Report by the union section of the district leadership Halle-Merseburg, 19 December 1924, date-stamp).
59. SAPMO Ry 1/I 3/11/16, fols. 75–76 (Report of the district leadership Halle-Merseburg for March/April 1927); SAPMO Ry 1/I 3/11/52, fols. 86–100 (Report of the union division Halle-Merseburg, 5 March 1928). See Leidigkeit and Herrmann, *Leninistischer Kurs,* 233.
60. SAPMO Ry 1/I 3/11/52, fols. 124–126 (Report by the union section Halle-Merseburg, 13 August 1929), the quotes fols. 124 and 125. On the 12th Party Congress see Weber, *Wandlung,* vol. 1, 223–232.
61. This is also the overall verdict of Mallmann, *Kommunisten,* 312–326. See Weitz, *German Communism,* 141–159, who downplays the importance of the KPD's vacillating course on the union question and who also fails to make an adequate distinction between the middle Weimar years, when the party was not yet primarily a party of the unemployed, and the years after 1929.
62. Author's calculations based on *Stat. Dt. R,. N. F.,* vol. 372, II, 20–27 (Reichstag elections of 20 May 1928) and *Stat. Dt. R., N. F.,* vol. 315, IV, 18–25 (Reichstag elections of 7 December 1924). On the results of the Reichstag elections of 1928 overall see Winkler, *Schein,* 520–527. Special conditions applied to the result in Schleusingen: because the KPD in Suhl opposed the course of the party as a whole, it had joined, first, the Lenin League, and then the SPD (Mallmann, *Kommunisten,* 354).
63. "Yellow" unions sought to pursue workers' interests through cooperation with employers, hence denouncing strikes. They were particularly promoted by heavy industry as a countervailing force against the Social Democratic trade unions and party and comprised 280,000 members on the eve of the First World War. See Klaus Mattheier, *Die Gelben: Nationale Arbeiter zwischen Wirtschaftsfrieden und Streik* (Düsseldorf, 1973).
64. On the organization see esp. Klotzbücher, "Stahlhelm," 31–50; Berghahn, *Stahlhelm,* 33, 64. As Klotzbücher shows (49f.), the precise number of members cannot be determined, given the very different estimates made by the national and the state leadership. In mid February 1927, the police president of Magdeburg sent a confidential memo to his Regierungspräsident with the result of an internal membership count by the Stahlhelm, of which he had learned through informants. According to his information, the organization, inclusive of the Jungstahlhelm, comprised 613,000 members: LHAM C 20 Ib 1991/IV, fol. 12 (PP Magdeburg to RP Magdeburg, 19 February 1927).
65. Finker, *Wehrverbände,* 316f., 327–330, 355, 365; idem, "Wehrwolf. Bund deutscher Männer und Frontkrieger 1923–1933," in D. Fricke, ed., *Die bürgerlichen Parteien in Deutschland: Handbuch der Geschichte der bürgerlichen Parteien und anderer bürgerlicher Interessenorganisationen vom Vormärz bis zum Jahre 1945,* vol. II (Leipzig, 1970), 835–840.
66. Berghahn, *Stahlhelm,* 66f.
67. Ibid., 103–114.
68. *MZ* no. 38, 21 January 1924 (number mentioned by Seldte in his speech); LHAM C 20 Ib 1991/II, fol. 90 (PP Magdeburg to OP, 20 January 1925); Berghahn, *Stahlhelm,* 105, 112.
69. LHAM C 20 Ib 1991/III, fols. 32f. (RP Magdeburg to the Prussian Ministry of the Interior, 18 January 1926); fol. 419 (PP Magdeburg to OP, 22 January 1927); LHAM C 20 Ib 1991/IV, fols. 198f. (PP Magdeburg to RP Magdeburg, 23 January 1928).
70. LHAM C 20 Ib 2002/I, fols. 94–308, passim.
71. LHAM C 20 Ib 2002/II, fols. 196–202 (RP Magdeburg to the Prussian Ministry of the Interior, September 1926, n.d.), the quotes fols. 199 and 201; fols. 205–207 (RP Merseburg to the Prussian Ministry of the Interior, 21 September 1926).
72. Ibid., fols. 214–217 (OP to the Prussian Ministry of the Interior, 16 October 1926).
73. LHAM C 20 Ib 2002/III, fol. 24 (LR Delitzsch to OP, 5 March 1927); see Rohe, *Reichsbanner,* 166–169, who points to the relatively minor importance of the Reich cartel.
74. LHAM C 20 Ib 1991/II, fol. 186 (PP Magdeburg to Magdeburg Reichswehr commander, 18 February 1925); fol. 192 (Magdeburg Reichswehr commander to PP Magdeburg, 6

April 1925); LHAM C 20 Ib 1991/III, fols. 156–183 (Reports and records of interrogations concerning the exercise near Wernigerode), fols. 217–225 (Reports of police commissioner Glienke, 26 April and 21 April 1926). On the discovery of further weapons caches in 1926/27 in the administrative districts of Magdeburg and Erfurt that were under the supervision of the Reichswehr see the reports and interrogations records in LHAM C 20 Ib 4120/I, fols. 287f., 308f., 314–318, 324, 328, 331–339. On the promotion of paramilitary exercises in the Stahlhelm see Klotzbücher, "Stahlhelm," 38f.

75. LHAM C 20 Ib 1991/III, fols. 72f. (PP Magdeburg to OP, 10 May 1926); fols. 244–303, 304, 306 (Reports, correspondence, and records of interrogations concerning the exercise near Magdeburg). On the role of the Stahlhelm in the secret arming of the Reichswehr see Berghahn, *Stahlhelm,* 55–63. In May 1926, the police president of Halle noted a general waning of Wehrwolf activities, but an increase in paramilitary exercises: LHAM C 20 Ib 1991/III, fols. 329f. (PP Halle to OP, 12 May 1926).
76. LHAM C 20 Ib 1914/IV, fols. 1f. (PP Magdeburg to RP Magdeburg, 14 January 1926).
77. LHAM C 20 Ib 1913/IV, fol. 30 (RP Magdeburg an OP, 29 March 1926); fol. 31 (RP Erfurt to OP, 28 March 1926); fol. 34 (RP Merseburg to OP, 27 March 1926).
78. Ibid., fol. 222 (RP Erfurt to OP, 7 June 1927).
79. Ibid., fol. 36 (RP Magdeburg to OP, 1 April 1926). In the administrative district of Merseburg, the Bund der Sturmsoldaten (League of Storm Soldiers) tried to woo members away from the Stahlhelm, also without success: ibid., fols. 82f., 85 (RP Merseburg to OP, 13 March and 31 July 1926).
80. Ibid., fol. 299f. (RP Merseburg to Prussian Ministry of the Interior, 4 November 1927 and 7 January 1928).
81. On the failure of the political plans of the Stahlhelm and the other organizations see Diehl, *Paramilitary Politics,* 200–243. See also Fritzsche, *Rehearsals,* 178–189, who points to the decrease in the Stahlhelm's influence among the younger members, who felt that it was not radical enough and too close to the traditional parties.
82. The percentages are the author's own calculations based on *Stat. Dt. R., N. F.*, vol. 315, II, 20–27. See Falter et al., *Wahlen,* 69.
83. The result of the elections in December in *Stat. Dt. R., N. F.,* vol. 315, IV, 18–25; see Falter et al., *Wahlen,* 70.
84. Election results are found in *Stat. Dt. R., N. F.,* vol. 372, II, 20–27; see Falter et al., *Wahlen,* 71.
85. LHAM C 20 Ib 1913/V, fols. 259f. (RP Magdeburg to the Prussian Ministry of the Interior, 4 November 1928); fol. 278 (RP Magdeburg to OP, 21 March 1929), here the quote.
86. Ibid., fol. 289 (RP Magdeburg to OP, 21 March 1929), here the second quote; fol. 316 (RP Magdeburg to OP, 25 September 1929), here the first quote; fol. 318 (RP Magdeburg to OP, 30 September 1929); fols. 308f. (RP Merseburg to OP, 27 April 1929). At the same time, the officials also noted the financial weakness of the new party, which lacked large donors.
87. On the social structure of the NSDAP before its electoral triumph in September 1930 see Michael Kater, *The Nazi Party: A Social Profile of its Members and Leaders 1919–1945* (Cambridge, MA, 1983), 31–50, 244–247. The considerable percentage of workers in the NSDAP before 1930 is emphasized even more by Detlef Mühlberger, *Hitler's Followers: Studies in the Sociology of the Nazi Movement* (London, 1991).
88. LHAM C 20 Ib 1913/V, fol. 318 (RP Magdeburg to OP, 30 September 1929); fols. 308f. (RP Merseburg to OP, 27 April 1929); fol. 311 (RP Magdeburg to OP, 21 March 1929).
89. Winkler, *Schein,* 738.
90. Falter et al., *Wahlen,* 105; *MZ* no. 634, 18 November 1929; *SZ* no. 271, 19 November 1929. Further strongholds of the NSDAP were in Naumburg and in the cities at the edge of the Harz, like Halberstadt, Wernigerode, and Quedlinburg, where the party now had more than ten seats in the city council and thus only one less than the SPD.
91. The law was intended to draw a line under the postwar period and meant freedom for Max Hoelz, among others. For details see Christoph, *Reichsamnestien,* 219–281. This was the sec-

ond nationwide amnesty after July 1922 and the first that provided for mitigation of punishments for crimes resulting in a death. See also Irmela Nagel, *Fememorde und Fememordprozesse in der Weimarer Republik* (Cologne, 1991).

92. LHAM C 20 Ib 1913/V, fol. 352f. (PP Halle to RP Merseburg, 11 January 1930).

Chapter 7

The Continuity of Violence

The political violence behind the rise of the Combat Leagues in the middle years of the Weimar Republic has so far remained largely unexamined, leaving aside the fighting between the police and the Communists in Berlin during the first days of May 1929, the so-called Bloody May.[1] In fact, the violent events were less dramatic than in the previous years, involved a comparatively smaller number of participants, and left fewer casualties than the confrontations in the years both before and after. Yet they were more than merely scattered clashes, and were not limited to a small number of locations. Political violence had become an endemic phenomenon that reflected characteristic features of the political culture.

Clashes with the Police

Unlike in the years 1919–1923, violent confrontations in which state security forces were one of the two parties to conflicts that did not involve a third party now took a back seat to clashes between members of the Combat Leagues. The "battle of Böllberg" of 11 May 1924 was not typical, given its scale, but it does show that the police continued to regard the Communists as their chief adversary. Clashes between the police and members of right-wing organizations were correspondingly rare, but they were not entirely absent and demonstrated a growing willingness on that end of the political spectrum to resort to violence toward state security forces. The strikes of the middle Weimar years took place for the most part without violence.[2]

The military review on the occasion of the restored Kaiser Wilhelm monument in Halle on 11 May 1924 was not the first time the new self-confidence of the right wing was on display. Between 18 and 20 January 1924, that is, still under the conditions of the state of emergency, the Stahlhelm held its Fifth Front Line Veterans' Day, which drew about 10,000 participants to the city. A "military

Notes from this chapter begin on page 183.

religious service" was scheduled for 20 January, a Sunday. The night before, the train station, amidst the throngs of uniformed and steel helmet–wearing association members, had already come to look like a "rear-echelon station"; a few groups had formed smaller columns and, ignoring a prohibition, had marched to the site of the meeting carrying black-white-red banners and singing the Erhardt song. Columns of this kind formed again on the way to the cathedral and after the service, when banners were unfurled again as members filed out. In response, the police—including mounted officers—moved against the train of demonstrators (though not all policemen showed the same enthusiasm—the police president observed "among some of the local police ... even a certain passive resistance, a reluctance to take action"). Eventually the police were able to break up the column and confiscate the unfurled banners; however, some of the officers had to brandish their guns and arrest several participants. Still, larger clashes or injuries did not occur.[3] Quite clearly, some in the Stahlhelm wanted to test how far one could push against official decrees, and in the process they did not shy from using open, if very circumscribed, violence against the police. This was a new type of behavior that had not been seen before.

It soon became clear that these were not negligible isolated incidents, but a test of strength. The *Magdeburgische Zeitung* downplayed the behavior of the members of the Stahlhelm, reporting seeing only a "vast crowd of people" but no march. It was also willing to grant that some of those involved in the clashes with the police were unaware of the prohibition against unfurled banners, and even though it reproached them for their "lack of discipline" overall, it acquitted the national Stahlhelm leadership of any responsibility. Seldte himself, who laid no blame on the members of the group, complained to the Regierungspräsident about the actions of the police, claiming that the officers, allegedly equipped with hand grenades and machine guns, had ridden ruthlessly into the crowd while the Social Democratic police president, pistol in hand, was approaching the site of the incident in his open car at high speed—accusations that could not be confirmed subsequently and were vehemently denied.[4] Without a doubt, the previously moderate Seldte had moved a bit to the right.

However, soon it was no longer members of the Stahlhelm who took the lead in acts of violence against policemen, but National Socialists. When a deceased member of the Stahlhelm was buried in Halle at the end of July 1926, a band from the NSDAP also participated. After the end of the memorial service, a member of the NSDAP and a spectator got into an argument, and the police stepped in. In response, the other National Socialists turned on the police, first shouting insults like "dogs" and "pigs," and then attacking the officers with sticks; they were supported by members of the Stahlhelm, one of whom called out: "Pull the dogs off the horses, kill the pigs." The police saw itself confronted by a hostile "crowd" and had to call in the riot squad to help disperse it; one policeman brandished his gun.[5] The National Socialists and the Stahlhelm members were displaying a new aggressiveness and a language that had previously been heard only from Communist demonstrators.

The relationship between the police and the KPD did not grow more tense with the establishment of the RFB. Harsh and bloody confrontations such as those in May 1924 in Halle remained rare exceptions, but they revealed that on both sides images of the enemy had hardened, and that under certain conditions they could lead to an escalation of violence. Such an incident, which left a number of dead, occurred on 13 March 1925 in Halle, in the middle of the election campaign for the Reich presidency. The way it unfolded shows how the concatenation of unfortunate circumstances and specific assumptions and anticipations on the part of those involved could have terrible consequences.

The KPD had scheduled a rally with its candidate Thälmann for the evening of 13 March in the Volkspark, its large meeting hall. An English and a French Communist were also slated to speak, but the police president, invoking an older directive from the Oberpräsident, issued an order prohibiting their participation. The KPD did not file a protest, but then allowed the foreigners to speak after all. The police did not intervene at this point because the officer in charge, Police Lieutenant Pietzker, happened to be outside the hall on the phone to his superior asking for further instructions. When he returned to the hall, the speeches had just finished and were now supposed to be translated. Pietzker climbed onto a table and ordered the interpreter to be quiet. Unfriendly catcalls came from the audience, the chairman made no effort to support Pietzker, and the agitation in the hall grew. The lieutenant now summoned the officers posted in front of the hall to remove the interpreter from the stage, but the RFB marshals stationed there and equipped with batons blocked the entrance. Pietzker then tried to disperse the meeting—unsuccessfully, even though he repeated his order and threatened to resort to the use of weapons. By now the police officers had reached the front of the stage and pulled out their clubs and, on Pietzker's orders, their pistols. At first the clearing of the stage met with no resistance, but when the crowed surged against the policemen a physical altercation ensued, and the clubs were used. Chairs and beer mugs were suddenly hurled at the police. Pietzker went down with injuries to his neck and shoulder and saw, as did other officers, someone shooting at him from the gallery. Without any further orders the police fired for about a minute. When the hall had finally emptied out, six bodies were found. More than twenty people were seriously hurt, and three subsequently died. Two of the dead were women; three others had been crushed by the panicked crowd. None of the police officers had any serious injuries or bullet wounds.[6]

The official investigation could not prove that any of the officers, or Pietzker, had done anything wrong in terms of criminal law. However, the shortcomings with respect to coordination on the evening of the deployment were criticized. The chief criticism was directed at Police President Runge, who was faulted not only for having prohibited the foreign speakers on the basis of a directive that had long ceased to be valid, but also for having left Halle on 13 March on official business. A few days later he was therefore dismissed by Interior Minister Severing.[7] The most explosive questions remained unanswered: Who had fired the first shot? Had the officers in fact been fired upon? The court's expert witness was able to find only two areas near the stage with traces that could be identified as bullet marks, and to identify one with certainty as having been produced by a small-caliber projectile. No firearms were found on any of the dead or injured. However, one RFB member stated during questioning that he could "not state which side had fired first." A woman who was a member of the KPD suspected that the first shot came from the police, but she was not sure. Another woman, a member of the DNVP, was also unable to state with certainty which side had opened fire; one NSDAP member as well as one member of the Reichsbanner had seen the first shot coming from the crowd.[8] Taking all these statements and findings together, one cannot rule out the possibility that a few shots from small-caliber weapons were fired at the policemen. However, it is very unlikely that the intention was to trigger the bloodbath that happened next. To be sure, in view of the "battle of Böllberg" ten months earlier this possibility cannot be rejected out of hand, but there are no other indications that it was in fact the case. It is more likely that a few of the RFB members spontaneously pulled their small-caliber firearms when it became apparent that the police were going to use force to disperse the meeting, for a reason that was not evident to the listeners. That the policemen responded on such a massive scale was surely in part the result of the circumstances—the tightly packed hall, which gave them hardly any possibility of retreat, and the sudden bombardment with chairs and beer mugs—but in part undoubtedly also of a certain image they had of "the Communists." By contrast, up to that point the audience in the hall and the RFB marshals, who merely pushed the police back, had behaved with considerable restraint. Pietzker himself evidently was close to the German Nationals.[9]

The exploitation of the event for propaganda purposes was not long in coming. On 19 March, the day the victims were buried, the *Klassenkampf* headlined its lead article with "Oath of Revenge!" The actions of the "bestialized policemen" merely showed how close the SPD had moved toward the German Nationals. The eight dead were part of a long line of victims that had been killed in March time and again in the proletariat's struggle to end the capitalist system. The answer, we are told, could not be complaining, but only a redoubled struggle—in concrete terms, a vote for Thälmann ten days later.[10] The *Saale-Zeitung*, by contrast, saw in the events merely a confirmation of its image of the KPD and warned against a "new wave of Communist terror." The police could not be blamed, for they had acted conscientiously with means that were unfortunately unavoidable; the real blame rested with the "thousands of Communists whipped into a frenzy."[11]

The incident in the Volkspark made its way into the political vocabulary of the KPD in Halle as the "Pietzker murders (*Pietzkermord*)." When the party held a rally at the end of August 1927 to protest the death sentences for Sacco and Vanzetti in the United States, the speaker—who had chaired the meeting in the Volkspark in 1925—warned against provocations by the police, accusing them of wanting to set off a bloodbath, just as they had done back then. When a column of demonstrators marched through downtown Halle after the end of the rally, RFB members who were acting as marshals used their fists to attack police offers who were trying to get the slowing column to keep moving. The officers could extract themselves only by using their swords. Small scuffles, accompanied by insults hurled at the officers, broke out also with non-uniformed participants at various locations on the march. The clashes continued into the evening, when a "crowd" of about a thousand gathered several times at the Hall Market, where police headquarters were located, pelted the police with rocks and sand, and even tried to force its way into the building. The police finally dispersed the crowd with rubber truncheons, and evidently there were no serious injuries. Charges were filed against sixty-eight individuals, among them nine women; however, they did not include any leading representatives of the KPD or the RFB, as the police president explicitly emphasized. In his view, the "main instigators and wire-pullers" had been "young, fanatical lads from the extreme left-radical organizations." He also underscored that the demonstrations by the KPD and the RFB "over the last few years have generally gone smoothly in terms of street policing." Yet ever since May 1927, when the police had drastically reduced the size of the contingents that accompanied the demonstrations, one could observe that the KPD was increasingly asserting the claim to be its own police and was less and less willing to comply with the orders of police officers. The "persistent, rude incitement of the masses" was doing its part to bring about excesses of this kind.[12]

The remarks of the police president indicate that in the phase of Communist realpolitik, the KPD was able to show itself in the street in a way that avoided conflicts with the security forces by adhering to the rules. However, this certainly did not mean that the latent hostility toward the police, nursed by many different experiences and certainly reciprocated, had disappeared. The mutual relationship contained enough fuel for an escalation. This was especially true when young KPD followers, who had been socialized in a culture of manhood that emphasized struggle and fighting, clashed with the police.[13]

Clashes between Political Opponents

Political violence in the middle years of Weimar was dominated not by clashes with the police, but by violent confrontations between members of the right-wing Combat Leagues and the NSDAP on one side, and members of the RFB, other Communist organizations, and the Reichsbanner on the other. These confrontations were especially numerous during election campaigns and the run-up to the referendums of 1926 and 1929, but they also occurred outside of such phases of intense mobilization, as James Diehl has pointed out.[14] In spite of some countervailing forces, the course was being set for the escalation during the later years of the Weimar Republic.

The run-up to the Reichstag elections in May 1924 was still without larger confrontations in the province of Saxony, even though, as the *Volksstimme* noted afterward, "the election campaign this time was fought to a large extent in the street."[15] Except for the vandalizing of election posters, there were no incidents worth recording.[16] More clashes were registered before the second Reichstag elections of the year, at the beginning of December. The *Saale-Zeitung* counted eighteen incidents on the weekend of the elections, though it reported only one case of serious injuries: during a confrontation between a member of the Reichsbanner and a follower of the Stahlhelm, one received a blow from a rubber truncheon, the other a penetrating wound to the lungs. According to the *Volksstimme*, there was a veritable storm of "swastika men" on the union building, though only a few windows were broken.[17] The relative stabilization of the political situation indicated by the results of the December elections was thus not tantamount to a decline in violence. Rather, the incidents merely indicate that the growing number of uniform-wearing activists on all sides created targets for verbal and physical attacks that were more visible than before, with the inevitable consequences.

The political polarization reached a new high point in March and April 1925, when a new Reich president was elected following the sudden death of Friedrich Ebert. The *Volksstimme* reported attempts by right-wing opponents to interfere with the propaganda trip of the Reichsbanner car through the villages around Magdeburg—a new form of political agitation—but also two unsuccessful attempts by Stahlhelm members to break up meetings of the SPD, as well as a hall brawl between Reichsbanner men and Communists in the county of Calbe.[18] The police president of Halle noted that during the last days of the election campaign there had been "almost daily clashes between the members of the various organizations," though (with but a single exception) the police had intervened in a timely manner. This had stretched the police forces to the breaking point: in the long run more officers were needed, especially since the heightened political tension had not abated after the election.[19] The police in Zeitz reported a near-clash on the occasion of two "reveilles" of the right-wing Combat Leagues and the RFB on 26 April, a few days before the second round of balloting. Because the police were able to interpose themselves in a timely fashion between the two columns of demonstrators (comprising 300 and 80 people, respectively), the situation did not progress beyond verbal insults and raised walking sticks. The chief blame was affixed to the Stahlhelm, which had departed from the assigned route and had displayed—and not only on that day—"conspicuous, provocative behavior."[20]

Numerous clashes were also recorded before the referendum on the expropriation of the nobility on 20 June 1926. The police of Magdeburg alone noted more than forty incidents during the day of the referendum and the previous night: people hanging posters were attacked, units of the Reichsbanner or the RFB clashed with those from the Stahlhelm, and individual members of the organizations who chanced upon one another in the street started brawls upon recognizing each other's uniforms or insignia.[21] Things were relatively quiet on the whole during the provincial parliamentary elections in mid November and the referendum on the Young Plan shortly before Christmas 1929.[22] In most clashes the goal was to show oneself and to defend or win public space. The threshold to the use of massive, potentially deadly violence was rarely crossed.

However, violence also occurred outside of the election campaigns, and it was here that the radical right was showing a growing willingness to resort to violence. The first incident of this kind consisted of clashes at the margins of a torch parade in honor of the newly elected Reich President Hindenburg, which the Stahlhelm organized in Magdeburg on the evening of 29 April 1925. Since the police expected that many opponents of this organization would be gathering along the route, it escorted the arriving trains. The Wehrwolf had not announced its own demonstration, so its 150 members were without a police escort as they began to march into the center of town. When the crowd greeted them with calls of "Heil Moscow," some of them attacked the spectators with flaming torches. At two places, groups of Communists tried to place themselves in front of the column of the Stahlhelm, but they were pushed aside by the police. By contrast, the Reichsbanner, which was present in large numbers, was stopped from getting involved by its leaders, who still could not prevent some minor scuffles between individual Stahlhelm members and Republicans. In the worst of these, one member of the Stahlhelm suffered several knife wounds.[23]

A new aggressiveness on the part of the right was evident not only in the large city of Magdeburg, but also in remote locations. The second chairman of the local Reichsbanner group in a farming village in the rural county of Weißenfels complained to the Regierungspräsident that since the beginning of 1924 there had been a number of assaults on supporters of the Republic. After the war, a Republican Gymnastics Club had been established with participation from the teacher as well as the priest, and it was causing financial losses for one of the two innkeepers in the village. In response, the birthday party of the teacher's daughter had been interrupted by shouting, the windows of the schoolhouse had been smashed, trees belonging to the innkeeper of the Gymnastics Club had been cut down, and children had been pelted with rocks. Without a doubt, economic tensions merged here with traditional lines of village conflict, and the ways in which the conflict was carried out also resembled those of earlier times. What was new was their political overtone. The complaint referred to the incidents as an "outflow of terror" that was being waged "by Stahlhelm and Wehrwolf people against the local Republican population." Evidently this argumentation was not merely a tactical move to gain the support of the officials, for the Landrat, too, saw the incidents as the consequence of the "sharp opposition" between the Reichsbanner and the "so-called national associations." He then added:

"Such incidents are not rare in the towns and villages of the present county located around Weißenfels and Zeitz and in the middle of the brown coal region, and they are in line with the tenor of the times. What is striking, however, is that these antagonisms are now also emerging in such purely agricultural communities."[24]

Political violence was becoming an increasingly endemic phenomenon that was spreading also to areas that had previously been quiet. But changes were noted even where the political polarization—as reflected in the election results—had been strong for some time. On 25 July, the Landrat of Ammendorf reported excesses by RFB men in the town and the surrounding Saalkreis—one of the KPD strongholds in the administrative district of Merseburg, where the DNVP had results that were only slightly below the party's average. A bicycling group of 70–80 RFB men, on their way home from Veterans' Day observations in Schkeuditz, had passed a village in which the bourgeois singing club was celebrating the anniversary of its founding. First, black-white-red garlands were pulled down and dragged across the street, then the passengers of a car, all of them members of the singing club, were beaten with clubs. On the evening of the same day, a uniformed Stahlhelm member on his way to the *Schützenfest* in Ammendorf was stopped by several RFB men and assaulted with fists and sticks. He defended himself with his firearm, fortunately causing only minor injuries.[25] As the chief gendarme of Ammendorf noted, these symbolic battles and fights over terrain were merely the last events in a long chain. "Frictions" between both groups had existed as early as the summer of 1924, but for the most part it was only "mutual ragging."

According to the gendarme, however, all this changed profoundly with the campaign leading up to the Reichstag elections in December, for the Stahlhelm was now "rather active" as a propagandist for the DNVP. It began with the vandalizing of posters, but there were also "physical altercations. And the Stahlhelm was the first to engage in this." On a Sunday in November, twenty Stahlhelm members had forced their way into a tavern and beaten up a Communist without any prior quarrel. Even the local Stahlhelm leader had to concede to the police that, "the Stahlhelm men had behaved rudely." Other fights of this kind occurred the night before the election of the Reich president, followed by corresponding counteractions by the men of the RFB, who now repeatedly insulted and also beat their adversaries, often on the way to and from work. The gendarme by no means wanted to assign blame for the development only to the members of the Stahlhelm, though he underscored that among them were "elements who use every opportunity to start a fight with the Red Front Fighters," for example, by visiting, on the occasion of the Stahlhelm Days, taverns that were frequented mostly by Communists.[26] From a different locality in the county, the gendarme reported on a troop of seventeen Wehrwolf members who had mocked and ever more rudely insulted the driver of a car decorated with small black-red-gold flags; eventually, when three policemen intervened, they had attacked them—with an infantry shovel among other things—at the command "Storm troop advance!" They had behaved like "wild animals," and calmed down only when a crowd of onlookers that had gathered in the meantime wanted to take the side of the policemen.[27] In all of this, the willingness to engage in violence that became visible among the right-wing organizations was still noticeably contained. But to the same extent the Stahlhelm and Wehrwolf were no longer content to display their own strength and became "more political," as it were, placing themselves openly in service to the German Nationals. After the election of the honorary Stahlhelm member Hindenburg, when they seemed to be harvesting the fruits of their efforts, resistance to the security forces was no longer far off.

New on the part of the right wing in the province of Saxony was also the combination of anti-Semitism and violence against people. On 18 May 1924, a Sunday, the Halle Gymnastics Club of 1904, whose membership was largely Jewish, held a gymnastics exhibition in the Reform Realgymnasium; before it began, the various groups were supposed to be photographed in the school's courtyard. After the first few pictures had been taken, two young lads in "Hitler uniform" suddenly appeared, jeered at the gymnasts, and refused to leave the courtyard. Two leaders of the club initially managed to push them out into the street, but then the young anti-Semites received reinforcement from the *völkisch* Siegfried Hiking Club, which was holding a gymnastics class at the same time in a school across the street. About thirty young men attacked the Jewish gymnasts, not only with fists, but with a total of twenty oak clubs, which suggests that the attack had been planned. Still the *völkisch* assailants were driven out of the school courtyard, and the police were called and took down their personal information. No one had suffered any serious injuries.[28]

It must have been not least incidents like this that prompted the Prussian Interior Minister Severing to pass the so-called "stick prohibition" (*Stockverbot*) a year later, after the election campaign for the Reich presidency. In a decree at the end of May 1925, he lamented the growing radicalization of both right-wing and left-wing organizations, and especially of their youthful members, who were no longer content to insult their adversaries but attacked them with dangerous objects. That is why the police had to take action against the "carrying of uniformly heavy, gnarled sticks, numerous rubber truncheons, and especially striking and stabbing weapons."[29] The reaction of the Stahlhelm was not long in coming. Shortly after the Regierungspräsident of Merseburg had issued even more restrictive implementing regulations for Severing's decree at the beginning of September—the carrying of lightweight sticks was now also prohibited—and had informed the organizations, the Reich Interior Minister, at this time still the German National Schiele, received a letter of protest from the Stahlhelm. It complained about a rash of assaults on Stahlhelm members ever since the prohibition; the Reichsbanner and its chairman, Hörsing, were responsible for the fact that five national members had been killed and twenty-one seriously injured.[30] Oexle, the new police president of Halle (where most attacks were said to have occurred), could not see any connection to the stick prohibition, however. The majority of the incidents, many of them clustered around the election campaign in the spring, predated his decree; of several others only the account of the Stahlhelm existed, since no report had been made to the police.[31]

What the official then went on to say reveals fundamental aspects of the political violence in Halle and elsewhere. He did not hide his skepticism about the stick prohibition, even if its implementation had not encountered any problems so far, since it would not put an end to the violence. It would be preferable, Oexle continued, "if political disagreements are fought out with sticks, instead of, as expected and as has already happened, with knives, brass knuckles, and other such implements, which are not so easy to detect for the police, but are far more dangerous." The clashes were taking place only where the police were not present, and the participants for the most quickly disappeared once the police arrived. The "most frequent cause of the clashes" was the wearing of the insignia of the various organizations, "because they had an inciting effect," although the adversaries were by no means always members of the organizations whose insignia they wore; "young lads" were pinning them on "quite frequently," which was true not least for badges of the RFB. The members of the RFB especially were in other respects "generally well-disciplined" because they feared either particularly harsh punishment from the courts or the dissolution of their organization. Still, they and members of the KPD on the one side, members of the Stahlhelm and the Wehrwolf, on the other, were those most frequently involved in violent confrontations, while members of the Reichsbanner and the Jungdo rarely participated, "at least in the most recent period." At the end of his letter, the police president gave a cautious all-clear signal. He noted that most public events in Halle had occurred without any disturbances; fights usually happened at night once the events were over, as participants were returning home alone or in smaller groups. He had therefore instructed the police to step up their night patrols.[32]

Oexle very accurately described the Janus-face of the activities of the Combat Leagues. Their chief purpose was to make their presence felt in the street, in the public sphere, and thereby assert their own claim to power. This did not invariably imply violence, especially not if the threat of harsh sanctions was hanging over such behavior. However, the nighttime violence was no accidental by-product, in two regards. First, it served to test the strength of the other side, if the police happened not to be looking, and darkness lessened the danger of being recognized and arrested and made it easier for the actors—sometimes under the influence of alcohol—to cross the threshold of violence more quickly. Second, the heightened recognizability thanks to the wearing of insignia offered a chance to prove one's "manhood" in physical combat also to those young men who were not, or not yet, members of these organizations. For youth from the lower classes, limited physical violence was part of their "street socialization,"[33] whereas it represented something new in this form to those from bourgeois families. It is difficult to determine how "political" the youths from either group perceived the violence they perpetrated to be. In any case, their environment perceived them in political terms, and they were seen as part of the general confrontation between the Combat Leagues.

As before, however, the political violence was not primarily youth violence. Of the actors from the province of Saxony during the middle Weimar years of whom we have more detailed information, about one-fifth had been born prior to 1890, one-fourth belonged to the actual front line age groups, and just under half were born after 1900 and had therefore been too young to participate in the war. But only one-tenth of them had not yet attained the age of majority at the time when they became involved in a violent confrontation.[34] This age profile largely matches that of the period from 1919 to 1923, if one leaves out the fighting in March 1921. In those years, as well, only one-third belonged to the actual front line age groups of those born between 1890 and 1899, while a third each was born earlier or later.[35] Although workers were also involved in such confrontations on the side of the right-wing organizations in the middle Weimar years, shopkeepers and other members of the middle class participated at least in equal numbers.[36] Once again, this matches the occupational data we have for the years 1919–1923.[37] Even if the Stahlhelm and the Wehrwolf were not purely bourgeois organizations in terms of their social structure, the battle being waged in the streets was a "proxy war" not merely between "right-wing" and "left-wing" workers, but also between representatives of the bourgeoisie and the workers over supremacy in the public realm.

As the police president of Halle had feared, Severing's stick prohibition did not fundamentally ease the tension in the political atmosphere. Severing himself felt compelled, in two decrees at the end of August 1926 and in March 1929, to call once again for resolute action against acts of political violence and the abuse of the right of assembly through the use of violence.[38] However, for a while it was possible to calm the situation during rallies and demonstrations by using the measures suggested by the police president of Halle. In May 1927, his colleague in Magdeburg decided to drastically reduce the police presence at these events. In 1926, more than 12,000 policemen were deployed at over 250 larger events. The costs of doing this were simply too high, especially since these activities in Magdeburg, the headquarters of the Stahlhelm and the Reichsbanner, surpassed even those in Berlin. Henceforth there would only be the usual measures to ensure safe traffic. The police president was able to obtain the more or less explicit approval of the organizations and parties; the representatives of the NSDAP were the only ones who refrained from an official statement, though they did not contradict the declarations issued by the others. At the beginning of January 1928, a positive result was reported in response to an inquiry by police officials from Bremen. Between June and November 1927, there had been 142 marches in Magdeburg with nearly 30,000 participants, with no negative experiences concerning the new kind of police escort.[39]

Outside of political demonstrations, however, the violence was not contained, and each encounter between hostile organizations of the right and the left could lead to violent confrontations. On 2 July 1927, the local Halle group of the Teno sailed to Wettin/Saale to celebrate a summer fest in together with the town's shooting club. The local Halle group of the RFB had rented premises there for the same day and the same purpose. The police presence was limited to two gendarmes. Both celebrations, which took place at taverns located far apart, went off without disturbances. However, as night set in, RFB troops were moving about the town stopping passersby, searching them for insignia of right-wing organizations, and assaulting several—whom they considered political enemies because of their Stahlhelm or shooting club uniforms—with fists and drumsticks. At around three in the morning, the Teno section tried to reach their ship's dock in closed formation, but the column broke up and further attacks took place, which now also involved clubs and rubber truncheons. When one Teno member pulled out a pistol with blank cartridges and fired a shot at the attackers, without causing any damage, the situation escalated further. The shooter and several other Teno members fled into a house that was soon virtually besieged by a "crowd," composed for the most part of RFB men. The agitated crowd, which could not be calmed down even by an RFB leader, eventually forced its way into the house, searched it for weapons, and beat one of the Teno members unconscious. All along calls were heard like "We have the power today, not the police!" and "Bring them out, shoot them dead, the butchers!" However, once it seemed that a riot squad from Halle was about to arrive, the RFB men dispersed quickly.[40]

This incident combined well-known behavior patterns with new ones. As was true before 1923, the use of a firearm marked for the "crowd" the point at which the threshold had been crossed to a form of self-defense that was no longer regarded as legitimate. New, however, was the verbal claim by the RFB men that they were now acting as the police, as it were. Officials had already noted something similar in connection with the street demonstrations, not only among the RFB, but also with the Wehrwolf.

The NSDAP also acted in a provocative fashion. One example involved Gregor Straßer, who at an event in Magdeburg in May 1927 found himself confronted by about 150 Communists in an audience of 600. Following insulting comments about Liebknecht and Luxemburg and the "red mob" in front of him, Straßer was shouted down and attacked by the supporters of the KPD. However, the police brought a quick end to the brawl that was about to erupt, and only a few suffered minor injuries. For the police president of Magdeburg the attack by the Communists was not a well-planned act, but largely the result of Straßer's provocation. He also emphasized that "in contrast to the excesses of the National Socialists in Berlin, which have developed almost into a permanent state," this was an isolated incident, since "the local Communists and RFB men have for some time now provided no reason for any police intervention."[41] Six months later, at a Social Democratic event in Jessen, a small community in the rural northeast of the administrative district of Merseburg, there was a brawl with the local NSDAP group. As the Regierungspräsident reported, this incident marked a new stage in the relationship between these two parties. Before, that relationship had only been "tense," with no reason for the police to intervene; now, however, the NSDAP had deliberately sought out the confrontation.[42] This did not let the KPD and the RFB off the hook, for their members, outside of the political events that the police kept a special eye on, certainly did take the offense against their enemies on the right. It does illustrate, though, that in the middle years of Weimar, violence emanated above all from the right-wing Combat Leagues and the NSDAP.

Notes

1. On this see Thomas Kurz, *Blutmai: Sozialdemokraten und Kommunisten im Brennpunkt der Berliner Ereignisse von 1929* (Berlin, 1988).
2. See LHAM C 20 Ib 1952/I, 1953/I, 1954, passim. Larger clashes occurred in Madgeburg during a strike of streetcar workers at the beginning of October 1925, when first strikebreakers were beaten up, and then the police found itself confronted by a hostile "crowd" that was made up largely of "young people": LHAM C 20 Ib 1952/I, fols. 315f. (Police president to RP Magdeburg, 7 October 1925).
3. LHAM C 20 Ib 4665/III, fols. 18–21 (PP Magdeburg to RP Magdeburg, 22 January 1924), the quote fol. 20. The *Volksstimme* claimed in its report of the events, though without giving details, that some policeman had been beaten with umbrellas and sticks and emphasized that "hysterical women were screeching, spitting" and had behaved "as though half mad" (*VS* no. 18, 22 January 1924).
4. *MZ* no. 38, 21 January 1924; LHAM C 20 Ib 4665/III, fols. 77–79 (Seldte to RP Magdeburg, 25 January 1924); fols. 74–76 (Reply by PP Magdeburg to RP Magdeburg, 29 January 1924). In the days after the incidents the *Magdeburgische Zeitung* looked for victims of the alleged misbehavior of the police, but the matter soon disappeared from the headlines.
5. LHAM C 20 Ib 1913/V, fols. 80–84 (Copy of the verdict of the trial before the Lay Assessors' Court Halle, 19 September 1927). Of four defendants, one was acquitted and three received jail terms of three to six months.
6. LHAM C 20 Ib 2043/I, fols. 11–19 (RP Merseburg to the Prussian Ministry of the Interior, 17 March 1925) and passim (Interrogation records). The account of the incident is based not only on the report by the Regierungspräsident, but also on statements by other witnesses, including those from the ranks of the Communists.
7. Ibid., fols. 18f. (Criticism by RP); fols. 265–270 (Notice of dismissal by the prosecutor, 3 July 1926); *MZ* no. 142, 19 March; no. 145, 20 March 1925 (Report about the debate of the incident in the Prussian Landtag).
8. LHAM C 20 Ib 2043/I, fols. 81f., 175, 84, 199, 182 (Records of police interrogations).
9. *VS* no. 63, 15 March 1925.
10. *KK* no. 52, 19 March; no. 53, 20 March 1925; see the eulogy by Otto Kilian at the Gertrauden cemetery in LHAM C 20 Ib 2043/I, fol. 100 (PP Halle to RP Merseburg, 19 March 1925).
11. *SZ* no. 65, 18 March 1925.
12. LHAM C 20 Ib 2041/I, fols. 150–164 (PP Halle to RP Merseburg, 24 August 1927), the quotes fols. 158, 159, 162. The police president quotes insults such as "You butchers, it won't be long now and we'll take your place, and you'll all hang from the gallows," or "You green scoundrels, soon you'll be replaced, then we'll take the guns out of your hands, and you'll be lined up against the wall and slaughtered" (fol. 164).
13. On this see the following chapter.
14. Diehl, *Paramilitary Politics,* 190–198. His characterization of the situation as "a state of latent civil war" (194), however, seems to be an overstatement, given the clear limits of the actual violence.
15. *VS* no. 106, 7 May 1924.
16. *VS* no. 105, 6 May 1924.
17. *SZ* no. 288a, 9 December 1924; *VS* no. 288, 9 December 1924. In addition, unknown perpetrators made an attempt on the life of Georg Bernhard, the editor-in-chief of the *Vossische Zeitung.* On his way back from an election rally for the DDP in Merseburg, he lost control of his car and flipped over because someone had loosened the bolts on one of the rear wheels. Fortunately, neither Bernhard nor anyone else was injured. Two days before, two adherents of the radical right who had been persistently interrupting a speech by Bernhard were arrested by the police. A search turned up a loaded revolver, which one of the two men confessed was to be used to kill Bernhard. On the incident in Halle see *MZ* no. 625, 9 December 1924.

18. *MZ* no. 164, 31 March; no. 217, 30 April 1925; *VS* no. 92, 21 April; no. 93, 22 April; no. 97, 26 April 1925.
19. LAMe C 48 Ie 948, fols. 235f. (PP Halle to RP Merseburg, 14 May 1925); see *SZ*, special edition, 27 April 1925.
20. LAMe C 48 Ie 948, fol. 42 (Police administration of Zeitz to RP Merseburg, 27 April 1925).
21. LHAM C 20 Ib 1991/III, fols. 148–155 (RP Magdeburg to the Prussian Ministry of the Interior, 19 October 1926). The letter is a response to a list of alleged attacks on members of the Stahlhelm sent to the interior minister by the organization. In many cases it was impossible to get a clear account of what had happened, so many proceedings had to be dismissed. To the writer of the report, the claims of the Stahlhelm seemed "exaggerated in many cases." See also *VS* no. 49, 27 February 1927; no. 51, 2 March 1927, about two trials for breach of the public peace, which resulted from incidents in Burg near Magdeburg and in Magdeburg itself. In one case, an attack on 18 June 1926 by Reichsbanner men on members of the Bismarck Youth, who were soundly beaten, the primary responsibility of the Reichsbanner men was undeniable.
22. *VS* no. 271, 19 November; no. 300, 21 December 1929.
23. LHAM C 20 Ib 1895/V, fols. 71f. (PP Magdeburg to RP Magdeburg, 30 April 1925); see *VS* no. 101, 1 May 1925; *MZ* no. 221, 3 May 1925. It was characteristic of the justice system in Magdeburg—which at the beginning of the year had rendered the notorious verdict in the charge of slander brought by Reich President Ebert against the editor Rothardt—that in the subsequent trial charges were brought only against four Reichsbanner men and one Communist who had assaulted participants in the parade only after the incident at Breiter Weg; they received jail terms of six months to a year for serious breach of the public peace (*VS* no. 160, 11 July 1925).
24. LAMe C 48 Ie 948, fols. 241f. (Mayor Thielicke to RP Merseburg, 11 March 1925), Thielicke was mayor of the neighboring town; fol. 248 (LR Weißenfels to RP, 6 May 1925). In the village of Prittwitz, villagers and members of the Communist youth got into a brawl on 8 June 1924 after the young Communists had torn off the insignia of Gymnasts: LAMe C 48 Ie 134/XIV, fol. 248 (Schupo Weißenfels to RP Merseburg, 10 June 1924). See also LHAM C 20 Ib 1991/II, fol. 134 (RP Erfurt to the Prussian Ministry of the Interior, 26 February 1925), where we hear of a clash between working-class athletes and a Stahlhelm/Wehrwolf group on 31 August 1924 in County Hohenstein near Nordhausen: a brawl broke out when the military group, singing the old imperial hymn "Hail to thee in the victor's wreath," marched past a tavern where the workers were socializing.
25. LAMe C 48 Ie 948, fols. 470f. (LR Saalkreis to RP Merseburg, 15 July 1925).
26. Ibid., fols. 475–478 (Gendarme division of Ammendorf to LR Saalkreis, 5 August 1925). The officials also emphasized that in recent times there had been several cases of "vicious maltreatment of Stahlhelm men" before and after the elections for Reich president, though they also reported a case from the beginning of February when Stahlhelm men had beaten three members of the RFB in a tavern without reason after first locking all exits.
27. Ibid., fol. 524 (Gendarme office Niemberg to LR Saalkreis, 13 July 1925). See also LHAM C 20 Ib 1991/II, fols. 237f. (RP Merseburg to OP, 24 July 1925) and LHAM C 20 Ib 1991/III, fol. 67 (RP Merseburg to OP, 29 June 1925): on the night of 20/21 June 1925, Stahlhelm men had attacked Reichsbanner men with clubs and had stolen black-red-gold flags.
28. LHAM C 20 Ib 1913/III, fols. 209f. (PP Halle to OP, 16 May 1924). The *Saale-Zeitung*, no. 118, 21 May 1924, limited itself to a report of three lines, which did not lay blame and thus painted a false picture. See also LHAM C 20 Ib 4120/I, fol. 333 (PP Erfurt to RP Erfurt, 16 March 1926): here we hear about the desecration of a Jewish cemetery perpetrated during the night of 12/13 March 1926 by three members of the Viking League, who had overturned ninety-five headstones. On the less conspicuous but numerous acts of anti-Semitic violence in the mid 1920s see Walter, *Antisemitische Gewalt*, 200–221; Hecht, *Deutsche Juden*, 187–205.
29. LAG Reg. Erfurt Präsidialabteilung no. 10995, fol. 151 (Circular decree, 26 May 1925).

30. LHAM C 20 Ib 1991/II, fol. 247 (Telegram, 9 October 1925). During a protest rally against the stick prohibition, the Halle teacher Dennhardt, leader of the Jungstahlhelm, made the astonishing statement that the Stahlhelm members carried their sticks merely "to support themselves after long marches." He added that they were "always the ones attacked" and threatened that they would resort to "self-defense" if they were not protected from attacks by their enemies: LAMe C 48 Ie 948, fols. 570f. (Police record, 11 October 1925). On similar reactions in Berlin see Wirsching, *Weltkrieg*, 438f., who represents them as a natural response to Communist violence without paying adequate attention to the radical right's inherent willingness to engage in violence.
31. LHAM C 20 Ib 1991/II, fols. 250–252 (PP Halle to OP, 10 October 1925).
32. Ibid., fols. 252–255 (PP Halle to OP, 10 October 1925).
33. See Jürgen Zinnecker, "Straßensozialisation: Versuch, einen unterschätzten Lernort zu thematisieren," *Zeitschrift für Pädagogik* 25, no. 5 (1979): 727–746; Rolf Lindner, "Straße—Straßenjunge—Straßenbande," *Zeitschrift für Volkskunde* 79, no. 2 (1983): 192–208.
34. We have information for about sixty-seven actors. They come from the following sources: LHAM C 141 Halberstadt nos. 282, 290, 299; LHAM C 20 Ib 1913/V, 1960/II, 1991/V, 2041/II.
35. We have data on about 100 persons in fourteen cases of violent clashes between 1919 and 1923 (not counting the fighting in March 1921) both with state security forces and between members of right-wing and left-wing organizations. It comes from the following sources: LHAM C 141 Halberstadt nos. 243, 246, 251; LAMe C 141 Naumburg nos. 14, 21, 26, 28, 30, 39, 41, 42; GSTA PK I. HA Rep. 84 no. 11673.
36. We have occupational information for 30 of the actors that belonged to right-wing organizations: 10 were simple "workers" and three were skilled workers, but 14 identified themselves as merchants, white-collar workers, master artisans, or lower civil servants; 3 others who presented themselves as "bakers" or "locksmiths" cannot be precisely classified. The other data regarding the social profile is too fragmentary to allow for meaningful statements.
37. Of the twelve members of right-wing organizations known for this period, only one was employed as a "worker" without any further identifying information and two were bakers, but the others were farmers, merchants, and mid- and low-level civil servants. By contrast, a little more than half of the other actors, a total of forty-four, can be identified as unskilled or semi-skilled workers, the majority of the others had learned a trade, and only five were merchants or white-collar workers. Occupational data is available for ninety-seven individuals.
38. LAG Reg. Erfurt Präsidialabteilung no. 10995, fol. 171 (Circular decree of 24 August 1926); fol. 195 (Circular decree, 21 March 1929).
39. Report about a press conference by the police president, in *Magdeburger Generalanzeiger* no. 116, 19 May 1927 (in LHAM C 20 Ib 1859/IV, fols. 214f.). However, officials in the Prussian Ministry of the Interior were skeptical. Similar agreements had already occurred previously in Düsseldorf, Bonn, Wuppertal, and in early 1927 also in Cologne. Especially in the Düsseldorf region, that is, part of the Ruhr region, the experiences had not been positive: GSTA PK I. HA Rep. 77 MInn Tit. 4042 no. 119, fol. 8 (Note by the Minister of the Interior, 24 June 1927).
40. LHAM C 20 Ib 1960/II, fols. 277–286 (Declaratory part of the decision of the Lay Assessors' Court Halle, 21 January 1928). Sixteen defendants were sentenced to jail terms between three and twenty-one months.
41. Ibid., fols. 210–212 (PP Magdeburg to RP Magdeburg, 6 May 1927).
42. LHAM C 20 Ib 1859/VI, fols. 235f. (RP Merseburg to OP, 3 February 1928).

Chapter 8

A PARADE OF MEN
Violence in the Political Culture

Scholars have frequently emphasized that the political culture of the Weimar Republic was characterized by fragmentation. There was no minimum consensus shared by all camps and currents; not even the opposition to the Versailles Treaty generated sufficient commonalities.[1] This fragmentation thesis, however, relates only to the culture of political interpretation. It overlooks the similar forms of political self-representation and the concordance of values and behaviors to which they gave rise. Such commonalities have been described via the concepts of "militarization" or "militarism." It is quite obvious that the right-wing and left-wing Combat Leagues imported a growing number of military elements into the sociopolitical culture of the Weimar Republic. What is unclear, however, is whether the military symbols and rituals on all sides led to a substantive change in how politics was conceived, or whether the left-wing formations, especially the Reichsbanner, filled military forms with what was in the final analysis antimilitarist content. It is also unclear whether the mere adoption of relevant forms or only violence itself should be seen as the touchstone for a thorough and pervasive militarization.[2]

The outward militarization of the political culture had its breakthrough in 1921, when the Free Corps and the Home Guards disappeared for good and the rise of the Combat Leagues began.[3] Now, military ways of behavior and values could be brought to bear in a sustained way in new organizational forms. This triggered a surge of mobilization among the population. The Combat Leagues were not clubs of notables, but were intended to reach the masses. As a result, the way in which they were set up involved the founding of many local groups, which was always combined with a flag consecration, an act of considerable public relations value. This alone had a mobilizing effect on the group's own followers as well as its adversaries. Added to this was that uniforms and—at times when there

Notes from this chapter begin on page 206.

was no actual event—insignia allowed members to recognize each other. This became a potential source of violence, especially where Stahlhelm local groups were set up deliberately in Communist strongholds.

The new "street politics" was not limited to the founding period of these organizations between 1921 and 1924, however. The years 1924–1929 certainly did not lack for election campaigns: three Reichstag elections and two simultaneous elections for the Prussian Landtag, two rounds of balloting to elect the Reich president, the referenda on the expropriation of the nobility and on the Young Plan, along with elections for provincial assemblies and local government—all this offered a wealth of opportunities for political self-representation. Political adversaries were more likely to wear the insignia of their organizations during election campaigns than at other times; as they returned home from events at nighttime, they could physically experience their own claims to the street without much fear of the police. Another such opportunity came when people hanging posters ran into each other, or when members went out to check that their own posters had not been vandalized. A further potential for violence lay in the practice—not an invention of the Weimar Republic—of sending speakers to the events of political adversaries. The presence of uniformed Combat League groups heightened the conflictual elements of this practice, since strength was now being demonstrated and terrain was being symbolically and physically occupied also in indoor spaces. If a speaker was not given permission to speak or was suddenly cut off, a "hall brawl" (*Saalschlacht*) was imminent.

Another novelty during the middle Weimar years was the increased mobility of the election campaigners due to the use of trucks and cars. It would seem that the Reichsbanner was the first organization in the province of Saxony to use this kind of transportation on a larger scale. The election of the Reich president in 1925 was the first time that members of the organization traveled through the counties adjoining Magdeburg in "black-red-gold fighting trucks," which were greeted in all the villages by local units of the organization and cheered by crowds of onlookers, among whom there were sometimes also political adversaries.[4] The decoration with banners made the trucks visible from afar, and the chance to have the same speaker appear in many locations in a short period of time boosted the group's presence. Politics was now taking place increasingly in the streets. The number of encounters with outwardly identifiable opponents surged and increased the likelihood of violent confrontations. Still, the activities of the Combat Leagues were not primarily aimed at the use of violence. Their public appearances were rituals in which a political concept was presented not in its argumentative, but in its affective and symbolic aspects.[5] This suggested a limited use of violence, since massive use would have proved counterproductive to the image an organization sought to present as well as to its legal survival. However, the willingness to engage in violence was—with characteristic differences—kept alive and furthered by the forms these appearances took and the values they conveyed.

Political Fests

This willingness to engage in violence was sustained, not least, at the political fests. After the initial years of the Weimar Republic, these events were given new forms and new elements. Above all, May Day was imported from the *Kaiserreich* period into the new state by the workers' movement as its own celebratory tradition. However, the competition between the KPD and the SPD gave rise not only to separate May Day fests, but also—especially in the KPD—to a separate calendar of festivals, a separate "church calendar."[6] It began in January with commemorative ceremonies for Rosa Luxemburg and Karl Liebknecht, with Lenin added as a third in 1924 (the "LLL Commemorations"), and continued with the commemoration of the March dead, which combined the memory of the victims of the Revolution of 1848 and the Paris Commune with those of the fighting in 1919, 1920, and 1921. The next date in the calendar was 1 May, 3 August was Anti-War Day, and the final event was the commemoration of the Russian Revolution on 7 November, two days before the SPD celebrated "its" Revolution Day. Added to this were other get-togethers like International Women's Day and especially the Red Days, analogous to the German Days held by the right.[7] The LLL Commemorations and Revolution Day, in particular, called for interpretations that embedded the fighting to date and the victims into a larger political perspective and referred to the "new Jerusalem" in Moscow.

While the SPD placed its interpretation of the Revolution against that of the Communists on 9 November, and sought to impress the accomplishment of the Weimar Republic upon the public's awareness, with the help of the bourgeoisie in its ever shrinking role, on 11 August, Constitution Day, the right wing developed its own calendar of festivities. The most prominent was the Reich Founding Day in the middle of January, which simultaneously celebrated the founding of the Stahlhelm. Important was also Bismarck's birthday on 1 April and the German Days, which were held mostly during the warmer months.[8] Together with the Stahlhelm, the "national" part of the bourgeoisie could now undertake on these occasions precisely what had been until now the prerogative of the workers' movement—namely, making a bold and visible statement of its own claim to the street.[9]

There are remarkable similarities in how these festivities unfolded. Above all, military elements became a fixed component. The Stahlhelm took the lead in this regard: its Front Line Veterans' Day offered an elaborate program, which in 1925 extended over three days. During the course of Saturday, groups of participants from all over the country, several tens of thousands in all, arrived in Magdeburg and, with singing, marched in closed formation to their lodgings. The evening began with a dinner for the extended leadership of the organization and a number of honorary guests, among them Admiral Scheer and *Forstrat* Escherich. Seldte gave a programmatic speech followed by three other, brief addresses, one of which was delivered by Duesterberg. In the meantime, the Stahlhelm rank and file had gathered in front of the hall. Afterward, accompanied by their leadership cadre, they marched through the city to the circus building, where taps was sounded in the usual military forms, including the joint singing of the final hymn. This was followed by two acts of the drama *York* by the war poet Ernst Lissauer; the play was introduced by musical pieces and followed by another speech from Seldte. While the play was still going on, the sociable part of the festivities, known as German Evenings, were already getting under way in seven Magdeburg taverns.

Endurance was called for on Sunday, Reich Founding Day. As early as 9 AM, the first Stahlhelm groups marched through downtown Magdeburg, first to a mass at the cathedral, then to restaurants for lunch. After 12 PM, the men moved in larger formations back to the Stadt und Land hall, where the play *Frederick the Great* was performed, followed once again by two brief speeches from Seldte and Duesterberg. The day was concluded with more German Evenings. The following day was devoted to another round of "drinking and coffees," which, according to the police, were "heavily attended."[10] The year before, the program had included as another element the joint pronouncement of the Rütli Oath (Rütli was the legendary birthplace of the Swiss Confederacy) and the singing of the German national anthem; in the final scene of the final play *The Somme,* Frederick the Great had made another appearance, this time to the tune of the "Hohenfriedberger [March]."[11]

Elaborate festivities were staged not only in the Stahlhelm metropolis of Magdeburg. At the beginning of August 1924, the Kyffhäuser Jugendbund (Kyffhäuser Youth League), the new youth organization of the veterans' group, presented itself to the public with a German Day in Nordhausen and on Kyffhäuser, a nearby mountain that was crowned by a monument to Barbarossa. Here the Jungdo marched out and presented a torch parade to the guests of honor, among them Hindenburg. Gymnastic exercises were put on, and patriotic presentations could be admired. *Germany, Awake!,* written by a newspaper editor from Nordhausen, was performed on the evening of the first day. The celebration was concluded with the consecratory play *Honoring the Hero:* masses came marching out and the dead hero was solemnly cremated. That morning, participants had had a chance to attend, at the Nordhaus stadium, the "Presentation of Events from the Ur-Germanic Life of the People," which a retired lieutenant colonel had "created most effectively on the basis of the best research of Old Germanic scholarship."[12] This work followed in the footsteps of the "living tableaux," for instance those presented on the Völkisch County Day in August 1925, when visitors to Gardelegen were entertained by groups of figures who embodied, successively, the period of the Germanic tribes, lansquenets, the era of Louis XIV, the founding of the Reich, and soldiers of the Reichswehr, accompanied by the recitation of poems. "Then"—the step from the sublime to the ridiculous was a small one—"the wife of a shoemaker from Bösdorf, dressed like an ancient priestess, performed the consecration of the Cheruscians." During a commemoration of Schlageter put on by the Wehrwolf in Halle, members of the organization depicted Schlageter's execution by shooting, then the Rütli Oath, and finally Frenchmen attacked by Wehrwolf men with rifles.[13]

These staged events in the city and the province adopted many elements from the veterans' fests, the festivities for the emperor's birthday, and historical anniversaries that people had celebrated during the *Kaiserreich,*[14] though now that the monarchy had ended they were missing the central point of reference. As on previous occasions, many laypeople participated in the performances. This intensified the individual experience of the play and suggested equality in the propagated "*Volk* community." However, what actually happened during the Front Line Veterans' Day made clear that this was a hierarchically constructed community. The leadership cadre of the Stahlhelm and its guests of honor met away from the simple members. Only afterward were the latter included in the program of festivities, at first purely as a marching column. Here one can see that the appellation "comrade," introduced in the Stahlhelm and seeming to ignore differences of military rank, was relative.

The plays that were put on—whose content has not survived—and the living tableaux created historical references that could be assigned to three different categories. In addition to references to the mythical Germanic past (already common during the *Kaiserreich*) and to concrete historical figures and events after this period, there was now the memory of the recent world war and the continuing conflict with France. In the process, a tradition was constructed whose purpose—unlike before—was no longer to legitimize current conditions, but to emphasize the virtues and attitudes that were now necessary. A prime model for this was Prussia, wellspring of first, the canon of old Prussian virtues, and second, specific historical figures like Frederick the Great, who was depicted not only as an exemplary monarch but also a war hero and savior of his state from a seemingly hopeless situation. The common oath expressed the constantly propagated desire for "unity," while at the same time sacralizing it and thereby elevating it to a higher level.

Like the Stahlhelm, the Reichsbanner also employed military forms at its public appearances. During the organization's founding phase in 1924, the flag consecrations offered the new local groups ample opportunity for doing so. For example, on 19 and 20 July 1924, the Reichsbanner Neuhaldensleben gathered for a Republican Day that the *Volksstimme* described in detail. The festivities began on Saturday evening with a festive drink, which, after an "effective prologue," led to the official speech by "Comrade Tramp," a local. This was followed by a pledge of the Republicans in verse form, affirmed by the assembled guests with a call of "Free Heil!" and the singing of the third stanza of the national anthem; solo and choral singing brought the evening to a close. On Sunday morning, Reichsbanner delegations from the surrounding communities and from Magdeburg arrived in Neuhaldensleben, which was decked out in black-red-gold banners. Throngs of people began to form, but as the *Volksstimme* emphasized, the fest was soon given "its strict order, which was carried out in exemplary fashion" as the Reichsbanner groups moved "in closed formations" to the banner consecration at the festival grounds, where they formed "an immense block" surrounded by the other guests, women, and children. The separation of the genders was just as clear here as it was among the adversaries on the right. The singing club "Unity (*Einigkeit*)" intoned the banner song, and Ernst Brandenburg from the national board gave the consecration speech, at the end of which "a sea of hands" rose for the oath of loyalty to the Republic. Words of greeting followed, after which, to the accompaniment of the "sounds of a fife-and-drum corps and two bands," celebrants marched through the town, of course once again in "exemplary orderliness" and "tight formation"; then, finally, came "joyous and festive happenings" at the taverns surrounding the festival grounds.[15]

A good deal of marching was also done at the national meeting of the Reichsbanner around the end of February 1925, when well over 100,000 members assembled in Magdeburg. However, there were no consecration plays, oath, or taps as at Stahlhelm events, and thus none of the excessive emotionalism. The celebration centered around the march to the cathedral square in separate groups—"a splendid picture of voluntary discipline and great courage for sacrifice"—and the joint march (lasting several hours) through the center of town as an impressive demonstration of strength. The verbal contributions had a more sober framework. The previous evening, the delegations from all parts of Germany and Austria had been received at their taverns with words of greeting; in the morning, Federal Chairman Hörsing delivered a speech in the city theater to delegations of the various Gaue.[16] But a military veneer was now also given to the annual celebration of the Weimar Constitution on 11 August, when the Reichsbanner marched with music and banners, in exemplary order.[17]

To be sure, the Reichsbanner avoided an excessively "militaristic" display and the adoption of certain military rituals like taps; moreover, the high level of the organization's order and discipline was specially emphasized only during the first two years after its founding. However, the descriptions of the organization's public appearances by the *Volksstimme* give the impression that an effort was being made to demonstrate to Social Democratic supporters and to the right-wing Combat Leagues that the Reichsbanner was, basically, just as good as they at moving about in military formation.[18] The Republican Days shared central staging elements with the German Days: the uniforms worn by the male participants, the military arrangement, and the march through the town, as well as the joint swearing of the oath. The group's own strength and fighting power were to appear equal to the other side. The adoption of forms previously disapproved of brought with it the partial adoption of military values, an emphatic assertion of the polarity of gender roles, and the targeted appeal to the emotions. However, this development had distinct boundaries, which became evident in the program of the national meeting and at other celebrations of the Social Democrats.

The SPD retained traditional forms from the workers' movement in celebrating its new Revolution Day on 9 November, enthusiasm for which was not so readily shared by the Republicans among the bourgeoisie. There was no parade by the Reichsbanner—probably also to avoid making the organization appear too much like an appendage of the party. The festivities were held in a hall and centered around the ceremonial address, framed by music and choral pieces from the repertoire of the old workers' movement. In 1928, on the ten-year anniversary of the Revolution, masses in formation appeared for the first time in Magdeburg in the speaking chorus of *The Fiery Drum;* the final scene of the play, which depicted the road of the working class "out of factory enslavement to liberated humanity," led into the joint singing of the Socialist march.[19] The speaking chorus—a genre that was developed only after 1919, experienced its first flowering in the immediate postwar years, and became the chief element of the new mass plays on both wings of the workers' movement[20]—reinforced the pathos-laden traits of the SPD's celebratory culture. The "masses" that appeared on stage were in formation, but not in uniform; this, and the "inwardly" focused commemorations of the Revolution marked the limits of the militarization among Social Democrats.

The Communists, too, adopted military elements into their celebratory repertoire with the RFB, but they likewise did not let its influence become too strong. As a counterpart to the German Days of the right wing and the Republican Days of the Reichsbanner, the Communists put on Red Days, at which the RFB played the lead role. Bitterfeld was the location for such a meeting on 7 March 1925; it centered around the banner consecration, or *Fahnenweihe*—the *Klassenkampf* used this word explicitly—for the RFB of the subdistrict of Bitterfeld. On the morning of that day, the Halle delegation marched to its vehicles "in military order." Here, too, there was "exemplary order" when, following the welcome in Bitterfeld, the first demonstration was held, which, drawn up by the marshals of the RFB, could "hardly be surpassed in military orderliness and discipline." Afterward everyone gathered in a large square, the Workers' Singing Club sang a "revolutionary song," and then the chairman of the Halle RFB Gau, "Comrade Richter," delivered some brief words of welcome and solemnly handed over the banner. The men of the Bitterfeld RFB responded by swearing never to abandon it. Next came the fighting song of the RFB performed by a band, words of greeting from the national leadership, and a joint oath from all participants to support Thälmann in the election for Reich president. Afterward, the RFB men marched through the streets of Bitterfeld, which had been decorated with red cloth. When the delegation from Halle returned home, working women with red kerchiefs were allowed to greet them.[21] Here, too, the salutation "comrade" (*Kamerad*) invoked the community of experience constituted by the veterans, excluded women, and appealed to the emotions connected with the military rituals. However, the link to the goals of the party was too obvious for the RFB's pretended independence from the KPD to seem credible.

Much larger in scale, and comparable to the Stahlhelm meetings, was the Thomas Müntzer Day that the KPD held on the weekend of Pentecost in 1925 in Eisleben, 400 years after the Peasants' War. On the first evening, two scenes from an older Müntzer play were put on in the garden of the Volkshaus, framed by recitations and choral singing. There were also speeches by two KPD parliamentarians, Hoernle and Kilian, who reviewed the history of the Mansfelder Land up to the March fighting in 1921, without neglecting to properly condemn Luther, who was born in Eisleben, as a traitor to the peasants. During intermission, red signal fires burned in the hills surrounding Eisleben. The evening concluded with the singing of "Brothers, to the Sun, to Freedom." The morning of Pentecost Sunday was dominated by a "historical-political demonstration march" through the streets of the city; in the afternoon, a "red mass meeting" was held in the large field on the outskirts of town. Only now did the RFB swing into action, opening the remainder of the program with a parade. A long trumpet signal announced the "consecration and handing over of the red banner, given to the revolutionary proletariat of Mansfeld by Russian workers and peasants of the Ural region," followed by two songs. Then came what was conceived as the high point of the meeting, a performance of the mass play *Thomas Müntzer,* written by Berta Lask specifically for this occasion; Lask would later cause a stir with her pieces *Leuna 1921* and *Poison Gas Cloud over Soviet Russia.* This was followed by several brief speeches, after which the men of the RFB and worker athletes formed the sign of the hammer and sickle, and everyone sang the "International." Finally, after five hours, participants were able to move on to the sociable part of the evening. On Pentecost Monday, the Red Youth met for a rally and a parade through the city, after which there was a fair with amusing presentations on the outdoor stage.[22]

During the May demonstrations, only music groups of the RFB participated in a prominent way. The RFB also took a back seat at the new Revolution Day festivities and the LLL Commemorations. Speaking choruses and recitations, effectively staged with elaborate lighting, dominated the festivities to commemorate the great "dead of the proletariat." The festivities in Halle in 1926 began with a solemn, muffled drum roll in a hall draped in black. A speaking chorus in the hall and the galleries called for turning the days of commemoration into "days of struggle," and the curtain slowly rose to reveal a triangle with the names of the three heroes. Liebknecht's name was illuminated first, and texts about him and then about Rosa Luxemburg were recited by an actress. After intermission, speaking choruses of children and youngsters alternated the calls "Lenin is dead" and "His work must live." The joint singing of "Brothers, to the Sun, to Freedom" provided the transition to the address; at the end, the participants intoned the "International."[23]

The KPD, too, tried to underscore its strength and fighting power to the public by adopting military forms. However, in spite of the militancy of its own propaganda, which I will discuss later, the public appearances of the RFB remained just one element of Communist celebratory culture and never assumed a dominant role.[24] Both the Reichsbanner and the RFB were a response to the occupation of public space by right-wing organizations. Their public appearances had three functions: to demonstrate their readiness to fight to their opponents, to mobilize their own supporters, and to recruit workers who were still politically uncommitted or woo members away from competing organizations.[25] But their influence did not go so far as to fundamentally alter the representational style of the Social Democrats and Communists. In the final analysis, they imparted an incisive form above all to the defensive preparedness of the party rank and file that had developed in the years since 1921. For the SPD, the Reichsbanner was an element of its organizational network meant to guarantee the defense of the Republic by its sheer size, while for the KPD, the RFB was connected with an interpretation of the political struggle, an interpretation that ascribed a preeminent role to the dead heroes and martyrs of the proletariat and the associated virtues.

Values and Methods of Struggle

The speeches and recitations at the celebrations were concerned not only with visions of a new state and a new society, but also with values and qualities that were indispensable on the road to achieving these goals, with the characteristics of the enemy, and with the ways and means of fighting him. In the bourgeois public of the province, which lacked a committed Republican voice of wide reach after the *Saale-Zeitung* moved to the right, "unity" continued to represent the highest good.[26] The word meant two things: the unity/unanimity of the bourgeoisie, and the unity of the nation. Given the growing fragmentation of the landscape of bourgeois parties—the differences over the Dawes Plan, Stresemann's Locarno policy, and the Young Plan, which affected especially the DNVP as the largest party on the right—the call for unity among the bourgeoisie is understandable, especially since it seemed within grasp for a brief moment, in the run-up to Hindenburg's election as Reich president.

Thus the moderate *Magdeburgische Zeitung* could issue an appeal in April of 1925 to bring about a "bourgeois unity front" against the Weimar Coalition and its candidate, Marx, because Hindenburg—and this is where the second connotation of the unity idea came into play—was in a position "to unite the entire German people behind himself across all parties and classes."[27] At a rally in March 1924, the "*völkisch*-social block" spoke of unity as the precondition for saving Germany from "chaos"; shortly afterward, at a celebration commemorating Bismarck put on by the Stahlhelm, General Maercker stated that "unity must be achieved first" before one could turn once again to the acquisition of colonies. In May 1926, the cathedral preacher in Magdeburg, Martin, lamented the new deepening of the rift within the German people caused by the most recent flag decree of the Reich government, though he expressed his optimism that the bourgeoisie, in the face of the smear campaign against the old princes, would find its unity under the monarchic banner, after which it would move toward its salvation under the leadership of the German Nationals. "Unity and togetherness" is how the *Saale-Zeitung* summed up its general impression of the Reich Founding Celebration of the Halle Stahlhelm in 1928, where Admiral Scheer had called for "a return to Bismarck" as a way of achieving the necessary unity.[28] There was hardly an occasion when the unity motif could not be used—whether in historical recollections or in relation to political questions of current or future relevance. By contrast, the concept played no comparable role in the political rhetoric of either the Communists of the SPD. On the right, this was more than the usual invocation of the unity of one's own organization: first, because no organization existed; second, because the emphatic and emotional way in which this demand was voiced reflected also the vehement rejection of both the idea of class struggle and the concept of a clash of interests that was mediated through parliament and was, in the final analysis, unavoidable in a modern society.[29]

What virtues would help achieve the precarious unity and lead Germany to new power and glory? A leader in the Bismarckean mold was needed, on this there was agreement on the right.[30] But the chief quality that this leader—like all Germans—should possess was emphatically invoked not only by the right, but also by the left, though with different connotations: manliness. For the right, the model of this manliness was the front line soldier. Seldte had already articulated this demand in 1922 at the Front Line Veterans' Day of the Stahlhelm: "We want the idea of the Stahlhelm to become the common property of the entire German people: the idea of manliness." Cathedral preacher Martin, whose pathos could hardly be surpassed by anyone, decried the lack of manliness two years later, on the same occasion: "Nowhere do we have men anymore"; "much too much softness" was in the German people, while what was needed were "men of steel" like the world war veterans assembled before him. In the present emergency men should not complain so much but leave the whining to "wailing women" instead; faith, too, should be "something masculine, something hard as steel, not something maudlin." The Jungnationaler Bund (Young National League), too, should be made up of "tough men"; no one wanted anything to do with "effeminate Mama's boys."[31] "Manliness" was defined here in strict separation from female qualities that carried negative connotations, which meant that gender roles were clearly separated. For example, the Jungnationaler Bund regarded each of its female members as a "future wife and mother," and Seldte, in his speech at the Front Line Veterans' Day events in 1924, underscored that Germany could only be rebuilt by "men of battle and women who are mothers."[32]

The ideal of manliness could be given a variety of different accents. In his speech at the rededication of the Kaiser Wilhelm monument in Halle in 1924, Duesterberg listed the Prussian catalogue of virtues as he defined it: alongside loyalty and diligence he mentioned "selfless devotion, courage, voluntary discipline," also "exemplary social conduct" and "passionate love of the fatherland." The first issue of *Alter Dessauer*, the paper of his faction within the Stahlhelm, called for "self-control, discipline of the old Prussian kind" as cardinal values in addition to loyalty.[33] Loyalty and comradeship were emphasized by the "Erhardt Song" (part of the standard repertoire of the Stahlhelm); willingness to fight, vigilance, and "strength and heroic courage" by the "Hitler Song," the text of which was noted down by the Magdeburg police on Veterans' Day in 1924.[34] This catalogue of chiefly military virtues was taken much further still by the "Wehrwolf Song," sung to the tune of the "Hohenfriedberg March." Seven times in four verses we hear of death and the willingness to die, three times of heroism; in addition, the Wehrwolf banner showed a death's head against a black background. What this means is that the willingness to sacrifice and thus the willingness to take radical action were emphasized most strongly in the Combat Leagues with the youngest members, most of whom later switched over to the National Socialists.[35]

To be sure, it is not surprising that Combat Leagues and the youth organizations affiliated with them offered military values as the concrete manifestations of the ideal of manhood they propagated. But one must not underestimate their influence outside of the organizations themselves, not least because the bourgeois papers devoted much space to reporting on the meetings of these organizations; Seldte's speeches at the Front Line Veterans' Days were reprinted at length in the *Magdeburgische Zeitung*. When the paper, in a lead article on the presidential campaign in 1925 titled "Hindenburg our leader!" quoted the candidate's reference to "labor and thrift," "honesty and faith in God" as guiding values, these were admittedly—comparatively speaking—civilian values, but they came from the mouth of a war hero and imperial general field marshal.[36] However, it was precisely the emphasis on "labor," which had been heard ever since the Versailles Treaty at the latest—Seldte, too, spoke of the Germans as the "people of labor"[37]—that made it possible to connect with "manliness." For example, for a while in 1924 the *Saale-Zeitung* published a paper of its own under the title *Wir Volk* (We the People), which was clearly aimed at a non-bourgeois readership. Its heading showed, between the two words, the frontal figure of a worker with unbuttoned shirt and sleeves rolled up, who has placed a heavy hammer on the ground next to himself and is holding its handle with his right hand.[38] The strong male manual laborer appears here as the incarnation of the laboring nation. Anyone who was pursuing the "national community" also had to adopt guiding images from outside the bourgeois horizon. The paper was thus clearly trying to pick up the pictorial language not least of the Communist press.

While the KPD did not use the concept of "manliness" explicitly in its political rhetoric, its iconography in particular shows beyond doubt that men played the main part in the revolutionary struggle of the working class. The main figure of Communist pictorial propaganda was the muscular "Giant Proletariat," whose gender is obvious from his bare chest. The workers' movement had been using this image since the turn of the century, though now it was given unmistakably aggressive traits on the Communist side.[39] For example, on the day before a right-wing parade in Halle in May 1924, the *Klassenkampf* added a large cartoon to its lead article entitled "To Hell with the Fascist Menace"; in it, this same giant, with a grim countenance, strikes the ground between two factory chimneys with his fist, forcing a crowd of smaller figures wearing Stahlhelm uniforms and swastikas to flee helter-skelter.[40] A poster announcing a Red Day in Belgern (County Torgau) combined the masculine motif with advertising for the RFB: two sturdy men face the viewer with legs apart and resolute faces. The man on the left is a worker with his sleeves rolled up and his right hand curled into a fist, while on the right an RFB fighter in uniform sounds a signal on his trumpet, which visually underscores the appeal of the caption: "Join the Red Front." Between them, the two men are holding a red banner with the Soviet star (Figure 8.1).[41]

Figure 8.1 Recruitment Poster for Red Day, 1925

Toughness, determination, and the readiness to fight spoke from such images. These were virtues of the party activist committed to the revolution, but also of the soldier. Reference to the October Revolution made this link even tighter. A poster for the 10th International Youth Day featuring the slogan "Young Workers! Onto the barricades!" depicted a group of Russian peasants carrying rifles with mounted bayonets and with hands raised as though for an oath.[42] In fact, alongside the fist,[43] the hand raised for an oath, especially for an oath of revenge, was a central motif of Communist pictorial language. Revenge—not individual revenge, of course, but "class revenge," as the KPD emphasized—had to be exacted for the great dead leaders Karl Liebknecht and Rosa Luxemburg and for the many less prominent victims killed in the March fighting during the previous years or, as in 1925 in the Volkspark in Halle, by new police tyranny.[44] On 15 January 1926, the *Klassenkampf* provided its lead article, titled "Our Revenge: Completion of Your Work!" with a woodcut showing a worker with Lenin's features standing at the bier of Liebknecht, the left hand on the dead man's chest, the right raised for the oath of revenge, while behind him crowd the masses of the proletariat (the men in the foreground); above all of them flies a large red flag against a large sun (Figure 8.2).[45] Through the sworn promise of revenge for the dead of his class, the (male) proletarian acquired the soldier-like strength to become a fighter for world revolution.

In essence, all of life was a struggle, and the class struggle was not only an abstract political concept. The featured speaker at the May rally in Halle in 1924, the KPD functionary Bowitzki, one of the military organizers of the "March action" in 1921, commemorated the victims killed "in the daily struggle of the production process," along with those who have had to give up their lives "in the tough resistance" to capitalism and militarism.[46] In the end, the motifs of struggle, sacrifice, and revenge could be transfigured in a quasi-religious way. Hardly anyone did this as compellingly as the poet Oskar Kanehl, whose "Red Soldiers" were paraded out at the founding meeting of the RFB in Erfurt:

> "Geheiligt ist unser Krieg.
> Gesegnet sind unsere Waffen ...
>
> Der Besten Blut ist mordend hingeflossen.
> Wir sind die Rächer. Sind die Erben ...
> Rennt an, ihr Weißen, gegen unseren Opfermut.
> Wir werden siegen. Oder sterben ...
>
> Bei unsern Weibern: Brüder, Waffen!
> Bei unsern Kindern: Waffen, Waffen!
> mit unsern Leibern decken wir die Freiheit ..."
>
> [Sacred is our war.
> Blessed are our weapons ...
>
> The blood of the best was shed in murder.
> We are the avengers. We are the heirs. ...
> Throw yourselves against our courage of sacrifice, You Whites.
> We shall win. Or die ...
>
> With our women: brothers, arms!
> With our children: arms, arms!
> With our bodies we shield liberty...][47]

Figure 8.2 Oath of Revenge for Karl Liebknecht, 1926

Here, men fight and sacrifice themselves for a Socialist society to be won in a new revolution, even though Kanehl's poem resounds more with the pathos of heroic defenders than the optimism of world reformers. The virtues that were demanded of the fighters were essentially no different from those the Stahlhelm and others of like mind expected from their followers—namely those of the soldier.

The SPD also paid tribute to the advance of military values, though only up to a point. At a celebration of the Reichsbanner in February 1930, shortly before the breakup of the Grand Coalition on the Reich level ushered in the final phase of the Weimar Republic, Erik Nölting underscored that the organization had demonstrated that in the new democracy there was no place for "effeminacy and lack of discipline," and it had "given leadership and direction to the inner longing of the undecided masses."[48] This was one way of describing the result of soldierly training, but, as the *Volksstimme* underscored, the Reichsbanner was precisely a "civil army for the defense of the Republic."[49] The last election appeal for the Republican presidential candidate Marx on the front page of the *Volksstimme* in 1925 showed the silhouette of a chiseled warrior holding a long sword in his right hand and a banner with the Reich eagle in his outstretched left. "Long live the Republic! Vote Wilhelm Marx!" could be read between the sword and the banner. The political enemy, however, was not depicted (Figure 8.3).[50]

Another SPD warrior on a campaign poster for the Reichstag elections in 1924 was swinging an axe against a hydra, whose three heads were meant to represent the monarchists, the *völkisch* parties, and the "rowdy KPD."[51] However, such a direct depiction of the enemy as the target of the attack was the exception. The "Reichsbanner Song" (by Bruno Georges) called upon the "brothers" to close ranks, infused the three new colors of the Reich with meaning and importance, and closed with the verse: "Through the black night red leads victoriously, To golden paths to liberty, Storm troop of the German Republic, the black-red-gold banners." The enemies of the Republic were not mentioned directly. Karl Bröger, the prominent workers' poet, also dedicated a "Republican Flag Song" to the organization: "He who is a real man, let him join the ranks," the lyrics read, and "For these colors we will die," though once again without any reference to the enemy.[52] The military elements and allusions are obvious, but they were turned "inward," as it were, directed at one's own organization and members, not at an enemy explicitly identified.

The conceptions of the enemy articulated in word and image provide further insights into the attitude that was to be taken in fighting the respective enemy. For the right, the Communists remained the chief opponent. Only its extreme edge, especially the NSDAP, which was slowly gaining influence, aimed its incitement during the middle Weimar years mainly against the Jews. Still, even at a DNVP rally at the beginning of 1924 in Halle, in an electoral atmosphere dominated by agitation against the Dawes Plan, professor of medicine Hermann Stieve could proclaim, without challenge, that Jews had no love for the fatherland, were "inferior, fat, and sluggish," and had a "predisposition to softening of the brain."[53] Opinions diverged as to the threat posed by the Communists. To the *Saale-Zeitung*, which had by now moved close to the German Nationals, they were "red hordes that are only waiting for the moment when they can bash in the heads of peaceful citizens with impunity and rob them," as it wrote in an article in mid March 1925 about the bloodbath in the Volkspark. Needless to say, from this perspective the Communists bore most of the responsibility for the events,

Figure 8.3 Campaign Poster for Wilhelm Marx, 1925

as they did for the fighting in Berlin in May 1929, a "wild orgy of hatred against the existing order." Moreover, the paper argued that at the "Lighthouse" trial, which had placed brawling Stahlhelm members in the dock, insufficient attention had been given to the responsibility of the KPD, even though everyone knew that "the Communists incite violence at *all* events put on by the Stahlhelm."[54] The picture of Communists as demonic criminals was continued here, even though the determination with which the Communists advocated their beliefs was accorded some respect. Because the Communists were willing to die for their ideas, the *Saale-Zeitung* emphasized, they seemed "a thousand times more sympathetic than all the Socialist and other 'republican' nobility governing today."[55] The bourgeois paper criticized the bourgeoisie for its lack of a radical disposition, and in so doing it made clear how much it was already defining the political situation as a final struggle even before the outbreak of the great crisis in the fall of 1929.

The *Magdeburgische Zeitung*, too, spoke of the "subversive doings" of the KPD, which had to be opposed "with all of the state's instruments of power," but it avoided the emotionalism of the Halle paper. Following the fighting in May 1929, it underscored the difference from the situation ten years earlier: today, it was no longer possible "for a small, radical minority to assume control through a surprise attack on the state." It was therefore "absolutely wrong to paint the specter of Bolshevism for the middle classes."[56] The paper also called for a sober, interest-driven attitude toward the Communist motherland, the Soviet Union. It was important to gain access to the market in that country, and one should therefore not allow oneself to be pulled into a defensive political front. "We are fully aware," the article continued, "that the social conditions currently prevailing in Russia and the forms of the state and the economy … form a serious threat to west European culture, the magnitude of which depends on the degree of resistance" the Communists encountered; however, in this regard one should have confidence "in the moral powers of the German people." At the end of 1925 the *Saale-Zeitung*, too, after the elimination of Trotsky and Zinoviev, had argued that Communism was dead both in Russia and outside, and would "remain behind hollow and empty like an empty container."[57] An all-overshadowing fear of Bolshevism that would have regarded any countermeasure as ultimately legitimate cannot be inferred from such pronouncements.[58] German Communists were considered violent troublemakers interfering with the rebuilding of the nation or political criminals with more or less demonic traits (depending on one's stance), but the Soviet Union was seen as a state that was at least on the path toward becoming a normal European large power and should therefore be assessed in principle with the same criteria that were applied to other such powers.

In Communist pictorial language, a new enemy appeared in 1924 with the Reichsbanner. Still, the KPD devoted less space to elaborating images of the enemy than it did to discussing the qualities and behaviors of a class-conscious proletariat that was loyal to the party. The Reichsbanner was accused of being the "protective troops of capital," which had to be treated as "enemies of the proletariat." The organization was held up to ridicule in a pictorial broadsheet intended for children: the Reichsbanner as a horde of monkeys confronted the Communist lion, who merely had to let out a roar to garner respect; the colors black, red, and gold were here derived from the elongated monkey back. The Stahlhelm, meanwhile, was presented as a "shit pot," while those who wore the steel helmet were associated not only with "toadying and kicking," but also with "murder of workers."[59] As of 1923, however, the symbol for the militant enemies on the right was the easily identifiable swastika.[60] The "butchers" of the Schupo also remained clear enemies, in spite of some attempt to woo them: "police brutes" had fired on workers in the Halle Volkspark, a long-prepared "murder of workers" was committed in Berlin in May 1929.[61]

The SPD and the Reichsbanner were fighting on two fronts, as it were. That the chief enemies were to be found on the right was also reflected in the portrayal of the enemy. When it came to the Communists, the criticism was focused on the party as a whole, accusing it, for example, of continuing to seek power through violence after the events of May 1929. Approval was also expressed for the outlawing of the RFB, since the purpose of the organization had been to recruit members "who are willing to engage in armed struggle against the democratic state and its supporters." But the Social Democrats avoided personally demeaning the Communist "footsoldiers."[62] By contrast, the Stahlhelm had behaved "like wild beasts" when they broke up an election rally by the SPD in November 1924: they were "the definitive criminal type" and also "pumped full of alcohol." Other "intoxicated front-line heroes" who did something similar in April 1925 behaved "like a band of thugs." "Fascist murderous rabble" had attacked a Reichsbanner man in Neuhaldensleben during the referendum on the expropriation of the nobility.[63] And while the KPD was not genuinely seen as a potential partner of the Social Democrats, its simple supporters were certainly "prodigal sons" that could be wooed away for one's own party; by contrast, such hopes did not seem realistic when it came to the members of the Stahlhelm and the other Combat Leagues.

The increasingly military appearance of political events, and the images of the enemy this entailed, went hand in hand with a growing propagation of violence as a way of engaging in conflict. But here, too, there are revealing differences. In March 1926, an NSDAP speaker demanded that the political enemies had to be opposed with "radical brutality," employing language that was becoming typical for his party, though it was also picking up on statements by the moderate bourgeois press in the fall of 1923.[64] The Stahlhelm did not necessarily go that far, at least not in public. But during his speech at the rededication of the Moltke monument in May 1924, Duesterberg did praise the commitment of his comrades in the "fight for equality in the streets," which had been waged victoriously in the end. Even the more moderate Seldte underscored, at the celebration of the founding of the Reich in Magdeburg in 1927, that the organization had been founded "to combat the internal enemy, who then had control over the street," a goal that had now been achieved. And when Seldte had proclaimed a year before on the same occasion that some had sought to strip the Germans of "freedom, honor, fatherland," which, if they could not be reclaimed peacefully, "we shall have the strength to take back by force," his words were, at the least, ambiguous in meaning and referred not only to international politics.[65]

The language was harsher still behind closed doors. At a members-only meeting of the Magdeburg Stahlhelm at the end of 1926, at which the entire national leadership was present with the exception of Seldte, the former Free Corps leader Friedrich Wilhelm Heinz was able to demand without challenge that the enemy had to be "brutally fought against," namely in the spirit of the Erzberger murderers Schulz and Tillessen.[66] The leader of the Jungstahlhelm, the Halle primary school teacher Dennhardt, made such statements also in public. At an election rally in December 1924, he declared that the murders of Erzberger and Rathenau had been "committed out of a youthful, passionate love of the fatherland," words that—according to the police record—triggered "a storm of enthusiasm among many youthful listeners." A year later, Dennhardt, at a protest rally against Severing's prohibition against sticks, threatened "self-help" if the government did not do more against the attacks on members of right-wing organizations.[67] It is not difficult to see that little about such statements was meant to be defensive, especially given the behavior of the right-wing Combat Leagues in clashes with their enemies. On their part, there was thus certainly no decline in the readiness to resort to violence during the relative calm of the middle years of Weimar. The expansion of their organizational apparatus and the elaboration of their rites of self-presentation went hand in hand with the openly articulated readiness to fight for the "right to the street" with violence, if necessary. The growing penchant by the radical right to take the offensive—described above—had its roots also in the conscious affirmation and propagation of violence.

The KPD continued to propagate violence as a legitimate offensive tool in the political struggle in keeping with the state of the class conflict. The "bloodiest of revolutions" was better than a slow wasting away, noted the *Klassenkampf* on the anniversary of the October Revolution in 1925. A few years later, a lead article in the paper about the events in Berlin stated that on 1 May 1929, the proletariat of Berlin had resumed the struggle against the bourgeoisie "in its highest forms" for the first time since 1923, even though the party had not directly called upon it to do so.[68] Even during the more moderate phase of the KPD in 1926/27, when Georg Schumann declared that Lenin's most important doctrine was that the party stand up "also for the small needs of the workers," there was no doubt that only "revolutionary violence" could break the resistance of the bourgeoisie and would have to lead initially to the dictatorship of the proletariat.[69] The notion of "civil war" as the appropriate form for the final conflict between bourgeoisie and proletariat remained alive, even if the phrase itself was no longer explicitly used after 1925.[70] A slogan for Anti-War Day in 1924 proclaimed that only "civil war against capital" could prevent a new world war.[71] And Oskar Kanehl composed these lines: "Leap onto the barricades, Come out for the civil war, Fix the Soviet banners, For the red victory."[72] No less bold were the words of Boleslaw Strzelewicz, who appeared as a reciter at many KPD festivities:

"...Laßt ab von Eurer Menschlichkeit -
Humanität ist nicht am Platze,
Wo die entmenschte Bestienfratze
Den Giftzahn fletscht, uns zu vernichten.
Ihr müßt den heil'gen Haß aufrichten!
Euch selbst, der ganzen Welt zur Liebe,
Um die verruchten Freiheitsdiebe,
Um die Verräter, die Euch drücken,
Für alle Zeiten zu ersticken.
So dienen wir der Menschlichkeit!"

[... Take leave of your humanity –
Humanity is out of place,
Where the beastly and inhuman face
Bares the poisoned tooth to destroy us.
You must arouse the sacred hatred!
For your sake, for love of the entire world,
To smoother for eternity
The wicked thieves of liberty,
The traitors that oppress you.
Thus we serve humanity!][73]

The Social Democrats distanced themselves emphatically from such positions, in spite of the military phrases that entered into their political rhetoric. For example, during the presidential election campaign in 1925, the people were called "onto the barricades" for an "offensive against Hindenburg"; the Reichsbanner traveled about in the "black-red-gold war vehicle," heading for the "decisive battle."[74] Following the "defensive battle" of the referendum in 1926, the "light cavalry of the proletariat" was seen in action "in the election campaign" alongside "tanks," referring to party members on bicycles and in a bus transporting campaign material.[75] The verbal borrowings from the military were not always meant to be entirely serious, but the fact that they were used shows how accustomed people had grown to them.

Moderate physical violence against the political enemy from the right and the left did not seem a problem, provided it was applied in a purely defensive way. In a report on Constitution Day in 1925 in the "reactionary stronghold" of Halle, where there had been small scuffles, the *Volksstimme* voiced its impression "that it is impossible to fight the enemy of the Republic in Halle with the weapons of the intellect. The only remedy against the insults and insolence of this nationalistic-Communistic crowd in Halle is a good thrashing. Those types can still be taught some manners this way."[76] Elsewhere, subunits of the Reichsbanner threatened to resort to "self-help" if the authorities failed to take sufficiently vigorous steps against the provocations from Stahlhelm members.[77] And when a blustering Hörsing declared, during the festivities on the anniversary of the founding of the Reichsbanner in 1925, that while the organization rejected violence as well as any illegal arms, it would "fight every attacker with the same means, beat him, and, if necessary, destroy him,"[78] this did not sound all that different from Seldte's and

Duesterberg's pronouncements about the successes of the Stahlhelm in the battle for the street.

Meanwhile, "Women, prevent the civil war!" an appeal from the *Volksstimme* to its readers during the Reichstag election campaign in May 1924, expressed a concern that the Social Democrats voiced repeatedly in the middle years of the Weimar Republic.[79] The accusation of working toward a civil war was aimed at both the Communists—they sought power "only through and in a civil war," it was said in connection with the Berlin "Bloody May" in 1929—and, even more emphatically, at the radical right. In its commentary on Constitution Day in 1926, the *Volksstimme* did not rule out that the struggle between enemies and supporters of the Republic "will one day escalate into the horrors of a civil war after all. The more fascist currents spread throughout Europe, the more serious is the danger that the democratic polity in Germany, as well, must fight once more for its survival."[80] Statements like these mark a clear distance between the SPD and both the Communists, for whom civil war was *not* a horror scenario, and the radical right; although the latter did not, of course, approve of the idea, its openly expressed willingness to employ violence offensively did not, in the final analysis, rule out this possibility.

As far as the Reichsbanner was concerned, only defensive force was acceptable. This was the limit that the "militarization" of politics encountered in the Republican veterans' organization.[81] With the Communists and the extreme right, however, this "militarization" went further. Among them, the uniforms, the rituals, and the values that were propagated combined to legitimate and promote offensive political violence as well.

Notes

1. Lehnert and Megerle, "Teilkulturen"; idem, "Identitäts- und Konsensprobleme in einer fragmentierten Gesellschaft. Zur politischen Kultur in der Weimarer Republik," in D. Berg-Schlosser and J. Schissler, eds., *Politische Kultur in Deutschland: Bilanz und Perspektiven der Forschung* (Opladen, 1987), 80–95.
2. Mommsen, "Militär," uses the concept of militarization in the broadest sense; Richard Bessel, "Militarismus im innenpolitischen Leben der Weimarer Republik: Von den Freikorps zur SA," in K.-J. Müller and E. Opitz, eds., *Militär und Militarismus in der Weimarer Republik* (Düsseldorf, 1978), 193–222, here 220, applies it to the right-wing Combat Leagues; Eve Rosenhaft, "Gewalt in der Politik: Zum Problem des 'sozialen Militarismus,'" in Müller and Opitz, *Militär und Militarismus,* 237–259, here 238, sees the violent behavior in political conflicts as the crucial characteristic.
3. Unlike Michael Geyer, "Nation, Klasse und Macht: Zur Organisation von Herrschaft in der Weimarer Republik," *AfS* 26 (1986): 27–48, I see *this* as the central development that set the course, not the establishment of the Home Guards in 1919, whose importance—as I have shown above—was limited, and which did not yet articulate the claim to a symbolic dominance of public space.
4. *VS* no. 93, 22 April 1925; see also *VS* no. 113, 15 May and no. 117, 20 May 1928.

5. See Murray Edelman, *Politics as Symbolic Action* (Chicago, 1972), esp. 12ff.
6. This is the argument of Mallmann, *Kommunisten,* 225.
7. On this, and especially May Day, see Mallmann, *Kommunisten,* 220–226. On the "escape from the German past" in the development of the KPD's intellectual tradition see Wirsching, *Weltkrieg,* 342–348.
8. See Fritzsche, *Rehearsals,* 83–92.
9. Ibid., 169–177.
10. LHAM C 20 Ib 1991/II, fols. 89–91 (PP Magdeburg to OP, 20 January 1925); *MZ* no. 32, 18 January 1925.
11. *MZ* no. 38, 21 January 1924.
12. *SZ* no. 187, 12 August 1924. Incidentally, Hindenburg, an honorary citizen of Nordhausen, was given a special reception that included an honorary drink at City Hall, where he delivered two brief speeches. He was also called out onto the balcony of his hotel by the crowd, from where the "warrior figure of the hero" returned a greeting of "Hurrah!"
13. LHAM C 20 Ib 1913/III, fols. 315–317 (Gendarme to LR Gardelegen, 24 August 1925); LAMe C 48 Ie 134/XIII, fols. 96–98 (PP Halle to RP Merseburg, 28 May 1924).
14. Rohkrämer, *Militarismus,* 55–69; Monika Wienfort, "Kaisergeburtstagsfeiern am 27. Januar 1907. Bürgerliche Feste in den Städten des Kaiserreichs," in M. Hettling and P. Nolte, eds., *Bürgerliche Feste: Symbolische Formen politischen Handelns im 19. Jahrhundert* (Göttingen, 1993), 157–191; Charlotte Tacke, "Die 1900-Jahrfeier im Teutoburger Wald 1909. Von der 'klassenlosen Bürgergesellschaft' zur 'klassenlosen Volksgemeinschaft'?" in Hettling and Nolte, *Bürgerliche Feste,* 192–230.
15. *VS* no. 169, 22 July 1924; see *VS* no. 128, 3 June 1924; nos. 46–48, 24–26 February 1925.
16. *VS* no. 46, 24 February 1925.
17. *VS* no. 187, 12 August 1924; no. 185, 11 August 1925; no. 187, 13 August 1926; no. 188, 13 August 1927; no. 187, 13 August 1929; see LAMe C 48 Ie 134/XIII, fols. 254f. (PP Halle to RP Merseburg, 12 August 1924).
18. See Rohe, *Reichsbanner,* 96–109, esp. 108f., who perhaps overemphasizes the distance from old military customs.
19. *VS* no. 266, 11 November 1928. A lot of things about the new form struck the reporter as not yet successful; he criticized the long pauses and the lack of speaking discipline on the part of the participants. See also no. 263, 10 November 1925; no. 265, 11 November 1927.
20. See Henning Eichberg, "Thing-, Fest- und Weihespiele in Nationalsozialismus, Arbeiterkultur und Olympismus: Zur Geschichte des politischen Verhaltens in der Epoche des Faschismus," in H. Eichberg et al., *Massenspiele: NS-Thingspiel, Arbeiterweihespiel und olympisches Zeremoniell* (Stuttgart, 1977), 19–180, here 71–94; Uwe Hornauer, *Laienspiel und Massenchor: Das Arbeitertheater der Kultursozialisten in der Weimarer Republik* (Cologne, 1985), 160ff.
21. *KK* no. 43, 9 March 1925.
22. LAMe C 48 Ie 948, fols. 201–203 (Police of Eisleben to RP Merseburg, 3 June 1925). According to police information, only 5,000 participants showed up, rather than the 30–40,000 expected by the KPD. The police report also noted a "striking absence of interest" during the performance, even though it "lacked any refinement … and one could follow the play's train of thought without any mental exertion." On Berta Lask see Ludwig Hoffmann and Daniel Hoffmann-Ostwald, *Deutsches Arbeitertheater 1918–1933,* 2 vols. 2nd ed. (Munich, 1973), vol. 1, 87, 224–239; Rüdiger Safranski and Walter Fähnders, "Proletarisch-revolutionäre Literatur," in B. Weygraf, ed., *Literatur der Weimarer Republik* (Munich, 1995), 174–231, here 202f. Ilse Berend-Groa, the play's director, and Gustav von Wangenheim, who played the role of Müntzer, were two of the most prominent figures in Communist cultural work.
23. *KK* no. 19, 23 January 1926. The actress was the already mentioned Ilse Berend-Groa, member of the KPD since 1920, who had been engaged in pioneering efforts for the KPD cultural work since 1923 with its lay group in Kassel, called the Proletkult Kassel: see Hoffmann, *Arbeitertheater,* vol.1, 225. On the May Day festivities see *KK* no. 88, 2 May 1925; no. 102, 2 May

1929. Forty-four LLL Commemorations took place in the district Halle-Merseburg in 1927: SAPMO Ry 1/I 3/11/16, fol. 61 (Report by the district leadership for Dec. 1926/Jan. 1927, 11 February 1927). On the commemoration of the Revolution see *KK* no. 263, 8 November 1927; no. 246, 8 November 1929.

24. Of course, one must not directly compare the celebrations of the KPD I have just described with the Front Line Veterans' Days of the Stahlhelm. For one, the Stahlhelm was *not* an advance organization of a party; for another, the Reich meetings of the RFB in Berlin were, to be sure, also marked by parades and uniforms (see Finker, *Geschichte,* passim).
25. In addition, one must not forget their fourth function, which Ziemann, "Kriegserinnerung," has noted, namely as a medium for the exchange of war memories and thus for the processing of the war experience.
26. A detailed account in Schumann, "Einheitssehnsucht."
27. *MZ* no. 183, 10 April; no. 209, 26 April 1925.
28. LHAM C 20 Ib 1859/III, fols. 250f. (Police of Quedlinburg to RP Magdeburg, 26 March 1924); LHAM C 20 Ib 4685, fol. 141 (PP Magdeburg to RP Magdeburg, 4 April 1924); LHAM C 20 Ib 1859/IV, fols. 151f. (PP Magdeburg to RP Magdeburg, 10 May 1926); *SZ* no. 16, 19 January 1928. The emphasis on "unity" of the "other," non-Socialist Germany as the basis for an offensive political strategy is pointed out in Lapp's description of similar events in the Free State of Saxony: Lapp, *Revolution*, 138–141.
29. The central work on the criticism of parties and parliamentarism under Weimar is still Kurt Sontheimer, *Antidemokratisches Denken in der Weimarer Republik: Die politischen Ideen des deutschen Nationalismus zwischen 1918 und 1933* (Munich, 1968; reprint 1992), 141–192, 250–252. The importance of the unity motif in the thinking about politics and society during the 1920s and its relationship to the concept of *Volksgemeinschaft* (national community) are examined at length by Paul Nolte, *Die Ordnung der deutschen Gesellschaft: Selbstentwurf und Selbstbeschreibung im 20. Jahrhundert* (Munich, 2000), 159–183.
30. For a detailed discussion, especially of the religious connotation of the *Führer* ideas, see Klaus Schreiner, "'Wann kommt der Retter Deutschlands?' Formen und Funktionen von politischem Messianismus in der Weimarer Republik," *Saeculum* 49 (1998): 107–160, esp. 124ff.
31. *MZ* no. 32, 18 January 1922; also see *MZ* no. 32, 18 January 1925 (Speech by Seldte at the Veterans' Day 1925 with the call for a "German kind of man"); LHAM C 20 Ib 4665/III, fols. 33f. (Addendum 5 to the report of PP Magdeburg to RP Magdeburg, 22 January 1924); LHAM C 20 Ib 4687, fol. 176 (Recruitment flyer of the Jungnationaler Bund, 1921). On the high esteem in which military values were held by Protestantism in Württemberg during the Weimar period see Trauthig, *Kampf,* 141ff.
32. LHAM C 20 Ib 4687, fol. 175; *MZ* no. 38, 21 January 1924.
33. Stahlhelm, *Sechs Jahre Stahlhelm,* Appendix 16; *Alter Dessauer* no. 1, 13 September 1924, in LAMe C 48 Ie 134/XIII, fol. 428.
34. LHAM C 20 Ib 4665/III, fols. 142f. The chorus of the Erhardt Song mentioned the "swastika on the steel helmet"; it thus contained a constant reminder of the NSDAP, even during the time it was outlawed and when it was reconstituting itself, which surely made its revival easier. In the Hitler Song, "Hitler's courageous troops" march through all of Germany. It emphasizes the readiness to fight and to follow and points explicitly to the old colors of the Reich: "The slogan black-white-red. Always faithful to the land of the Aryans, to Hitler goods and blood (*Gut und Blut*)."
35. LHAM C 20 Ib 4689, fol. 460. It says, for example:

    Zum Tor zieht hinaus die todesmutge Schar
    Die Brust hoch gereckt, das Auge blitzend hell und klar
    Mit treudeutschem Trutze und zum Tode bereit ...

    Die Wehrwölfe ziehen aus ins Todesfeld
    Nicht Tod sie fürchten, erhoffen nichts von dieser Welt ...
    Unser Tod bringt den Sieg und macht das Vaterland frei ...

[The death-defying band leaves through the gates
The chest held high, the eye shining bright and clear
With true German defiance and ready to die ...

The Werewolves march out into the field of death
They fear not death, hope for nothing from this world ...
Our death brings victory and sets the fatherland free...]

On the type of the "fraternity song" of the 1920s, which conveyed the conquest of the soldier's melancholy by taking refuge in male heroism and thus offered an interpretation of the recent war experience, see the instructive comments by Jürgen Reulecke, "'Wir reiten die Sehnsucht tot' oder: Melancholie als Droge: Anmerkungen zum bündischen Liedgut," in T. Kühne, ed., *Männergeschichte—Geschlechtergeschichte: Männlichkeit im Wandel der Moderne* (Frankfurt, 1996) 155–173, esp. 159f. On the connection between the cult of masculinity and the readiness to resort to violence among the radical political right of Weimar see Bernd Weisbrod, "Kriegerische Gewalt und männlicher Fundamentalismus: Ernst Jüngers Beitrag zur Konservativen Revolution," *GWU* 49, no. 9 (1998): 544–560.

36. *MZ* no. 209, 26 April 1925.
37. *MZ* no. 32, 18 January 1925.
38. *Wir Volk* no. 40, 2 June 1924.
39. Noted by Mallmann, *Kommunisten,* 236f.
40. *KK* no. 58, 10 May 1924; similar accounts in LAMe C 48 Ie 134/XIII, fol. 226 (Leaflet of August 1924 against the Dawes Plan; a giant stomps down an enemy); *KK* no. 211, 7 November 1924 (7 Years SU; a giant with a hammer behind a globe); additional references in Mallmann, *Kommunisten,* 236f.
41. LAMe C 48 Ie 948, fol. 46 (Recruitment poster from the summer of 1925).
42. LAMe C 48 Ie 134/XIII, fol. 311 (7 September 1924).
43. For a detailed account see Gottfried Korff, "Rote Fahnen und geballte Faust: Zur Symbolik der Arbeiterbewegung in der Weimarer Republik," in D. Petzina, ed., *Fahnen, Fäuste, Körper: Symbolik und Kultur der Arbeiterbewegung* (Essen, 1986), 27–60, esp. 30–43; see Mallmann, *Kommunisten,* 237.
44. *KK* nos. 51–53, 18–20 March 1925; LHAM C 20 Ib 2043, fol. 100 (PP Halle to RP Merseburg, 19 March 1925, report about the funeral of the Volkspark victims at Getrauden cemetery); *KK* no. 12, 15 January 1926; see LHAM C 20 Ib 5218/II, fol. 161 (Gendarme to LR Kölleda, 31 July 1922, report about the consecration of a memorial stone for the fighters of the 1921 "March action" killed near Bachra). Mallmann does not mention the motif of revenge in his analysis of Communist pictorial language.
45. *KK* no. 12, 15 January 1926. On the emphasis on masculinity in the propaganda of the KPD see also Weitz, *German Communism,* 188ff.
46. *KK* no. 51, 2 May 1924.
47. LHAM C 20 Ib 1960/I, fol. 21 (Addendum to the report of PP Erfurt to RP Erfurt, 18 August 1924). On Kahnel see Safranski and Fähnders, "Literatur," 188–190.
48. *VS* no. 47, 23 February 1930. On the "softer" aspects of the ideal of comradeship in Weimar political culture, not only on the left, see Birthe Kundrus, "The First World War and the Construction of Gender Relations in the Weimar Republic," in K. Hagemann and S. Schüler-Springorum, eds., *Home/Front: The Military, War, and Gender in Twentieth-Century Germany* (Oxford, 2002), 159–180, and Thomas Kühne, "Gender Confusion and Gender Order in the German Military, 1918–1945," in Hagemann and Schüler-Springorum, *Home/Front,* 233–254.
49. *VS* no. 113, 15 May 1924.
50. *VS* no. 97, 26 April 1925.
51. *VS* no. 286, 6 December 1924. On the tenth anniversary of the Revolution, 9 November 1928, the *Volksstimme* published a cartoon showing the gigantic figure of a proletarian holding a hammer in the right hand and taking a large step forward. Scampering out of his way are Lilliputians, some of whom can be identified as a pastor, a policeman, an officer, and an

entrepreneur. However, the giant has such a kindly look on his face that one is loath to believe that he might put his hammer to any evil purpose (*VS* no. 264, 9 November 1928).

52. *VS* no. 179, 2 August; no. 187, 12 August 1924. On the importance of the Republican colors to the self-conception of the Reichsbanner see Benjamin Ziemann "'Gedanken eines Reichsbannermannes auf Grund von Erlebnissen und Erfahrungen': Politische Kultur, Flaggensymbolik und Kriegserinnerung in Schmalkalden 1926. Dokumentation." *Zeitschrift des Vereins für Thüringische Geschichte* 53 (1999): 201-232, esp. 207–210.
53. LHAM C 20 Ib 1859/IV, fols. 210-212 (PP Magdeburg to RP Magdeburg, 6 May 1927, report about a Nazi meeting with Gregor Straßer); LHAM C 20 Ib 1913/V, fol. 319 (RP Magdeburg to OP, 14 October 1929, report about a Nazi event in Magdeburg with a speaker Gengler from Nuremberg); LHAM C 20 Ib 4663, fols. 206f. (PP Halle to RP Merseburg, 11 March 1924). Stieve also acquainted his listeners with a proposal that Hitler supposedly made in a conversation with Duesterberg, namely "to kill half of the Jews and put the other half into camps." This, Stieve went on, "sounds pretty good," but it was "not feasible," because "it would bring all economic life to a half and we would be finished." He did not express any fundamental critique of Hitler's position, nor was any voiced from others at the meeting. On the rise of "voyeuristic anti-Semitism" in the second half of the 1920s see Walter, *Antisemitische Gewalt,* 177–199.
54. *SZ* nos. 64 and 65, 17 and 18 March 1925; no. 256, 30 October 1928; no. 103, 2 May 1929.
55. *SZ* no. 195, 4 May 1929. Pastor Martin could well imagine an intellectual engagement with the KPD, but not with the SPD or the DDP, because, as Martin commented with words that were also prompted by a general criticism of the bourgeoisie, "some of them are pretty fat members of the bourgeoisie": LHAM C 20 Ib 1859/IV, fol. 151f. (PP Halle to RP Merseburg, 10 May 1926). Other examples of a bourgeois criticism of the bourgeoisie: LHAM C 20 Ib 4663, fol. 77f. (Police of Halle to OP, 7 November 1922, report about a speech by the former head of the central office of the Home Guards in Berlin, Runkel, at a commemoration of the day of Roßbach, where we hear of the sleeping bourgeoisie); LHAM C 20 Ib 1913/II, fol. 64 (Text of the "Scharnhorst Song," which criticizes "the bourgeoisie that is losing its vigor").
56. *MZ* no. 243, 5 May 1929.
57. *MZ* no. 235, 30 April 1929; *SZ* no. 305, 31 December 1925. Incidentally, the words that the *Magdeburgische Zeitung* used against the by now irrelevant Rhenish Separatists were even more vitriolic than those against the Communists. A lead article on Germany's foreign policy stated with frightening brutality: "The Rhenish *Volk* rose up … with clubs, axes, old rifles, and bare fists against the separatists, killed the vermin, threw it back into the flames of the burning town halls, and affirmed with its blood the will to remain German" (*MZ* no. 164, 31 March 1925).
58. Trauthig, *Kampf,* 261–285, notes a weakening of the fear of Bolshevism within Württembergean Protestantism, but not a fundamental correction.
59. *KK* no. 118, 22 July 1924; LAMe C 48 Ie 948, fol. 394 (Pictorial broadsheet of 1925); LAMe C 48 Ie 134/XIII, fol. 270 (Sticker of 1924).
60. LHAM C 20 Ib 5217/II, fol. 325 (Cartoons against the Ruhr policy of 1923, in which, among other things, swastika men dressed in Bavarian fashion shoot workers); LAMe C 48 Ie 134/XIII, fol. 227 (Poster for Anti-War Day 1924, which depicts a skull wearing a spiked helmet, iron cross, and swastika). In addition, the fat capitalist with top hat and cigar naturally makes his appearance in the pictorial language; see Mallmann, *Kommunisten,* 237; Weitz, *German Communism,* 263–270.
61. *KK* no. 48, 14 March 1925; no. 104, 4 May 1929. On the KPD's agitative work among the Schupo see Leßmann, *Schutzpolizei,* 295–301.
62. *VS* no. 102, 3 May; no. 105, 7 May 1929. By contrast, the top Communist candidate in the electoral district of Magdeburg in the Landtag elections in December 1924, who at the end of August that year had started a brawl in the assembly hall as a member of the Reichstag, was

heavily criticized; his behavior reflected the "beer-joint spirit" of the Communist parliamentarians (*VS* no. 281, 30 November 1924).

63. *VS* no. 281, 30 November 1924; no. 101, 1 May 1925; no. 141, 20 June 1926.
64. LHAM C 20 Ib 1913/IV, fol. 32 (PP Magdeburg to RP Magdeburg, 22 March 1926).
65. Stahlhelm, *Sechs Jahre Stahlhelm,* Appendix 16; LHAM C 20 Ib 1991/III, fol. 423 (PP Magdeburg to RP Magdeburg, 23 January 1927); fol. 36 (Appendix to RP Magdeburg to Prussian Ministry of the Interior, 20 January 1926).
66. LHAM C 20 Ib 1991/III, fols. 386f. (Informant report about a meeting at the beginning of December 1926, passed on by RP Magdeburg to OP, 14 December 1926). Heinz supposedly said, amidst "general laughter," that it was better for Erzberger to have been shot than to have died from "fatty degeneration of the heart." The Regierungspräsident explicitly did not regard Heinz's statements as representative of the organization.
67. LAMe C 48 Ie 134/XIV, fol. 332 (PP Halle to RP Merseburg, 11 December 1924); 948, LAMe C 48 Ie fols. 570f. (Police record, 11 October 1925).
68. *KK* no. 248, 7 November 1925; no. 104, 4 May 1929; see also no. 105, 6 May 1929.
69. *KK* no. 18, 22 January 1927; no. 262, 6 November 1926.
70. On the KPD's ideas and plans for armed struggle during the middle Weimar years, which were aimed against both Blanquist activism and hope in the spontaneity of the masses, see Wirsching, *Weltkrieg,* 240–256, esp. 254–256.
71. LAMe 134/XIII, fol. 226; see also ibid., fol. 274 (Sticker against the Stahlhelm: "Hurrah for civil war against capital!"); fol. 328 (Leaflet of the Communist Youth: "For civil war and revolution!").
72. LHAM C 20 Ib 5213/II, fols. 145f. (Poem titled "Young Guard," found during a house search in Halberstadt in November 1923). See also *KK* no. 248, 7 November 1925.
73. LHAM C 20 Ib 5213/I, fol. 103 (Poem "Be Ready!"). On Strzelewicz see Hoffmann, *Arbeitertheater,* vol. 1, S. 398. See also Weitz, *German Communism,* 249–255.
74. *VS* no. 75, 29 March; no. 91, 19 April; no. 92, 21 April; no. 93, 22 April 1925.
75. *VS* no. 50, 28 February 1926; no. 113, 15 May; no. 117, 20 May 1928.
76. *VS* no. 185, 11 August 1925.
77. LHAM C 20 Ib 1913/III, fols. 203f. (Reichsbanner Magdeburg to OP, 7 October 1924); LHAM C 20 Ib 1859/III, fols. 409f. (Reichsbanner Thüringen to the Prussian Ministry of the Interior, 5 September 1924); see *VS* no. 22, 26 January 1924.
78. *VS* no. 46, 24 February 1925.
79. *VS* no. 104, 4 May 1924.
80. *VS* no. 102, 3 May 1929; no. 186, 12 August 1926; see also no. 113, 15 May 1924; no. 91, 19 April 1925; no. 262, 9 November 1926.
81. On the commonalities and differences between the Reichsbanner and the RFB as well as the right-wing Combat Leagues see the apt and very detailed discussion in Rohe, *Reichsbanner,* 110–116, 222–226.

Part IV

The Escalation of Violence: 1929/30–1933

In the last years of the Weimar Republic, above all in 1932, a far greater number of people were perpetrators and victims of political violence than during the middle years. The primary responsibility lies with the Nazi movement. Modern in its propaganda techniques and in its status as a "people's party" that was aimed, in principle, at all social strata, it picked up the forms and substance of political self-representation that the anti-Republican right had developed chiefly since 1924, but radicalized them in a way that accorded violence a key role. These brutal new methods of political struggle were tolerated and supported by those voices of the bourgeois public who believed that the time had arrived for a fundamental revision of the political system. Added to this was the fact that the course that the KPD pursued, and its supporters' behavior during the political fighting in the streets, seemed to confirm in every respect the picture that had been painted of the Communist as enemy.

Chapter 9

The Rise of the Nazi Movement and the Persistent Weakness of the Communists

Profile and Successes of the Nazi Movement

The NSDAP had already attained considerable strength in the province of Saxony before the Reichstag elections in September 1930. In July 1930, it had 161 local groups with nearly ten thousand members, which made up about one-tenth of the membership in the Reich.[1] Detailed reports from the three administrative districts in the summer of 1930 described the NSDAP unanimously as a party that was drawing members "from all circles of the population," though it was recruiting "chiefly from bourgeois society," as the Regierungspräsident of Merseburg wrote—in other words, it was drawing in primarily the commercial middle class, white-collar employees, and civil servants in the cities. His colleague in Magdeburg, whose territory had 3,400 party members, noted that in the cities, supporters of the DNVP and the DVP were the chief source of recruits for the NSDAP; he also mentioned workers, though it was only those who "are unemployed or economically dissatisfied and do not wish to join the KPD" that joined the National Socialists. In the countryside, too, the NSDAP was strongly on the rise, but here there was still a shortage of local leadership figures, especially in the Altmark, which continued to be dominated by the DNVP and the Landbund. But an additional influx, we are told, was to be expected from the Stahlhelm, especially the Jungstahlhelm, many of whose members disapproved of attempts by the national leadership to distance itself from the NSDAP after the failure of the referendum against the Young Plan.[2] As strongholds of the party the report mentioned once again Quedlinburg and Wernigerode.[3]

The Regierungspräsident of Merseburg saw in the NSDAP's intensive propaganda activities—above all in the countryside and especially for the campaign against the Young Plan—the chief reason behind the party's success in his district,

Notes from this chapter begin on page 241.

where 4,700 members were organized into 85 local groups, that is, nearly half of the membership of the province. He did not provide an analysis of social structure, but he did underscore the key role that the economic crisis played in the growth of the NSDAP. The party had made the most gains among students; one-third of the students in Halle had most recently voted for the Nazi list.[4] Among workers there was "a larger number of radical elements, who have already done all they could with the KPD," that had joined the NSDAP. However, the mass of NSDAP members do not seem to have come from the working class. Apart from the city of Halle itself (800 members), the strongest local groups were in the counties of Liebenwerda (513), Eckartsberga (366), Querfurt (358), and the city of Naumburg (350), while KPD strongholds like the Saalkreis (52), the Mansfelder Gebirgskreis (100), and County Bitterfeld (101) had noticeably smaller membership numbers. This suggests that the NSDAP won the support of workers where the KPD had never had a dominant influence, or where, as in the Geisel Valley of County Querfurt, industrialists in conjunction with the Stahlhelm had been trying for a long time to move their workers and employees to the right.[5]

In the smallest administrative district of Erfurt, the NSDAP counted 1,600 members in 29 local groups. Here it was above all the rural population in the Catholic counties that proved rather unreceptive, as it did in other German regions. The workers in the counties with old Social Democratic and free union traditions were also resistant. In the city of Erfurt, it was "chiefly small business people and artisans, and some workers" who joined the NSDAP, with only "a scattering of Communists." The strongholds of the NSDAP in the district of Erfurt were, after the city itself (370 members) the rural, protestant county of Hohenstein (375), and the county of Mühlhausen (223), which adjoined the now National Socialist town of Gotha.[6]

On the whole, these findings confirm the picture that scholarship has painted of the membership of the NSDAP during its growth into a mass party.[7] In terms of its social profile, the NSDAP in the province of Saxony as elsewhere was a kind of people's party, in which, however, the middle classes were clearly overrepresented and the lower classes clearly underrepresented, and which did not succeed in recruiting to any meaningful extent members from either the Catholic milieu or the Social Democratic and Communist working-class circles. At the time the reports were written, the farmers in the province of Saxony were not yet drawn in as clearly as the urban middle classes, but that would soon change. The official reports do not allow us to make further differentiations about the share of membership by the respective social strata. The Regierungspräsident of Magdeburg pointed out that at many meetings of the NSDAP in his city, half of those attending were civil servants, who, partly out of fear of disciplinary action against them, did not register as members at all or did so under the occupational cover of "commercial clerks." It also comes as no surprise that officials of the Reich and municipal government were more likely to join the party than Prussian civil servants, who, at any rate, had the most to fear from disciplinary consequences until 20 July 1932.[8] The reports also leave unanswered the question of whether academics had already joined the NSDAP in larger numbers. However, it would seem that they accounted for a small part of membership, since the relevant professional organizations of the party had barely established a foothold in the province by the summer of 1930. Only Halle had recently established a local group of the Nationalsozialistischer Ärztebund (National Socialist Physicians' League), though so far with only ten members.[9]

Where did the workers in the National Socialist German *Workers'* Party come from? Those former Communists who migrated to the NSDAP in the province of Saxony most likely had had only tenuous ties to the KPD and had been motivated to join primarily by their radical rejection of the Weimar system, rather than by a deeply rooted Marxist class consciousness. As for the remainder of the workers, they were presumably largely those who had been previously unorganized politically or had been reached by the Stahlhelm or the successors of the "Yellows." That interpretation seems to be supported by the fact that the party had not yet succeeded in setting up a Nationalsozialistische Betriebszellen-Organisation (NSBO, National Socialist Organization of Factory Cells) in the administrative district of Magdeburg, while in the district of Merseburg, the NSBO had "made little headway." Only Halle itself had a few smaller cells in factories and one in the municipal streetcar department, with 60 members. In Suhl, a cell was founded in a weapons factory at the beginning of 1930.[10] Long after the great electoral success of the NSDAP in October 1931, there had still been "no meaningful progress" in setting up cells in the industrial heartland of the province. A rare exception was the cell in Leuna with about 50 members, which still was rather modest in size, compared to the total number of workers.[11]

Internal KPD sources also do not reveal that the NSDAP was seen as dangerous competition at the factory level in the district of Halle-Merseburg. In its organizational report from August/September 1932—when, in spite of the KPD leadership's identification of "Social Fascism" as the prime target, the danger from the right was impossible to overlook—the district leadership provided an overview of the balance of political power in the important large enterprises. It revealed that while the NSDAP had attained some influence, it was far from emerging as the chief competition. For example, at the Bitterfeld plant of IG Farben with its 2,600 workers and 500 white-collar employees, the survey counted 30 members of the NSDAP, compared to 40 members of the SPD or the Reichsbanner and 31 Communists. At the Piesteritz nitrogen plant (1,100 workers, 200 white-collar employees) there were 35 National Socialists, as against 35 Communists and 60 Social Democrats or members of the Reichsbanner. The Lauchhammer power plant (120 workers, 20 employees) had only 1 NSDAP member, as against 7 Communists and 10 members of the Reichsbanner. At the municipal works in Merseburg, the KPD works cell had 10 members, while only 1 member of the workforce was in the NSDAP, compared to 12 in the SPD or the Reichsbanner. No National Socialists are listed in any other enterprises.[12]

Of course this is not a representative overview of the situation in the factories and enterprises in the summer of 1932, and the report is no doubt likely to have over- rather than underestimated the strength of the KPD's own cells and may not have included all the members of the other organizations. Still, it creates the impression that at a point when the economic crisis in Germany had reached its nadir and management was therefore in a favorable position in terms of its ability to dismiss Communists and enforce good behavior in the workplace, the National Socialists had not been able to establish any strongholds. One must also bear in mind that a good number of the listed Nazi party members were probably white-collar employees, not workers.[13] A look at the results of the works council elections in Leuna underscores this finding: not a single vote was cast for the National Socialists in 1930, in 1931 they won 10.5 percent as against 34.9 percent for the Communist list, and even in the spring of 1933, only 28.7 percent of the workers and employees voted for the Nazis—which was still a relatively good result compared to the nationwide showing of the NSBO, which was far below the party's expectations.[14] As elsewhere in Germany, the NSBO in the province of Saxony does not seem to have succeeded in breaking into the core of the KPD membership or into the ranks of the Social Democratic workers with longstanding ties to the free unions and their party.[15]

The NSDAP had varied, though on the whole moderate, success in its efforts to recruit the youth in the middle of 1930, leaving aside for a moment the abovementioned students. As of yet there was no Nationalsozialistischer Schülerbund (National Socialist Pupil League) in the administrative district of Magdeburg, while initial steps in Quedlinburg had bogged down after the provincial school board issued a prohibition against joining this organization. Only a few vocational schools left indications of Nazi members among their students. Hitler Youth groups existed only in Magdeburg itself, where— its group having been refounded in 1929 after a failed attempt in 1927—members had increased from 16 to 120, most of them *Gymnasium* students, and in Oschersleben (no more than 20 members).[16]

The administrative district of Merseburg presents a different picture. Local groups of the Nazi Schülerbund already existed in Halle and, once again, Naumburg, with 150 and 100 members, respectively; another group existed in Torgau, whose members came chiefly from the *Gymnasien.* The Hitler Youth, too, had been able to set up local groups in several towns since 1929, eight in total, of which that in Naumburg was the largest with 150 members. In the view of the Regierungspräsident, some of the teachers, especially at the higher secondary schools, lacked the necessary commitment to oppose these organizational efforts, and a few were already known to be members of the NSDAP, which makes sense in a NSDAP Gau headed by the former teacher Paul Hinkler.[17] In the administrative district of Erfurt, once again, a Nazi Schülerbund is known to have existed only in the capital city; the teachers, we are told, were generally "opposed" to the party. The Hitler Youth had no more than 60 members in the entire administrative district; aside from Erfurt, local groups existed in Nordhausen and Mühlhausen.[18] This information is not enough for an exhaustive description for the province of Saxony of the social profile of the Hitler Youth prior to its reorganization throughout the Reich in 1931, but at least it indicates that here, too, the middle-class presence was strong.[19]

The official reports do not reveal how the social profile of the NSDAP in the province of Saxony changed during the subsequent years. The interest of these reports was increasingly focused on the SA as the most immediately dangerous part of the Nazi movement. However, it was obvious that the party itself grew rapidly after its stunning success in the Reichstag elections in September 1930. By February 1931, its membership in the administrative district of Magdeburg had more than doubled from the previous summer to nearly 8,000, and by early October it stood at nearly 10,000.[20] Growth was even more explosive in the administrative district of Erfurt. By the time of the Reichstag elections, more than 2,700 members were organized in the Prussian part of the Gau Thuringia, an increase of a thousand since that summer. Thirteen months later the number had nearly doubled to 5,300. After the city of Erfurt (700 members), the strongest local groups continued to be found in the medium-sized cities of Mühlhausen (350) and Nordhausen (240), while in Sömmerda, home to a Rheinmetall plant, the local group was only 30 strong at this time, and in the weapons-manufacturing city of Suhl, which was about half the size of Mühlhausen and Nordhausen, there were no more than 135 members, in spite of the support from a local factory owner.[21]

Our sources do not reveal who these new party members were. Indications can be found in the reports about the occupations of the party functionaries at the middle and lower levels down to the local group leaders (Table 9.1). According to this data, workers—both skilled and unskilled—made up barely one-fifth of this leadership personnel in the administrative district of Magdeburg in 1930, and a year later they were only slightly more; in the administrative district of Erfurt, meanwhile, their share even dropped to slightly below one-fifth. In the province of Saxony, as in Germany on the whole, workers were thus clearly underrepresented in a party that advertised itself as a *Workers'* Party, especially in comparison with the other radical workers' party, the KPD.[22] The vast majority of functionaries belonged to the middle class. Merchants, master artisans, white-collar workers, and civil servants made up about half in both administrative districts. The largest single group was farmers, whose share rose from about one-fifth to more than a quarter. The local "elite" of entrepreneurs and a small group of self-employed, former officers, and teachers made up about one-tenth, with the trend pointing down.[23] This meant that the lower leadership positions were in the hands of the very same groups—and, incidentally, staffed exclusively by men—that had formed the backbone and leadership of the Home Guards in 1919. At its leadership level, the NSDAP presented itself less as a people's party than a movement embracing the middle class and farmers and including a not inconsiderable—though not very large—portion of the working class.[24]

The electoral results for the NSDAP in 1930 and 1932 point in the same direction as the findings regarding its membership structure. In the province of Saxony, the Reichstag elections in September 1930 led to its breakthrough as

Table 9.1 Social Profile of the NSDAP Leadership 1930/31 (Province of Saxony)

Occupation/Class	Party leadership, adm. dist. Magdeburg, Sept. 1930	Party leadership, adm. dist. Magdeburg, Oct. 1931	Party leadership, adm. dist. Erfurt, Sept.1930	Party leadership, adm. dist. Erfurt, Oct. 1931	SA leadership, adm. dist. Erfurt, July 1931
Worker					
Semi- and unskilled workers	9.5%	8.3%	7.8%	8.5%	14.0%
Skilled workers	9.5%	11.9%	12.2%	10.7%	16.0%
Workers total	19.0%	21.2%	20.0%	19.2%	30.0%
Middle Class					
Master artisans	12.4%	10.1%	12.2%	12.8%	12.0%
White-collar employees	6.7%	10.1%	15.6%	9.2%	14.0%
Merchants	20.0%	18.3%	20.0%	17.0%	6.0%
Low- and mid-level civil servants	8.6%	4.7%	2.2%	4.3%	6.0%
Farmers	22.9%	27.8%	18.9%	26.2%	20.0%
Middle class total	70.6%	71.0%	68.7%	69.5%	58.0%
"Elite"					
Entrepreneurs	4.8%	5.3%	6.7%	7.8%	6.0%
Self-employed (academics)	3.8%	2.4%	1.1%	2.1%	6.0%
Higher civil servants	1.9%	0.6%	–	–	–
Former officers	–	0.6%	2.2%	1.4%	–
Editors-in-chief	–	–	1.1%	–	–
"Elite" total	10.5%	8.9%	11.1%	11.3%	12.0%
Grand total	100.1%	100.1%	100.0%	100.0%	100.0%
N =	105	169	90	141	50

Sources: In LHAM C 20 Ib: 2049/I, fols. 65–89; 2049/II, fols. 24–50 (RP Magdeburg to OP, 10 October 1931); 2052/I, fols. 51–59 (RP Erfurt to OP, 25 September 1930), fols. 205–218 (RP Erfurt to OP, 1 October 1931), fols. 186–191 (RP Erfurt to OP, 2 July 1931).

the second-largest party, though not with the same kind of outstanding results it achieved in the Prussian eastern provinces or in Schleswig-Holstein. Still, apart from the Catholic Eichsfeld county of Heiligenstadt, it now commanded a voter potential of more than 10 percent in all urban and rural counties, including Communist strongholds like the Saalkreis or County Bitterfeld. However, the available data suggest that the party was *not* able to make significant inroads into the Communist electorate.

The NSDAP's electoral strongholds in 1930 (Table 9.2) were in part medium-sized towns like Naumburg and Quedlinburg, where the party had enjoyed a

Table 9.2 NSDAP (KPD/SPD) Strongholds 1930/32 I (Province of Saxony)

County	NSDAP 1930 1932 I	NSDAP gains 1930/1928 1932 I/1930	Bourgeois parties 1930/1928 (DNVP) 1932 I/1930	SPD/KPD 1930/1928 1932 I/1930	New voters 1930/1928 1932 I/1930
RC Naumburg	36.7 %	+ 2771	– 1657 (– 2054)	– 58	+ 1056
	56.4 %	+ 2045	– 1716	+ 168	+ 497
RC Eckartsberga	31.9 %	+ 5127	– 2303 (– 5131)	+ 1145	+ 3969
	63.1 %	+ 7571	– 5330	– 498	+ 1743
Quedlinburg City	31.5 %	+ 3881	– 2491 (– 720)	– 185	+ 1205
	31.6 %	+ 3500	– 2271	– 740	+ 489
Naumburg City	31.3 %	+ 4850	– 3422 (– 1308)	+ 236	+ 1664
	45.9 %	+ 2937	– 2615	+ 87	+ 409
RC Langensalza	30.3 %	+ 6138	– 4405 (– 3263)	+ 466	+ 2199
	58.0 %	+ 7239	– 4656	– 555	+ 2028
RC Querfurt	29.5 %	+ 9220	– 4895 (– 4606)	+ 42	+ 4667
	46.6 %	+ 7191	– 6461	+ 832	+ 1562
RC Torgau	28.5 %	+ 8535	– 3764 (– 5569)	+ 1743	+ 6414
	54.6 %	+ 8762	– 7777	– 388	+ 597
RC Gardelegen	27.7 %	+ 8473	– 5270 (– 1952)	+ 205	+ 3408
	57.2 %	+ 12114	– 7255	– 625	+ 4234
Eisleben City	27.7 %	+ 3579	– 2247 (– 813)	– 189	+ 1143
	45.1 %	+ 2570	– 2192	– 8	+ 370
Halle City	25.4 %	+ 28923	– 15009 (– 8818)	– 470	+ 13444
	41.4 %	+ 19756	– 22536	+ 2231	– 549
KPD strongholds					
Weißenfels City	17.8 %	+ 3497	– 1450 (– 1149)	+ 208	+ 2255
	38.0 %	+ 4887	– 4428	– 24	+ 435
Saalkreis	16.5 %	+ 8101	– 4010 (– 3854)	+ 125	+ 4216
	34.1 %	+ 9366	– 9830	+ 1528	+ 1064
Bitterfeld	14.3 %	+ 7713	– 2632 (– 5260)	+ 3151	+ 8232
	35.0 %	+ 12501	– 12813	+ 1515	+ 1203
SPD strongholds					
Neuhaldensleben	17.4 %	+ 6459	– 4088 (– 3196)	– 422	+ 1949
	42.0 %	+ 10343	– 7349	– 1209	+ 1785
Wanzleben	17.3 %	+ 6304	– 4051 (– 2361)	– 1088	+ 1165
	36.7 %	+ 8289	– 5396	– 1184	+ 1709
Wolmirstedt	17.1 %	+ 5131	– 3782 (– 2473)	+ 343	+ 1692
	37.8 %	+ 6971	– 4855	– 581	+ 1535

RC = rural county
Sources: *Stat. Dt. R., N. F.,* vol. 372, II, 20–27; vol. 382, II, 20–27; vol. 434, 48–50.

certain influence for some time, in part decidedly rural areas, where it was already able to attract the votes especially of those who had left the DNVP, and County Querfurt and the Geisel Valley, where the industrialists had repeatedly tried to have a sizable number of Stahlhelm members among the miners of the brown coal pits. The large city of Halle was the exception, and it is possible that here the militancy of the right-leaning Stahlhelm wing played a mobilizing role.[25] In all cases, the losses of the (other) bourgeois parties were massive. It was especially the DNVP that suffered steep losses, which—with the exception of Halle—were not absorbed by another bourgeois party, while in the countryside the Christian-National Peasants and Farmers' Party (CNBLP) posted strong gains and presumably attracted part of the DNVP voters. The two workers' parties together either suffered relatively minor losses or were even able to post gains, especially in the Communist strongholds. Only in the Börde counties of Wanzleben and Neuhaldensleben, Social Democratic strongholds, did the SPD lose more votes than the Communists gained.[26] Because of a rise in the number of eligible voters and the simultaneous rise in voter turnout, the number of valid ballots in 1930 was significantly higher than in 1928. The existing data indicate that in most cases the loss of votes by the bourgeois parties was greater than the votes added by new voters, which leads to the assumption that the better part of the votes picked up by the NSDAP came from the bourgeois parties. However, the pure numbers of how much was gained or lost by whom generally conceals a high degree of crossover movement between the parties.[27] The figures for the three Communist strongholds suggest that here it was especially many first-time and new voters who cast their ballots for the NSDAP. It must remain speculation, however, whether these voters were predominantly politically uncommitted workers, or rural or middle-class residents of the counties.

In July 1932, the NSDAP scored another clear victory. This time, as the numbers indicate, the National Socialists attracted new voters to a much smaller extent than in 1930; instead, they received an influx above all from the voter reservoir of the bourgeois parties, in the countryside especially from the CNBLP, which had been strong in 1930 but was now, as elsewhere in Germany, sinking into obscurity just as rapidly as it had arisen.[28] The renewed losses of both workers' parties together in the Börde counties suggest that a number of rural workers who previously had voted chiefly for the Social Democrats now cast their ballots for the National Socialists. In the Communist strongholds, by contrast, the SPD gained across the board (except in the Mansfelder Gebirgskreis), but so did the KPD. This also changed the ranking list of the NSDAP strongholds. After the CNBLP ceased to play a role, the ten counties with the strongest showing for the NSDAP were exclusively rural: Eckartsberga (63.1 percent), Schweinitz (60.7 percent), Salzwedel (60.5 percent), Langensalza (58.0 percent), Gardelegen (57.2 percent), the rural counties Naumburg and Weißensee (56.4 percent each), Osterburg (55.4 percent), Torgau (54.6 percent), and the rural county Erfurt (53.9 percent). Judging from the numbers, in the counties of Weißensee (with the industrial town of Sömmerda) and Erfurt it was chiefly former voters of the DNVP, DVP, and the CNBLP, as well as new voters, who turned toward the National Socialists.[29] Of these strongholds, in 1919 five had been among the ten counties with the largest Home Guards (in relative terms). Here we see a long continuity of the radical turn of farmers against the left and the Republic.

Of course, the unique thing about the NSDAP was the fact that in addition to this farmer extremism (not a general rural extremism, for in the Börde counties the NSDAP had below-average results), it was able to win a great many votes also in the cities, especially small and medium-sized cities. On the whole, the results of the Reichstag elections of 1930 and July 1932 accord with the findings on the membership structure of the NSDAP. Its supporters came from all strata of the population, but chiefly from the farming and commercial middle class, as well as from among workers who were previously uncommitted politically or had voted for a "national" party—but only to a limited extent from among the voters of the SPD and the KPD.[30] In the long run, the radical nature of the NSDAP and the readiness of its SA to resort to violence proved attractive especially where the left had always been viewed as the enemy, but not where people had undergone powerful experiences with political violence in the early 1920s.

On the eve of the Reichstag elections in 1930, the SA as a whole was not very important in the province. Halle was the seat of one SA *Standarte* (regiment), which had recently also acquired a motorized unit with twelve vehicles. The recruitment of *Unterführer* (subleaders) in the administrative district there targeted especially former noncommissioned officers. In the south of the province there were SA units in Mühlhausen, Nordhausen, and Erfurt itself, though with 115 members Erfurt's was much smaller than the membership of the local party group. The SA seems to have been strongest in the administrative district of Magdeburg, where the establishment of four new *Standarten* and eight *Stürmen* (assault units) was imminent in counties of the Börde and the Altmark.[31] Moreover, henceforth all members of the SA were to receive "police training" (by two former police officers) and had to procure a pistol (to be kept at home), the cost of which would be borne by the party, however.[32] This shows very clearly that the SA was staking out a very different territory than the older Combat Leagues of the right wing. It saw itself not merely as an army of the party and not as a veterans' organization, in spite of the wooing of former soldiers, nor was it out to establish a largely symbolic presence in the streets like the Reichsbanner; instead, it was already presenting itself to its members as a future force of order.

The contrast to the Combat Leagues was also generational, as James Diehl has noted.[33] Since the end of 1928, the Stahlhelm, by setting up military exercise groups for men aged 21–30, had tried once again to demonstrate its superiority to the competition on the left and to retain its attractiveness in the face of the new competition from the right. This attempt was a total failure. The great majority of local groups dominated by older members refused to follow the plans of the national leadership and could be persuaded, at most, to increase their sport activities. At the beginning of April 1930, the officials noted the failure of this undertaking. No small number of Jungstahlhelm members left their organization and joined the National Socialists.[34] On the whole, the relative youthfulness of the SA members in the province of Saxony as elsewhere shows that the organization cannot be seen as the direct continuation of the Home Guards or the right-wing Combat Leagues. More than two-thirds were too young to have served in the war, and most of them had presumably not been members of the Free Corps, either. The argument that the members of the SA had become accustomed to using violence in war and the immediate postwar years thus contributes little to explaining their willingness to resort to violence, even though the leadership corps was made up largely of former soldiers and Free Corps fighters.[35]

More detailed information about the composition of the SA in the province was compiled in February 1931, shortly after Röhm's appointment as Chief of the SA (Table 9.3). In the administrative district of Magdeburg, "artisans and artisan apprentices" together with "commercial clerks and apprentices" made up more than half of the membership; farmers and "agricultural employees" accounted for less than one-tenth, industrial workers for one-tenth, and rural workers for nearly one-fifth. More than half of the members were between the ages of 20 and 30, another quarter was younger than 20, and only the remaining fifth belonged to the "front line generation." A somewhat different picture emerges in the district of Merseburg. Artisans and merchants together made up not quite half of all SA men, while farmers accounted for a little more than one-tenth. The share of industrial workers was much higher, one-fourth, and that of rural workers just under one-tenth; "others" made up the same share as in Magdeburg. The age relationships were very similar, though the SA men in Merseburg were even a little younger. The corresponding data for the administrative district of Erfurt come

Table 9.3 Social Profile of the SA 1930/31 (Province of Saxony)

Occupational group[37]	Members in the adm. dist. of Magdeburg Feb. 1931	Members in the adm. dist. of Merseburg Feb. 1931	Members in the adm. dist. of Erfurt Nov. 1930	Leadership personnel, adm. dist. of Erfurt June 1931[38]
"Industrial worker"	10.6%	24.5%	36.5%	
"Rural worker"	18.3%	9.3%	6%	30%
"Artisans and apprentices"	33.1%	23.4%	12%	14%
"Commercial clerks and apprentices"	20.2%	20.4%	(34%)[39]	12%
"Farmers, young farmers, agr. employees"	8.9%	13.3%	11%	20%
"Civil servants and employees of public authorities"	0.5%	0.6%	0.5%	6%
"Members of technical and other professions"	8.4%	8.5%	?	18%
Total	100.0%	100.0%	100.0%	100%
N =	?	?	?	50

Sources: LHAM C 20 Ib 2048/II, fol. 63f. (Survey by PP Magdeburg, 1 February 1931); fol. 5 (Survey by PP Merseburg, 18 February 1931); LHAM C 20 Ib 2052/I, fol. 40 (RP Erfurt to OP, 1 November 1930); fols. 186–191 (RP Erfurt to OP, 2 July 1931).

from November 1930. Here, industrial workers made up the largest group in relative terms at one-third, while rural workers were substantially below one-tenth; the share of the other groups corresponded approximately to tallies for the district of Merseburg. The SA men in Erfurt were somewhat older, three-tenths being over the age of 30. All told, the Erfurt SA had 787 men. The first numbers we have for the other two administrative districts come from the fall of 1931. In November 1931, the SA had 5,865 members in Magdeburg-Anhalt and 4,214 in Halle-Merseburg. The organization had evidently grown substantially everywhere since the beginning of the year.[36]

Since these data cannot be compared with similar data on the social profile of NSDAP membership in the province or with SA membership on the Reich level, any statements on the social profile of the organization must be made with a good deal of caution. It would at least appear that the SA in the province of Saxony was on the whole "more proletarian" than the party itself, though one must bear in mind that the local make-up of the SA could be very different from place to place. For example, in Halle and in the Mansfelder Seekreis, more than half of the SA *Stürme* were recruited from among industrial workers, while in the countryside they were mostly composed of farmers and rural workers.[40] It is striking, moreover, that industrial workers in the administrative district of Magdeburg had joined the SA only in relatively small numbers by the beginning of 1931, and that they also did not form the majority in a single county. The highest percentage was reached in the counties of Quedlinburg and Oschersleben with 28 percent, while in Magdeburg itself they accounted for less than 13 percent. This at least suggests that the skilled metalworkers in the district, with their long Social Democratic tradition and membership in the Reichsbanner, were relatively unreceptive to the SA. The situation was different with rural workers: they made up 75 percent of the SA in the county of Osterburg and 60 percent in the two counties of Jerichow. However, these were—revealingly enough—farming counties, whereas in the Börde counties with their large estates there either were no SA units, or rural workers made up less than one-tenth of the membership, as in the county of Calbe.[41]

The occupational data do not reveal how many skilled workers were included in the category "industrial workers," do not distinguish between apprentices and artisans already engaged in their profession, and, most of all, provide no information about how many artisans were self-employed and how many were working as skilled workers. Only this information would allow us to determine precisely the share of workers. Nor do the data say anything about the share of the unemployed among the SA men, which could not have been small, given the organization's age profile. All in all, workers were probably not overrepresented—in fact were likely to have been even somewhat underrepresented—in the SA in the province of Saxony. The middle class furnished a considerable number of members, and together with the farmers they made up the majority in the province as a whole, which means that the SA—of course with local differences—also had a "bourgeois" character, especially since the ratio of members with higher technical or academic training was not negligible. This conclusion, while contradicting

Conan Fischer's claim that the SA was predominantly a working-class organization, is in line with the arguments of Peter Longerich and, most recently, Sven Reichardt, who have compared in detail the findings of previous studies on the SA membership profile. Both underscore the occupational as well as regional heterogeneity of the SA.[42]

The subsequent development of the SA's social profile can be traced only in part. We do have a survey for the administrative district of Erfurt (dated June 1931)—incomplete, though—about the SA structure and leadership personnel, especially the *Sturm- und Scharführer* (leaders of assault units and troops). At that point, the organization had 1,500 members, that is, about twice as many as the previous fall. The lion's share was found in the city of Erfurt, which was by now the headquarters of a *Sturmbann* (battalion) with 600 men. The size of the SA *Sturm* in Suhl, however, had remained at 55 men. Apart from the city of Erfurt, the SA had grown chiefly in the countryside. One-fifth of its leadership positions were now filled by farmers, whereas a year earlier farmers had accounted for only one-tenth of the entire SA membership in the district. Workers made up very nearly a third of the leadership corps, lower than their share of membership overall the previous year, but still significantly higher than under the leadership of the party as a whole in the administrative district of Erfurt. The share of the "elite" was the same in both cases at a little over one-tenth, while the ratio of the middle class to workers corresponded roughly to that among the membership, meaning that the share of SA leadership positions held by the middle class was somewhat smaller than it was within the party leadership.[43] Another brief survey shows the state of the SA in March 1932. The SA *Untergruppe* (Sub-Group) Magdeburg-Anhalt with six *Standarten* was estimated at about 5,900 men and the *Untergruppe* Halle-Merseburg (three *Standarten*) at about 4,250; the members in the administrative district of Erfurt, now allocated differently administratively, were unchanged at about 1,500.[44]

The SA not only grew in number, it also continued to expand and consolidate its organization. In addition to medical and musical divisions, which the RFB also had, motorized units were established starting in early 1931. For example, in February 1931, Halle already had 15 vehicles at its disposal, Eisleben 12, and Bitterfeld 8. Erfurt, too, had set up an automobile unit with ten men. When the SA was outlawed by the Brüning government in April 1932, the police in Erfurt were not able to get their hands on the membership lists, which had been removed quickly enough, but it did find the correspondence of the leadership of the Gau's motorized unit. According to these documents, in this city the SA had at its disposal 396 motorcycles, 180 passenger cars, and 53 trucks, operated and maintained by 700 men.[45] Such an impressive array of motor vehicles made it easy to be omnipresent during an election campaign, and it also meant that raiding squads could be quickly moved from the larger SA locations to remote areas to break up meetings and support other SA units. Such a capacity for mobility contributed to the escalation of violence in ways that must not be underestimated, as Richard Bessel has pointed out.[46]

This mobility could also be fully exploited because the SA invented something the other organizations did not have: the SA Home. Placing SA men into such quasi-barracks helped the unemployed among them, allowed for their rapid mobilization, and created the precondition for a way of life of male bonding and cult of violence that Sven Reichardt has described in vivid detail for Berlin.[47] Neither the Stahlhelm nor the Wehrwolf nor the RFB nor the Reichsbanner had created anything like it. In Magdeburg, the SA had had a "Storm Tavern (*Sturmlokal*)," where members met regularly and from where they were deployed, since the end of 1929. The following year an SA Home was set up, with room for 30 men and the ability to produce 250 meals; in addition, it was equipped with a phone and kept a car at the ready. By November 1932, 180 men could be housed in another SA Home in Magdeburg. At this time there were no other homes in the administrative district, but when the SA was outlawed the following April, there were homes in Halberstadt, Oschersleben, Wernigerode, and Schönebeck. In the fall of 1931, the two other administrative districts had SA Homes only in Halle and Nordhausen.[48] That was not a great number of these quasi-barracks, so their importance in these districts should not be exaggerated. True, they were undoubtedly very important in the larger cities, especially Berlin, since here the SA men housed in them were deployed more frequently than others and therefore may have had fewer qualms when it came to the use of violence against their opponents. But the rural SA members, too, were violent. The SA had different faces; its violence emanated not only from the male society of the SA Homes.

The Permanent Weakness of the Communists

During the years of the worldwide economic crisis, the KPD was once again able to attract new members and also many new voters. However, unlike its de facto main opponent, the NSDAP, its true strength was less than it might have appeared to be. The threat of being outlawed hung over its head, it recruited its supporters increasingly among the unemployed, which took the potential weapon of a mass strike out of its hands, and after the prohibition of the RFB it found it much more difficult to establish a new Combat League unhampered by state repression and to show a uniformed presence analogous to the SA in public spaces.

In all three KPD districts of the province, the trendline of membership was pointed upward. The district of Magdeburg saw a steady increase from 3,000 members in 1929 to nearly 7,000 at the end of 1931. The district of Thuringia (in which the administrative district of Erfurt made up about two-thirds of the population) grew from 5,000 to over 9,000, and the district of Halle-Merseburg from nearly 11,000 to over 13,000, with strong fluctuations occurring again in 1930.[49] This was robust growth, but in none of the three districts was it sufficient to even approach the numbers of the period before 1932, even though the adult population had grown substantially. Even in the tension-filled year 1932, only 1,000 new members were added in the district of Halle-Merseburg.[50] This still made the district one of the party's strongest, but a membership of 14,000 was a far cry from the 66,000 on the eve of the "March action" or the well over 20,000 at the turn of 1922/23.

Moreover, party membership remained subject to strong fluctuations. Detailed information is available for the district Halle-Merseburg for several months in 1932. Only in March, a phase of intense political mobilization in anticipation of the Reich presidential elections, did membership rise on balance by 1,000, while it declined in June and August by about 50 each month; in the process, the number of those leaving was between around 120 and 300. More than half of the departing members had belonged to the party for less than a year, with less than one-tenth having an affiliation of ten years or more.[51] It would thus seem that the core of long-term members was hardly affected by the fluctuations.[52] This is also supported by the known reasons why members left, some of which were taken down in February 1932. These records suggest that it tended to be problems with coming up with membership dues or, vaguely, a lack of interest in party work that led to the departure, rather than clearly articulated, divergent political opinions resulting in exclusion.[53]

A report by the district to the central office in May 1930 examined why the party was not able to exhaust the pool of potential recruits and what was behind the strong fluctuations. Apart from organizational shortcomings—in the collection of dues, in the works cells, in political campaigns—the criticism was aimed chiefly at the "obvious sectarian attitude of the better part of our members and functionaries." This attitude expressed itself at times in an almost open reluctance to accept new members, leading to the isolation of the party from its surrounding environment and to an unwillingness to ponder tactical questions; instead, everything was elevated into a fundamental problem of principle.[54] This was not the conflict—emphasized by Mallmann—between an unrealistic leadership avant-garde of the Leninist kind and a party base that was closer to real life and its demands and therefore inertial, but a conflict that ran through the base itself. A considerable part of the base looked back upon many years of membership in the KPD and preferred cultivating a "correct" consciousness over engaging in the drudgery of daily party work, while the other, fluctuating part had joined the KPD because of its radical positions, without establishing a closer bond to the party. Neither camp was much able to engage in pragmatic and consistent party work.[55]

The KPD was not able to acquire larger, sustained influence in factories and enterprises. The works cells remained the stillbirth they had essentially always been. Even the RGO, the new union in opposition to the ADGB, could achieve only temporary successes. In its former stronghold of Leuna, where it had won more than half of all votes at the works council elections in 1929, it garnered only a third of the votes in 1930; that figure shrank further in 1931 and by 1933 had evaporated to less than one-tenth. The free unions, by contrast, improved their position again, overtook the RGO in 1930, and in the spring of 1933 polled over 40 percent of the votes, only slightly less than the combined lists of the Stahlhelm and the NSBO, which did very well here after power changed hands at the Reich level.[56] Of course, what stood behind these results was not so much a political reorientation of the workforce as—in addition to massive pressure and harassment by management—massive layoffs, which were intended, not least, to hurt Communist supporters.[57] In other centers of the chemical industry, however, among them Wolfen, Bitterfeld, and Greppin, the RGO was able to further expand its position in 1931, thus accounting for the bare or substantial majority in the works councils of the three large enterprises. In the Mansfeld regions, as well, following the great strike of 1930, and in the Kali mining industry, the RGO posted a growth in votes over 1930, though it was far from a majority.[58]

In 1932, the works council elections were canceled because of an emergency decree. However, the already mentioned report about the work cells and the RGO group in select enterprises conveys a sense of its strength in the summer of that year. According to this report, the RGO for the most part had only a few more members than the Communist work cells—all told, leaving aside two smaller enterprises, no more than 3 percent of the workforce, that is, only a small minority. In the Wolfen film factory, for example, the RGO had a grand total of 94 members, whereas it had only 30 in the IG Farben factory in Bitterfeld, which was similar in size, a number that was equal to the NSDAP membership there.[59] In the chemical industry and, less so, in mining, where the workers' ties to the free unions were less well-developed than in other sectors, the RGO succeeded in keeping a stable following, though it was not able to make use of the gains that the KPD enjoyed during elections. The reasons for this were, first, the RGO's neglect of the classic union work or—as in the work cells—its representatives' failure to make appearances, and second, the counterwork done by the free unions and the repression by management.[60]

However, even outside factories and enterprises, the RGO, as an organization of growing numbers of the unemployed, was anything but a stellar success. Neither the "official" membership numbers nor the more realistic unofficial ones were higher than the KPD membership in the districts in questions; in fact, the opposite was the case. At the end of 1932, the unofficial numbers were below 10,000 in the district of Halle-Merseburg, below 4,000 in Magdeburg-Anhalt, and below 9,000 in Thuringia. The "official" numbers were not much higher.[61] On the whole, the RGO was not able to make any inroads into that segment of the workers who had hitherto remained aloof from the KPD.[62]

The KPD was far more successful as an electoral party. In spite of some setbacks, for instance during the election of the Reich president in 1932, until November 1932 it was able to steadily increase its votes (absolute and percentage-wise) also in the province of Saxony. In the electoral district of Magdeburg, for example, it added about 30,000 votes in the Reichstag elections in September 1930, in July 1932 it added another 14,000, and in November another 18,000, in both the cities and the countryside. In its consistently strong electoral district of Merseburg it was also able to tack on about 30,000 votes in 1930, and while it lost about 1,000 in July 1932 (with the SPD gaining steadily), in November it posted another gain of 16,000. This gave the party 27.1 percent, which was the third-best result in the Reich and—in absolute terms—far more votes than in its triumphant Landtag elections in 1921. Still, since then it had lost its dominant position as the majority party in the electoral district and as the majority party in over half of all counties. It held first place only in the Saalkreis and in the county of Bitterfeld, while the NSDAP was ahead in all others, as well as in the whole electoral district. Unlike in the early 1920s, however, the KPD was now represented more evenly in the various counties, especially in the countryside, where it moved much closer to its chief competitor especially in the SPD strongholds of the Magdeburger Börde. For example, in County Wolmirstedt it won more than a third and in County Wanzleben more than half as many votes as those cast for the SPD in the November elections in 1932. In the administrative district of Erfurt as well, the KPD gained overall, while the SPD suffered losses on the whole both here and in the other two electoral districts, losses that were, on balance, smaller than the gains of the KPD.[63]

Not easy to answer is the question of how many votes flowed from the NSDAP back to the workers' parties, especially the KPD, in November 1932. This would provide a clearer picture of the extent to which the KPD and the NSDAP were competing for workers with a weak union tradition, for example rural workers and those in the chemical industry. The purely arithmetical numbers offer no precise information about the real extent of the voter currents, though they do provide clues that accord with the findings regarding the other elections (Table 9.4). In

Table 9.4 Losses of the NSDAP in the Reichstag Elections of November 1932 (Province of Saxony)

County	NS losses 1932 II/1932 I	Gains/losses by the SPD/KPD together (KPD alone)	Gains by bourgeois parties	Voter turnout
KPD strongholds				
Bitterfeld	– 4384	+ 491 (+ 1083)	+ 2400	– 1493
Saalkreis	– 5011	+ 703 (+ 1317)	+ 2440	– 1868
City of Weißenfels	– 1607	– 38 (+ 19)	+ 758	– 887
SPD strongholds				
Neuhaldensleben	– 1757	– 500 (+ 676)	+ 1115	– 1142
Wanzleben	– 1861	– 13 (+ 462)	+ 470	– 1404
Wolmirstedt	– 1346	– 540 (+ 536)	+ 630	– 1256
NSDAP strongholds				
Eckartsberga	– 2856	+ 398 (+ 310)	+ 1150	– 1308
Langensalza	– 2338	+ 400 (+ 382)	+ 1156	– 782
Querfurt	– 3532	+ 171 (+ 744)	+ 1665	– 1696
Halle	– 11860	+ 1286 (+ 3202)	+ 9595	– 979

Source: *Stat. Dt. R., N. F.*, vol. 434, 48–50, 116–118.

the strongholds of the KPD and SPD, as well as those of the NSDAP, far more votes flowed to the bourgeois parties than to the working parties; moreover, the number of nonvoters was greater than the number of ballots cast for the workers' parties. Most of the losses of the SPD probably benefited the KPD. That about one-sixth of the NSDAP vote went to the workers' parties—as happened in County Langensalza—was the exception. In farming areas as well as here and in County Eckartsberga, where both the KPD and the SPD posted gains, a large part of this influx must have come from the National Socialists, but it was rather modest compared to the votes that migrated from the Nazis back to the bourgeois parties. Other than that, the KPD owed most of its gains to the losses of the Social Democrats. We can conclude from these findings, as well, that while a direct competition between the workers' parties and the NSDAP did exist, in both rural and industrial counties, its effects were not profound in either place.[64]

Was the KPD's success in rebuilding its combat organizations similar to its success as an electoral party? The outlawing of the RFB had pushed the party onto the defensive in the struggle over public terrain, at least initially. The organization continued to exist illegally, though it lost about half of its members throughout the Reich and developed increasingly into a military cadre force that was to assume leadership in a possible armed insurrection.[65] The RFB's original main function, that of demonstrating a readiness to fight in public, was to be assumed by a new organization, the Kampfbund gegen den Faschismus (Fighting League Against Fascism), which was set up at the end of the September 1930, following the surprising electoral success of the NSDAP. Another incentive came from the decision by the Reichsbanner to establish the Schutzformationen (Schufo, Protective Formations), potent fighting units that were supposed to be ready to confront the SA and were trained accordingly, but were not given arms.[66] In the summer of 1931, the Kampfbund had about 100,000 members throughout the Reich, which was substantially less than the RFB during its heyday. At the beginning of 1932, the party's central office did not rate the organization as highly effective. A particular problem was its relationship to the RFB, many of whose members had joined the Kampfbund: some of them saw their old group as superfluous, while others tried to continue its work in the Kampfbund and thereby threatened its status as a legitimate organization.[67]

Police authorities in the province of Saxony noted the illegal continuation of RFB activities, chiefly in the form of "paramilitary exercises," field training, and firing exercises with small-caliber weapons, but they did not see this as a serious source of danger. At the beginning of December 1932, the police, in a well-planned action, swooped down on the Erfurt RFB organization during nightly firing training and arrested its members.[68] The development of the Kampfbund was already in decline after a brief surge. For example, while it still had 3,500 members in July 1931 in the KPD district of Magdeburg-Anhalt, according to information from the party, a year later there were only 300 left, though by November 1932 the number had risen again to 1,000.[69] The Regierungspräsident of Erfurt reported in the middle of April 1932 that membership—leaving aside Erfurt itself and Suhl—"has declined considerably in nearly all other local groups," and that all its meetings "have been very poorly attended in the last months"—a remarkable statement, given the high political tension of the campaign for the presidential elections. Moreover, the paramilitary exercises and the weapons training begun the previous year had fallen "completely dormant." The reason for this sad state of affairs—expressed also in statements by KPD members—lay in the over-organization of the KPD and the heavy burden placed by the party on the party itself at the expense of its auxiliary organizations.[70] The source makes it very clear that the Kampfbund was in fact—much like the RFB and other organizations like it—nothing more than a minor appendage of the KPD that could not live up to its claim of appealing to wide segments of the working class.

The same holds true for the Roter Massenselbstschutz (Red Mass Self-Defense), whose establishment the KPD had called for after the first round of balloting in the presidential elections and the various attendant clashes; its model was the Iron Front led by the SPD. This new organization, too, was aimed at winning over workers who had hitherto remained at arm's length from the KPD, and once again "it generally failed to be successful," as the Oberpräsident of the province of Saxony reported to Berlin at the end of October 1932. Individual units of the new organization had made an appearance in Weißenfels and Halle, though only during the Reichstag elections in July, and they did not seem to be very tightly organized. Smaller units to which "only proven members of the KPD" were admitted, totaling probably no more than one hundred men, existed in Suhl, Mühlhausen, and Nordhausen. This was evidently a pure self-defense force for the party.[71]

Whatever the KPD attempted, after the outlawing of the RFB it was not able to create a potent mass organization that could have stood up to the SA both as an instrument for demonstrations and a fighting unit. As it was, its efforts did not go beyond its own members and supporters, and the party was unable to pull even them together into a solid organization. It was therefore to be expected that those KPD members and sympathizers who had a penchant for militancy were more difficult to control and had a greater tendency to engage in individual action than would have been the case if they had been integrated into the discipline of a larger organization. Moreover, their frustration grew in the face of the massive growth of the SA.[72] The threat of violent insurrection by the KPD and its auxiliary organizations, however, was virtually nonexistent even at the height of the economic crisis and political tension in the summer and fall of 1932—and even weaker than it had been in the fall of 1923, when the Communists in Saxony and Thuringia had had a certain potential for violence at their disposal, at least briefly. The illegal military apparatus of the KPD was unable to make up for the lack of a mass basis. Prussian officials were well aware of this, especially after the putsch of 20 July 1932 in Prussia had brought committed enemies of the Republic into leadership positions.[73]

The Mansfeld Strike, Social Protest, and Communist Violence

The limits of the KPD's influence were also apparent from its attempts to exploit for its own benefit the social protest in the years of the economic crisis. This social protest was different from what it had been during the years of inflation: it centered not on subsistence protests against "rising prices," but on protests against unemployment. Since this protest emanated from "workers" instead of "consumers," it offered the KPD a greater chance of becoming involved. At the same time, against the backdrop of rising unemployment the strike lost its potency as a threat and an instrument for exerting pressure. That is the reason, not least, why the province of Saxony during these years, in spite of an increasingly tense economic and political situation, witnessed only a single large labor struggle, the Mansfeld strike. This nearly eight-week-long confrontation against the Mansfeld AG, carried on by almost 13,000 miners and workers at smelting plants in June and July 1930, shortly after the formation of the first Brüning government, attracted attention far beyond the borders of the province of Saxony. It was the first time that the Communist RGO sought to play an independent role vis-à-vis the free unions in a larger conflict, in this case against the miners' union.[74] This strike and the protests of the unemployed in the years of the Great Depression also show how violent social protest could turn into political violence. While the Communists did not shy away from advocating violence, the police did not act with restraint. Despite its gains among the electorate, the KPD remained in a ghetto.

Since 1929 the Mansfeld AG had been confronted by a collapse in copper prices, and in the months leading up to the strike it sought to respond to the problem with drastic wage cuts. Negotiations to that effect had been going on with union representatives since the end of January. After another precipitous drop in the price of copper in the middle of April, the company stepped up its demands. It called for a 15 percent reduction in wages beginning 1 June and threatened to shut down the company unless a sufficient number of workers were willing to continue their employment under the proposed terms or adequate state subsidies were forthcoming. The free and Christian unions were willing to accommodate management, to the point of accepting wage cuts in several steps, but then a meeting of functionaries at the end of April rejected any cutback in contractual wages. A proposal by a mediator on 20 May—wage cuts between 8 percent and 10 percent—was turned down by both sides. Management then went back to its old demands, and all signs pointed to a gathering storm.[75]

In this situation, the Free Miners' Union made a tactical error. At another conference of functionaries on 26 May, it was decided to define the shutdown of the company as a lockout and to simply call upon workers to stay at home. A course of total confrontation with the Mansfeld AG was to be avoided, but this shifted the initiative to the Communists for now. After mediation had failed, the RGO began a campaign of meetings, especially in the towns and villages of the Mansfelder Land. But six meetings also took place in plants of the Mansfeld AG, the first since the days of the "March action" in 1921. On 29 May in Helbra, the campaign reached its high point at a meeting of plant delegates that called for an immediate strike, adopted a catalogue of demands that included a wage hike of 2 percent, and elected a strike committee with a Communist chairman. On 2 June (1 June was a Sunday) the overwhelming majority of Mansfeld workers did in fact fail to report for work. At the Wolf mine, the largest mine in the district, only 140 of 2,100 miners descended into the pit, while only 19 of 600 workers reported at the Krug smelting works. The turnout was similar at other mines and plants, forcing management to close down all operations and have only the most essential work performed. Only now did the non-Communist unions also establish strike committees.[76]

It appeared that the RGO had in fact succeeded in gaining the support of the mass of workers, but a closer look reveals that its success rested on weak foundations. From the start, its meeting activity in the run-up to the strike can be interpreted in part as compensation for previous missteps. In the year and a half before the strike, the KPD had expelled sixty full-time union functionaries from the party because they were unwilling to support the RGO's confrontational course. That included all nine works council chairmen in the larger plants of the Mansfeld AG, who had been expelled prior to the works council elections in March. The RGO did not do well in the elections: it could furnish only 16 of 166 members of the works councils in all of the company's plants and was faced with the unpleasant fact that a number of party comrades were campaigning on the lists of the free unions.[77] The "reconcilers" within the party organization, by now defeated within the party organization of the district of Halle-Merseburg, evidently still had some influence in the unions. The RGO thus had to assert itself in the struggle against the Mansfeld AG if it wanted to be a serious rival to the other unions.

That so many workers had joined the strike by 2 June was not least an outcome of the general wage conditions in the Mansfeld region. The wages that the company paid its miners continued to be far lower than those in other mining districts.[78] The kind of sacrifice that was being demanded from the workers therefore seemed even less tolerable here than elsewhere. The fact that the conflict with the company revolved chiefly around pay is also a major reason why the wives of workers, as the keepers of the family budget, were especially conspicuous in the first days of the strike. Large numbers of them appeared at the factory gates to intercept strikebreakers, block the path of cars, and push strollers that bore signs reading "Strikebreakers are being transported here." Perhaps it was owing more to them than to the strikingly large number of pickets (especially young workers)—700 at the Wolf mine, alone—that so few strikebreakers went to work on 2 June, whereupon the Mansfeld AG ordered the temporary shutdown of all operations. In spite of what the police president of Halle described as a testy mood among the strikers, there were no violent clashes with those "willing to work"; only the window of one of their buses was smashed.[79]

However, the weakness of the Communists was revealed during the first few days. The women gathered outside the factory gates were almost exclusively party members, while the "cordon of unaffiliated women … is still very weak," as the emissary from party headquarters had to concede.[80] In other respects, as well, the Communists remained relatively isolated. Initially (and into July), its central strike committee was made up almost entirely of party comrades, as were the strike committees at the individual plants, which took shape only slowly. Moreover, the central strike committee lacked the necessary energy and commitment: it made too little effort to mobilize the strikers in meetings, was slow to issue strike coupons, and took its time setting up the promised strike kitchens. In addition, there were tactical mistakes. For example, as early as the strike's first days, the delegate from the central office criticized the demand for a wage hike of 2 marks that was part of the call for the strike as unrealistically high. There was no way one could say that the "masses" in fact stood behind the KPD and the RGO. This became very obvious on 26 June, when the KPD in central Germany organized a "Day of the Party" and held eight public meetings in the strike area, at which, despite the events of the preceding days (discussed below), only 251 new members were signed up. "With better work by the party," the author of the report noted, the success of the recruitment effort could "invariably have been greater."[81]

The first three weeks of the strike passed without any meaningful incidents on the strike front itself. Numerous pickets remained outside the mines and the other plants. The police were steadily reinforced, but the authorities pulled in only additional gendarmes from neighboring counties and regions, and no Schupo. This decision was clearly motivated by the fear that their deployment could massively exacerbate the situation. Several units of the gendarmes were housed on company grounds, not least to prevent acts of sabotage. The police thus did not offer a clear target as they had back in March of 1921 in the seminary building in Eisleben, though they did create the impression that they were taking the side of the company. But in contrast to 1921, the number of deployed officers was much smaller: by the middle of June there were only 132 gendarmes, to which we must add the twenty municipal police officers from Eisleben. By the end of the strike another twenty-five gendarmes had been added, but no Schupo officers.[82] All told, this was anything but an imposing force, nor did it command the kind of warlike equipment it had in 1921. It would appear that the police leadership, in response to the events in March 1921, had also developed some deployment strategies aimed at avoiding an escalation.[83]

Violent clashes occurred at the union meetings. The responsibility clearly lay with the Communists: at the beginning of the strike they had formed a "self-defense force" composed chiefly of young workers and former RFB men, which they now used to break up the meetings of the free and Christian unions, with success especially in Eisleben. Moreover, Communist pickets tried to prevent essential maintenance work from being performed.[84] Other than that, however, life in the Mansfelder Land continued as normal. After a trip by car through the area on 24 June, *Regierungsrat* Freyseng from the office of the Regierungspräsident in Merseburg noted that the strikers were "not agitated and not embittered," though they hoped for a speedy resolution.[85]

That same day, however, the situation grew more explosive. The responsibility lay with the management of the Mansfeld AG. The company tried to resume operations at the brass plant in Hettstedt, which was probably intended as a test of how solid the strike front was. About 240 strikebreakers, some of them members of the Stahlhelm, managed to slip into the factory past some inattentive pickets, but at the end of the shift the police had to protect them against a now larger crowd of pickets. There were a number of smaller scuffles with the gendarmes. The next day the conflict escalated. Although the number of "those willing to work" had already dropped by a third, those who remained were now confronted with an unmistakably more massive use of violence. The cars in which they were riding and the escort vehicles of the police were pelted with stones, and the strikebreakers themselves were insulted, threatened, and a few so badly beaten that they "required medical attention." Their names were publicly posted in their home towns, some were pursued to their homes, and others had the crops harvested and stolen from the fields they were cultivating.[86]

The police also came under attack, and they struck back. Their uncontrolled use of rubber truncheons in some instances not only prompted several SPD parliamentarians to raise the issue in the Landtag, but also led the Prussian Minister of the Interior to demand a detailed report. The Regierungspräsident of Merseburg rejected the criticism of the behavior of the police, though he did concede that "on occasion persons not directly involved" had also received blows because they happened to be in the crowd that was moving against the officers. The Regierungspräsident accused the KPD of having called for acts of violence, though in his first report he referred only to an article in the *Klassenkampf*; a few days later, however, we read that "under the leadership of Communist functionaries ... numerous outsiders" had also been involved in the excesses.[87] The names of these leaders were not given; moreover, the police had arrested only eight individuals, which raises questions about the basis for its claim that "numerous outsiders" had been present. The *Klassenkampf*, too, could not be accused of having directly called for violence against strikebreakers. The paper devoted prominent coverage every day to the events in the Mansfeld area, though it limited itself to an abstract rhetoric of struggle, which juxtaposed the successes of the "red battlefront" against what it claimed was a repeated "offensive to break the strike." However, on 25 June the KPD organ did note with satisfaction that the workers had fallen upon the strikebreakers "to give them what they deserved," namely, "a sound beating."[88]

There is no doubt that the KPD and RGO did nothing on 24 and 25 June to keep their supporters and the "self-defense force" from taking violent action against strikebreakers and the police. But the actions of the pickets and of the population in the towns required no special planning and preparation; instead, it emerged spontaneously from the situation, followed old patterns, and was triggered by the conduct of the Mansfeld AG. The police, with their weak forces, were not able to prevent the excesses; their own excesses were the result of being set upon and of their image of the Communist foe. After the incidents in Hettstedt, the Mansfeld AG gave up its effort to resume regular operations for the time being. At the same time, the Free Miners' Union tried to regain the leadership of the strike. On 30 June, the union organized a rally with its national chairman, Husemann, to which only members were admitted. Still, the RGO was able to show up in considerable strength and even attack Husemann physically, who was saved from being badly beaten.[89] The pattern of conduct in the coming weeks had thus been laid down. The non-Communist unions tried to achieve a solution to the conflict under their leadership, while the KPD and RGO sought to prevent an end to the strike at all costs and did not shrink from using violence.

On 10 July, representatives of the company and the unions met in the Reich Labor Ministry for new talks, during which the granting of subsidies was raised again. Five days later the negotiators reached an agreement that largely bore the handwriting of company management. An accord signed by both sides stipulated a 9.5 percent cut in contractual wages and called for subsidies from the Reich and Prussia. In addition, union representatives did not object to the Mansfeld AG's intention to cut pay exceeding the contractual rate by another 2.5 percent, though this was not put in writing. A conference of functionaries approved the agreement with 75 to 51 votes, though it also decided to officially end the strike only after the subsidies were granted. Meetings of union members confirmed the announced result of the negotiations, also in Hettstedt and the surrounding area, where the RGO managed to break up one meeting. While the course of the unions seemed to be moving toward success, the RGO made new efforts to turn things around in its favor. It appears to have drawn in a substantial number of previously unorganized workers, and it also succeeded in expanding its own strike committee with the addition of several members of the Free Miners' Union and the DMV. On 17 July it called for a political mass strike against the government. However, a day later the non-Communist unions withdrew their pickets, and on 23 July the Reich government and Prussia concluded a subsidy agreement with the Mansfeld AG. As far as the free and Christian unions were concerned, this put an end to the strike. The workers now returned to the mines and plants in large numbers, protected by the police, which became increasingly embroiled in physical altercations with the Communist pickets. Even when company management publicized the cut in piecework wages in public postings on 24 July and the unions, as agreed, did not protest, there was no new strike movement. The Regierungspräsident of Magdeburg reported that the workforce had "descended in full" into the mines, and in the smelting plants "the part of the workforce intended for the resumption of operations" had reported for work.[90]

The Communists made one final attempt to regain the initiative. On the evening of 24 July, the KPD organized a demonstration march to Hettstedt, in which about 1,000 participated. The hope was that banners and chants would change the minds of smelting plant workers ready to return to work. On the outskirts of town, the police that had been notified in the meantime tried to place a squad car at the head of the procession, but when the car had to stop, the officers were verbally insulted and then pelted with rocks. The demonstrators surged against the officers and engaged them in a street battle, with the demonstrators wielding flagpoles and the police their rubber truncheons. According to statements by the policemen, three pistol shots were also fired at them, but there were no serious injuries. The next day in a farmer's barn, officers arrested eight men who later in court admitted to having participated in the clash the previous night. All came from Halle, and all were members of the KPD and explained their presence in the Mansfeld region with the very believable explanation that they had wanted to visit their uncle.[91] That same day around noon, the police dispersed a crowd of about 2,000 that had gathered outside the tavern of the free union strike committee in Helbra; similar scenes occurred in Wimmelburg and in Eisleben itself, but otherwise things were quiet throughout the region. The police, however, do not seem to have imposed any special restraint on themselves in the actions they took.[92] The RGO quickly realized its defeat. On 25 July, its central strike leadership decided to recommend the resumption of work, though not without denouncing this as the unavoidable outcome of the "stab-in-the-back by the social-fascist functionaries."[93]

All told, the Mansfeld strike, and not least its unspectacular end, revealed the weakness of the RGO, its initial successes notwithstanding. It was not able, either in terms of personnel or organizationally, to convert the workers' massive discontent over the company's moves into a lasting gain in mobilization, even though it received strong support from the central party office in Berlin.[94] Unlike the excesses against strikebreakers, the offensive acts of violence during the final phase of the strike did not meet with any resonance, not even when the police, as was probably expected, took tough action. In the end, it did not take a large deployment of the police to make the resumption of work possible.[95] Many workers had been worn down by the long weeks of the strike and accepted the less-than-satisfactory result of the negotiations. Even though the RGO now drew in some new supporters, most members of the other unions continued to back their leaders. The author of the report by the KPD district leadership therefore concluded that the strike failed not because of the unorganized workers, but because of the "strikebreaking by the organized ones."[96]

The social protest after 1930 was, on the whole, no longer the consumer protest of the inflation period, which had united participants of various social status, mobilized in particular women as those in charge of providing for their families, and not taken on a clear political thrust. For the years of the Great Depression, we have no reports from the province of Saxony about the forced sale of foodstuffs at lower prices, which had been a typical form of protest during the inflation. The looting of entire stores or the more or less forceful removal of food became a more broadly discussed problem only in 1932, as did the plundering of fields, for the protection of which the farmers discussed plans for setting up a field guard in the summer of 1932.[97] The crisis that had grown more acute since the turn of 1929/30 did not lead to prices that were out of control, but to reduced income, and it affected precisely the surging number of the unemployed. To that extent it was "more proletarian" and "more male" than in 1923 and intensified the tensions between Communists and Social Democrats, especially since the jobless included a disproportionately large number of young men—one-quarter of the registered male unemployed in 1932 were between 18 and 25 years old[98]—who were less rooted in the Social Democratic workers' movement than their fathers. Moreover, Communists were more likely to be laid off than workers with no ties to the party.

The unemployed responded in very different ways to their situation, however. Some interpreted it chiefly as an individual fate and sank into apathy or even committed suicide out of despair. Others, especially the younger ones, crossed the threshold into criminal behavior or found an outlet for their frustration in "small" violence toward the representatives of the disintegrating welfare states in their offices. A closer bond to a clique of youths or to one of the Combat Leagues, where one could reaffirm a sense of masculinity damaged by the lack of employment, was only one possible response, as was political activity.[99] Violence was by no means an inevitable consequence of joblessness.[100] However, the political causes of the economic and social crisis now seemed clearer than in 1923. The emergency decrees of the presidential governments, which reduced wages and subsidies and interfered massively in the right of collective bargaining, now pointed to identifiable authorities and individuals as the culprits responsible for the situation of the workers and the unemployed, whereas the earlier hyperinflation seemed to have swept over the country like a natural catastrophe. As a result, the KPD propaganda could now fall on more fertile soil than in the early years of the Republic.

Foremost among the protests that it initiated among the jobless were street demonstrations. They took place on a large scale for the first time at the beginning of March 1930, since the Communist International had proclaimed 6 March the worldwide Day of Struggle against Joblessness. After clashes during a rally of unemployed workers in Berlin at the beginning of the year, the Prussian Minister of the Interior had outlawed outdoor meetings, but the KPD called upon all to ignore the prohibition from the "social-fascist Grzesinski." "We put force against force" declared a circular from the Halle-Merseburg Committee of the Unemployed to the local KPD groups in the district. Attempts were made in a number of places to hold demonstrations, especially in the Communist strongholds, most of which drew several hundred people, sometimes more than 1,000. According to police reports, workers in the factories and plants did not participate, even though committees of the jobless in front of the gates to the plants called upon them to do so. Youngsters made up a large portion of the demonstrators, "often half," and women, too, were observed "in larger numbers." All in all, in the verdict of the Regierungspräsident, the participants were "almost entirely supporters of the KPD."[101]

Since the police had to break up the demonstrations, there were smaller scuffles with the officers in many places, and sometimes also kicks, punches, and thrown rocks, though this did not lead to serious injuries among the police. A more serious clash took place in Ammendorf near Halle. A first attempt to organize a train of demonstrators after a meeting of unemployed workers was thwarted by a Schupo unit that arrested several leaders; during a second action against the crowd, which had grown to between 200 and 300, three police officers were knocked to the ground and kicked. Two others who rushed to their aid also went down and were stripped of their rubber truncheons, but they still managed to draw their guns and fire, first in warning, and then at their attackers. One assailant was killed on the spot, and another died shortly after from his wounds. Both men—a 40-year-old disabled veteran and a 22-year-old worker—were members of the (now banned) RFB. There was no reasonable doubt that the police had acted out of self-defense. Even the *Klassenkampf* conceded that the shots had been fired only "after the workers surrounded a Schupo."[102]

Similar incidents happened over the next two years. During the Reich Day of the Jobless that the KPD called for at the end of February 1931, clashes with police occurred in Magdeburg and Halberstadt, triggered by police attempts to break up a public meeting in the one instance, and redirect a column of demonstrators in the other. Rocks and pieces of iron were hurled against the officers, a few suffered minor stab wounds; in return, they used their rubber batons.[103] Further confrontations occurred in the wake of the emergency decree of 5 June 1931, which drastically cut payments to the jobless. The police in Suhl used their rubber truncheons to break up an illegal demonstration march to the Simson Works. In Aken (near Dessau), the police were attacked from within a demonstration and gained the upper hand only after they readied their weapons for firing. Following the end of a KPD rally in Magdeburg, police arrested a man who had called for violence against them; when they took him away, a "crowd" moved in on them and they fired shots in self-defense. One 22-year-old worker was fatally shot, and one young woman was wounded in the foot.[104]

Similar scenes occurred in 1932. One hot spot was the county of Bitterfeld, where unmarried unemployed received smaller assistance payments if they lived with their parents; since this rule was often circumvented, the county administration decided that from the beginning of July it would pay out only the lower rates. After the magistrate in Greppin, under pressure from a delegation of unemployed workers, kept the higher rates, the KPD tried to overturn the regulation in a neighboring town as well. Several pickets blocked the door to the municipal office, where the payout had initially begun without any problems. In front of the office, a "crowd" continued to grow with the influx of people from the surrounding area, and the mood became increasingly testy. Nine gendarmes, who were supervising the payout inside the office, climbed out of a window and cleared the door. The crowd, in the front ranks of which stood women and children, showered them with rocks and bottles and may have fired on them, so that the officers eventually opened fire themselves. Three people were injured, and a leading functionary of the local KPD group was killed when he was hit from behind and the bullet lodged in his lung; it may not have been fired from a police pistol.[105]

These accounts do not create the impression that the unemployed developed forms of protest independent of KPD guidance. The actions of the jobless were concentrated where the KPD had its strongholds or where—as in the large city of Magdeburg—it could at least mobilize more than merely a handful of its own supporters. The protests were led by Communist activists. Although the participation of women and children suggests similarities to the food protests of the inflation years, those similarities were much more tenuous than might seem at first glance. Women and children were not simply present in larger numbers: they were deliberately placed in front when the demonstrators expected a confrontation with the police.[106] The violence during the demonstrations was only in part spontaneous. Because of its declining influence in factories, the KPD was increasingly dependent on the street as its sphere for action.[107] At the same time, this sphere was massively restricted by the official prohibitions against rallies. The police were determined to enforce these prohibitions and, given who their enemy was, did not impose any particular restraint on themselves. For that reason alone, the violence was predictable. The KPD, for its part, deliberately fueled the confrontations, for example, by calling for resistance to the police in its public pronouncements.[108] When its supporters used projectiles like iron hooks or even fired on the police, especially from a distance and shielded by women and children, this shows the heightened degree of planning behind such actions and a growing willingness to resort to violence on the part of those engaged in them. The party leadership was also trying in this way to incorporate into its tactics the increasing edginess of many unemployed workers,[109] but it miscalculated. The more massive violence toward police officers was not simply a continuation of the "small" violence toward employees in administrative offices.

With its violent tactics, the KPD leadership bound the hard core of its base—which included also the women and children among the demonstrators—more closely to itself, but beyond that it gained few supporters and also scared away many unemployed from involvement with the Communists. As Dick Geary and Andreas Wirsching have argued, the tactics of the KPD contributed to a fracturing of the unemployed and to the "self-ghettoization" of the party.[110] The steady increase in the number of voters who backed the KPD did not signal approval of its actions, and certainly not a generally higher readiness to engage in violence on the part of the workers, but a fundamental protest against the policies of the Reich governments and against a helplessly floundering SPD.

Notes

1. LHAM C 20 Ib 2048/I, fols. 181–187 (OP to the Prussian Ministry of the Interior, July 1930, undated draft); according to this document there were 9,629 members; Kater, *Nazi Party,* 263.
2. For details see Berghahn, *Stalhelm,* 143–156.
3. LHAM C 20 Ib 2048/I, fols. 49–60 (RP Magdeburg to OP, 5 July and 26 July 1930).
4. This put Halle more or less in the middle range of German universities; see Geoffrey Giles, *Students and National Socialism in Germany* (Princeton, 1985), 54. For a general discussion of

the reasons why many students turned toward the NSDAP early on see Michael Kater, *Studentenschaft und Rechtsradikalismus in Deutschland 1918–1933: Eine sozialgeschichtliche Studie zur Bildungskrise in der Weimarer Republik* (Hamburg, 1975); Anselm Faust, *Der Nationalsozialistische Deutsche Studentenbund: Studenten und Nationalsozialismus in der Weimarer Republik,* 2 vols. (Düsseldorf, 1973), esp. vol. 1, 112ff.

5. LHAM C 20 Ib 2048/I, fols. 68–72 (RP Merseburg to OP, 5 July 1930); fols. 132–138 (RP Merseburg to OP, 29 July 1930).
6. Ibid., fols. 173–177 (Office of the state criminal police to OP, 26 July 1930). Raßloff, *Flucht,* 333, 364–367, points out that the NSDAP in Erfurt did not attract any members of the local bourgeois elite prior to 1933. On the difficulties the NSDAP had in organizing local branches in predominantly Catholic regions see Heilbronner, *Catholicism, Political Culture, and the Countryside.*
7. Kater, *Nazi Party,* 32–71, 244–251; Peter Manstein, *Die Mitglieder und Wähler der NSDAP 1919–1933: Untersuchungen zu ihrer schichtmäßigen Zusammensetzung* (Frankfurt, 1988), 129–142; Mühlberger, *Hitler's Followers,* 48f., 80–83, 121–123, 155–158.
8. LHAM C 20 Ib 2048/I, fols. 49f. (RP Magdeburg to OP, 5 July 1930); fols. 133, 137 (RP Merseburg to OP, 29 July 1930). If we relied on the comment by the head of the Magdeburg office as a source, we would have to peg the ratio of civil servants even higher than Kater does, which means that civil servants would be even more overrepresented.
9. Ibid., fol. 136 (RP Merseburg to OP, 29 July 1930).
10. Ibid., fol. 52 (RP Erfurt to OP, 13 March 1930); fol. 68 (RP Merseburg to OP, 5 March 1930). Suhl was part of County Schleusingen, which was surrounded by Thuringia, in whose government the Nazis had been represented since 1930. The agitation by the party was correspondingly intense there, although its membership in the stronghold of the Communists or the leftist SPD, at 199, made it only the fourth-largest party in the administrative district of Erfurt.
11. LHAM C 20 Ib 2051/II, fol. 139 (RP Merseburg to OP, 24 October 1931).
12. SAPMO Ry 1/I 3/11/18, fols. 44–49 (Organizational report by the district Halle-Merseburg, undated).
13. Conan Fischer, *The German Communists and the Rise of Nazism* (New York, 1991), 162–188, here esp. 177, pays little attention to this, or to the role of layoffs in the decline of votes for the RGO lists. One indication for the growing influence of the NSBO among workers, however, is his reference to the change in the RGO's strategy vis-à-vis the National Socialists: as of the summer of 1932, they were no longer to be driven out of the factories with blows, but brought into one's own camp through a "a united front from below." Yet Fischer is not able to show that this new approach had any larger success, and it remains unclear, in the end, to what extent Communists and National Socialists were in fact direct rivals in the factories.
14. Weitz, *German Communism,* 150; see Wolfgang Zollitzsch, *Arbeiter zwischen Weltwirtschaftskrise und Nationalsozialismus: Ein Beitrag zur Sozialgeschichte der Jahre 1928 bis 1936* (Göttingen, 1990), 195–201, who sees a major reason for the relative success of the NSBO in the Leuna works in the agrarian roots of many workers, which made close ties to a union difficult from the outset.
15. See Volker Kratzenberg, *Arbeiter auf dem Weg zu Hitler? Die nationalsozialistische Betriebszellen-organisation. Ihre Entstehung, ihre Programmatik, ihr Scheitern 1927–1934* (Frankfurt, 1987), esp. 175ff., who describes the "lack of ties and roots" as the main characteristic of the NSBO members. According to Kratzenberg, in Berlin, the example of his study, the members were—apart from white-collar workers—chiefly younger workers from smaller cities and towns, former members of right-wing union organizations, the previously non-organized, and workers in the public sector, as well as the jobless who had previously belonged to the KPD, although none of this can be quantified with any greater precision. In the rank list of the NSBO Gaue (in terms of membership size) in the summer of 1931, Magdeburg (18th of 36) and Halle-Merseburg (23rd) held only middling to lower rank; ibid., 209f. A similar tenor is found in

Jeremy Noakes, *The Nazi Party in Lower Saxony, 1921–1933* (Oxford, 1971), 174–182. In the works council elections at the beginning of February 1933, the RGO in the film factory Wolfen was even able to win a majority and once more substantially boost its votes over the 1931 results, while the ADGB lost about the same number of votes, with the NSBO list benefiting from the losses of the Stahlhelm and reaching a quarter of the RGO's votes (*KK* no. 28, 2 February 1933).

16. LHAM C 20 Ib 2048/I, fol. 49 (RP Magdeburg to OP, 5 July 1930).
17. LHAM C 20 Ib 2048/I, fol. 133 (RP Merseburg to OP, 29 July 1930). Hinkler, who would sometimes lend a hand to help break up a meeting, continued his career after 1930 as the manager of the NSDAP group in the Prussian Landtag. His successor was another former teacher, Rudolf Jordan, who came from a town near Fulda. Beginning in 1928, the Magdeburg Gau was headed by the retired captain Wilhelm Friedrich Loeper, a former career officer who had to leave the Reichswehr in 1924 because of his involvement in the Hitler putsch. Beginning in 1927, Fritz Sauckel was the Gau chief in Thuringia, which had authority over the Nazi organization in the administrative district of Erfurt; Sauckel was later made Plenipoteniary-General for Labor Deployment and the man chiefly responsible for the fate of forced laborers during the war. On the biographies of the Gau chiefs see Peter Hüttenberger, *Die Gauleiter: Studie zum Wandel der Machtgefüge in der NSDAP* (Stuttgart, 1969).
18. LHAM C 20 Ib 2048/I, fol. 24 (RP Erfurt to OP, 15 May 1930); fols. 174, 176 (Report by state criminal police office, 26 July 1930). According to these documents, there was in the district of Merseburg also a smaller local group of the Freischar Schill (in Eisleben), an organization that originally had been part of the Deutschvölkische Freiheitsbewegung (German-*Völkisch* Freedom Movement) but was now leaning more and more toward the National Socialists: LHAM C 20 Ib 2048/I, fol. 136 (RP Merseburg to OP, 29 July 1930); see also Peter D. Stachura, *Nazi Youth in the Weimar Republic* (Santa Barbara, CA, 1975), 113.
19. Stachura, *Nazi Youth*, 57–62, emphasizes by contrast that the membership of the Hitler Youth before 1930 was "predominantly working class."
20. LHAM C 20 Ib 2048/II, fol. 35 (Survey by RP Magdeburg, 1 February 1931) and LHAM C 20 Ib 2049/II, fol. 25 (Survey, 10 October 1931) document 7,889 and 9,887 members, respectively.
21. Author's calculations based on LHAM C 20 Ib 2052/I, fols. 51–59 (Survey by RP Erfurt, 25 September 1930); fols. 205–218 (Survey, 1 October 1931). Neither survey lists membership figures for the various local groups, which is why the total number is slightly higher than the one produced by the calculation. Incidentally, in Sömmerda the local group had not grown since the previous year, and the group in Suhl grew only by 15 members. Unfortunately we do not have a survey for the administrative district of Merseburg.
22. Methodologically, especially in dividing up the artisans without a more detailed identification, I am following Kater, *Nazi Party*, 8 (using this method 36.6% should be assigned to the middle class). According to Weber, *Wandlung*, vol. 2, 27f., two-thirds of the leading functionaries of the KPD were recruited from among skilled and other workers; it is likely that the ratio was even higher at the lower levels.
23. Following Kater (*Nazi Party*, 10), I have assigned 2.6% each of the "merchants" and the "farmers" to the class of entrepreneurs. The category of civil servants also includes former civil servants. As noted above, the total share of civil servants may be higher than indicated.
24. See Kater, *Nazi Party*, 174, 256f., who, on the basis of a sample, also points out that workers may have been underrepresented on the local level. Wirsching (*Weltkrieg*, 452) has emphasized the middle-class character of the Berlin NSDAP; for Saxony, Claus-Christian W. Szejnmann, *Nazism in Central Germany: The Brownshirts in 'Red' Saxony* (New York, 1999), 111ff. and 211ff. (a chapter written by Mühlberger) emphasizes the character of the NSDAP as a people's party, though he notes the trouble it had establishing itself in the strongholds of the SPD and the KPD. On the membership development of the NSDAP overall, on the basis of new data, see most recently Jürgen W. Falter, "Die "Märzgefallenen" von 1933: Neue Forschungsergeb-

nisse zum sozialen Wandel innerhalb der NSDAP-Mitgliedschaft während der Machtergreifungsphase," *GG* 24, no. 4 (1998): 595–616, esp. 611f., who by contrast notes a "remarkably high" worker ratio of 40% before 1933 and regards these workers as by no means atypical in terms of occupational profile. Of course, this observation does not yet clarify their political and social background.

25. Revealingly enough, Duesterberg failed to beat Hitler or Hindenburg during the first round of the Reich president elections even in his home town; with 17,000 votes, he garnered not even half as many votes as Hitler. During the second round, Hindenburg received here—and only here—fewer votes than during the first round; most of the Duesterberg ballots of the first round are therefore likely to have moved over to Hitler; *Stat. Dt. R., N. F.,* vol. 427, II, 18f.
26. An electoral analysis of the KPD district of Magdeburg-Anhalt attributed the defeat of the SPD in County Wanzleben to the fact that the municipal magistrates of the SPD newly elected in 1929 had approved large salaries for themselves, which was not well received. In the eyes of the KPD, the electoral success of the NDSAP in the district was due in equal measure to newly mobilized voters and to defectors from the bourgeois parties. In Magdeburg, the NSDAP had polled an especially large number of votes in Wilhelmstadt, the section of town that housed civil servants and white-collar workers, but few votes in the working-class areas. Industrial workers had thus hardly voted for the NSDAP, except in the small town of Schönebeck, where the management of the local radiator factory had systematically hired members of the Stahlhelm and the NSDAP: SAPMO Ry 1/I 3/12/33, fols. 89–92 (Analysis of election results, 1930, undated).
27. On these methodological problems see Falter, *Hitlers Wähler,* 75–80.
28. On the penetration of the NSDAP into the countryside in Protestant Germany as a whole see Wolfram Pyta, *Dorfgemeinschaft und Parteipolitik 1918–1933: Die Verschränkung von Milieu und Parteien in den protestantischen Landgebieten Deutschlands in der Weimarer Republik* (Düsseldorf, 1996).
29. In the rural county Erfurt the loss was only 80 votes, but in County Weißensee it was 576. The biggest loss, of 625 votes, occurred in County Ziegenrück. Still, the losses in the administrative district of Erfurt were less than 10% on average and thus made up only a relatively small part of the gains by the NSDAP, with the exception of Ziegenrück, where the share was around 15%. See Heinrich August Winkler, *Der Weg in die Katastrophe: Arbeiter und Arbeiterbewegung in der Weimarer Republik 1930 bis 1933* (Bonn, 1990), 689, who mentions these losses but does not clarify how they relate to the gains of the NSDAP.
30. Raßloff, *Flucht,* 149f., reaches in essence the same conclusion for the city of Erfurt. For a general discussion of NSDAP voters see Falter, *Hitlers Wähler,* here esp. 101ff., 194ff.; Manstein, *Wähler,* 165ff. The best-known theories about the provenance of Nazi voters, which are controversial especially as they relate to the elections of 1930—which was higher, the share of former voters from bourgeois parties other than the DNVP (the class-theory approach) or the share of first-time and new voters as well as voters of the DNVP (the mass theory approach)?—are reviewed by Falter, *Hitlers Wähler,* 42ff. Falter, who has presented what is to date the cleanest election analysis in terms of methodology, though one that is difficult to follow for the statistical layman, does not take a clear position, though he does not attribute central importance to the increased voter participation (*Hitlers Wähler,* 101). Jürgen R. Winkler, *Sozialstruktur, politische Traditionen und Liberalismus: Eine empirische Längsschnittstudie zur Wahlentwicklung in Deutschland 1871–1933* (Opladen, 1995), esp. 309ff., concludes that the electoral successes of the NSDAP had a strong link with conservative electoral traditions, and a weaker one with liberal traditions.
31. A *Standarte* comprised 1,000–3,000 men, a *Sturm* 70–200; see Longerich, *Braunen Bataillone,* 112.
32. LHAM C 20 Ib 2048/I, fols. 51f. (RP Magdeburg to OP, 5 July 1930); fol. 134 (RP Merseburg to OP, 29 July 1930); fol. 174 (Report by state criminal police office, 26 July 1930).
33. Diehl, *Paramilitary Politics,* 284f.

34. LHAM C 20 Ib 1991/V, fol. 317 (RP Erfurt to OP, 10 September 1929); fol. 318 (RP Magdeburg to OP, 22 September 1929); fols. 319f. (RP Merseburg to OP, 22 September 1929); fol. 328 (RP Merseburg to OP, 4 April 1930). The comments by Berghahn, *Stahlhelm,* 134f., are only very brief. For details on the switchover movement see Götz von Olenhusen, "Jungstahlhelm," 155ff., 166ff. On the minor importance of paramilitary exercises in the Reichsbanner before 1930 see Rohe, *Reichsbanner,* 158–165.
35. Longerich, *Braunen Bataillone,* 85–91. Free Corps fighters and the bourgeoisie were explicitly addressed by a recruitment poster of the SA that the police president of Magdeburg sent to the Oberpräsident at the end of March 1931 (LHAM C 20 Ib 1860/X, fol. 128e). It borrowed directly from the language used to recruit the Free Corps in 1919, though it made it harsher in specific ways through the use of the word "subhumanness": "Volunteers step forward! It is not only the borders of the state that are in danger, life and property are also being threatened daily by the organized criminality of the Reichsbanner and the Communists. This organized subhumanness must be opposed. We therefore call upon all German men and youngsters to join the SA."
36. LHAM C 20 Ib 2048/II, fols. 63f. (Survey of PP Magdeburg, 1 February 1931); fol. 5 (Survey of RP Merseburg, 18 February 1931); LHAM C 20 Ib 2052/I, fol. 40 (RP Erfurt to OP, 1 November 1930). Andreas Werner, "SA: 'Wehrverband,' 'Parteitruppe' oder 'Revolutionsarmee'? Studien zur Geschichte der SA und der NSDAP 1920–1933," PhD diss., University of Erlangen-Nuremberg, 1964, 547, on the strong growth 544–546. According to this data, membership in the SA group "Middle," which included, apart from the two large administrative districts of the province, also the entire Free State of Saxony, had risen steadily between 1 March and 1 November 1931 from 14,558 to 31,022.
37. The category designations are taken from the sources on Magdeburg and Merseburg.
38. The vocational data of the source was converted into the categories of the other sources on membership.
39. This presumably includes the "members of technical and related occupations," which is why they no longer appear as a separate category.
40. LHAM C 20 Ib 2048/II, fol. 4 (RP Merseburg to OP, 18 February 1931).
41. LHAM C 20 Ib 2048/II, fols. 63f. (Survey of PP Magdeburg, 1 February 1931).
42. See the exhaustive analysis in Reichardt, *Kampfbünde,* 311–317; Longerich, *Braune Bataillone,* 81–85. See also Bessel, *Political Violence,* 33–39, who points out that in the rural East of Prussia the SA was mainly a middle-class organization in which farmers and sons of farmers made up the largest single group. Conan Fischer's most important study in this regards is *Stormtroopers,* here 24–81.
43. LHAM C 20 Ib 2052/I, fols. 186–191 (Survey, 15 June 1931); fols. 42–47 (Survey of 25 September 1930). The data refer to the 50 leadership members; occupational information is missing for another 14. See Mathilde Jamin, *Zwischen den Klassen: Zur Sozialstruktur der SA-Führerschaft* (Wuppertal, 1984), 200f., who arrives at similar figures for a nearly comparable sample of the lower SA leaders on the Reich level. Here the share of the working class is 26.1%; that of the middle class, 68.1%. See also Reichardt, *Kampfbünde,* 317–323; Bessel, *Political Violence,* 39–43.
44. GSTA PK I. HA Rep. 77 Tit. 4043 no. 310, fol. 374 (PP Berlin to the Prussian Ministry of the Interior, 18 March 1932). According to this report, since July 1931 the SA had grown in all of Prussia from 81,300 to 138,300 men. If we compare these figures to those given by Werner, "Studien," 549–551, who draws on internal reports of the top SA echelons, the group "Middle," from which the Free State of Saxony had now been removed, grew by nearly 10,000 to 20,964 members between December 1931 and August 1932, which means it nearly doubled again.
45. LHAM C 20 Ib 2048/II, fol. 4 (RP Merseburg to OP, 18 February 1931); LHAM C 20 Ib 2052/I, fol. 111 (RP Erfurt to OP, 10 April 1931); LHAM C 20 Ib 2048/II, fols. 352–354 (RP Erfurt to OP, 15 April 1932).

46. Bessel, *Political Violence,* 48f.
47. Reichardt, *Kampfbünde,* 449–461; see also Bessel, *Political Violence,* 49–53.
48. LHAM C 20 Ib 2048/II, fols. 163–165 (RP Magdeburg to OP, 31 October 1931); fol. 159 (RP Merseburg to OP, 24 September 1931); fol. 161 (RP Erfurt to OP, 22 September 1931); fol. 355 (RP Magdeburg to OP, 19 April 1932). See Longerich, *Braune Bataillone,* 126–130.
49. Weber, *Wandlung,* vol. 1, 379, 376f., 370f.; SAPMO Ry 1/I 3/11/21 (Chart on the membership trend 1926–1930, presumably drawn up at the end of 1930, unpaginated). The figure given by Weber for 1929 would thus constitute the average figure for 1929.
50. Leidigkeit and Herrmann, *Leninistischer Kurs,* 400; see Mallmann, *Kommunisten,* 90; on the membership movement as a whole see also Winkler, *Weg,* 595. According to a report by an informant, Duddins, a KPD member of the Landtag, at a conference of party workers in Erfurt in October 1932, pegged the strength of the "KPD movement" in the district of Thuringia at "around 14,000 members," to which were added another 3,000 Young Communists. This would have been another clear increase over the number for 1931. Duddins underscored, however, that this was not sufficient for larger actions, since only 11% of the members were still employed in factories: LHAM C 20 Ib 2041/III, fol. 204 (Informant's report, 23 October 1932).
51. SAPMO Ry 1/I 3/11/32, fol. 28 (Survey of the fluctuation in the party district Halle-Merseburg until 31 March 1932, undated); fol. 40 (Survey of the fluctuation in the district Halle-Merseburg from 1 to 30 June 1932, undated); fol. 56 (Survey of the fluctuation in the district Halle-Merseburg from 1 to 31 August 1932, undated). In March, 1,164 members joined, 124 left; in June the same figures were 267 and 305, in August 120 and 172.
52. See Mallmann, *Kommunisten,* 87–93, esp. 91.
53. SAPMO Ry 1/I 3/11/32, fols. 1–21 (Surveys of the fluctuation in the subdistricts from 1 to 29 February 1932, undated). However, the information refers only to a minority of 79 of the 376 who left, and it is also not clear why the information was not gathered in some cases or not passed on. One member was expelled from the party because he did not give up his membership in the Stahlhelm.
54. SAPMO Ry 1/I 3/11/16, fols. 154–165 (Report of May 1930, author unknown).
55. See Mallmann, *Kommunisten,* 147–154, who does not adequately address this conflict within the party.
56. Weitz, *German Communism,* 150, based on sources from the Leuna company archives. Winkler, *Weg,* 959, and Werner Müller, *Lohnkampf, Massenstreik, Sowjetmacht: Ziele und Grenzen der „Revolutionären Gewerkschaftsopposition (RGO) in Deutschland 1928 bis 1933* (Cologne, 1988), 368, who draw on employer and Communist sources, respectively, report, in contrast, that the RGO share in 1931 rose again to over 38% and was thus higher than that of the free unions. See Zollitzsch, *Arbeiter,* 195–201.
57. Report about the Communist Reich Conference for the Chemical Industry on 18 April 1930: LHAM C 20 Ib 2041/I, fols. 47–51 (PP Weißenfels to RP Merseburg, 24 April 1930); also see *Kämpfendes Leuna,* 507.
58. Winkler, *Weg,* 956, 959. Because of an emergency decree, works council elections generally did not take place in 1932. In Greppin, which did have an election, the RGO lost more than a quarter of its votes and dropped just below the ADGB list. The *Klassenkampf* saw massive layoffs as one reason for the defeat, though it conceded that this was not a sufficient explanation (*KK* no. 72, 26 March 1932).
59. SAPMO Ry 1/I 3/11/28, fols. 44–49 (Report of the district leadership Halle-Merseburg of August/September 1932). The two smaller companies with large RGO cells were the Metal Factory Dicker & Werneburg in Halle (41 workers, 13 RGO members) and the Municipal Works Merseburg (146 workers, 20 RGO members). The report does not indicate how many of the workers belonged to one of the free unions.
60. See the report by the subdistrict of Weißenfels from the end of 1930 (SAPMO Ry 1/I, 3/11/21, fol. 327), which lists all of these factors to explain the defeat in the works council elections especially in the brown coal mining industry. A similar argumentation was heard at a meeting

of the District Industry Group Leadership Mining in Halle on 3 April 1931 (SAPMO Ry 1/I 3/11/52, fol. 142f.) on the reasons behind the lack of success in the elections a year later. It also singled out the weak party work in the mining sector, with too much emphasis having been placed on the chemical industry. On the general causes for the failure of the RGO see Müller, "Lohnkampf," 393–414. However, whether the RGO, as Müller believes, led to the "complete fracturing of the previously still largely unified proletarian milieu" (395) is doubtful.

61. Müller, "Lohnkampf," 345, 342.
62. See the overall assessment of the RGO in Winkler, *Weg,* 597–600.
63. Author's calculations based on *Stat. Dt. R., N. F.,* vol. 372, II, 20–27; vol. 382, II, 20–27; vol. 434, 48–50.
64. On the Communist electoral successes in 1932 see Fischer, *Communists,* 124–129, who points at length to the overlaps between the voter potential of the NSDAP and the KPD but gives inadequate consideration to their limits. The supposition of Wolfram Pyta, *Gegen Hitler und für die Republik: Die Auseinandersetzung der deutschen Sozialdemokratie mit der NSDAP in der Weimarer Republik* (Düsseldorf, 1989), 130, that a considerable portion of former Thälmann voters cast their ballots for Hitler in the second round of the Reich president elections in 1932, is not borne out by the figures for the district of Halle-Merseburg. It is true that the Communist candidate lost votes in all counties. However, either the turnout dropped even more, or Hindenburg gained votes in excess of the loss of the Communists and the decline in voter participation, which means that in purely mathematical terms, there is no evidence of a transfer of votes. See also Winkler, *Weg,* 528–530.
65. Siegfried Bahne, *Die KPD und das Ende von Weimar: Das Scheitern einer Politik 1932–1935* (Frankfurt, 1976), 21; Rosenhaft, *Beating the Fascists,* 88–91, 100–106; Finker, *Geschichte,* 203ff.
66. On the development of the Schufo, which subsequently shaped the appearance of the Reichsbanner more and more, see Rohe, *Reichsbanner,* 365–379.
67. Bahne, *KPD,* 21; Finker, *Geschichte,* 223.
68. LHAM C 20 Ib 1960/IV, fols. 54–68 (PP Erfurt to OP, 17 December 1932).
69. Report on the party congress of the KPD on 3 and 4 December, 1932: LHAM C 20 Ib 2041/III, fols. 208f. (RP Magdeburg to OP, 19 December 1932).
70. Ibid., fol. 102 (RP Erfurt to OP, 12 April 1932).
71. GSTA PK I. HA Rep. 77 Tit. 4043 no. 225, fols. 231–233 (OP to the Prussian Ministry of the Interior, 29 October 1932). The statement about the weak fighting effectiveness of the new organization is all the more credible as the reporting Oberpräsident was now the new official installed by Reich Commissioner Papen. The other reports in the file, which come largely from the Rhineland and Westphalia, also convey the impression of an organization that was on the whole rather insignificant, in spite of a few local successes. See Detlef Schmiechen-Ackermann, *Nationalsozialismus und Arbeitermilieus: Der nationalsozialistische Angriff auf die proletarischen Wohnquartiere und die Reaktion in den sozialistischen Vereinen* (Bonn, 1998), 386–396, who regards all successor organizations of the RFB as weak, while Wirsching, *Weltkrieg,* 568–570, arrives at the same conclusion for the Kampfbund in Berlin, though he believes that the influx into the Roter Massenselbstschutz was somewhat larger, also because of the simpler criteria of admission.
72. Against Rosenhaft, *Beating the Fascists,* 110, it is likely that this structural inferiority of the KPD to the NSDAP must be seen as the reason for the barely containable "individual terror," not the rivalry of the various Communist fighting organizations, some of which had different tasks, after all.
73. This is overlooked by Striefler, *Kampf,* 221–260; although he substantiates a number of examples of preparations for an uprising by the KPD, he does not in any way deal with the question of how many Communists would have been ready and able to follow the call of an uprising. As a result, he severely overestimates the threat emanating from the KPD.
74. Müller, *Lohnkampf,* 140f. Weitz does not mention this conflict.

75. LHAM C 20 Ib 1953/I, fols. 174–179 (several letters by RP Merseburg and the Mansfeld AG of May 1930); Hoffmann, *Kupferschieferbergbau,* 65f.; Jonas, *Mansfeld-Arbeiter,* 252–261; Imig, *Streik,* 82–101.
76. LHAM C 20 Ib 1953/I, fol. 181 (Radio message by PP Halle to OP, 2 June 1930); SAPMO Ry 1/I 3/11/17, fol. 37 (Final report on the strike of the Mansfeld workers by Jan Groden [pseudonym?], 1 August 1930); Imig, *Streik,* 101–123, 131–137.
77. SAPMO Ry 1/I 3/11/17, fol. 26 (Report about the situation of the strike, 17 June 1930); fol. 37; Imig, *Streik,* 79–81. The massive extent of the changes within the party is revealed by the conclusion of the reporter on 17 June: "One can say that in the entire region an entirely new party is now arising."
78. For example, the average wage for a Mansfeld pikeman was 5.70 marks, compared to 8.08 marks in the Dortmund mining district; in 1929 it was 9.17 marks vs. 10.19 marks, in 1930 8.66 marks vs. 10.27 marks. See Jonas, *Mansfeld-Arbeiter,* 132, who draws on information from management.
79. SAPMO Ry 1/I 3/11/17, fol. 4 (Schubert to Kasper, Berlin, 7 June 1930); LHAM C 20 Ib 1953/I, fol. 181 (Radio message by PP Halle to OP, 2 June 1930).
80. SAPMO Ry 1/I 3/11/17, fol. 4 (Schubert to Kasper, Berlin, 7 June 1930).
81. Ibid., fols. 5–7; fol. 32 (Report, 17 June 1930); fol. 40 (Final report by Jan Groden, 1 August 1930), here the quote; see fol. 14 (Report, 11 June 1930), according to which after ten days of striking, "not even 1/10 of the workers participating in the strike" had signed up in the RGO lists
82. LHAM C 20 Ib 1953/I, fol. 237 (RP Merseburg to OP, 9 July 1930); fol. 253 (RP Merseburg to OP, 3 September 1930); fols. 280–282 (RP Merseburg to OP, 14 March 1931).
83. To that extent, the thesis by Leßmann, *Schutzpolizei,* esp. 231–238, according to which during the entire Weimar period the Schupo focused its training on a military model guided by the events of 1921, must be verified as it applies to the gendarmes, for whom no separate study exists.
84. SAPMO Ry 1/I 3/11/17, fol. 16 (Report by Kasper and Schubert, June 1930, n.d.); fol. 31 (Report, 17 June 1930); LHAM C 20 Ib 1953/I, fol. 205 (RP Merseburg to OP, 3 June 1930); fol. 238 (RP Merseburg to OP, 9 July 1930).
85. LHAM C 20 Ib 1953/I, fol. 216 (handwritten note).
86. LHAM C 20 Ib 1953/I, fol. 217 (RP Merseburg to OP, 26 June 1930); SAPMO Ry 1/I 3/11/17, fol. 39 (Final report by Jan Groden, 1 August 1930), here the quote.
87. LHAM C 20 Ib, fol. 218 (Interpellation no. 1463 by the delegates Christange und Drescher, SPD, 26 June 1930); fols. 220f. (Prussian Ministry of the Interior to RP Merseburg, 5 July 1930); fols. 237–239 (RP Merseburg to OP, 9 July 1930), here the first quote; fols. 228–230 (RP Merseburg to OP, 15 July 1930), here the second quote. The article in the *Klassenkampf,* no. 147, 26 June 1930, was a report about the events in Hettstedt, it was thus written after the fact.
88. For example in *KK* no. 138, 16 June; no. 143, 21 June; no. 144, 23 June; the quotes from no. 147, 26 June 1930, the article criticized by the Regierungspräsident.
89. SAPMO Ry 1/I 3/11/17, fols. 39f. (Final report by Jan Groden, 1 August 1930); see *KK* no. 151, 1 July 1930.
90. LHAM C 20 Ib 1953/I, fol. 243 (RP Merseburg to OP, 19 July 1930); fol. 250 (RP Merseburg to OP, 25 July 1930); SAPMO Ry 1/I 3/11/17, fol. 41(Final report by Jan Groden, 1 August 1930); Imig, *Streik,* 192–235.
91. LHAM C 20 Ib 1953/I, fols. 259–264 (Verdict of Lay Assessors' Court Eisleben, 4 September 1930).
92. Ibid., fol. 250. That the *Klassenkampf* in the final phase of the strike repeatedly spoke of "police terror," which revealed just how far things had gone in terms of "social Fascism," is not surprising; however, the presumption of excessive severity on the part of the police during this phase is supported above all by the fact that Interior Minister Severing, against the opinion of the Regierungspräsident of Merseburg and the Oberpräsident Dr. Falck, explicitly rejected a

public commendation for the policemen involved: LHAM C 20 Ib 1953/I, fol. 275 (Prussian Ministry of the Interior to OP, 10 February 1931).

93. *KK* no. 173, 26 July 1930; see Imig, *Streik,* 236f.
94. See the list of high-ranking advisors in SAPMO Ry 1/I 3/11/17, fols. 13 and 17 (Report by Kaspar and Schubert, June 1930, n.d.).
95. To that extent Winkler, *Weg,* 155f., is in error, as he relies too heavily here on the work of Jonas and Imig.
96. SAPMO Ry 1/I 3/11/17, fol. 42 (Final report by Jan Groden, 1 August 1930).
97. *MZ* no. 104, 22 February 1932 (on a request in the Landtag concerning the securing of food stores); *SZ* no. 187, 12 August 1930; no. 147, 25 June 1932; *MZ* no. 341, 24 June; no. 355, 1 July 1932. Various aspects of social protest in Berlin are described in Swett, *Neighbors,* 194–207, 213–231.
98. For details see Peter D. Stachura, *The Weimar Republic and the Younger Proletariat: An Economic and Social Analysis* (New York, 1989), 114ff., here 118.
99. For a detailed discussion see Rose-Marie Huber-Koller, *Gewerkschaften und Arbeitslose: Erfahrungen der Massenerwerbslosigkeit und Aspekte freigewerkschaftlicher Arbeitslosenpolitik in der Endphase der Weimarer Republik,* 2 vols. (Pfaffenweiler, 1992), vol. 1, 223ff., 290ff.; Wolfgang Russ, "Zwischen Protest und Resignation: Arbeitslose und Arbeitslosenbewegung in der Zeit der Weltwirtschaftskrise," *ÖZG* 1, no. 2 (1990): 23–52; Detlev Peukert, "The Lost Generation: Youth Unemployment at the End of the Weimar Republic," in R. J. Evans and D. Geary, eds., *The German Unemployed: Experiences and Consequences of Mass Unemployment from the Weimar Republic to the Third Reich* (London, 1987), 172–193; Stachura, *Republic,* 133ff.; see also the essays in Peter D. Stachura, ed., *Unemployment and the Great Depression in Weimar Germany* (Basingstoke, 1986), including those by Stachura himself, Falter, and Conan Fischer.
100. Specifically on the violence (with a critique especially of the theory of "relative deprivation") see Russ, *Protest,* 35–40; on the violence against welfare officials see David F. Crew, *Germans on Welfare: From Weimar to Hitler* (Oxford, 1998), 157–165.
101. LHAM C 20 Ib 2041/II, fol. 29 (RP Merseburg to OP, 24 March 1930).
102. Ibid., fols. 30f. (RP Merseburg to OP, 24 March 1930); fol. 1f. (RP Merseburg to OP, 7 March 1930); *SZ* no. 56, 7 March 1930; *KK* no. 56, 7 March 1930; *VS* no. 57, 8 March 1930.
103. LHAM C 20 Ib 2041/II, fols. 171f. (RP Magdeburg to OP, 5 March 1931).
104. Ibid., fols. 247f. (RP Erfurt to OP, 14 July 1931, on the incident of 27 June 1931); fols. 253f. (RP Magdeburg to OP, 15 July 1931); fol. 229 (RP Magdeburg to OP, 24 June 1931, incident of 22 June 1931); for a similar incident in Erfurt of 15 July 1931 see LHAM C 20 Ib 2041/III, fol. 18 (RP Erfurt to OP, 18 July 1931).
105. GSTA PK I. HA Rep. 77 Tit. 4043 no. 234, fols. 246f., 250f. (RP Merseburg to the Prussian Ministry of the Interior, 7 and 8 July 1932); *KK* no. 158, 8 July 1932. According to the autopsy report, the dead demonstrator was hit by a bullet that was smaller in caliber than the police pistols. The *Klassenkampf* also did not dispute that he was shot in the back. On other clashes with a less serious outcome see *MZ* no. 363, 5 July 1932; Schmidtke, "Sozialdemokratie," 254f.; *MZ* no. 332, 19 June 1932; *SZ* no. 153, 2 July; no. 152, 1 July 1932.
106. See LHAM C 20 Ib 2041/III, fol. 1 (RP Merseburg to OP, 7 October 1930). According to this document, the KPD engaged in strong agitation again in the Mansfeld area after the long strike; shortly before, unemployed workers had stormed the local municipal offices in Helbra. "When clashes with the police are expected, women and children are systematically placed in the front," noted the official. See also *SZ* no. 152, 1 July 1932, for the assault on the town hall in Dommitzsch.
107. Rosenhaft, *Beating the Fascists,* 37–41, points out that during its demonstrations the KPD generally placed the emphasis on the action itself and less on the demands that were put forth, which made clashes with the police even more likely.
108. During a rally by unemployed workers, a member of the provincial Landtag called upon his listeners to deal with the police by following the example of the Reich Youth Day in Leipzig,

where on Easter 1930 two policemen had been shot to death and several had been seriously injured: LHAM C 20 Ib 2041/II, fol. 122 (RP Merseburg to OP, 22 August 1930). For a case of an attempt in Tangermünde to free prisoners with rocks prepared ahead of time see LHAM C 20 Ib 2041/III, fols. 44f. (RP Magdeburg to OP, 21 November 1931).

109. On this see the essay by David F. Crew, "Gewalt 'auf dem Amt.' Wohlfahrtsbehörden und ihre Klienten in der Weimarer Republik," in Lindenberger and Lüdtke, *Physische Gewalt,* 213–237.

110. See Dick Geary, "Unemployment and Working-Class Solidarity: The German Experience 1929–1933," in Evans and Geary, *German Unemployed,* 261–280; Wirsching, *Weltkrieg,* 401–410. In light of the findings presented here, the thesis by Anthony McElligott, "Mobilising the Unemployed: The KPD and the Unemployed Workers' Movement in Hamburg-Altona during the Weimar Republic," in Evans and Geary, *German Unemployed,* 228–260, here 247–254, according to whom there were two movements of the unemployed, a "party-defined and imposed movement, with its emphasis on organizational discipline," and a "more spontaneous movement which jelled into form to confront the state only at particular moments," is not convincing. See also Huber-Koller, *Gewerkschaften,* vol.1, 416–435, who points to a number of seemingly independent self-help actions but then concedes that "many of these actions" took place "within the framework of Communist unemployment policy." On the very vigorous meeting activity of the KPD among the unemployed see also Tenfelde, *Provinz,* 209–212.

Chapter 10

Escalation without Limits?

Political Violence in the Final Phase of the Weimar Republic

It was not only the protests by the unemployed, orchestrated by the KPD, that aggravated the political climate during the years of the global economic crisis. Contemporary observers followed the rise in politically motivated acts of violence with dismay. "You have to go back twenty years in your mind," noted the *Deutsche Allgemeine Zeitung* in the fall of 1931, "to properly judge where we have come in this regard: the murder of a political opponent was something that seemed hardly conceivable in Imperial Germany. Today, however, it is part of everyday occurrences." The far-right paper also knew what to do about it: take harsh measures against the "murderous Communist plague."[1] While the comparison pointed to an undeniable difference in the political climate, the identification of those allegedly responsibility was driven by political bias, and the description of the state of affairs also proves skewed upon closer examination. Is it true that political murders were "everyday occurrences" in the last years of the Weimar Republic, that, as a recent study has claimed, they were "the order of the day,"[2] which means that only drastic measures could effect a remedy?

The Growth in Political Violence 1930–1931

The increase in violent political clashes since the turn of 1929/30 was impossible to miss. In the middle of October 1931, the left-liberal *Welt am Montag* published statistics on those killed and injured during political clashes in Germany; they were based on official sources and newspapers and extended to the end of July 1931.[3] According to these data, 457 people had been killed and 1,154 injured since the beginning of 1923. However, more than half of the fatalities (236) and more than one-third of the injuries (462) occurred in 1923 alone. 66 had died

---

Notes from this chapter begin on page 271.

and 266 had been injured between 1924 and 1928, but since 1929 the number was already 155 dead and 426 injured. That violence was on the rise was unmistakable, but it certainly did not reach the level of the first postwar years or of the year of hyperinflation with its diffuse violence, and definitely not the level of 1919 and 1920, which saw the scattered eruption of civil war. If the paper saw Germany in an "era of latent civil war" since 1929, the numbers alone—as bad as they were—hardly provided sufficient justification for such a view.

The survey in the *Welt am Montag* also revealed which side had suffered the most victims. The number of "left-radical" dead stood at 323, 108 of which had lost their lives since 1929. Two-thirds of the fatalities in the "latent civil war" thus came from the ranks of the Communists. "Right-radical" organizations had suffered 31 dead during the last few years, while 8 fatalities occurred in the "Republican" camp and 10 among the police. This alone indicates that the Reichsbanner and the SPD were not among the main participants in the violent confrontations. The ratios among the injured also point in this direction. Only 31 had been injured since 1929 on the side of pro-Republican organizations, compared with 165 among the Communists, 194 among right-wing radicals, and 35 among the police. From these figures we may conclude that the vast majority of clashes involved Communists and National Socialists.[4]

This picture can be confirmed and described in greater detail with the help of statistical surveys of meetings and demonstrations in the province of Saxony where the police had intervened to quell disturbances.[5] In 1929, the total number of such deployments reached 51, a year later it jumped to 172, and it hit 229 in 1931, with those at indoor meetings being in the clear majority in 1930 and 1931. The chief adversaries of the police were clearly the NSDAP in the one camp and the KPD in the other. Members of other right-wing organizations and members of the Reichsbanner hardly played a role. In 1929 they drew attention as "troublemakers" in only 2 cases, in 1930 in only 6, in 1931 in 14 (in 11 of which the culprits were Stahlhelm members). The police took action against Communists far more frequently than they did against the National Socialists. In 1929 the ratio was 30:11, in 1930 it was 121:32, and a year later 140:63. Since the numbers also include unauthorized meetings and the NSDAP, unlike the KPD, generally did not attempt to enforce the "right to the street" in defiance of police bans, the ratio of mutual disturbances of meetings was less imbalanced than it might appear at first glance. Still, there is little doubt that even during authorized meetings, the KPD provided cause for police intervention more often than the NSDAP, even though the NSDAP was catching up, so to speak. Of course it was not always violence that prompted police action; moreover, the numbers by themselves say nothing about how the escalation unfolded in a particular case and thus about where the real responsibility lay.

Finally, of note is the information in the surveys about weapons confiscated by the police. In 1929, the police found only 2 firearms and 8 striking and stabbing weapons or other dangerous objects among participants at meetings. In 1930 it confiscated 17 firearms and 181 other weapons, but the following year, despite a further rise in disturbances, the numbers (5 and 78) were closer to the levels for 1929. Although one should not forget that members of the SA or the RFB who were ready for violence must have known how to hide some of their weapons from the police—this was one of the functions of the "SA brides," for example[6]—the numbers do not suggest that an entire arsenal of weapons would have been encountered at every unruly meeting.[7] In addition to fists, the objects one found in a tavern were adequate as weapons, at least as long as the intent was to let the enemy feel one's own strength.

Other official summary reports that include also nighttime assaults or more or less accidental clashes likewise support the assumption that violence was deliberately limited and contained. In none of the three administrative districts had confrontations between National Socialists and their enemies led to fatalities in 1930 or 1931. In 1930, incidents with serious consequences occurred only in the administrative district of Merseburg, where five people were gravely injured. In 1931 there were four such cases in the administrative district of Magdeburg and five in the administrative district of Merseburg; as for the district of Erfurt, no clashes with serious consequences were reported in either 1930 or 1931.[8] As bad as it was for those affected by violence, there was no development under way that was in danger of getting out of control.

The front lines in the confrontations continued to be very distinct. In spite of the continuous, vehement polemic in their press against the SPD, Communists rarely took action against the Social Democrats. As before, this happened mostly when the SPD made a public display on a larger scale. For example, at the national meeting of the Reichsbanner at Pentecost in 1930 in Magdeburg, members of the group were pelted several times with rocks and bottles thrown from passing trucks by members of the organization of Communist sportsmen, who were returning from a similarly large athletic meet in Erfurt; in the evening, one Reichsbanner man received a stab wound. In August of the same year, members of the Sozialistische Arbeiterjugend (Socialist Workers' Youth) who were driving back from a youth day in Eisleben were assaulted with pickets and sticks by Communist rivals during a passing maneuver.[9] Other than that, there were never more than minor scuffles when KPD members tried to interrupt Social Democratic meetings.[10] When it came to the SPD, the chief enemy of Communists who were ready and willing to engage in violence was the Social Democratic–led police.[11] Regular events put on by the SPD and the Reichsbanner did not become the target of systematic attacks by the KPD. The front lines in the battle for control of the public sphere clearly ran between a right-wing camp, now represented almost exclusively by the SA and NSDAP, and a left-wing camp, now made up—almost just as exclusively—by the KPD, though now and then it was joined by individual members of the Reichsbanner and the SPD.

The repertoire of ways in which this struggle was waged was not very extensive. Conflicts over highly visible symbols, which had played a large role at the beginning of the 1920s, for example after the murders of Erzberger and Rathenau, now receded entirely into the background. Occasionally we hear of the nighttime theft of a black-red-gold banner,[12] though only in one instance did the attack on a symbol of this kind trigger a larger clash. The incident also happened at one of the Pentecost Days in 1930. While driving to Erfurt, a group of Communist sportsmen noticed a black-white-red flag outside a tavern in a village near Naumburg, where the Wehrwolf was holding its own national meeting. The flag was taken down, the innkeeper who pleaded for restraint was beaten, and then a truck bearing twenty Wehrwolf men who had been summoned from a neighboring village appeared on the scene. Soon a fight with sticks, rocks, and knives was under way, during which the Communists, who had likewise received reinforcement, showed themselves far more aggressive and injured five of their enemies, some of them seriously. Two of the Communists were later sentenced to six months and one year in prison for committing a serious breach of the public peace.[13]

"Small" symbols like the insignia on a jacket and the uniform continued to be important, for they identified friend and foe and assured membership in a larger unit and thus one's own strength; there was good reason why the Prussian and later the Reich Ministry of the Interior hoped to contain the National Socialist violence by outlawing uniforms. "Large" symbols like flags and banners achieved their effect in the public sphere of streets and squares. It was here that the military associations had been able to exert their greatest propagandistic influence in the middle Weimar years, when the NSDAP had made successful use of this stage during the campaign against the Young Plan. This was therefore the natural place for the police to start in their measures against the violence of both the SA/NSDAP and the KPD.

The governments of Prussia and the Reich issued a series of regulations in an effort to counter the increasingly violent political confrontations—on the whole with only limited success, though with crucial consequences for the image of this violence that was created among the public. The most important instrument was the ban on marches and outdoor meetings. Following excesses in January 1930, the Prussian Minister of the Interior had issued such a ban for the entire state. It was lifted at the end of March 1930 when a new Law for the Protection of the Republic—the first had expired in July 1929—once again provided greater legal leeway for prohibitions against meetings.[14] As early as the middle of June 1930, the police president of Magdeburg outlawed all marches and outdoor meetings of the NSDAP and the KPD for two weeks after there had been clashes during several marches by both parties, but especially the NSDAP, following the lifting of the ban in Prussia. Four weeks earlier, following disruptions during NSDAP recruitment drives in the county of Wanzleben, the Regierungspräsident had also prohibited a larger meeting that would have included a large march through several villages; the Nazis honored the prohibition.[15]

On 11 June 1930, the Prussian government attempted to deprive the party's public displays of a good part of their impact by issuing a decree prohibiting the NSDAP and its auxiliary organizations from wearing uniforms. The prohibition was only partly upheld in court and was repealed in its original form a year later, but by then it had been incorporated into the catalogue of measures in the new emergency decree of 28 March 1931 "to fight political excesses." Drafted at Severing's initiative in cooperation with Reich Interior Minister Wirth (formerly the Reich chancellor in 1921/1922), the law made it easier to issue—in addition to a ban on uniforms for political organizations—prohibitions against anti-Republic meetings, to confiscate printed matter, and to suspend the publication of newspapers for a limited time. The unauthorized carrying of firearms was made a punishable offense. Lastly, an important provision was the duty to register truck convoys, which were now subject to the same criteria as political meetings.[16] Finally, as part of the emergency decree of 8 December 1931, the wearing of uniform clothing as an identifying mark of membership in a political organization was forbidden.[17]

The Prussian police authorities thus had at their disposal a broad spectrum of tools to curtail the public effectiveness of the NSDAP and KPD alike. And in places—such as Magdeburg—where the top bureaucrats were clearly on the side of the Republic, these tools were used. In addition, sweeping bans on demonstrations were issued, for example, on 31 October 1931 for all of Prussia.[18] These were easier to enforce and police than prohibitions on uniforms, which individual SA members could violate—especially in the countryside—without fear of sanctions, and toward which the NSDAP developed strategies of circumvention that sometimes made the police look ridiculous. Banning indoor meetings was also more difficult, especially if the speakers adhered to certain conditions.[19] Since in most cases the NSDAP honored the official bans on demonstrations, it had to accept a noticeable curtailment of its effectiveness in the public sphere. But it benefited from the behavior of the KPD, for the Communists ignored the bans much more frequently than their enemies and then put up staunch resistance to the police.[20] As a result, they appeared in the public as *the* troublemakers par excellence, providing all anti-Republican forces on the right with the best arguments for increasingly harsh actions against the Communists and allowing them to level severe criticism at the Social Democratic–led state government, which was denounced as weak and incompetent.

It therefore comes as no surprise that, apart from the already mentioned clashes between Communist demonstrators and the police, violent confrontations during public rallies and marches made up only a very small part of the many acts of violence in the years 1930 and 1931. Moreover, they cluster in the period before the summer of 1930, when the official measures were not yet having much effect. Thereafter, such confrontations occurred largely in places that had not previously been noted for an especially tense atmosphere. In the otherwise quiet NSDAP stronghold of Langensalza, Communist counterdemonstrators interrupted an NSDAP rally at the beginning of December 1930 and provoked a brawl that caused some minor injuries. In March 1931, Social Democrats and Communists used loud singing in an effort to keep the Thuringian Gau chief Sauckel from giving a speech in the market square of the Center Party stronghold of Heiligenstadt. When the police proceeded to push back the noisemakers, the shout "SA advance!" suddenly rang out, the police cordon was broken, and the previously peaceful counterdemonstrators were violently assaulted. A trial for breach of the public peace that was sought against eleven National Socialists had to be dismissed for lack of evidence.[21]

Reports of similar events in Halle or Magdeburg, in counties like Bitterfeld or the Mansfeld region, and in the other Börde counties are almost impossible to find. They are also absent for the intense phase of the Reichstag election campaign in September 1930 and for the weeks prior to the referendum on the dissolution of the Prussian Landtag in August of 1931. This is not to say that these regions and periods were free of violence; rather, the violence did not develop within the framework of large outdoor events because such rallies and marches hardly took place, least of all where the authorities expected things to get out of hand.[22] But this also means that the image of the SA—as a force "conquering" the proletarian sections of town with ever larger marching columns and demonstrating its growing strength until even the last insecure bourgeois had realized which side to back—was a myth constructed after the fact. The SA was able to operate relatively unimpeded in the public sphere at most in the brief span between the fall of 1929 and January 1930, that is, during the campaign over the Young Plan and municipal elections, when the old Law for the Protection of the Republic was no longer in force and the new one had not taken effect yet, and then once again the first half of 1930. Judging from the numbers, however, the marching columns it brought out could not have been very impressive.[23] Thus, the fascination with ranks of marching men—even if it could be manifested among observers in the presence of SA men who were not completely uniform in appearance and did not always keep in step—could exert its influence only to a very limited extent during the period of the great surge of the NSDAP.[24] At the end of July 1930, the Regierungspräsident of Magdeburg looked back at a virtually closed chapter when he noted that "the National Socialists for a while had the deliberate intent of marching through heavily working-class districts in a provocative form in order to draw out the Communists." Their provocation had succeeded, but "in all these instances," the officials continued, "they were always the ones being attacked."[25] This form of street fighting was now largely a thing of the past. During the campaigns for Reichstag elections in the summer of 1930 and in 1931, the NSDAP employed public meetings in taverns as the chief propaganda instruments, though they held these in large numbers.[26]

As a result, the violent clashes between National Socialists and their enemies on the left for the most part now took a form that could be described as small-scale meeting warfare (*Versammlungskleinkrieg*). Indoor meetings in closed rooms led to brawls, and on the way to and from them, participants were attacked by members of the opposing camp—Communists, in most instances. In Thale, a small town in County Quedlinburg and home to an iron smelting plant, the NSDAP held a public meeting on 31 May 1930. A large portion of the attendees were Social Democrats and Communists. The meeting had barely begun when a member of the KPD made a motion about the agenda but was rebuffed. In response the man climbed onto a table and called upon those present "to drive this Nazi rabble, which had no business in Thale, out of Thale." A commotion arose, during which the Communists sang "several verses of a song." For a brief moment quiet returned, and the speaker, an NSDAP man from Merseburg, began his speech but was soon interrupted by hecklers. The noise increased when "about 50 National Socialists in uniform suddenly marched into the hall in formation." Calls like "Out with the rabble!" and "Look at those greenhorns!" were heard. The police officers in attendance now considered the situation so dangerous that they dissolved the meeting. The Communists then attacked the uniformed Nazis without warning, using chairs and beer mugs to assault their opponents, who in turn fought back. Swinging rubber truncheons, the police eventually separated the two groups. Several of those involved suffered serious head injuries. The SA troops marched off in formation.[27]

A month later in Schwanebeck, a small, inconspicuous town near Halberstadt, the KPD members intent on breaking up the meeting did not wait long, shoving aside the ticket seller with the words "Stop blathering, out of the way" and seizing the first chairs they could find. In Artern (rural county Sangerhausen) at the end of April 1930, the Communists were not allowed to speak in the discussion, whereupon a brawl erupted. In March 1931in Bockwitz, a small city in the brown coal region of County Liebenwerda, 200–300 KPD members crowded around the entrance to a meeting hall when the ticket-taker would not allow them to enter because they refused to pay. Informed that an SA group was approaching, some of them turned around and ran toward the SA men, followed by several police officers, who were able to put a quick stop to the brawl that ensued. One SA man was stabbed, which landed the assailant in jail for seven months.[28]

The violence in these cases was not spontaneous but part of a strategy by the KPD that was intended to demonstrate to the National Socialists its superiority physically as well as at the ballot box, and to show Social Democratic followers who was taking the most resolute action against the danger from the right. In an analysis of the Reichstag elections in 1930, the Magdeburg KPD leadership boasted of having made sure in Thale that every National Socialist meeting was disrupted, and could in fact point out that the number of Communist votes had doubled. The KPD did in fact win more votes than the SPD lost, but that did not change the fact that here, too, the NSDAP was able to increase its votes from 32 to 1,116—largely through an influx of bourgeois voters—and although it was still second to the KPD (1,908 votes), the margin was much smaller than before. The KPD had even less success with its strategy of violence in County Wanzleben, where (as mentioned above), after a series of clashes in May 1930, all outdoor rallies and marches were banned. Here, according to the KPD district leadership, persons engaged in business had even assured their party in writing that they had nothing to do with the NSDAP. In September 1930, the two workers' parties combined lost over 1,000 votes (the KPD itself added 1,100) while the NSDAP gained more than 6,000, most of which came once again from the bourgeois parties. If the KPD used offensive violence against the NSDAP, it was able at best to win over some SPD voters; meanwhile, this strategy reinforced among bourgeois voters the very picture of the Communists and the defensive reflexes against them that the KPD had always given plenty of opportunity to cultivate and practice.[29]

The incidents I have described identify typical triggers of these small-scale meeting wars: not being allowed to speak and refusing to pay admission. These incidents reveal—as in Thale, for example—a ritual of escalation and attest that it was simple weapons available at the moment that were usually used in the fighting. In essence this is also true of the violence initiated by the NSDAP. At a Nazi meeting in the small town of Osterwieck (rural county Halberstadt) a few days before the elections in September 1930, the speaker provoked the listeners with harsh words, and when the atmosphere in the hall became increasingly agitated, he warned the enemies of the National Socialists: "If you don't behave, you'll get a thrashing today." When the supervising police commissioner, because of the growing turmoil that could no longer be contained, declared that the meeting was dissolved, "the assault squad of the National Socialists of 25 to 30 men, which had been kept concealed, stormed into the hall" and virtually trampled those attending the meeting. The ensuing brawl, which the police quickly brought under control, left several participants with minor injuries. A blackjack, a wire whip, and a stick were found among the SA men.[30]

The attendees at an election rally by the Staatspartei at the end of August in Halle included a sizeable number of Nazis, who had dispersed themselves throughout the hall. Their constant heckling prompted the chairman to declare the meeting was over immediately after the speaker had finished his comments. A wild brawl was the result: several NSDAP members suddenly appeared on the stage to shouts of "Heil!," whereupon their Gau chief, standing on a table, tried to turn the meeting into a National Socialist one. During the ensuing fight, chairs, beer mugs, and other projectiles were used. The Gau chief Hinkler and six of his men were put on trial for breach of the public peace. Their sentences were outrageously "harsh": three acquittals, three fines of 50 marks.[31] These incidents also reveal a particular pattern of escalation. The Nazis first caused a commotion, which they then put down with their usual means and demonstrated their physical strength. In most instances, the NSDAP, very much unlike the Communists, could expect to find lenient judges.

Of course, in many cases even the police officers on the scene could not determine which side had prompted the brawl. Before an NSDAP meeting in the small town of Kirchmöser (rural county Jerichow II) in November 1930, the police searched all 250 attendees for weapons, finding them on a dozen members of the Reichsbanner and the KPD and confiscating rubber clubs and rubber hoses hidden in trouser legs. A little later, forty NSDAP men from neighboring Brandenburg appeared outside the tavern. The police noticed that they were carrying walking sticks and were able to take them away without resistance, but they were unable to prevent the usual scenario with tables, chairs, and glasses flying through the air as soon as the Nazis had entered the hall. Thirteen members of the NSDAP and six Reichsbanner men suffered minor injuries.[32]

Hall brawls of this kind made up the better part of the small-scale meeting warfare as of the beginning of 1930. Another form was nighttime attacks on the enemy as they were returning home from a rally. By contrast, targeted attacks on prominent representatives of the other camp were rare.[33] The injuries caused by such clashes were mostly minor. A "normal" political atmosphere, in which arguments could have been exchanged with a certain calm, no longer existed, of this there could be no doubt. By the same token, it would be wrong to speak of a climate of bloody terror with numerous victims. However, political violence was now virtually omnipresent, even if it was only the limited violence of interrupted meetings. It was triggered by the frequency of rallies held by the NSDAP, which was trying to carry its propaganda into the remotest corner of the province and in the process encountered resistance not only from the KPD, but also the SPD and the Reichsbanner. It is revealing that most of the above-mentioned towns and many other locations had not previously attracted attention through political violence. The countryside in large sections of the Altmark and in other purely farming counties, where the few Social Democrats and Communists were sorely outnumbered from the beginning, was largely spared the violence. But any place that was home to large numbers of industrial workers and miners resisted the advance of the NSDAP.

Violence emanated also from the SA Homes and taverns. Eve Rosenhaft has seen in them a major source of the confrontations between Communists and National Socialists in Berlin. According to her analysis, the SA deliberately made taverns in working-class sections, whose owners were in economic difficulties, into its headquarters and base for "conquering" the neighborhood; the KPD supporters responded with a series of attacks on these taverns. The result was small-scale warfare that was all but uncontrollable from the top.[34] In the summer of 1931, Magdeburg witnessed a spectacular conflict over an SA Home. On their way home from a celebration of Constitution Day on 11 August 1931 (and a few days after the failure of the referendum to dissolve the Prussian Landtag, of which the NSDAP had been one initiating party), larger groups of Reichsbanner men marched past the Insleber Schloß, an SA tavern where SA men and Stahlhelm members were sitting in the garden. An exchange of words, during which the Reichsbanner men heard insults like "blockheads" and "drummer fools," prompted them to attack the garden and the terrace. The police soon appeared and put an end to the brawl. Because the officers believed someone from the tavern had fired at them, they fired back, but nobody was hit. This did not settle the matter, however. Excesses by SA men had occurred that evening (and previously) in the area around the SA Home in Wilhelmstadt, a bourgeois suburb, so the police now set out to search the house. At first, the officers found themselves confronted by an SA man threatening them with a pistol and saber; next, they discovered, in addition to two firearms, an entire arsenal of striking and stabbing weapons. Police President Baerensprung thereupon ordered the immediate closure of the house.[35]

The conflict now entered into its second phase. The German National *Magdeburger Tageszeitung* attacked the police president sharply in several articles that accused him of incompetence for supposedly losing control of the police and allowing "order-loving bourgeoisie"—meaning, SA men—to be treated like "prison inmates" for no good reason; finally, it held him responsible if "somebody loses control" because of the conduct of the police. The *Magdeburgische Zeitung* lent a hand by calling—though much more moderately in tone—for a thorough investigation, and printed reports from eyewitnesses who described the Reichsbanner as the aggressor, claimed that they had not heard a shot from the Insleber Schloß, and accused the police of completely disproportionate behavior. The *Saale-Zeitung* adopted the version of its German National sister paper and also gave extensive coverage to what SA Leader Stucken had to say.[36] Preliminary investigative proceedings into all three parties were eventually suspended since there was no proof of punishable conduct by an individual person. Oberpräsident Dr. Falck, who in a letter to Severing decried the "planned smear campaign" by the right-wing press against the police, even had to exert some influence on the prosecutor's office, whose order to suspend the preliminary proceedings had created the impression that the SA men had found themselves in a situation of self-defense. Although there was no denying at the end of the investigation that the Reichsbanner men had not exactly avoided the conflict and that the police had acted in haste, neither finding could gloss over the fact that acts of violence had repeatedly emanated from the SA Home in Wilhelmstadt—not least because of a flying squad (*Matrazensturm*) of "very strong persons" kept in readiness there—and that the authorities had therefore shut it down with good reason.[37]

The handling of the incident showed the predicament Republican civil servants faced if they chose to arrange for robust police action against the SA. But the outrage in the German National press was not over the fact that the authorities had sought to prevent the SA from defending itself appropriately against its opponents on the left. Rather, it was focused entirely on the police president, who, as a severely wounded recipient of the Iron Cross First Class and the holder of a doctorate in law, simply did not fit the cliché of the unqualified SPD politician interested only in his material well-being and was therefore persecuted by the press of the radical right with all the more hatred.

The sources do not reveal that the SA Home, like another one that was closed down in Magdeburg at the beginning of February 1932, was part of the kind of strategy Rosenhaft has described in Berlin. Also in contrast to the German capital, where a network of SA Homes and taverns sustained a culture of male camaraderie that bred violence,[38] there were not very many SA "storm taverns (*Sturmlokale*)" in Magdeburg or other cities of the province. Magdeburg itself had had one since the end of 1929, though later it was absorbed by the Insleber Schloß after the authorities had set its closing hours at 6 PM. Until the end of October 1931, other taverns existed in the administrative district of Magdeburg only in Gardelegen and Salzwedel, plus two in Stendal.[39] There could not have been too many more in the other parts of the province, since the numerous reports about clashes and attacks do not reveal a pattern of violence and counterviolence connected with them. This may have been in part due to the fact that even Halle and

Magdeburg hardly had self-contained proletarian or even Communist sections as large as those that existed in the Prussian capital. It is also important to note that such a fighting strategy for the SA was very costly both organizationally and physically, which is why it may have been an option only for a Gau leader as fanatical and "competent" as Goebbels, especially since every "battle" won or lost in the small-scale war in Berlin carried a very different symbolic significance than it did in the Prussian province.

As far as Communist violence was concerned, Magdeburg and Halle were not Berlin, either. For the KPD in the province of Saxony there was no need to take any steps when the Central Committee of the party, in November 1931, denounced "individual terror"—premeditated attacks on enemies with unrestrained violence that had not been approved by the party leadership. Violence—*limited* violence, which is the important point—was something the KPD here, as in Berlin, saw as a legitimate instrument to break through police cordons or give SA men a good thrashing. By contrast, attempts to kill policemen or arson attacks on SA taverns that left dead and injured in their wake were not found here. Only fanatical party activists of the likes of Erich Mielke[40] displayed a willingness to engage in violence to the point of unscrupulous murder. This kind of violence developed chiefly in Berlin, not least because of the National Socialists' strategy of conquest, which is why it should be discussed primarily within the context of the fighting that took place there. It was most likely not typical of the attitude of the Communist rank and file.[41]

The Bloody Year, 1932

The number of victims claimed by political violence reached a new high in 1932. A survey by the Prussian Ministry of the Interior recorded 155 dead for the entire year, the same number that the *Welt am Montag* had given for the period 1929 to 1931. Of these, fifty-five belonged to the NSDAP, fifty-four to the KPD, and twelve to the Reichsbanner or the SPD, while thirty-three, among them most of the victims of the "Altona Bloody Sunday"[42] in July, could not be assigned to a party. One policeman was killed that year during political clashes. The gender distribution of the victims attests once again to the male character of political violence: only seven were women, four of whom died in Altona. By far the majority of the fatalities, 105, occurred between the lifting of the SA ban in the middle of June and the Reichstag elections at the end of July, while in April and May, that is, with the ban still in place but in the tense atmosphere of the decision in the Reich presidential election and the election campaign for the Prussian Landtag, thirteen people had died. Of the 105 victims of the bloody summer, leaving aside those killed in clashes with the police, twenty-four came from the NSDAP, thirty from the KPD, and seven from the Reichsbanner, while eleven cannot be assigned to a party. The SA's heightened willingness to resort to violence, especially after it became legal again, was unmistakable.[43] This impression is confirmed by the Prussian Ministry of Justice's statistics from July 1932: in the period between September 1930 and March 1932, twice as many preliminary investigative proceedings were launched against perpetrators from the political left for crimes of political killing than against right-wing perpetrators; now, the ratio was balanced.[44]

This development was also evident in the province of Saxony, though not as clearly. Here, according to the data from the Ministry of Justice, the clashes in 1932 left nine dead. Four members of the KPD and one Reichsbanner man were killed by police bullets; the others were a Communist and three National Socialists.[45] Apart from the confrontations between the KPD and the police, there had been no fatalities in the previous two years; in that regard, the numbers show a serious surge in violence. However, relative to the many political rallies that took place in 1932, with its five large-scale elections, this was—as cynical as it may sound—not a dramatically elevated number. Moreover, compared to 1931, the police had intervened in only a few more cases of disturbances, namely 234; the previous year it had done so on 229 occasions. Nearly three-quarters of the cases were indoor meetings, an indication that outdoor rallies continued to be restricted, even if the restrictions were somewhat loosened during the election campaigns.[46] Incidentally, rallies that led to violence peaked early on, in the first four months of the year, with a total of 132 events, the largest number (thirty-four) occurring in April, while there were only fifty-eight in June and July combined. The ratio of disturbances remained virtually unchanged compared to 1931: KPD members provided the reason for intervention in 135 cases and the NSDAP did so in sixty-four cases, while the Reichsbanner, with twelve cases clustered largely in the months from January to March, had a somewhat larger share than before. Notable is the number and kind of weapons that were confiscated. The total for 1932 stood at 388, forty-three of which were firearms. This undoubtedly reflected a heightened willingness to engage in more dangerous violence that also accepted the possible death of the enemy in its calculus.[47]

The palpable escalation in violence since the beginning of the year could be attributed to a substantial degree to the SA. In the fall and winter of 1931/32, when the unemployment rate surged again and the NSDAP leadership was entertaining hopes for an imminent takeover of power following marches in Bad Harzburg and Braunschweig, its membership showed a massive increase.[48] The behavior of leaders and followers created the impression that the SA was also ready for a putsch, should the other ways of capturing political power fail. In October 1931, the Regierungspräsident of Magdeburg reported that only *Standartenführer* were now allowed to enter the office of SA *Oberführer* Stucken. During a search of SA members, the authorities had found combat-ready packs. Steel helmets were procured, and each SA man was equipped with an "iron ration" and a first aid kit.[49] At the end of December and the beginning of January, the National Socialist biweekly *Der Kampf* in Halle and local Nazi leaders in Naumburg and the surrounding area disseminated rumors about an imminent Communist putsch.[50]

During the Reich presidential elections on 13 March, the activities of the SA created a tense situation. Halle Gau Chief Jordan had declared two days previously, at a rally in County Eckartsberga, that the party would take command of the Reichswehr at midnight on 14 March. Then, on the afternoon of election day, SA men were seen in counties Eckartsberga and Weißenfels gathering at various sites in marching gear. The police that were presently alerted set up roadblocks and carried out searches that turned up a number of pistols and many striking weapons. Observers in other counties noted "a certain movement and readiness" by the SA. According to the Regierungspräsident of Merseburg, the concentration of SA men had "unsettled large sections of the population." In Stendal, too, there were concerns among the Republican citizens over several hundred National Socialists that had been "put in quarters" with party friends in the week before the elections. Searches during the following days found an entire arsenal of weapons in the house of a *Sturmbannführer,* a dentist with a practice in Düben; reports about field exercises, layout maps, and alarm orders were turned up by the police in the possession of a barber in Weißenfels, and in Magdeburg.[51] While these should not be seen as preparations for a well-planned attempt at a coup in all parts of Germany, the SA men themselves were made to believe (or were reinforced in their belief) that things were about to happen, and the opponents of the National Socialists had no reason to regard the activities of the SA as a ruse.

These concerns were also fed by the real violence experienced at the hands of the SA. Clashes and a knife attack emanating from an SA Home in Magdeburg led to its closure at the beginning of February.[52] At the end of January, the NSDAP organized a public meeting in a Börde village of County Wolmirstedt, which initially went off quietly. Shortly before the end of his speech, an SA man handed the speaker a slip of paper and then declared that an SA man had just been beaten to death in Magdeburg outside the offices of the *Volksstimme;* to honor the slain comrade, the speaker called upon everyone to rise. His party comrades did so immediately, and after some hesitation so did the other half of the attendees, once a union secretary from Magdeburg had declared that the dead should be honored regardless of their party affiliation. The subsequent discussion proceeded calmly until, shortly before the closing words, ten SA men led by a "known troublemaker" suddenly entered the hall, jostled attendees, and then, after a whistle signal and the cry "Go to it!," joined the thirty SA men posted in front of the stage in an assault on the listeners from the opposing camp. Three Reichsbanner men, one member of the SPD, and three unaffiliated attendees suffered injuries, none of them life-threatening. The report of the man killed outside the office of the *Volksstimme* was pure fiction; evidently, the thugs from Magdeburg had been summoned via telephone after the first provocation had failed to work.[53]

At a Nazi meeting in Eilsleben (County Neuhaldensleben) at the beginning of March, attended by about 50 National Socialists and about 250 of their political opponents, thirty to thirty-five SA men from the SA Home in Helmstedt suddenly appeared and lined up in front of the stage. Until then, the meeting had been relatively calm, but now the unrest mounted. When the first participants tried to leave the hall, SA men smashed tables and chairs and attacked the attendees with table and chair legs. One SA man and two members of the Reichsbanner suffered serious head injuries. The four gendarmes present at the meeting proved powerless to do anything.[54] Such cases of offensive violence against peaceful participants at rallies and meetings, during which outside and therefore difficult-to-identify SA men were especially conspicuous, increased the sense of threat that emanated from the SA.

But even more than these "hall battles," it was ambushes and more or less accidental clashes on the street, against which the police were largely unable to take effective action, that characterized political excesses until the Reichstag elections in July. In Salzwedel one night in March, about forty Reichsbanner men damaged the party office of the NSDAP by ripping off the shutters and smashing the windows with an axe. One member of the NSDAP suffered injuries to his face. The local Reichsbanner leader later explained that the reason for this targeted "violence against objects" had been the discovery of a heavy machine gun and several infantry rifles in the house of the Nazi district leader.[55] Other attacks were more serious. Following a party meeting (*Kameradschaftsabend*) in a village near Langensalza at the end of January, several NSDAP members were attacked by a group of local Communists, who had received reinforcement from Langensalza. The attackers, brandishing firearms, knives, and blackjacks, killed an SS man, while another was seriously wounded by a bullet.[56] In Bockwitz (County Liebenwerda) in the middle of February, "several hundred Communists" attacked a tavern in which a public meeting of the NSDAP was about to get under way. Windows were broken, the entrance was occupied, and six Landjäger were unable to disperse the crowd even with the help of rubber truncheons. They were threatened and pelted with rocks, and when warning shots had no effect they fired into the crowd. Five members of the KPD, only two of whom came from Bockwitz itself, were wounded, three seriously.[57]

Fortunately, these attacks on groups of political enemies and their meeting places seldom had such a bloody outcome, but in view of the weapons that were now being used, it is clear that dangerous consequences were part of the calculus more so than had been the case before. When the Reichsbanner confronted the NSDAP it did so with limited instruments of violence, unlike the KPD attackers near Langensalza. Targeted assaults of this kind were typical of Communist tactics. Moreover, "crowds" like the one that became active in Bockwitz expressed Communist resistance against the advances of the NSDAP. Not least the aggression toward the police, who in this case ended up unwittingly caught in the middle, indicates that the attackers at Nazi meetings represented the active core of the KPD. In contrast to the bloody protests of the unemployed, however, this core excluded women.[58] The goal was to prevent the NSDAP meetings, and the police were not accorded the right to intervene.

The ban on the SA and the SS, which the Reich government issued immediately after Hindenburg's reelection on 13 April, was generally accepted calmly; only Magdeburg saw minor scuffles between smaller groups of SA men and the police. For now there were no more large-scale, violent clashes; the ban was effective.[59] But when the new Papen government made an important concession to its potential partner on the extreme right by lifting the ban on 16 June, violence erupted again. Just how important a symbol the uniform was to the SA had already become apparent days before the lifting of the ban in Magdeburg. On the morning of 8 June, a week after the formation of the Papen cabinet, uniformed SA men appeared on the streets of downtown Magdeburg, their numbers growing by the hour. Word had supposedly come from group command that the prohibition had been repealed, and that members were to show themselves in the city in their uniforms. Around noon, the police intervened, arrested SA men, and had them take off their uniform. In the center of the city, however, the situation grew tenser: "Everywhere larger and smaller groups were milling about, namely National Socialists and Communists." When a larger group of the Reichsbanner marched to a meeting with Ernst Lemmer, the National Socialists seemed intent on attacking them but were pushed back by the police. Later, the police escorted the Reichsbanner men home, but they were unable to prevent smaller fights with Nazis at various locations in the city, though they all ended without any serious injuries. The cause of the entire unrest, according to a statement by the police president, "was entirely the fact that members of the SA suddenly appeared everywhere in uniform."[60]

In the following six weeks leading up to the Reichstag elections, the violent scenes from the spring were repeated, without escalating the way they did in Berlin or the Ruhr region, however. They now shifted more into the street, not least because of the time of year. In the early morning hours of 24 June, clashes broke out in Eisleben. Thanks to stringent police surveillance, meetings of the NSDAP and the KPD on the prior evening had gone off without incident, but half an hour past midnight the calm came to an end. First, several Communists pulled a motorcyclist off his bike; when a policeman appeared on the scene, both sides accused the other of having fired shots. A little while later, "a Communist was shot in the abdomen. The shooter could not be identified." Members of the NSDAP congregated in front of the gymnasium, the meeting place of the Communists. Although the police were able to prevent an assault on the building, they were not able to stop the Nazis from attacking, "without any apparent cause, a person allegedly belonging to the KPD," who suffered serious head injuries. Shortly before 2 AM, a group of Communists stopped cars in the center of the city and searched them for members of the NSDAP, though "they were no longer seen." Eventually, the police surrounded the gymnasium, searched the KPD members for weapons, and found a loaded pistol; when the police were clearing the road in front of the gymnasium, where "60–70 Communists armed with clubs and sticks had by now gathered," one officer fired a warning shot to defend himself against an attack. Although the question of responsibility could not be definitively settled, per the conclusion of the Regierungspräsident, this was probably an attempt by the National Socialists to take revenge for the breakup of one of their meetings in the neighboring village of Bornstedt two days earlier.[61]

Clashes in Staßfurt took on even more dangerous dimensions. The day before the Reich presidential elections in April had already seen rocks thrown at an SA band and scuffles between Communists and National Socialists.[62] After smaller clashes had occurred for several days between the two groups, about 100 Communists had gathered at the entrance to town on the evening of 23 June to await a well-known National Socialist, who usually returned home by car at this time with an escort from the SA Home in neighboring Leopoldshall, which was part of Nazi-governed Anhalt. When the car appeared the crowd surged forward, calls like "Thrash the cutthroats!" were heard, and eight shots were fired in rapid succession. One Communist was fatally shot in the back and another was hit in the arm, while those in the car remained unharmed. The subsequent investigation determined that the shots had not been fired from the car.[63] During the funeral five days later, more shots were fired, this time from police rifles. The memorial service itself at the cemetery passed without incident. Three thousand supporters of the KPD gathered, among them many from neighboring communities; the police were reinforced with gendarmes and were present with twenty-five men. A procession after the service had been prohibited, but when it began to form, made up especially of men from out of town, and the police tried to stop it, the situation escalated in the usual way. Following insults hurled at the officers—"Butchers," "Down with the Blood Cossacks"—one participant from the crowd was arrested. In response the others moved toward the police, and one man planted himself in front of the officers, tore open his shirt, and called out "Stop! Shoot here!" One of the Landjäger was surrounded, a scuffle ensued, and warning shots were fired, followed by shots at the marchers. When the crowd finally retreated, three lay dead and four others were seriously injured. All were men, only two of whom came from Staßfurt.[64] Until the end of the July, the city continued to see smaller clashes between National Socialists on the one side, and Communists—but also Social Democrats—on the other.[65]

The terrible bloodbath of Staßfurt was not the only—though it was the worst—clash between the police and a crowd made up largely of supporters of the KPD.[66] The situation in Staßfurt, in Eisleben, and elsewhere created the impression of a state of affairs the police were barely able to control any longer. Was this the civil war–like unrest that, as the Papen government suggested after the horrendous "Bloody Sunday of Altona," made intervention by the Reich unavoidable? Certainly not. To be sure, the police were exhausted and extremely tense from being deployed at countless election events, and they made mistakes, but they managed to defuse dangerous situations in the nick of time. The battles over the public space were being waged more ruthlessly than in the years before, but they remained battles over territory; the goal was not—not yet—the physical destruction of the enemy. He was to be taught a lesson, and his room to move about was to be curtailed. The use of firearms was often symbolic, intended to underscore one's own strength and impress the enemy, though admittedly their use could also have more dangerous consequences.

Still, none of this could truly be described as a "civil war," at least not by comparison with the fighting in 1919 and 1920. An escalation in that direction could not be ruled out, but for now certain boundaries in the battle over public space were still being respected, as Richard Bessel has pointed out.[67] If the picture of a civil war was created in the public mind, this was largely due to the endemic character of the violence, which seemed to be erupting everywhere and thus appeared impossible to control any longer.[68] The real danger for the state, however, lay in the potential for a putsch on the part of the constantly growing and increasingly well-equipped SA, against whom the proper measure was not police intervention on a small scale, but an outright ban like the one that had just recently been lifted. The small group of activists in the KPD's military apparatus was not even close to being able to attempt a coup. Their forces were just sufficient to mobilize an adequate number of supporters short-term to disrupt meetings by the other side or attack small groups of National Socialists. The KPD's resources were simply too weak to build up a strong Combat League or a secret organization capable of a putsch from among the growing ranks of unemployed workers.

After the Reichstag elections on 31 July, the violence in the province of Saxony receded noticeably. A wave of terror by the SA like the one that swept through East Prussia and Swabia at the beginning of August did not occur here. As a result, there was no need for the draconian emergency decree against political excesses—first used against the murderers of Potempa[69]—to quell the violence. No matter how great the frustration of members of the NSDAP and the SA may have been over the failure to assume power after the party's new electoral success, it was not vented in attacks on political enemies. Evidently, the violence during the weeks of the election campaign was closely connected with the mobilization of party supporters on all sides and the large number of meetings. Although violence could break out anywhere, it did so only within the framework of specific situational constellations. Political violence had not become an everyday phenomenon—though it may have seemed that way in the hot summer of 1932.

Although violence flared up again in the run-up to the second Reichstag elections, it was nowhere close to what it had been during the summer. The worst incident occurred once again in Staßfurt, an exchange of gunfire between National Socialists and Communists on election day that left several participants with serious and one with minor injuries.[70] However, when the emergency terror decree from the beginning of August was lifted again at the end of the year, the worst seemed to be over; political violence seemed to have become once again a manageable phenomenon, especially since the frustration of the SA men over the failed takeover of power expressed itself not in uncontrolled violence directed outward, but in conflicts with the party leadership and an exodus from the party.[71]

Young and Unemployed? The Social Profile of the Actors

Variously detailed data could be found for 106 participants in violent confrontations between 1930 and 1932.[72] One-third belonged to the SA, the NSDAP, or some other organization of the radical right, half appeared before the courts as defendants, and the others gave evidence as witnesses (directly involved in a brawl). Nearly two-thirds were Communists, but only three were members of the Reichsbanner; all Communists and Reichsbanner men had to answer as defendants.[73] This underscores the impression that most of the confrontations were fought out by supporters of the NSDAP and the KPD while members of the Reichsbanner had only a secondary role, and it supports the assumption that charges were brought chiefly against "leftist" perpetrators of violence. Incidentally, we know of only four actors—two in each camp—who switched sides.[74]

Only 3 of the 106 actors were women,[75] the rest men. A solid third had been born prior to 1900, two-thirds after, which means that the vast majority had not experienced the war as soldiers. Only a little over one-tenth had been born in 1910 or later, the youngest in 1914.[76] At least twenty-two were married.[77] Most of the participants in clashes with political opponents were thus neither young people nor former soldiers possibly brutalized by their participation in the war. Whether the actors were unemployed or not can be conclusively determined only for forty-one, of whom twenty-six had no work, fourteen had a job, and one received a pension. This finding does not allow for a clear interpretation. Given the age structure of those involved, a high ratio of unemployed would not be surprising; on the other hand, it would appear that deriving a willingness to engage in violence merely from the "relative deprivation" of joblessness is not tenable. More revealing are the data about prior criminal records, which were available for forty-six of the participants: fifteen had been previously found guilty of bodily injury and eighteen merely of offenses against property; thirteen had no previous record. This is yet more evidence against the notion that political violence was perpetrated chiefly by men with a particular penchant for violence. With some caution, one can conclude from the data that the typical violent offender of the last years of the Weimar Republic was male, relatively young but not a youth, and that his willingness to engage in violence resulted above all from his radical political convictions, against which other factors receded into the background.[78]

The occupational profiles of the actors from the two camps show characteristic differences. Of the sixty KPD and Reichsbanner members for whom data exist, thirty-three—that is, more than half—were unskilled or semi-skilled workers, twenty-four were qualified as skilled workers or craftsmen (three in a service profession), and only three could be clearly classified as not being workers. Among their twenty-nine identifiable opponents were only one unskilled laborer and eighteen trained craftsmen (none in service professions), while the other ten were clearly middle-class. If one reckons that a third of the craftsmen belonged to the middle class, the latter is even the majority. As small as this sample is, it does support the existing findings on the social profile of the SA. During violent confrontations, as well, it was not largely workers with the same qualifications who confronted each other, but quite different social groups, with the extreme right showing once again a predominantly middle-class/bourgeois profile.[79]

The SA Unleashed: Terror after 30 January 1933

Power was transferred to the new government headed by Hitler on 30 January 1933, and once Göring assumed control over the Prussian police and another election campaign got under way, the pattern of political violence changed within a few days. This had nothing to do with the Communists, who made no attempt to rise up against the new government or step up their efforts in the battle for terrain against the other side. On the contrary: it became clear very quickly that no violent resistance would be coming from either the Communists or the Reichsbanner.

What changed was the behavior of the SA. On 4 February, a march was staged in Staßfurt by the Stahlhelm and various other veterans' associations—alongside the NSDAP and the SA/SS—to celebrate the new government. At the edge of the march, a uniformed Worker Samaritan, who was on his way to his assignment at a movie theater, was beaten by the local SA leader and suffered serious head injuries. After witnesses had confirmed the identity of the assailant, Mayor Kasten had him arrested, but then ordered his release following an intervention by two leading members of the Staßfurt NSDAP. SA men who had been alerted dispersed again. Shortly after ten that night, Kasten left the town hall and headed for home. Upon reaching his house he was cut down by two bullets and so seriously injured that he died the following day. He was still able to recognize the killer—who called out to him with the words "Just wait, you scoundrel, now the score will be settled!"—from his school uniform: a *Gymnasium* student who, as it was quickly ascertained, belonged to the SA.[80]

Previously, on the very day of Hitler's appointment as Reich chancellor, a worker walking with his wife in a village near Delitzsch had been beaten up and fatally injured after he passed some SA men stationed in front of a tavern.[81] In Eisleben on 12 February, during an SA march that led past the headquarters of the local KPD, a larger number of SA and SS men stormed—unprovoked—into the adjoining sports hall, where the functionaries of the subdistrict were meeting at the time. The attackers assaulted their opponents with the gymnastics equipment and fired wildly; three Communists and one assailant were killed, and the KPD functionary Bernhard Koenen lost an eye.[82] On 19 February near Tangermünde, a troop of SA men shot at members of the Reichsbanner on their way home from a meeting; a young Reichsbanner man suffered life-threatening injuries when a bullet hit him in the eye.[83]

All this happened even before Göring made the SA into an auxiliary police on 22 February, before the Reichstag fire and the subsequent imposition of a state of emergency and passage of the Enabling Act, which once and for all removed all the barriers enacted by the constitutional state that had still constrained the use of violence against the enemies of the new regime. The cases I have described were not about personal vendettas. If anyone had a score to settle in Staßfurt, it should have been the Communists following the bloodbath in June 1932, since the Social Democrat Kasten, as mayor, was responsible for the local police. The action of the young man who killed him, like the unrestrained shooting by his SA comrades, was aimed at the Weimar "system" that was now irrevocably doomed, and whose representatives and symbols were to be dealt the death blow.

In the context of this process, only at first glance does the indiscriminate shooting by the SA seem like a break with the violence of the struggle over terrain during the previous year. It merely continued the "arming" of 1932 and the violence that had already been on the rise then, though under completely altered circumstances. Now that the threat of a ban no longer hung over the SA, the police—willingly or under coercion—were on the SA's side. The terror that now unfolded was not ordered "from the top"; instead, it broke out once there were no more restraints in its way and was curtailed by the leadership of the NSDAP and the SA only when it began to endanger the public standing of the new regime. It was also not merely an unbridled eruption of violence, but a campaign that intensified step by step from the deadly shots at individual enemies of the regime to organized manhunts and brutalization in improvised torture chambers and "spontaneous" concentration camps in the months after passage of the Enabling Act. The special and continually rising brutality of this violence was not simply a consequence of the violence-promoting subculture in the male fraternity of the SA, nor was it merely a safety valve for the frustrations of unemployed young men who had been systematically trained to be violent.[84] It was above all also a result of the discrepancy between the pretensions and the reality of the SA's image of itself. Over the last few years, the SA had *not*—as it later liked to pretend—marched into proletarian areas as a conqueror that harvested the fruit of its actions on 30 January 1933. Instead, its provocations and attacks notwithstanding, in the final analysis it had waged its struggle from a defensive position, which it wanted to give up but could not because of official restrictions and for reasons of political opportunism. Its conduct had not been particularly heroic, and now it tried to make up for it with that much more brutality.

The gradual intensification of this "compensatory" violence cannot be traced here in detail. Its next stage became apparent in Magdeburg on 8 March when, with Nazi flags flying from public buildings, SA men forced their way into the house of the Reichsbanner and shot up the place, while others demolished the office of the KPD. Three days later the Reichsbanner house was occupied again—its occupants had left in time after a warning from police headquarters—and the SA posted guards and mounted a machine gun on the balcony. A short time later, an SA unit marched to city hall, forced its way into the office of Lord Mayor Ernst Reuter,[85] and compelled him to accompany them, whereupon a Schupo officer intervened and took Reuter into protective custody for the time being, thus keeping him from further harm. His deputy, Goldschmidt, was less fortunate: the SA led him through the city to the Reichsbanner house, where they forced him to salute the party flag with the Hitler greeting. It was here that the police were able to take Goldschmidt to safety.

That 8 March, the violence was turned on those who would be its chief victims in the future. Around eleven at night, several people wearing NSDAP party insignia stormed into the Hotel Amsterdam—SA men were standing guard outside—and fell upon the roughly twenty-five guests with the cry "Jewish gang, you should be killed!"; among the guests were several foreigners and two Fascists from Italy. Eight were injured, one Polish man seriously. The next day, SA men occupied shops "whose owners were believed to be of the Jewish faith." Customers were forced to leave, some of them along with several employees were maltreated, and the shops were closed.[86]

This was indeed a new stage of violence, for in spite of verbal anti-Semitic excesses, the province had until then been largely spared violent attacks against Jews and Jewish property.[87] Now that the SA saw itself engaged in an unrestrained offensive and no longer had to concentrate its forces on the struggle against the potent enemy on the left, it directed its potential for violence increasingly against the Jews, whom Nazi ideology had declared the quintessential enemy.

Notes

1. *Deutsche Allgemeine Zeitung,* no. 525, 13 November 1931.
2. Striefler, *Kampf,* 9.
3. *Welt am Montag,* no. 41, 12 October 1931 (in GSTA PK I. HA Rep. 77 Tit. 4043 no. 120, fol. 301).
4. This is confirmed by Reichardt, *Kampfbünde,* 55–75, in particular 65–69.
5. LHAM C 20 Ib 1859/V, fol. 47 (Survey, December 1929, n.d.); fol. 241 (Survey, 27 December 1930); fol. 286 (Survey, December 1931, n.d.). On the increase in political violence since 1929 in the Free State of Saxony see Lapp, *Revolution,* 206f.
6. Marie-Luise Ehls, *Protest und Propaganda: Demonstrationen in Berlin zur Zeit der Weimarer Republik* (Berlin, 1997), 383.
7. According to statements by the Regierungspräsident of Merseburg, however, the police had adjusted to the tactic of both the KPD and the NSDAP to pass weapons to women at meetings prior to being searched as early as the spring of 1930. Women were now also searched, whereupon such efforts ceased, and no special resistance was offered to the police. LAMe C 48 Ie 1165, fol. 142 (RP to all Landräte, 11 April 1930). As for Berlin, Wirsching, *Weltkrieg,* 601f., indicates a more massive arming on both sides. Reichardt, *Kampfbünde,* 82–84, emphasizes the low number of weapons found among Communists and National Socialists as opposed to those found among the Squadristi in Italy.
8. LHAM C 20 Ib 2054, fols. 6f. (RP Merseburg to OP, July 1930, n.d.); fols. 22f. (RP Magdeburg to OP, April 1931, n.d.); fols. 25f. (RP Merseburg to OP, April 1931, n.d.); fols. 36f. (RP Magdeburg to OP, January 1932, n.d.).
9. LHAM C 20 Ib 1859/V, fols. 132f. (PP Magdeburg to RP Magdeburg, 10 June 1930); LHAM C 20 Ib 2041/II, fol. 80 (RP Merseburg to OP, 15 August 1930).

10. LHAM C 20 Ib 2041/II, fols. 97f. (two incidents at the end of August/beginning of September 1930 in County Weißenfels, where the SPD retained its status as the majority party at the elections a few weeks later); fol. 162f. (two incidents in County Merseburg). After a recruitment evening put on by the Reichsbanner in County Neuhaldensleben in March 1931, a brawl broke out that left several badly hurt; however, the two injured Communists were known as "ruffians": ibid., fols. 177f. (RP Magdeburg to OP, 3 April 1931).
11. The exception that proves the rule was an incident during the Reich Day of the Jobless on 25 February 1931 in Staßfurt. Members of the KPD attacked a procession of the Reichsbanner that was returning from a funeral. In the ensuing brawl, four people were badly hurt on both sides, several suffered minor injuries: LHAM C 20 Ib 2041/II, fol. 172 (RP Magdeburg to OP, 5 March 1931).
12. For example, on Constitution Day 1930 in the Saalkreis, where members of the Germania Soccer Club were identified as the culprits, or during the night preceding Constitution Day 1931 at the house of a merchant in Nordhausen, the culprits being several members of the NSDAP: LHAM C 20 Ib 1913/VI, fols. 95f. (RP Merseburg to OP, 21 August 1930); LHAM C 20 Ib 2052/I, fol. 227 (RP Erfurt to OP, 23 September 1931).
13. LHAM C 20 Ib 1991/V, fol. 279 (RP Merseburg to OP, 21 July 1930).
14. For details see Pyta, *Hitler,* 296–303. The new law was weaker than the old one, but still better than no law at all. It allowed for prohibiting meetings not only on the grounds that they had the potential for being violent (as already provided for in Article 123 of the Reich Constitution and §10 II 17 of the Prussian General Law (Preussisches Landrecht), but also on the grounds of seditious agitation against the Republic. However, the threshold for this cause was set much higher than Interior Minister Severing, for example, had wanted.
15. LHAM C 20 Ib 1859/V, fols. 137f. (PP Magdeburg to OP, 14 June 1930); LHAM C 20 Ib 2051/I (not pag., RP Magdeburg to OP, 22 May 1930).
16. Pyta, *Hitler,* 329–335. On the analogous decree in Bavaria see Geoffrey Pridham, *Hitler's Rise to Power: The Nazi Movement in Bavaria, 1923–1933* (New York, 1973), 126f., 260. See also the criticism of the bans by the Brüning government in 1931 as biased against the left by Dirk Blasius, *Weimars Ende: Bürgerkrieg und Politik 1930–1933* (Göttingen, 2005), 28–32.
17. Pyta, *Hitler,* 340.
18. Ibid., 340–353; Ehls, *Protest,* 181.
19. See Pyta, *Hitler,* 348–351; on the prohibition against uniforms see Leßmann, *Schutzpolizei,* 336–341. See also the discussion in Reichardt, *Kampfbünde,* 231f.
20. Examples of this in Berlin in Ehls, *Protest,* 164ff., 178ff.
21. LHAM C 20 Ib 2052/I, fol. 77 (RP Erfurt to OP, 16 December 1930); fol. 178 (RP Erfurt to OP, 7 April 1931). As it later turned out, perjury by a secondary school teacher (*Studienrat*) was crucial to the outcome of the proceedings. He had accused the police of passivity and thus accorded the SA a kind of right of self-defense.
22. Examples of bans on marches in LHAM C 20 Ib 2051/II, fol. 125 (a planned Nazi march in Wetting, parallel to a union celebration, 27/28 June 1931); fol. 131 (marches by the NSDAP and KPD in Artern, 24 July 1931); LHAM C 20 Ib 2041/II, fol. 279 (meeting of the Communist Youth in Zeitz and Wittenberg, 6 September 1931). In rural county Delitzsch (which also included Eilenburg), the local NSDAP group applied for the first time at the end of February 1931 for permission to hold a march, which was granted on the condition that the marchers not wear uniform clothing; 500 persons participated, there were no incidents. In the middle of September, permission was granted for a march of the SA-Sturmbann with 350 participants; once again, the event was free of incidents. After that, the NSDAP reappears only during the campaign for the presidential election in March/April 1932 with two outdoor rallies: LAMe C 50 Delitzsch A no. 377, fol. 96 (NSDAP Eilenburg to police administration of Eilenburg, 27 February 1931); fol. 144 (Police report, 16 March 1931); fol. 276 (Schupo Halle to LR, 14 September 1931); fol. 469 (Police administration of Eilenburg to LR, 10 March 1931); fol. 539 (Note by LR, 7 April 1932). After the emergency decree of March 1931, the NSDAP

applied only once for permission to hold a march in the rural county of Eckartsberga, which was granted: LAMe C 50 Eckartsberga no. 412, fol. 11 (LR to NSDAP Eckartsberga, 7 August 1931). The files that were compiled in the wake of the obligatory permissions for truck convoys that were in force since April 1931 also do not reveal that the NSDAP was trying to hold numerous large meetings. By the end of 1931, the Oberpräsident, who was the authority in charge of permissions for any event that crossed the borders of the administrative district, had received only one application from the party; it concerned the participation in a march in Braunschweig in the middle of October. None of the requested trips (among others from Halle, Torgau, Erfurt, Bitterfeld, Delitzsch, Nordhausen) was granted: LHAM C 20 Ib 1964/II, fols. 75, 76, 80, 97, 102, 104, 106, 118, 126, 139, 150.

23. Even for Berlin itself, the image of SA columns marching boldly and aggressively through working-class sections in formation—an image carefully cultivated by the SA's own literature of remembrance—has come to be called into question. Most marches here occurred in the summer and fall of 1929; thereafter, bans by the police president severely curtailed their activities and brought them largely to a halt in 1931 and 1932; see Ehls, *Protest,* 144ff., 160ff., 176ff., 189ff. Reichardt, *Kampfbünde,* 514f., mentions propaganda marches in enemy territory as the symbolic and emotional high point of SA activities in Communist neighborhoods but does not provide examples.
24. The limits of this fascination have been emphasized by Gerhard Paul, *Aufstand der Bilder: Die NS-Propaganda vor 1933* (Bonn, 1990), 133–142; confirmed by Ehls, *Protest,* 386. See also Schmiechen-Ackermann, *Nationalsozialismus,* esp. 429ff., who emphasizes that only after 30 January 1933 did the SA succeed in "conquering" the Social Democratic and Communist sections, if they still possessed an intact network of associations encompassing members from both parties. By contrast, the old picture is painted by Longerich, *Braune Bataillone,* 116–120, in his otherwise excellent study, on the basis of recollections by the SA. Entirely taken in by this source is Thomas Balistier, *Gewalt und Ordnung: Kalkül und Faszination der SA* (Münster, 1989).
25. LHAM C 20 Ib 2054, fol. 9 (RP Magdeburg to OP, 24 July 1930).
26. In the rural county of Delitzsch, thirty such meetings by the NSDAP took place before the September elections, far more than were held by any of the other parties, among which only the KPD organized a large number. Beyond that, the NSDAP made a public appearance only on 9 November, when 41 members in Eilenburg marched to the memorial to the war dead (without music, flags, or uniforms) and laid three wreaths there. See numerous police reports in LAMe C 50 Delitzsch no. 375, fols. 720-760. The only larger march that took place in the county that year was a torch parade by the Wehrwolf with 250 participants on 8 October, on the occasion of a Gau Sports Day in Eilenburg: LAMe C 50 Delitzsch no. 375, fol. 690 (Police administration of Eilenburg to LR, 8 October 1930). On the meeting activity of the NSDAP in the Free State of Saxony, which overshadowed that of all other parties, see Lapp, *Revolution,* 204–206.
27. LHAM C 20 Ib 2049/I, fol. 39f. (RP Magdeburg to OP, 5 June 1930). A good description of a similar case in Bavaria in late 1929 is provided by Pridham, *Hitler's Rise,* 128–130.
28. LHAM C 20 Ib 2049/I, fols. 23f. (Police administration of Schwanebeck to LR Oschersleben, 2 July 1930); LHAM C 20 Ib 2051/I (not pag., RP Merseburg to OP, 14 May 1930; RP Merseburg to OP, 17 March 1931). For other typical cases see LHAM C 20 Ib 2049/I, fols. 255f. (KPD assault units at the Nazi Gau Party Day in Dessau on 30/31 August 1931); LHAM C 20 Ib 2051/I (RP Merseburg to OP, 18 December 1930, hall brawl at a Nazi meeting in Altenburg near Naumburg on 15 December 1930; RP Merseburg to OP, 20 December 1930, meeting broken up in Diemitz, Saalkreis, on 19 November 1930); LHAM C 20 Ib 2052/I, fol. 8 (hall brawl at a Nazi meeting in Dingelstädt in the Eichsfeld, begun by Reichsbanner men).
29. SAPMO Ry 1/I 3/12/33, fol. 89 (Report of the district leadership Magdeburg-Anhalt, no date); the results of the elections based on *Stat. Dt. R., N. F.,* vol. 372, II, 21; vol. 382, II, 21; see Chapter 9 of this volume, Table 9.2. At the beginning of June 1930, the KPD in Lützen

reported to the district leadership in Halle about the beginnings of the Nazi organization in their town. A local group had just been established with the help of National Socialists from the Geisel Valley and planned to hold a public meeting in the near future. "We will, in any case, break up the meeting and ... organize an assault troop," the writer in Lützen reported. In addition, members were daily on the lookout "to catch these heroes in the act of putting up posters ... in order to give them a thrashing": SAPMO Ry 1/I 3/11/21, fol. 315 (Local group Lützen to organizational division of the district Halle-Merseburg, 6 June 1930). On the connection between political violence and the election results of 1930 and 1932 I see Richard Dee Wernette, "Political Violence and German Elections: 1930 and July 1932," PhD diss., University of Michigan (Ann Arbor), 1974, who concludes from a quantitative analysis of the overly narrow and one-sided *Kölnische Zeitung* that the violence on the whole brought the NSDAP additional votes.

30. LHAM C 20 Ib 2049/I, fol. 53 (RP Magdeburg to OP, 9 September 1930).
31. LHAM C 20 Ib 2051/I (RP Merseburg to OP, 26 August 1930; PP Halle to OP, 9 September 1930). The presiding judge was interested only in the formal question of who had thrown the first chair, but the clerk keeping the record sympathized with the defendants, which was reflected in inadequacies in his notes. Other, similar cases, all in LHAM C 20 Ib 2051/I: RP Merseburg to OP, 4 April 1930 (disruption of a meeting by the Friedensgesellschaft [Peace Association] in Halle on 1 April 1930); RP Merseburg to OP, 19 April 1930 (disruption of an SPD meeting in Freyburg a. Unstrut under the leadership of Hinkler on 10 April 1930); RP Merseburg to OP, 24 January 1931 (SA troop against hecklers during a Nazi meeting in Herzberg a. Elbe, rural county Schweinitz, on 15 January 1931); RP Merseburg to OP, 17 March 1931 (attack on attendees of a meeting on 20 January 1931 in Schraplau, Mansfelder Seekreis).
32. LHAM C 20 Ib 2049/I, fol. 3 (RP Magdeburg to OP, 14 November 1930). See other cases in ibid., fol. 28 (smaller brawl between National Socialists and Communists during a Nazi meeting in Magdeburg on 13 August 1930); fol. 30 (the same during a search for weapons outside a Nazi meeting on 18 August 1930 in Tangermünde); fols. 158–160 (clash at a Nazi meeting in Wernigerode between National Socialists and counterdemonstrators from the Reichsbanner and the Communists); LHAM C 20 Ib 2051/I, RP Merseburg to OP, 29 April 1930 (brawl during a Nazi meeting in Könnern, Saalkreis, on 9 April and in Delitzsch on 12 April 1930); RP Merseburg to OP, 19 June 1930 (the same at a Nazi meeting in Eisleben on 23 May 1930); RP Merseburg to OP, 12 January 1931 (the same at a Nazi meeting in Merseburg on 17 December 1930); LHAM C 20 Ib 2051/II, fols. 3f. (hall brawl at a Nazi meeting in Pratau, rural county Wittenberg, on 23 March 1931); fols. 47f. (the same at a Nazi meeting in Mühlberg a. Elbe, rural county Torgau, on 29 March 1931).
33. Rocks thrown at departing National Socialists, beatings, and occasionally also stab wounds were the most common forms of these clashes. See, for example, LHAM C 20 Ib 2051/I, RP Merseburg to OP, 5 July 1930 (incident in County Torgau on 1 July 1930, five Communists were later given jail terms of several months for breach of the public peace); RP Merseburg to OP, 6 February 1931 (similar incident in Teuchern on 23 December 1930; RP Merseburg to OP, 11 September 1930 (attack by 15 NSDAP men on 3 members of the SPD following a celebration of Constitution Day in Halle); LHAM C 20 Ib 2049/I, fol. 31 (rocks thrown at members of the NSDAP in Salzwedel on 22 July 1930). One of the rare, targeted attacks on a specific person occurred in Halle on 22 July 1930, when two National Socialists assaulted the Gau secretary of the Reichsbanner; the victim was thrown to the ground and beaten with a steel rod but suffered only minor injuries: LHAM C 20 Ib 2051/I (RP Merseburg to OP, 31 July 1930).
34. Rosenhaft, *Beating the Fascists,* 111ff.; idem, "Links," 238–275, esp. 243ff. The same approach is taken by Anthony McElligott, *Contested City: Municipal Politics and the Rise of Nazism in Altona, 1917–1937* (Ann Arbor, MI, 1998), 178–191; for a more detailed discussion see his "'...und so kam es zu einer schweren Schlägerei.' Straßenschlachten in Altona und Hamburg," in M. Bruhns et al., eds., *'Hier war doch alles nicht so schlimm.' Wie die Nazis in Hamburg den*

Alltag eroberten (Hamburg, 1984), 58–85. The importance of the taverns for the National Socialist strategy of conquest is also highlighted by Wirsching, *Weltkrieg,* 590–594. His argument that both sides pursued a "totalitarian claim to a virtual monopoly of news and opinion" (ibid., 591) is problematic, since such claims obviously did not extend to the bourgeois sections of Berlin. Reichardt, *Kampfbünde,* 465–467, also stresses the importance of SA and Communist taverns as places where violence was planned and cultivated.

35. LHAM C 20 Ib 2050, fols. 44f. (RP Magdeburg to OP, 13 August 1931). The weapons arsenal consisted of 21 daggers, 3 clubs of steel, rubber, and bone, 12 striking tools of iron and wood, 1 hatchet, 1 hand grenade, 1 spade, and 2 steel helmets.
36. *Magdeburger Tageszeitung,* no. 187, 13 August; no. 188, 14 August; no. 189, 15 August 1931; *MZ* no. 438, 13 August; no. 440, 14 August; no. 444, 16 August; no. 448, 18 August; no. 450, 19 August 1931; *SZ* no. 189, 15 August 1931.
37. LHAM C 20 Ib 2050, fols. 60f. (OP to the Prussian Ministry of the Interior, 27 August 1931); fols. 111–121 (Note by the chief prosecutor about the witness statements, 6 January 1932); fols. 124–127 (Note about a meeting between the Oberpräsident and the police president and members of the state prosecutor's office, 5 December 1931). The matter eventually drew the attention even of the Berlin press: the *Vossische Zeitung* (no. 207, 30 August 1931) dealt with the "*Kasernenzauber* of the SA" and reported about SA Homes in Berlin; right-wing papers like the *Deutsche Zeitung* (no. 241, 14 October 1931) were critical of the police.
38. See the detailed and convincing description of this culture of violence in Reichardt, *Kampfbünde,* 416–432, 454–474.
39. LHAM C 20 Ib 2048/II, fols. 163–165 (RP Magdeburg to OP, 31 October 1931).
40. Mielke murdered a Berlin police captain in August 1931 in a carefully planned action and fled to Russia immediately after the crime. In 1957 he became East German Minister for State Security and remained in this position as head of the Stasi until the fall of 1989.
41. See Winkler, *Weg,* 442f.; for a detailed discussion of the resolution see Rosenhaft, *Beating the Fascists,* 57–87, who does not distinguish adequately here between stages of violence and has her eye only on the Berlin party base. In that sense it is also questionable to what extent the radicalization of the Berlin KPD base noted by Wirsching, *Weltkrieg,* 580–583, can be generalized.
42. On this incident, which offered the Papen government the pretext for deposing the Prussian government, see McElligott, *Contested City,* 191–194; Léon Schirmann, *Altonaer Blutsonntag 17. Juli 1932: Dichtungen und Wahrheit* (Hamburg, 1994). On the acts of violence before and after Altona see also Wolfgang Kopitzsch, "Politische Gewalttaten in Schleswig-Holstein in der Endphase der Weimarer Republik," in E. Hoffmann and P. Wulf, eds., *"Wir bauen das Reich." Aufstieg und erste Herrschaftsjahre des Nationalsozialismus in Schleswig-Holstein* (Neumünster, 1983), 19–39.
43. GSTA PK I. HA Rep. 77 Tit. 4043 no. 122, fols. 325–328 (Survey of victims of political violence in 1932, undated). See also Reichardt, *Kampfbünde,* 56, 59f., who draws upon a similar but less detailed list. The survey was presumably prepared only after the beginning of 1933. On the whole it probably conveys an accurate picture, though it contains obvious lacunae. It does not include a number of casualties from the draft version of the survey that resulted from the use of weapons by the police and from other causes, such as being killed by another member of one's own group. If all these cases are included, the total stands at 189 for the entire year. The Reichsbanner pointed out (*VS* no. 233, 3 October 1932) that between January and September, 17 Reichsbanner men had been killed in clashes with National Socialists, not 10, as given in the ministry's published figures, which later found their way into the statistic. Incidentally, most fatalities occurred in Berlin and the Ruhr region.
44. GSTA PK I. HA Rep. 84a no. 11770, fol. 1 (Survey of preliminary proceedings, 1932, n.d.).
45. However, a Communist killed in Staßfurt on 24 June is missing; the case is examined in more detail below. There is no additional evidence of further errors—deliberate or not—in the survey, as far as the province of Saxony is concerned.

46. See Ehls, *Protest,* 218–221.
47. LHAM C 20 Ib 1859/VI, fols. 1f. (Survey, 3 January 1933).
48. Werner, "SA," 549f.; Longerich, *Braune Bataillone,* 152f.
49. LHAM C 20 Ib 2049/I, fol. 301 (RP Magdeburg to OP, 6 October 1931).
50. LHAM C 20 Ib 2051/II, fol. 269 (RP Merseburg to OP, 26 January 1932).
51. LHAM C 20 Ib 2048/II, fols. 240f. (RP Merseburg to OP, 6 April 1932); fols. 245–257 (RP Merseburg to OP, 11 April 1932); fols. 263–265 (PP Magdeburg to OP, 18 March 1932); LHAM C 20 Ib 2049/II, fol. 215f. (*Kampfleitung* [fighting leadership] of the Iron Front Stendal to OP, RP, and PP Magdeburg, 8 March 1932); *VS* no. 67, 18 March 1932. On the alerting of the SA on 13 March see Longerich, *Braune Bataillone,* 153.
52. LHAM C 20 Ib 2049/II, fols. 212f. (PP Magdeburg to the SA *Gauführer,* 2 February 1932, copy).
53. LHAM C 20 Ib 2049/II, fols. 271–275 (RP Magdeburg to OP, 25 January and 25 February 1932).
54. Ibid., fols. 266f. (RP Magdeburg to OP, 4 March 1932).
55. Ibid., fol. 224 (RP Magdeburg to OP, 11 March 1932); fol. 227 (Note by OP, 18 March 1932).
56. LHAM C 20 Ib 2052/I, fol. 282 (RP Erfurt to OP, 6 February 1932).
57. LHAM C 20 Ib 2041/III, fol. 82 (RP Merseburg to OP, 19 February 1932); fols. 85–90 (Report by the gendarme division Mückenberg, 19 February 1932).
58. Other cases in the spring of 1932: LHAM C 20 Ib 2041/III, fol. 81 (attack on a meeting tavern in Wansleben, Mansfelder Seekreis, on 18 February); LHAM C 20 Ib 2049/II, fol. 186 (the same in County Calbe at the end of February); LHAM C 20 Ib 2051/II, fol. 305 (the same in Bitterfeld on 10 February). On the difficult relationship between the SPD and the KPD in Nordhausen see Schmidtke, "Sozialdemokratie," 254f.
59. On this see the coverage in the *Volksstimme,* no. 88, 14 April; no. 89, 15 April; no. 90, 16/17 April; no. 91, 18 April; no. 95, 22 April; no. 97, 25 April 1932, which also reports a few minor scuffles with Communists. Blasius (*Weimars Ende,* 32–47) fails to acknowledge the effectiveness of the ban.
60. LHAM C 20 Ib 2049/III, fols. 15f. (PP Magdeburg to OP, 9 June 1932); fol. 24 (PP Magdeburg to OP, 13 June 1932), according to which there continued to be almost daily clashes for the same reason.
61. LHAM C 20 Ib 2051/III, fol. 15 (RP Merseburg to OP, 23 June 1932); fols. 113f. (RP Merseburg to OP, 27 June 1932). Similar incidents: LHAM C 20 Ib 2051/III, fol. 137 (brawl after an SA meeting in Eilenburg on 17 July); LHAM C 20 Ib 2052/I, fol. 311 (Communist attack on NSDAP members on 31 July on a country road near Erfurt, one serious injury); LHAM C 20 Ib 2049/III, fol. 42 (shots fired in Magdeburg on 3/4 July at NSDAP members returning from Dessau); fol. 66 (Social Democratic workers against participants at a NSDAP meeting on 17 July in Neuhaldensleben); fol. 54 (Communists against participants returning home from an NSDAP event on 13 July in Fermersleben near Magdeburg). When more than 100 SA men disrupted an SPD meeting in County Stendal at the end of July, their attack left twelve with minor injuries and two with serious injuries. At the beginning of October, a trial before the *Landgericht* (district court) in Stendal sentenced 25 SA men for serious breach of the public peace—but not for bodily harm—to jail terms between three and fifteen months: LHAM C 20 Ib 2049/III, fols. 73f. (RP Magdeburg to OP, 5 August 1932), fol. 123; also see *MZ* no. 544, 8 October 1932. For criticism of the comparatively lenient sentences see *VS* no. 238, 8/9 October 1932.
62. *MZ* no. 198, 11 April 1932; *VS* no. 85, 11 April 1932.
63. LHAM C 20 Ib 2049/II, fols. 30–32 (RP Magdeburg to OP, 21 and 27 June 1932). The finding of the investigation—that the shots had been fired by the Communists, which means the bullet that killed the Communist was fired by his fellow Communists—at first gives cause for skepticism. However, the investigation was conducted not by the local police, but by the state

criminal police based in Magdeburg, who, given their closeness to the Republican officials of the provincial capital, presumably had even less sympathy—if any—for the NSDAP than did the Staßfurt police. The report of 27 June contains no marginal comments questioning the findings by Oberpräsident Dr. Falck, who likewise had no reason to let the Nazi who fired the deadly bullet get away scot-free. As late as 5 February 1933, the state police conducted trustworthy investigations following the assassination of the Social Democratic mayor of Staßfurt (see below). In its reporting, the *Volksstimme* originally assumed a "Nazi murder," but then was remarkably restrained (*VS* no. 147, 24 June; no. 148, 25/26 June; no. 151, 29 June; no. 152, 30 June 1932). It is most likely that the Communist crowd had wanted to teach the National Socialist a lesson and scared him with shots fired into the air, since the large number of demonstrators would have merely gotten in the way in a planned assassination; the shots fired in the tumultuous situation then ended up hitting the wrong target. On this symbolic use of weapons see Rosenhaft, "Links," 249; Reichardt, *Kampfbünde,* 83f.

64. LHAM C 20 Ib 2049/III, fols. 34–36 (RP Magdeburg to OP, 29 June 1932).
65. Ibid., fols. 75f. (RP Magdeburg to OP, 5 August 1932).
66. During an athletic meeting of the KPD in County Osterburg, gendarmes fired into the crowd when the participants wanted to form a forbidden march and attacked the officers; two men were injured: LHAM C 20 Ib 2041/III, fols. 143f. (RP Magdeburg to OP, 29 June 1932). One member of the Reichsbanner (!) died when the police opened fire in Wittenberg on a protest march by the Antifaschistische Aktion (Anti-Fascist Action), whose participants attacked an office of the NSDAP and also assaulted police officers who were escorting the march: ibid., fol. 147 (RP Merseburg to OP, 16 July 1932).
67. See Bessel, *Political Violence,* 96: "On the whole, considering the political philosophies and the size of the organisations involved, the number of dead and seriously injured ... seems evidence less of uncontrolled civil war ... than of a series of incidents in which the rules of the game generally were understood and respected." See also his "Violence as Propaganda: The Role of the Storm Troopers in the Rise of National Socialism," in T. Childers, ed., *The Formation of the Nazi Constituency 1919—1933* (London, 1986), 131–146, here 135. Of course, one still needs to emphasize the increase in violence in 1932 compared to the previous years. An exaggeration is the statement by Striefler, *Kampf,* 370, that in the summer of 1932 the country was "repeatedly at the verge of an unbridled civil war." See also the descriptions of clashes in July 1932 by Bessel, *Political Violence,* 85–87 (Ohlau and Greifswald) and William Sheridan Allen, *The Nazi Seizure of Power: The Experience of a Single German Town* (London, 1965), 96, 115, 137f. (in the town of Northeim, Lower Saxony).
68. Dirk Blasius, who puts forth a number of different and confusing definitions of "civil war," fails to draw this distinction. See Blasius, *Weimars Ende,* 15, 20, 30, 55, 69.
69. On this murder, committed with unprecedented brutality by several SA men, see Bessel, "Potempa." On the wave of terror in East Prussia see idem, *Political Violence,* 87–92.
70. LHAM C 20 Ib 2049/III, fol. 128 (RP Magdeburg to OP, 9 November 1932). The reporting *Regierungsrat* Dr. Stier and the *Regierungsvizepräsident* Berthold, who lost his job a little time later, had held their positions before 20 July. On the other, smaller clashes see *VS* no. 234, 4 October; no. 239, 10 October; no. 245, 17 October; no. 249, 21 October; no. 254, 27 October; no. 256, 29/30 October; no. 257, 31 October; no. 258, 1 November; no. 259, 2 November; no. 261, 4 November; no. 262, 5/6 November; no. 263, 7 November 1932.
71. LHAM C 20 Ib 2051/III, fol. 178 (RP Merseburg to OP, 4 October 1932). According to this document, the leader of the Weißenfels SA had just left the party. He had run the local NSDAP group until 1928, was then SA leader for two years, and had drawn close to the movement around Otto Straßer in 1930 but was then readmitted into the party. This time he was leaving because the party would not give him the kind of leadership position to which he believed himself entitled, and he now intended to join the KPD (!). "The incident is symptomatic of the strong tension between the leadership of the party and the SA that has been observed recently at various locations in this district, and for the strong turnover (*Verbrauch*) of *Unterführer* of

the SA that this entailed." On the conflicts in and around the SA after the summer of 1932 see Longerich, *Braune Bataillone,* 158–164, who points to the explosive mood among segments of the SA, a mood that was pushing for putsch-like actions. Clear evidence for this does not exist for the province of Saxony. See also Pridham, *Hitler's Rise,* 291–294; Bessel, *Political Violence,* 92–95.

72. The data come from LHAM C 20 Ib 2041/II–III, 2049/I–III, 2051/I–III, 2054, and LHAM C 141 Halberstadt nos. 309, 328, 343, 352/1–2, 379, 417.
73. We have information for 93 persons (of a total of 106).
74. Reichardt (*Kampfbünde,* 521–25) also points out that members of the Combat Leagues rarely switched sides.
75. These were three Communist women who were sentenced to three months each for their participation in attacks on Nazi leaflet distributors in Quedlinburg on 22 September 1930: LHAM C 141 Halberstadt no. 352, fols. 1–5 (Verdict of Lay Assessors' Court Halberstadt, 9 December 1930).
76. We have information for 104 cases. The oldest actors had been born in 1877, the youngest in 1914. Participation in the war is documented with certainty for only one person. However, we lack any information for one-third of the individuals.
77. Six were definitely single, but there is no information for 67.
78. See the profile of the Communist street fighters in Rosenhaft, *Beating the Fascists,* 167ff. According to her research, young adults between 19 and 22 made up the largest group, 80 percent were thus younger than 30; in my sample, the percentage under 30 comes to a little under 70 percent. The explanation for the younger average age in Berlin may lie with the inclusion of youth gangs in the struggle over sovereignty in the sections of the city and the lower spatial mobility of the fighters here. Reichardt (*Kampfbünde,* 428f.) also points out the lack of criminal records for most of the SA men in his sample.
79. On this see the findings by Merkl, *Stormtrooper,* 96–99, according to whom just under 60 percent of the SA dead were skilled workers or workers in service profession, while 25 percent belonged to the middle class. This would mean that the intense violent clashes involved a substantially higher ratio of workers among the SA men than is found in the SA overall, but still far fewer than on the other side. Of course, Merkl's figures are not directly comparable to the ones presented here, which is even more true of his other findings on the social profile of the SA, which he drew from 581 biographies of SA men collected after 1933 by the American sociologist Theodore Abel. In this collection, SA men who joined before 1930 are overrepresented, as are those from Berlin and other large cities. To what extent their statements about their motives for joining the SA and their experiences fighting came from later projection, and to what extent they reflect attitudes of the period before 1933 is impossible to determine. Therefore, Abel's source is of limited value for the pre-1933 period.
80. LHAM C 20 Ib 2049/III, fols. 208f. (Report by the state criminal police office IA, 5 February 1933).
81. LHAM C 20 Ib 2051/III, fol. 260 (RP Merseburg to OP, 31 January 1933).
82. *VB* no. 37, 13 February; no. 38, 14 February 1933 (with the impressions of the events gathered by Friedrich Stampfer, the editor-in-chief of the *Vorwärts* who happened to be in Eisleben); *KK* no. 38, 14 February; *SZ* no. 37, 18 February; no. 38, 14 February 1933; see Leidigkeit and Herrmann, *Leninistischer Kurs,* 444.
83. LHAM C 20 Ib 2049/III, fol. 191 (RP Magdeburg to OP, 21 February 1933). That same day in Erfurt saw the death of an inebriated KPD functionary who had gotten into an argument with an SA man and been shot in the abdomen without having attacked his opponent: LHAM C 20 Ib 2052/I, fol. 327 (RP Erfurt to OP, 21 February 1933). On similar incidents in eastern Prussia see Bessel, *Political Violence,* 98–105, 116–118.
84. Longerich, *Braune Bataillone,* 176, places this point at the center of his interpretation of the terror that accompanied the assumption of power.

85. Reuter, one of the coming men of the SPD in the final years of the Weimar Republic and lord mayor of Magdeburg since 1931, was put in a concentration camp until 1934 and then emigrated to Turkey, where he spent the war years. In 1947 he was elected lord mayor of Berlin and became famous for his courageous leadership during the Berlin blockade a year later.
86. LHAM C 20 Ib 2049/III, fols. 218–220 (RP Magdeburg to OP, 18 March 1933). This document and the already cited police reports are, incidentally, clear and unambiguous in assigning blame. On numerous excesses and attacks by the Schönebeck SA in March/April 1933 under its leader Karpe, who had already attracted attention previously, see fols. 236–241, 252, 263. On similar incidents in Silesia see Bessel, *Political Violence,* 105–109.
87. The official files for the years 1930–1932 contain only one notice about excesses in Eisleben. In February 1931, a local shop owner complained that anti-Semitic graffiti like "*Juda verrecke*" and swastikas on Jewish stores were "a daily occurrence," with no intervention by the police. Recently some had tried to prevent a Jewish shop owner from driving his car. If the Oberpräsident would not ensure protection, the Reichsbanner would resort to "self-help." In his response, the Regierungspräsident of Merseburg emphasized that the problem was not a shortage of police officers but mistakes in their training and leadership, which is why he had assigned a Schupo lieutenant colonel to the local police: LHAM C 20 Ib 2051/I (not pag., Letter to OP, passed on to RP on 7 February 1931; response by RP, 10 February 1931). The reaction by the Regierungspräsident can be interpreted only as an admission that in Eisleben, and no doubt elsewhere as well, some police officers ignored anti-Semitic insults and threats if they did not lead to open violence. By contrast, larger attacks like that on the Jewish gymnastics club in 1924 could not go unnoticed, not least because the Social Democratic and Communist press would have immediately addressed the issue. To be sure, one must not underestimate the latent menace of the almost quotidian anti-Semitism or fail to see it as part of the prehistory of the Holocaust. Still, it must be noted that until the *Machtergreifung,* the physical violence of the SA was directed largely against its political enemies on the left. See also Bessel, *Political Violence,* 77–83; Longerich, *Braune Bataillone,* 121; Moshe Zimmermann, *Die deutschen Juden 1914–1945* (Munich, 1997), 43. On the violence against Jews as part of the wave of terror in August 1932 and after see Walter, *Antisemitische Gewalt,* 236–242.

Chapter 11

MISJUDGMENT, DOWNPLAYING, APPROVAL

Interpretations of Political Violence 1930–1933

It was not great marches and outdoor rallies with tens of thousands of participants and elaborate programs that characterized how political parties presented themselves in public at the end of the Weimar Republic, but the waves of meetings that crested during election campaigns and the small-scale warfare that developed around them. There is no question that the style of meetings held in halls changed in the process. They became—at least in the cities—increasingly martial, replaced the give-and-take of argumentative speech and counter speech with rough attacks on the enemy and bold appeals to one's own followers, and brought the militarization of politics once and for all into the closed meeting hall.[1] The public realm of the street, if Republican officials could have their way, was to be stripped once again of its military appearance through bans on demonstrations and uniforms and thus be pacified. In the end, however, the clashing political courses in Prussia and on the Reich level engendered the opposite: the small-scale warfare in and around meetings made the street into a terrain pervaded by violence. Half-hearted repression did not contain the violence, thereby adding fodder for feelings of being under threat.

With the partial closing of the street as a place for potent self-representation and the growth in meetings, the spoken word—as an instrument of propaganda, not as a rational argument—took on great weight in relationship to the symbolic presentation of politics, especially within the NSDAP. By contrast, the National Socialist press was of only secondary importance, which in the province of Saxony was reflected not least in the fact that the party did not control any daily papers until 1 April 1932, that is, at a time when it had nearly achieved the high point of its mobilization of electoral support.[2] Since the Nazi press is all but unavailable and the meeting reports by the police contain hardly any detailed information about the content of speeches at events put on by the NSDAP, the oral presentation of its politics in the province is, in essence, accessible only

Notes from this chapter begin on page 300.

through the mirror of the reactions by its political enemies and allies. Especially the attitude of the bourgeois public, however, provides insight into why the rise of National Socialism was so impetuous, and why the transfer of power to Hitler met with so little opposition and resistance.

Revisionists' Hopes and Fear of Civil War

In their descriptions of domestic political conditions from 1930 on, the *Magdeburgische Zeitung* and the *Saale-Zeitung* vacillated between the hope that the unloved parliamentary democracy would come to an end, and the fear that the path to an authoritarian political system could be blocked if the country descended into civil war. On New Year's Day 1930, the *Magdeburgische Zeitung* presented a list of urgently needed reforms in all areas—the constitution, culture, penal law, social welfare legislation. A year later the paper noted: "The time of partial reforms is over, everything is now at stake." Anxiety moved to the fore in 1932. People were in a "state of inner uncertainty," we are told; "like a sick person, Germany is in danger of losing its head and opting for radical solutions," it will "either recover" or "succumb to enervation."[3] Once again, the argument invoked the image of the sick body of the nation—an image that was hostile to pluralism—and the importance of "nerve," which carried male connotations. At the turn of 1932/33, this fear had given way to a new optimism, however. The *Saale-Zeitung* saw the emergence of a "new front of level-headedness," and for the Magdeburg paper, "the entire German *Volk* stands ready in unanimity"—at least when it came to the ongoing fight against the Versailles Treaty, the revision of which continued to be a central political goal, all the fixation on domestic politics notwithstanding.[4] The return of this optimistic tenor was based, especially for the *Magdeburgische Zeitung,* on the 1932 reelection of Hindenburg, who was seen as a guarantor of "non-partisanship" and "internal unity," on the end of the National Socialist surge in the November elections, and on the potential split within the Nazi party, which seemed a distinct possibility at the end of 1932. But the *Magdeburgische Zeitung*'s call for the "cooperation of all constructive forces" was aimed not at a collaboration between the Social Democrats and the bourgeois parties, but at an alliance between the Straßer wing of the NSDAP and the Center Party as well as the other bourgeois parties. By contrast, the paper expected only obstructionism from the "Marxist group" in the Reichstag, meaning the SPD and the KPD, with no fundamental distinction made between the two parties.[5]

By the time political violence had noticeably receded, fear of a civil war had waned. That fear had been articulated clearly for the first time at the end of 1930. "Among us, people are no longer pursuing intellectual conquests, but seek to force through their views with terror," the Magdeburg paper noted in the middle of December.[6] The harsh criticism was still aimed at all sides, though its concrete occasion was the behavior of the Reichsbanner in the run-up to a large NSDAP meeting in the city at which Hitler was supposed to appear, and which was eventually prohibited after the Republican group announced a counter-rally and there was reason for fear violence.[7] By the middle of August 1931, the paper noted that the country had been "in a civil war … for years," even if it varied in intensity; the only ones denounced by name, though, were the Communists. Shortly before the first round of balloting in the Reich president elections in 1932, we read of "two peoples (*Völker*) in one country" fighting "with a bitterness hardly ever seen before," "each of whom would prefer to visit war upon the other." Only Hindenburg could overcome the "dissension" and create unity after the model of 1914.[8]

After the outbreak of violence in the wake of the lifting of the ban on the SA, Germany was seen back "on the road to civil war," and an editorial on 9 August expressed profound concern when the wave of SA terror swept through East Prussia and Silesia: this was now "the open blood terror of a crowd gone wild, at the end of which will be civil war" unless the government intervened resolutely (which it did the following day with an emergency decree that provided for draconian punishments). In spite of the unmistakable criticism of the NSDAP, there was more than one culprit, as the finger-pointing of the Magdeburg paper made clear: "It must be said that the political terror began with the bloody deeds of the Communists. That these doings over a number of years had to push the political enemy to take countermeasures is understandable. On the other hand, it is not legitimate to derive from this fact a right of revenge by the same means."[9] The very real fear of civil war was indeed combined with different assessments of how responsibility for it was to be assigned, but this assessment was not persuasive—especially with regard to the SA terror in the first half of August, for it was clearly not self-defense against Communist attacks. The entrenched image of the Communist enemy blurred the contours of the violence emanating from the other side, which was in this case much more brutal.

The *Volksstimme,* too, articulated a growing fear of civil war. "We no longer have to invoke the image of civil war, we are in the middle of it," the Social Democratic paper underscored in November 1931, following larger clashes over the SA Home in Schönebeck. A few days later, at the festivities in Magdeburg commemorating the Revolution, Paul Löbe spoke of "drifting into a civil war," and at the beginning of 1932, the *Volksstimme* noted the sense "that we are no longer standing on solid ground, but on a plank that is drifting about in the sea. The feeling of uncertainty, of terror haunts people."[10] The "outlines of a civil war" were supposedly becoming apparent after the lifting of the ban on the SA, and shortly before the Reichstag elections at the end of July we read: "The terror is here, the end of democracy … everything is all too true, and too true are the hundreds of fresh graves of SA murders and civil war."[11] In both the *Volksstimme* and the bourgeois papers, this vague notion of civil war served to put the fears engendered by the development of domestic politics into a nutshell. It seemed that the country was falling back into the bloody chaos of 1919/20.

After the July elections, the *Volksstimme* saw a "sigh of relief" pass through the middle class, which still believed "in culture and human dignity," because the advance of the NSDAP seemed to have been arrested, in spite of its electoral success compared to the Reich president elections. As the reason for this the paper identified the "Socialist worker" who stood before the Nazi movement "upright and victorious"; one could "feel once again the power of unity – the Iron Front," which Hitler would "never" defeat.[12] This peculiar commentary on the elections—which had, after all, brought the SPD further losses—made no mention of the Communists and their gains. The optimistic tenor—as far as fending off Hitler was concerned, not with respect to the SPD's own political influence—was certainly not feigned, and it was reiterated before the November elections.[13] But as far as this "reasonable" middle class was concerned, it expressed no more than a hope, for after the almost complete disappearance of centrist bourgeois parties, in that camp there were no longer any partners for an alliance to be found. While the *Volksstimme* therefore believed only a strong Iron Front could prevent civil war, and thus called for a withdrawal to the organizational pillar of the Social Democratic milieu, the *Magdeburgische Zeitung* placed its hopes on a very different strategy: cooperation between the bourgeois parties and sections of the NSDAP against the "Marxist group" in parliament. Here there was no longer any common ground.[14]

Always the Aggressor? The Communists and the Social Democrats

Unlike the rest of the public, the Communists discussed civil war not as a threat, but as a possibly unavoidable stage in the class struggle, especially in a period of class conflicts that were becoming more intense around the world. Ever since the ultra-left turn in 1929, there was no doubt that this "third period" had been entered.[15] However, the phrase "civil war," though propagated only a few years earlier, ceased to appear in the reports and commentaries of the party organ from Halle. Instead, right up to Hitler's appointment as chancellor, the view of the political situation proclaimed in the *Klassenkampf* was characterized by a boundless optimism of eventual victory. Looking back at 1929, manifestations of capitalism's "disintegration" seemed increasingly evident, with the "front lines of class clearly ripped open," and the optimism justified that the coming year would "advance the dictatorship of the proletariat a long way." In April 1931, the paper saw the "contradictions of class heightened to the utmost" and Germany "filled with elements … of the proletarian Revolution," which, of course, had to be organized now. On Revolution Day in November, the paper detected not only the "collapse of capitalism," but also the "collapse of the influence of socio-fascist parties" as well as the "bankruptcy of fascism in the countries of fascist dictatorships."[16] The following year, after a temporary setback in view of the slight pullback during the Reich presidential elections, which was, however, attributed in the final analysis only to organizational shortcomings (the "extra-parliamentary mobilization of the masses" had been "inadequately carried out"[17]), the KPD was able to celebrate "its greatest electoral victory since its inception" in the Reichstag elections on 31 July and then sweep to complete triumph in November: the "splendid electoral victory" proved, according to the *Klassenkampf*, "that the forces of the revolutionary class front are constantly growing at an accelerating pace, whereas the disintegration of the mass basis has begun in the fascist camp." On the way to final victory there could be, at most, obstacles like the "intensified murderous and terroristic agitation" of the National Socialists, but there could be no doubt about the eventual outcome.[18]

Although this optimism devoid of nuance may have invoked the impressive electoral successes of the party, it concealed its organizational stagnation. Meanwhile, it could be used by the bourgeois press as an argument against the Communists. In early 1930, the *Magdeburgische Zeitung* condemned the "open or insidious acts of violence by the Communists toward people of dissenting opinions," which had recently been noted again in Berlin. Evidently the KPD, because of unemployment and economic crisis, believed that this was a favorable time "to incite the masses to acts of violence." Following clashes at the Day of Struggle against Joblessness in Ammendorf, the *Saale-Zeitung* seconded that opinion with reference to the "instigators of the extreme left," who alone bore the guilt for the fatal shots; at the same time, it interpreted the failure of these actions in mobilizing the masses as "clear proof that the peoples of the world want nothing to do with Communism," including the German people, which had given "another demonstration of its levelheadedness and its calm judgment."[19]

Halle's *Saale-Zeitung* sounded a different tone on the eve of Reichstag elections on 14 September 1930. Communism was "the worst enemy that has hitherto arisen for the entire civilized world, and its victory would undoubtedly mean the 'Fall of the West,'" the paper warned its readers. But then it went on to say that "at the moment … it is not yet the worst enemy," not as bad as the "Socialism of a Scheidemann and comrades," who could prepare the way for "Bolshevism" after the example of Russia—"with the help of blind members of the bourgeoisie," for whom one should therefore never cast one's ballot.[20] For reasons of electoral tactics, the paper was reviving ur-images of the Communist enemy that dated back to 1919, while at the same time relativizing them to serve the goal of closing the ranks of the bourgeoisie against the entire left. This shows that while there was a certain stock of deep-seated fears about "Bolshevism," they could be subordinated to other arguments and thus lose their fundamental character. For example, the *Saale-Zeitung*, in a review of 1931—that is, in a situation when social and political tensions had heightened even more—noted an "epochal change": the entire world was becoming "nationalistic," even Communism, for "in Russia itself it has long since become as nationalistic as one can possibly imagine," and in all other countries it would "become ineluctably nationalistic and absorbed by nationalism through the instinct of self-preservation by the various peoples."[21] This expressed what was in fact a longer-term conviction—not least with respect to the evolution of the NSDAP, into whose ranks the paper no doubt saw the "nationalized" Communists streaming—that presented no problem for the *Saale-Zeitung*, in contrast to the *Magdeburgische Zeitung*, which was still insisting emphatically on specifically bourgeois values. If the Communists were attacked, it was generally with reference to the threat they posed not to German culture as such, but to the life and limb of the people in Germany. What was being continued was the topos of the political "criminals," not a general fear of being overwhelmed by "Bolshevism."

But the Communists did not simply commit acts of violence; they also operated with particularly insidious methods. The "sinister face of the red civil war," the *Magdeburgische Zeitung* wrote in an editorial on the murder of two police officers at the Bülowplatz in Berlin in 1931, was revealed by the fact that "no open, honest fight" was taking place: "Here death sneaks about in the dark against the keepers of peace and order." But the police were not the only targets: if there was a clash with National Socialists, both papers generally assumed that the actions of the Communists were "planned" and presumed that "in the vast majority of all cases the bloody confrontations were begun by the Communist side."[22] Those incidents in which the violence had clearly emanated from the National Socialists were almost never reported, unless they attracted the kind of attention that the wave of terror did in August 1932, and even then—as will be seen—the papers came up with relativizing formulations.

By contrast, the instigators of Communist acts of violence were vehemently denounced. Their "bestialities" were leading to a "general civil war," not least, according to the *Magdeburgische Zeitung,* "because the hatred for the authors of the ongoing street battles that is accumulating in all strata of the population could one day discharge itself explosively."[23] Not only did this lay the blame for the violence-prone domestic political atmosphere on the Communists, it also asserted that the victims of this violence had a right to self-defense independent of the actions of the state. It was only a small step from this kind of finger-pointing to the kind of characterization of the Communists penned by the Magdeburg paper after the "Bloody Sunday of Altona": by their behavior they had turned themselves into "subhumans in the truest sense of the word."[24] Much like the label of "vermin" in the context of the March fighting of 1921, this verdict opened the door to a realm of thinking and acting that made room for violent measures that were, in essence, no longer constrained.[25]

The *Volksstimme,* too, voiced sharp criticism of the KPD, but it imbued that criticism with different connotations and was noticeably restrained after the end of 1931. After the clashes with the police in Magdeburg and Ammendorf, the paper spoke of "a political crime" by the Communists and of their "blood guilt," but more harmless attributes like "bandit romanticism" (*Räuberromantik*) and "revolutionary hullabaloo" (*Revolutionsklamauk*) also seemed like appropriate labels. Following a confrontation between Reichsbanner men and Communists in Neuhaldensleben, the latter were reproached for being "the worthy avant-garde of political hooliganism," and as "faithful comrades of these mattress stormers [!]" (referring to the Magdeburg SA Home) and "fraternity brothers of Swastika and Soviet star" they were put on the same level as the SA.[26] But these verdicts lacked the vitriol and especially the contempt for humanity displayed by the bourgeois press. The *Volksstimme* did not engage in a closer examination of the behavior of the Communists. It would appear that in 1932, in spite of the profound political differences, the paper wanted to avoid drawing too sharp a line of separation against the left so as not to lose even more votes to the "political children" Severing had once mocked, and to avoid blocking on the side of the SPD every possibility of cooperation in the name of fighting the National Socialists.[27]

The *Klassenkampf*, for its part, left no doubt about its verdict on the SPD. The position of a "unity front from below" that was aimed explicitly against the leadership of the SPD was—smaller fluctuations in the party line notwithstanding[28]—propagated until the very end. The only thing that was toned down was the harshness of the attacks on the Social Democrats. In connection with the Mansfeld strike they were attacked as "social fascists" (*Sozialfaschisten*), and at the end of the strike we even hear of the "stab in the back by the social fascist functionaries." On the occasion of the LLL Commemoration in January 1932, the *Klassenkampf* was still describing the path of the SPD as leading "from reconciliatory opportunism to social fascism" and accusing it of "mortal enmity" toward the proletarian revolution.[29] The paper, an organ of the district leadership, regarded the ban on the SA as merely a maneuver, with the help of which a "gang of political desperados, the SPD leadership," was endeavoring to "do the business of Fascism more quickly." By contrast, the goal of the KPD, we read a few days later, was to form "a unity front with all honest workers" but not with the SPD, a "pioneer for Fascism."[30] Although the verdict of "social fascism" was no longer pronounced, the accusations aimed at the SPD, and not only explicitly at its leadership, remained harsh. Its leaders had become "pillars of the Papen regime, pillars of murderous Fascism," because they wanted to respond to the government's legalization of the SA at the ballet box and not in the streets; thus it was now imperative to establish the Roter Massenselbstschutz. At the turn of the year, the paper spoke of the "class traitor SPD."[31]

The day after Hitler's appointment, the *Klassenkampf* called upon its readers not to fight the new government jointly with the SPD leadership, since the latter, unwilling to depart from the constitution, was merely spouting "pseudo-radical phrases." The paper boldly declared: "Judas Iscariot at work! The class betrayal of the SPD. They want to deliver the working class into the hands of Fascism."[32] Even after the SA attack in Eisleben in the middle of February, when contact was established in Halle between the KPD-dominated unity committee of the local works councils and the Social Democratic leadership of the local cartel of the ADGB, the *Klassenkampf* clung to its old line. Because the ADGB representatives did not immediately agree to the formation of joint mass self-defense units, the paper called for a "unity of action" against such "sabotage." "Now more than ever," the important thing was "to form the unity front over the heads of the ADGB leaders."[33] In the face of this massive attack—moderated only in tone, not in substance—it was hard to imagine any cooperation between the KPD and the SPD, unless the SPD, already a minority in the district Halle-Merseburg, was willing to cease existing. The KPD propaganda did not prevent occasional cooperation between members of the two parties, but it could not provide a basis for their organizational consolidation. In the end, the KPD district leadership would not be given the chance to publicly change its course: the day after the publication of the article on Eisleben, the *Klassenkampf* was banned.

For the bourgeois papers, meanwhile, the differences between the SPD and the KPD were far less significant than their supposed commonalities. In the conflict over the Hitler meeting in Magdeburg at the end of 1930, the *Magdeburgische Zeitung* accused the SPD of having worked with the "means of terror" and noted a general "state of war" between the NSDAP, on the one side, and the Reichsbanner and the SPD, on the other. The paper could not see any fundamental difference between Social Democrats and National Socialists. At this time the *Saale-Zeitung* struck a harsher tone when it accused the leadership of the Reichsbanner, following its decision to set up "protective formations," of "flirting" with "threats of civil war" and addressed the chairman of the organization directly: "Hörsing is calling for civil war."[34] Thus the Reichsbanner was equated with the KPD. It therefore made sense that the *Saale-Zeitung* also accused the Republican organization of having committed "premeditated" attacks on National Socialists.[35] The logical upshot was that after the outlawing of the SA, the paper called for an additional ban on the Reichsbanner as the "private army of Social Democracy" and a similar measure against the Iron Front and its "agitators for civil war."[36] In essence, these were the same accusations that were leveled against the Communists: preparations for civil war and planned, premeditated attacks. From such a perspective, the differences between Social Democrats and Communists seemed on the whole smaller than those between the National Socialists and the older bourgeois parties.

Justified Self-Defense? The National Socialists

> This is simply the activated beer bench. But as the common saying goes, there is nothing so stupid and idiotic that it does not find supporters ... It would be foolish in an election to cast one's vote for one party only to annoy the other. It would be dangerous to give it to the National Socialists, who, once in power, would prove incapable of leading the Reich, and who would bring the German *Volk* revolution and war, economic collapse and general joblessness, in short, death and destruction.[37]

This apt, almost prophetic characterization of the NSDAP and its politics is not from the *Volksstimme* but from an editorial in the *Magdeburgische Zeitung*, published on the eve of Reichstag elections on 14 September 1930. In keeping with the occasion, the words were suitably dramatic, but there is no doubt that they still expressed massive opposition to the NSDAP. This opposition concerned the program and the public actions of the party in equal measure. However, over the next two years this opposition weakened so drastically on both points, and especially the latter, that no fundamental arguments were put forth any longer against the participation of the National Socialists in the government.

We know of the skepticism with which bourgeois circles regarded the economic program of the National Socialists.[38] A few days after the September elections, the Magdeburg paper saw the "ruin of the German bourgeoisie" on the horizon, should this program be put into practice. At the turn of 1930/31, the *Magdeburgische Zeitung* was still not sure whether the NSDAP should be placed in the right wing or the Socialist camp. During the Reichstag elections a year later, the paper put the emphasis once again on "Workers' party" and issued yet another urgent warning after the second round of balloting: "If it has been noted so frequently that Hitler is the only rival candidate to Bolshevism," his voters "from bourgeois circles" should ponder how many Communist votes had most recently flocked to Hitler.[39]

Socialist tendencies within the NSDAP were less of a concern to the *Saale-Zeitung,* which was part of Hugenberg's media empire. By the end of 1930 its assessment of the party was essentially positive. Before the presidential elections in 1932, the paper singled out as Hitler's chief accomplishment that he had succeeded in keeping many millions of Germans away from "purely negative, destructive radicalism, from Communism." Only after a takeover of power by the two parties of the Harzburg Front, which seemed within reach, had been thwarted in the middle of August by Hitler's intransigent behavior, did the paper briefly assume a clear defensive posture. An "atmosphere of class warfare" had been created by the Berlin transportation strike, declared an editorial on the eve of the November elections, and the NSDAP bore the chief responsibility. The country was therefore once again in a situation like the one shortly after the Revolution of 1918—the voters had to choose either "Socialism or the state of the *Volk* community."[40] Since the economic ideas of the NSDAP remained problematic, its possible usefulness in the battle against the KPD and the SPD was therefore impossible to calculate precisely, but in the end it seemed significant enough that a closer discussion of the program was avoided.

The methods with which the NSDAP proceeded against its political opponents were dealt with less critically. Only in the *Magdeburgische Zeitung* did they initially meet with clear disapproval. However, this position was soon relativized and increasingly watered down, quite in contrast to the verdict on the behavior of the Communists. The above-quoted lead article on the September elections in 1930 aimed its criticism of the party explicitly at Hitler's statement that "heads will roll in the sand" after a takeover of power.[41] Before the second round of voting in the presidential elections, the paper—in keeping with the occasion—again found strong words to drive home the threat posed by the NSDAP and to elevate a vote for Hindenburg into the duty of every citizen: "Whoever exercises civic responsibility will protect order and the organic development against revolution and the rule of the strongest … [H]e has no choice between the mindset of the conquistador, demagoguery, and propaganda genius, on the one side, and the quiet greatness of incorruptible fulfillment of duty, on the other."[42]

However, what sounded like a rejection on principle in fact contained far more tactical moves than had been the case a year and a half earlier. Only two days before declaring its support for Hindenburg, the *Magdeburgische Zeitung* had taken up the actions of Prussian Minister of the Interior Severing, who, after a large-scale investigation, had so much incriminating material on the SA that he argued for a ban of the organization, which was then issued a few days after Hindenburg's re-election. To be sure, the article opposed all "private armies" and conceded that "a number of SA leaders" had apparently "taken organizational measures" that could lead "to the most serious conflicts with the power of the state and to open civil war." But the paper qualified its remarks by asserting that the militarily structured "private force" of the SA would become "a danger to the state ... only if that is what the leader of the party wants."[43] When the ban was announced a week later, the paper criticized it as being incomprehensible "to the broadest segments of the German *Volk*," for "in the hands of a legal, that is to say, constitution-abiding leader," the SA "might one day have acquired strong and great national-political importance." In this perspective, the SA—substantially larger by now—no longer seemed a menacing civil war force, but above all a valuable recruitment reservoir for the future establishment of an army that was appropriate to the great power Germany, a role that these observers were not willing to accord to the Reichsbanner.

At the same time, once the leadership structure of the SA became the chief element in assessing it, Hitler himself moved into a key position; everyone knew that during the Reichswehr trial in Ulm in September 1930, Hitler had sworn an "oath of legality" and publicly renounced any further plans for a putsch. On the basis of this oath, the *Magdeburgische Zeitung* argued, one should have asked Hitler to establish order within the SA.[44] The expectations about the potential future uses of the SA now pushed the actual experiences with its behavior into the background—even though the *Magdeburgische Zeitung* and the paper from Halle could have discovered from the speeches by Nazi speakers that Hitler's oath notwithstanding, nothing had changed about the NSDAP's willingness to engage in violence. In spite of the threat of a ban on meetings, the police repeatedly noted blatant proclamations that brutal violence would be used on "the day of reckoning" with all the enemies. One speaker wanted all children to learn the craft of rope making, so that plenty of rope would be available on the "day of revenge"—implied was that enemies would he hanged from lampposts. Gau Chief Jordan from Halle wanted to use the SA and the SS to "crush" all opponents, while Loeper, his comrade from Magdeburg, would have recalcitrant policeman "shot down with the canons of the Reichswehr" after the takeover of power.[45] The *Magdeburgische Zeitung* preferred not to look closely at such verbal outbursts.

It was therefore perfectly consistent when the paper avoided clearly identifying the perpetrators of violence in the first week of August 1932. It admitted a "certain system" reminiscent of the Communists and also underscored that these were "'political' methods of a terrifying immorality and dreadful brutality," against which harsh measures would have to be taken because this case "by far exceeds earlier events in its seriousness." But as the culprits it identified only "members of extreme right-wing circles," without any further qualification.[46] The crime of Potempa, too, received little reportage, in contrast to the verdict by the special court in Beuthen, though this was covered together with the verdict by another Silesian court against several Reichsbanner men who had seriously injured several National Socialists during massive clashes in Ohlau. The cases, in no way comparable—a deliberate attack in Potempa, an unplanned clash in Ohlau—were placed on the same level. While the Magdeburg paper considered the jail terms imposed in the Ohlau trial as too lenient, it rejected the imposition of the death penalty for the murderers of Potempa as disproportional and expressed limited understanding for the provocative reaction of the Nazi leadership, whose tenor can also be found in a statement by the Halle SA.[47]

There is no question that the *Magdeburgische Zeitung*'s concern about the domestic political situation, which seemed to be drifting toward civil war, was genuine, and that the paper did not blame only one side. At the same time it was clear that the paper was relativizing that responsibility through its choice of words in identifying perpetrators, through the space that was devoted to the various incidents, and through the weight it gave them. Even the ghastly deed of Potempa did not prompt a return to the politically clear and morally unambiguous position taken at the end of 1930. The NSDAP and the SA, eyed with skepticism but no longer with complete rejection, had by now acquired so much political weight in the eyes of the *Magdeburgische Zeitung*, and had so much potential for the future in spite of all concerns, that unbridled criticism no longer seemed appropriate. The fact is that the respected Magdeburg paper could have afforded blunt criticism more so than all the other papers, since it was still owned by the founder's family and did not have to make any compromises with financiers linked to a specific party. However, throughout the entire bourgeois public, including Republican circles, there were hardly any models left for an uncompromising rejection of the National Socialists, since even the great left-liberal dailies believed that the NSDAP's participation in the government seemed all but unavoidable.[48]

The *Saale-Zeitung* had no major concerns about the fighting methods of the National Socialists. Describing their actions in a retrospective of the year 1930, it found the positively connoted terms "will" and "storming ahead," and the only thing it criticized was that the movement still lacked "direction and a goal." Thereafter, the paper was strikingly restrained when it came to acts of violence perpetrated by the National Socialists. A long report about the meeting of the Harzburg Front in October 1931 (the largest part of which was devoted to Hugenberg's speech) mentioned this issue, revealingly enough with the thrust aimed against the critics of the NSDAP. Hitler's public appearance, noted the paper, "stood in striking contrast to the portrayal by anti-Hitler circles … who are intent on portraying this man as the leader of a violent movement," for his speech showed that for him, "the real struggle … is a struggle of the soul for the soul of our *Volk*." Groener's ban on the SA found a negative echo, with the criticism clearly aimed at Reich President Hindenburg himself.[49] The violent acts of

1932 where blamed—in the harsh language I have described—on the Communists; the paper had nothing to say about the wave of terror in August or about Potempa, reporting on them only in a very limited way and with no reference to the political background. The paper devoted only an editorial to the Terror Emergency Decree of 9 August; still, it did not address the background of the decree, but merely noted—with a mixture of helplessness and distance—that in a time characterized by "the will to fight," change could come about at most through long-term educational work. This was not a policing task, but a matter "of the soul." The resemblance in word choice to the characterization of Hitler the previous year is revealing, even though the National Socialists were not directly mentioned among the educational institutions the paper identified: alongside church and school it listed "the great patriotic (*vaterländische*) organizations like the Stahlhelm." No clear condemnation of National Socialist acts of violence appeared in the *Saale-Zeitung*.[50]

The *Klassenkampf* did not deal at length with the public conduct of the NSDAP and its SA. The front lines seemed clear from the very beginning. One was dealing with "fascist cutthroats," "cowardly murderers," "Nazi bandits," and "provocative gangs of murderers," who were to blame for a "bestial murder of workers" in Potempa.[51] It was imperative to form self-defense leagues against them; moreover, given the growing strength of the Communists, there was reason to believe that many voters of the NSDAP would find their way into the other camp at some time or another. Of course, any exhaustive examination of the violence perpetrated by the NSDAP would have invariably raised questions about the KPD's attitude toward violence. Its print organ preferred not to face these questions, especially, as I have shown earlier, because the problem had certainly not been solved with the party leadership's official rejection of "individual terror" in November of 1931.[52]

The *Volksstimme* dealt with the NSDAP's willingness to engage in violence at greater length, seeing this as a crucial aspect in its analysis of the new political enemy. The vocabulary it employed to characterize the Nazis was not very different from the one it applied to the Communists. We hear of "Nazi hordes," of "bloodlust," and a "murderous gang" following clashes in Stendal in August 1931; those who attacked the Insleber Schloß were "a gang of bandits ... no better than the terror gangs of the Berlin Communists;" "rabble," "adolescent Nazi scoundrels," while "Nazi hordes" were roaming about the Breiter Weg in Magdeburg after the ban on the SA.[53] The topos of the "criminal" was not missing, either. "The small thugs are incited with great slogans about rolling heads ... This is a degradation of political morals, which is being cultivated only in the circles of the underworld and in Hitler's SA leadership," the paper wrote in October 1931 in response to a verdict against an SA men who had struck down a member of the Reichsbanner.[54] An even more robust tone was struck in a commentary on the incidents at the Insleber Schloß: "Anyone who wanted to describe human degeneration and depravity of the highest sort," no longer had to draw "his examples from Hamburg's dock area or the breeding grounds of Berlin's underworld," but could find them in his own city.[55] Connecting politics and criminality was a potent agitative instrument, to be sure, but words like "subhumans," which the bourgeois press employed against the Communists, did not appear in the Social Democratic paper. And there was another threshold that was not crossed: in its response to the verdict in the Potempa case, the *Volksstimme* opposed the imposition of the death penalty, for no matter how "despicable" the crime, the fundamental opposition to the death penalty would not be relinquished; moreover, the real responsibility lay with those who for years had been cultivating the spirit of political murder in Germany.[56]

The *Volksstimme* did not rely only on bold verbal attacks, which were occasionally laced with satire, as for example in the cartoon of a bull-necked SA comrade with the caption: "The tough Hitler fighter. The new ideal of manhood."[57] It also drew a connection between the terror methods of the NSDAP and the behavior of the bourgeoisie. "The Camorra movement of the National Socialists," we read in one lead article on the discussion over a Hitler rally in Magdeburg in December of 1930, which was eventually banned, had "won an electoral victory on 14 September that is without question a major disgrace to the German bourgeoisie."[58] The Social Democratic paper was blunter in its commentary on a trial of SA men who had knifed several members of the Reichsbanner at the end of November 1931. It noted in the reporting of the bourgeois press the "bankruptcy of any sense of morals and respect for the law, not only among the Nazis, but in wide circles of the 'respectable citizenry.' … Acts of violence, brutality, cowardice, unscrupulousness, and mendacity are glorified; everything is good and heroic—if it is aimed against the workers' movement."[59] Shortly thereafter, the *Volksstimme* looked back at the period of the Revolution: "The justified bourgeois pride had no place for the 'saddler's apprentice.' Now the justified bourgeois pride is licking the boots of a decorative painter from Bohemia, who has not achieved anything politically. Republicans were murdered. Nothing stirred in the moral bourgeoisie. It lost all leadership, all moral precepts. Only hatred against the Socialist workers."[60]

These biting words touched exactly the point where the criticism of Hitler and the NSDAP by the anti-Republican though not decidedly National Socialist public stopped and diluted moral standards in favor of strategic political considerations. In a special section titled "Political murder. Looking ahead to the Third Reich," published at the end of February 1932, the *Volksstimme* drew an even larger framework, placing the terror it feared next to the persecution of heretics in the Middle Ages, from where it drew a line to the bloody suppression of the Paris Commune and the "white terror" after World War I. From this perspective, the war itself appeared as the great destroyer of civilization and humanity; it had set humanity back "more than 400 years."[61] This also meant that the rule of the National Socialists would have consequences for the workers' movement that were even direr than the oppression it suffered under the Anti-Socialist Law. The repressive methods of the Bismarck period, supported by a large segment of the bourgeoisie, were thus qualitatively very different from the blatant violence of the NSDAP, which included political murder in its calculus;[62] however, given the growing moral indifference among large sections of the middle class, such a distinction lost its political significance. That is why in the eyes of the *Volksstimme,* as well, the front lines in domestic politics were becoming more obvious. Cooperation was impossible with the National Socialists, and—the toleration policy notwithstanding—with the bourgeois parties if they formed coalitions with the NSDAP. Still, at the end of 1932, the terror that emanated from such prospects for the future seemed to wane. In his review of the year, the chairman of the Magdeburg SPD, Ernst Wittmaack, commented on the NSDAP's prospects for success: "Just as he has emerged, this clay colossus, he will collapse again upon himself."[63] The electoral defeat of the National Socialists on 6 November nourished the fateful belief that the worst was already over.[64]

The Willingness to Fight and "State Authority": The Road to the Emergency Law

As far as the district organ of the SPD was concerned, the response to the National Socialist violence was clear: "Where the enemy of the Republic uses terror and attacks against Republicans, it is necessary to answer in kind," we read in an appeal to the Reichsbanner published by the *Volksstimme* shortly before the elections in September 1930. Such martial tones grew stronger still once the Schufo of the Reichsbanner were set up in response to the success of the NSDAP. The national conference that made this decision adopted an "attack resolution" and called upon all Gau leaders to engage in "activism to the point of fanaticism." "Violence triggers violence!" the *Volksstimme* declared in a commentary on a Reichsbanner rally at the beginning of December, and the appearance of the new Schufo had shown to all the world "that the workers in the district of Magdeburg-Anhalt are determined and able to answer violence with violence." Gustav Ferl, an SPD member of parliament and member of the national board of the Reichsbanner, who had stepped to the speaker's platform dressed in his Schufo uniform, was quoted as saying that his party would "fight for the victory of truth ... with a never-before-seen fanaticism," and would "defend democracy and parliament with bodies and fists." Preparations were also under way "in case the Nazis should provoke civil war. Our weapons then will not be only rotten eggs." Otto Hörsing, no master of refined rhetoric, spoke even more bluntly in January of 1931. The Reichsbanner did not want "civil war and the rolling of heads," he declared, but should "the enemies of the Republic have the gall to lift their dirty fingers against the Republic, they can rest assured that the front of our column will not be holding bouquets of roses in their hands when it opposes them."[65] Such statements and commentaries were surely not suited to calm the domestic political atmosphere. They put the horror scenario of civil war on the table and threatened the use of violence; however, their harshness should also be understood as a result of the shock triggered by the unexpected electoral victory of the NSDAP, the threats made by the party, and the fears of a putsch this engendered.[66]

It is striking, however, that such pronouncements of a willingness to fight back, which put one's own instruments of violence front and center without hesitation, are focused on the first months after 14 September. To be sure, the rest of 1931 also saw references to the possibility that "self-defense" against National Socialists might be necessary, but for now it was the police that were called upon to take robust measures. And while the Schufo, which had been "put on leave" after the ban of the SA, was reconstituted when the ban was lifted, the lead article in the *Volksstimme* avoided pointing to the party's fighting organization, placing the emphasis instead on the duty of the state to ensure the security and safety of its citizens.[67] The martial vocabulary did not disappear, but after the establishment of the Iron Front in the winter of 1931/32, it was elevated to a more abstract level. The willingness of the Iron Front to march and fight was repeatedly emphasized—in words, in symbols like the hammer, and in pictures and campaign posters depicting muscular proletarians with their fists raised ready to strike an enemy who was still not shown, behind them three arrows, the new symbol in the fight against the enemies of the Republic.[68]

But in the face of further massive electoral gains by the NSDAP and the end of the Social Democrats' power in Prussia, resignation and despair were mixed in with the constant emphasis on the willingness to fight. At the same time, there was to be no doubt that the real battle against the National Socialists had to be waged not in the street, but at the ballot box. In an editorial on 23 July 1932, the *Volksstimme* declared that the Reichstag elections would decide "whether we want to be hammer or anvil, free Germans or starving slaves without rights." This battle had to be fought "with sacred passion, with total courage of sacrifice."[69] At the end of the year, when the National Socialist threat seemed to be receding markedly, the rhetoric had returned to the traditional demand concerned with strengthening one's own organization. In a New Year's editorial, SPD Chairman Otto Wels wrote in the *Volksstimme* that this was the time "to bring the striking power of the strongest German workers' party to its highest perfection." "Discipline and the willingness to fight" had always been the "best weapons" of the SPD; they had to be solidified also in 1933. Ernst Wittmaack praised the defensive accomplishments of the Iron Front in the previous year, though he dispensed with any new threats of violence directed against the National Socialists, whom he essentially saw as defeated.[70] Even after Hitler's appointment as Reich chancellor, this line was not abandoned. "The civil war is beginning," the paper declared on 31 January, but the important thing was still to strengthen the Iron Front, to be ready to defend oneself, and beyond that to maintain discipline and "keep one's nerve."[71]

Communist propaganda and the *Klassenkampf* continued to be dominated by fighting words borrowed from military language. The Mansfeld strike was intended as a "successful counterattack" against the capitalist exploiters, and in March 1931 "we will charge forward again in the works council elections." A year later we read: "Let us take Leuna by assault," and during the Reich presidential elections: "Fall into step for Thälmann!" "Advance along the entire line!"[72] Although we hear of the "People's Revolution" (*Volksrevolution*), it seemed like a very distant prospect. The first task was to continue consolidating the "revolutionary mass party," not least through a "revolutionary unity front from below." The more immediate goal was to prepare the "political mass strike that must open the way for the decisive conflict with the capitalist class," but that also, as the "strongest weapon" of all "anti-Fascists," should be used to fend off a takeover of power by the National Socialists.[73]

The conditions and limits to the use of violence were not discussed in this perspective focused on organizational matters. Such a discussion would have been dangerous to the paper's ability to publish, given the attentive readers in the police offices. However, implicit indications of the KPD's understanding of violence could certainly be found. In a commentary on the demonstrations on the occasion of Day of Struggle against Joblessness in March 1930, the *Klassenkampf* praised the behavior of the workers who had "enforced the right to the street"—a success that, as we have seen, was won in violent clashes with the police and cost the lives of two demonstrators in Ammendorf. A month later, a KPD member of the provincial Landtag demanded, at an unemployment rally, that workers must "strike the government and its armed Fascists ruffians wherever you encounter them, after the model of the Reich Youth Day in Leipzig."[74] This was clearly an encouragement to engage in massive violence, for in Leipzig at Easter 1930, two police officers had been shot and killed in clashes with Communists; others had been seriously injured. The choice of words referred to the slogan revived in 1929 by Heinz Neumann, a member of the party's Polbüro: "Strike the Fascists wherever you encounter them!"[75]

Although the party leadership in Berlin soon regarded Neumann's motto as unusable, because it was hoping over the long term to attract voters away from the NSDAP and to the KPD,[76] supporters of the KPD continued to be encouraged to fight for the "right to the street"—if necessary by force—against the police and of course against the SA. "Break the Fascist terror in the Mansfeld region," demanded the *Klassenkampf* in July 1932, later declaring "War against Hitler and Goebbels" after a hall brawl in the middle of January 1933.[77] In the process, the transition from defense to offense could not be clearly identified. The KPD leadership did not issue an unambiguous pronouncement against offensive—and sometimes massive—violence. When the *Klassenkampf* in March 1931 took a look back at the uprising in the industrial region of central Germany ten years earlier, it spoke once again about the provocation by the authorities and the spontaneous resistance of the workers; the only mistake that was conceded on the party's part was that the mobilization had not yet been adequate for a large-scale uprising.[78] The offensive struggle pursued by force of arms in pursuit of a new political order appeared as the final link in a chain of actions that looked essentially no different than it had in the past. This amounted to more than mere toleration of the violence that the rank and file regarded as legitimate.

The *Klassenkampf* responded to Hitler's appointment as Reich chancellor with a call for a heightened readiness to fight. There was no talk of a massive use of force, however. Factories had to be made "strike ready" and "anti-Fascist self-defense units" were to be set up everywhere. "The utmost is now at stake!" we read, but there was no call for resistance by any means or preparation for it.[79] The danger emanating from the new regime was underestimated, while the KPD's own forces were realistically judged to be too weak. What the KPD leadership was preparing for was a certain period of illegality or semi-legality, which would be followed—after the bankruptcy of Hitler's cabinet—by the hour of the KPD.[80] No matter how dangerous the rest of the public believed the Communists to be, their reaction, for all its verbal militancy, gave no indication that a large-scale uprising of workers centrally directed by the Berlin leadership was imminent.

The bourgeois press came out in favor of harsh measures against every form of terror and violence, but we must set their proposals into the context of their ideas about what needed to be changed in domestic politics. To the *Magdeburgische Zeitung* it was clear what fundamental mistakes needed correcting to put a stop to the violence: "The street belongs to traffic and not politics," it tersely stated in December 1930.[81] This pronouncement picked up on the infamous dictum of the former police president of Berlin, Jagow, which he had used in 1910 to publicly threaten the use of force against voting rights demonstrations by the SPD. It betrayed an outdated attitude from the early nineteenth century, which understood politics as communication within circles of notables, while at the same time it regarded "the courage to profess an independent opinion" and the "intellectual struggle for the best opinion" as indispensable. The paper advocated this position as late as March 1933 without recognizing the contradictions in which it had become entangled through its stance vis-à-vis the NSDAP.[82]

Concretely, the first thing that had to be done was to preserve the "authority of the state," to proceed with even-handed toughness against "all asocial elements, no matter the political camp to which they belong or are close to"; on this the paper from Magdeburg and the *Saale-Zeitung* were in agreement. This meant curtailing the right to demonstrate, using the "state's instruments of power" to enforce the ban on uniforms, considering the declaration of a state of emergency when violence kept rising in June/July 1932, and welcoming as a "redemption" (*Erlösung*) the government's announcement at the beginning of August that it intended to execute violent offenders under certain circumstances.[83] Reich President Hindenburg could be relied upon as a "guarantor for peace and order in the land."[84] But the demand for a "uniform authority," articulated by the *Magdeburgische Zeitung* on 17 July in light of the tensions between the Reich, Prussia, and the southern German *Länder*,[85] reveals the political thrust of this seemingly neutral formula. It was aimed at replacing the Prussian state government—which was now acting only in a managing capacity—with a cabinet of the right that pursued the same course as the Reich government. How to get there was open for debate; the *Magdeburgische Zeitung* was not happy about Papen's putsch-like approach and would have preferred an agreement between the NSDAP and the

Center Party in the Prussian Landtag, but neither did it conceal its satisfaction that the "party book civil servants," the greatest evil of the old coalition governments, had finally been done away with.[86] The *Saale-Zeitung* was triumphant, considering 20 July 1932 the "most important day" since 9 November 1918: "Finally there is in postwar Germany once again a firm, manly will and a clear, planned intervention to create state order."[87] The call for the enforcement of "state authority"—which carried male connotations—and for a right-leaning course were inextricably intertwined.

As a result, the condemnation of National Socialist violence lacked the edge of finality. The *Magdeburgische Zeitung* and the paper from Halle, too, for all their sympathy for an authoritarian style of governing and in spite of their mental orientation toward a vanished political culture, could not avoid the recognition that a truly effective cabinet would need broad support in parliament and a mass base if there was to be no "open breach of the constitution." "National concentration" was the title of an editorial in the *Magdeburgische Zeitung* after the elections in November 1932; the chief political task now was the "great coalition of the right from the National Socialists to the Center Party." "Plenary power" for the NSDAP, that is, all power to Hitler's party, was still to be rejected, but after Hitler's oath of legality there was no more reason to place him and his party "under a parliamentary law of exception."[88] Thus the same paper that had issued a scathing verdict of National Socialism in September 1930 was able to acknowledge Hitler's appointment on 30 January 1933 as the logical outcome of a longer process; this was "the conclusion of a development that began eight months ago with the fall of then-Reich Chancellor Brüning ... The parliamentary principle that the opposition must assume responsibility once it has become strong enough for it has now prevailed." The *Magdeburgische Zeitung* had "always been among those who regarded this development as necessary in the interest of clearing up the political atmosphere in Germany."[89] By refraining from simply equating Hitler with his party, it was possible not only to suppress concerns about the programmatic ideas of the NSDAP, but also to portray the perpetrators of violence from within its ranks as marginal phenomena, or at any rate, as nonrepresentative of the NSDAP and the SA. A revision of domestic political conditions seemed possible without dangerous ruptures, now that—as the *Saale-Zeitung* happily noted—the spirit of Harzburg had returned to German politics with the coalition cabinet of 30 January.[90] Other possibilities for resolving the stalemated situation after Schleicher's failure—for example, plebiscitary approval for a governing program over the head of the parliament, which the paper from Halle had still contemplated in the middle of July 1932[91]—were no longer discussed at all. The change to the system that now seemed within easy reach made all earlier concerns melt away.

No restraint was to be shown toward the Communists. In the summer of 1932, when the *Saale-Zeitung* was calling for a state of emergency throughout the Reich to put an end to the civil war–like conditions, it did not fail to point to the "Bolshevist wave" that was supposedly washing across Europe at the time.[92] Both papers had already called for draconian measures against the KPD following the murders at Bülow Square in Berlin in August 1931. "Towards those who have brought about this red civil war one must resort to the instruments of war!" the *Magdeburgische Zeitung* demanded, and the *Saale-Zeitung* wanted to see "the penal law applied to the Communists freed of all political considerations," though it also advocated a response "with all means."[93] When new excesses leading to fatalities and injuries occurred in Germany at the beginning of January 1933, the *Saale-Zeitung* again called upon the government to take "vigorous steps" and pointed to the countries of Italy, Hungary, and Poland, who had succeeded in "destroying Communism." A ban on the KPD should also be considered, whereupon it might be necessary to pass through a "brief zone of fire," though with good preparation this could be managed.[94] The idea of banning the KPD was not entirely new, but the reference to other countries as a model certainly was, especially since it was no secret what kind of bloody methods of repression some of them had used. That the position here had hardened is evident also in the attitude toward Fascist Italy, which struck both papers as worthy of emulation at the end of 1930. While the *Magdeburgische Zeitung* at least still identified the "almost complete absence of public criticism" as the chief fault of the Mussolini regime, the Roman correspondent of the *Saale-Zeitung* would not voice any criticism; he did emphasize, though, that there was no anti-Semitism in Italy—because of the small Jewish share of the population there was "naturally no Jewish question at all"—and expressed the hope "that the Brown Shirts, too, will gradually cast off their anti-Semitism."[95]

While the excesses of the SA after 30 January 1933 were ignored, downplayed, or presented as still unproven, the tone grew even harsher toward the Communists after the Reichstag fire. The *Magdeburgische Zeitung* demanded that the "strike that is now clearly to be carried out by the Communist side against order in the state … must be fended off with all the instruments of power at the state's disposal," though when it came to the followers of the Communists—the "misled mass"—the "instrument of persuasion" should also be used. As for the *Saale-Zeitung,* "the most radical measure is just harsh enough." The new emergency decree, which substantially curtailed basic rights, including freedom of the press, was welcomed, for it would "set in motion the campaign of annihilation—which can no longer be put off—against a party and movement … which have by now turned into a gigantic national political threat." The Magdeburg paper also saw no problem with the emergency decree, since it had already existed in similar form under Stresemann, and it even expressed regret that the government had not decided to once again set up special courts as it had done the previous August.[96]

Only a few days later, the danger had passed. When the results of the Reichstag elections had come in, the *Magdeburgische Zeitung* called upon its readers, "now that the Communist enemy has been defeated, to turn the gaze outward. There is the national front, on which all forces must concentrate!" And the *Saale-Zeitung* emphasized with satisfaction "that it is to the credit of the turning point during these days that on the whole it has so far been as devoid of bloodshed as one could possibly imagine." The enemy was not coming out to fight. "The clay colossus of Marxism has suffered a blow and, crumbling, has collapsed in upon itself like a rotten jug."[97] The lack of surprise reveals that the threat emanating from the KPD was seen, in the end, as a disturbance of "peace and order," which, while very menacing at times, could be controlled by the state's security forces and had not shaken Germany at its foundations. The Communists were criminals and internal enemies, but there were even worse enemies, namely those of the last war, against whom all forces had to be marshaled.

Warnings against the terror perpetrated by the SA were formulated only very cautiously. It was understandable, according to the Magdeburg paper, if, in response to the conduct of the Communists, "the popular will expresses itself spontaneously in demonstrations and sometimes even acts of violence," although it was imperative to return now to a state under the rule of law. These warnings were prompted above all by anti-Semitic excesses in Magdeburg department stores.[98] The *Saale-Zeitung,* as well, did not hide a certain degree of concern, especially in view of the way power had been taken over in the states of southern Germany, but it placed all of this within a larger perspective. The country was in the midst of a "legal revolution," a situation in which there were only two choices: one could be either "hammer or anvil." The race "for the towers and flagpoles" that was being run at the moment against the NSDAP, according to the Hugenberg paper, could not take place without an occasional "collision" and "must not be measured with the yardstick of bourgeois, safe times." After this trivialization of the events in the south and the renunciation of earlier middle-class ideas of the kind the *Magdeburgische Zeitung* was still trying to defend, the *Saale-Zeitung* then employed a medical image: "The 'German case' has been transferred from the internist to the department of surgery. Now cuts are being made, and a light narcosis cannot be avoided. Of course, the boundary against anarchic conditions must also be severely drawn."[99] Here the mental construct of the "national body" (*Volkskörper*) was picked up again, stripping the political enemy of his human character and turning violent measures into "interventions" that were objectively necessary. That the violent perpetrators of the SA, the object of cautious criticism, were not clearly identified here may already be an indication of the paper's own fear of excesses and the censorship that was coming. However, its basic notion that the new revolution undid the Revolution of 1918 and might cause casualties was merely a logical continuation of the ideas about revising the domestic political conditions that had developed up to that point.

When the Enabling Act was finally passed, the *Magdeburgische Zeitung,* too, was unable to cling any longer to its old ideas about the state under the rule of law. It noted a "coordination of the national will in an astonishingly quick period," though it still warned against "confusing this with a uniformization of convictions." It did not name any institutions that could still intervene in this process in a controlling manner. "The men of 30 January no longer have anything controlling them, the only control now is inside of them: their conscience, to which they are responsible for carrying out the work of liberation successfully."[100]

The new regime had established itself. Hardly anything could express more clearly the political and moral bankruptcy of those who prepared the way for it within the bourgeoisie than this helpless appeal to an authority—conscience—that may well have been important to the bourgeois individual of the nineteenth century, but had no meaning whatsoever to the new masters.

Notes

1. Hermann Balle, "Die propagandistische Auseinandersetzung des Nationalsozialismus mit der Weimarer Republik und ihre Bedeutung für den Aufstieg des Nationalsozialismus," PhD diss., University of Erlangen-Nürnberg, 1963, 241–252; Paul, *Aufstand der Bilder,* 120–127; for a general discussion of the change in Social Democratic party work in public see Pyta, *Hitler,* 468–485; Rohe, *Reichsbanner,* 403–417.
2. Balle, "Auseinandersetzung," 253–264; Peter Stein, *Die NS-Gaupresse 1925–1933: Forschungsbericht—Quellenkritik—neue Bestandsaufnahme* (Munich, 1987), specifically on the press in the province of Saxony, 197, 205, 215.
3. *MZ* no. 1, 1 January 1930; no. 1, 1 January 1931; no. 1, 1 January 1932. The paper expressed its position on the revision of the Reich constitution unambiguously on Constitution Day 1931: "The constitution certainly cannot remain in its present form, unless there is to be in the future a persistent discrepancy between written and actual constitutional law." "The monopolistic position of the popular representative body that is found nowhere else in the world" had to be cut back "to a reasonable measure," and "broader authority" had to be given to the Reich president (*MZ* no. 434, 11 August 1931).
4. See, for example, *MZ* no. 1, 1 January 1930.
5. *MZ* no. 1, 1 January 1933; *SZ* no. 307, 31 December 1932.
6. *MZ* no. 690, 18 December 1930.
7. The rally was to take place on 18 December 1930; it was banned by Police President Baerensprung, as was the planned counter-rally by the Reichsbanner.
8. *MZ* no. 436, 12 August; no. 129, 6 March; no. 141, 12 March 1932.
9. *MZ* no. 335, 21 June; no. 401, 24 July; no. 418, 2 August; no. 431, 9 August 1932.
10. *VS* no. 263, 10 November; no. 264, 11 November 1931; no. 1, 1 January 1932. See also the reporting about a rally to commemorate the defeat of the Kapp Putsch with Prussian Minister President Otto Braun in Magdeburg in March 1930 (*VS* no. 65, 18 March 1930).
11. *VS* no. 152, 30 June; no. 172, 23/24 July 1932.
12. *VS* no. 179, 1 August 1932.
13. *VS* no. 263, 7 November 1932. See Winkler, *Weg,* 694, 782, who also points out that after 6 November the SPD leadership was completely at a loss over what to do.
14. Combining elements of both concepts was not very promising, as Schleicher's plans for a "cross front" (*Querfront*) and their rapid failure attest. On this see Axel Schildt, *Militärdiktatur mit Massenbasis? Die Querfrontkonzeption der Reichswehr-Führung um General von Schleicher am Ende der Weimarer Republik* (Frankfurt, 1981), esp. 158ff.; Winkler, *Weg,* 810ff. More recently, Henry A. Turner, *Hitler's Thirty Days to Power: January 1933* (Reading, MA, 1996), in particular 79ff., puts forth the notion that Schleicher's intention was not at all to split the NSDAP but to exert additional pressure on it, and underscores the illusions on which Schleicher's approach was based. Blasius, *Weimars Ende,* 68–78, 116–122, 137–142, shows how Papen and Schleicher used the looming civil war as an argument in their political maneuvering during the final months of the Weimar Republic.
15. For a detailed account see Wirsching, *Weltkrieg,* 419–431.

16. *KK* no. 268, 31 December 1929; no. 100, 30 April; no. 204, 7 November 1931.
17. *KK* no. 84, 11 April 1932.
18. *KK* no. 259, 8 November; no. 194, 20 August 1932. See Winkler, *Weg*, 693f., 780–782.
19. *MZ* no. 36, 19 January 1930; *SZ* no. 56, 7 March 1930. On the clashes themselves see Chapter 9 of this volume.
20. *SZ* no. 215, 13 September 1930.
21. *SZ* no. 306, 31 December 1931. However, see Trauthig, *Kampf*, 286ff., who noted in Protestantism in Württemberg during the final years of Weimar a rise in anti-Bolshevism under the influence of eschatological visions.
22. *MZ* no. 436, 12 August 1931; *SZ* no. 173, 26 July 1930; *MZ* no. 363, 5 July 1932.
23. *SZ* no. 54, 4 March; no. 161, 12 July; no. 166, 18 July 1932; *MZ* no. 363, 5 July 1932.
24. *MZ* no. 393, 20 July 1932. A few days before, the paper had described the Communist with a metaphor from the animal world as "political hyenas of the economic crisis."
25. For a history of the term "subhuman" (*Untermensch*) and its consequences see Reinhart Koselleck, "Zur historisch-politischen Semantik asymmetrischer Gegenbegriffe," in his *Vergangene Zukunft: Zur Semantik geschichtlicher Zeiten* (Frankfurt, 1979), 211–259, here 253–258. On the word *Schädlinge* (pests, vermin), see Chapter 3 of this volume.
26. *VS* no. 56, 7 March; no. 57, 8 March; no. 58, 9 March; no. 132, 8 June; no. 205, 3 September; no. 187, 13 August; no. 193, 20 August 1931.
27. See Winkler, *Weg*, 444–446, 619–626.
28. For a detailed account see Winkler, *Weg*, 444f., 553–555, 618f., 754f., 867f.; Bahne, *KPD*, 22–42.
29. *KK* no. 159, 10 July; no. 166, 18 July; no. 167, 19 July; no. 173, 26 July 1930; no. 12, 15 January 1932.
30. *KK* no. 87, 14 April; no. 96, 25 April 1932.
31. *KK* no. 141, 18 June; no. 302, 31 December 1932.
32. *KK* no. 26, 31 January 1933.
33. *KK* no. 38, 14 February 1933. On the contacts between the SPD and the KPD after Hitler's appointment see Winkler, *Weg*, 867–875.
34. *MZ* no. 690, 18 December; no. 688, 17 December 1930; *SZ* no. 223, 23 September; no. 228, 29 September 1930.
35. *MZ* no. 433, 10 August 1931; *SZ* no. 14, 17 January 1931.
36. *MZ* no. 205, 15 April; no. 209, 17 April 1932; *SZ* no. 61, 12 March 1932. Incidentally, the *MZ* believed that the Stahlhelm should be assessed "very differently" from the Reichsbanner and the SA.
37. *MZ* no. 500, 13 September 1930.
38. For a detailed account see Henry A. Turner, *Big Business and the Rise of Hitler* (New York, 1985).
39. *MZ* no. 506, 16 September 1930; no. 1, 1 January 1931; no. 145, 14 March (emphasis original); no. 198, 11 April; no. 199, 12 April 1932.
40. *SZ* no. 305, 31 December 1930; no. 55, 5 March; no. 261, 5 November 1932.
41. *MZ* no. 500, 13 September 1930.
42. *MZ* no. 193, 9 April 1932.
43. *MZ* no. 189, 7 April 1932; also see no. 155, 9 March 1932, where the suspicion is voiced that this could also be simply "electioneering" on Severing's part.
44. *MZ* no. 205, 15 April 1932.
45. LHAM C 20 Ib 2051/II, fol. 202 (The NS county leader in the Mansfelder Seekreis, Alvensleben, end of October 1931); LHAM C 20 Ib 2049/II, fol. 4 (Speaker Mohr in Wolmirstedt in September 1931); fol. 20 (Jordan on 11 November 1931 in Quedlinburg); fol. 179 (Loeper in Schönebeck on 19 February 1932). For a detailed discussion of the content and defamatory style of Nazi propaganda see Balle, *Auseinandersetzung*, esp. 58ff.; Paul, *Aufstand*, 223ff.
46. *MZ* no. 420, 3 August 1932.

47. *MZ* no. 435, 11 August; no. 438, 12 August; no. 459, 24 August 1932; LHAM C 20 Ib 2051/III, fol. 158 (*Sturmbann* order, 23 August 1932). According to this latter document, the SA comrades in Potempa had, "in their desperation, removed a vile Marxist inciter." On Ohlau see Bessel, *Political Violence,* 85f. The serious clashes, which at times turned into veritable street battles, developed after several hundred SA and Reichsbanner men who were returning from larger rallies encountered each other in Ohlau. It could not be determined who had begun the violence, and injuries occurred on both sides. One SA man drowned after he was thrown, injured, into a body of water; the perpetrator could not be found. On the whole, the Ohlau incident is therefore in no way comparable to the Potempa case, which was clearly a targeted killing. On silence and (restrained) approval as predominant responses within Württemberg Protestantism to the murder of Potempa, see Trauthig, *Kampf,* 47–52.
48. On the gradual erosion of enmity toward the NSDAP in the supra-regional liberal press see Modris Eksteins, *The Limits of Reason: The German Democratic Press and the Collapse of Weimar Democracy* (Oxford, 1975), 213ff., who describes this process as the result of changes in the ownership structure at the various papers, growing disillusionment over the capacity of the Weimar Constitution to function, and an underestimation of how dangerous the National Socialists were. A similar argument was made by Michael Bosch, *Liberale Presse in der Krise: Die Innenpolitik der Jahre 1930 bis 1933 im Spiegel des "Berliner Tageblatts," der "Frankfurter Zeitung" und der "Vossischen Zeitung"* (Frankfurt, 1976), esp. 279ff. By contrast, the continuity in the basic positions is emphasized by Bernd Sösemann, *Das Ende der Weimarer Republik in der Kritik demokratischer Publizisten: Theodor Wolff, Ernst Feder, Julius Elbau, Leopold Schwarzschild* (Berlin, 1976).
49. *SZ* no. 305, 31 December 1930; no. 240, 12 October 1931; no. 89, 16 April 1932. Before the first round of balloting, the paper had supported Duesterberg, before the second it withheld its endorsement.
50. *SZ* no. 186, 10 August 1932. The *Magdeburger Tageszeitung*—close to Hugenberg like the *Saale-Zeitung* but with a smaller circulation than the *Magdeburgische Zeitung*—went even further. The brief reporting about the acts of terror in East Prussia and Silesia culminated in the headline "Attacks and more attacks. Secret orders by the central leadership of the Red Front?" which all but blamed the victims (*Magdeburger Tageszeitung,* no. 185, 9 August 1932). Also revealing was the commentary—both exaggerated and downplaying—on the reaction of the Nazi leadership to the verdict in the Potempa case. The government must not tolerate such behavior, we read; however: "We certainly understand the agitation of the National Socialists, who have suffered hundreds of dead, victims of cowardly murder. All the more reason why the leaders should remain calm and not incite the people with such appeals" (*Magdeburger Tageszeitung,* no. 198, 24 August 1932). On the relativization of Nazi violence in Württemberg Protestantism see Trauthig, *Kampf,* 69–75.
51. *KK* no. 133, 10 June 1930; no. 62, 14 March; no. 143, 21 June; no. 154, 3 July 1932; no. 30, 4 February 1933; no. 183, 11 August 1932.
52. See also Rosenhaft, *Beating the Fascists,* 81–87; Fischer, *Communism,* 102–117.
53. *VS* no. 187, 13 August; no. 191, 18 August; no. 192, 19 August 1931; no. 44, 20/21 February; no. 89, 15 May 1932.
54. *VS* no. 249, 24 October 1931.
55. *VS* no. 187, 13 August 1931.
56. *VS* no. 198, 23 August 1932.
57. *VS* no. 202, 27/28 August 1932.
58. *VS* no. 291, 13 December 1930.
59. *VS* no. 54, 3 March 1932.
60. *VS* no. 99, 27 April 1932.
61. *VS* no. 44, 20/21 February 1932. Of all the papers examined here, the *Volksstimme* was also the only one that commemorated in detail the tenth anniversary of the murder of Walter Rathenau (*VS* no. 147, 24 June 1932).

62. On the SPD's ideas of what a National Socialist–led Germany would look like, see Pyta, *Hitler,* 91–109.
63. *VS* no. 308, 31 December 1932.
64. See Pyta, *Hitler,* 181–193, who sees the persistent perception of the NSDAP as, in the final analysis, a bourgeois class party as the chief reason why the majority of the SPD underestimated the danger posed by the NSDAP and its chances of success in the fall and winter of 1932/33.
65. *VS* no. 207, 5 September; no. 222, 23 September; no. 281, 2 December 1930; no. 15, 18 January 1931.
66. See Winkler, *Weg,* 216; Rohe, *Reichsbanner,* 365ff.; Pyta, *Hitler,* 485–492, who, strangely enough, does not mention the formation of the Schufo. Into this context we should also place the blocking of the NSDAP rally with Hitler in Magdeburg in the middle of December 1930. If Hitler did not permit any other speakers, the Reichsbanner—which had been denied the chance to offer a counter speech at previous meetings—threatened to prevent the rally. When the *Volksstimme* presented the eventual ban as a "democratic lesson" for Hitler and his men, this certainly trivialized the behavior of its own side. Of course, the following comment was to the point: "If a gang of burglars were to undertake to organize itself to the point were it felt strong to keep the police at bay or even make one of the gang police president, it would not occur to any citizen that this represented anything more than the "legal exploitation of democracy" (no. 291, 13 December 1930). Rohe's statement (*Reichsbanner,* 364) that this move to prevent the meeting meant a "conscious transition to counter-terror" goes too far.
67. *VS* no. 187, 13 August 1931; no. 66, 17 March; no. 147, 24 June 1932.
68. *VS* no. 295, 18 December 1931; no. 44, 20/21 February; no. 202, 27/28 August 1932. For an instructive and detailed discussion of the modernization of the SPD propaganda and its limits see Pyta, *Hitler,* 468–485; also see Rohe, *Reichsbanner,* 403–417.
69. *VS* no. 172, 23/24 July 1932.
70. *VS* no. 308, 31 December 1932. On the vacillating mood in the Reichsbanner after 20 July 1932, when the paramilitary activities were stepped up, the leadership pursued a course of greater distance from the SPD, while resignation and passivity grew among many members; see Rohe, *Reichsbanner,* 438–461.
71. *VB* no. 26, 31 January; no. 29, 3 February; no. 35, 10 February 1933. The *Volksstimme* is no longer available for the period after 31 December 1932, but its sister paper from Halle advocated positions that were no different. The *Volksblatt* was banned on 24 February 1933.
72. *KK* no. 133, 10 June 1930; no. 63, 16 March 1931; no. 68, 18 March; no. 79, 5 April; no. 80, 6 April 1932.
73. *KK* no. 12, 15 January; no. 58, 10 March 1930; no. 14, 17 January; no. 63, 16 March; no. 100, 30 April 1931; no. 166, 18 July 1932.
74. *KK* no. 56, 7 March 1930; LHAM C 20 Ib 2041/II, fols. 29–31 (RP Merseburg to OP, 24 March 1930); fol. 122 (Gendarme of Lochau to RP Merseburg, 22 August 1930), the quote from the record of the gendarme. The parliamentarian was later given a jail term of three months in keeping with the Law for the Protection of the Republic.
75. Max Lademann, for example, a leading member of the KPD in the district, was fined in June 1930 for using it: LHAM C 20 Ib 2041/II, fols. 100–103 (Verdict of the Lay Assessors' Court Halle, 23 June 1930).
76. Winkler, *Weg,* 184f.; Rosenhaft, *Beating the Fascists,* 57–81, esp. 64f.
77. *KK* no. 153, 2 July 1932; no. 12, 14 January 1933. An example from January 1932 in LHAM C 20 Ib 2041/III, fol. 74 (RP Magdeburg to OP, 22 January 1932). According to this document, during a meeting of jobless in Aken/Elbe a KPD speaker pointed to the unemployed in Magdeburg who, by throwing rocks in front of city hall, had pushed through the acceptance of their demands. One could learn from them about the fight against the police and the parties, who were all against the KPD.
78. *KK* no. 63, 16 March 1931.

79. *KK* no. 26, 31 January; no. 27, 1 February 1933.
80. Bahne, *KPD*, 41f.
81. *MZ* no. 668, 7 December 1930.
82. *MZ* no. 387, 17 July; no. 418, 2 August 1932; no. 118, 5 March 1933.
83. *MZ* no. 688, 17 December; no. 690, 18 December 1930; no. 313, 10 June; no. 355, 1 July 1932; *SZ* no. 165, 16 July 1932; *MZ* no. 387, 17 July; no. 393, 20 July; no. 420, 3 August 1932; *SZ* no. 186, 10 August 1932.
84. *MZ* no. 329, 18 June 1932.
85. *MZ* no. 387, 17 July 1932.
86. *MZ* no. 397, 22 July 1932.
87. *SZ* no. 169, 21 July 1932.
88. *MZ* no. 411, 29 July; no. 697, 6 November; no. 600, 8 November; no. 602, 9 November 1932; no. 56, 31 January 1933.
89. *MZ* no. 56, 31 January 1933.
90. *SZ* no. 26, 31 January 1933. On the image of Hitler in supra-regional, right-leaning dailies see Eva Pfeifer, "Das Hitlerbild im Spiegel einiger konservativer Zeitungen in den Jahren 1929–1933," PhD diss., University of Heidelberg, 1966. According to Pfeifer, certain concerns about Hitler's competence did not disappear, but they were given less weight than his ability to mobilize the masses.
91. *SZ* no. 162, 13 July 1932.
92. *SZ* no. 165, 16 July 1932.
93. *MZ* no. 436, 12 August 1931; *SZ* no. 192, 17 August 1931.
94. *SZ* no. 2, 3 January; similarly no. 22, 26 January 1933.
95. *MZ* no. 668, 7 December 1930; *SZ* no. 227, 27 September 1930. Otherwise, however, a detailed engagement with the anti-Semitism of the NSDAP is missing from the two papers, which did not use anti-Semitic arguments themselves. Nazi anti-Semitism was bothersome, but it was not perceived as a major problem of the new movement. On the discussion of the Fascist system carried on in Germany at the end of the Weimar Republic see most recently Wolfgang Schieder, "Das italienische Experiment: Der Faschismus als Vorbild in der Krise der Weimarer Republik," *HZ* 262 (1996): 73–125. Schieder points out that even some liberal writers considered using the Fascist model of government against the NSDAP in Germany.
96. *MZ* no. 110, 1 March; no. 112, 2 March 1933; *SZ* no. 51, 1 March 1933.
97. *MZ* no. 120, 6 March 1933; *SZ* no. 58, 9 March 1933.
98. *MZ* no. 128, 10 March; no. 129, 11 March 1933.
99. *SZ* no. 58, 9 March 1933. For a detailed discussion of Württemberg Protestantism's trivialization of the terror that accompanied the *Machtergreifung* see Trauthig, *Kampf*, 385ff., esp. 396ff.
100. *MZ* no. 155, 25 March 1933.

Conclusion

Political Violence and the Weimar Republic's Chances of Survival

Murders and civil war–like fighting were not typical of the political violence of the Weimar Republic as a whole, even though it may seem that way at first glance. Rather, the present study has shown that the violence between 1921 and 1933 took the form of a struggle over public terrain and symbols, which often assumed ritualistic features and was characterized by the use of limited methods and instruments. This "small" violence of street fighting and hall brawls reflected the absence of a basic political consensus and the partial loss of the state's monopoly of force.[1] In that respect, the violence was a constant burden on the political process and prevented political conflicts in the Weimar Republic from taking a "normal"—that is, essentially peaceful—course. At the same time, because the violence was largely ritualized in nature until the onset of the Great Depression, it was impossible to predict whether it would escalate further or recede. The main contention of this study is that the political violence of the ritualized struggle over terrain gradually became, after 1921, an endemic but not uncontrollable phenomenon. There were two reasons behind this development. First, the rise of the right-wing Combat Leagues and their claim to the public sphere of the street galvanized Social Democrats and Communists into mobilizing and organizing their followers in a similar fashion. Second, "masculinity," though with connotations that varied in their aggressiveness, became a central value in all political subcultures.

This is not to say that the political violence in the Weimar Republic can be reduced simply to brawls between the Stahlhelm and the Communist RFB. It began with the circumscribed civil war between 1919 and 1921. However, the political relevance of this civil war becomes apparent only in a long-term perspective—one that includes the prewar period, inquires into the chances of alternative developments in the early years of the Republic, and does not see the years after 1921 determined a priori by what had come before. This is the

Notes from this chapter begin on page 314.

perspective I have taken in this book. That is why the circumscribed civil war fighting of 1919–1921 cannot be understood merely as the result of a widespread "brutalization" as a result of the experience of World War I. Brutalization through exposure to violence while fighting on the front lines might have affected at most a minority of front-line soldiers. This is suggested, above all, by the finding that the behavior of the Landesjägerkorps, the Home Guards, the Reichswehr, and the Schutzpolizei was, on the whole, measured and restrained between 1919 and 1921. Responsibility for the atrocities in 1920 and 1921 lay chiefly with former fighters in the Baltic region. It would appear that the ideologically charged war against the Bolshevik troops in the Baltic, conducted with no regard for the traditional laws of war, had a brutalizing effect, which is also reflected in the violent careers of later SA and SS leaders[2]—but it involved a comparatively small number of German soldiers. If the left-leaning workers among the demobilized soldiers picked up arms again, as was the case in March 1920, they did so for the most part not because they enjoyed fighting, but in an act of self-defense against the imminent counterrevolution. It is not coincident that those who moved against the Schutzpolizei with more offensive motives a year later had a noticeably younger average age, which means that among their ranks were far more fighters who had not served in the war.

What was important in the end—and this is the crucial point—was not the war experience itself, but the way in which it was interpreted in the political conflict of the postwar period.[3] No small number of those involved in the violent clashes then and in subsequent years were already married and had children. Most were adults, had completed their education, and—in the early years—probably had a job as well, though one cannot identify a particular occupational profile. Also, most of them did not have a prior criminal record. It is therefore difficult to explain the political violence of the first as well as later years of the Weimar Republic with the help of specific characteristics of those who perpetrated it. An important role on the left was no doubt the absence of socialization into the Social Democratic workers' movement, while on the right fears of losing social status weighed heavily; in the final years unemployment was added as an important factor. The crucial element, however, was the way in which such factors were transformed by processes of mobilization and interpretation within the political culture.

It would therefore be too simplistic to see a deep-seated and lasting traumatization of the bourgeoisie through military defeat, revolution, and inflation as the primary cause behind the political violence in the early years of the Weimar Republic and subsequently. And this violence was even less the inescapable result of attempted uprisings by the Communists.[4] For one, on the bourgeois side the fighting of the early years was rooted in its old fears about the Social Democratic workers' movement; after November 1918 and in view of the reality of Bolshevik rule in Russia, these fears were transferred to the radical left in Germany and were, without a doubt, massively intensified. Before 1914, the bourgeois press had reproached the leaders of the SPD for turning the street into the stage of politics, thereby conjuring up the danger that the "rabble" would disturb the public order and criminals would have an easier playing field. After 1918, the radical left was also accused of making deals with criminals, and eventually it was equated with the latter. The use of the military against the strike movement in the spring of 1919 met with approval from the bourgeoisie because—whether pro-Republican or not—it saw the strike as a pure test of strength by the radical left.

For another, in the early years of the Republic, the fear of the workers' movement that haunted the bourgeoisie was by no means so deep that it saw any form of violence against it, including extralegal measures, as legitimate. Within the bourgeois public—shaped in the province of Saxony not by conservative, but fundamentally liberal papers—the workers' resistance to the Kapp Putsch was not unanimously rejected but met with understanding and even a certain measure of approval. And the food protests of the years of inflation, a source of unrest and violence that flared up time and again, were certainly not seen as the work of Communist manipulators, but recognized for having a dynamic of their own.

Above all, however, the passivity of the Home Guards is a persuasive argument for the need to reassess the fear of Bolshevism among urban dwellers and farmers—the "bourgeoisie" in the political sense. In 1919/20, the Home Guards in the province of Saxony, as elsewhere, were organized throughout the province and massively armed; by far the vast majority of their members belonged to the propertied class in city and countryside. But all these thousands of armed men barely lifted a finger when Kapp and his followers attempted to overthrow the government in Berlin in March 1920, or when fighting subsequently broke out between the military and armed workers in many places, including the province of Saxony. In fact, in most cases the guards allowed themselves to be disarmed almost without resistance. Had the bourgeoisie, after the Revolution and the spring unrest and fighting in 1919, been truly haunted by a deep-seated, highly emotional fear of Bolshevism that completely dominated its political worldview, it would have had the opportunity now to "settle the score" with the radical left and at the same time bring down the unloved Republic. Nothing of the sort happened. The Home Guards had neither prepared for deployment in support of the revolution of the Berlin putschists, which perhaps was owing to logistical problem, nor did they intervene in the fighting on a broad front, which they could have done with the simple justification that they were ensuring "peace and order." They did not stage a "night of the long knives," nor did they move against the leading representatives of the radical left with deliberate measures of violence. The Home Guards therefore did not play the key role many scholars have assigned to them: that of habituating large segments of the bourgeoisie to the use of violence—including extralegal violence—against the left.[5]

Instead, the Home Guards reveal the limits to how highly charged the old hostile image of the Socialist workers' movement could become, and to its continuation on the prewar pattern. Those rural counties in which the Home Guards had especially high membership were mostly strongholds of rural-farming conservatism, whose basic positions had always included a pronounced hostility toward the city and its industrial working class. And *this* is also where the strongholds of the German Nationals were in the Reichstag elections of 1920 just as in 1919, not in those towns and counties that had experienced the violence of the circumscribed civil war first hand, where, as in Halle itself, the DNVP, as the toughest opponent of the left, did not achieve above-average rates of growth in 1920. The primary concern of the bourgeoisie in 1919/20 was not the imminent destruction of bourgeois society and culture, which one had to fend off with all one's power (such fears were articulated only in a brief phase at the beginning of 1919), but the lasting disruption of Germany's revival by the activities of the radical left. For this revival, especially after the Versailles Treaty, the "unity" of all Germans was indispensable. The radical left posed a threat because it upset this unity, not because it was capable of shaking German society and culture to their foundations. The German workers—the "masses" that were necessary for another revolution—seemed on the whole too level-headed to foment a full-scale upheaval. To be sure, a number of burghers wanted to have a paramilitary organization—the Orgesch—at their disposal in order to exert pressure on the left, but for most burghers the deployment of the state's security forces seemed adequate to deal with the saboteurs of the required unity.

The reason why the bourgeois public demanded toughness from these forces and was willing to overlook atrocities lies chiefly in the combination of two factors: the hostile image of the "party of rebellion," used against the SPD prior to 1914 and now applied to the radical left, and the primacy of "order" in Germany, considered absolute at least since the Versailles Treaty and now also embraced by the governing SPD. The course pursued by the USPD or KPD leadership played only a secondary role. However, the leaders of the radical left *did* bear some responsibility because they took an unclear stance toward offensive violence—not directly calling for it, but describing it as a legitimate instrument—and because, after the merger of the leftist USDP with the KPD, they endowed the notion of civil war, hitherto used by all sides as a metaphor for the greatest imaginable horror, with positive connotations. The propaganda and behavior of the KPD leadership in March 1921, and especially the fighting methods of a man like Max Hoelz, then fit seamlessly into a perceptual pattern that defined the Communists as political criminals who destroyed property and spread chaos. It is therefore difficult to imagine anything more disastrous for the young mass party than that half-hearted and completely miscarried putsch attempt, during which a man rose to prominence who was in no way representative of the party as a whole. On the one hand, it permanently lost the membership "mass" it had just succeeded in bringing into its fold, who wanted nothing to do with putschist adventures. On the other hand, the image of the Communist Party was now firmly established among the bourgeoisie. Had Hoelz not intervened in the conflict, most likely it would not have gone beyond a few skirmishes in and around Eisleben.

The findings for the years 1918 to 1921 that I have summarized here once again, especially the relative unimportance of the Home Guards, raise the more general question of whether there were missed opportunities and alternative possibilities of development that cast the fate of the Weimar Republic in a less deterministic light. To be sure, the findings for the province of Saxony can be applied to other parts of Germany only with qualifications. The civil war fighting in the spring of 1919 in Berlin, the Ruhr region, and in Munich undoubtedly was carried on with far greater intensity, and involved more brutality on the part of the Free Corps, than was the case in the province of Saxony. To that extent, it left deeper chasms and may have led to a stronger radicalization of everyone involved. The same is true for some of the clashes in the wake of the Kapp Putsch, especially for the renewed fighting in the Ruhr region and the fighting in Gotha, for example.[6] But as important as these places and regions were, the passivity of the Home Guards seems to have been, on the whole, the rule and not the exception—leaving aside the special case of Bavaria and parts of Prussia east of the Elbe. It is also likely that outside of the province of Saxony, as well, the food protests, which followed in the footsteps of nineteenth-century forms and displayed a strikingly high participation by women, were not immediately attributed to left-radical machinations, but interpreted as a phenomenon with roots of its own, though also with potentially dangerous consequences for the political order.[7] Moreover, there is no need to assume that the local and regional climate of the press in the bourgeois camp was thoroughly dominated by anti-Republican papers as early as 1919–1921.

Therefore a good deal of evidence spurs us to take the political maneuvering room offered especially in the "dreamland of the truce," i.e., at the turn of 1918/19, very seriously. The possibilities for changes in the bureaucracy and the judicial system, in the military and the economy, were far more extensive than the changes that actually occurred—this has often been emphasized.[8] But the findings presented here also indicate that the shock of revolution and the fear of Bolshevism were not so deeply ingrained in the bourgeoisie as to form an ineradicable political constant at the turn of 1918/19. If those individuals and political forces in Germany who were responsible for war and defeat had been clearly named and harshly criticized, there would have been a much better chance of more staunchly reinforcing the left-liberal currents within the German bourgeoisie, which had gained strength on the eve of the war, and providing a more solid foundation for the Republic. The circumscribed civil war in the spring of 1919 would have impeded such a development, but it would not have blocked it entirely. As it was, radical nationalism was able to consolidate once more the influence it had won in the late *Kaiserreich* and to slowly—though not without help from the radical left—impose its interpretation of the war and the defeat on the bourgeois-national camp.

One of the nationalists' most important instruments after 1921 was the Combat Leagues, chief among them the Stahlhelm, which in their own way proved to be a brilliant political innovation. Their chief accomplishment was to open up the street to the bourgeoisie as a sphere of political action. In so doing they picked up on the models from the *Kaiserreich,* its veterans' organizations and military parades, even as they expanded their functional radius. On the outside, the Stahlhelm and the other leagues presented themselves as a reserve army that proved to recent foes that Germany was able to defend itself; on the inside they styled themselves as a model of a seemingly classless national community led by its leaders in accordance with the principle of command and obedience. They embodied the "unity" of the German nation that one should aspire to, as well as the initially absent "unity" of the bourgeois parties—in Protestant Germany, to be more precise.[9] Their legitimacy lay in the conviction that their recollection and interpretation of the war was the "correct" one. With this general goal of promoting unity, the Stahlhelm and like-minded associations enjoyed prospects for success in both the cities and the countryside and thus were able to find supporters within the entire bourgeois-national camp.

Because the right-wing Combat Leagues used the public realm of the street as a political stage, they competed with the workers' movement, which had previously claimed this space as its own. Since the leagues acted out martial manliness with a counterrevolutionary thrust in this public venue, the concrete demonstration of that manliness in the form of physical violence was a possible consequence of such displays, especially when they were deliberately staged in the strongholds of the workers' movement. It was not inevitable that these public displays would spawn violence, as the relative calm during the marches and parades of the middle Weimar years demonstrates; rather, it happened only gradually as the Stahlhelm and the other associations established their organizational network. However, without the Combat Leagues on the right, political violence would not have turned into a permanent phenomenon.

The left did not react right away. Neither the assassination of Matthias Erzberger nor the murder of Walther Rathenau prompted the SPD to begin setting up its own Combat League, and even as late as 1923 only initial steps had been taken. It was not until 1924, after the Hitler putsch had demonstrated just how dangerous the right-wing extremists gathering in Bavaria were, that the Reichsbanner was established by the Social Democrats and bourgeois Republicans. The KPD leadership tried to set up paramilitary formations in 1923 in the context of a new offensive course, but once again it was thwarted by its own supporters, alongside the ban of the Prussian government. Hyperinflation ratcheted up the political crisis as high as it could go, but at the same time it led to a confusing fragmentation as the society was thrown back into the daily struggle for survival, a situation that was bound to impede the formation of potent armies of civil war. Only the RFB would prove a success—even if its attractiveness failed to extend beyond party members—because it imitated the other associations in promoting the cult of manly military readiness, but it did not prepare for concrete violent actions. If a real threat of civil war emanated from any side prior to 1923, it came from the radical right, not from the radical left.

The Communists did not exist, in any case. There was constant tension between the party leadership and the party base, which manifested itself not least in the question of the use of violence. The starting position was the same for both sides: the radical left, and then the KPD as a whole, saw itself confronted by a "coalition of order" (Weitz) made of industrialists, the bureaucracy, the military, and the police, for which Social Democrats often bore the political responsibility and which found whatever support it needed among the bourgeois and Social Democratic public. In the early years of the Weimar Republic, this coalition of order had employed disproportionately massive force to keep the radical left at bay, and thereafter it was always quick, in cases of conflict, to put the continuing threat of violence into practice. Responding to this with violence seemed only natural, but there remained some room for maneuver. To fight the advance of the right-wing military associations and of the political forces allied with them, the Communist base (and parts of the Social Democratic base) resorted to the instrument of "small" violence after the model of the "street politics" (Lindenberger) of the prewar period. It was intended to let one's own strength be felt by the enemy, who was to be taught a lesson, without inflicting any serious, let alone lethal, injuries. Only when the other side clearly transgressed such boundaries through the use of firearms—as happened in Sommerschenburg in July 1922, for example—was it possible for the situation to escalate.

Attacks on the police were generally along these same lines. Assassination attempts were not part of the repertoire of the Communist rank and file. The KPD leadership, by contrast, always regarded offensive violence as a possible form of action; however, its attempts to create potent paramilitary formations or an efficient military apparatus were supported only by a small circle of committed activists, while most party members looked upon them with incomprehension and rejected them. The violent measures of the "coalition of order" turned many workers into Communists who remained loyal to the party because they wanted radically different politics, for which the paradise in the East seemed to be the model, but what they did *not* want were violent adventures in which they were "burned up" by the party leadership for its own purposes. Those Communists in Halle who, on 11 May 1924, responded very indifferently to the call for a demonstration by their leadership knew full well why they would not allow themselves to be driven in front of the guns of the police.

The KPD leadership thus bore some responsibility for the disastrous situation in which the party eventually found itself at the end of the Weimar Republic. Its propaganda of violence in word and image, which had reached its first high point in the agitation for "civil war" in 1924, kept providing the grateful bourgeois public with further confirmation of its image of the Communist enemy. Every act of "small" violence against Stahlhelm members and, later, SA men added more evidence, even though the threats of civil war issued by the KPD leadership had little or nothing to do with the beatings meted out by its members. In the brief phase of realpolitik in 1926/27, the KPD pursued a somewhat different course, taking seriously the immediate interests of the workers in the factories and toning down its polemic against the SPD. At that time the police noted little violence surrounding the marches of the RFB and the other Combat Leagues. It is doubtful and remains a point of speculation whether the continuation of this course would have substantially altered the image of the KPD among the public, and if so, how long it would have taken. At least there was an opportunity, through work in the factories (as well as in the various parliamentary committees, from the local parliaments on up) to achieve practical successes and to hold on to members this way, rather than through verbal radicalism. A continuation of this course would presumably also have had a dampening effect on violence by the rank and file. Although the "order coalition" tended over the long term to push the KPD out of the factories, by the middle of the 1920s the party still had sufficient strongholds and was by no means consigned to the street as its chief sphere of action.[10] At any rate, the turn to the extreme left in 1928/29 was, in spite of the events of May 1929, not forced upon the party by its enemies, but brought about largely by the now completely Stalinized and Moscow-dependent party leadership under Thälmann.

The seeds of the escalation of violence in the last years of Weimar were sown during the supposedly calm middle years. The sought-after unity of the (Protestant) bourgeoisie, which as a whole was moving increasingly toward the right, seemed to have been briefly attained with Hindenburg's election in 1925, but the concrete political results were disappointing. Now the Stahlhelm—alongside the other, similarly positioned right-wing Combat Leagues—could try to hold onto its members by displaying greater radicalness and violence in its public appearances, or by becoming directly involved in politics. As is attested by the establishment of small-caliber shooting clubs and the conflict over the "stick ban," steps were taken to pursue the first strategy; the second was also pursued, though in the end unsuccessfully. In any case, the move to ratchet up the violence called out the opposing groups and contributed to the spread of violence. The Stahlhelm made yet another attempt to hold on to its younger members by creating military sports groups, but with no success. In the SA and the NSDAP, the Stahlhelm and the bourgeois parties now faced competition that was hard to beat against the backdrop of the Great Depression. The NSDAP radicalized the concept of the united "national community" (*Volksgemeinschaft*) by issuing threats against the Communists and Jews who were to be expelled from it, and by crudely attacking the Weimar "system" as such; the SA radicalized the concept of the Combat Leagues by defining itself as no longer a veterans' organization but a fighting force against the political system, by taking the activism of the old organizations to a new level, and by displaying greater brutality.

Still, even in 1932 Germany was not in imminent danger of drowning in an uncontainable flood of violence, let alone a real civil war. As is indicated above, the seeds of an escalation of violence in the confrontations between the Combat Leagues had already been sown in the middle years. In the new crisis the belligerence picked up pace, leading to an increased use of firearms and a rising number of those seriously injured or killed. However, the SA could not cross certain boundaries, lest it become embroiled in serious conflicts with the state and no longer be able to maintain a credible reputation as a reserve force for order. Although the Communist rank and file, the chief enemy of the SA, found itself in a structurally inferior situation, it still did not resort to fighting methods that were generally harsher than before. The KPD as a whole was once again in a disastrous position. After its Combat League had been outlawed, it was not able to create a potent alternative against the backdrop of the economic crisis, while at the same time it was confronted by an NSDAP/SA that was continually gaining strength. When the KPD leadership tried to commit the rank and file to a new, ultra-left course and in the process abandoned realistic, day-to-day politics—the results of which were driven home not least in the Mansfeld strike—it provided at least indirect encouragement of the violence committed by its supporters. The police responded to this with often lethal harshness, picking up on patterns of behavior from the early Weimar years and continuing its "militarization," which had become apparent back then. However, police tactics during the demonstrations in the middle years, police conduct during the Mansfeld strike, and countless interventions to contain the violence of brawls during the later years attest that there were alternatives to this tough response.

With the requisite political will, the violence of the final phase of the Weimar Republic could at least have been brought under control. The ban on the SA that was initiated by the Prussian government proved potent and effective, especially since the Communists, too, remained largely quiet after it took effect. Consistently enforced, it could have prevented the terrible escalation of violence in the summer of 1932 and in this regard calm the political situation. But the path chosen by the new Reich government met with support from a bourgeois public that should have known—at the latest after the murder in Potempa and Hitler's response to the subsequent verdict of the special court—whom it was dealing with. In the end, the failure to see the threat posed by the National Socialists was not grounded in a deep-rooted fear of the Communists, even though that fear had grown again since 1929, but in the hope placed in the political and future military potential offered by this rapidly rising mass movement. A "coalition to break up the Republic" had been forming since 1924, and its radical wing was now pushing increasingly to the fore.[11] It was not the case that the extremes on either side of the political spectrum drove each other forward, leaving the bourgeoisie in the end with no choice but to pick one side or the other. Rather, National Socialism stood in a tradition of bourgeois-national opposition to the Weimar Republic, which it radicalized so successfully against the backdrop of crisis that voters flocked to it in large numbers.

While the Communists were not entirely blameless in this, they were not the chief cause. Back in the middle Weimar years, the boundary between the bourgeois-national and the Socialist camps had rigidified, which was reflected not least in the way political violence developed. While Communists and Social Democrats hardly ever clashed in physical confrontations, both appeared on the scene as enemies of the right-wing groups. Without the Great Depression, the Weimar state would presumably not have been delivered into the hands of the National Socialists. But precisely the history of the Combat Leagues suggests that the course for an authoritarian revision of the political system had already been set in the middle years; and while this revision need not have assumed the dimensions of the Third Reich, it would have led to the partial return of the power structures that had existed under the *Kaiserreich*.[12] The history of political violence in the Weimar Republic is one piece of evidence that the Republic failed, in the final analysis, because large segments of the bourgeoisie were unable to free themselves of their outdated authoritarian frame of mind.[13]

For the growing number of bourgeois opponents of the Republic, the Communists and eventually the Social Democrats as well were troublemakers who stood in the way of the desired "unity" of the national community. As my discussion of the positions of the (right-) liberal to the national-conservative press in Saxony has demonstrated, this anti-Communism was not necessarily combined with anti-Semitism, and was conceivable also without it. Without question, explicit anti-Semitism became more important and radical, as evidenced, for example, by the rise of the DVP and the exclusion of Jewish members from the Stahlhelm, but for now it was still a minority phenomenon. The extreme anti-Semitism of the National Socialists was clearly rejected by the moderate bourgeois public, which is probably why it did not lead to violent actions on a larger scale, as they would have merely hurt the party. But this opposition was not sufficiently committed or sustained to form the basis of tough resistance to Nazi policies. When the SA—following the rapid victory over the Communists that it achieved with brutal violence, a victory it used to restore its damaged self-image—turned against the next enemy, it was predictable that its actions would encounter vigorous opposition only at the beginning. Once Communists and Social Democrats were no longer able to impede the desired unity, a new scapegoat for all problems had to be found. The Communists were replaced by the Jews, this time with consequences that were far more horrendous.

Notes

1. See Norbert Elias, "Die Zersetzung des staatlichen Gewaltmonopols in der Weimarer Republic," in his *Studien über die Deutschen: Machtkämpfe und Habitusentwicklung im 19. und 20. Jahrhundert* (Frankfurt, 1989), 282–294.
2. See Waite, *Vanguard,* 285ff.
3. There is no doubt that soldiers can be brutalized while serving at the front line, as has been demonstrated, for example, for German soldiers on the Eastern Front during World War II; see Omer Bartov, *Hitler's Army: Soldiers, Nazis, and War in the Third Reich* (Oxford, 1992). An entirely different question, however, is what happens to this brutalization after the war, how rapidly and under what conditions it "disappears," as it were, or under what conditions it acquires lasting political influence. This, precisely, is central to the question I am discussing here. Reinhart Koselleck already pointed to the methodological problem of trying to determine the relative importance of war experiences, prior proclivities, and later processing: "Der Einfluß der beiden Weltkriege auf das soziale Bewußtsein," in W. Wette, ed., *Der Krieg des kleinen Mannes: Eine Militärgeschichte von unten* (Munich, 1992), 324–343. A comparison with the development of England after 1918 or Germany after 1945 would make this point even more

clearly. An attempt to make such a comparison for the years after 1918 in Europe is Andreas Wirsching and Dirk Schumann, eds., *Violence and Society after the First World War,* published in Munich as *Journal of Modern European History* 1, no. 1 (2003) with contributions by Adrian Gregory (on Britain), Benjamin Ziemann (on Germany), Andreas Wirsching (on France and Italy), Dietrich Beyrau (on Russia), and Pjotr Wrobel (on Eastern Europe), and featuring a comparative essay by Dirk Schumann.

4. This is the old thesis, found, for example, in Karl-Dietrich Erdmann, *Die Weimarer Republik* (Munich, 1980), 80ff.; Schulze, *Freikorps,* 69ff.
5. This was still assumed by Weisbrod, *Gewalt,* 393f.; Diehl, *Paramilitary Politics,* 55ff., 75ff.; Geyer, "Nation," 35.
6. See Matthiesen, "Radikalisierungen"; idem, *Bürgertum.*
7. See Geyer, *Verkehrte Welt,* 167ff.
8. Concisely summarized in Kolb, *Die Weimarer Republik,* 157–163; Winkler, *Weimar,* 67f.
9. In addition to Fritzsche, *Rehearsals,* and Lapp, *Revolution,* esp. 131ff., see on this Fritzsche, *Germans into Nazis,* esp. 83ff., a brilliant essay on the influence of populist political conceptions after 1914, though he exaggerates the dissolution of the traditional milieu under the banner of the *Volksgemeinschaft.*
10. In this regard, Weitz is wrong, *Communists,* 160ff.
11. M. Rainer Lepsius, "Machtübernahme und Machtübergabe: Zur Strategie des Regimewechsels 1918/19 und 1932/33," in his *Demokratie in Deutschland: Soziologisch-historische Konstellationsanalysen. Ausgewählte Aufsätze* (Göttingen, 1993), 80–94, the quote on 86.
12. In disagreement with Wirsching, *Weltkrieg,* esp. 6ff., 21, it must be said that his model of two competing totalitarian movements fails to cast adequate light onto the prewar roots of the radical right and the right-wing Combat Leagues, as well as the new elements of the political culture they developed, as a precondition for the rise of the NSDAP. See also his essay "Kommunistischer 'Antifaschismus' in Berlin und Paris zwischen the Weltkriegen," in D. Schmiechen-Ackermann, ed., *Anpassung, Verweigerung, Widerstand: Soziale Milieus, Politische Kultur und der Widerstand gegen den Nationalsozialismus in Deutschland im regionalen Vergleich* (Berlin, 1997), 201–220.
13. On this argument, which picks up on the thesis of the "*Sonderweg*" (special path) (even if the notion of a *Sonderweg* no longer appears tenable, since it logically presupposes a "normal path" that is impossible to define, in the final analysis), see most recently Gerald D. Feldman, "Der 30. Januar 1933 und die politische Kultur von Weimar," in H. A. Winkler, ed., *Die deutsche Staatskrise 1930–33: Handlungsspielräume und Alternativen* (Munich, 1992), 263–276; also see his "The Weimar Republic: A Problem of Modernization?" *AfS* 26 (1986): 1–26; Ian Kershaw, "Der 30. Januar 1933: Ausweg aus der Staatskrise und Anfang des Staatsverfalls," in Winkler, *Staatskrise,* 277–284, 290f.

Bibliography

Archives

Bundesarchiv Koblenz

Reichskommissar für Überwachung der öffentlichen Ordnung, Lageberichte (microfiches, accompanying volume by Ernst Ritter. Munich, 1979)

Stiftung Archiv der Parteien und Massenorganisationen der DDR im Bundesarchiv (SAPMO)

ZK Militärpolitische Arbeit (Ry 1/I 2/705)
KPD-Bezirk Halle-Merseburg (Ry 1/I 3/11)
KPD-Bezirk Magdeburg-Anhalt (Ry 1/I 3/12)
KPD-Bezirk Thüringen (Ry 1/I 3/13)
Erinnerungen (Sq Y 30)

Geheimes Staatsarchiv Preußischer Kulturbesitz in Berlin-Dahlem, I. Hauptabteilung (GSTA PK I. HA)

Preußisches Staatsministerium (Rep. 90a)
Innenministerium (Rep. 77) (previously at Merseburg)
Justizministerium (Rep. 84a)

Landeshauptarchiv Sachsen-Anhalt in Magdeburg (LHAM)

Oberpräsidium (Rep. C 20 Ib)
Regierung Magdeburg (Rep. C 28 If)
Landratsämter (Rep. C 30)
Staatsanwaltschaft Halberstadt (Rep. C 141 Halberstadt)

Landesarchiv Gotha (LAG)

Regierung Erfurt (Rep. Reg. Erfurt)
Landratsamt Schleusingen (Rep. Landratsamt Schleusingen)

Landesarchiv Merseburg (LAMe)

Regierung Merseburg (Rep. C 48 Ia and Ie)
Landratsämter (Rep. C 50)
Außerordentliche Gerichte des Reiches (Rep. C 133)
Staatsanwaltschaft Naumburg (Rep. C 141 Naumburg)
Betriebsarchive (Rep. Mansfeldsche Kaliwerke AG Eisleben)

Newspapers

Deutsche Allgemeine Zeitung (Berlin)
Klassenkampf (Halle)
Saale-Zeitung (Halle)
Magdeburger Tageszeitung (Magdeburg)
Magdeburgische Zeitung (Magdeburg)
Volksblatt (Halle)
Volksstimme (Magdeburg)

Statistics and Other Primary Sources

Akten der Reichskanzlei. Weimarer Republik: Das Kabinett Fehrenbach, 25. Juni bis 4. Mai 1921. Ed. Peter Wulf. Boppard, 1972.

Arbeiterklasse siegt über Kapp und Lüttwitz. Sources selected and edited by Erwin Könnemann, Brigitte Berthold, and Gerhard Schulze. East Berlin, 1971.

"Bericht des Untersuchungsausschusses über die Unruhen in Mitteldeutschland vom November 1918 bis zum 19. März 1919." *Sammlung der Drucksachen der verfassunggebenden preußischen Landesversammlung,* Tagung 1919/21, vol. 10, no. 3227. Berlin, 1921.

Falter, Jürgen, Thomas Lindenberger, and Siegfried Schumann. *Wahlen und Abstimmungen in der Weimarer Republik: Materialien zum Wahlverhalten 1919–1933.* Munich, 1986.

Geyer, Curt. *Die revolutionäre Illusion: Zur Geschichte des linken Flügels der USPD. Erinnerungen.* Ed. Wolfgang Benz and Hermann Graml. Stuttgart, 1976.

Haneke, Erwin. "Die Bodennutzung, das Personal, die Vieh- und Maschinenhaltung der landwirtschaftlichen Betriebe im Freistaat Preußen, in seinen Provinzen, Regierungsbezirken und Kreisen nach den Ergebnissen der landwirtschaftlichen Betriebszählung vom 16. Juni 1925." *Zeitschrift des preußischen statistischen Landesamtes* 68 (1929): 89–219.

Hoelz, Max. *Vom 'Weißen Kreuz' zur roten Fahne: Jugend-, Kampf- und Zuchthauserlebnisse.* Berlin, 1929; reprint Leizpig, 1984.

Jahresberichte der preußischen Regierungs- und Gewerberäte und Bergbehörden für 1914–1918. Berlin, 1919.

Leopoldt, Adolf. *Rote Chronik der Kreise Zeitz, Weißenfels, Naumburg.* Zeitz, 1931.

Maercker, Georg. *Vom Kaiserheer zur Reichswehr: Geschichte des freiwilligen Landesjägerkorps. Ein Beitrag zur Geschichte der deutschen Revolution.* Leipzig, 1921.

"Niederschriften über die von dem Untersuchungsausschuß zur Nachprüfung der Ursachen, des Umfangs und der Wirkungen des kommunistischen Aufstandes in Mitteldeutschland im März 1921 in mündlicher Verhandlung erhobenen Beweise." *Sammlung der Drucksachen des Preußischen Landtages,* 1. Wahlperiode, 1. Tagung, vol. 8, no. 4140.

Preußische Statistik. Vol. 251.

Reichskommissar für Überwachung der öffentlichen Ordnung. *Denkschrift über die Märzunruhen im Jahre 1921.* Berlin, no date (1921?)].

Schneider, Joseph. *Die blutige Osterwoche im Mansfelder Land: Tatsachenmaterial aus der Märzaktion.* Vienna, 1922.

Stahlhelm, ed. *Sechs Jahre Stahlhelm in Mitteldeutschland.* 2nd ed. Halle, 1926.

Sperlings Zeitschriften- und Zeitungsadreßbuch: Handbuch der deutschen Presse. Leipzig, 1926/27, 1929, 1931.

Statistik des Deutschen Reiches, Neue Folge. Vols. 250, 291, 315, 372, 382, 401, 403, 412, 427, 434.

Secondary Sources

Albertin, Lothar. *Liberalismus und Demokratie am Anfang der Weimarer Republik: Eine vergleichende Analyse der Deutschen Demokratischen Partei und der Deutschen Volkspartei.* Düsseldorf, 1972.

Allen, William Sheridan. *The Nazi Seizure of Power: The Experience of a Single German Town.* London, 1965.

Angress, Werner T. *Stillborn Revolution: The Communist Bid for Power in Germany, 1921–1923.* Princeton, NJ, 1963.

Asmuss, Burkhard. *Republik ohne Chance? Akzeptanz und Legitimation der Weimarer Republik in der deutschen Tagespresse zwischen 1918 und 1923.* Berlin, 1994.

Bahne, Siegfried. *Die KPD und das Ende von Weimar: Das Scheitern einer Politik 1932–1935.* Frankfurt, 1976.

Balistier, Thomas. *Gewalt und Ordnung: Kalkül und Faszination der SA.* Münster, 1989.

Balle, Hermann. "Die propagandistische Auseinandersetzung des Nationalsozialismus mit der Weimarer Republik und ihre Bedeutung für den Aufstieg des Nationalsozialismus." PhD diss., University of Erlangen-Nürnberg, 1963.

Bandoly, Sieglinde. "Veränderungen der sozialökonomischen Struktur in der Magdeburger Börde vor dem ersten Weltkrieg." In Hans-Jürgen Rach and Bernhard Weissel, eds., *Landwirtschaft und Kapitalismus: Zur Entwicklung der ökonomischen und sozialen Verhältnisse in der Magdeburger Börde vom Ausgang des 18. Jahrhunderts bis zum Ende des Ersten Weltkrieges.* Vol. 1, East Berlin, 1978, 233–262.

Barth, Boris. *Dolchstoßlegenden und politische Desintegration: Das Trauma der deutschen Niederlage im Ersten Weltkrieg 1914–1933.* Düsseldorf, 2003.

Bartov, Omer. *Hitler's Army: Soldiers, Nazis, and War in the Third Reich.* Oxford, 1992.

Berghahn, Volker R. *Der Stahlhelm, Bund der Frontsoldaten 1918–1935.* Düsseldorf, 1966.

Berg-Schlosser, Dirk, and Jakob Schissler, eds. *Politische Kultur in Deutschland: Bilanz und Perspektiven der Forschung.* Opladen, 1987.

Bessel, Richard. "The Potempa Murder." *CEH* 10, no. 3 (1977): 241–254.

———. "Militarismus im innenpolitischen Leben der Weimarer Republik: Von den Freikorps zur SA." In Klaus-Jürgen Müller and Eckart Opitz, eds., *Militär und Militarismus in der Weimarer Republik,* Düsseldorf, 1978, 193–222.

———. *Political Violence and the Rise of Nazism: The Storm Troopers in Eastern Germany, 1925–1934.* New York, 1984.

———. "Violence as Propaganda: The Role of the Storm Troopers in the Rise of National Socialism." In Thomas Childers, ed., *The Formation of the Nazi Constituency 1919–1933,* London, 1986, 131–146.

———. "Militarisierung und Modernisierung: Polizeiliches Handeln in der Weimarer Republik." In Alf Lüdtke, ed., *"Sicherheit" und "Wohlfahrt": Polizei, Gesellschaft und Herrschaft im 19. und 20. Jahrhundert,* Frankfurt, 1992, 323–343.

———. *Germany after the First World War.* Oxford, 1993.

Bieber, Hans-Joachim. *Bürgertum in der Revolution: Bürgerräte und Bürgerstreiks in Deutschland 1918–1920.* Hamburg, 1992.

Birk, Gerhard. "Das regionale Kriegervereinswesen bis zum ersten Weltkrieg, unter besonderer Berücksichtigung des Kreises Wanzleben." In Hans-Jürgen Rach and

Bernhard Weissel, eds., *Bauer und Landarbeiter im Kapitalismus in der Magdeburger Börde: Zur Geschichte des dörflichen Alltags vom Ausgang des 18. Jahrhunderts bis zum Beginn des 20. Jahrhunderts,* East Berlin, 1982, 265–297.

Blasius, Dirk. *Weimars Ende: Bürgerkrieg und Politik 1930–1933.* Göttingen, 2005.

Bleiber, Helmut. "Zum Anteil der Landarbeiter an den Bewegungen der Dorfbevölkerung in der deutschen Revolution 1848/49." *JbW* 4 (1975): 65–81.

Bock, Hans-Manfred. *Syndikalismus und Linkskommunismus von 1918 bis 1923: Ein Beitrag zur Sozial- und Ideengeschichte der frühen Weimarer Republik.* New ed. Darmstadt, 1993 (1st ed. 1969).

Bosch, Michael. *Liberale Presse in der Krise: Die Innenpolitik der Jahre 1930 bis 1933 im Spiegel des "Berliner Tageblatts", der "Frankfurter Zeitung" und der "Vossischen Zeitung."* Frankfurt, 1976.

Botz, Gerhard. *Gewalt in der Politik: Attentate, Zusammenstöße, Putschversuche, Unruhen in Österreich 1918 bis 1938.* 2nd ed. Munich, 1983.

Bourke, Joanna. *Dismembering the Male: Men's Bodies, Britain, and the Great War.* Chicago, 1996.

Bucher, Peter. "Zur Geschichte der Einwohnerwehren in Preußen 1918–1921." *MGM* 9, no. 1 (1971): 15–59.

Buder, Johannes. *Die Reorganisation der preußischen Polizei 1918–1923.* Frankfurt, 1986.

Bues, Alfred. "Die ökonomische und politische Rolle Carl Wentzels (9.12.1876–20.12.1944) als Agrarkapitalist und Monopolist." PhD diss., University of Halle-Wittenberg, 1972.

Calließ, Jörg, ed. *Gewalt in der Geschichte: Beiträge zur Friedenserziehung.* Düsseldorf, 1983.

Chickering, Roger. *We Men Who Feel Most German: A Cultural Study of the Pan-German League, 1886–1914.* Boston, 1984.

———. *Imperial Germany and the Great War, 1914–1918. Cambridge, 1998.*

Childers, Thomas. "The Social Language of Politics in Germany: The Sociology of Political Discourse in the Weimar Republic." *AHR* 95, no. 2 (1990): 331–358.

Christoph, Jürgen. *Die politischen Reichsamnestien 1918–1933.* Frankfurt, 1988.

Crew, David F. "Gewalt 'auf dem Amt': Wohlfahrtsbehörden und ihre Klienten in der Weimarer Republik." In Thomas Lindenberger and Alf Lüdtke, eds., *Physische Gewalt: Studien zur Geschichte der Neuzeit,* Frankfurt, 1995, 213–237.

———. *Germans on Welfare: From Weimar to Hitler.* Oxford, 1998.

Daniel, Ute. *Arbeiterfrauen in der Kriegsgesellschaft: Beruf, Familie und Politik im Ersten Weltkrieg.* Göttingen, 1989. English edition, *The War from Within: German Working-Class Women in the First World War,* trans. Margaret Ries. Oxford, 1997.

Daniel, Ute. *Kompendium Kulturgeschichte: Theorien, Praxis, Schlüsselwörter.* Frankfurt, 2001.

Davis, Belinda J. *Home Fires Burning: Food, Politics, and Everyday Life in World War I Berlin.* Chapel Hill, NC, 2000.

Diehl, James M. *Paramilitary Politics in Weimar Germany.* Bloomington, IN, 1977.

Die Märzkämpfe 1921. Ed. Marx-Engels-Lenin-Stalin Institut. East Berlin, 1956.

Dörner, Andreas. *Politischer Mythos und symbolische Politik: Der Hermannmythos. Zur Entstehung des Nationalbewußtseins der Deutschen.* Reinbek, 1996.

Döser, Ute. "Das bolschewistische Rußland im Urteil der deutschen Rechtspresse 1918–1925." PhD diss., Free University of Berlin, 1961.

Drechsler, Ingrun. "Die Magdeburger Sozialdemokratie vor dem Ersten Weltkrieg." PhD diss., University of Magdeburg, 1992.

———. "Von Fehden und Kämpfen: Der schwierige Weg der Magdeburger Arbeiter bis zur Gründung einer sozialdemokratischen Partei 1900." In Helga Grebing, Hans Mommsen, and Karsten Rudolph, eds., *Demokratie und Emanzipation zwischen Elbe und Saale: Beiträge zur Geschichte der sozialdemokratischen Arbeiterbewegung bis 1933,* Essen 1993, 42–53.

———. "Die Rote Stadt im Roten Land: Die Magdeburger Sozialdemokratie unter besonderer Berücksichtigung ihrer Gründungsphase und Entwicklung vor dem Ersten Weltkrieg, als sozialdemokratische Hochburg im Spiegel ihrer Wahlergebnisse während der Weimarer Republik und ihrer erfolgreichen kommunalen Wohnungsbaupolitik." *IWK* 29, no. 2 (1993): 177–194.

Drobnig, [Walter]. *Der mitteldeutsche Aufstand 1921: Seine Bekämpfung durch die Polizei.* Lübeck, 1929.

Eckstein, Harry. "Theoretical Approaches to Explaining Collective Political Violence." In Ted Robert Gurr, ed., *Handbook of Political Conflict,* New York, 1980, 135–166.

Edelman, Murray. *Politics as Symbolic Action.* Chicago, 1972.

Ehls, Marie-Luise. *Protest und Propaganda: Demonstrationen in Berlin zur Zeit der Weimarer Republik.* Berlin, 1997.

Eichberg, Henning. "Thing-, Fest- und Weihespiele in Nationalsozialismus, Arbeiterkultur und Olympismus: Zur Geschichte des politischen Verhaltens in der Epoche des Faschismus." In Henning Eichberg et al., *Massenspiele: NS-Thingspiel, Arbeiterweihespiel und olympisches Zeremoniell,* Stuttgart, 1977, 19–180.

Eksteins, Modris. *The Limits of Reason: The German Democratic Press and the Collapse of Weimar Democracy.* Oxford, 1975.

Elias, Norbert. "Die Zersetzung des staatlichen Gewaltmonopols in der Weimarer Republik." In Norbert Elias, *Studien über die Deutschen: Machtkämpfe und Habitusentwicklung im 19. und 20. Jahrhundert,* Frankfurt, 1989, 282–294.

Elkins, David J., and Richard E. B. Simeon. "A Cause in Search of Its Effect, or What Does Political Culture Explain?" *Comparative Politics* 11, no. 2 (1979): 127–145.

Engelmann, Dieter, and Horst Naumann. *Zwischen Spaltung und Vereinigung: Die Unabhängige Sozialdemokratische Partei Deutschlands in den Jahren 1917–1922.* Berlin, 1993.

Erdmann, Karl-Dietrich. *Die Weimarer Republik.* Munich, 1980.

Erger, Johannes. *Der Kapp-Lüttwitz-Putsch.* Düsseldorf, 1967.

Ersil, Wihelm. *Aktionseinheit gegen Cuno: Zur Geschichte des Massenkampfes gegen die Cuno-Regierung 1923 in Mitteldeutschland.* Berlin, 1963.

Exner, Franz. *Krieg und Kriminalität.* Leipzig, 1926.

Faber, Fritz. "Magdeburgische Zeitung, Magdeburg (1664–1945)." In Heinz-Dietrich Fischer, ed., *Deutsche Zeitungen des 17. bis 20. Jahrhunderts,* vol. 2, Pullach, 1972, 57–73.

Falter, Jürgen W. *Hitlers Wähler.* Munich, 1991.

———. "Die 'Märzgefallenen' von 1933: Neue Forschungsergebnisse zum sozialen Wandel innerhalb der NSDAP-Mitgliedschaft während der Machtergreifungsphase." *GG* 24, no. 4 (1998): 595–616.

Faust, Anselm. *Der Nationalsozialistische Deutsche Studentenbund: Studenten und Nationalsozialismus in der Weimarer Republik.* 2 vols. Düsseldorf, 1973.

Feldman, Gerald D. "Bayern und Sachsen in der Hyperinflation 1922/23." *HZ* 238 (1984): 569–609.

———. "The Weimar Republic: A Problem of Modernization?" *AfS* 26 (1986): 1–26.

———. "Der 30. Januar 1933 und die politische Kultur von Weimar." In Heinrich August Winkler, ed., *Die deutsche Staatskrise 1930–33: Handlungsspielräume und Alternativen,* Munich, 1992, 263–276.

———. *The Great Disorder: Politics, Economics, and Society in the German Inflation, 1914–1924.* New York, 1993.

Feldman, Gerald D., Eberhard Kolb, and Reinhard Rürup. "Die Massenbewegungen der Arbeiterschaft in Deutschland am Ende des Ersten Weltkrieges (1917–1920)." *PVS* 13, no. 3 (1972): 84–105.

Finker, Kurt. "Die militaristischen Wehrverbände in der Weimarer Republik und ihre Rolle bei der Unterdrückung der Arbeiterklasse und bei der Vorbereitung eines neuen imperialistischen Krieges (1924–1929)." Habilitation thesis, Pädagogische Hochschule Potsdam, 1964.

———. "Wehrwolf: Bund deutscher Männer und Frontkrieger 1923–1933." In Dieter Fricke, ed., *Die bürgerlichen Parteien in Deutschland: Handbuch der Geschichte der bürgerlichen Parteien und anderer bürgerlicher Interessenorganisationen vom Vormärz bis zum Jahre 1945,* vol. 2. Leipzig, 1970, 835–840.

———. *Geschichte des Roten Frontkämpferbundes.* East Berlin, 1981.

Fischer, Conan. *Stormtroopers: A Social, Economic and Ideological Analysis, 1929–1935.* London, 1983.

———. *The German Communists and the Rise of Nazism.* New York, 1991.

Flemming, Jens. "Die Bewaffnung des 'Landvolks': Ländliche Schutzwehren und agrarischer Konservatismus in der Anfangsphase der Weimarer Republik." *MGM* 26, no. 2 (1979): 7–36.

Frevert, Ute. *Ehrenmänner: Das Duell in der bürgerlichen Gesellschaft.* Munich, 1991. English edition, *Men of Honour: A Social and Cultural History of the Duel,* trans. Anthony Williams. Cambridge, MA, 1995.

Friedeburg, Robert von. "Klassen–, Geschlechter–, oder Nationalidentität? Handwerker und Tagelöhner in den Kriegervereinen der neupreußischen Provinz Hessen–Nassau 1890–1914." In Ute Frevert, ed., *Militär und Gesellschaft im 19. und 20. Jahrhundert,* Stuttgart, 1997, 229–244.

Fritzsche, Peter. *Rehearsals for Fascism: Populism and Political Mobilization in Weimar Germany.* New York, 1990.

———. *Germans into Nazis.* Cambridge, MA, 1998.

Gailus, Manfred. *Straße und Brot: Sozialer Protest in den deutschen Staaten unter besonderer Berücksichtigung Preußens, 1857–1849.* Göttingen, 1990.

———. "Food Riots in Großbritannien, Frankreich und Deutschland: Anmerkungen zu neueren Forschungsergebnissen." *AfS* 33 (1993): 586–604.

Gailus, Manfred, and Thomas Lindenberger. "Zwanzig Jahre 'moralische Ökonomie.' Ein sozialhistorisches Konzept ist volljährig geworden." *GG* 20, no. 3 (1994): 469–477.

Gailus, Manfred, and Heinrich Volkmann, eds. *Der Kampf um das tägliche Brot: Nahrungsmangel, Versorgungspolitik und Protest 1770–1990.* Opladen, 1994.

Galtung, Johan. *Strukturelle Gewalt: Beiträge zur Friedens- und Konfliktforschung.* Reinbek, 1975.

Gast, Helmut. "Die proletarischen Hundertschaften als Organe der Einheitsfront im Jahre 1923." *ZfG* 4, no. 3 (1956): 439–465.

Geary, Dick. "Unemployment and Working-Class Solidarity: The German Experience 1929–1933." In Richard J. Evans and Dick Geary, eds., *The German Unemployed: Experiences and Consequences of Mass Unemployment from the Weimar Republic to the Third Reich,* London, 1987, 261–280.

Geinitz, Christian. *Kriegsfurcht und Kampfbereitschaft: Das Augusterlebnis in Freiburg. Eine Studie zum Kriegsbeginn 1914.* Essen, 1998.

Geinitz, Christian, and Uta Hinz. "Das Augusterlebnis in Südbaden: Ambivalente Reaktionen der deutschen Öffentlichkeit auf den Kriegsbeginn 1914." In Gerhard Hirschfeld et al., eds., *Kriegserfahrungen: Studien zur Sozial- und Mentalitätsgeschichte des Ersten Weltkriegs,* Essen, 1997, 20–35.

Geyer, Martin H. "Teuerungsprotest und Teuerungsunruhen 1914–1923: Selbsthilfegesellschaft und Geldentwertung." In Manfred Gailus and Heinrich Volkmann, eds., *Der Kampf um das tägliche Brot: Nahrungsmangel, Versorgungspolitik und Protest 1770–1990,* Opladen, 1994, 319–345.

———. *Verkehrte Welt: Revolution, Inflation und Moderne. München 1914–1924.* Göttingen, 1998.
Geyer, Michael. "Nation, Klasse und Macht: Zur Organisation von Herrschaft in der Weimarer Republik." *AfS* 26 (1986): 27–48.
Giles, Geoffrey J. *Students and National Socialism in Germany.* Princeton, NJ, 1985.
Goltermann, Svenja. *Körper der Nation: Habitusformierung und die Politik des Turnens 1860–1890.* Göttingen, 1998.
Gordon, Harold J. *Hitler and the Beer Hall Putsch.* Princeton, NJ, 1972.
Gorlas, Johannes and Detlev J. K. Peukert, eds. *Ruhrkampf 1920.* Essen, 1986.
Götz von Olenhusen, Irmtraud. "Vom Jungstahlhelm zur SA: Die junge Nachkriegsgeneration in den paramilitärischen Verbänden der Weimarer Republik." In Wolfgang R. Krabbe, ed., *Politische Jugend in der Weimarer Republik,* Bochum, 1993, 146–182.
Grill, Johnpeter Horst. *The Nazi Movement in Baden, 1920–1945.* Chapel Hill, NC, 1983.
Groh, Dieter. *Negative Integration und revolutionärer Attentismus: Die deutsche Sozialdemokratie am Vorabend des Ersten Weltkrieges.* Frankfurt, 1973.
Gumbel, Emil J. *Vier Jahre politischer Mord.* Berlin, 1922.
Gurr, Ted Robert. *Why Men Rebel.* Princeton, NJ, 1970.
Gutsche, Willibald. *Die revolutionäre Bewegung in Erfurt während des 1. imperialistischen Weltkrieges und der Novemberrevolution.* Erfurt, 1963.
———. "Übergang zum Imperialismus und Erster Weltkrieg (1897/98 bis 1917)." In Willibald Gutsche, ed., *Geschichte der Stadt Erfurt,* Weimar, 1986, 321–358.
Hanisch, Wilfried. *Die Hundertschaften der Arbeiterwehr: Die proletarischen Hundertschaften in Sachsen.* East Berlin, 1958.
Hardtwig, Wolfgang and Hans-Ulrich Wehler, eds. *Kulturgeschichte heute.* Göttingen, 1996.
Hartenstein, Wolfgang. *Die Anfänge der deutschen Volkspartei 1918–1920.* Düsseldorf, 1962.
Hartewig, Karin. *Das unberechenbare Jahrzehnt: Bergarbeiter und ihre Familien im Ruhrgebiet 1914–1924.* Munich, 1993.
Hausen, Karin. "Schwierigkeiten mit dem 'sozialen Protest': Kritische Anmerkungen zu einem historischen Forschungsansatz." *GG* 3, no. 2 (1977): 257–263.
Hecht, Cornelia. *Deutsche Juden und Antisemitismus in der Weimarer Republik.* Bonn, 2003.
Heer-Kleinert, Lore. *Die Gewerkschaftspolitik der KPD in der Weimarer Republik.* Frankfurt, 1983.
Heilbronner, Oded. *Catholicism, Political Culture, and the Countryside: A Social History of the Nazi Party in South Germany.* Ann Arbor, MI, 1998.
Henning, Friedrich-Wilhelm. "Ansätze der industriellen Entwicklung in Sachsen–Anhalt im 19. und 20. Jahrhundert." *Forschungen zur Brandenburgischen und Preußischen Geschichte, Neue Folge* 4, no. 1 (1994): 1–30.
Hering, Rainer. *Konstruierte Nation: Der Alldeutsche Verband 1890 bis 1939.* Hamburg, 2003.
Heß, Ulrich. "Entwicklung zur Industriestadt und zu einem Zentrum der Arbeiterbewegung (1871 bis 1897/98)." In Willibald Gutsche, ed., *Geschichte der Stadt Erfurt,* Weimar, 1986, 281–320.
Hibbs, Douglas A. *Mass Political Violence: A Cross-National Causal Analysis.* New York, 1973.
Hinrichs, Ernst. "Le charivari et les usages de réprimande en Allemagne: État et perspectives de la recherche." In Jacques Le Goff and Jean-Claude Schmitt, eds., *Le Charivari: Actes de la table ronde organisée à Paris,* Paris, 1981, 297–306.
Hobsbawm, Eric J. *The Age of Extremes: A History of the World, 1914–1991.* New York, 1994.
Höffler, Felix. "Kriegserfahrungen in der Heimat: Kriegsverlauf, Kriegsschuld und Kriegsende in württembergischen Stimmungsbildern des Ersten Weltkriegs." In Gerhard

Hirschfeld et al., eds., *Kriegserfahrungen: Studien zur Sozial- und Mentalitätsgeschichte des Ersten Weltkriegs,* Essen, 1997, 68–82.
Hoffmann, Ludwig, and Daniel Hoffmann-Ostwald. *Deutsches Arbeitertheater 1918–1933.* 2 vols. 2nd ed. Munich, 1973.
Hoffmann, Walter. *Der Mansfelder Kupferschieferbergbau: Ein Beitrag zur mitteldeutschen Wirtschaftsgeschichte.* Meisenheim a. Gl., 1957.
Holtfrerich, Carl-Ludwig. *Die deutsche Inflation 1914–1923.* Berlin, 1980.
Holzbach, Heidrun. *Das "System Hugenberg": Die Organisation bürgerlicher Sammlungspolitik vor dem Aufstieg der NSDAP.* Stuttgart, 1981.
Hornauer, Uwe. *Laienspiel und Massenchor: Das Arbeitertheater der Kultursozialisten in der Weimarer Republik.* Cologne, 1985.
Hornung, Klaus. *Der Jungdeutsche Orden.* Düsseldorf, 1958.
Huber-Koller, Rosemarie. *Gewerkschaften und Arbeitslose: Erfahrungen der Massenerwerbslosigkeit und Aspekte freigewerkschaftlicher Arbeitslosenpolitik in der Endphase der Weimarer Republik.* 2 vols. Pfaffenweiler, 1992.
Hüttenberger, Peter. *Die Gauleiter: Studie zum Wandel der Machtgefüge in der NSDAP.* Stuttgart, 1969.
Imig, Werner. *Streik bei Mansfeld 1930: Der Streik der Mansfeld-Arbeiter im Jahre 1930 und seine Unterdrückung mit Hilfe des Staatsapparates der Weimarer Republik.* East Berlin, 1958.
Iwand, Wolf M. *Paradigma Politische Kultur: Konzepte, Methoden, Ergebnisse der Political-Culture Forschung in der Bundesrepublik. Ein Forschungsbericht.* Opladen, 1985.
Jamin, Mathilde. *Zwischen den Klassen: Zur Sozialstruktur der SA-Führerschaft.* Wuppertal, 1984.
Jasper, Gotthard. *Der Schutz der Republik: Studien zur staatlichen Sicherung der Demokratie in der Weimarer Republik 1922–1930.* Tübingen, 1963.
Jessen, Ralph. *Polizei im Industrierevier: Modernisierung und Herrschaftspraxis im westfälischen Ruhrgebiet 1848–1914.* Göttingen, 1991.
Jochmann, Werner. "Die Ausbreitung des Antisemitismus in Deutschland 1914–1923." In Werner Jochmann, *Gesellschaftskrise und Judenfeindschaft in Deutschland 1870–1945,* Hamburg, 1988, 99–170.
Jonas, Wolfgang. *Das Leben der Mansfeld-Arbeiter, 1924 bis 1945.* East Berlin, 1957.
Jones, Larry Eugene. *German Liberalism and the Dissolution of the Weimar Party System, 1918–1933.* Chapel Hill, NC, 1988.
Kaase, Max. "Sinn oder Unsinn des Konzepts Politische Kultur für die vergleichende Politikforschung, oder auch: Der Versuch, einen Pudding an die Wand zu nageln." In Max Kaase and Hans Dieter Klingmann, eds., *Wahlen und Politisches System: Analysen aus Anlaß der Bundestagswahl 1980,* Opladen, 1983, 144–172.
Kämpfendes Leuna: Die Geschichte des Kampfes der Leuna-Arbeiter. Part I, vol. 1 (1916–1933). East Berlin, 1961.
Kater, Michael. *Studentenschaft und Rechtsradikalismus in Deutschland 1918–1933: Eine sozialgeschichtliche Studie zur Bildungskrise in der Weimarer Republik.* Hamburg, 1975.
———. *The Nazi Party: A Social Profile of Its Members and Leaders 1919–1945.* Cambridge, MA, 1983.
Kaufmann, Doris. *Katholisches Milieu in Münster 1928–1933: Politische Aktionsformen and geschlechtsspezifische Verhaltensräume.* Düsseldorf, 1984.
Kershaw, Ian. "Der 30. Januar 1933: Ausweg aus der Staatskrise und Anfang des Staatsverfalls." In Heinrich August Winkler, ed., *Die deutsche Staatskrise 1930–33: Handlungsspielräume und Alternativen,* Munich, 1992, 277–284.
———, ed. *Weimar: Why Did German Democracy Fail?* New York, 1990.

Klein, Hans-Dieter. "Zwischen Burgfrieden und Komintern: Die Unabhängige Sozialdemokratie in Halle-Merseburg 1917–1920." In Helga Grebing, Hans Mommsen, and Karsten Rudolph, eds., *Demokratie und Emanzipation zwischen Elbe und Saale: Beiträge zur Geschichte der sozialdemokratischen Arbeiterbewegung bis 1933,* Essen, 1993, 181–195.

Kling, Gertrud. *Die Rolle des Arbeiter- und Soldatenrats von Halle in der Novemberrevolution (November 1918 bis März 1919).* Halle, 1960.

Klotzbücher, Alois. "Der politische Weg des Stahlhelm, Bund der Frontsoldaten in der Weimarer Republik: Ein Beitrag zur Geschichte der 'Nationalen Opposition' 1918–1933." PhD diss., University of Erlangen-Nürnberg, 1964.

Kluge, Ulrich. *Die deutsche Revolution 1918/19: Staat, Politik und Gesellschaft zwischen Weltkrieg und Kapp-Putsch.* Frankfurt, 1985.

Knabe, Erich. "Die mitteldeutsche chemische Industrie in ihrer standortmäßigen Bedingtheit." PhD diss., University of Halle, 1927.

Knatz, Christian. "Ein Sieg über Aufrührer und Reformer: Der Mitteldeutsche Aufstand von 1921 als verpaßte Chance der preußischen Schutzpolizei." *ZfG* 46, no. 1 (1998): 28–39.

Koch-Baumgarten, Sigrid. *Aufstand der Avantgarde: Die Märzaktion der KPD 1921.* Frankfurt, 1986.

Kocka, Jürgen. *Klassengesellschaft im Krieg: Deutsche Sozialgeschichte 1914–1918.* 2nd ed. Göttingen, 1978.

Kolb, Eberhard. *Die Arbeiterräte in der deutschen Innenpolitik 1918–1919.* Düsseldorf, 1962.

———. *Die Weimarer Republik.* 6th ed. Munich, 2002. English edition, *The Weimar Republic,* trans. P.S. Falla, 2nd ed. New York, 2004.

Könnemann, Erwin. *Einwohnerwehren und Zeitfreiwilligenverbände: Ihre Funktion beim Aufbau eines neuen imperialistischen Militärsystems (November 1918 bis 1920).* East Berlin, 1971.

Könnemann, Erwin, and Hans-Joachim Krusch. *Aktionseinheit contra Kapp-Putsch: Der Kapp-Putsch im März 1920 und der Kampf der deutschen Arbeiterklasse sowie anderer Werktätiger gegen die Errichtung der Militärdiktatur und für demokratische Verhältnisse.* East Berlin, 1972.

Kopitzsch, Wolfgang. "Politische Gewalttaten in Schleswig-Holstein in der Endphase der Weimarer Republik." In Erich Hoffmann and Peter Wulf, eds., *"Wir bauen das Reich": Aufstieg und erste Herrschaftsjahre des Nationalsozialismus in Schleswig-Holstein,* Neumünster, 1983, 19–39.

Korff, Gottfried. "Rote Fahnen und geballte Faust: Zur Symbolik der Arbeiterbewegung in der Weimarer Republik." In Dietmar Petzina, ed., *Fahnen, Fäuste, Körper: Symbolik und Kultur der Arbeiterbewegung,* Essen, 1986, 27–60.

Koselleck, Reinhart. "Zur historisch-politischen Semantik asymmetrischer Gegenbegriffe." In Reinhart Koselleck, *Vergangene Zukunft: Zur Semantik geschichtlicher Zeiten,* Frankfurt, 1979, 211–259.

———. "Der Einfluß der beiden Weltkriege auf das soziale Bewußtsein." In Wolfram Wette, ed., *Der Krieg des kleinen Mannes: Eine Militärgeschichte von unten,* Munich, 1992, 324–343.

Koshar, Rudy. *Social Life, Local Politics, and Nazism: Bourgeois Marburg 1880–1935.* Chapel Hill, NC, 1986.

Kratzenberg, Volker. *Arbeiter auf dem Weg zu Hitler? Die nationalsozialistische Betriebszellenorganisation. Ihre Entstehung, ihre Programmatik, ihr Scheitern 1927–1934.* Frankfurt, 1987.

Krause, Hartfried. *USPD: Zur Geschichte der Unabhängigen Sozialdemokratischen Partei Deutschlands.* Frankfurt, 1975.

Kruse, Wolfgang. "Die Kriegsbegeisterung in Deutschen Reich zu Beginn des Ersten Weltkriegs: Entstehungszusammenhänge, Grenzen und ideologische Strukturen." In Gottfried Mergner and Marcel van der Linden, eds., *Kriegsbegeisterung und mentale Kriegsvorbereitung,* Berlin, 1991, 73–81.

———. *Krieg und nationale Integration: Eine Neuinterpretation des sozialdemokratischen Burgfriedensschlusses 1914/15.* Essen, 1993.

Kühne, Thomas, ed. *Männergeschichte – Geschlechtergeschichte: Männlichkeit im Wandel der Moderne.* Frankfurt, 1996.

———. "Gender Confusion and Gender Order in the German Military, 1918–1945." In Karen Hagemann and Stefanie Schüler-Springorum, eds., *Home/Front: The Military, War, and Gender in Twentieth-Century Germany,* Oxford, 2002, 233–254.

Kundrus, Birthe. "The First World War and the Construction of Gender Relations in the Weimar Republic." In Karen Hagemann and Stefanie Schüler-Springorum, eds., *Home/ Front: The Military, War, and Gender in Twentieth-Century Germany,* Oxford, 2002, 159–180.

Kurz, Thomas. *Blutmai: Sozialdemokraten und Kommunisten im Brennpunkt der Berliner Ereignisse von 1929.* Berlin, 1988.

Lapp, Benjamin Nathan. *Revolution from the Right: Politics, Class, and the Rise of Nazism in Saxony, 1919–1933.* Atlantic Highlands, NJ, 1997.

Large, David Clay. *The Politics of Law and Order: A History of the Bavarian Einwohnerwehr, 1918–1921* (= Transactions of the American Philosophical Society, vol. 70, part 2). Philadelphia, PA, 1980.

Lärmer, Karl. *Vom Arbeitszwang zur Zwangsarbeit: Die Arbeitsordnungen im Mansfelder Kupferschieferbergbau von 1673–1945.* East Berlin, 1961.

Lederer, Emil. "Soziologie der Gewalt: Ein Beitrag zur Theorie der gesellschaftsbildenden Kräfte." In Emil Lederer, ed., *Soziologische Probleme der Gegenwart,* Berlin, 1921, 16–29.

Lehnert, Detlef. "Propaganda des Bürgerkriegs? Politische Feindbilder in der Novemberrevolution als mentale Destabilisierung der Weimarer Demokratie." In Detlef Lehnert and Klaus Megerle, eds., *Politische Teilkulturen zwischen Integration und Polarisierung: Zur politischen Kultur der Weimarer Republik,* Opladen, 1990, 61–101.

Lehnert, Detlef, and Klaus Megerle. "Identitäts- und Konsensprobleme in einer fragmentierten Gesellschaft: Zur politischen Kultur in der Weimarer Republik." In Dirk Berg-Schlosser and Jakob Schissler, eds., *Politische Kultur in Deutschland: Bilanz und Perspektiven der Forschung,* Opladen, 1987, 80–95.

Lehnert, Detlef, and Klaus Megerle, eds. *Politische Identität und nationale Gedenktage: Zur politischen Kultur in der Weimarer Republik.* Opladen, 1984.

———, eds. *Politische Teilkulturen zwischen Integration und Polarisierung: Zur politischen Kultur in der Weimarer Republik.* Opladen, 1990.

Leidigkeit, Karl-Heinz, and Jürgen Herrmann. *Auf leninistischem Kurs: Geschichte der KPD–Bezirksorganisation Halle-Merseburg bis 1933.* Halle, 1979.

Lepsius, M. Rainer. "Parteiensystem und Sozialstruktur: Zum Problem der Demokratisierung der deutschen Gesellschaft." In M. Rainer Lepsius, *Demokratie in Deutschland: Soziologisch–historische Konstellationsanalysen. Ausgewählte Aufsätze,* Göttingen, 1993, 25–50 [1966].

———. "Machtübernahme und Machtübergabe: Zur Strategie des Regimewechsels 1918/19 und 1932/33." In M. Rainer Lepsius, *Demokratie in Deutschland: Soziologisch–historische Konstellationsanalysen. Ausgewählte Aufsätze,* Göttingen, 1993, 80–94 [1971].

Leßmann, Peter. *Die preußische Schutzpolizei in der Weimarer Republik: Streifendienst und Straßenkampf.* Düsseldorf, 1989.

Liang, His-Huey. *Die Berliner Polizei in der Weimarer Republik.* Berlin, 1977.

Lichtenberg, Martin. "Entwicklungstendenzen in der Magdeburger Industrie." PhD diss., University of Jena, 1934.

Liepmann, Moritz. *Krieg und Kriminalität in Deutschland.* Stuttgart, 1930.

Lindenberger, Thomas. *Straßenpolitik: Zur Sozialgeschichte der öffentlichen Ordnung in Berlin 1900 bis 1914.* Bonn, 1995.

Lindenberger, Thomas, and Alf Lüdtke. "Die 'verdiente Tracht Prügel': Ein kurzes Kapitel über das Lynchen im wilhelminischen Berlin." In Thomas Lindenberger and Alf Lüdtke, eds., *Physische Gewalt: Studien zur Geschichte der Neuzeit,* Frankfurt, 1995, 190–212.

———, eds. *Physische Gewalt: Studien zur Geschichte der Neuzeit.* Frankfurt, 1995.

Lindner, Rolf. "Straße – Straßenjunge – Straßenbande." *Zeitschrift für Volkskunde* 79, no. 2 (1983): 192–208.

Lipp, Carola. "Politische Kultur oder das Politische und Gesellschaftliche in der Kultur." In Wolfgang Hardtwig and Hans-Ulrich Wehler, eds., *Kulturgeschichte heute,* Göttingen, 1996, 78–110.

Lohalm, Uwe. *Völkischer Radikalismus: Die Geschichte des Deutschvölkischen Schutz– und Trutz-Bundes 1919–1923.* Hamburg, 1970.

Longerich, Peter. *Die braunen Bataillone: Geschichte der SA.* Munich, 1989.

Lösche, Peter. *Der Bolschewismus im Urteil der deutschen Sozialdemokratie 1903–1920.* Berlin, 1967.

Lucas, Erhard. *Märzrevolution im Ruhrgebiet: Vom Generalstreik gegen den Militärputsch zum bewaffneten Arbeiteraufstand März-April 1920.* 3 vols. Frankfurt, 1970–1978.

Ludewig, Hans-Ulrich. *Arbeiterbewegung und Aufstand: Eine Untersuchung zum Verhalten der Arbeiterparteien in den Aufstandsbewegungen der frühen Weimarer Republik 1920–1923.* Husum, 1978.

———. "Unruhen, Aufstand und Bürgerkrieg 1918–1923 im mitteldeutschen Raum." In Werner Freitag, Klaus Erich Pollmann, and Matthias Puhle, eds., *Politische, soziale und kulturelle Konflikte in der Geschichte von Sachsen-Anhalt,* Halle, 1999, 164–174.

Lüdtke, Alf. "Trauerritual und politische Manifestation: Zu den Begräbnisumzügen der Sozialdemokratie im frühen Kaiserreich." In Bernd Jürgen Warnecken, ed., *Massenmedium Straße: Zur Kulturgeschichte der Demonstration,* Frankfurt, 1991, 120–148.

Maier, Charles. *Recasting Bourgeois Europe: Stabilization in France, Germany, and Italy in the Decade after World War I.* Princeton, NJ, 1975.

Mallmann, Klaus-Michael. *Kommunisten in der Weimarer Republik: Sozialgeschichte einer revolutionären Bewegung.* Darmstadt, 1996.

Manstein, Peter. *Die Mitglieder und Wähler der NSDAP 1919–1933: Untersuchungen zu ihrer schichtmäßigen Zusammensetzung.* Frankfurt, 1988.

Mattheier, Klaus. *Die Gelben: Nationale Arbeiter zwischen Wirtschaftsfrieden und Streik.* Düsseldorf, 1973.

Matthiesen, Helge. *Bürgertum und Nationalsozialismus in Thüringen: Das bürgerliche Gotha von 1918 bis 1930.* Jena, 1994.

———. "Zwei Radikalisierungen – Bürgertum und Arbeiterschaft in Gotha 1918–1923." *GG* 21, no. 1 (1995): 32–62.

Mauch, Hans-Joachim. *Nationalistische Wehrorganisation in der Weimarer Republik: Zur Entwicklung und Ideologie des "Paramilitarismus."* Frankfurt, 1982.

McElligott, Anthony. "'… und so kam es zu einer schweren Schlägerei': Straßenschlachten in Altona und Hamburg." In Maike Bruhns et al., *"Hier war doch alles nicht so schlimm." Wie die Nazis in Hamburg, den Alltag eroberten,* Hamburg, 1984, 58–85.

———. "Petty Complaints, Plunder and Police in Altona 1917–1920: Towards an Interpretation of Community and Conflict." In Peter Assion, ed., *Transformationen der Arbeiterkultur,* Marburg, 1985, 110–125.

———. "Mobilising the Unemployed: The KPD and the Unemployed Workers' Movement in Hamburg,-Altona during the Weimar Republic." In Richard J. Evans and Dick Geary, eds., *The German Unemployed: Experiences and Consequences of Mass Unemployment from the Weimar Republic to the Third Reich,* London, 1987, 228–260.

———. *Contested City: Municipal Politics and the Rise of Nazism in Altona, 1917–1937.* Ann Arbor, MI, 1998.

Mende, Roswitha. "Geschichte der Sozialdemokratie im Regierungsbezirk Merseburg von der Jahrhundertwende bis 1917." PhD diss. (B), University of Halle, 1984.

Mergel, Thomas, and Thomas Welskopp, eds. *Geschichte zwischen Kultur und Gesellschaft: Beiträge zur Theoriedebatte.* Munich, 1997.

Merkl, Peter H. *Political Violence under the Swastika: 581 Early Nazis.* Princeton, NJ, 1975.

———. *The Making of a Stormtrooper.* Princeton, NJ, 1980.

Merz, Kai-Uwe. *Das Schreckbild: Deutschland und der Bolschewismus 1917 bis 1921.* Berlin, 1995.

Miller, Susanne. *Burgfrieden und Klassenkampf: Die deutsche Sozialdemokratie im Ersten Weltkrieg.* Düsseldorf, 1974.

———. *Die Bürde der Macht: Die deutsche Sozialdemokratie 1918–1920.* Düsseldorf, 1978.

Moeller, Robert G. *German Peasants and Agrarian Politics, 1914–1924: The Rhineland and Westphalia.* Chapel Hill, NC, 1986.

Mommsen, Hans. "Militär und zivile Militarisierung in Deutschland 1914 bis 1938." In Ute Frevert, ed., *Militär und Gesellschaft im 19. und 20. Jahrhundert,* Stuttgart, 1997, 265–276.

Mommsen, Wolfgang J. "Die deutsche Revolution 1918–1920: Politische Revolution und soziale Protestbewegung." *GG* 4, no. 3 (1978): 362–391.

Morgan, David. *The Socialist Left and the German Revolution: A History of the German Independent Social Democratic Party, 1917–1922.* Ithaca, NY, 1975.

Mosse, George L. *Fallen Soldiers: Reshaping the Memory of the World Wars.* Oxford, 1990.

Mühlberger, Detlef. *Hitler's Followers: Studies in the Sociology of the Nazi Movement.* London, 1991.

Müller, Werner. *Lohnkampf, Massenstreik, Sowjetmacht: Ziele und Grenzen der "Revolutionären Gewerkschaftsopposition" (RGO) in Deutschland 1928 bis 1933.* Cologne, 1988.

Nabert, Thomas. *Der Großgrundbesitz in der preußischen Provinz Sachsen 1913–1933: Soziale Struktur, ökonomische Position und politische Rolle.* Cologne, 1992.

Nagel, Irmela. *Fememorde und Fememordprozesse in der Weimarer Republik.* Cologne, 1991.

Nardin, Terry. "Conflicting Conceptions of Political Violence." In Cornelius P. Cotter, ed., *Political Science Annual: An International Review,* vol. 4, Indianapolis, IN, 1973, 75–126.

Narr, Wolf Dieter. "Gewalt und Legitimität." *Leviathan* 1, no. 1 (1973): 7–42 (reprinted in Otthein Rammstedt, ed., *Gewaltverhältnisse und die Ohnmacht der Kritik,* Frankfurt, 1974, 9–58).

Neidhardt, Friedhelm. "Gewalt: Soziale Bedeutungen und sozialwissenschaftliche Bestimmung des Begriffs." In Bundeskriminalamt, ed., *Was ist Gewalt?* vol. 1., Wiesbaden, 1986, 109–147.

Nieburg, Harold L. *Political Violence: The Behavioral Process.* New York, 1969.

Nipperdey, Thomas: *Deutsche Geschichte 1866–1918,* vol. 2: *Machtstaat vor der Demokratie.* Munich, 1992.

Noakes, Jeremy. *The Nazi Party in Lower Saxony, 1921–1933.* Oxford, 1971.

Nolte, Ernst. *Der europäische Bürgerkrieg 1917–1945: Nationalsozialismus und Bolschewismus.* Berlin, 1987.

Nolte, Paul. *Die Ordnung der deutschen Gesellschaft: Selbstentwurf und Selbstbeschreibung im 20. Jahrhundert.* Munich, 2000.

Nußer, Horst G. W. *Konservative Wehrverbände in Bayern, Preußen und Österreich 1918–1933, mit einer Biographie von Forstrat Georg Escherich 1870–1941.* 2 vols. Munich, 1973.
Oeckel, Heinz. *Die revolutionäre Volkswehr 1918/19: Die deutsche Arbeiterklasse im Kampf um die revolutionäre Volkswehr, November 1918 bis Mai 1919.* East Berlin, 1968.
Oertzen, Peter von. *Betriebsräte in der Novemberrevolution: Eine politikwissenschaftliche Untersuchung über Ideengehalt und Struktur der betrieblichen und wirtschaftlichen Arbeiterräte in der deutschen Revolution 1918/19.* 2nd ed. Berlin, 1976.
Paul, Gerhard. *Aufstand der Bilder: Die NS-Propaganda vor 1933.* Bonn, 1990.
Peukert, Detlev J. K. *Die Weimarer Republik: Krisenjahre der klassischen Moderne.* Frankfurt, 1987. English edition, *The Weimar Republic: The Crisis of Classical Modernity,* trans. Richard Deveson, New York, 1992.
———. "The Lost Generation: Youth Unemployment at the End of the Weimar Republic." In Richard J. Evans and Dick Geary, eds., *The German Unemployed: Experiences and Consequences of Mass Unemployment from the Weimar Republic to the Third Reich,* London, 1987, 172–193.
Pfeifer, Eva. "Das Hitlerbild im Spiegel einiger konservativer Zeitungen in den Jahren 1929–1933." PhD diss., University of Heidelberg, 1966.
Pridham, Geoffrey. *Hitler's Rise to Power: The Nazi Movement in Bavaria, 1923–1933.* New York, 1973.
Pyta, Wolfram. *Gegen Hitler und für die Republik: Die Auseinandersetzung der deutschen Sozialdemokratie mit der NSDAP in der Weimarer Republik.* Düsseldorf, 1989.
———. *Dorfgemeinschaft und Parteipolitik 1918–1933: Die Verschränkung von Milieu und Parteien in den protestantischen Landgebieten Deutschlands in der Weimarer Republik.* Düsseldorf, 1996.
Rach, Hans-Jürgen, and Bernhard Weissel, eds. *Landwirtschaft und Kapitalismus: Zur Entwicklung der ökonomischen und sozialen Verhältnisse in der Magdeburger Börde vom Ausgang des 18. Jahrhunderts bis zum Ende des Ersten Weltkrieges.* 2 vols. East Berlin, 1978–1979.
———, eds. *Bauer und Landarbeiter im Kapitalismus in der Magdeburger Börde: Zur Geschichte des dörflichen Alltags vom Ausgang des 18. Jahrhunderts bis zum Beginn des 20. Jahrhunderts.* East Berlin, 1982.
Rach, Hans-Jürgen, Bernhard Weissel, and Hainer Plaul, eds. *Die werktätige Dorfbevölkerung in der Magdeburger Börde: Studien zum dörflichen Alltag vom Beginn des 20. Jahrhunderts bis zum Anfang der 60er Jahre.* 2 vols. East Berlin, 1986–1987.
Radkau, Joachim. *Das Zeitalter der Nervosität: Deutschland zwischen Bismarck und Hitler.* Munich, 1998.
Raithel, Thomas. *Das "Wunder" der inneren Einheit: Studien zur deutschen und französischen Öffentlichkeit bei Beginn des Ersten Weltkriegs.* Bonn, 1996.
Raßloff, Steffen. *Flucht in die nationale Volksgemeinschaft: Das Erfurter Bürgertum zwischen Kaiserreich und NS-Diktatur.* Cologne, 2003.
Rauchfleisch, Udo. *Allgegenwart der Gewalt.* Göttingen, 1992.
Rauh-Kühne, Cornelia. *Katholisches Milieu und Kleinstadtgesellschaft: Ettlingen 1918–1939.* Sigmaringen, 1991.
Reichardt, Sven. *Faschistische Kampfbünde: Gewalt und Gemeinschaft im italienischen Squadrismus und in der deutschen SA.* Cologne, 2002.
Reulecke, Jürgen. "'Wir reiten die Sehnsucht tot' oder: Melancholie als Droge. Anmerkungen zum bündischen Liedgut." In Thomas Kühne, ed., *Männergeschichte – Geschlechtergeschichte: Männlichkeit im Wandel der Moderne,* Frankfurt, 1996, 155–173.
Ritter, Gerhard A., and Klaus Tenfelde. *Arbeiter im deutschen Kaiserreich 1871 bis 1914.* Bonn, 1992.

Robbe, Waltraud. *Die Knappschaftsfessel von Mansfeld: Ein Beitrag zur Geschichte der Lage und des Kampfes der deutschen Arbeiterklasse in der Zeit von 1850 bis 1900.* East Berlin, 1958.

Rohe, Karl. *Das Reichsbanner Schwarz-Rot-Gold: Ein Beitrag zur Geschichte und Struktur der politischen Kampfverbände zur Zeit der Weimarer Republik.* Düsseldorf, 1966.

———. "Regionalkultur, regionale Identität und Regionalismus im Ruhrgebiet." In Wolfgang Lipp, ed., *Industriegesellschaft und Regionalkultur,* Munich, 1984, 123–154.

———. "Politische Kultur und der kulturelle Aspekt von politischer Wirklichkeit: Konzeptionelle und typologische Überlegungen zu Gegenstand und Fragestellung Politischer Kulturforschung." In Dirk Berg-Schlosser and Jakob Schissler, eds., *Politische Kultur in Deutschland: Bilanz und Perspektiven der Forschung,* Opladen, 1987, 39–48.

———. "Politische Kultur und ihre Analyse: Probleme und Perspektiven der politischen Kulturforschung." *HZ* 250 (1990): 321–346.

———. *Wahlen und Wählertraditionen in Deutschland: Kulturelle Grundlagen deutscher Parteien und Parteiensysteme im 19. und 20. Jahrhundert.* Frankfurt, 1992.

Rohkrämer, Thomas. *Der Militarismus der "kleinen Leute": Die Kriegervereine im Deutschen Kaiserreich 1871–1914.* Munich, 1990.

Rohrbacher, Stefan. *Gewalt im Biedermeier: antijüdische Ausschreitungen in Vormärz und Revolution (1815–1848/49).* Frankfurt, 1993.

Rosenhaft, Eve. "Gewalt in der Politik: Zum Problem des 'sozialen Militarismus'." In Klaus-Jürgen Müller and Eckart Opitz, eds., *Militär und Militarismus in der Weimarer Republik,* Düsseldorf, 1978, 237–259.

———. *Beating the Fascists? The German Communists and Political Violence, 1929–1933.* London, 1983.

———. "Links gleich rechts? Militante Straßengewalt um 1930." In Thomas Lindenberger and Alf Lüdtke, eds., *Physische Gewalt: Studien zur Geschichte der Neuzeit,* Frankfurt, 1995, 238–275.

Russ, Wolfgang. "Zwischen Protest und Resignation: Arbeitslose und Arbeitslosenbewegung in der Zeit der Weltwirtschaftskrise." *ÖZG* 1, no. 2 (1990): 23–52.

Sabrow, Martin. *Der Rathenaumord: Rekonstruktion einer Verschwörung gegen die Republik von Weimar.* Munich, 1994.

Safranski, Rüdiger, and Walter Fähnders. "Proletarisch-revolutionäre Literatur." In Bernd Weyergraf, ed., *Literatur der Weimarer Republik,* Munich, 1995, 174–231.

Salewski, Michael. *Entwaffung und Militärkontrolle in Deutschland, 1919–1927.* Munich, 1966.

Schieder, Wolfgang. "Das italienische Experiment: Der Faschismus als Vorbild in der Krise der Weimarer Republik." *HZ* 262 (1996): 73–125.

Schildt, Axel. *Militärdiktatur mit Massenbasis? Die Querfrontkonzeption der Reichswehr-Führung um General von Schleicher am Ende der Weimarer Republik.* Frankfurt, 1981.

Schirmann, Léon. *Altonaer Blutsonntag, 17. Juli 1932: Dichtungen und Wahrheit.* Hamburg, 1994.

Schirmer, Dietmar. *Mythos – Heilshoffnung – Modernität: Politisch–kulturelle Deutungscodes in der Weimarer Republik.* Opladen, 1992.

Schmidtke, Klaus. "Die Sozialdemokratie in Nordhausen und Salza – Bürgerstadt und Arbeiterdorf zwischen Kaiserreich und DDR." In Franz Walter, Tobias Dürr, and Klaus Schmidtke, *Die SPD in Sachsen und Thüringen zwischen Hochburg und Diaspora: Untersuchungen auf lokaler Ebene vom Kaiserreich bis zur Gegenwart,* Bonn, 1993, 183–286.

Schmiechen-Ackermann, Detlef. *Nationalsozialismus und Arbeitermilieus: Der nationalsozialistische Angriff auf die proletarischen Wohnquartiere und die Reaktion in den sozialistischen Vereinen.* Bonn, 1998.

Schölzel, Christian. *Walther Rathenau: Eine Biographie.* Paderborn, 2005.
Schorske, Carl E.. *Die große Spaltung: Die deutsche Sozialdemokratie 1905–1917.* Berlin, 1981.
Schreiner, Klaus. "'Wann kommt der Retter Deutschlands?' Formen und Funktionen von politischem Messianismus in der Weimarer Republik." *Saeculum* 49 (1998): 107–160.
Schubert, Helga. "Der mitteldeutsche Generalstreik 1919." PhD diss., University of Leipzig, 1963.
Schultz, Eberhard. "Rolle und Anteil des linken Flügels der USPD im ehemaligen Regierungsbezirk Halle–Merseburg bei der Herausbildung und Entwicklung der KPD zur revolutionären Massenpartei (1917–1920)." PhD diss., University of Halle, 1969.
Schulze, Hagen. *Freikorps und Republik 1918–1920.* Boppard, 1969.
Schumacher, Martin. *Land und Politik: Eine Untersuchung über politische Parteien und agrarische Interessen 1914–1923.* Düsseldorf, 1978.
Schumann, Dirk. "Der aufgeschobene Bürgerkrieg: Sozialer Protest und Politische Gewalt in Deutschland 1923." *ZfG* 44, no. 6 (1996): 526–544.
———. "Gewalt als Grenzüberschreitung: Überlegungen zur Sozialgeschichte der Gewalt im 19. und 20. Jahrhundert." *AfS* 37 (1997): 366–386.
———. "Einheitssehnsucht und Gewaltakzeptanz: Politische Grundpositionen des deutschen Bürgertums nach 1918 (mit vergleichenden Überlegungen zu den britischen 'middle classes')." In Hans Mommsen, ed., *Der Große Krieg und die Nachkriegsordnung: Politischer und kultureller Wandel in Europa 1914–1924,* Stuttgart, 2000, 83–105.
———. "Europa, der Erste Weltkrieg und die Nachkriegszeit: Eine Kontinuität der Gewalt?" *Journal of Modern European History* 1, no. 1 (2003), 24–43.
Schunke, Joachim. *Schlacht um Halle.* East Berlin, 1956.
Schuster, Kurt G. P. *Der Rote Frontkämpferbund 1924–1929: Beiträge zur Geschichte und Organisationsstruktur eines politischen Kampfbundes.* Düsseldorf, 1975.
Schwarze, Johannes. *Die bayerische Polizei und ihre historische Funktion bei der Aufrechterhaltung der öffentlichen Sicherheit in Bayern von 1919–1933.* Munich, 1977.
Sewell, William H. "The Concept of Culture." In Victoria E. Bonnell and Lynn Hunt, eds., *Beyond the Cultural Turn: New Directions in the Study of Society and Culture,* Berkeley, 1999, 35–60.
Siggemann, Jürgen. *Die kasernierte Polizei und das Problem der inneren Sicherheit in der Weimarer Republik: Eine Studie zum Auf- und Ausbau des innerstaatlichen Sicherheitssystems in Deutschland 1918/19–1933.* Frankfurt, 1980.
Sneeringer, Julia. *Winning Women's Votes: Propaganda and Politics in Weimar Germany.* Chapel Hill, NC, 2002.
Sofsky, Wolfgang. *Traktat über die Gewalt.* Frankfurt, 1996. English edition, *Violence: Terrorism, Genocide, War,* trans. Anthea Bell. London, 2003.
Sontheimer, Kurt. *Antidemokratisches Denken in der Weimarer Republik: Die politischen Ideen des deutschen Nationalismus zwischen 1918 und 1933.* Munich, 1968 (repr. 1992).
Sösemann, Bernd. *Das Ende der Weimarer Republik in der Kritik demokratischer Publizisten: Theodor Wolff, Ernst Feder, Julius Elbau, Leopold Schwarzschild.* Berlin, 1976.
Speitkamp, Winfried. *Jugend in der Neuzeit: Deutschland vom 16. bis zum 20. Jahrhundert.* Göttingen, 1998.
Stachura, Peter D. *Nazi Youth in the Weimar Republic.* Santa Barbara, CA, 1975.
———. *The Weimar Republic and the Younger Proletariat: An Economic and Social Analysis.* New York, 1989.
———, ed. *Unemployment and the Great Depression in Weimar Germany.* Basingstoke, 1986.
Stang, Joachim. *Die Deutsche Demokratische Partei in Preußen, 1918–1933.* Düsseldorf, 1994.
Stein, Peter. *Die NS-Gaupresse 1925–1933: Forschungsbericht – Quellenkritik – neue Bestandsaufnahme.* Munich, 1987.

Striefler, Christian. *Kampf um die Macht: Kommunisten und Nationalsozialisten am Ende der Weimarer Republik.* Berlin, 1993.

Swett, Pamela. *Neighbors and Enemies: The Culture of Radicalism in Berlin, 1929–1933.* Cambridge, 2004.

Szejnmann, Claus-Christian W. *Nazism in Central Germany: The Brownshirts in 'Red' Saxony.* New York, 1999.

Tacke, Charlotte. "Die 1900-Jahrfeier im Teutoburger Wald 1909: Von der 'klassenlosen Bürgergesellschaft' zu 'klassenlosen Volksgemeinschaft'?" In Manfred Hettling and Paul Nolte, eds., *Bürgerliche Feste: Symbolische Formen politischen Handelns im 19. Jahrhundert,* Göttingen, 1993, 192–230.

Tarrow, Sidney. *Power in Movement: Social Movements, Collective Action, and Politics.* New York, 1994.

Tenfelde, Klaus. *Proletarische Provinz: Radikalisierung und Widerstand in Penzberg/Oberbayern 1900–1945.* Munich, 1982.

———. "La riscoperta dell' 'autodifesa colletiva': Protesta sociale in Germania durante l'inflazione del 1923." *Annali dell' Istituto Storico Italo-Germanico Quaderno* 11 (1983): 379–422.

———. "Stadt und Land in Krisenzeiten: München und das Münchener Umland zwischen Revolution und Inflation 1918 bis 1923." In Klaus Tenfelde and Wolfgang Hardtwig, eds., *Soziale Räume in der Urbanisierung: Studien zur Geschichte Münchens im Vergleich 1850 bis 1933,* Munich, 1990, 37–57.

Thormann, Hans, and Erich Staab. *Der mitteldeutsche Raum: Seine natürlichen geschichtlichen und wirtschaftlichen Grenzen.* Merseburg 1929.

Tilly, Charles. "Review of Ted Robert Gurr, *Why Men Rebel.*" *Journal of Social History* 4, no. 4 (1971): 416–420.

———. *From Mobilization to Revolution.* Reading, MA, 1978.

Tilly, Charles, Louise Tilly, and Richard Tilly. *The Rebellious Century, 1830–1930.* Cambridge, MA, 1975.

Tonn, Willi. "Der Kampf der KPD um die Aktionseinheit der Arbeiterklasse im Bezirk Merseburg in den Jahren 1921–1923." PhD diss. (A), Martin Luther University, Halle–Wittenberg, 1973.

Trauthig, Michael. *Im Kampf um Glauben und Kirche: Eine Studie über Gewaltakzeptanz und Krisenmentalität der württembergischen Protestanten zwischen 1918 und 1933.* Leinfelden-Echterdingen, 1999.

Trotha, Trutz von, ed. *Soziologie der Gewalt.* Cologne, 1997.

Turner, Henry A. *Big Business and the Rise of Hitler.* New York, 1985.

———. *Hitler's Thirty Days to Power: January 1933.* Reading, MA, 1996.

Verhey, Jeffrey. *The Spirit of 1914: Militarism, Myth, and Mobilization in Germany.* Cambridge, 2000.

Vogler, Wilhelm. "Probleme des Klassenkampfes zwischen den Landarbeitern und Gutsbesitzern im Regierungsbezirk Merseburg (1918–1923)." PhD diss. (A), Martin Luther University, Halle–Wittenberg, 1973.

Volkmann, Heinrich, and Jürgen Bergmann, eds. *Sozialer Protest: Studien zu traditioneller Resistenz und kollektiver Gewalt in Deutschland vom Vormärz bis zur Reichsgründung.* Opladen, 1980.

Voss, Eberhard. "Revolutionäre Ereignisse und Probleme des Klassenkampfes zwischen Landarbeitern und Gutsbesitzern in den Jahren 1921 bis 1923 in Deutschland." PhD diss. (A), University of Rostock, 1964.

Waite, Robert G. L. *Vanguard of Nazism: The Free Corps Movement in Postwar Germany.* Cambridge, MA, 1952.

Walter, Dirk. *Antisemitische Gewalt und Kriminalität: Judenfeindschaft in der Weimarer Republik.* Bonn, 1999.

Walter, Franz. "Sachsen und Thüringen: Von Mutterländern der Arbeiterbewegung zu Sorgenkindern der SPD. Einführung und Überblick." In Franz Walter, Tobias Dürr, and Klaus Schmidtke, eds., *Die SPD in Sachsen und Thüringen zwischen Hochburg und Diaspora: Untersuchungen auf lokaler Ebene vom Kaiserreich bis zur Gegenwart,* Bonn, 1993, 11–38.

Ward, Janet. *Weimar Surfaces: Urban Visual Culture in 1920s Germany.* Berkeley, 2001.

Warneken, Bernd Jürgen. *Als die Deutschen demonstrieren lernten: Das Kulturmuster "friedliche Straßendemonstration" im preußischen Wahlrechtskampf 1908–1910.* Tübingen, 1986.

———. "Die friedliche Gewalt des Volkes: Muster und Deutungsmuster von Demonstrationen im deutschen Kaiserreich." In Bernd Jürgen Warneken, ed., *Massenmedium Straße: Zur Kulturgeschichte der Demonstration,* Frankfurt, 1991, 97–119.

Weber, Hermann. *Die Wandlung des deutschen Kommunismus: Die Stalinisierung der KPD in der Weimarer Republik.* 2 vols. Frankfurt, 1969.

Weber, Stefan. *Ein kommunistischer Putsch? Märzaktion 1921 in Mitteldeutschland.* Berlin, 1991.

Weede, Erich, and Edward N. Muller. "Rationalität, Repression und Gewalt." *KZfSS* 42, no. 2 (1990): 232–247.

Wehler, Hans-Ulrich. *Deutsche Gesellschaftsgeschichte, vol. 3: Von der "Deutschen Doppelrevolution" bis zum Beginn des Ersten Weltkriegs, 1849–1914.* Munich, 1995.

Weichlein, Siegfried. *Sozialmilieus und politische Kultur in der Weimarer Republik: Lebenswelt, Vereinskultur, Politik in Hessen.* Göttingen, 1996.

Weisbrod, Bernd. "Gewalt in der Politik: Zur politischen Kultur in Deutschland zwischen den beiden Weltkriegen." *GWU* 43, no. 6 (1992): 391–404.

———. "Kriegerische Gewalt und männlicher Fundamentalismus: Ernst Jüngers Beitrag zur Konservativen Revolution." *GWU* 49, no. 9 (1998): 544–560.

Weitz, Eric D. *Creating German Communism, 1890–1990: From Popular Protests to Socialist State.* Princeton, NJ, 1997.

———. *Weimar Germany: Promise and Tragedy.* Princeton, NJ, 2007.

Wenzel, Otto. "Die kommunistische Partei Deutschlands im Jahre 1923." PhD diss., Free University of Berlin, 1955.

Werner, Andreas. "SA: 'Wehrverband', 'Parteitruppe' oder 'Revolutionsarmee'? Studien zur Geschichte der SA und der NSDAP 1920–1933." PhD diss., University of Erlangen–Nürnberg, 1964.

Wernette, Richard Dee. "Political Violence and German Election 1930 and July 1932." PhD. diss., University of Michigan, Ann Arbor, 1974.

Wheeler, Robert F. *USPD und Internationale: Sozialistischer Internationalismus in der Zeit der Revolution.* Frankfurt, 1975.

Widdig, Bernd. *Culture and Inflation in Weimar Germany.* Berkeley, 2001.

Wienfort, Monika. "Kaisergeburtstagsfeiern am 27. Januar 1907: Bürgerliche Feste in den Städten des Kaiserreichs." In Manfred Hettling and Paul Nolte, eds., *Bürgerliche Feste: Symbolische Formen politischen Handelns im 19. Jahrhundert,* Göttingen, 1993, 157–191.

Wille, Manfred. "Grundzüge der Entwicklung Magdeburgs von 1917 bis 1945." In Hans-Jürgen Rach, Bernhard Weissel, and Hainer Plaul, eds., *Die werktätige Dorfbevölkerung in der Magdeburger Börde: Studien zum dörflichen Alltag vom Beginn des 20. Jahrhunderts bis zum Anfang der 60er Jahre,* vol. 2, East Berlin, 1987, 255–279.

Winkler, Heinrich August. *Von der Revolution zur Stabilisierung: Arbeiter und Arbeiterbewegung in der Weimarer Republik 1918 bis 1924.* 2nd ed. Berlin, 1985.

———. *Der Schein der Normalität: Arbeiter und Arbeiterbewegung in der Weimarer Republik 1924 bis 1930.* 2nd ed. Berlin, 1988.

———. *Der Weg in die Katastrophe: Arbeiter und Arbeiterbewegung in der Weimarer Republik 1930 bis 1933.* Bonn, 1990.

———. *Weimar, 1918–1933: Die Geschichte der ersten deutschen Demokratie.* Munich, 1993.

Winkler, Jürgen R. *Sozialstruktur, politische Traditionen und Liberalismus: Eine empirische Längsschnittstudie zur Wahlentwicklung in Deutschland 1871–1933.* Opladen, 1995.

Wirsching, Andreas. "Kommunistischer 'Antifaschismus' in Berlin und Paris zwischen den Weltkriegen." In Detlef Schmiechen-Ackermann, ed., *Anpassung, Verweigerung, Widerstand: Soziale Milieus, Politische Kultur und der Widerstand gegen den Nationalsozialismus in Deutschland im regionalen Vergleich*, Berlin, 1997, 201–220.

———. *Vom Weltkrieg zum Bürgerkrieg? Politischer Extremismus in Deutschland und Frankreich 1918–1933/39: Berlin und Paris im Vergleich.* Munich, 1999.

———, and Dirk Schumann, eds. *Violence and Society after the First World War* (= *Journal of Modern European History* 1, no. 1 [2003]).

Zarusky, Jürgen. *Die deutschen Sozialdemokraten und das sowjetische Modell: Ideologische Auseinandersetzung und außenpolitische Konzeptionen 1917–1933.* Munich, 1992.

Ziemann, Benjamin. *Front und Heimat: Ländliche Kriegserfahrungen im südlichen Bayern 1914–1923.* Essen, 1997. English edition, *War Experiences in Rural Germany, 1916–1923,* trans. Alex Shinnen. Oxford, 2007.

———. "Republikanische Kriegserinnerung in einer polarisierten Öffentlichkeit: Das Reichsbanner Schwarz-Rot-Gold als Veteranenverband der sozialistischen Arbeiterschaft." *HZ* 267 (1998): 357–398.

———. "'Gedanken eines Reichsbannermannes auf Grund von Erlebnissen und Erfahrungen': Politische Kultur, Flaggensymbolik und Kriegserinnerung in Schmalkalden 1926. Dokumentation." *Zeitschrift des Vereins für Thüringische Geschichte* 53 (1999): 201–232.

Zimmermann, Ekkart. *Political Violence, Crises and Revolution: Theories and Research.* Cambridge, MA, 1983.

Zimmermann, Moshe. *Die deutschen Juden 1914–1945.* Munich, 1997.

Zinnecker, Jürgen. "Straßensozialisation: Versuch, einen unterschätzten Lernort zu thematisieren." *Zeitschrift für Pädagogik* 25, no. 5 (1979): 727–746.

Zollitzsch, Wolfgang. *Arbeiter zwischen Weltwirtschaftskrise und Nationalsozialismus: Ein Beitrag zur Sozialgeschichte der Jahre 1928 bis 1936.* Göttingen, 1990.

Subject Index

Index of People and Places

(Note: Erfurt, Halle, Magdeburg, and Merseburg are not included)

CPSIA information can be obtained
at www.ICGtesting.com
Printed in the USA
JSHW041547280720
6968JS00007B/123

9 780857 453143